Venizelos

Venizelos at his desk (1920s)

Institute for Neohellenic Research
National Hellenic Research Foundation

Eleftherios Venizelos

The Trials of Statesmanship

Edited by Paschalis M. Kitromilides

Edinburgh University Press

Transferred to digital print 2013

First published in hardback in 2006 by
Edinburgh University Press Ltd
22 George Square, Edinburgh

This paperback edition published 2008

Typeset in 10.5/13 Sabon
by Servis Filmsetting Ltd, Stockport, Cheshire, and
printed and bound by CPI Group (UK) Ltd
Croydon, CR0 4YY

A CIP record for this book is available from the British Library

ISBN 978 0 7486 3364 7 (paperback)

Contents

Foreword vii
George David

Acknowledgements viii

Note on Transliteration; Abbreviations x

Plates to be found between pages 212 and 213

Introduction: Perspectives on a Leader 1
Paschalis M. Kitromilides

I: Setting the Stage

1. A Century of Revolutions: The Cretan Question between European and Near Eastern Politics 11
Leonidas Kallivretakis

2. Venizelos' Early Life and Political Career in Crete, 1864–1910 37
A. Lilly Macrakis

II: The Drama of High Politics

3. Venizelos' Advent in Greek Politics, 1909–12 87
Helen Gardikas-Katsiadakis

4. Protagonist in Politics, 1912–20 115
Thanos Veremis and Helen Gardikas-Katsiadakis

5. Venizelos' Diplomacy, 1910–23: From Balkan Alliance to Greek–Turkish Settlement 134
Michael Llewellyn Smith

6. Reconstructing Greece as a European State: Venizelos' Last Premiership, 1928–32 193
Ioannis D. Stefanidis

7. The Last Years, 1933–6 234
Ioannis S. Koliopoulos

III: The Content of Political Action

8. The Experiment of Inclusive Constitutionalism, 1909–32 251
Ioannis Tassopoulos

9. Venizelos and Civil–Military Relations 273
Thanos Veremis

10. Venizelos and Economic Policy 284
Christine Agriantoni

11. Modernisation and Reaction in Greek Education during the Venizelos Era 319
Alexis Dimaras

12. Venizelos and Church–State Relations 346
Andreas Nanakis

IV: Offstage

13. Venizelos' Intellectual Projects and Cultural Interests 377
Paschalis M. Kitromilides

List of Contributors 389

Index 390

Foreword

George David

The idea of this book originated in a conversation I had several years ago at a Bilderberg meeting in Scotland with Margaret MacMillan, Professor of History at the University of Toronto. Margaret, a great scholar of the 1919 Paris Peace Conference, was keenly aware of the role played by Eleftherios Venizelos in the meetings that redrew the political map of Europe and expressed an interest in reading more about him and his policies. I promised to send her books in English to satisfy her curiosity, which I understood had also to do with the close personal friendship between Venizelos and her great grandfather David Lloyd George.

When I returned to Greece I called a close friend, Paschalis Kitromilides, Professor of Political Science at the University of Athens and asked him to suggest some works on Venizelos in English. He chuckled on the phone and told me that the latest book in English on Venizelos had been published by our Cypriot compatriot Doros Alastos as far back as 1942. I was both slightly shocked and amused by the revelation. This gave me the idea that under the aegis of the A. G. Leventis Foundation a new book presenting a profile of Venizelos as leader, statesman and reformer of Greek society could be published. For this undertaking I thought there was no one better than Professor Kitromilides himself, a well-established and respected authority on modern Greek history and politics. I therefore asked him to organise the project in his capacity as Director of the Institute for Neohellenic Research at the National Hellenic Research Foundation. The present book is the result of his strenuous effort to co-ordinate a group of distinguished authorities on Venizelos in the community of scholars on Greece.

On behalf of the A. G. Leventis Foundation I am pleased and proud that we have contributed to the filling of a serious gap in the knowledge of modern Greece of English-reading scholars and of a broader cultivated international public interested in the history, politics and biography of twentieth-century Europe. I wish to express my appreciation to all those who have contributed to turning into reality this vision to honour the man who has strong claims to be considered Greece's greatest statesman of the twentieth century.

Acknowledgements

This book has been long in the making and the debts incurred in this period of gestation are too many even to be adequately recalled and properly recorded here. The work has been transacted in the Institute for Neohellenic Research of the National Hellenic Research Foundation, which has provided the operational base for co-ordinating and putting together the collection.

The Eleftherios Venizelos Research Foundation in Chania, Crete has been instrumental in supplying most of the illustrations from its photographic archive. The Liberal Club in Athens has been equally generous in its help to the editor. The National Centre for Maps and Cartographic Heritage in Thessaloniki has expertly produced the maps.

In working on the collection I benefited greatly from the advice of Thanos Veremis and Helen Gardikas-Katsiadakis and from the assistance of Leonidas Kallivretakis. Alexandra Doumas, David Hardy and Mary Kitroeff have helped with the translation of parts of the project. Constantina Simonetatou at the phototypesetting section of the Institute for Neohellenic Research has worked with patience and skill on the production of the manuscript.

My old teacher in America, Professor Fred I. Greenstein of Princeton University, has helped me to introduce the personality and politics perspective in the understanding of Venizelos' leadership. Professor Theodore Skaltsas of the University of Edinburgh has been very encouraging and supportive throughout the project. Two anonymous referees for Edinburgh University Press have greatly contributed with their comments but also with their enthusiasm to the improvement of the final product.

The A. G. Leventis Foundation has generously funded the project at all its stages. Without its support this, like many other worthy projects in contemporary scholarship, would not have been possible.

The greatest debt of all is owed to George David, a distinguished leader in business and a man of vision for culture and scholarship. The idea of this book is his brain child and his forbearance and enthusiasm has been a great support for the editor at moments of doubt and anxiety.

To stress our debt to him we wanted the book to be published by the publishing house of his own alma mater, the University of Edinburgh, an institution that is so dear to his heart. We are delighted this has been made possible and we are grateful to Edinburgh University Press for helping us to render the appropriate homage to a great alumnus of the University of Edinburgh.

P. M. K.

Note on Transliteration

The only standard system for the transliteration of the Greek alphabet into languages written in Latin characters is that used for the transliteration of classical Greek. The transliteration of ancient Greek, however, is quite inappropriate for rendering the spelling and especially the phonetics of modern Greek. Accordingly the following modifications have been introduced to make it conform more to the modern morphology and sound of the language. Diphthongs have generally been retained, except in those cases where the modern pronunciation of Greek requires a consonant to be adequately rendered (e.g., 'aftou,' not 'autou'). The Greek vowels η and ι have been uniformly rendered with 'i', and similarly ο and ω have been rendered with 'o'. The Greek υ has been rendered with 'y', except when it forms part of a diphthong; then it is rendered by 'u' (e.g., 'tou'). The rough breathing has been dropped.

Consonants have generally been rendered phonetically. Thus the Greek β has been rendered by the Latin 'v' rather than 'b'. The Greek consonant φ is rendered by 'ph' in all words with an ancient Greek root. Conversely, Greek names with Latin roots (e.g., Constantinos) have been transliterated as closely as possible to their original form.

The names of modern Greek authors appear in the form used by the authors themselves if they have published work in a foreign language. Inevitably some inconsistencies will remain, but I hope the reader will find this understandable in a book of this nature. Place names have been used in their standard forms in the English language, otherwise they have been transliterated following the general rules adopted in this book.

ABBREVIATIONS

AF [=Affaires Etrangères]	French Foreign Ministry
AMF [=Archives du Ministère des Finances]	Archives of the French Ministry of Finance
AMO [=Archeio Moatsou]	E. Moatsos Papers, Archives of the University of Crete, Rethymnon

AN [=Archives Nationales]	French National Archives
AYE [=Archeion Ypourgeiou Exoterikon]	Historical Archives of the Greek Foreign Ministry
DBFP	Documents on British Foreign Policy
FO	Foreign Office
PRO	British Public Record Office

Introduction: Perspectives on a Leader

Paschalis M. Kitromilides

At the dawn of the twenty-first century a more or less general consensus in Greek politics acclaims Eleftherios Venizelos (1864–1936) as the most important statesman in Greek political history and the creator of contemporary Greece. Although it would be rash to dismiss this as plain mythology about the man and his political achievements, there can be at the same time little doubt that a Venizelos cult is growing in Greek political thought. Recognition extends far beyond the intellectual sphere and permeates public opinion at large, as evinced by innumerable avenues and squares named after him in Greek towns and cities. Statues and monuments are multiplying throughout the country and, in a decision of telling significance, the new major international airport, built in Athens in the 1990s, has been named the 'El. Venizelos Airport'.

All this is a rather recent development. The general adulatory consensus concerning Venizelos emerged in the late twentieth century, in the wake of earlier strong passions and divisions about the man and his politics that had dominated political debate and public feeling in Greece for most of that century. Throughout his active political life and during several decades following his death Venizelos had been the object of the deepest admiration and devotion, as well as of the strongest contempt and hatred on the part of his respective followers and opponents. These feelings at times ran so high that they led to profound divisions in Greek politics. The divisiveness around Venizelos' personality and politics pervaded all writing about him as well. Until about the 1980s, most writing about Venizelos had remained partisan, reflecting the respective positions of devoted friends or sworn enemies. Some of the most influential literature on the subject had been quite critical and severe in its judgement on the man and his work, whereas most positive appraisals suffered from sentimentality and unconditional admiration. Partisan motivations in the literature on Venizelos are not limited to writing in Greek but colour also whatever has appeared on him in other languages, including English.

Writing on Venizelos in English includes mostly adulatory accounts by his followers and supporters during the period of Greece's great diplomatic ventures in the 1910s and 1920s.[1] Other than that, the last major book-length study in English appeared as far back as 1942 and was the work of the London-based Cypriot publicist Doros Alastos.[2] In scholarly writing Venizelos makes an occasional transient appearance in the diplomatic historiography of the Paris peace settlement of the First World War, but generally his role in the negotiations remains a secondary concern for most writers. It is characteristic of the neglect to which Venizelos has been relegated in mainstream historiography in English that in the authoritative two-volume collection *The Diplomats 1919–1939*, which surveys international diplomacy in the 1920s and 1930s through in-depth studies, an important chapter is devoted to 'Turkish diplomacy from Mudros to Lausanne' and its protagonists, but Venizelos is only incidentally and rather superficially accorded one passing reference.[3]

Since the 1980s a new climate has been evident in Greek historiography on Venizelos. A succession of remarkable collective volumes and some important monographic works which have appeared since that period have established Venizelos, his life and political activity as a growing research field and have consequently allowed more balanced and all-rounded judgements to emerge.[4] This new research and the interpretative perspectives it makes possible for a critical understanding of the man, his policies and his contribution to the making of contemporary Greece are presupposed by the present collection. In the following pages twelve authors, all of them recognised scholars in Modern Greek politics and history, present a rounded perspective on Eleftherios Venizelos as a Cretan revolutionary leader, as a reforming prime minister of Greece, as a European diplomat, and as a protagonist in the deep division in Greek society provoked by his modernising policies. The most significant policy areas upon which he left his mark as a statesman are also analysed in specialised essays.

One of the distinctive features of the collection is the encounter of scholarly generations in its pages. Some of the authors are senior authorities in their respective fields of research and bring the benefit of their long experience to this collection. Others belong to a younger generation and contribute a fresh perspective and the benefit of novel research to some of the subjects treated in the volume. It will be noticed that the methodological logic guiding the composition of the collection is informed by inter-disciplinary principles: our chosen approach to Venizelos is shaped by an interplay of perspectives from biography, political science and diplomatic history, but our study is broadened in scope and outlook by invoking the contribution of constitutional theory, and economic, ecclesiastical and intellectual history. In fact, the interdisciplinary approach allows certain little-known aspects of Venizelos' politics to be explored systematically for the first time in the present collection: his policies toward the Orthodox Churches form a case in point.

The attempt at a systematic study of Venizelos' political personality and political career in the context of the critical historical period during which he dominated Greek politics inevitably raises certain broader questions of political analysis. If serious historical research in the last quarter century has rescued Venizelos from the ideological controversies of the past, still some fundamental political questions remain to be probed. It may sound iconoclastic to all those for whom Venizelos is just the hero of a growing cult in Greek political culture, but I believe that the critical perspectives emerging from all the essays in this collection, both those surveying the trajectories of the political leader and those appraising aspects of his major policies, force upon the reader the question of Venizelos' statesmanship.

The character of Venizelos' style of leadership, as illustrated by the strong and persisting feelings of devotion he elicited from his followers, could be quite plausibly described as a form of charismatic authority,[5] but was he a statesman in the Weberian sense of the responsible management of politics?[6] This is the question invited by the accounts of his politics in the present collection. He was certainly a great strategist, and most of the time he also proved a skilful tactitian in promoting the goals he set for his policies. His finest hour as a strategist came with his achievement of the integration of internal reform and the pursuit of irredentist goals in a unified policy blueprint for the Greek state, upon assuming the premiership in 1910. He thus accomplished the transcendence of the fundamental dilemma besieging Greek political thought from the 1840s to the 1890s over the relative advantages and the priority to be accorded between internal reform and external expansion. Venizelos managed to persuade his followers that the two objectives could go together into a consistent programme of modernisation, whereby internal reform would release the necessary energies for the successful pursuit of the irredentist goals of Greece. When he signed the Treaty of Sèvres in August 1920, Venizelos could feel that this overall strategy had been vindicated.

The classic distinctions about leadership proposed by Max Weber apply to Venizelos in two different ways: he was a man of passion but also a man with a feeling of responsibility. His passion for politics transpired in his single-minded devotion to the overall strategy he devised for the transformation of Greece. His responsible management of politics became quite often apparent in his diplomacy. He employed his remarkable tactical skills in the diplomatic field in order to harness and tame nationalist emotions. His greatest feat consisted perhaps in the forging of the Balkan alliance in 1912. He thereby transformed the lethal hatreds of inter-Balkan politics into a common front against the Ottoman Empire, tempering mutual irredentist maximalisms among Balkan states in favour of a realist programme of liberation of territories whose ethnic profiles legitimately attached them to the claimant states. Two subsequent phases of Venizelos' diplomacy confirmed his tactical ingenuity: his skill at promoting Greek national objectives at the Paris Peace Conference in 1919 and 1920 and his ability at bringing about a Greek–Turkish rapprochement in 1930 after the strain of decades of enmity and war between the two countries. The way he could bring himself to teach his political community to transcend the traumas of war, defeat and uprooting, and to elaborate a vision of peace that appeared credible on the other side of the Aegean as well was Venizelos' greatest substantive achievement in inter-state relations, whereby he could be judged to meet John Rawls' criteria of statesmanship. In bringing about the required adjustments in Greek public philosophy that made the Greek–Turkish 'treaty of friendship' possible, Venizelos manifested the 'strength, wisdom and courage' that define not 'the politician who looks to the next election, but the statesman, who looks to the next generation'.[7]

Despite these achievements, Venizelos' statesmanship had its limits. Either a failure of nerve or a surrender to the expediencies of political passions led Venizelos to his most controversial political decisions, the 'misguided' Greek intervention in Asia Minor in 1919,[8] and the condonement of the military coup in March 1935. His attitude toward the military coup in March 1935 certainly represented a failure of nerve. Greece's 'Anatolian venture',[9] however, which he initiated, despite serious warnings to the contrary,[10] was the product of grave political miscalculation that led to a failure of political judgement. Both of these actions eventually resulted in fundamental reversals of some of Venizelos' most characteristic achievements on the levels respectively of territorial gains and institutional change.

How could these failures of political judgement be interpreted? It is perhaps at this point that a consideration of Venizelos in the context of contemporary studies of political leadership might prove relevant for a fuller understanding of the more perplexing aspects of his policies and the deciphering of some dark episodes of his politics, such as the violence of his Cretan guards against political opponents. As a matter of fact, Venizelos is a notable absence in studies of leadership in relevant international scholarship, in which the inclusion of his case might broaden the basis and scope of comparative analysis. Venizelos' career in Greek politics illustrates very well the interplay between the leader's character and the expectations of his contemporaries, and the patterns of communication between the two which led to the political outcomes on the historical record.[11]

Thanks to the more recent elaboration of a precise and systematic methodology for the study of leadership, Venizelos' political personality and accomplishments could now be appraised on a scale of criteria that allow a clearer analytic understanding: public communication, organisational capacity, political skill, vision, cognitive style and emotional intelligence.[12] The studies that make up the present collection provide considerable evidence on Venizelos as an effective public communicator and on his competence in harnessing his considerable skills in political management to his overriding vision of transforming Greece into a modern liberal European state. To a considerable extent his vision was dictated by his cognitive style, which gleaned from his deep experience of Cretan politics in particular and Greek national politics in general the types of understanding necessary to cement his conviction in the modernising imperatives he set for his country. His emotional intelligence – or in Weber's terms 'the sense of proportion and the firm taming of the soul'[13] – was his greatest weapon: it supplied him with the ability to manage his emotions and turn them to constructive uses rather than allow them to dominate him and undermine his capacity to exercise leadership.[14] His most serious political failures, in fact, arose when his emotional intelligence failed him, as happened with the 1935 coup. It is in this direction I believe that meaningful further research on Venizelos as a political leader can be undertaken.

The best way to appraise Venizelos as a statesman would be to place his politics in a comparative perspective. Two comparisons readily present themselves to the student of twentieth-century politics and diplomacy. One obvious comparison, already suggested by Harold Nicolson a long time ago, is between Venizelos and his Romanian counterpart at the Paris Peace Conference, Ioan Bratianu.[15] Bratianu, who was ostensibly also a liberal, was much more successful than the Greek prime minister in obtaining for Romania 'all and more than all' at the eventual settlement. Furthermore the 'Greater Romania' that emerged from the Peace Conference proved much more durable than the 'Greece of two continents and five seas' that was Venizelos' transient achievement. Yet this 'territorial' aspect of their respective strategies cannot really be considered as the decisive criterion for the judgement of the two leaders as statesmen. On this level two other criteria might be considered more pertinent yardsticks of judgement: one was the mastery of the art of compromise whereby Venizelos in 1923 and in 1930 showed himself capable of taking a truly responsible long-term perspective on his country's national interests; the second criterion of statesmanship was the consistency with which Venizelos tried to harness the pursuit of nationalist goals towards the building of a modern liberal political society within Greece. His philosophy of modernisation through liberalism proved to be his lasting legacy to Greek politics. On the grounds of these two principles, compromise and modernisation through liberalism, it would appear that Venizelos fares better as a statesman than Bratianu.

A second obvious comparison is between Venizelos and the founder of the modern Turkish republic, Mustafa Kemal Ataturk. The comparison has often been attempted in scholarly literature.[16] In the case of this comparison, too, Ataturk could be considered much more successful than Venizelos in achieving the goals of Turkish nationalism and in putting an imprint on the future of his country that is proving almost unshakeable. But does this make him a greater statesman than Venizelos? This is a truly hard question to answer. If one takes a long-term perspective, however, appraising, as John Rawls requires to do, the extent to which the interests of future generations might be served by a leader's options and strategies, the comparison between Ataturk and Venizelos might be cast in a different light: the authoritarianism that remained inextricably intertwined with Ataturk's legacy of modernisation from above is proving, at the beginning of the twenty-first century, the most serious obstacle to Turkey's European trajectory, whereas Venizelism's liberal legacy has been one of the weapons that has sustained Greece's accession and integration in united Europe.

Obviously these are just hints toward a comparative perspective on Venizelos' statesmanship. In-depth comparative studies along the lines suggested above should certainly contribute to a fuller understanding of the subject. In turn, such comparative historical studies might conduce to the futher elaboration of the theory of leadership by enriching its substantive basis and by sharpening its critical edge. For the moment, in the following pages we map out the historical territory upon which this further political research could be meaningfully attempted.

NOTES

1. E.g. S. B. Chester (1921), *Life of Venizelos*, London: Constable and C. Kerofilas (1915), *Eleutherios Venizelos. His Life and Work*, London.
2. Doros Alastos (1942), *Venizelos. Patriot Statesman Revolutionary*, London.

3. Gordon A. Craig and Felix Gilbert (eds), *The Diplomats* (1953), Princeton, vol. I, p. 175. By contrast Venizelos' diplomacy is accorded a substantial chapter by Margaret MacMillan (2001), in *Peacemakers: The Paris Conference of 1919 and its Attempt to End War*, London, pp. 357–76.
4. Most notably, Odysseas Dimitrakopoulos and Thanos Veremis (eds) (1980), *Meletimata gyro ston Venizelo kai tin epochi tou* [*Studies on Venizelos and his Time*], Athens; and Thanos Veremis and Youla Goulimi (eds) (1989), *Eleftherios Venizelos. Koinonia, oikonomia kai politiki stin epochi tou* [*Eleftherios Venizelos. Society, Economy and Politics in his Age*], Athens. Also G. Th. Mavrogordatos and Ch. Hadjiiosif (eds) (1988), *Venizelismos kai astikos eksynchronismos* [*Venizelism and Bourgeois Modernisation*], Irakleio.
5. As convincingly suggested by G. Th. Mavrogordatos (1983), *Stillborn Republic. Social Coalitions and Party Strategies in Greece, 1922–1936*, Berkeley, pp. 55–64. One of the earliest observers authoritatively to recognise Venizelos' charisma was the great Romanian historian and statesman Nicolae Iorga in a perceptive obituary originally published on 20 March 1936. See N. Iorga (1939), *Oameni cari au fost*, Bucharest, pp. 158–9.
6. Max Weber (1946), 'Politics as a Vocation', in H. H. Gerth and C. Wright Mills (eds), *From Max Weber. Essays in Sociology*, New York, p. 98.
7. John Rawls (1999), *The Law of Peoples*, Cambridge, Mass., p. 97.
8. According to the authoritative judgement of John S. Koliopoulos and Thanos Veremis (2002), *Greece. The Modern Sequel from 1831 to the Present*, London, p. 129. See also the critical appraisal by MacMillan, pp. 361–4 (see Note 3).
9. Cf. A. A. Pallis (1937), *Greece's Anatolian Venture – and After*, London: Methuen, pp. 194–201. On this critical and tragic question cf. also G. B. Leontaritis (1990), *Greece and the First World War: From Neutrality to Intervention, 1917–1918*, Boulder, pp. xi–xv, 427–8.
10. Pallis, *Greece's Anatolian Venture*, pp. 20–7 (see Note 9).
11. Cf. Dankwart A. Rustow (1970), 'The Study of Leadership', in D. A. Rustow (ed.), *Philosophers and Kings. Studies in Leadership*, New York, pp. 1–32.
12. Fred I. Greenstein (2000), *The Presidential Difference. Leadership Style from FDR to Clinton*, Princeton: Princeton University Press, pp. 5–6, 194–200. These latest approaches to political leadership presuppose considerable earlier theoretical and experimental work, surveyed in F. I. Greenstein and Michael Learner (eds) (1971), *A Sourcebook for the Study of Personality and Politics*, Chicago: Markham.
13. Weber, 'Politics as a Vocation', in Gerth and Mills (eds), *Essays*, p. 115 (see Note 6).
14. Cf. Greenstein, *Presidential Difference*, p. 6 (see Note 12).
15. Harold Nicolson (1965), *Peacemaking 1919*, New York: Grosset's Universal Library, pp. 135–7. On Bratianu's diplomacy, see also Sherman David Spector (1995), *Romania at the Paris Peace Conference: A Study of the*

Diplomacy of Ioan I. C. Bratianu, Iaşi: The Romanian Cultural Foundation, esp. pp. 289–98 for a general appraisal.

16. Cf. the judgement by Arnold Toynbee (1931), 'The Graeco-Turkish Settlement', in A. Toynbee, *Survey of International Affairs 1930*, London: Oxford University Press, pp. 157–68.

PART I

Setting the Stage

1

A Century of Revolutions: The Cretan Question between European and Near Eastern Politics

Leonidas Kallivretakis

The island of Crete was the last Greek region to be subjugated by the Ottoman Turks,[1] falling after a long and bloody war that lasted from 1645 to 1669.[2] Following the example of mainland Greece, the island rose against Ottoman domination in 1821 but, despite some early successes, the struggle made little or no progress for three years. No major urban centre was captured by the insurgents, who were restricted to the possession of two forts of limited importance – those of Kisamos and Gramvousa. The presence of a solid Muslim population – almost half the population were Tourkokritikoi (i.e. Turco-Cretans), most of whom sided with the sultan – was certainly one of the reasons for this situation. Another factor in this was the isolation of the island, on account of its distance from the main theatre of the revolution, to overcome which, 'special commissioners', unacquainted with local conditions and characteristics, were sent from Greece. Finally, the lack of a fleet of any size accounts for the Cretans' failure to counter the steady arrival of Ottoman reinforcements. With the aid of the Egyptians, who landed on Crete in 1822 and 1823, long before Ibrahim Pasha's intervention in the Peloponnese, the uprising was quickly restricted to the western provinces, where it smouldered until it was finally extinguished.

The international treaties of 1829, 1830 and 1832 excluded Crete from the new Greek kingdom,[3] a development that provoked strong, though ineffective, protests in both Crete and Greece. The majority of the Cretans were obliged to accept this *fait accompli*, though some, mainly those whose activities on the island had exposed them to reprisals and a number of families of victims of the struggle, chose to remain in Greece, where they had fled after the crushing of the uprising. These and their descendants were to form an influential Cretan lobby, which was to play an important role in Greek political affairs throughout the nineteenth century.

Meanwhile, the vali of Egypt, Mohamed Ali, judging that the services rendered by him in suppressing the Greek uprising had not been appropriately recompensed by the Sublime Porte, decided to claim actively what had not been granted him voluntarily. In 1831, Egyptian forces successfully invaded Syria and one year later the sultan was compelled to cede the administration of Crete to Mohamed Ali. During the period of Egyptian rule (1831–40), the administration of the island was assigned to Mustafa Pasha, a man of Albanian descent who had been on the island with the Egyptian armies since 1822 and had run the pashalik of Chania since 1824.[4]

The contradictions between the centripetal desires of the Sublime Porte and the centrifugal manoeuvrings of Mohamed Ali were soon sharpened once again. Constantinople became increasingly sensitive to the danger posed for the future of her empire by the fact that the Egyptian, Arabic, Syrian and Cretan provinces were effectively in the hands of the ambitious vali of Cairo. For his part, Mohamed Ali wished to consolidate his position and achieve recognition of his right to bequeath his pashalik to his descendants. A fresh breach was inevitable, and in 1839 the Ottoman armies crossed the Euphrates, but were once more defeated by the Egyptians. Sultan Mahmud died a week later, while the admiral of the Ottoman fleet took his ships to Alexandria and surrendered them to the vali of Egypt. Faced with the vigorous reaction of the Great Powers to the possibility of the complete overthrow of the status quo in the Near East, and under the threat of the bombardment of Alexandria by the European fleets, Mohamed Ali was compelled to back down. In accordance with the Treaty of London, signed in 1840 by Britain, Russia, Austria and Prussia, 'acting at the request of the Sultan', Mohamed Ali retained Egypt for himself and his descendants, but on condition that he returned the other provinces.[5] After the restoration in Crete of direct rule from Constantinople, the Sublime Porte kept Mustafa Pasha in his position, and the change was not greatly felt by the population. Mustafa Pasha remained on the island for almost thirty years, until September 1851, adding to his name the surname *Giritli* ('the Cretan').[6]

During this period important changes took place in Cretan society, the consequences of which were not long in making themselves felt. The end of the uprising in the 1820s found Crete full of 'ruins and widows'. A good part of the population had either been killed or had abandoned the island, and the unremitting struggle had led to the virtually total annihilation of the men-folk in some regions. The average population density had fallen to about thirteen inhabitants per square kilometre.[7]

In an attempt to bring peace to the island, Mustafa Pasha installed his own administrative machinery, refusing to give important offices to local Muslims. Observing rudimentary principles of equality, he appointed mixed councils in each Sanjak and introduced the use of the Greek language in public documents.[8]

The Albanian gendarmerie brought from Egypt attempted to enforce law and order, often intervening in support of the Christians and restraining, not without savagery, the arbitrary actions and resistance of the Turco-Cretans: 'Many of the insubordinate Muslims were either beheaded or incarcerated at that time in the prison of the Gramvousa fort.'[9]

Before this period, tax collection was mainly under the control of local agas, who had contracted the right to collect taxes in bulk (mukataa). In most cases they secured this right for life (malikiane aghasi) and converted it into a hereditary activity, in this way expropriating a large part of the agricultural output. The authoritarian structure of this machinery was completed both at the economic level, through the process of lending and bankruptcy, and at the political level, to the extent that the owner of the mukataa usually belonged to the dominant Muslim majority and was supported by its administrative structures. Applying the policy successfully implemented in Egypt by Mohamed Ali twenty years earlier,[10] Mustafa Pasha removed a large part of the mukataas from the agas, thereby depriving them of an important source of economic and social power.[11]

The reorganisation of the Ottoman timar system also caused disturbance. In 1828 the Sublime Porte decided that the military service obligations of the timar-holders should be brought up to date and obliged them to enrol in new battalions in the regular army, at the same time discouraging the right to use a substitute; this led in practice to the gradual removal during the 1830s of timars from those who were not in a position, or did not wish, to fulfil their new obligations and conform with the new regulations.[12]

In conclusion, on the morrow of the rebellion, the Muslim community of Crete was not only decimated, but its access to the machinery of power was reduced, and at the same time the ruling class was largely deprived of its ability to appropriate a significant proportion of the wealth produced by the conquered society. The disenchantment that arose in these circumstances led to the emergence of two phenomena within the Muslim community. A number of Muslim Cretans reverted to Christianity, and many of the rest gradually abandoned the countryside and withdrew to the towns and their environs.

In speaking of a reversion to Christianity, it should be borne in mind that the great mass of Cretan Muslims were descended not from Turkish settlers – the conquest of Crete in the late seventeenth century had taken place at a period when the initial impulse of Ottoman colonisation had run itself out – but from native Christians who had converted to Islam, basically of their own free will, during the first century of the conquest. It is indicative that these 'Turco-Cretans', as they came to be called, continued to speak Greek and drink the wine produced by their vineyards, contenting themselves with learning by rote some of the verses from the Koran to meet their new religious needs.[13] Occasionally, the conversion to Islam was feigned and there are references to families who continued to baptise their children for two centuries and to take part in parallel religious ceremonies ('crypto-Christians'), but these tended to be isolated cases.[14]

Cases of Turco-Cretans who reverted to Christianity are occasionally found as early as the time of the 1821 uprising. A typical example is that of the Kourmoulides who, led by the chief of the clan Husein Pasha, abandoned Islam *en masse* – over sixty men – and played a leading role in the rebellion.[15] The phenomenon became more common later, during the 1850s, especially after the signing of the Hatti Humayun charter, to which we shall return below. Examples are known of entire villages being baptised en masse in the provinces of Mylopotamos and Pediada.[16]

Although we do not have the complete quantitative evidence to calculate the dimensions of the phenomenon, it is indicative that the percentage increase of the Christian community between 1834 and 1881 was more than double that of the Muslim community. Even when account is taken of the gradual return of the refugees of 1821, who were mainly Christians, an increase of this scale in the Christian community can hardly be interpreted as the result only of internal demographic growth. The Ottoman administration attempted to cut off this stream by passing a number of restrictive measures, though these led to a rebellion by the people and were the main reason for the removal of the then governor general, Veli Pasha.[17] This incident was an important indication of the decline of the Ottoman regime in Crete.

During the course of the nineteenth century, the countryside gradually became Christian (in 1881, 82.4 per cent of the rural population was Christian) and tightly enclosed the Muslim towns (Muslims made up 70 per cent of the urban population).[18] The steady flight of Muslims from the countryside, and especially from regions remote from the castles, was the result both of the changed terms of exploitation of the land and of the sense of insecurity created within the ranks of the Muslim population.

This development was accompanied by another significant phenomenon – the purchase of land by Christians. 'After 1829, a large part of the land then under Muslim ownership in the most fertile plains, came into the hands of Christians. The complete deprivation of the Turks through this peaceful revolution,' wrote Georges Perrot in 1867, 'is a question of time. Agas and beys, stripped of their estates . . . for a cheap price, inundate the towns, seeking to survive by renting some of the land that the Turkish administration is wasting, though it is unable to satisfy all the idlers that implore it.' At this point, the comment of the governor general of the island, Ismail Hakim Pasha, is revealing: that while forty years earlier, Christian estates had accounted for one fifth of the total, they had already (by 1866) reached three fifths, according to his calculations; he ends his comment with the estimation that if the Christians persisted systematically, they would ultimately buy Crete from the Turks, without the need for a rebellion.[19]

This systematic mass purchase of land by Christians was perhaps the most characteristic sign of the social change in the making in nineteenth-century Crete. 'Cases are rare,' stresses the man in charge of the official census of the island in 1881, 'of a Cretan villager who does not possess his own house and a larger or smaller, fairly productive, piece of agricultural land.'[20]

This growth of small- and medium-scale property ownership, which was interlinked with the fact that large landed estates based on çiflik-type relations were not created on the island (with the exception of a few examples of Church properties) meant that the situation in Crete was very similar to the one that pertained in what was then free Greece. It is revealing that, when it was annexed to Greece in 1912, the island did not bring in its baggage problems of land distribution like those posed in the cases of Thessaly or Epirus.

At the same time, the contracting of taxes, now removed from the hands of the owners of the mukataa, passed largely under the control of Christians, especially the recognized kapetanei (i.e. chieftains) of the provinces, who mainly undertook to collect the tithe and the poll tax (the military tax after 1856).[21]

It may be noted, in conclusion, that in 1881 the majority (60.4 per cent) of the Muslims on the island lived in eastern Crete: in Lasithi and above all in Irakleion and the two provinces of Rethymnon that bordered with Irakleion, Mylopotamos and Amari. Twenty per cent of the Muslims lived in the countryside of western Crete, in the administrative regions of Rethymnon and Chania, where they formed only 15.4 per cent of the rural population.[22]

All these developments gave Crete a distinctive character within the Ottoman Empire, defined by the following characteristics: in a region that was geographically demarcated by its character (an island), a population was formed that was for the most part homogeneous with respect to its language (Greek), religion (Orthodox Christian) and its clear consciousness of belonging to a particular national group that already existed as an independent state a few dozen miles away. The censuses of the period before 1881, though rarely agreeing with each other on the precise numbers, nevertheless concur in attesting to a clear and steadily increasing Christian majority that fluctuated between 62.5 per cent and 77.4 per cent, depending on the decade and the source of information. It was a population firmly rooted in their land which had, moreover, officially acquired the right to possess arms.[23]

These facts help us to understand the phenomenon of the successive rebellions of varying range and intensity that broke out throughout the whole of the nineteenth century (1821, 1833, 1841, 1858, 1866, 1878, 1889, 1895, 1897), mainly in western Crete – on occasion with the backing of the Greek government but frequently, as we shall see below, even against the wishes of the official Greek state. This phenomenon is not encountered in other Ottoman provinces, where the subject populations were not solid and were not marked by homogeneity of religion, language or collective consciousness, and where the political, social and economic conditions had developed in different directions.

This population was faced with the Muslim community and the Ottoman authority. The former, once very strong numerically, politically and economically, fought a rearguard battle throughout the century, until it was reduced towards its end to the role of a disenchanted minority of 11 per cent, confined to the towns and their immediate environs and cut off from the hinterland and productive activity. The Ottoman authority, on the other hand, was in a state of continual crisis after the middle of the century, incapable of establishing and following a consistent policy, sometimes dangerously compliant and sometimes inappropriately autocratic, as moderation and arrogance succeeded each other with the same frequency that the rulers of the day were sent out – thirty-seven governors succeeded each other in the space of forty-six years, with an average term of office of fifteen months.

THE UPRISINGS OF 1833 AND 1841

The first Cretan rebellion after the Greek War of Independence of 1821 took place as early as 1833, when thousands of Christians assembled, unarmed, in the village of Mournies near Chania to protest against the taxation measures and other arbitrary actions of Mustafa Pasha. Despite the peaceful character of the demonstration, the authorities reacted violently, and forty-one of the leaders of the movement and several other Christians throughout the island were arrested and hanged, as an example to the rest.[24]

The next rebellion took place in 1839 to 1841. The crisis between the Ottoman Empire and Egypt led, as already mentioned, to the end of Egyptian occupation and the restoration of direct Ottoman rule on the island, and several Cretans, mainly those who had settled in Greece, considered that the time was ripe to raise the Cretan question once more. Through a series of memoranda addressed to the Great Powers, the Cretan Committee sought the unification of the island with Greece or, failing that, the granting of internal autonomy. Placing their hopes in the intervention of the Powers, or at least of Great Britain, which was rumoured to be interested in taking the island under its 'protection', the Cretans arose in a rebellion that began in February 1841 and lasted about five months. During this period, a number of bloody clashes took place, initially in Western Crete and then in the rest of the island, though without a substantial outcome.[25] This was followed by a fairly long period of peace, which, remarkably, was not disturbed even during the great crisis of the Eastern Question that broke out in the 1850s and culminated in the Crimean War (1854–6).

THE HATTI HUMAYUN AND THE FIRMAN OF 1858

On the basis of article 7 of the Treaty of Paris, signed on 30 March 1856 after the Crimean War, France, Britain, Prussia, Russia and the Kingdom of Piedmont-Sardinia undertook jointly to guarantee the territorial integrity of the Ottoman Empire. In the spirit of this principle, any conflict in the East would be a matter of European interest. The same treaty also envisaged the improvement of the living standards of the Christian subjects of the porte. After persistent démarches by the Allies, the sultan had already issued an imperial decree (Hatti Şerif), the text of which had, in effect, been dictated by Allied ambassadors in Constantinople. In an attempt to give this document the force of an obligation undertaken to the Great Powers, the countries that had signed the Treaty of Paris made explicit reference to it in article 9 of that treaty. 'The firman,' it comments, 'was communicated to the Powers, who noted the great importance of this act of communication.'[26]

The Hatti Şerif of 1856, more widely known as the Hatti Humayun, ratified and consolidated the reforms for which it had assumed an obligation with the Gul Hane charter of 1839. It provided guarantees for the safety of the persons and property of all the subjects of the empire 'without distinction of class or religion', and confirmed all the privileges that had been granted 'from very ancient times' to all the non-Muslim communities settled in the empire. Any distinction that was intended to make any population group inferior to another on grounds of religion, language or race 'was struck from the administrative record', and all subjects were to be accepted without discrimination into the public services and the political and military schools. All commercial, political and legal differences between Muslims and non-Muslims were to be referred to joint courts, and freedom of representation on provincial and community councils was to be secured for the various religious communities, as, too, was the principle of equal taxation for all. Other provisions promised the construction of roads, the promotion of public works, the reform of the monetary and finance system, and the founding of banks.[27]

In 1858, many thousands of Cretans assembled in Pervolia near Chania and threatened to take to arms if the administration did not pass the appropriate measures to carry out the programme of promised reforms. The Sublime Porte, which was then experiencing difficulties in Montenegro, capitulated to these demands and issued a firman which reduced taxes and guaranteed free elections to the councils of elders. The implementation of this firman, however, was blocked by the incompetence of the administrative machinery and the hostility of the Muslim population to any reform. The appointment of Ismail Pasha as governor general of the island in 1861 did not improve the situation. A former minister of trade in Constantinople, and of Greek extraction, Ismail attempted to please everyone, 'promising everything to everyone, without ever keeping his promises'. In this way, he increased the numbers of the disaffected. Relations between Christians and Muslims became increasingly tense. At the end of 1866, the disaffection assumed fearful dimensions and conflict seemed inevitable.

THE UPRISING OF 1866

In May 1866, several leading figures in the Christian population of the island gathered at Aghia Kyriaki near Chania and sent a long report to Ismail Pasha, asking him to convey it to the sultan. In it, ten requests were 'respectfully' submitted, including relief from the inflated taxation, improvement of public transport, free elections to the councils of elders, the creation of a loan bank, improvement of the juridical system and the reintroduction of the Greek language in legal transactions, the securing of guarantees of personal liberty, the creation of schools and hospitals, permission to trade freely from all the ports on the island and, finally, a general amnesty for those who had participated 'in the general uprising in our Homeland'.[28]

At the same time as submitting this report to the sultan, those assembled in Aghia Kyriaki also put their signatures to a confidential memorandum intended for the three Powers protecting Greece, in which, after referring to their part in the Greek War of Independence of 1821 and, despite this, 'their subjugation once more to the Ottoman yoke', they called upon the Powers to consent to their unification 'with their Greek brothers' or, 'if this is not possible at the present time', at least to the granting of a form of political organisation that would ensure 'Christian and humane' governance.[29] After these documents were signed, the assembly was dissolved, leaving a committee to await the official reply.

Before carrying out their plans, the Cretans had been in contact with the Russian and Greek consuls in Chania. The former, though declaring himself 'opposed to revolutionary movements', nevertheless counselled them to pursue certain reforms by peaceful means, including the abolition of the new taxes, free elections to the councils of elders, and so on, promising his 'probable support'. The Greek consul 'avoided giving them encouragement', since the government in Athens strongly disapproved of a Cretan uprising at that point in time, observing that the current political situation in Europe was 'not favourable to a serious enterprise of this nature', and advising the Cretans to content themselves with seeking 'with moderation, relief from some of the unbearable taxes, and nothing more'.[30]

The situation was already deteriorating, however. The Muslims and their families sought refuge in the fortified towns, while the Christians armed themselves and gathered in the mountains and Ismail Pasha called upon the committee to disband, stating that he regarded its continued existence as a revolutionary act. The Sublime Porte's answer, publicly posted on 20 July, rejected the demands with menaces. 'More than all the subjects of the empire,' it noted, 'the Cretans enjoy benefits,' and 'they have no right or reason to request the abolition of taxes,' while 'with regard to roads, schools, hospitals, etc.,' improvements 'cannot be implemented forthwith, but very gradually'. On the other hand, by advancing these demands, the Cretans 'have risen in revolt, arranged gatherings, and behaved in a way that could not but be described as rebellion'. The governor general of the island was ordered to send forces to arrest the leaders of the 'rebellion', and disperse the rest 'by force', unless they 'submitted and provided written guarantees of their submission in the future'.[31]

After this, the insurgents, who had already formed themselves into a 'General Assembly of Cretans', gathered at Askyphou near Sphakia where, on 21 August 1866, they voted in favour of the dissolution of

Turkish authority and 'the unbroken and eternal unification of Crete and all her dependencies with Mother Greece'. The implementation of the vote was assigned 'to the bravery of the courageous people of Crete, to the assistance of Greeks throughout the world and all philhellenes, to the Mighty intervention of the Protecting and Guarantor Great Powers, and to the omnipotence of God on High'.[32]

The insurrection was proclaimed on paper through this vote, and in practice through armed struggle. Five days later, the insurgents laid siege to the Ottoman forces in Vryses near Apokoronas, obliging them to withdraw. In every area of the island the rebels came face to face with the regular army and Turkish Cretan irregulars, who shut themselves up in the forts and made frequent sallies to strike at the surrounding villages.

There followed the longest and most bloody of all the Cretan uprisings of the nineteenth century. It lasted about three years, during which Egyptian forces landed once again on the island to reinforce the Turkish efforts, while on the other side, a large number of volunteers from Greece and also from Europe and America hastened to fight on the side of the rebels.[33] During the same period, five successive Ottoman governors were replaced, in an endeavour to quell the insurrection, and six Greek governments followed one upon the other as a result of the reverberations of their policies on the Cretan question. The kingdom of Greece and the Ottoman Empire broke off diplomatic relations and came to the verge of open military conflict, which was averted at the last moment through the intervention of an international conference convened in Paris to determine the terms on which the crisis could be resolved. During the course of the rebellion thousands were killed on both sides, hundreds of villages were torched and looted, and the productive base of the island suffered a severe blow, while 50,000 women and children fled to Greece as refugees. Amongst them were the seven members of the family of the Cretan merchant Kyriakos Venizelos, who fled from Chania to Kythira and thence to Syros, taking with them their last-born child, Eleftherios Venizelos, then only three years old.

Despite the subsequent isolation of the maximalist supporters of unification with Greece and the predominance of the moderate group that favoured an autonomous principality of Crete within the Ottoman Empire,[34] and despite the global sympathy elicited by the struggles and sacrifices, the insurrection failed to influence the prevailing attitude of international diplomacy, which favoured the maintenance of the status quo in the Ottoman Empire.[35] After a series of desperate battles, most of the revolutionaries retreated before the superiority of the enemy forces and, having neither food nor munitions, submitted to the Turks or fled to

Greece, though a few isolated groups continued to wander in the gorges, becoming involved in minor skirmishes until the spring of 1869.[36]

THE ORGANIC STATUTE OF 1868 AND ITS IMPLEMENTATION

Despite the failure to achieve its immediate aims, the uprising of 1866 to 1869 nevertheless had a side-effect, the true dimensions and consequences of which were not appreciated at the time. In November 1867, in an attempt to undermine the insurrection by removing the basis for its claims, the Ottoman government announced, through the mouth of the grand vizier Ali Pasha himself, who had gone to Crete for this purpose and was personally handling the entire affair, a special administrative regulation, which was signed by the sultan in January 1868 and became known as the Organic Statute of Crete.[37] In addition to the restructuring of the administration of the island, this law provided for the involvement of Christians at every level of the administrative machinery and in the composition of the courts, for the equal use of the Turkish and Greek languages in the administration, for the creation of a local bank and, perhaps most importantly of all, for the election of a general assembly with legislative competence at local level.

These measures might have relieved the atmosphere somewhat, had they been passed in good time in response to the original Cretan demands, but now, after a year of bloody conflict, they appeared to come too late and were predictably rejected outright by the rebels, who had by this time entered on a struggle with broader aims.

Once the insurrection was suppressed, however, the implementation of the Organic Statute ushered in a new period in nineteenth-century Cretan history, though in the end this was not in the direction hoped for by its inspirers.

Probably the most important feature of all was the role played by the institution of the General Assembly. With a mixed membership drawn from both ethnic groups on the island, and elected indirectly by the local elders, this assembly was to meet forty days each year in closed sessions, to pass measures relating to local issues such as transport, public works, the credit system, trade, farming, education, and so on, though its decisions had to be ratified by the governor general and the Ottoman government.

In the early years, this assembly functioned in only a rudimentary manner: the administration interfered in the election process, which was in any case indirect, the representation of the ethnic groups was unbalanced (the Christians, who formed 74 per cent of the population, had a majority of two and later only one seat), the debates were conducted in an authoritarian manner by the governor general, who was ex officio chairman, the assembly was frequently dissolved before the forty days had elapsed and very few of its substantive decisions were in fact ratified. Even in these adverse circumstances, however, its operation created a forum for debate about the basic problems of the people of Crete and revealed the dynamism of the Christian element, but at the same time demonstrated that a basically rational approach to even the simplest of local issues, conflicted de facto with the very nature of the Ottoman regime.

THE CHALEPA PACT OF 1878

The sequence of international events in the Balkans from the middle of the 1870s onwards (revolt of Bosnia-Herzegovina in 1875 to 1876, intervention of Serbia and Montenegro on the side of the rebels in 1876, the Russo-Turkish War of 1877 to 1878),[38] created a highly charged atmosphere in Crete. While not leading directly to an uprising aimed at secession, this encouraged in the ranks of the Christian community on the island the growth of a strong reform movement, to which the General Assembly gave expression. A factor that is perhaps not unconnected with this development is that the original social composition of the body, which was overwhelmingly rural in nature, had begun to change after 1875, when the first new Christian representatives took their seats, most of them doctors and lawyers who had trained at the University of Athens.[39]

Already in the assembly of 1876, the Christians refused to discuss the usual current affairs and made an issue not only of the unfettered implementation of the Organic Statute, but also of its amendment to conform with the requirements of the principle of equality. Their long memorandum, submitted on 22 May 1876 and conveyed to Constantinople by the governor general, Reuf Pasha, demanded fairer representation of the Christian population in the assembly, the administration and the judiciary, the right to draw up a local budget, the prohibition of incarceration without a previous judicial decision, and the freedom to build churches.

The response of the Sublime Porte, which was publicly posted on 2 August, rejected the demands submitted, apart from a few, such as the founding of a bank, the institution of compulsory public education, the law specifying rules for holding municipal elections, and the right to establish printing presses and publish newspapers.[40] This attitude, while satisfying the Muslims, gave rise to intense anger amongst the Christian population. Christian officials, administrative counsellors and judges continued to abstain from their duties, since the assembly, which had been dissolved prematurely, had not had time to renew their period of office; meanwhile, the first armed bands had already made their appearance in the mountains, and the Cretan lobby in Athens was collecting money and munitions. The Ottoman administration attempted to strangle the movement at birth by arresting, without any specific charge, the lawyer Constantinos Mitsotakis, representative of Kydonia and a leading figure in the Christian community. However, it was obliged in the end to set him free, when the electors refused to vote for a replacement and, for the first time in history, a popular demonstration took place in the centre of Chania, in front of the governor general's residence.[41] These events illustrated the profound psychological change in the morale of the Christians and the irreversible decline of Ottoman control over the island.

Meanwhile, in a desperate attempt to forestall the rapid general developments that threatened the cohesion of the entire edifice of the Ottoman Empire, the new sultan, Abdul Hamid II (the third in three months, after a series of coups d'état and resignations) announced the granting of a constitution and the impending election of an Ottoman parliament for the first time.[42]

This is not the place to examine this political movement in depth, which in any case swiftly proved ephemeral and of no consequence. The Cretans, who were called upon to send two members of parliament to Constantinople, one Christian and one Muslim, treated the entire matter as a threat to their albeit rudimentary autonomy and to any improvements they had managed to bring about in the affairs of their island, and as a retrograde step that restored Crete to the status of merely an Ottoman province, subjected, with no special provisions, to the general institutional framework of the empire. Despite the appeals and the asphyxiating pressure applied by the administration, no more than five Christian electors could be persuaded to take part in the electoral process in March 1877,[43] while the two Christian 'members of parliament' who were 'elected' one after the other to represent their fellow islanders in the Ottoman parliament, refused the office.[44]

Meanwhile, the insurrection proceeded, the movements of armed bands about the countryside intensified, and the kapetanei who had lived in exile in Greece since 1868 continued to return to the island. All this culminated in January 1878 in the convening of the 'Pan-Cretan Revolutionary Assembly' at the village of Fres in the province of Apokoronas. Having become embroiled in the war with Russia, the Sublime Porte was not in a position to mobilise enough forces to suppress the uprising, and was obliged to come to terms with the insurgents. In any case, defeat on the battlefield soon followed,[45] and the Treaty of Berlin in July 1878 ordained that 'the Sublime Porte is obliged strictly to implement in the island of Crete the Organic Statute of 1868, after such amendments as may be judged necessary'.[46]

Almost relieved that it did not have to cede Crete, like Thessaly and Arta, to Greece, the Ottoman government entered into negotiations, and in October 1878 the Pact of Chalepa was signed in the suburb of this name in Chania and was ratified by a firman of the sultan on 9 November 1878.

The Chalepa Pact brought to the Organic Statute some notable changes which, as was explicitly stated, 'cannot be modified by the [Ottoman] Constitution'. An obligatory term of five years was fixed for the governors of the island, in order to give continuity to the administration, and explicit reference was made, albeit only to the possibility, to his being of Christian descent; and, in either case, he was to be assisted by a counsellor of the other religion. A local gendarmerie was created, in which both ethnic communities participated. Administrative correspondence and judicial decisions were to be composed in both languages, while Greek was to be the only official language for sessions of the courts and the General Assembly. The latter was to consist of eighty members, with a clear Christian majority (forty-nine against thirty-one).[47]

THE UNUSUAL 'PARLIAMENTARY' SYSTEM OF CRETE UNDER TURKISH RULE (1878–89)

The Pact of Chalepa was immediately put into practice with the appointment as governor general of Alexandros Karatheodori Pasha, one of the numerous eminent Christians holding high office in the Ottoman administration. The first violation of the treaty occurred a mere fourteen days later, when, instead of serving for a five-year period, Karatheodori was suddenly replaced by his colleague Ioannis Photiadis Pasha.[48] Photiadis was the first, and only, governor who not only remained in his post for five years, but whose period of office was renewed, ending ingloriously in 1885.[49] He was followed by a series of three governors, up to 1889, Ioannis Savvas Pasha for twenty months, Kostakis Anthopoulos Pasha for fifteen months, and Nikolakis Sardinski Pasha for sixteen months. It is notable that the Sublime Porte appeared more prepared to appoint governors of Christian origin (which was only envisaged as a possibility in the Chalepa Pact) than to keep them in post for five years (which was an express obligation).

This decade is marked by the longest attempt to apply in Crete a regime that had some, albeit rudimentary, liberal and parliamentary features. Its implementation threw into relief the contradictions and limitations of the regime.

At that period, the division of Cretan society into two political groups – that of the liberals or 'barefooted' (xypolitoi) and that of the conservatives or karavanades – had become consolidated. The division, whose roots lay in the distant past, had been established as early as the time of the Organic Statute, which created a complicated administrative machine and an attendant plethora of administrative posts. To capture these a solid political faction was formed, which was on good terms with the administration. This faction included a wide variety of individuals, ranging from those who had taken part in the 1866 events as spies, informers and collaborators of the Turks to the naturally conservative property owners (who were opposed to subversive movements and the attendant dangers), a large part of the senior clergy, and ordinary opportunists who had an eye on financial or other gains.[50] This faction often formed a de facto alliance with the corresponding Muslim party of the beys, in which eminent, wealthy Muslim notables were to be found alongside senior administrative officials and army officers, members of the fanatical religious brotherhoods, the sub-proletariat of Muslim settlers,[51] and ordinary fortune-seekers. The major characteristic shared by these was their steadfast opposition to even the simple reform measures put forward by the Sublime Porte, and their systematic undermining of the governors who attempted to implement them.[52]

'The only positive distinction that one could confirm between the two fighting factions,' notes the young, rising politician, Eleftherios Venizelos, with studied moderation, in one of his first political writings:

> was that the one – which consisted from the very beginning of the most vital elements of the land and included almost all the scholars of the day, invariably took the initiative, proved itself more vigorous than the other, played a leading role and invariably fought for various reforms – was more exposed to the wrath of the government and was therefore persecuted and crushed by it, despite often being in a majority, while the other – which contained more conservative elements and consisted mainly of those who had been politically active in the past – was rather reserved in the present and served as the moderating tool of the impulsive power of the first faction.
>
> In this state of affairs, it is very natural that the vigorous faction claimed for itself the title of progressive or Liberal Party and attributed the title conservative to the other, which the latter was quite happy to accept without protest .[53]

In practice, things were not quite so simple, however, and the rivalry between the two factions had reached the point where it could spark fierce passions, igniting spirits to a level that posed a danger to the cohesion of the island's population. The electoral system was a factor contributing to this atmosphere: half the representatives were replaced every year, being chosen by the electors, who were themselves selected through an indirect method. Moreover, the assembly also served as an electoral court, a circumstance that enabled the (usually conservative) majority of the day arbitrarily to form the political landscape, taking up almost half the parliamentary session of forty days in a usually successful endeavour to invalidate the election of their liberal rivals.[54] At the same time, the Pact of Chalepa introduced the condition that the majority of public offices should be filled by elections instead of through arbitrary appointment by the Ottoman authorities (the method used hitherto), thus going from one extreme to the other and turning the island into an unending electoral battlefield.[55]

At the end of the 1880s the two parties prepared for a final confrontation. In the spring of 1888, the liberal faction won the elections for the first time. There followed a spate of objections by their rivals, but ultimately the General Assembly proceeded with its task and, in the very short period left between the review of the elections and the end of the session, managed to vote in some important laws relating to the organisation of the municipalities, the organisation of the gendarmerie, the founding of a bank, and so on. One of the new measures involved a revised electoral law that introduced into Crete for the first time the principle of universal (male, of course) secret suffrage.[56]

The following elections, held on 2 April 1889 under this new system, led to a crushing defeat for the conservatives, who managed to return only eleven representatives, and the triumph of the liberal faction, with forty representatives elected. One of these was Eleftherios Venizelos, who had recently (1887) graduated from the law school of Athens University,[57] and was returned for the first time as representative of Kydonia, in place of his retiring brother-in-law Constantinos Mitsotakis,[58] who also made over to him the newspaper *Lefka Ori* (*White Mountains*), which he had published since 1880. The newspaper was republished in 1888 by Venizelos, C. Foumis, Ch. Poloyiorgis and I. Moatsos, who formed a modernising group within the Liberal Party that became known as the *Lefkoreites*, after the name of their newspaper.

The side of each of the two conflicting parties of the Christian community was taken by the corresponding factions of the Muslim representatives. As was to be expected, the first sessions of the new General

Assembly were inundated with objections to the elections, further igniting the already strong party passions.

THE 'REVOLUTION' OF 1889 AND ITS CONSEQUENCES

While the review of the elections was still in progress, however, five of the representatives of the conservative faction suddenly submitted a memorandum in which they declared it to be their judgement that no improvement could be made in the affairs of the island under the present regime and that they considered the only solution to be the unification of Crete with Greece; accordingly, they decided to abstain from the work of the assembly, and were followed in this by the other minority members.[59]

This unexpected action took place despite the efforts of the Greek consul in Chania to avert it. The consul's attitude was giving explicit expression to the total opposition of the Greek government under Charilaos Trikoupis to any movement in Crete. The majority were now faced with a terrible dilemma, for if they failed to declare themselves in favour of this untimely conservative initiative, they risked being accused of betraying the national cause.

On 5 June 1889, the General Assembly submitted to the extraordinary imperial emissary Mahmud Pasha a series of economic demands, amongst them the incorporation of customs revenues into the local budget, and the founding of an agricultural bank with the right to issue banknotes. The assembled opposition supporters abandoned completely their demand for unification with Greece and submitted a memorandum in which they sought the replacement of the governor general Sardinski Pasha (the only governor who had not taken the side of the conservative faction but had collaborated with the liberal majority), the invalidation of all the acts of the General Assembly and the dismissal of all civil servants, adding, in a purely demagogic spirit, the cancellation of debts to the state and fairer administration of justice, amongst other things. The Party of the Beys made similar demands in a corresponding memorandum.[60]

The response of the imperial emissary was publicly posted on 22 June. While offering a temporary solution to the financial problems and promising the future creation of a bank, it rejected the other demands, since they had not been submitted through the official assembly but had been formulated by a gathering that did not legally represent the province. This development initially discouraged the assembled representatives, but it was then decided to force the issue by moving to Boutsounaria, the usual venue for revolutionary gatherings near Chania, it being known that, as Venizelos observed, 'The mere name of this place caused Christian breasts to beat with a sacred pulse, and sent a corresponding chill down Turkish spines.'[61] Rejecting any discussions with their party rivals and all the admonitions of the Greek government, the supporters of the insurrection sought to create a fait accompli by terrorising the Muslims of the countryside, in the hope that this would strengthen their final negotiating position.

At the same time, while the imperial emissary was recalled to Constantinople, signs of a hardening of respective attitudes became apparent, with the first armed clashes between Christians and Muslims, and also between Christians of rival factions, while the usual attacks by aggressive Muslim crowds on the Christian inhabitants of the towns also began. Faced with a deteriorating situation, the leaders of the two Christian factions concluded an agreement in principle with the liberals agreeing to consent to the demand for the replacement of Sardinski Pasha, on condition that the armed gatherings of conservatives should be dissolved forthwith. Although the Ottoman government agreed to the now joint demand and hastened to dismiss the governor general on 16 July 1889, the conservative grouping failed to observe the agreement. The dynamic of the situation had made them captives of their own armed bands, who refused to disband and rejected any compromise. This gave the local Turkish governors a pretext for arming the paramilitary Muslim bands which were intensifying their activities against the Christians, whose families rushed once more to the shores of the island in order to flee to Greece by whatever means possible. Already 'armed bands of both religious groups were polluting the country, raping, burning and murdering'.[62]

In this climate, the Greek government issued a communiqué to the Great Powers declaring its intention to intervene to protect the Christian population, while Constantinople appointed Shakir Pasha as military governor and locum tenens of the governor general, with instructions to restore order swiftly. When he arrived in Crete, Shakir Pasha at once proclaimed martial law and succeeded in a short time in restricting the activities of the intransigent Muslims and driving the armed Christians into the mountains. The majority of the leading politicians, irrespective of party, fled to Greece, Eleftherios Venizelos amongst them.

The most important consequence of the 'revolution of 1889', however, was that it provided the Ottoman government with a pretext for arbitrarily revoking most of the reforms that had been achieved by the Pact of Chalepa, eleven years earlier. A firman issued by the sultan on 17 November 1889 abolished a series of regulations, such as the obligatory five-year term of the governor general, the limited term of presiding judges and public prosecutors (who were now to be appointed for life by the government), and the practice of giving preference to locals in appointments to the gendarmerie. At the same time it was ordained that in the appointment of civil servants, preference would be given henceforth to those who spoke Turkish, and the number of members of the General Assembly was reduced from eighty to fifty-seven (thirty-five Christians and twenty-two Muslims), who were not to be elected by universal male suffrage but indirectly by electors from each province. An amnesty was proclaimed in theory, though exceptions were made in the case of leaders of the insurgents who had already been condemned by courts martial and politicians who were considered to have played a leading role in the recent 'troubles'. Amongst the latter was included Eleftherios Venizelos who, despite his clear opposition to the recent events, was thus recognised by his rivals in the most official manner as the undisputed leader of the Cretan people.[63]

THE UPRISING OF 1895

Martial law was lifted and persecutions ceased in 1890. The broader consequences of the events of 1889 were still felt, however, as arbitrary actions by the Ottoman authorities continued and all traces of self-administration were, in essence, effaced: the majority of Christians refused to accept appointment to public office or to participate in the elections that would have given a veneer of legality to the new regime. Sardinski was succeeded by five Muslim pashas, none of whose terms of office exceeded fourteen months.

In March 1895, Alexandros Karatheodori Pasha was put in place as governor general for the second time in his career. Although the experienced former minister of foreign affairs managed to persuade the Christians to end their abstention from public life and to send representatives to the General Assembly, his policy soon led to an impasse. The intransigent Muslims turned to acts of violence, designed to create an unsettled situation that would lead to the recall of Karatheodori to Constantinople, Christian bands proceeded to exact reprisals and also the question was raised of restoring the special regulations of the Pact of Chalepa.

The pasha dissolved the General Assembly, while Manousos Koundouros, a judge from Sphakia, took the initiative in forming a committee known as the Metapoliteftiki (change-of-government) and proceeded to draw up a memorandum, which was approved by the General Assembly that met at Krapi in Apokoronas in September 1895. This memorandum sought the granting of partial autonomy to Crete under a

Christian governor, who would hold office for five years, and the restoration of the Chalepa privileges in an improved and expanded form. This was the first time that an insurrection had not begun with the standard demand for union with Greece, but from the start set itself 'reformist' objectives. Its activities were nevertheless regarded as revolutionary and Karatheodori, having attempted in vain to arrest its leaders, was recalled in February 1896. The general amnesty proffered by his successor, Turhan Pasha, also appointed governor of the island for the second time, met with no response and hostilities intensified, culminating in the siege of Vamos Apokoronou by the insurgents in May 1896.

After these developments, the Ottoman government sent out the former ruler of Samos, Georgios Verovic Pasha, as new governor, and on 31 July, under pressure from the Great Powers, was obliged to cede a new Organic Statute. This provided for the appointment of a Christian as governor general for a period of five years, with the approval of the Powers, for the creation of a Cretan gendarmerie organised and staffed at officer level by Europeans, for the filling of public offices by local Christians and Muslims in the proportions of two to one, and for guarantees of judicial and economic independence.[64]

TOWARDS AN AUTONOMOUS CRETAN STATE

The acceptance of the new charter by the rebels calmed passions for a time, but a fresh impasse soon emerged, when the intransigent Muslims of the island, in collaboration with hard-core circles of the Ottoman government, put into practice a fresh plan to undermine the new regime by creating a climate of terror. This rapidly escalated from the isolated murders of leading Christians to the mass slaughter of the Christian populations of the towns and the torching of Christian neighbourhoods.[65]

The Christians also formed armed bands, escalating their activities in their turn, and the Great Powers sought for ways out of the crisis, finally deciding on international intervention. Meanwhile, the Greek government of Theodoros Diliyannis decided to forestall them by sending an expeditionary force to capture the island (1 February 1897). This decision, taken under the pressure of the intransigents (intransigent political elements and extreme nationalist groups) and public opinion, with no military preparation or diplomatic groundwork, was to lead to the so-called 'unfortunate' Greek-Turkish War of 1897, which ended disastrously for Greece. At the same time, however, it accelerated the development of events in Crete by forcing the decision on an international occupation of the island, leading thereafter to its proclamation as an autonomous principality. This brought to an end over three centuries of occupation by the Ottoman Empire, the last soldier of which departed the island on 12 November 1898.[66]

NOTES

1. With the exception of the island of Tinos, that was subjugated in 1715.
2. See e.g. W. Bigge (1899), *Der Kampf von Candia in den Jahren 1667–1669*, Berlin; W. Bigge (1901), *La Guerra di Candia*, Turin; R. C. Anderson (1952), *Naval Wars in the Levant 1559–1853*, Princeton; Marinos Tzane Bounialis [1681] (1979), *Diigisis dia stichon tou deinou polemou tou en ti niso Kriti genomenou [A Narrative in Verses of the Terrible War that Took Place in the Island of Crete]*, Athens; Th. Detorakis (1990), *Istoria tis Kritis [History of Crete]*, Irakleio, pp. 251–70.
3. See e.g. K. Kritovoulidis (1859), *Apomnimonevmata tou peri aftonomias tis Ellados polemou ton Kriton [Memoirs of the Cretans' War for the Autonomy of Greece]*, Athens; N. Stavrakis (1890), *Statistiki tou plithysmou tis Kritis [Statistics of the Population of Crete]*, Athens, pp. 155–8; I. P. Mamalakis (1983), *I Kritiki Epanastasis tou 1866–1869 [The Cretan Revolution of 1866 to 1869]*, Athens, pp. 21–4; Detorakis, *Istoria,* pp. 318–50 (see Note 2).
4. J. C. B. Richmond (1977), *Egypt 1798–1952*, London, pp. 45–54; Stavrakis, *Statistiki*, pp. 148–52 (see Note 3); Detorakis, *Istoria,* pp. 351–8 (see Note 3).
5. A. Cahuet (1905), *La Question d' Orient*, Paris p. 99; Stavrakis, *Statistiki* (see Note 3); Mamalakis, *Epanastasis*, pp. 24–7 (see Note 3).
6. Consideration was given, indeed, to appointing him vali of Crete for life, but the proposal aroused strong British objections, and the Sublime Porte was negatively influenced by the example of Egypt; see R. Pashley (1837), *Travels in Crete*, London, vol. I, pp. xxi–xi; Stavrakis, *Statistiki*, pp. 158–9 (see Note 3).
7. See e.g. Pashley, vol. I, p. xxiv, vol. II, p. 325 (see Note 6); M. Chourmouzis Byzantios (1842), *Kritika [Cretan Affairs]*, Athens, p. 104.
8. Pashley *Travels* (see Note 6); Stavrakis, p. 156 (see Note 3); Mamalakis *Epanastasis*, p. 24 (see Note 3).
9. Stavrakis *Statistiki*, p. 157 (see Note 3).
10. Richmond, *Egypt*, pp. 45–54 (see Note 4); Stavrakis, *Statistiki*, pp. 148–52 (see Note 3).
11. Pashley, *Travels*, pp. xxv–xxvi (see Note 6); Stavrakis, *Statistiki*, pp. 152–7 (see Note 3).
12. S. J. Shaw and E. K. Shaw (1977), *History of the Ottoman Empire and Modern Turkey*, Cambridge, vol. II, p. 43.
13. Pashley (see Note 6); T. A. B. Spratt (1865), *Travels and Researches in Crete*, London; Stavrakis, *Statistiki*, pp. 148–52 (see Note 3).

14. F. W. Sieber (1823), *Travels in the Island of Crete in the Year 1817*, London, pp. 56–8.
15. Pashley, *Travels* vol. I, pp. 105–8 (see Note 6); Kritovoulidis, *Apomnimonevmata*, pp. 8–13, 28, 100–2 (see Note 3).
16. Mamalakis, *Epanastasis*, p. 30 (see Note 3).
17. Mamalakis, *Epanastasis*, p. 31 (see Note 3); N. A. Tsirintanis (1950), *I politiki kai diplomatiki istoria tis en Kriti ethnikis epanastaseos 1866–1868* [*The Political and Diplomatic History of the National Revolution in Crete 1866–1868*], Athens, vol. I, p. 29.
18. Stavrakis, *Statistiki* (see Note 3).
19. Tsirintanis, *I politiki kai diplomatiki Istoria*, vol. I, p. 62 (see Note 17).
20. Stavrakis, *Statistiki*, p. 198 (see Note 3); I. P. Mamalakis, *Epanastasis*, pp. 24–5 (see Note 3).
21. Stavrakis, *Statistiki*, p. 158 (see Note 3).
22. Ibid., generally.
23. Tsirintanis, *I politiki kai diplomatiki Istoria*, vol. I, pp. 30–1 (see Note 17).
24. Detorakis, *Istoria*, pp. 352–5 (see Note 2).
25. For a detailed presentation of the movement in its international setting, see Miranda Stavrinou (1986), *I Aggliki politiki kai to Kritiko zitima, 1839–1841* [*English Policy and the Cretan Question, 1839–1841*], Athens.
26. Cahuet, *La Question*, p. 170 (see Note 5).
27. Ibid., p. 191. The Hatti Humayun was simply a theoretical document promising reforms and laying down their principles. It had no practical significance without the passing of laws that would have ensured its implementation. This, however, presupposed the political will to do so. Even if the sultan had wished to implement reforms of this nature, and even if politicians with renovating attitudes had surrounded him, he would still have been confronted by the ethics and beliefs of the Muslims and by the countless civil servants who adhered to the old state of affairs. Their resistance would have vitiated all efforts at reform.
28. Domna N. Dontas (1966), *Greece and the Great Powers, 1863–1875*, Thessaloniki, pp. 65–71; Tsirintanis, *I politiki kai diplomatiki Istoria*, vol. I, pp. 114–22, 159–65 (see Note 17).
29. Tsirintanis, *I politiki kai diplomatiki Istoria*, vol. I, pp. 168–75 (see Note 17).
30. Academy of Athens (1957), *Mnimeia tis Ellinikis istorias: I Kritiki epanastasis 1866–1869* [*Monuments of Greek History: The Cretan Revolution of 1866–1869*], Athens, vol. VI, no. 1, pp. 5–9, 12, 33; Tsirintanis, pp. 114–22 (see Note 17).
31. Academy of Athens, *Mnimeia*, p. 39 (see Note 30); Tsirintanis, vol. I, pp. 202–5, 262–5 (see Note 17).
32. Tsirintanis, vol. I, pp. 370–1 (see Note 17).
33. For the activities and the adventures of the foreign volunteers, see, for example, J. E. Hilary Skinner (1868), *Roughing it in Crete in 1867*, London;

E. Desmaze (1878), *Études et souvenirs helléniques*, Lyon; L. F. Callivretakis (1987), 'Les Garibaldiens à l' insurrection de 1866 en Crète (le jeu des chiffres)', in *Indipendenza e Unità Nazionale in Italia ed in Grecia*, Florence, pp. 163–79.

34. Tsirintanis, vol. I, pp. 294–308 (see Note 17).
35. On the attitude of the Great Powers toward the Cretan question during that period, see, for example, A. S. Byzantios (1867), *L' Insurrection de Candie et le gouvernement français*, Leipzig; J. Missotaki (1867), *La politique anglaise et l' annexion de la Crète à la Grèce*, Paris; J. Cartwright (1867), *The Eastern Question*, London; J. Cartwright (1867), *The Insurrection in Candia and the Public Press*, London; J. Cartwright (1869), *Turkish Rule in Europe since the Treaty of Paris (1856)*, London; E. Driault (1898), *La Question d' Orient depuis ses origines jusqu' à nos jours*, Paris; K. Bourne (1956), 'Great Britain and the Cretan Revolt, 1866–1869', *The Slavonic and East European Review* 35, pp. 74–94; A. E. Mange (1940), *The Near Eastern Policy of the Emperor Napoleon III*, Urbana; Domna N. Dontas (1966), *Greece and the Great Powers, 1863–1875*, Thessaloniki.
36. Tsirintanis, vol. III, pp. 528–31 (see Note 17); Detorakis, *Istoria*, pp. 361–77 (see Note 2). For a detailed account of the insurrection by an independent observer, see the book published by the US Consul in Chania, William J. Stillman [1874] (1966), *The Cretan Insurrection of 1866–1869*, Austin.
37. For a detailed presentation of the Organic Law and its implementation, see Kallia Kalliataki-Mertikopoulou (1988), *Ellinikos alytrotismos kai othomanikes metarrythmiseis – I periptosi tis Kritis, 1868–1877* [*Greek Irredentism and Ottoman Reforms – The Cretan Case, 1868–1877*], Athens; and for the broader background R. H. Davison (1963), *Reform in the Ottoman Empire, 1856–1876*, Princeton.
38. For these events and the Eastern question crisis in the 1870s, see, for example, S. T. Lascaris (1924), *La politique extérieure de la Grèce avant et après le congrès de Berlin*, Paris; D. Harris (1936), *A Diplomatic History of the Balkan Crisis of 1875 to 1878*, Stanford; M. D. Stoyanović (1938), *Great Powers and the Balkans 1875–1878*, Cambridge; S. Goriainov (1948), *La Question d' Orient à la veille du traité de Berlin, 1870–1878, d' après les archives russes*, Paris; L. S. Stavrianos (1963), *The Balkans since 1453*, New York, pp. 396–412; R. Millman (1979), *Britain and the Eastern Question, 1875–1878*, Oxford.
39. Kalliataki-Mertikopoulou, *Ellinikos alytrotismos*, p. 238 (see Note 37).
40. Ibid., pp. 267–88.
41. K. G. Fournarakis (1929), *Dioikisis kai Dikaiosyni epi Tourkokratias en Kriti* [*Administration and Justice during the Turkish occupation in Crete*], Chania, p. 58.
42. H. Temperley (1933), 'British Policy towards Parliamentary Rule and Constitutionalism in Turkey', *Cambridge Historical Journal* 4, pp. 156–91; R. Devereux (1963), *The First Ottoman Constitutional Period: A Study of*

the Midhat Constitution and Parliament, Baltimore; R. H. Davison, *Reform in the Ottoman Empire*, pp. 383–6 (see Note 37).

43. While, even under the provisions of Ottoman law, more than fifty were required.
44. Kalliataki-Mertikopoulou, *Ellinikos alytrotismos*, pp. 314–18 (see Note 37).
45. F. V. Greene (1879), *The Russian Army and its Campaigns in Turkey in 1877–1878*, London.
46. W. N. Medlicott (1938), *The Congress of Berlin and After: History of the Near East Settlement 1878–1880*, London; B. H. Sumner (1937), *Russia and the Balkans, 1870–1880*, Oxford; E. K. Venizelos (1971), *I Kritiki epanastasis tou 1889* [*The Cretan Revolution of 1889*], ed. I. Manolikakis, Athens, p. 322.
47. Venizelos, *I Kritiki epanastasis*, pp. 324–6 (see Note 46); E. Prevelakis (1963), 'To kathestos tis Chalepas kai to firmani tou 1889' ['The Regime of Chalepa and the Firman of 1889'], *Kritika Chronika* 17, pp. 163–82; Detorakis, *Istoria*, pp. 385–6 (see Note 2).
48. Being appointed instead as minister for foreign affairs.
49. He was replaced after being censured by the General Assembly.
50. Kalliataki-Mertikopoulou, *Ellinikos alytrotismos*, pp. 154–5, 161 (see Note 37).
51. A population composed of very poor Circassians, Kurds and, mainly, Benghazi immigrants, the so-called Chalikoutides, small groups of which were transported to the island, mainly during the period of Egyptian rule and installed in the suburbs of the main cities, working as porters and so on.
52. Kalliataki-Mertikopoulou, *Ellinikos alytrotismos*, p. 158 (see Note 37).
53. Venizelos, *I Kritiki epanastasis*, p. 42 (see Note 46).
54. The fact that the elections were validated by the old members of the assembly and by those new members whose election was not contested, instigated a massive raising of objections, the so-called 'strategic objections', in order to reshape the composition of the assembly that was going to decide on them; see Venizelos, *I Kritiki epanastasis*, p. 91 (see Note 46).
55. 'If we take account of three successive years,' commented the governor general, Savvas Pasha, in 1886:

> we shall see that, in addition to the supplementary elections for representatives held annually, the following elections are held in quick succession: for mayors, mayor's deputies and counsellors, for municipal, provincial and departmental inspectors, for the councils of elders of the towns and villages, for the electors of the departments of the councils of elders, for the electors of the administrators of the vakuf [religious welfare institutions], for the deputies of courts of first instance and magistrate's courts, for provincial and administrative counsellors, etc., etc. I believe that for any people, a similar electoral system would have given rise to passions much stronger than those amongst us, and parties that would fight each other much more persistently – see Venizelos, *I Kritiki epanastasis*, p. 44 (see Note 46).

56. Chania newspaper *Lefka Ori*, 2 January 1889; Venizelos, *I Kritiki epanastasis*, pp. 50, 90–2 (see Note 46).
57. During his stay in Athens, the twenty-three-year-old Venizelos had a chance to make his first contact with international politics, when he met Joseph Chamberlain (1836–1914) on a visit to Athens, and revealed to him the real situation of the Cretan people. The impression made by the young Cretan student on the British politician seemed quite strong, since Chamberlain was persuaded of the rightness of his views; see reports on this meeting in the Athens newspaper *Nea Ephimeris*, 3 and 5 November 1886. A less well-known meeting, but even more characteristic of the impression that Venizelos was making on his interlocutors, even before becoming famous, is the one with the French politician Georges Clemenceau (1841–1929), who visited Crete a few years later. Asked back in France what impressed him the most – antiquities, monuments and so on – Clemenceau supposedly replied, 'The biggest impression I got was from a young lawyer of Chania, whose name I forget, but it sounds something like Venezuela.' The conversation is supposed to have taken place in the Comtesse de Noailles' literary salon, in the year 1899; see D. Kaklamanos, 'Venizelos', Athens newspaper *Eleftheron Vima*, 5 April 1936; and see P. S. Delta (1978), *Eleftherios K. Venizelos*, Athens, p. 8.
58. Constantinos Mitsotakis married Venizelos' elder sister, Aikaterini, in 1880.
59. The five leading protagonists of this action were A. Kriaris, N. Zouridis, I. Mygiakis, A. Kakouris and I. Anastasakis. See Venizelos, *I Kritiki epanastasis*, pp. 52, 244 (see Note 46).
60. Venizelos, *I Kritiki epanastasis*, pp. 60–3 (see Note 46).
61. Ibid., p. 72.
62. Ibid., p. 384.
63. Ibid., pp. 411, 476–9, 496–501.
64. See, for example, I. Pikros (1977), 'Pros ton polemo tou 1897' ['Towards the War of 1897'], in G. Christopoulos and I. Bastias (eds), *Istoria tou Ellinikou Ethnous* [*History of the Greek Nation*], vol. xiv, Athens, pp. 106–16; Detorakis, *Istoria*, pp. 390–4 (see Note 2).
65. See, for example, Pikros, 'Pros ton polemo', in *Istoria*, pp. 116–18 (see Note 64); Th. Detorakis (2001), 'Ta Eleftheria tis Kritis-Oi megaloi stathmoi tou Kritikou zitimatos' ['The Liberation of Crete – The Main Milestones of the Cretan Question'], in Th. Detorakis and Al. Kalokairinos (eds), *I teleftaia phasi tou Kritikou zitimatos* [*The Last Phase of the Cretan Question*], Irakleio, p. 24.
66. Although the autonomy of the Cretan state from the Ottoman government was complete, as suggested by the existence of its own currency, stamps and even its own flag, a metal Turkish flag remained standing on Suda islet, as a reminder of the sultan's suzerainty. The final de jure abolition of this suzerainty in international law came in 1912, during the First Balkan War, when the Cretan deputies were received in the Greek Parliament and a governor general was sent from Athens to the island.

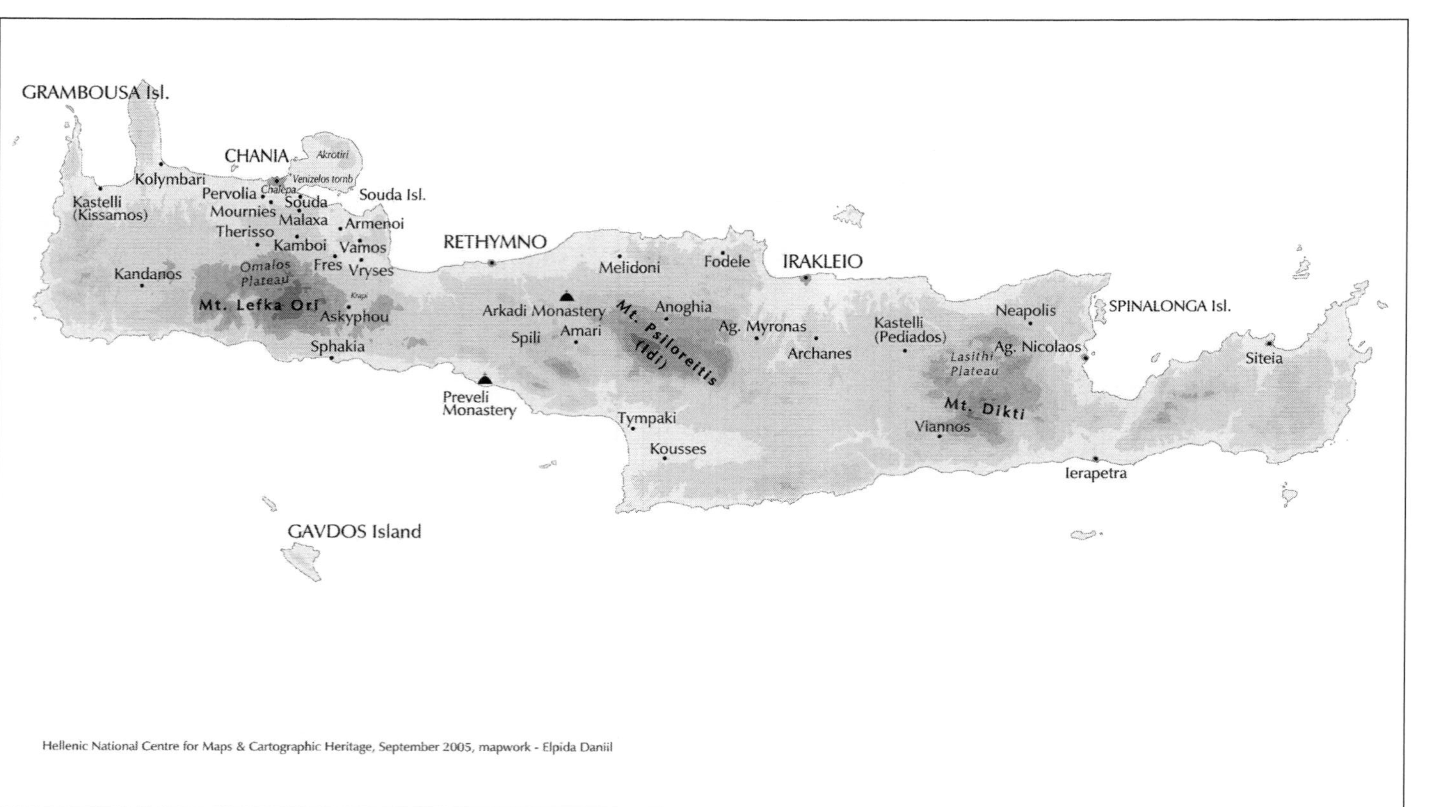

Crete in the Age of Revolutions

2

Venizelos' Early Life and Political Career in Crete, 1864–1910

A. Lilly Macrakis

ORIGINS

There is little consensus among historians on the ancestry of Eleftherios Venizelos. The document most relied on by Venizelos' biographers is an extract from a letter sent by Venizelos to the Cretan chieftain Constantinos Diyenakis or Daskaloyannis, who had asked him (on 19 August 1899) to recount his origins. Of his father Kyriakos, Venizelos wrote:

> While still very young, he participated in the great struggle of 1821 as the secretary of Koumis, the chieftain of Selino, with whom he endured the siege of Monemvasia. He was later awarded the medal of the revolutionary struggle. Three of his brothers were killed during the revolution, while another, Hadji Nikolos Venizelos, was sent with two other Cretans to negotiate with the chieftains in Greece at the start of the Greek Revolution . . . Exiled in 1843 by the Turkish government, which confiscated his shop and his land, Kyriakos remained outlawed but was again exiled during the 1886 revolution; he finally received permission to return to Chania in 1874.[1]

Kyriakos was a remarkable young man, bright, ambitious and resilient. Born in poverty during the most bloody upheaval in Greek history, he survived deportations, exiles, bankruptcies and persecutions to become a man of importance and distinction in his native country.

The Venizelos family is first recorded in the village of Mournies; later they moved to Chania, where Kyriakos carried on his father's business, touring the province of Chania selling household goods. He was known as a dependable merchant to the peasants of the Chania area and soon built up a modest personal fortune.

It is difficult to follow the private life of Kyriakos from the mid-1830s to the mid-1840s, although a part of it can be reconstructed from a series of letters written beginning in 1846, which bridge the gap with references to earlier events.[2]

In 1846 Kyriakos met and married Styliani Ploumidaki from the village of Therisso, at the time a girl in her mid-twenties. According to the Cretan biographers of Venizelos, this marriage was a major social advancement for the young salesman, since Styliani Ploumidaki was, supposedly, the granddaughter of the famous general Vasilios Chalis, a hero of the 1821 revolution. In fact, Vasilios Chalis had only a remote relationship with the Ploumidakis family. It was nevertheless a highly respected family of Therisso and Styliani's father, Ioannis Ploumidakis, was a well-known leader in the area.

Kyriakos' wife is still one of the most shadowy figures in the Venizelos family and is seldom mentioned in the letters of her son Eleftherios. Although of a strong and even opinionated character, she accepted a secondary role in the patriarchal society of her time. The father is a much more vivid figure than this homely, heavy-set woman who in all her photographs looks plain, stoical and determined. It appears that Styliani Ploumidaki was illiterate and dressed like a peasant all her life; she bore at least nine children, of whom six survived. She spent most of her time taking care of her retarded child Agathoklis and her houses in Chania, Mournies and later Chalepa. She survived her husband by fifteen years and died in July 1898 on the Aegean island of Milos during the upheaval of that year on Crete. Her death passed practically unnoticed at the time, as had her life.[3] Be that as it may, Kyriakos endured a series of exiles for the next fifteen years, to Syros, Athens and Missolonghi, but was finally able to return to Chania. Between 1861 and 1866, he worked hard to rebuild his shop and clientele, and to raise his family which by now consisted of five young children.[4] He was also active in philanthropic and educational affairs, first as a trustee of the Greek school of Chania and later as the president of the 'Minos' Association of Chania, an educational and social club. He wielded considerable authority locally and was respected as a talented businessman and as a leader of the Christian community.[5]

During the winter, the Venizelos family made its home not far from the shop, in the Topanas section of town, one of the best quarters of Chania and the centre of the Greek community. In the summer months the family moved away from Chania to Mournies, the favoured summer resort of the wealthy Chaniots. It was there that Eleftherios was born.

Although later in his career Eleftherios Venizelos moved in circles far removed from his provincial beginnings, he never cut himself off from his family or from his Cretan friends. Indeed, he was closely attached to them throughout his life and always spoke of the influence of his family with great approval and gratitude. In fact, Venizelos' family loyalty was one of the most important elements of his Cretan heritage. Although there is a good deal of uncertainty, of legend and of fantasy regarding his origins, there is no doubt that his was a strong-willed tightly knit family of high ideals and intense patriotism, 'values to be inherited by young Eleftherios and later used both in his private and public life'.[6]

CHILDHOOD AND YOUTH

Eleftherios Kyriakou Venizelos was probably born on 11 August 1864, in the small village of Mournies, whilst his family was on summer vacation.[7] Mournies is a beautiful Cretan village, surrounded by vineyards and olive groves with terraced gardens and fruit trees. To the north lies the wide sweep of the Bay of Chania, to the south are the White Mountains, and far to the east the high peak of Psiloritis.

He was the fifth surviving child of Kyriakos and Styliani Venizelos. Three daughters – Mariyo, Eleni and Katingo – and four sons were born earlier to the family.[8] Of the four sons already born, three had died in childbirth or infancy; the fourth, Agathoklis, had contracted typhoid fever at the age of two and remained mentally and physically handicapped. Agathoklis was a source of constant anxiety to his father and even more to his mother. He died in his late twenties. Another girl, Evanthia, was born later. All the sources consulted speak of Kyriakos Venizelos' deep wish for a son to carry on his name and business. The wish was fulfilled in August 1864.

It is understandable that all kinds of legends have surrounded the birth of the 'saviour' of Greece. All the ingredients are there: the bright light in the sky at the moment of birth,[9] the priest praying over the pregnant woman;[10] even the Muslim hodja was summoned from the village by Venizelos' father to appease the spirit of Mohammed himself![11] 'Don't repeat such nonsense,' Eleftherios Venizelos later used to say, 'people will think I was God!'

Two years after Lefterakis' birth the next upheaval occurred, the serious and protracted Cretan Revolution of 1866. It has been thought that Kyriakos Venizelos was one of the instigators of this revolution, that his part in it was the reason for his exile by the Turkish government. In fact Kyriakos had tried desperately to persuade his fellow Cretans to abstain from such a risky enterprise, to listen to the voice of moderation of the Great Powers and the Greek government, and to be patient until circumstances allowed them to move.[12] In fear of being implicated, Kyriakos had no choice but to leave Crete once more. Late in August, together with his family and the families of his friends Costis Foumis, Spyros and Antonis Markantonakis and Ioannis Markoulakis, he sailed for the island of Kythira.

This was the first of many exiles for Eleftherios Venizelos. The families stayed in Kythira for three years and it was here that the young Venizelos became a friend of Costis Foumis, three years his senior, his future collaborator in the government of autonomous Crete and comrade-in-arms in the Therisso revolt. When the revolution ended in 1869, many families could not return to Crete or did not feel that it was safe to do so. The Venizelos family then left Kythira and moved to the island of Syros, where they stayed for another three years, returning to Chania most probably in 1872.

So, as N. Tomadakis aptly puts it: 'Venizelos started to perceive life not in Chania, but in the friendly environment of Ermoupolis, with its many Cretan refugees. It is here that he came in contact with the educational world of the time and with free Greece.'[13]

Venizelos was eight years old when he returned – as a Greek citizen – to Turkish-occupied Chania.[14] His father, closely supervising the education of his young son, immediately enrolled him in a co-operative elementary school, Aghioi Anargyroi, the best school in the area. There Venizelos attended the last classes of the four-year elementary school. Most probably, Venizelos then had three years of middle school and the first year of high school in Chania. His training was good, especially in French, but his father later criticized the competence of his teachers in mathematics and Latin. Apart from this information, gathered from the exchange of letters between Kyriakos Venizelos and his son's teachers,[15] there is no other record of Venizelos' early school years. However, from private interviews with Venizelos' relatives and friends one can follow the boy Venizelos at school, at home and at play with his young Cretan friends.

Those who knew him personally or through his parents speak of him as bright, interesting and extremely active, a boy who could be arrogant and belligerent, while always commanding the respect of his fellow playmates, who were willing to follow him despite the repeated warnings of their elders to avoid him. He was often ruthless but seldom rancorous. His contemporaries admired his daredevilry,[16] but they also liked him for his high spirits and companionship, and although wilful and difficult on occasion he possessed a charm that made up for his offences.[17]

By 1877 Venizelos had changed, playing less and reading more – poetry as well as prose. He had become 'something of a bookworm', a fact which made his practical father remark one day: 'Crete does not need any more songs and guns. It already has plenty.' At fifteen he flirted with the idea of joining the Greek army and becoming a career officer. But the consul of Greece in Chania, George Zygomalas, persuaded him that he would help his country more by educating himself than by going into the military.[18]

The summer of 1877 was a transitional period for Venizelos. In September, among the rumours of a new Balkan crisis due to the Russo-Turkish war, young Eleftherios left for Athens to attend a private school, entering the second form of gymnasium (grammar school).

The Lykeion Antoniadis, where Venizelos became a boarder, was a private school of commercial studies, with a good reputation and first-rate teachers. Since Kyriakos intended Eleftherios to succeed him in business, he saw to it that his son was educated accordingly. This does not mean that he ignored the importance of a broader education. On the contrary, with Kyriakos' encouragement, Eleftherios embarked on an academic programme which included mathematics, ancient Greek, history, Latin, religion and French, besides commercial studies, calligraphy and gymnastics. Later, his father even asked him to add German to his curriculum, since he considered languages, 'important from a social and practical point of view'.[19]

His school education was enriched during his long stay in Athens, and strong political figures left an indelible mark on this lively adolescent mind. Venizelos felt a strong sympathy towards Prime Minister Koumoundouros and later developed an admiration for Prime Minister Trikoupis, for his advanced social and economic measures as well as for his moderate foreign policy. His father seemed at times annoyed by his son's interest in Greek politics. 'Don't read the nonsense of the newspapers there,' he said, 'read your Children's Digest, which is educational and fun at your age.'[20]

For his last school year it was decided that Venizelos would not return to the Lykeion Antoniadis in Athens. Instead he was enrolled in the public school of Syros, whose reputation was very good thanks to an excellent teaching staff. In June 1880 he passed his senior examinations and graduated with honours from high school in July. On the certificate, though, his conduct was graded as only 'Fair'![21]

Eleftherios Venizelos was sixteen by this time. The end of his schooldays would mean the permanent return to Crete and the beginning of a business career in his father's shop. He was far from certain that this was the course he wanted to pursue, but his father insisted. The misguided goodwill of parents often pushed bright young men into paths they did not choose, and Venizelos' father was no exception in trying to regulate his son's future. Although Eleftherios may have felt the desire to take his career into his own hands, he was hampered by filial loyalty and prevailing norms. For the present, he had to mark time.[22]

Eleftherios eventually managed to persuade his father to let him pursue a legal training; but first he served for sixteen months as the merchant son his father wanted him to be. From June 1880 to October 1881, he served his apprenticeship in his father's shop, learning the trade, stock-taking, buying, selling, bargaining – sometimes with feeling but more often out of duty. People who observed him then say that he actually made an excellent merchant, never letting his clients go without a purchase, always cheerful and affable. In this way he got to know his future constituency, as a junior salesman. Some of his biographers believe that his background in trade was apparent throughout his career. Other biographers disagree and see this period as a waste of time. They report that Venizelos was bored, resentful of his father, whom he considered too strict and demanding; 'an eagle in a cage'.[23]

Most of his friends had already left for Athens, where they were attending the School of Law or of Medicine at the University of Athens, as was the frequent practice of members of the middle class during the period of Turkish rule in Crete.[24] Some had remained in Chania though. He often went for long walks with them discussing his plans and his dreams for the future. They were an important source of support and encouragement, and they were involved with many of the literary groups and educational associations of the city. His friends commiserated, his mother advised patience. So, Eleftherios would come back to the Chalepa house every evening and spend most of his time reading. He liked to read modern Greek poetry; he learned whole passages by heart, which he would later recite to his friends with passion, perched on the rocks of Prophitis Ilias. He was studying foreign languages too. It was at this time that he perfected his French and worked less successfully on his German.[25]

In September 1881 a critical meeting took place between Kyriakos Venizelos and the consul general of Greece, George Zygomalas. The consul, who was a personal friend of Kyriakos Venizelos, and who had been aware of the preoccupations of his intelligent and sensitive son, tried again to convince the father to put aside his fears and send his son to Athens for higher studies. Aware of the patriotism of the elder Venizelos, he emphasised the fact that a young man with qualities of leadership should not be asked to tend shop in Crete for the rest of his life. He should study law and become a leader of his community. This was a powerful appeal to Kyriakos' patriotism, and it was successful.[26] Eleftherios was given permission to leave immediately for Athens, where he enrolled in the Law School of the University of Athens, in October 1881. Most of his friends were by then second-or third-year law students and he had to bear some teasing for his limited experience of Athenian life and his 'provincial view point'. The Cretan group roomed together in a large house near Omonia Square, but the active social life was too much for Venizelos, who, during his second year, rented rooms near the Law School by himself.

Politics entered more and more into his discussion of Athenian life. When the ex prime minister Alexandros Koumoundouros died in March of 1883, Venizelos sent a letter to his father trying to analyse the present political leadership in Greece:

> Forty to fifty thousand people attended the funeral and for good cause . . . Clearly Koumoundouros was right in avoiding war [against Turkey], a war we could have never won . . . if at times he seemed tolerant towards his friends' abuses . . . he is not to blame; it is our governmental system that is at fault, a system that lends itself to the abuses of the deputies . . .[27]

This is one of the last letters Venizelos wrote to his father. Towards the end of his second year of studies he was asked by his family to come home at once. His father's health had deteriorated and he had been taken to Mournies, where he died a few days after the arrival of his son.[28]

Now, at nineteen, young Venizelos found himself head of a family, financially responsible for a widowed mother and an unmarried sister. So he opted to stay in Chania for the time being and put his father's shop in order. The next two years have left little documentary evidence. Certainly the role of a provincial merchant never appealed to him; he had made clear to his friends that his goal was not to remain, like his father, a useful and respected citizen of his community living quietly in the Turkish-occupied city of Chania.

Although Venizelos stayed in Chania from 1883 to 1885, he continued renewing his registration at the Law School, attending classes, often by combining business and study trips to Athens, and passing the required examinations. Finally, two years after his father's death, he came to the conclusion that, with his family's finances in acceptable condition, he could resume his studies full time and liquidate the store. His short business career was over.

During his second stay in Athens as a student, Venizelos was at last free to devote himself to his own priorities. He showed boundless energy in his intellectual life, his social life and in the widening circle of acquaintances and friends he now associated with. It was Venizelos, his friends testify, who, although among the youngest, drew the group together and it was under his leadership that the Cretan problems were analysed and presented to the Greek public. Most probably, it was in these years at the

University of Athens that Venizelos became convinced of his political vocation; it was there that he had begun to form his views on Greece and its future course.[29]

The young Venizelos first emerged as a spokesman for the cause of Crete in November 1886, as a result of his well-known interview with the British statesman Joseph Chamberlain, later secretary of state for the colonies. Chamberlain, passing through Athens on his return from a long trip to the East, gave an interview to the Athenian newspaper *Akropolis* on the political situation in Greece,[30] in which he said that a well-known Greek in Constantinople had told him that the Cretans wished to secede from Turkey but were against union with Greece. This declaration brought protests from Cretans in Athens and particularly from the students, who appointed a five-member delegation to ask for an interview with the British statesman in order to explain the Cretan issue to him. The delegation first published a protest in the 3 November edition of the Athenian newspaper *Nea Ephimeris*, strongly reiterating that 'the aim of the Cretan people was union with Greece, to which aim the many past revolts had given ample testimony'.[31] The five students chosen to represent their fellow Cretans were Lilimbakis, Andreadakis, Maris, Kapsalis and Venizelos. According to the report of *Nea Ephimeris*, the delegation met for an hour at the Hotel d'Angleterre with Chamberlain, who asked questions regarding the state of affairs in Crete. It was, most probably, Venizelos who led the delegation and acted as its spokesman. After the meeting the delegation published the whole text of the interview in *Nea Ephimeris* and also circulated it among the Cretan students in Athens. This is a remarkable document for its eloquence, tone of authority, and powerful arguments. It reflects not only patriotic fervour but also a deep knowledge of the island. It seems that Chamberlain was much impressed by the thorough knowledge of local affairs displayed by the students, and by the judicious soberness with which they spoke. It is said that the next day, when Markos Renieris, then the governor of the National Bank of Greece and a native of Crete, asked him for his help on the Cretan problem, Chamberlain replied: 'With men like those who visited me yesterday you should not be afraid that your country will not be liberated from the Turks.'[32]

The interview made a profound and lasting impression in Athens. From then on both Venizelos' own circle and the journalists of the capital considered him the informal spokesman for young Crete. Men like Kanellidis, editor-in-chief of the Athenian newspaper *Kairoi*, would not print his news and editorials on Crete without consulting Venizelos.

Two and a half months later, on 15 January 1887, Venizelos passed his final examinations and received his law degree with the grade 'Very Good', a rather disappointing mark, short of the grade 'Excellent' he expected. Characteristically, this was due to his self-assured and provocative attitude in challenging one of his professor's interpretation of the law in the oral examination.[33]

On 10 March 1887, Venizelos finally returned to Chania, ready to start his law career in his native island.

THE LAWYER

Venizelos was already fully equipped for a career in law and probably in politics, since law was then the most common occupation and preparation of aspiring politicians.[34] His friends welcomed him as the 'new rising star' among the few available lawyers in Crete. His old friend and future political collaborator Foumis had already sent him a telegram in Athens, immediately after his examinations. 'My dear Lefteri,' it said, 'let me shake your hand and congratulate you warmly on your great success.'[35]

Venizelos, however, was not in a hurry to start his law career. He was seeking a way to make the best use of his capabilities. He had come to the conclusion that advanced law studied abroad, most probably in Germany, would be necessary to a successful career as a lawyer or a judge. To that end he continued his study of foreign languages and tried to put his financial affairs in order. On the whole, though, the first months of his stay in Chania were rather quiet, a kind of convalescence after a serious illness in Athens. But they also contained seeds of the future. For the first time, he toured the district of Kydonia, and these trips with his friends took him into the heart of the constituency which he was to represent later in the Cretan Assembly.

Besides frequent excursions and games (he was an expert at bridge), Venizelos regularly visited relatives and friends and strolled along the quay of Chania, where Greek 'society' gathered in the evening. This was how Venizelos met his future wife.[36]

Maria Eleftheriou Katelouzou was the daughter of a well-established merchant from Chania, Sophoklis Eleftheriou Katelouzos. Venizelos had known her since 1885, when he was twenty-one and she, a friend of his sister, only fifteen. They had not met again since and Venizelos was surprised and charmed by her mature looks and lively nature. She was Venizelos' first real love and probably his only one.[37]

According to his friends, this infatuation was one of the main reasons he cancelled his projected studies abroad.[38] Openly he spoke only of an economic setback; whatever the reason, he chose to remain in Chania. Social gatherings and courtship followed, until Venizelos decided to propose. Sophoklis Katelouzos responded to Venizelos' approach with eagerness and the couple were formerly engaged in January 1889. But the marriage had to wait. Maria was too young and Venizelos had just opened his law office. Besides, only two months before, he had turned to journalism and two months later he was to become regularly involved in politics.

Any assessment of Venizelos' career as lawyer, journalist and politician must take account of the remarkable energy and breadth of vision that supported these activities. Since Venizelos' work as a lawyer is neither as accessible nor as glamorous as his political life, the study of his legal career has been generally neglected and only very recently has formed the object of a major conference.[39] Yet, his three careers complemented each other beautifully. The qualities required in political writing and legal analysis added to Venizelos' intellectual development in ways that are discernible in his later political career.

Many acquaintances expressed the view that Venizelos had at the time committed himself wholeheartedly to the Cretan wars of liberation and, that as a result he did not have the opportunity to give serious consideration to his law practice. Venizelos never denied this view but rather cultivated it. At the height of his career, he spoke at a banquet given in his honour by the foreign press at the Peace Conference in 1919:

> After I finished my studies in Athens I returned home and hung out my bandolier. I had not tried many cases in the court of my home island before it became necessary for me to take up arms against the Turkish government. Although my father was born in Greece, I was considered an Ottoman subject – therefore a rebel – because my mother was born under the Turkish flag. At the end of this revolution, I returned again to my hometown and resumed my practice. I did not have time, however, to go far with it, for I had to take up arms again and go to the mountains. I soon reached the point where I had to decide whether I ought to be a lawyer by profession and a revolutionary at intervals or a revolutionary by profession and a lawyer at intervals . . . I naturally became a revolutionary by profession.[40]

This is not entirely accurate. It is a rather dramatised account, its emphasis adjusted to suit the later stages of his story. The law practice of Venizelos, which began in 1888 and ended in 1909, can be usefully divided into three periods separated by episodes of political action: 1888–96; 1901–5; 1906–9. The first period spans eight years, from 1888 to 1896, and was active and productive with only a brief hiatus in 1889–90, when he was elected representative in the short-lived Cretan Assembly.[41]

In the beginning he was the assistant of the well-known lawyer Spyros Moatsos and later he collaborated with his old friend and future political collaborator Yangos Iliakis. But it was he who conducted the main business. Most of the contemporary briefs available in Crete today indicate that from the outset Venizelos was the one who drafted the legal documents, wrote the briefs and the motions, raised the lawsuits and wrote most of the reviews; he rewrote most of his partners' drafts as well. All the work was done in the beautiful, clear, longhand he always used, which never needed revision. Venizelos at that time worked continuously from eight in the morning until ten at night, except for brief visits to court and occasional business lunches. By 1896, he already had on file 2,321 cases, and by 1905 he had 3,460 per year, an amazing number by any standard. It is obvious that he never experienced the usual lean years and under-employment of most young lawyers. On the contrary, he was swamped by all kinds of cases and had to work overtime and ask for the collaboration of his colleagues in order to cope with an ever-increasing general practice. Later, the fact that his clients were both Christian and Muslim gave his enemies ammunition for accusing him of being a Turcophile.[42] His fees were quite high and his income well above that of his colleagues. Still, due to his family obligations, his political activities, and a habit of spending 'as if there were no tomorrow', he never became wealthy. Money did not interest him at the time.

Venizelos was extremely successful as a general practitioner of law. He also had a remarkable legal mind and an excellent formal education which, matched with his realism and practicality, were ideal components for a future politician. In his briefs, and the laws he introduced later, he is clearly not 'an intuitive man with instantaneous and empirical reactions' but rather a man who combined theory and practice, abstract ideas and their practical application. This is amply demonstrated by a study of his contributions to the committee to draw up the Cretan constitutions of the years 1899 and 1907, and also in his legislative work of the years 1899 and 1901 as councillor (minister) of justice under Prince George, an impressive work for its breadth of vision and also for its sheer volume.[43]

Although he never offered a written explanation of his legal views, Venizelos, in his various law cases and commentaries on laws, shows himself deeply committed to the idea that law must serve the changing interests of society. According to him, the major defect of Greek law in this respect was a result of its foundation in Roman traditions, which invariably put the interests of the state above those of the citizens. By the time Venizelos entered law school in Athens, it had already become clear to him that the laws of the state tended to make the adjustment between the citizen and the state difficult and unequal. This was particularly true in Crete where Ottoman civil law, together with the laws added by the

Cretan representatives after the Pact of Chalepa, made government arbitrary. But even after 1904, when Cretan civil law was introduced, family and inheritance laws were based on the antiquated Byzantine-Roman code. Venizelos tried to accelerate the liberalising trend that had begun among certain Greek legal experts who advocated that laws undergo constant change. The desire to protect the individual against the arbitrariness of government appears with great frequency in Venizelos' work in Crete and later in Greece. In this, as in his political orientation later, he shows his liberal and reformist leanings.[44]

Venizelos did not specialise in any particular area of law. He was equally at home with criminal, civil and commercial law; he was particularly versed in constitutional law. His tremendous dexterity in handling difficult cases swiftly gave him a position of prestige in his profession. He spent hours reading the documents for each legal case, and wrote the preliminary report, the motions, the legal procedures himself, with attention to detail but without superfluous digressions.[45]

During his early years of law practice some of the cases he undertook attracted public attention either because they dealt with inter-ethnic problems or because they dealt with problems of ethics. Few biographers of Venizelos mention his most notable and controversial case, which became a cause célèbre in Chania in the 1890s. This was the murder in 1894 of Tevfik Bedri Bey, in the village of Loutraki of the Kydonia district. Two Greeks, Yorgos Papadakis and Antonis Larentzakis, were accused of this murder. It was generally believed that the arrest was arbitrary and due to political motives; no Christian lawyer in Chania dared prosecute this case against two Christians except Venizelos. The outcry among the Cretans against his decision was unprecedented, and the passions deriving from this event are still being aired by the descendants of the accused and the detractors of Venizelos.[46] The two accused Christians were found guilty, condemned to death, and were hanged outside the fort at Chania on 7 January 1894. To many, the behaviour of Venizelos in lending his skills of persuasion to the enemy, 'selling them to the Turks', was indefensible if not treasonable. To others, it was proof that Venizelos could separate the claims of justice and decency from his loyalties as a patriot. The issue soon became part of the rhetoric against Venizelos, especially in the entourage of Prince George, who viewed the policies of Venizelos as self-serving and, by implication, as serving Turkish interests.[47]

At twenty-five, Venizelos was already a well-established and prominent lawyer. If there ever was a stage in his career when he might easily have settled into a bourgeois routine, this was it. He could have joined those whose youthful ambition and idealism subside before the realities of everyday life. But Venizelos' goal remained to contribute to shaping the political future of his island. Besides tending to his law practice, he now turned to political writing.

THE JOURNALIST

Many politicians of Venizelos' time had followed careers similar to his before their rise to power. Journalism was second only to law as the most common occupation of aspiring politicians. At a time when the character of most of the Greek press was overtly polemical, an able journalist could wield considerable political influence. Venizelos' ability to manipulate ideas and facts, and his powers of observation and analysis gave him a natural aptitude for the work.[48]

A few months after Venizelos had opened his law office, an opportunity presented itself. His brother-in-law, Costas Mitsotakis, a distinguished politician and journalist, had been elected judge of the Court of Appeals in the same elections in which Venizelos had lost as an alternate judge. Mitsotakis had for many years been the publisher and editor of the liberal newspaper *Lefka Ori*. Now he handed over the newspaper to Venizelos. Together with his close friends Costas Foumis, Iakovos Moatsos, and Charalambos Poloyorgis, he formed an editorial board, and the paper was launched under its new owners on 19 December 1888.

The association of Venizelos and his friends with one of the leading weekly papers of Chania lasted six months, until the end of June 1889. Venizelos' contributions to the paper were primarily on political and financial topics. Besides the introductory statement signed by all the editors and presenting their political views, Venizelos wrote the weekly article and the most important editorials, signing with the pseudonym *Lefkoritis*.[49]

As a proprietor and editor of *Lefka Ori*, Venizelos quickly earned a wide reputation as an outspoken critic of Turkish policies in Crete and of Cretan factionalism. In the eyes of his countrymen he represented the feelings and attitudes of the young, progressive element of the Cretan patriotic élite. To foreign representatives he seemed daring but sensible. To his Greek colleagues he looked fresh and persuasive.[50]

As a journalist, Venizelos deliberately restricted himself to the discussion of a few broad themes and used his position as leading editor to develop a carefully worked out policy for Crete. The central theme presented by him in his articles was the need for 'the development of the moral and material forces of the Cretan people' and co-operation between the warring parties.

In a long article entitled '1888' he wrote: 'It is our duty to advise the followers of both parties to give up fighting and jockeying for position and turn their competitive spirit to a discussion and recognition of the vital interests of the country.' He then gave a moving description of the tragic situation on the island where in-fighting among Cretan politicians and murders of Muslims and Christians were tearing the country apart.

Repeatedly in his articles and later in his speeches Venizelos returned to the theme of reconciliation and peace on the island, with enosis (union with Greece) as the ultimate goal. This aim could not be served by a feuding Christian community 'who quarrel among themselves and try to destroy each other'.

He also advocated active participation of all citizens in public affairs since, besides the political problem, the biggest obstacles to union with Greece were the apathy of the Christians and the lack of economic development on the island. In the first issue of the paper, he wrote: 'The worst attitude is that of stagnation, the refusal of betterment which leads to misery and internal dissension and which brings a quick corruption of character . . .'[51]

It is important to realise that at this early stage of his career, Venizelos had already developed a novel approach to the Cretan problem. This he was presenting in his editorials in *Lefka Ori*, forcefully and repeatedly; he was not merely advocating political reforms and union with the mother country; instead, he was writing both as a teacher and a reformer, trying to bring about deeper changes in Cretan society. He was advocating a real spiritual and intellectual revolution, a revolution that would overturn long-held historical traditions and popular superstitions, and that would reach the deep roots of the social system.

For his time and place, Venizelos was an exceptionally well-read man with wide cultural interests. Among the Greek classical writers who had a great influence on his thought one should single out Aristotle and Thucydides.[52] Not only did he read most of their work in the original, but he also scribbled pointed comments in the margins and entered additional comments in his private diary. Most importantly, he did finally make a translation of Thucydides into modern Greek, when he was out of office and living abroad between 1921 and 1924, 'not out of boredom but rather in order to freshen his mind and renew his thinking'.[53] He often referred to Aristotle's ideas directly or indirectly. He always insisted, for example, that politics is the means by which citizens become members of a community and arrive at a just society. 'I never separated morality from politics in public life,' he told the members of the French Academy of Moral and Political Science, when he was elected a member of this prestigious institution in 1919. 'For political men as well as nations, acceptance of a moral code, undistinguished from political laws, constitutes the best, nay, the surest way to success.'[54]

Many who have written about Venizelos have failed to emphasise his extraordinary precocity and the informed outlook of his editorials. They have tended to interpret his career as a gradual evolution from that of a narrow Cretan environment to that of world statesmanship. This interpretation is unjustified. Venizelos *started* with a broad outlook; as he began his own law practice simultaneously with the practice of political journalism, the techniques and interests of each field favourably reinforced the other. It is thus virtually impossible to separate Venizelos the lawyer from Venizelos the journalist. The two overlap, mainly because editorial polemics were regarded in Crete as acts of political defiance; well-publicized and well-reasoned unionist positions could rapidly propel an attorney and journalist to the status of a hero in Cretan eyes. A young man capable of expressing popular grievances, without at the same time losing sight of wider horizons, could hope to forge ahead almost as rapidly in Crete as another young provincial of genius had in late revolutionary France.

By the spring of 1889 and at the age of twenty-four, with only one year's standing as a lawyer and journalist, Venizelos took the big step into active politics. In the Cretan general elections of April 1889 he contested the province of Kydonia as a Liberal Party candidate and won. This was the beginning of his active participation in the political and national movement of his country and added to his two practising professions a third.

THE MAKING OF A POLITICIAN

In the six years following Venizelos' election to the Cretan Assembly in 1889, we are confronted with the most obscure period of his early life. We have no concrete record covering these years, except for an important analysis which he prepared on the subject of his political ideas and general views on the Cretan question. It is a short essay describing the abortive revolution of 1889 and written during his self-imposed exile in Athens, from September 1889 to May 1890. The manuscript describes with remarkable clarity and even-handedness the events of these turbulent days as he witnessed them as a deputy of the Liberal Party. The document was recovered quite recently among his law practice papers; it is the only known retrospective on political events from Venizelos' hand.[55]

The political thought of Venizelos was nurtured in the years following the Pact of Chalepa and its implementation. As Venizelos reflects in his manuscript on the 1889 revolution and as we can see in the interesting memoranda that the Greek general consul in Crete, Ioannis Gryparis, addressed to the Greek foreign minister, Stephanos Dragoumis,[56] four elements characterised the post-Chalepa period: first, Turkey showed a reluctance to implement the Pact of Chalepa;[57] second, the two main Cretan parties started intense in-fighting;[58] third, the Great Powers' position vis-à-vis Crete was confused and inconsistent;[59] and lastly, the Greek government, as well as the Greek parties on the mainland, played an increasingly important role in directing Cretan policies.[60] All these issues were analysed by Venizelos in his editorials between December 1888 and June 1889 as well as reviewed in his essay on the 1889 revolution, as mentioned above.

The reluctance of Turkey to implement the clauses of the Pact of Chalepa was due to its objections to three specific clauses which referred to religious toleration, freedom of the press, and the appropriation of the island's revenues and taxes. Venizelos had addressed these issues while still a law student, in the interview with Chamberlain in 1886. In early 1889, Venizelos reiterated his position regarding freedom of the press and the improvement of the financial situation on the island. In two of his articles in the *Lefka Ori* he demanded from the governor general the strict application of the provisions of the Pact of Chalepa, as they had been amended by the firman of 12 July 1887. In an article on the right of freedom of the press of 23 January 1889, he compared the existing system to the Spanish Inquisition. 'Censorship and the muzzling of the press are the products of the Papal Synods of the Middle Ages and of the Holy Inquisition.'

In his essay on the events of 1889, Venizelos spoke in broader terms about the situation in Crete from 1878 to 1888 and presented five 'burning problems' directly responsible for the Porte's lack of progress in internal affairs: the lack of (1) an enlightened administration which would show strength both towards the central government and towards the island; (2) economics that fulfilled the needs of that service and supported the development of the country; (3) an enlightened system of justice, independent of pressures and worthy of its high mission; (4) public safety; and (5) a tax system free from the bad features of the existing one.

Although Venizelos vigorously berated the Porte for its short-sighted policies and its venality, he was far more bitter when reviewing another post-Chalepa phenomenon, the intense in-fighting between the two parties of the island over the right to political spoils. Since 1878, the Cretans had been divided into two main parties, the conservatives, or karavanades, and the liberals, or xypolitoi, each with its own ideology and party line, but both agreeing in wishing for the union of Crete with Greece. The comments of Venizelos in his 1889 essay on the differences between the two parties are of some interest here:

> As concerns the burning desire of the Cretan people for its national freedom . . . there will never be any disagreement among the Cretans . . . The difference of opinion among the Cretan politicians is strictly due to reasons connected with the existing internal state of affairs.

Between March and April 1889, Venizelos gave most of his time and energy to the election campaign. He knew his district well and had close professional and political contacts with many of his constituents. He was already well known in the district of Kydonia and was much admired for his talents as a lawyer and as a public speaker. He was well aware that the most effective issue of his election campaign would be the issue of union with Greece which, as he noted in his retrospective analysis, cut across party lines. He chose not to use his talents as a public speaker to inflame the nationalistic fervour of his compatriots. Instead, he used all his energies to address the constitutional, administrative and economic crises that had prevailed in the island since 1878 and the need for peaceful co-existence of the two parties as well as of the two religious communities. Since his first editorial in the *Lefka Ori* he had urged Cretans to exploit to the full the political and economic advantages granted to them by the Pact of Chalepa and to wait for a more propitious time for their national aspirations.

Certainly, Venizelos' election addresses were skilfully adapted to the circumstances. There was always acknowledgement of the union issue, but this was coupled with the warning that 'action now would plunge the country, prematurely and inappropriately, into a doomed fight and would leave her weak and incapable of functioning'.

As the election campaign was ending, Venizelos and his collaborators in the *Lefka Ori* published their final policy statement re-emphasising the need for 'the development of the moral and material forces of the Cretan people' and spelling out their political platform. The editors reminded their readers, too, that such a programme would be effective only through the collaboration of the two political parties. This collaboration was, they said, 'a patriotic duty'.[61]

The elections were held on 2 April and the result was declared the following day. For the first time in the newly-constituted Cretan parliament, the Liberal Party was able to secure a large majority. Among its elected members were the three editors of *Lefka Ori*, Charalambos Poloyiorgis, Constantinos Foumis, and Eleftherios Venizelos.

In the new General Assembly there were thirty-eight liberals and eleven conservatives. Of the thirty-eight liberals, eight belonged to the group of the *Lefkorites*. This informal group of like-minded friends was very well described by Gryparis:

> a group of representatives from the districts of Chania and Sphakia, young professionals [connected with the *Lefka Ori*] who belong to the majority party of the liberals but who, through the media and their behaviour in the assembly . . . disapprove of the lowly acts of their colleagues from the East.[62]

From the very first session of the assembly on 27 April, Venizelos attacked his own party on several issues, since his campaign for parliamentary reform took precedence over solidarity. He succeeded in making the maximum impact on the parliamentary scene: he already had the bearing of a party leader and he behaved like an exemplary parliamentarian. He argued the cases he presented to the assembly one by one, patiently and painstakingly, elucidating procedural matters, underlining the letter of the law and reproaching his fellow liberals for their failure to behave better than the conservatives now that they were in the majority: 'A party should be founded not merely on numbers. It needs moral principles without which it can neither serve the land nor its own ends.'[63]

Venizelos may have soon realised that the fierce debates in the first meetings of the Cretan Assembly would end in the failure of all efforts for a reconciliation of the two parties. Immediately after the election results he had published a 'peace offering' editorial in the *Lefka Ori* of 28 April 1889. 'We once more come offering our hand to our political adversaries and we invite them, nay, beg them, for a common effort and co-operation for the sake of the fatherland.' It is interesting to note that during the first period of the assembly, most of the proposals by Venizelos were voted down. His inclination to pursue an independent course of action, regardless of party affiliation and personal loyalties, was resented by his party and misunderstood by the opposition. Venizelos persisted, however.

The Cretan Assembly of 1889 was short-lived. A major crisis occurred on 6 May when five conservative deputies introduced a motion for union of Crete with Greece, in order to embarrass their opponents and attract the sympathy of the Christian population.[64]

From the very first, Venizelos sided with the cautious policies of the Greek government which, under the leadership of Charilaos Trikoupis, was reluctant to engage in new adventures. Trikoupis' and Consul Gryparis asked the Christian deputies to refrain from any hasty action in view of an unfavourable international situation. But the conservative leaders left the assembly, took to the mountains, raised an armed band in the province of Apokoronas, and soon set up a provisional government called The Committee.

During these crucial weeks, Venizelos was in constant touch with Gryparis. Although he avoided any contact with the rebel forces, he did try, through intermediaries, to persuade the leading chiefs of the insurrection to lay down their arms and agree to peace. At the same time, he and his friends sent telegrams to the Greek government asking it to help in preventing direct confrontation between the rebels and the Turkish troops by dispatching Greek forces to the island.

Venizelos and some of his friends – all well-known political leaders – left for Athens at the end of September 1889. In the following month, it seems that Venizelos spent a lot of time writing and studying – composing his essay on the abortive revolt, sending love-letters to his fiancée, becoming proficient in French, and starting to study English. Moreover, he and his political friends made a fresh attempt to persuade Trikoupis of the need for immediate action. In the as-yet-unpublished manuscript of Costis Foumis, the author described this interview in some detail, relating the group's secret meeting with Trikoupis, which took place the very first night of their arrival in Athens. During the meeting, the prime minister explained the reasons for his negative stance regarding the Cretan revolt and told the four exiled leaders that, as Lefkorites, they were the only group not responsible for the in-fighting in Crete. He also told them how frustrated he was by the untimely revolt, since he had been preparing in various ways – material, diplomatic, military and moral – for an eventual Cretan revolt that could occur at a more favourable time.[65]

This meeting shows the moderate policies of Charilaos Trikoupis and at the same time explains Venizelos' cautious policies in the 1890s, policies strongly influenced by Trikoupis' views regarding the Cretan problem.

All armed resistance was finally eliminated, Shakir lifted martial law on 16 April 1890 and declared a general amnesty. All exiled leaders returned, including those excluded from amnesty; among them was Eleftherios Venizelos.[66]

In sum, Venizelos' role as a first-term deputy had been small but effective. In this brief engagement in the political affairs of his island he had revealed himself as a man of energy, determination and decisiveness. Although the youngest among his peers he had been able to build up a small following in the assembly, give some cohesion to the new group of the Lefkorites, and command the confidence of the liberal and conservative deputies in the Cretan assembly, because of his respect for the principles of constitutionalism and his meticulous attention to procedural matters.

Venizelos' political creed at that time was simple: (1) moderate liberalism; (2) devotion to Greece; and (3) keeping the peace on the island. His brand of liberalism combined hostility to radical moves with opposition to the arbitrariness of government; he was the advocate of gradual development – economic, educational, political – for all classes on the island. His devotion to Greece was demonstrated by his accepting the Trikoupis government's policies on Crete.

Without repudiating his commitment to the national cause, Venizelos shared the fears of Trikoupis concerning a premature insurrection in Crete, realising that Greece was handicapped by the lack of an adequate army and navy and by the absence of allies. His adherence to peace was a result of his belief that a war between Greece and Turkey would be disastrous and that Crete would be better served if the Greeks heeded the advice of the Powers and remained quiet.

MARKING TIME

In the aftermath of the 1889 revolution and Greece's passivity on the Cretan problem, Venizelos withdrew from political activity. But his personal, political and intellectual development continued, shaping and consolidating his future political choices. These years also included the happiest and the most tragic moments of his family life.

In the autumn of 1890 he married Maria Eleftheriou Katelouzou in an elaborate ceremony in Topanas, attended by well-known members of Chania society, the consuls, and the other representatives of the Powers. The first of their children, Kyriakos, was born in 1892. Two years later Maria died giving birth to a second son, Sofoklis.

Maria's death plunged Venizelos into terrible grief from which he was slow to recover. For many weeks, he was incapable of working. The steadying influences of his family and of his close friend Klearchos Markantonakis, and his inner strength, gradually brought him back to his legal and political activities, but, according to his friends, he was never the same again.

We do not have any reliable medical information on Venizelos' mental and psychological make-up. But that the death of his wife brought to the surface unusual and deeper problems is undeniable. Venizelos returned to his law practice in the autumn of 1894. Through his professional work, he was slowly able to transmute his emotional problems. By plunging once more into political journalism he could attain a sort of catharsis.

It would take him two years, however, to involve himself once again in the politics of Crete.

Although Venizelos abstained from Cretan politics between 1890 and 1896, he repeatedly expressed his satisfaction at the appointment of Karatheodori Pasha. Soon after meeting the new governor general he became part of his inner circle and visited him often at his home. Despite the appointment of a Christian governor, however, during September 1895 there developed among the Christians a renewed movement demanding autonomy for the island, which expressed itself through the newly formed Reform Committee, Metapoliteftiki Epitropi. The able Sphakiot leader Manousos Koundouros, was appointed president of the committee.

Koundouros, an Athens-trained lawyer in Vamos, was respected by the Turks and liked by Biliotti. He believed in revolution leading first to autonomy and then to union with Greece, but only when union was feasible. This programme was endorsed by a mass meeting at Klima, Apokoronas, on 3 September 1895.

But not all the leaders agreed with him. Venizelos, in particular, re-entered revolutionary politics at this moment with the dangerously contrary opinion that the time was not ripe for open revolution. At Kamboi on 18 August 1896, he appeared as the representative from Chalepa; he was initially excluded on account of his views. His life was threatened by some Cretan representatives, who demanded his trial and execution. But this may have been simply a personal vendetta. This tentative step into politics was inconclusive but indicated his interest in re-entering the political arena.[67]

In these several years outside the formal political arena Venizelos' social relations were principally with Cretan professionals and intellectuals, Western consuls and the circle of Karatheodori Pasha, which undoubtedly contributed to the growth of his political thought. Indeed, we should see them not as years of abandonment and neglect but rather of retrenchment, intellectual development and consolidation. During this period of contemplating the lessons of the failed revolutions of the past and the initiatives of the present which he could not fully support, he developed the foundations of the philosophy and tactics which served him well later.

To the Cretan leaders and the outside world, including the Athens papers which had followed his career, his silence must have seemed to indicate the end of his political activity. But his next step was to be the leadership of the successful revolt which finally ended Ottoman rule in Crete, and transformed Venizelos from an Ottoman Cretan into a Cretan Greek.

VENIZELOS TURNS TO REBELLION

On 23 January 1897, on the promontory of Akrotiri, Venizelos joined the armed rebellion. It is a step that has been heroically celebrated: Akrotiri has been seen, in hindsight, as a destined moment, the first expression of Venizelos' brilliant leadership – as if by finally espousing rebellion he had set off a chain-reaction leading to freedom and justice for Crete. But in fact the moment was not of Venizelos' choosing; he was neither the initiator nor the leader of the Akrotiri revolt; and although his years of legal analysis, political journalism and parliamentary action had prepared him better than most for the calculation that now seemed to warrant armed resistance, that calculation was extremely problematic. The immediate background was the failure of the new reforms proclaimed by the Turks – under pressure from the Powers – in the summer of 1896.

The Greek government, pressed by the Cretan Committee and the irredentist National Society, opposed the new round of promises, the Christian Cretans distrusted them, the Muslims feared them; both sides knew that, after the Armenian massacres, Constantinople was on the defensive and under tremendous pressure from the Powers, who had indeed helped to formulate and promote the reforms. At the end of 1896, there were many scattered incidences of violence between Christians and Muslims; Muslims were abandoning their farms and Christians were fleeing the cities. The Powers had jointly mounted a small fleet, which lay outside the Bay of Chania to monitor the situation. In January, attacks on the Christian quarters of Chania were of such scope and violence that every household had to consider flight. Able-bodied men began to form armed bands in the hills around the city, and – perhaps the most significant new development – it was known that they had received arms and agents from the organised Cretan patriots in exile, with the tacit support of the Greek government. On 27 January the Greek government decided to send ships and troops to the island.

During the Chania disturbance, Venizelos was away from the city, campaigning for a seat in the new assembly, which had been defined by the sultan's reforms. But on 23 January, when he saw smoke rising from the city, he joined a group of armed Christians at Malaxa, who decided to remove themselves to Akrotiri. This would provide a staging ground for an attack on the communications between Chania and Souda, while also leaving open the possibility of communication with both the Greek consul in Chalepa and possibly a Greek fleet supplying them from the water.[68]

Venizelos' subsequent actions at Akrotiri form a central set-piece in the Venizelos myth. Following the long tradition of political hagiography, his biographers have often searched for those revealing 'stigmata' which are thought to be the inevitable accompaniment of later greatness. Thus Kerofilas tells us: 'Venizelos took command of the band of insurgents then concentrated at Akrotiri . . . The insurgents rendered him the most absolute obedience.' Alastos makes it sound as though Venizelos were all alone in this enterprise: 'Venizelos assumed the leadership of the 'Cretan Christian Defence Force' and established *his* [my emphasis] headquarters in Akrotiri.' Others have composed poems on Akrotiri and the role of Venizelos there, while editorials and articles speak of his bravery, his vision, his diplomatic genius and his perseverance.

The mythologising becomes more pronounced when we come to the 'famous scene' of 9 February. Kerofilas describes it thus:

> Venizelos turned towards the port of Souda, where the warships were anchored, and exclaimed: 'You have cannon-balls – fire away! But our flag will not come down' . . . . [after the flag was hit] Venizelos ran forward; his friends stopped him; why expose a valuable life so uselessly?

Gibbons concurs: 'On 20 February, Venizelos was ordered by the admirals to lower the flag and disband his rebel force. He refused'. Leeper adds: 'There was that famous day of February 1897 when . . . he rejected the orders of the Protecting Powers, and, in the picturesque phrase of the Greek newspapers, "defied the navies of Europe".' A writer in the *New York Times* reminds her readers:

> Under the smooth diplomat of today is the revolutionist who prodded the Turks out of Crete and the bold chieftain who camped with a little band of rebels on a hilltop above Canea and there defied the consuls and the fleets of all the Powers.[69]

The Akrotiri incident, then, although a goldmine for the study of Venizelos' leadership, is also a minefield of half-truths and embellishments by his admirers and critics.

Close examination of documentary evidence and cross comparison of the less reliable secondary materials allows a more dispassionate view. Indeed, even Venizelos' participation in Akrotiri, while appearing perfectly natural to his hagiographers, is a subtle and initially puzzling move.

Venizelos' role in an armed revolt at Akrotiri appears to reverse his earlier policy of gradualism, as expressed during the revolutionary assembly at Kamboi in August 1896. But upon closer analysis, his specific political and diplomatic tactics at Akrotiri conform with his general intellectual approach. Akrotiri is a turning point in his development from a legalistic idealist to a diplomatic pragmatist. To show this we must examine his objectives and the new circumstances presented at that time.

The first apparent contradiction at Akrotiri is his joint action with the insurgents in favour of enosis. We have seen that Venizelos was a moderate and had been prepared up to that point to accept reforms from the Ottoman government as a substitute for enosis, his long-term goal: at Kamboi, for example, he argued for eventual enosis and against Koundouros' conception of autonomy through revolt. But he had not fought directly for enosis in the past because he had not seen it as attainable nor as tactically desirable to promote. Now, it appeared both tactically appropriate and possibly attainable. At the end of January, the Greek government, prodded by the Cretan Committee and the National Society, had adopted a much more dramatically pro-Cretan policy, precipitated by repeated telegrams from Nikolaos Yennadis, Greek consul general at Chania. The decision to send a fleet and soldiers to the island was certainly an inspiration to local insurgents.

Another factor in Venizelos' changing position was that by the end of January, the increasing violence and disorder on the island had polarised the population. Venizelos must have felt that he could no longer call for moderation without compromising his patriotism.

A third significant factor was the Great Powers' increasingly direct involvement in the political and military affairs of Crete: a large fleet sat just off the coast while the consuls continued their customary involvement.

Under these complex and unstable circumstances, however, Venizelos cannot have believed that the Akrotiri revolt would itself be successful in military terms. Let us see why.

1. The Great Powers continued to be opposed to Cretan union with Greece for different reasons. The situation was dangerous for Greece. If she received satisfaction in Crete, a case might be made for compensating Serbia and Bulgaria in Macedonia. All in all, the new armed revolt could not expect military support from anywhere but Greece, and even that was not necessarily reliable.
2. The internal rift between the autonomists and the unionists weakened the unified front that the Cretans would have liked to present to the outside world. This rift was regional as well as ideological; the more pragmatic and mercantile eastern Cretans were perfectly willing to accept almost any solution which would allow the resumption of normal life and trade. So, Akrotiri would not have the backing of the whole Christian population.
3. The Turks, having promulgated the reform edict under pressure from the Powers following unrest in Crete and Armenia, welcomed a pretext to impose their traditional forms of government by force; and the

> Turko-Cretans, seeking to defend their privileges and their lands, would have welcomed armed support from the mother country.

On the other hand, Venizelos must have believed that the Akrotiri revolt could be productive. There were arguments to support this view.

1. Under the changing diplomatic circumstances, Venizelos, as a shrewd tactician, must have seen that revolution, even with a proclaimed goal of enosis, would push the Powers to act, which could only be to the good. Venizelos made this burningly clear when one of the officers of the British fleet suggested that a better policy would be to work with the Powers instead of forcing their hand: 'European policy is invariably the maintenance of the status quo, and you will do nothing for the subject races unless we, by taking the initiative, make you realise that helping us against the Turks is the lesser of two evils.'[70]
2. The Greek government, as represented by Yennadis, was at the moment willing to support the revolt with arms and ships.
3. Venizelos was confident that his long acquaintance with the European consuls would facilitate communication during a crisis and let him bargain with their governments.
4. Venizelos knew and felt that he was not alone; not just the peasants and their chiefs were in revolt in the countryside, his own social circle of Chania professionals had also joined the revolutionary movement.
5. The Armenian massacres and the atrocities in Chania had inflamed European opinion, and benign proclamations from the sultan could not erase their memory. In the wake of the news from Crete, the great newspapers of Europe had sent their correspondents as had philhellenic organisations. Venizelos was confident that he could use this attention to benefit the cause.
6. Greek public opinion, urged on by the National Society and the Cretan Committee in Athens, had reached hysterical proportions, silencing the voices of caution and sobriety. So, although there were powerful reasons for doubting that revolt could prevail, there were also convincing arguments for making the commitment to participation.

A WIDER STAGE

Venizelos' great moment came in 1897. Starting as one of 700 insurgents at Akrotiri, he immediately joined the leadership and soon rose to preeminence, a 'leader of leaders' in Chester's phrase. This strikingly rapid rise has been largely explained through his charisma and great force of character. Although this explanation surely captures an essential part of the story, more concrete reasons can be adduced which complement the myth. An analysis of events should be based on the revolutionaries' *Imerologion Akrotiriou* (*Diary of Akrotiri*), the only full and first-hand account of events within the insurgents' camp.[71] Previous analyses have been based mainly on consular reports and other official documents and have been concerned more with the international and diplomatic repercussions than with the actions of the Cretan leaders.[72]

The crucial days at Akrotiri begin with the revolutionaries' landing by boat at Arathi, with 100 men, on 23 January 1897. From that day until 11 April 1897, the details of the revolutionaries' activities, and more particularly those of Venizelos, shed light on the process of revolution and the process of leadership.[73]

On 24 January, Y. Milonoyannakis, N. Pistolakis and E. Venizelos, with twenty men, proceeded across the peninsula towards the western side of Akrotiri. The Turkish troops retreated ahead of them, but later they met resistance and firing continued until sunset. This was Venizelos' so-called 'great show of heroism and contempt of death which amazed everybody'.

That afternoon, a secret telegram arrived from the Greek Foreign Ministry announcing the imminent arrival of the warships *Hydra* and *Mykali*. The leaders at the consulate sent word to the insurgents.

That evening, some of the Akrotiri leaders – C. Mitsotakis, A. Sifakas, N. Zouridis and C. Foumis – met with Consul Yennadis in Chalepa to plan their strategy. At the meeting they decided to proclaim enosis, to call the king to take possession of the island, and to request military supplies from Greece. Yennadis enthusiastically forwarded these requests to Athens, while the Cretan leaders reported them to the insurgents, who eagerly drew up a proclamation, and circulated it throughout Crete.

On 26 January, a committee was formed on Akrotiri to deliver the petition to the Powers' representatives. The consuls received the petition coolly and repeatedly discouraged the revolutionaries. Venizelos stayed in Chalepa, sending notes to the Akrotiri insurgents on the moves of the foreign and Greek consuls.

On 3 February, a force of almost 2,000 Greek soldiers, under the command of Colonel Timoleon Vasos, the king's aide-de-camp, landed at Kolymbari, some miles west of Chania, and began a march on Chania, proclaiming the occupation of the island to the acclamation of the population and the insurgents.

The next day, the Ottoman governor general announced that the Powers had taken the major cities of Crete under their direct protection and that they would enforce a cessation of hostilities under threat of military intervention.

At this time, Venizelos and Archbishop Tsepetakis, on behalf of the insurgents, went to meet the commander of the Greek fleet, A. Reineck, on board the *Hydra*. When they requested weapons, Reineck immediately gave them two cannon and 267 Gras rifles. With great ceremony, he presented Venizelos with the Greek royal flag and with the command of four gunners. On 7 February, Prophitis Ilias was finally taken by seventy revolutionaries led by a group of twelve, among whom was Venizelos, and they raised the Greek flag. On 9 February the Powers fired on the flag on Prophitis Ilias, on the pretext that the insurgents had violated a six-kilometre neutral zone:

> The Turks fired on [our] positions and we replied . . . Suddenly, we heard a heavy barrage from the port, followed by a heavy rain of bombardment on the rebels from the direction of the European ships. The bombardment continued relentlessly, with the goal not only of frightening them but of finishing them off . . . While the Christians, amazed, stopped defending themselves, a Russian shell knocked down the Greek flag . . .[74]

This version, presented to the Greek parliament, indicates that the heavy bombardment came as a complete surprise to the insurgents. Other observers vary in their account. *The Times*' correspondent mentions a warning blank; Reuters, in *The Times*, reports warning shells. As it turned out, the exchange of fire substantially helped the cause of Greece and the fighters for enosis. That the defenders of Christianity had fired on the Greek flag and their co-religionists struggling to free themselves from the Turkish yoke shocked liberals throughout Europe and America. Venizelos was not even in Akrotiri at the time. Instead he 'was having a nip with the commander during the bombardment', according to Foumis fils.[75] He had been invited, together with Foumis and Kotsabasis, to the *Hydra* that day to discuss events with Yennadis and Reineck.

So far, we have seen Venizelos as one of a group of Cretan insurgents involved in dealing with the Greeks and the Powers. It is not clear what his influence in these preceding events was, although, knowing his later tactics, we might read his cleverness into the announcement of the Akrotiri events.

The bombardment and its echoes in international opinion led to a new state of affairs in which, for the first time, the European powers were forced to negotiate with the insurgents, still encamped on Akrotiri; in effect they had won acknowledgement as the representatives of Christian Crete. It is at this juncture that Venizelos' influence on events begins to be traceable, for he immediately became the chief negotiator with the Powers. This position as the insurgents' diplomat gave him great flexibility in setting and implementing policies. But he was not, as far as we can tell, a leader at this point. He did not marshal the Cretans in support of policies; he did not define their agenda for the future. This came later.

Venizelos' entry into diplomacy came with a letter of outrage and defiance, dated 10 February, addressed to the admirals and signed by twelve insurgent leaders.

> Since man has the right to rise against sovereign rule which offends human nature, we have occupied a strategic position overlooking Chania. We prepared to bombard the capital of the island and to eradicate by force the rule of the sultan, when, to our great consternation and our great surprise, we saw the flags of Christian, civilised Europe flying over the ramparts of Chania, warning us that our planned attack was forbidden . . . [our] national flag, around which we had all rallied, was hit by a Christian shell, but we all rushed to raise it once again, always ready to die for it . . . we declare that we shall remain faithful to our aspirations to death. Long live the king! Long live Enosis.[76]

The next six months of intense negotiations between the insurgents and the Powers' representatives defined the framework for the Cretan autonomy which was to follow. The important events between February and August are not movements of men and material, nor of attacks and replies, but rather the exchange of representatives and correspondence among the involved parties and the issuing of proclamations and declarations to the Cretan people and the European public. The following letter of Venizelos is justly seen as Venizelos' entry into diplomacy:

> [W]e think it necessary to declare that the only proper solution, the only just, equitable, and definitive solution, is the union of Crete with Greece. Any other solution would be merely a palliative; it would not give the country the benefits of a durable peace and enlightened government, and it would be the cause of the renewal of the late catastrophes, when the time came for the provisional solution to be exchanged for the definitive solution.[77]

In legalistic yet vivid prose, Venizelos, almost condescendingly, presents the Cretan case. Far more characteristically than his mythical bravery at Akrotiri, the composition of this letter is a true indication of the launching of a statesman's career: '[T]he incontrovertible logic of facts forces us to recognise the impossibility of a regular administration, either by Ottoman despotism or by an autonomous and independent constitution.'[78]

Another major diplomatic step was the formalisation of the insurgents' governance in Akrotiri on 22 February. This stable and well-defined committee was crucial to the development of influence with foreign powers, and also established that this was no band of undisciplined rebels but a properly constituted, even if presumptuous, provisional government suitable for such dealings.

The rise in prestige of the Executive Committee and of Venizelos himself is reflected in the extensive correspondence and many meetings with European representatives between February and August; social relations between the insurgents and the admirals were surprisingly warm. The first direct, but low-key meeting of the admirals with the insurgents took place on 26 February. The next meeting had more substance. Sifakas, Venizelos, Milonoyannakis, Foumis, Pistolakis and Kotsabasis were invited to the Russian warship *Alexander II* on 7 March. No doubt Foumis' introduction of each as 'lawyer' or 'doctor' impressed the admirals, who received them and served them tea. At this meeting, each side politely but firmly presented its position. The meeting made it clear that no simple resolution would be possible. Venizelos, however, persuaded the admirals to send him, under their protection, on a tour of the island, in order to explore the people's opinions on the question of autonomy versus enosis.[79]

But the comfortable negotiations in the Bay of Chania could not much longer remain relevant, after the Great Powers began their own negotiations on the future of Crete and when, on 6 April, the National Society provoked the Turks in Thessaly with an attack, starting the catastrophic Greco-Turkish war of 1897, which ended precipitously on 6 May. In this crisis the Greek government recalled the occupying commander, Vasos, in April and the Powers blockaded Crete.[80]

With the success of the Turks in Thessaly and the increased pressure of the Powers for a solution to the Cretan problem, those Cretans who had always been willing to accept autonomy were joined by the larger group which had hoped for enosis but now became persuaded that it was unrealistic.

The ability of the Akrotiri Executive Committee to present a unified front to the outside was eroded and its leaders could no longer count on a monopoly of communications with the foreign powers in whose hands the future of the island lay. Thus the political direction of the island slipped from the virtually self-appointed Akrotiri Executive Committee and the parliamentary forms of revolutionary assemblies had to be revived.

The first small revolutionary assembly, which was to bring together representatives from all Crete, was held in Spili, roughly halfway between Chania and Irakleion, presumably beyond the influence of the European Powers.

And afterwards, at the Armenoi meeting, which lasted from 26 June to 10 July, it was decided not to discuss the question of union versus autonomy, but rather to confine discussion to internal matters, which were certainly pressing enough. A group of three – Venizelos, Tsouderos and Foumis – was selected to present this decision to Admiral Canevaro, the senior commander of the international fleet, who approved and promised them that the Great Powers would tend to the Cretan problem after a peace treaty between Greece and Turkey had been signed. The hand of the Venizelos faction can be discerned in the decision to discuss the political question, when the time came, near the admirals' headquarters – in Armenoi if they remained at Chania. But, presumably in compromise, the next meeting was held in Archanes, twelve kilometres from Irakleion, the easterners' city but beyond the Powers' influence.

The assembly convened at Archanes on 5 August. Venizelos brought a group of supporters and was elected the same day as president. There are two main accounts of what followed, Venizelos' own[81] and Koundouros'[82]. The two accounts begin by agreeing that Venizelos stubbornly insisted that there should be no discussion of autonomy versus union. Venizelos claims that the autonomists took advantage of the return of a number of delegates to their villages to turn the assembly to their own ends. Koundouros says simply: 'The agents of the [the Greek] consulate, [i.e. Venizelos et al.] [were] repulsed . . . The people, however, prevailed and the declaration was passed.' The proceedings were hardly as civil as Koundouros suggests. In fact, a shouting match started and a brawl broke out, Venizelos' party refusing to concede. In the midst of the violence, Venizelos was threatened: his opponents spoke of 'verbal abuse and cursing'; he and his supporters and myth-makers speak of an attempt on his life. Venizelos adjourned the assembly and, angered, refused to participate further in its deliberations. He was immediately stripped of his post as president and excluded from all future sessions, after only three days in office. The declaration for autonomy passed.

At Archanes, Venizelos remained stubbornly in the unionist camp, sacrificing his post as president and any hope of influencing the assembly by his strict adherence to a doomed policy. Is it possible that he was acting in obedience to the National Society or the Greek government? It is still not known to what extent his thoughts and actions were influenced by agents of the mainland, or whether he was a member of the National Society, this 'invisible power'. He was certainly frequently accused of it by his opponents and he certainly denied it himself. His frequent trips to Athens would have given him the opportunity, if he were indeed a member, to receive orders. He and his friends were also in constant communication with the Greek consul general at Chania, Nikolaos Yennadis, and their relations were exceedingly warm. The consul general's brother, Stephanos Yennadis, was a member of the National Society's 'Supreme Committee'.

Whatever the effect of the National Society or the pressures from the Greek government, Venizelos' intransigence may also have been driven by pure idealism. As discussed earlier, his newspaper writings before his active involvement in politics are almost utopian in their vision of a changed Cretan polity and society. It is true that ten years had passed since then. In an interview he gave in 1896, he exhibited considerable pragmatism in saying that 'small countries must adjust to the circumstances and accept the fulfilment of their national desires by degrees'. Finally, unless we are willing to join his enemies in attributing his entire political behaviour to greed and ambition, idealism must explain not only his positions but also the obstinacy with which he pursued them.

Venizelos' idealism and legal methodology, then, both help to account for his unproductive stance. If he was a member of the National Society, it is not likely that it dictated to him; it is more probable that their goals simply often coincided. He may also have overestimated the weight of his personal views as president, and his own persuasive powers.

After the dramatic rupture at Archanes, Venizelos left for Chania. A month later he travelled to Athens and in September he returned to Crete with Sphakianakis, whom he persuaded to return as an elder statesman and lead the assembly, which had now been legitimised by the Powers' promulgation of autonomy. Sfakianakis was elected president at Melidoni, Mylopotamos. Venizelos, too, was welcomed with cheers by his Western comrades. In his stirring and now conciliatory address to the assembly delegates, he movingly rejoined them in the long march towards the national ideal:

> Although the long years of slavery have created great divisions in our midst, we should now come together, united, and lift up our long-trampled fatherland (applause). And, indeed, our country was trampled. What we achieve today is *not* the vision of our fathers nor is it our dream of yesteryear (cheers and applause). But if our pursuit of a wise and upright policy can only lead to the realisation of the promises of the Great Powers, we shall see rising on our island our own free nation with its own flag and its own army, pursuing, unshackled, its destiny of culture and peace, bound only by the most nominal ties to its former sovereign. And, so, shall we march bravely forward towards the fulfilment of our National Destiny . . .[83]

FROM AUTONOMY TO UNION

For the rest of 1897 and through 1898, Venizelos was heavily involved in the deliberations of the Cretan Executive Committee which was responsible for negotiating the form of autonomy with representatives of the Powers.[84] The Powers' intent at first was to negotiate autonomy under Ottoman suzerainty and with the appointment of a Christian governor. However, in the wake of the Irakleion massacres of 25 August 1898, the Great Powers were finally persuaded that all Turkish influence had to cease. On 3 November, under orders from the Powers, the troops of the sultan started to withdraw from the island, marking the end of 253 years of Ottoman rule.

After long deliberations on substance and alternative candidates, Prince George of Greece was appointed high commissioner of the newly autonomous Crete on 18 November 1898. The prince was to act on behalf of the Powers while the Porte retained a nominal suzerainty over the island. The prince's arrival in Crete on 9 December of that year was greeted with wild enthusiasm by the Christian population, which interpreted his installation in the island as an indication that Cretan union with the mainland was drawing nearer.[85]

With autonomy, a new legal structure had to be drawn up, and, on 25 December a committee of sixteen was chosen to work out a constitution. Not surprisingly, given his political and legal background, Venizelos was made a member of the committee and played an important role in the drafting of the constitution.[86] In the elections of 24 January 1899, under the new regime, Venizelos won a seat as a representative of Chania in the Cretan Assembly; in March of that year the assembly voted in the constitution of the Cretan state.[87] Immediately thereafter, in April, he was appointed councillor for justice in the first cabinet of Prince George.

The contributions of Venizelos to the drafting of the constitution, to the deliberations of the Cretan Assembly, and to the reorganisation of the island's legal system in his capacity as councillor of justice were decisive for the future of the young state. Venizelos entered the scene as a leading figure in the sixteen-member committee and soon became the protagonist in the debates for the ratification of the constitution in the Cretan Assembly. As its principal author, he was later criticised for many of its articles. The constitution was called 'an extremely conservative document', 'a grave and inexcusable error'. Even Venizelos thought so. He wrote to a member of the Cretan Assembly a few years later: 'My responsibility [for the prince's autocratic behaviour] is great since my influence was strong in the writing of the conservative constitution of 1899.'[88]

The constitution, in fact, was rather loose and although conservative, quite unorthodox; as a consequence, it created serious problems in its application. For example, Prince George of Greece, the high commissioner, was the representative of the Great Powers on the island but also had 'a contract' with the Cretan people. He was the central agent of the state, *and* the main executive officer, *and* an important member of the legislature. As Sphakianakis, chairman of the committee, declared, the commissioner was the centre of all power. On the other hand, the members of the government were, according to the constitution, councillors to the prince, directly responsible to him rather than to the assembly. Concurrently however, they were elected representatives in the assembly. This fact would certainly have produced some confusion and conflicts of allegiance, although there was a a clause forbidding them to exercise their function as representatives while holding the post of councillor. The Cretan Assembly, which was elected through universal male suffrage every two years, was also not given enough powers: it was to meet only once during its two-year term and had a very limited jurisdiction, since the final ratification of laws was within the high commissioner's rights.

Was Venizelos responsible for the conservative character of the Cretan constitution? And was he, really, the main moulder of the constitution? On this, views differ. According to one theory, the constitution of the Cretan State was conservative because the Cretan people, as well as the committee, believed in a strong executive, free of parliamentary interference, as the best short-term solution to the political problems of the island. On the other hand, the Special Committee of Inquiry, which was sent to Crete in March 1906 to assess the situation on the island, concluded that the committee of sixteen who had drafted the constitution did not consider autonomy as a permanent solution, since it did not settle the nationalist aspirations of the Cretans; instead, they saw it as a short, transitional answer, a prelude to enosis. In the meantime, the island would be better served by a strong leader and a monarchical government.

In the meetings of the constitutional committee, Venizelos strongly advocated a liberal policy towards the Turko-Cretans in the island and made sure to insert clauses guaranteeing their complete religious freedom and political equality. We see him debating these issues point by point in the minutes, where he reminds the representatives of the Turko-Cretans that it would be to their advantage to seek equal treatment rather than set themselves apart from the community and the laws of the island.

The spirit of co-operation, apparent in the discussion of the draft of the constitution between Christians and Muslims, was largely due to Venizelos' firm but sympathetic handling of Muslim demands.

The constitution demonstrated the liberal leanings of its framers in other ways too. The strength of its articles dealing with the guaranteed freedoms of the individual was largely due to the insistence of Venizelos and his firm – almost intransigent – stance.

In sum, Venizelos and his colleagues in the committee framed a conservative document, fully aware of its shortcomings and its restrictive clauses. They did so in the hope that the status of autonomy for the island would be of short duration. With enosis, a separate Cretan constitution would become unnecessary. They also had reason to hope that the term of the prince would not exceed the three-year initial appointment. With such extensive powers he would be able to organise the island quickly and efficiently so that union with the motherland would soon follow and they trusted the prince to interpret and exercise his almost unlimited power in a broad, liberal way.

The framers were soon to be disappointed on all counts.

On 17 April 1899, Venizelos was appointed councillor for justice in the first cabinet of Prince George, which also included: Constantinos Foumis, Manoussos Koundouros, Nikolaos Yamalakis and Hussein Yanitsarakis, a Muslim. Dr Ioannis Sphakianakis declined the offer to serve the prince, claiming ill health but in fact having misgivings about the prince's intentions and his ability to govern properly. Moreover, no councillor for foreign affairs was appointed, since the conduct of foreign policy had traditionally been left in the hands of the royal family of Greece. This was to have disastrous effects, bringing about the grave political crisis of 1901–6.

Venizelos kept the post of councillor for Justice for almost two years (from April 1899 to March 1901). In a very short period of time he was able to accomplish a tremendous amount of work of the highest calibre: he reorganised the law courts, introduced an up-to-date judicial system, inaugurated a modern police system, and organised the gendarmerie. The high quality of work as well as the smooth internal reshaping of the courts surprised the Powers and was noted even by Prince George at the time.[89] In order to accomplish this difficult and demanding job, Venizelos worked long hours, continually consulting his rich library of books on law and political economy. Much later he told N. Avraam, who had been appointed minister of justice in his cabinet in 1930: 'When I was serving as councillor for justice in Crete . . . I once remained locked in the ministry for four consecutive days and nights without food or sleep, because I was in a hurry to finish the work.'[90] Due to Venizelos' tremendous effort, the working of justice made a smooth and effective transition. There was no possibility for political trade-offs under the new system of appointments. As Venizelos said later: 'It ceased to be a spider's web, which can easily catch the weak but is, in turn, easily destroyed by the strong.'[91]

Venizelos worked in all areas of law during his term of office and, according to experts, demonstrated 'real legal genius'. His most arduous legal work was the drafting of the 335 modifications of the Cretan legal procedures, which he wrote personally and which later became the basis for the reorganisation of the Greek judicial system as well. During his two-year term in office Venizelos was able completely to revise the civil, commercial and criminal codes as well as the code of procedure, install twenty-six justices of the peace, and organise five courts of first instance, one court of appeal, five police courts and two assize courts. All these courts functioned with impartiality and effectiveness.

He was also given the significant task of the restructuring of the gendarmerie. He staffed this service with experienced Italian officers. In a few months there was a complete change of attitude: the Cretans, who had earlier regarded the gendarmerie with fear and contempt, were now proud to serve in it. They were well drilled and did their job seriously and conscientiously.

Venizelos was at the height of his physical and intellectual powers at this time. In his mid-thirties, riding high in the aftermath of the successful Akrotiri revolt; the protégé of a widely respected politician, Ioannis Sphakianakis, whom he viewed as a mentor and friend; accepted by Chania society and the wider international milieu of the foreign consuls, foreign correspondents, merchants; respected by his colleagues for his deep knowledge of legal affairs; head of a law firm which was considered one of the most successful on the island – he had entered public office with all the vigour and enthusiasm he had displayed in his early years as a young journalist and politician. When the constitution was finally accepted by the Powers and the Cretan Assembly adopted it, he had every right to take credit. He had, however, to come to terms with the fact that the Cretans were at the time so unified in their attitudes towards the high commissioner, who was the symbol of national unity, the idol of the people who was to provide at least symbolic solutions to all their problems, that anything short of full support for the prince and personal devotion would have been interpreted as treason to the national cause. So, Venizelos, casting aside his uneasiness about the personality of the prince, elected to remain in the government where he worked with zeal and loyalty in the area he knew best: the formulation of new laws for the country. The clash was to come later; under the circumstances, it could hardly have been avoided.

VENIZELOS AND THERISSO: A STAGED REVOLT

With the revolution of 1897, the final rebellion of the Cretans against the Turks, Venizelos was recognised in Crete as a national hero. With the Great Powers, and among the Cretans, he established a reputation as a fighter and negotiator. But it was the Therisso coup which established his fame as a nationalist and a liberal and progressive political figure among his fellow Cretans and, more importantly, in mainland Greece.

Curiously, the Therisso episode has only been rather belatedly addressed by serious scholarship. Contemporary comment was highly partisan and, until the definitive study by Constantinos Svolopoulos, based on a thorough study of contemporary documents, partisan polemic remained the only discussion of the episode.[92]

On one hand, Venizelos' supporters have portrayed the prince as having abandoned his original promises to the Cretan people, and Venizelos as the realistic but firm leader towards national union. On the other, Prince George's supporters have seen only blind ambition and irresponsible mischief-making in Venizelos' actions.

The Therisso revolt started on 10 March 1905, but its origin was Venizelos' dismissal from office on 19–20 March 1901. The clash between Venizelos and the high commissioner was precipitated by the attitude of Prince George on foreign policy and his unwillingness to accept a real dialogue with his councillors and his constituents on the national question and on the internal affairs of the island.

In keeping with the traditional conception of foreign policy as the privileged domain of the monarchy, Prince George took it upon himself to work towards the annexation of the island to Greece, without consulting his councillors on how to go about it. He initiated direct personal discussions with the tsar of Russia and the foreign ministers of Russia, France, Britain and Italy.

Venizelos believed this move to be premature, since the form and nature of the Cretan government were still poorly defined and unstable. Instead, he now publicly advocated the creation of a Cretan army. The Powers were to be asked to withdraw their garrisons. He argued that, in this way, Crete would gradually shake off international control, and at the first opportunity she could declare for union with Greece. Few understood the intentions of this new approach. The majority interpreted it as an attempt to declare Crete an independent state and to dissociate her from Greece. The Athenian press, misinformed by the entourage of the prince, launched a vicious attack against what it termed 'a new treachery'.

Soon, however, Venizelos' proposal was no longer at issue; the whole discussion proved academic for on 9 February 1901 the Powers sent a note with their answer to the prince's initiative: 'The Powers . . . are unanimously of the opinion that they are unable, under present circumstances, to sanction any change whatsoever in the island's political status in the direction suggested by Prince George . . .' Even so, Venizelos was again the victim of editorial attacks in such widely-read Greek newspapers as *Estia*, *Asty* and *Kairoi*, which called him 'an enemy of union' and 'a traitor'.

No longer able to co-operate with his enemies, Venizelos submitted his resignation on 5 March, pleading ill-health. This the prince refused to accept, saying that leaving the task before the work of reorganisation was completed was high treason. Venizelos submitted his resignation a second time on 18 March, stating more explicitly he could no longer serve any useful purpose by remaining in the government, where he was in constant disagreement with his colleagues and the high commissioner. Again his resignation was refused. The prince preferred to dismiss Venizelos for insubordination, rather than allow him the symbolic value of his resignation. Thus, on 20 March, a broadside appeared on all the walls of Chania, which announced his dismissal by the prince.

Immediately thereafter, the prince launched a campaign of vilification, using a variety of means. A series of articles, written possibly by the private secretary of the high commissioner, called Venizelos 'the insolent councillor' and criticised his policies as being anti-union, anti-dynastic, and pro-Powers. Meanwhile, the prince's private secretary sent periodic reports to the Greek foreign ministry describing Venizelos' various activities, and portraying him as probably a puppet of French policy and certainly anti-union and anti-Greek. Meanwhile, King George's government, which continued to support the prince's positions through its diplomatic contacts, also fed the Athenian press with anti-Venizelist propaganda. Their insistence paid off: foreign representatives in Crete such as Bourchier, Reinach, Softazadé, van der Brule, and foreign newspapers such as *The Times*, *Le Temps* and *The Tribune*, declared their conviction that the only solution to the Cretan question was the ultimate union of the island to Greece. On this, however, they advocated patience.

How can we explain the virulence of the prince's continuing polemic against Venizelos? It really appears disproportionate to the threat. After all, all the parties involved were seeking enosis one way or another. There were, of course, real differences between the approach of the prince and that of Venizelos. But few understood them. Certainly the prince never understood Venizelos' position. It was not a matter of feigning; the prince was just not able to follow the distinction Venizelos was making between the present situation of the dynastic government in Crete under foreign tutelage and true autonomy, free of foreign interference, with a Cretan governor approved by the Greek government, that Venizelos was advocating as the best step toward the achievement of union. There was another reason for the prince's opposition. Fundamentally, it appears that Prince George jealously guarded his powers and not only refused real participation in decision-making but even resented outside discussion of what he considered to be his personal domain. Often, he was abusive and even violent towards old Cretan chieftains. 'He told us,' old Papayannakis said, 'that he will act independently and that he will kick away the constitution, the laws, and all the Cretans, if he so wishes.'[93]

So, for Prince George the only pressures that counted would come from the Great Powers; internal politics were, at best, irrelevant. He failed to recognise the importance of political mobilisation among the Cretans themselves, and their long-frustrated desire to control their own destiny after centuries of struggle against the Turks. By the same token he failed to take seriously the new political currents in the island and the young dynamic men represented by Venizelos and his group – the rising bourgeoisie of the cities: merchants, doctors, lawyers, professors, intellectuals and even the young farmers in the countryside, who were taking exception to their fathers' loyalty towards the Greek prince.

Following his dismissal, Venizelos seems to have remained politically inactive for a while. But in December 1901, in response to the continuing anti-Venizelist attacks from the Athenian and the Cretan press, he launched his famous series of five articles in the Cretan newspaper *Kiryx* (*Herald*) under the dramatic title ' Let there be Light'. Venizelos responded in a dry and rational style to the 'libels' made against him; first, rather than defending his own conduct, laying out a tactical chronicle of the prince's rule and declaring his own position by presenting a conceptual basis for his political actions. As the series continued, though, he became more aggressive: 'When authority takes the people's liberties away by force, this opens the path to legitimate revolution and once this path is taken the victor will always be the people.' In practice, Venizelos remained pragmatic and constructive. During 1902 he met with the Greek prime minister, Alexandros Zaimis, and tried in vain to resolve the situation. He made every effort, in fact, to escape from the impasse through discussion and compromise. But the prince's government took the opposite approach: it closed down the *Kiryx* and imprisoned Venizelos for libel. Finally, in March 1905, after four years of discussion, Venizelos took the drastic step of organising a coup, the so-called 'Revolt of Therisso'.[94] He had contracted in great secrecy, starting in February 1905, with seventeen Cretan leaders who made up his 'inner group'.

The 300 revolutionaries who joined the seventeen signatories in their revolt had an immediate impact. They constituted no great military threat – although they would prove hard to dislodge from their isolated sanctuary in Therisso – but their political impact was electric. The immediate result was an influx of sympathisers – about 7,000 supporters joined them at Therisso over a period of twenty days. This time, Venizelos was unequivocally their leader.

On 10 March, he announced through broadsheets directly to the people of Crete that there was no hope for enosis as long as Prince George remained high commissioner, and that the only solution was to incorporate Crete into the kingdom of Greece.

At that point the Great Powers began to take notice. On 25 March, Venizelos submitted a memorandum to them, in conciliatory tone. His purpose was to expose the high commissioner, exercise moral pressure, and avoid open conflict with the Powers. In this he succeeded brilliantly. The outbreak of the revolt brought Venizelos more dramatically than ever before into the limelight. The Greek press devoted columns to it and sent its best representatives to the island to meet the leaders of the revolt.[95] Public meetings were held in Crete and in Athens; Venizelos' name became known to the Greeks of the mainland. Amazingly enough, he was finally able to arrange to meet the representatives of the Powers to discuss Crete's political future, and, even more amazingly, he persuaded them to withdraw their support from the prince. The revolutionary camp was disbanded in November.

During 1906 control over Crete shifted from the prince to the Powers, who agreed to set up a board of inquiry to examine the internal problems of the island. Elections in May gave Venizelos' party a minority in the assembly, but Prince George finally left Crete in September. The victory at Therisso not only brought about substantial hopes for changes on the island but it also established Venizelos' reputation on mainland Greece. Venizelos' visit to Athens, immediately after the end of the hostilities, was greeted with enthusiasm by the Athenians and their political leaders, who called him the bearer of new ideas and political methods. As a negotiator he was seen as pragmatic and effective. As a politician he was viewed as a man who was trying to introduce a novel political methodology and bold thinking, a young leader willing to advance new positions and new solutions to old problems. In short, a man competent to settle not only the problems of Crete but perhaps those of mainland Greece as well.

ENVOI

In the wake of the Young Turk movement in 1908 and the loss of Bosnia-Herzegovina and Eastern Rumelia to Turkey, the Cretan Assembly attempted to proclaim union, but again the Powers vetoed it.

In March 1910, after elections, Venizelos became president and prime minister of Crete; but not for long. The leaders of the Military League in Greece, a reform group which had executed a coup d'état in August 1909, invited him to Athens. On 12 September 1910 he resigned his Cretan positions and on 5 October he became prime minister of Greece.

On 14 October 1913, Crete finally achieved union with Greece. At the fort of Firkas in Chania, on 6 December, King Constantine of Greece and Eleftherios Venizelos together ceremonially raised the Greek flag over Crete.

Venizelos the Cretan was at last a Greek, and a Greek leader, once more the young favourite from whom much was hoped and of whom much might be forgiven. New constraints and disappointments would attend his maturity as an international statesman, but our story ends at this moment of happiness restored.

NOTES

1. Nikolaos Tomadakis (1964), O *Venizelos ephivos* [*Venizelos as a Youth*], Athens, pp. 21–2, quoting from Giorgios Papantonakis (1928), *I politiki stadiodromia tou Eleftheriou Venizelou* [*The Political Career of Eleftherios Venizelos*], Athens, pp. 11–12; D. Alastos (1942), *Venizelos: Patriot Statesman Revolutionary,* London, pp. 7–8; D. Pournaras (1961), *Eleftherios Venizelos*, Athens, vol. I, p. 16; P. Yiparis (1955), *Eleftherios Venizelos, o megas dimiourgos* [*Eleftherios Venizelos, the Great Innovator*], Athens, p. 18; G. Ventiris (1931), *I Ellas tou 1910–20. Istoriki meleti* [*Greece 1910–20. A Historical Study*], Athens, vol. I, p. 51; S. B. Chester of Wethersfield and Blabby (1921), *Life of Venizelos,* London and New York. For a recent discussion on the above see: Lilly Macrakis (2001), *Eleftherios Venizelos 1864–1910. I diaplasi enos ethnikou igeti* [*Eleftherios Venizelos 1864–1910. The Formative Years of a National Leader*], Athens, pp. 97–103; Appendix B-1 (p. 443) presents a tentative family tree of the Venizelos family.
2. The whole series of letters, both official and family correspondence, was collected by Errikos Moatsos and covers the period 1846–83. They are now housed in the archives of the University of Crete, in Rethymnon (AMO). For the correspondence of the years 1876 to 1879 see also Tomadakis *O Venizelos* (see Note 1).
3. AMO; 30 April 1846. See also O. Dimitrakopoulos (1977), 'Dyo

Othomanika eggrapha yia ton patera tou Venizelou' ['Two Ottoman Documents Concerning the Father of Venizelos'], in O. Dimitrakopoulos and Th. Veremis (eds), *Meletimata gyro apo ton Venizelo kai tin epochi tou* [*Studies on Venizelos and His Time*], Athens, pp. 701–11.

4. See the Macrakis version of his family tree and also *Apographi Ellinon ypikoon Chanion* [*Census of Greek Subjects Residing in Chania*], 1862, Gennadius Library.
5. Letter of Bishop Gavriil, AMO, 7 August 1880.
6. S. Stephanou (1975), *O Venizelos opos ton ezisa apo konta* [*Venizelos, As I Knew Him From Nearby*], Athens, vol. I, pp. 21–3, 309.
7. There is uncertainty regarding the exact date of Venizelos' birth. However, two relevant documents are known: (1) a certificate issued on 4 July 1874, (2) a certificate issued in July 1880, equivalent to high school diploma, stating that Venizelos was sixteen years old at the time; see Tomadakis, *O Venizelos*, pp. 8, 93, 97 (see Note 1). His approximate date of birth is 23 August 1864, that is, 11 August in the old calendar. See Macrakis, *Eleftherios Venizelos*, p. 444 (see Note 1).
8. See the Macrakis version of the family tree, Appendix B, where details on the whole family can be checked.
9. Herbert Adams Gibbons (1923), *Venizelos*, Boston, 2nd edn, p. 3; I. Mourellos (1964), *Venizelos, oi agapes tou, oi chares tou, oi odynes tou* [*Venizelos, His Loves, His Joys, His Pains*], Athens, pp. 39–41.
10. Gibbons, *Venizelos*, pp. 1–2 (see Note 9); Yiparis, *Eleftherios Venizelos*, p. 2 (see Note 1); Th. A. Vaidis (1964), *Vivlos Eleftheriou Venizelou* [*The Eleftherios Venizelos Bible*], Athens, vol. I, p. 59.
11. Vaidis, *Vivlos*, vol. I, p. 59 (see Note 10); K. Kerofilas (1915), *Eleftherios Venizelos: His Life and Work*, London.
12. Vaidis, *Vivlos*, p. 63 (see Note 10); Yiparis, *Eleftherios Venizelos*, p. 20 (see Note 1); Pournaras, *Venizelos*, p. 17 (see Note 1).
13. Tomadakis, *O Venizelos*, pp. 94–5 (see Note 1).
14. Venizelos became a Greek citizen in Syros. His father had become a Greek citizen during his first exile in the 1820s.
15. Letter of Kyriakos Venizelos to Eleftherios Venizelos, 19 September 1877, AMO.
16. See Mourellos, *Venizelos*, pp. 2–28 (see Note 9), who claims that the 'town fathers' of Mournies were calling him a trouble-maker.
17. His best friends in the early days were Antonakakis, Kapsalis and Ioannidis; see Tomadakis, *O Venizelos*, p. 107 (see Note 1). Most of his childhood friends belonged to the same milieu as Venizelos and had careers in the professions, mostly law and medicine.
18. Yiparis, *Eleftherios Venizelos*, p. 26 (see Note 1); Mourellos, *Venizelos*, p. 32 (see Note 9).
19. The following teachers were part of its staff: in religion, the famous historiographer of the patriarchates, Manuel Gedeon; in Roman and medieval

history, Professor Papavasiliou of the Chalki School of Theology (Tomadakis, pp. 125–6; Kyriakos Venizelos to Eleftherios Venizelos, Chania 27 March 1878, AMO).

20. Kyriakos to Lefteris, Chania 13 March 1878, AMO.
21. For this year at the high school of Syros, see the articles of Vrasidas Tomakas (1936), 'Eleftherios Venizelos was a Student at the Gymnasium of Syros', *Anagennisis Tinou* [*Tinos Renaissance*], 9 April; and in (1962) *Chronika tou Gymnasiou Arrenon Syrou* [*Chronicle of the Syros Boys' High School*], Syros, pp. 89–90.
22. Yiparis, *Eleftherios Venizelos*, p. 31 (see Note 1); Mourellos, *Venizelos*, p. 51 (see Note 9); Gibbons, *Venizelos*, p. 4 (see Note 9).
23. S. Pallis (1965), 'O Venizelos os nomikos kai dikigoros' ['Venizelos as a Legal Expert and a Lawyer'], *Nomikon Vima* 10, p. 533; Alastos, *Patriot*, pp. 8, 9 (see Note 1); Gibbons, *Venizelos*, p. 5 (see Note 9); Mourellos, *Venizelos*, pp. 53–4 (see Note 9); I. Manolikakis (1971), *I Kritiki Epanastasis tou 1889* [*The Cretan Revolution of 1889*], Athens, p. 18.
24. Pallis, 'O *Venizelos os nomikos kai dikigoros*', p. 533 (see Note 23).
25. Mourellos, *Venizelos*, pp. 34–5, 58 (see Note 9); Manolikakis, *Epanastasis*, pp. 16–17 (see Note 23).
26. Mourellos, *Venizelos*, pp. 58–61 (see Note 9); Manolikakis, *Epanastasis*, pp. 21–3 (see Note 23); Alastos, *Venizelos*, p. 9 (see Note 1).
27. The letter of Venizelos is dated 6 March 1883, AMO.
28. Mourellos, *Venizelos*, p. 723 (see Note 9); Yiparis, *Eleftherios Venizelos*, p. 33 (see Note 1); Tomadakis, *O Venizelos*, p. 87 (see Note 1); Mourellos, pp. 72–3; Yiparis, p. 33; AMO.
29. Oral communications of M. Foumis, Th. Mitsotakis, E. Moatsos.
30. Manolikakis, *Epanastasis*, p. 22 (see Note 23); Yiparis, *El. Venizelos*, p. 33 (see Note 9).
31. *Akropolis*, 1 November 1866, no. 1,377. Many accounts of the Chamberlain interview survive: Pournaras, *El. Venizelos*, vol. I, pp. 20–4, n. 1 (see Note 1); Mourellos, *Venizelos*, pp. 75–86 (see Note 9); Papantonakis *Stadiodromia*, pp. 21–32 (see Note 1); Manolikakis, *Epanastasis*, pp. 26–34 (see Note 23); Yiparis, *El. Venizelos*, pp. 35–6 (see Note 1). At the time, only *Nea Ephimeris* [*New Journal*], 5 November 1886, published the entire interview. The interview was also mentioned later by the British Ambassador in Athens, S. Waterlow to J. Simon, 19 March 1935, PRO F. O. 371.
32. Papantonakis, *Stadiodromia*, p. 32 (see Note 1); Pournaras, *El. Venizelos*, pp. 20–2 (see Note 1); Mourellos, *Venizelos*, p. 85 (see Note 9).
33. See *Nea Ephimeris*, 17 January 1887; Papantonakis, *Stadiodromia*, p. 17 (see Note 1); Stephanou, *O Venizelos*, p. 14 (see Note 6).
34. See on this point the editorial of *The Times* correspondent, William Stillman, in the newspaper of Venizelos and his friends, *Lefka Ori* [*White Mountains*], Chania, 13 June 1889. The whole of Crete had sixty-eight lawyers, forty-nine Christian and nineteen Muslim: N. Stavrakis (1890),

Statistiki tou plythismou tis Kritis [*Statistics of the Population of Crete*], Athens, p. 146, table 15, column 16.

35. Private archives of Constantinos Foumis (AF).
36. Mourellos, *Venizelos*, pp. 93–103 (see Note 9), Yiparis, *El. Venizelos*, pp. 38–49 (see Note 1).
37. Mourellos, *Venizelos*, p. 98 (see Note 9).
38. Private communications of Constantinos and Themistoklis Mitsotakis, Errikos Moatsos, Stelios Pistolakis.
39. S. Pallis (1965), 'O Venizelos os nomikos kai dikigoros' ['Venizelos as Legal Expert and Lawyer'], *Nomikon Vima* 10, pp. 529–50; C. D. Triantaphyllopoulos (1965), 'O Eleftherios Venizelos os nomikos' ['Venizelos as a Legal Expert'], *Ephimeris ton Ellinon nomikon,* 32nd year, Athens, July–August; K. N. Avraam (1936), 'O Venizelos kai i dikaiosini' ['Venizelos and Justice'], *Ergasia,* 7th year, v. 326 (29 March), pp. 295–6. One of the latest articles on Venizelos as a legal expert is Andreas A. Gazis (1988), 'O Eleftherios Venizelos kai to idiotiko dikaio' ['Eleftherios Venizelos and Private Law'], in G. T. Mavrogordatos and Ch. Hadjiiosif (eds), *Venizelismos kai astikos eksynchronismos* [*Venizelism and Bourgeois Modernisation*], Irakleion 1988, pp. 45–66. See also the conference proceedings (2003) *O Eleftherios Venizelos os nomikos. I symvoli tou stin anamorphosi tou ellinikou dikaiou* [*Eleftherios Venizelos as a jurist. His contribution to the reform of Greek law*], Athens.
40. Alastos, *Patriot*, p. 38 (see Note 1); Gibbons, pp. 35–7 (see Note 9).
41. See Macrakis, *Venizelos,* pp. 233–82 (see Note 1).
42. Even Prince George alluded to this in his memoirs (1959). *The Cretan Drama: The Life and Memoirs of Prince George of Greece, High Commissioner in Crete (1898–1906)*, ed. A. A. Pallis, New York, p. 141.
43. All the originals of the laws promulgated between 1899 and 1901 are housed in the Historical Archives of Chania, Crete.
44. Regarding the Cretan laws, which differed markedly from the Greek laws of the time, see Ch. Benakis(1928), *Kritikos Astikos Kodix* [*Cretan Civil Code*], Chania; E. Mastrogamvrakis (1902), *Politikoi Kodikes Kritikis Politias* [*Political Codes of the Cretan State*], Chania, vols 1 and 2; also Pallis, 'O Venizelos os nomikos kai dikigoros', p. 537 (see Note 39).
45. C. D. Triantaphyllopoulos, 'O El. Venizelos os nomikos', esp. pp. 484–6 (see Note 39). See also the article by E. Kothris (1977), 'O Eleftherios Venizelos os dimiourgos tou neoellinikou kratous,' ['Eleftherios Venizelos as the Creator of the Modern Greek State'], *Tetradia Efthynis* II, Athens; esp. pp. 64–5; Pavlos M. Kontoyannopoulos (1968), 'O Venizelos nomikos' [Venizelos as a Jurist], *Elephtheros Kosmos,* 26 March.
46. According to the descendants of Papadakis the whole affair was fraudulent and Venizelos derived considerable monetary advantage from it. Author-Anthoula Papadakis interview, Chania, Crete, summer 1970.

47. S. Vistakis (1911), *To ergon tou Venizelou* [*The Work of Venizelos*], Irakleion; S. Papadakis (1912), *Kritika Apomnimonevmata* [*Cretan Memoirs*], Athens; A. Spiliotopoulos (1925), *Ta kakopoia pnevmata tis ellinikis Istorias* [*The Evil Spirits of Greek History*], Athens, p. 185; Prince George, *The Cretan Drama,* pp. 154–5 (see Note 42).
48. Y. Iliakis (1932), *O Venizelos os dimosiographos* [*Venizelos as a Journalist*], Athens; Stephanou, *Venizelos*, vol. II, pp. 345–92 (see Note 6); Stillmann, *The Times,* 4 January 1889.
49. *Lefka Ori*, published weekly – every Monday – from 19 December 1888 to 27 June 1889. The complete series of this newspaper is housed at the Historical Archives of Chania. The newspaper made a brief reappearance in 1906. For the main editorials written by Venizelos, see the table by Macrakis in *Venizelos*, p. 196 (see Note 1).
50. S. Stephanou (1969), *O Eleftherios Venizelos protoporos tis koinonikis politikis kai tou kratous evimerias eis ton Dytikon Kosmon* [*Eleftherios Venizelos, a Pioneer of Social Policy and the Welfare State in the Western World*], Athens; Stephanou, *Venizelos,* vol. I, pp. 350–2 (see Note 6); D. Kaklamanos (1936), *Eleftherios Venizelos, o iros* [*Eleftherios Venizelos the Hero*], Oxford.
51. *Lefka Ori*, 19 December 1988, 6 February 1889, 17 April 1889.
52. D. Kaklamanos (1948), 'Eleftherios Venizelos, o yperochos politikos kai dianooumenos' ['Eleftherios Venizelos, the Magnificent Politician and Intellectual'], *To Vima*, 18 March, where there is an excellent analysis of Venizelos' intellectual make-up.
53. *Thoukididou Istoriai* [*Thucydides Histories*], translated by E. K. Venizelos, Athens, n.d. The first edition has an introduction by Caclamanos (1940), Oxford. His commentaries on Thucydides have been published by Evi Zachariadi-Holdberg (1991), *Ta scholia tou Venizelou ston Thoukydidi* [*Venizelos' Commentary on Thucydides*], Athens. See also the contribution by P. M. Kitromilides (Chap. 13 in this volume).
54. Institut de France. Académie des Sciences Morales et Politiques, 'Installation de M. Venizelos', Séance du Samedi, 10–21 Juin 1919, Paris, MDCCC-CXIX.
55. Eleftherios Venizelos (1971), *I Kritiki Epanastasis tou 1889 [The Cretan Revolution of 1889]*, ed. I. Manolikakis, Athens, hereafter mentioned as Venizelos, *1889*. The unfinished manuscript of the essay consists of 146 pages.
56. See S. Dragoumis (1905), *Agorefseis Stephanou Dragoumi* [*Orations of Stephanos Dragoumis*], Athens.
57. Chester, *Life*, p. 10 (see Note 1); Alastos, *Patriot*, p. 15 (see Note 1); A. Softazadé (1902), *La Crète sous la donimation et la suzeraineté Ottomane,* Paris, pp. 109–10. The best exposé of the situation was given by Venizelos in the 5 November 1886 *Nea Ephimeris* interview.
58. Venizelos, *1889*, p. 42 (see Note 55); '1888', *Lefka Ori,* 2 January 1889.

59. See the correspondence of the British consul in Crete, Alfred Biliotti, with the British foreign minister, Lord Salisbury. FO *Consular Archives,* 197/55; PRO FO *General Correspondence,* 32/598. Also the reports of the correspondent of *The Times,* William Stillman, especially of 23 May and 12 June 1889, which caused quite a stir in Crete; *Lefka Ori*, see 13 June 1889.
60. See *Ephimeris ton Syzitiseon tis Voulis* [*Journal of Parliamentary Debates*], 1889, pp. 9–75.
61. *Lefka Ori*, 27 March 1889.
62. Confidential letter of Gryparis to Dragoumis, 4 May 1889, AD (classification indication in AYE) A/14.
63. *Kriti* [*Crete*], no. 1026, 5 May 1889.
64. Correspondence of Gryparis and Dragoumis, 5 May to 29 July 1889, AD A/14; the consular reports, esp. the reports of Biliotti to Monson and to Salisbury, FO 32/598, 197/55; General Correspondence Consular Archives, the reports of Blanc to Delcassé, *Crète: Politique Etrangère, Relations avec la Grèce,* NS 72, 1889. *Turkey, No. 2: Correspondence Respecting the Affairs of Crete,* London, 1889 and *Turkey, No. 3: Further Correspondence Respecting the Affairs in the East*, London, 1889. Also Assembly in *Kriti,* 5 May to 31 July 1889; and the Turkish point of view in A. Softazadé, *La Crète*, p. 114 (see Note 57).
65. *Imerologion Akrotiriou 1897* [*Diary of Akrotiri 1897*], marginalia by C. Foumis, p. 1 ff.
66. Ibid., p. 5 ff. According to Michalis Foumis, Syngros used a ruse to persuade the Porte to grant a general amnesty – he 'revealed' to the ambassador the imminent universalisation of the rising: author/Foumis interview, July 1981.
67. Manousos Koundouros (1921), *Imerologion, Istorikai kai diplomatikai apokalypseis* [*Diary. Historical and Diplomatic Revelations*], ed. S. Vardakis, Athens.
68. See *Imerologion Akrotiriou 1897* (see Note 65); Biliotti to Salisbury, 5 February. *Turkey,* No. 10, no. 57; Blanc to Hanotaux, 5 February. *Affaires d'Orient*, pp. 12, 15, 38.
69. Kerofilas, *Life and Work*, pp. 13–17 (see Note 11); Chester, *Life*, pp. 40–1 (see Note 1); Alastos, *Venizelos*, p. 27 (see Note 1), Gibbons, *Venizelos*, p. 24 (see Note 9); A. W. A. Leeper (1916), 'Allied Portraits: Eleftherios Venizelos', *The New Europe* I, pp. 183–4; Anne O'Hare McCormack (1928), 'Venizelos: the New Ulysses of Hellas', *The New York Times Magazine*, 2 September, p. 14.
70. Macrakis, *Venizelos*, pp. 330–1 (see Note 1).
71. *Imerologion Akrotiriou 1897* was shown to me by Michalis Foumis, the son of Constantinos Foumis, in manuscript form. Foumis' copy contains useful comments in the form of marginalia and an extensive introduction covering the period 1889–1897. The pamphlet contains letters and documents of the insurrection, many of which I have not found elsewhere.

72. For a full bibliography of the diplomacy of the Cretan question between 1896 and 1898, see Macrakis, *Venizelos*, pp. 77–8 and pp. 334–5.
73. For a detailed narrative of the Akrotiri revolt, see Macrakis, *Venizelos,* pp. 309–76 (see Note 1).
74. Macrakis, *Venizelos*, p. 343, Note 29 (see Note 1).
75. Author-M. Foumis interview, summer 1981.
76. Macrakis, *Venizelos*, pp. 354–5 (see Note 1).
77. Ibid., p. 357.
78. Ibid.
79. *Diary*, pp. 108–15; Biliotti to Salisbury, 20 March, Turkey, no. 10, no. 301.
80. See extensive coverage of these events in the April issues of *Le Temps, The New York Times, The Manchester Guardian* and *The Times.*
81. Venizelos' views of the Archanes assembly are set out in an anonymous article in the newspaper *Neologos Constantinoupoleos,* 29 August 1897, no. 8371. It was published later in an article (1933) 'I Epanastatiki Synelefsis ton Kriton to 1897 kai ta gegonota ton Archanon' ['The Cretan Revolutionary Assembly of 1897 and the Events of Archanes'], *Myson,* vol. II, pp. 113–22 (hereafter, *Myson,* II). The introduction to the article indicates that it is the work of Venizelos and that, indeed, when Venizelos himself was asked he acknowledged writing it. See the longhand original in Venizelos' unpublished papers of the Benaki Archives, BMW, env. 264.
82. Koundouros, *Imerologion,* pp. 227–30 (see Note 67).
83. *Kritika* (1901) [*Cretan Affairs*], ed. S. A. Papantonakis, Chania, p. 18. This is a free translation of the original text. In order to preserve the rhetorical flourish I have bent some of the details of phrasing.
84. For the Cretan settlement of 1898, see the following: Macrakis, *Venizelos,* pp. 377–87 and Henry Norman (1897), 'The Wreck of Greece', *Scribner's Magazine* XXII, pp. 399–426; Henri Couturier (1911), *I Kriti. I thesis aftis ex apopseos tou Diethnous Dikaiou* [*Crete. Its Position from the Perspective of International Law*], transl. H. Veneris, Irakleion; Koundouros, *Imerologion,* p. 254ff (see Note 67); Jean-Stanislav Dutskowski (1953), *L' Occupation de la Crète (1897–1909). Une expérience d' administration d'un territoire,* Paris 1953; and especially the several relevant studies in T. Detorakis and A. Kalokairinos (eds) (2001), *I teleftaia phasi tou Kritikou Zitimatos* [*The Last Phase of the Cretan Question*], Irakleion.
85. The best discussion on the selection of Prince George of Greece as high commissioner is the article of George J. Marcopoulos (1969), 'The Selection of Prince George of Greece as High Commissioner in Crete,' *Balkan Studies* 10, pp. 335–50; see also *The Times* (London), 1 April 1897, p. 5
86. Very little has been done lately regarding the study of Cretan constitutional law. We, therefore have to rely on the old but still good analysis of N. Saripolos (1902), *To Kritikon syntagmatikon dikaion en sygrisei pros to imeteron kai ta ton xenon kraton* [*Cretan Constitutional Law in Comparison to*

Our Own and to Those of Foreign States], Athens, and G. Streit (1897), 'La Question Crétoise . . . ', *Revue de Droit International Public* IV, p. 383ff.

87. *To Syntagma tis Kritikis Politeias os epsiphisthi ypo tis Synelefseos ton Kriton* [*The Constitution of the Cretan State as Voted by the Cretan Assembly*], (1899), Athens.
88. Macrakis, *Venizelos*, p. 380–1 (see Note 1).
89. Prince George, *The Cretan Drama* (see Note 42).
90. Avraam, 'O Venizelos', p. 295 (see Note 39); Pallis 'O Venizelos', p. 16 (see Note 39), says that Venizelos was able to establish and staff the law courts in fifty days!
91. Avraam, 'O Venizelos', p. 255 (see Note 39).
92. Constantinos D. Svolopoulos (1974), *O Eleftherios Venizelos kai i politiki krisis is tin aftonomon Kritin 1901–1906* [*Eleftherios Venizelos and the Political Crisis in Autonomous Crete, 1901–1906*], Athens. Here I present some points discussed in this study. See also: A. van Der Brule (1907), *L' Orient Hellène: Grèce, Crète, Macedoine,* Paris, with remarkable cameos of the main political leaders of the time; Couturier, *I Kriti* (see Note 84); Eothen (pseudonym of I. Gennadios) (1905), 'Crete under Prince George', *The Fortnightly Review,* September, pp. 538–51, written during the Therisso revolt; J. A. Reinach (1910), *La Question Crétoise vue de Crète,* Paris; and, above all, the historical novel of P. Prevelakis (1948–50), *O Kritikos* [*The Cretan*], Athens, and especially vol. 3 called *The State,* dealing almost exclusively with the actions of Venizelos between 1905 and 1910. Two recent articles by Robert Holland have greatly contributed to a fuller understanding of the broader context of the Therisso episode: (1999), 'Nationalism, Ethnicity and the Concert of Europe: The Case of the High Commissionership of Prince George of Greece in Crete, 1898–1906', *Journal of Modern Greek Studies* 17, pp. 253–76 and 'The Prince, the Powers and the "Unfortunate Regime": The High Commissionership of Prince George of Greece in Crete, 1898–1906', in Detorakis and Kalokairinos (eds), *I teleftaia phasi,* pp. 31–46 (see Note 84).
93. Macrakis, *Venizelos*, p. 402 (see Note 1).
94. For an in-depth discussion of the reasons that prompted Venizelos to this action, see Svolopoulos, *O El. Venizelos*, p. 72–94 (see Note 92) and A. M. Maris (1985), *O Eleftherios Venizelos kai to kinima tou Therisou* [*Eleftherios Venizelos and the Therisso Movement*], Chania, pp. 86–113, where are the most important excerpts from this series of articles.
95. Valuable interviews were given by the leaders of the revolt – Venizelos, Foumis and Manos – during that time. The best known interviews were taken by Vlasis Gravriilidis of the *Akropolis and* Spyros Nikolopoulos of *Oi Kairoi.* Many journalists joined Venizelos in Therisso or were now siding in their columns with the rebels – George Pop of *Athinai*, Dimitrios Caclamanos of *Asty,* Kalapothakis of *Embros* and others identified with his methods and his policies not only concerning Crete but mainland Greece as well.

PART II

The Drama of High Politics

3

Venizelos' Advent in Greek Politics, 1909–12

Helen Gardikas-Katsiadakis

For many years, following the bankruptcy of Greece in December 1893 and the disgraceful defeat of the Greek army during a short campaign against the Ottoman forces in Thessaly in April 1897, Greece underwent a period of prolonged international isolation and domestic stagnation. National expansionist aspirations, while continuing to be the principal concern of politicians, remained unfulfilled, whereas social and financial problems accumulated. All the main issues stemmed from the impasse of the traditional Great Idea (Megali Idea). A military solution of Greek expansionist aspirations was a utopian vision unless the country could meet the financial burden of increasing its strength by means of a costly military and naval reorganisation. Successive Greek governments had pursued several ineffective policies, which had all led to increased financial burdens and repeated national humiliation. The military, junior officers in particular, were disillusioned and restless. Some sought a solution by joining the ongoing struggle of Greek bands in Macedonia, while others tried to advance their career at home. Meanwhile, Crete had become a powder keg in the Eastern Mediterranean. The young Cretan state was balancing precariously between the vestiges of Ottoman sovereignty and full Greek statehood. Whether in order to further their political aims or in order to embarrass their opponents in power in Chania, often encouraged by Athens, impatient Cretan politicians clamoured for enosis, union of their autonomous island with Greece.

The most serious crisis occurred in 1908, when Crete had been left with no head of state. On 20 September of that year, the high commissioner appointed by the Protecting Powers in 1906 as the head of state in Crete, Alexandros Zaimis, left for a holiday in Greece, leaving as locum tenens his private secretary, the young diplomat Alexandros Rangabe. Rangabe remained in Chania in the somewhat vague capacity of liaison officer between the Cretan government and the Greek government, but had no executive authority in Cretan affairs. The plan of the Greek prime minister George Theotokis was to prepare to derive compensation in Crete, whenever the inevitable crisis in the Balkans occurred. When the opportunity arose, Crete would declare its union with Greece, taking all necessary precautions not to compromise the Greek government in the eyes of Europe. The plan was put into effect as soon as it became certain that the Porte would not declare war on Bulgaria. On 24 September, following the declaration of Bulgarian independence, and instructions to Rangabe, a public demonstration was organised in Chania which demanded union with Greece; and a few days later, after a brief domestic political crisis, on 1 October, a five-member executive committee was instituted, consisting of Antonios Michelidakis, as president and in charge of security, Eleftherios Venizelos in charge of justice and foreign affairs, Charalambos Poloyorgis in charge of internal affairs, Emmanuel Logiadis in charge of finances and Minos Petychakis in charge of education. This executive committee assumed the responsibility of running the administration of the island provisionally, according to the laws of the Greek state, 'until the Greek government assumed the administration of the island'.

Predictably, Theotokis hesitated to acknowledge the coup for fear of compromising the Greek government in the eyes of the Great Powers. Instead, he hoped to obtain his goal through diplomatic means by appealing to the Protecting Powers. Meanwhile, he assured them that 'pending this appeal no step of a military or administrative nature would be taken by the Greek government with regard to Crete'.[1]

The Cretans, however, adopted a policy of 'forcing' the union de facto by planning their elections to coincide with the elections on the mainland and sending their own representatives to Athens to join their 'colleagues' of the independent state. Meanwhile, pending the withdrawal of the international troops in July 1909 and the Greek elections in March 1910, Crete remained tranquil. In July 1909, according to schedule, the Powers withdrew their troops from the island, leaving only four warships in Suda to guard the Turkish flag on the islet at the entrance to the bay. No sooner had the troops withdrawn, than the Cretans had hoisted the flag of Greece. Venizelos, still in charge of Cretan foreign affairs in the five-member executive committee, refused to haul it down, but promised the consuls of the Protecting Powers that the Cretans would adhere to the status quo and that no Cretan deputies would be sent to the Greek parliament until March 1910, when the Cretan elections were to take place. The flag crisis had immediate repercussions in Athens. On 6 August the Porte made a démarche to the Greek government demanding a disavowal of the Cretan unionist movement. On 9 August the new Greek premier Dimitrios Rallis replied that, as Greece was in no way implicated in this movement, she would continue to observe the same correct attitude as in the past. Not satisfied with this reply, the Porte declared a commercial boycott against

Greece and demanded explanations not only for the activities of Greeks in Crete, but also for those of Greek bands in Macedonia. The Greek reply, dated 18 August, was far less conciliatory than the first. Whereas its reference to Cretan affairs was vague, it openly laid the blame for the Greek activity in Macedonia on the anarchy prevailing in the region. By then, however, in Crete, the executive committee had resigned over the question of the Greek flag and a provisional government, which had succeeded it, had let the troops from the international warships haul it down. The Porte was satisfied and the crisis subsided. Once again, Crete returned to tranquillity pending the elections of March 1910.[2]

At the height of the Cretan flag predicament, a serious political crisis erupted in Athens. Following the example set by the Young Turks in the Ottoman Empire, a group of disillusioned junior officers had formed a secret organisation, the Military League and, on 15 August 1909 staged a coup, which led to the resignation of the weak Rallis government and the formation of a puppet government led by the leader of the Diliyannist group, a minor politician belonging to a heroic family, Kyriakoulis Mavromichalis. The main long-term advantage of the coup was that it excited aspirations of national revival, of anorthosis (reconstruction), a vague notion which included the desire for the restoration of a lost self-esteem and national prestige and for social progress and financial recovery. The new government, however, was under the complete control of the League, which had no experience in administration and led the country to a political impasse and to the brink of financial disaster. Toward the end of 1909, relations between the League and King George I had reached breaking point, the mood of co-operation between the League and the Mavromichalis ministry had evaporated and the League had decided to replace it, but could not find a suitable successor among Greek politicians. At that point, one of the members of the League's ten-member council, Epameinondas Zymbrakakis, suggested Venizelos, whose views he shared. At the time, Venizelos was in charge of foreign affairs in the Cretan Executive Committee.[3]

The opinion that Venizelos could become the man of the hour, given the opportunity, had been voiced even before the coup. Early in the summer, Chairopoulos, the editor of the Athenian daily newspaper *Chronos* (*Time*), which was the mouthpiece of the League, had invited its readers, through what he called a 'panhellenic salvation plebiscite', to address an appeal to Venizelos. At the time, Venizelos had written to Chairopoulos to call off the plebiscite, for it was damaging his political position in Crete.[4] By advancing the name of Venizelos, Chairopoulos was merely reflecting the general discontent and uneasiness of the people and there is no evidence that Venizelos was privy to the conspiratorial movements of the Greek officers. Yet, early after the August coup, Venizelos had emerged as one of the most fervent supporters of the Military League. In a series of articles in his own paper, the *Kiryx* (*Herald*), he had hailed it as a 'revolution' originating not only in the army but also 'in the mind of the entire Greek people'.[5] He had been following events closely and had volunteered to become the public adviser of the League several months before it decided to invite him to Athens. He had immediately blamed the king and the political parties for the impasse, which had led to the 'revolution' and had concluded that:

> We must hope that the parties will profit from the situation to attempt to remedy as much as possible the harm that they themselves have created to a large extent and that the parliament which is about to convene, which on account of the circumstances is essentially an *assembly*, since it is convened following a revolution, and is intended to recreate the Greek state, will prove totally worthy of its great mission, and that the representatives of the Greek people will lay aside their personal and partisan and provincial and local interests and will have but one goal, that is, how to establish firm foundations for the creation of a New Hellas, worthy of its mission.
>
> But even if this noble hope is betrayed, the struggle undertaken by the League of Officers, with the applause of the entire nation, should not be abandoned. If the political decay, produced by the corruption of so many decades, is so advanced that the work of reconstruction cannot be undertaken by the present parties and by regular means, then the League of Officers must place its material and moral power at the service of this noble cause to attempt, if necessary by means of a temporary *dictatorship* of a few months and of a predetermined duration, to implement its programme and to summon the people after the end of this period to elections for an *assembly*, which will sanction previous decisions and will decide upon the way in which the state will be governed.[6]

Once Venizelos' name was suggested, it took several days for the League to come to a decision, for it was by no means a unanimous body. It included both conservative officers, such as its head Colonel Nikolaos Zorbas, or the Cretan cavalry captain Epameinondas Zymbrakakis, and extremists and radical anti-royalists, such as Lieutenant Theodoros Pangalos. After three weeks of deliberation the League's council adopted an initial decision, that Venizelos should be summoned to offer his mediation between the League and the old parties of Greece. However, the letter of invitation that was finally addressed to Venizelos stated that, if circumstances required it, he could assume the leadership of the country, an expression implying the imposition of a dictatorship. A member of the league, Captain I. Kontaratos, delivered the letter to Venizelos in Chania.

In his answer, headed Chalepa, 22 December 1909, Venizelos reserved his final decision until he had examined the situation at close hand and then decided to set off for Athens within the next few days.[7]

By that time, the political system had been entirely discredited, the country was at a standstill, and a restless military and disillusioned populace had become a threat to public order.[8]

On 27 December Venizelos arrived in Athens. Despite his original request that his visit be kept secret, his arrival became known, arousing great hopes among his supporters within the League and great suspicion among the political leaders and on the throne. Some of the extremist members of the League, who had taken the initiative to invite him, had done so in the hope that he would lead an anti-dynastic movement that would overthrow King George I or even the entire dynasty. On the other side, among the old parties, the fear alone that the League would appoint Venizelos as Mavromichalis' successor at the head of the Greek government sufficed to revive memories of his not-too-distant anti-dynastic conduct in Crete. After all, his quarrel with the high commissioner, Prince George, had not been the only sign of his alleged anti-dynastic feelings. Throughout the 1909 crisis, from the *Kiryx*, he had blamed King George I for the political crisis. But his criticism had never included an outright rejection of the regime:

> and obviously the best thing the king can do at this point is to hand over the throne to his heir. Because we refuse to believe that the king seriously considered leaving Greece with his entire family, as has been written. Even if after a reign of almost half a century it has not become possible to achieve the desired unanimity of ideas, spirit and desires of people and king, we refuse to believe that the latter considers not only himself but also his Greek-born and bred children to have become so foreign to the nation to intend earnestly to sever the links that bind their family with the Greek people.[9]

Aware of the commotion his appearance would cause, Venizelos had abstained from visiting Athens, even in a private capacity, before being invited by the League. But when he arrived he lost no time in appearing before a meeting of the League's council.[10] His views on the handling of the situation by the League prior to his arrival may have been of historical value at the time, but permit us to gauge his convictions and his intentions, and to see traits of the tactics he pursued thereafter with remarkable consistency.

He criticised the League for entrusting the administration of the state to one of the very politicians they had intended to overthrow, thus failing to carry through their 'revolution'. 'Revolutions ruin and rebuild, and only then are they revolutions,' he was reported to have remarked. He also noted that a revolution is a momentary event, a unique opportunity for radical actions. But what impressed them most was his sudden about-face with regard to the throne. One of King George's most severe critics seemed to have become overnight one of his staunchest supporters. This about-face invites comment. Throughout his career, Venizelos appears to have wavered repeatedly in his position vis-à-vis the throne. One is led, however, to assume that in his quarrels with the crown his motives were personal rather than political or to an even lesser extent ideological, that these quarrels stemmed from disagreement with the methods and options of the monarch, not with the institution of monarchy as such. In the midst of one of Greece's most serious political crises, he prevailed upon the anti-dynastic faction within the League's council with the argument that a change of regime was against the national interests of the country and its international stability.

The League had hoped that Venizelos would agree to form a government that would succeed where Mavromichalis had failed. But Venizelos was not a member of the political establishment of Greece. His non-institutional involvement in Greek politics would only rouse a fierce reaction among Greek politicians. A return to regular parliamentary practices required, in his view, the immediate summoning of a national assembly, a task that the successor of Mavromichalis would have to undertake. It did not prove difficult to convince the League that, in order to avoid the risk of radical changes to the regime, the assembly would be 'revisionary' and not 'constitutional', and that it would have a limited task: a mere revision of the non-fundamental articles of the constitution. His plan had two aims: one was to work out a return to normal parliamentary practices by means of parliamentary elections; the other was to do so in such a manner as not to incur the risk of provoking an international crisis either by re-opening the Cretan question or by unsettling the regime. After all, British and French warships were patrolling off Phaliron as a clear reminder that the dynasty should be respected. By convening a double constitutional assembly for the revision of the 1864 constitution he secured both his aims. The March 1910 elections were postponed, depriving his fellow countrymen of a pretext for sending deputies to Athens. At the same time, if all Greek party leaders agreed that the assembly would not revise the fundamental articles of the constitution, the stability of the regime had been guaranteed. These arrangements were not prescribed in the 107 articles of the 1864 constitution and therefore required the consent of all the political leaders and of the king. Relations between the League and the parties being what they were, Venizelos undertook to secure their concurrence in this solution. His task was extremely difficult and required extraordinary negotiating talents. From the outset, not only did Greek party leaders view him with suspicion, but he was also undermined from within the League itself. He therefore threatened that, if he was not given a written authorisation to negotiate with the political leaders and a pledge that the League would be dissolved once the decision for the assembly was adopted, he would withdraw to Crete. The League was coerced into acceptance of his terms.

Venizelos received support from two unexpected quarters: the details of the confidential meeting between the League's council and Venizelos were immediately 'leaked' to King George I, who realised that in Venizelos he had found not the anti-dynastic demagogue he had feared, but an able and practical politician. He could not, of course, overcome his fears that uncontrolled political forces in the assembly might threaten the regime. Ever since Venizelos had publicised his views on the Greek political situation, a new serious rift had occurred between the king and the Cretan politician, which had nothing to do with the latter's alleged anti-dynasticism. Venizelos had repeatedly advised that if parliament failed to implement a programme of financial and military reconstruction, the League should impose a dictatorship, a government by decrees, of several months at the end of which a national assembly would sanction the legality of these decrees and decide upon the means of the administration of the state.[11] The king had thwarted such designs by intimating that: 'Upon any tendency to violate the constitution of the country or to convene a national assembly by means of simple royal decrees, His Majesty has the firm and uncompromising determination to resign from the throne with his entire family.'[12] But it was clear that Venizelos was trying to work out a return to and not a departure from constitutional rule. Besides, the king continued to fear that Venizelos' involvement in Greek politics would dissatisfy the Porte and create an international crisis.

Venizelos also found an unexpected ally in the person of the leader of the second largest party, D. Rallis, who believed the assembly to be the only way to rid the country of the embarrassing and dangerous League. The leader of the majority party, G. Theotokis, was more difficult to convince. For several days he vacillated in his usual manner, while a letter he received from Venizelos pressing for an unequivocal statement only served to irritate him further.[13] By 10 January, embittered by the conduct of the party leaders and exasperated at the possibility of a failure of his mission, Venizelos anticipated either a new revolution or civil war and anarchy, and considered accepting the dictatorial powers that the League had offered him twelve days earlier. Rallis made one last effort to win Theotokis round, while Venizelos, in a move to test the tenacity of the League, resigned from his mission. The resignation produced the desired effect: the League's council convened to reaffirm its decisions. By 14 January Theotokis had acquiesced, once he was given additional reassurances that the League would be dissolved when the convocation of the assembly was proclaimed. A new round of negotiations was required in order to convince King George I. Here, it was Theotokis who played the key role. The king had been opposed to any departure from constitutional legitimacy, but Venizelos had made a clear case in favour of a transition with the consent of the parliamentary parties. The decision was sealed in a crown council on 16 January. With the thorny issue of the transition to regular parliamentary practices settled to the satisfaction of Venizelos, there remained the question of selecting the prime minister who would implement it. In this matter, too, Venizelos had his way. He succeeded in prevailing upon the League to select Stephanos Dragoumis rather than his rival candidate Stephanos Skouloudis by a majority of fourteen votes to four.[14]

With the arrangement concluded, a new government was formed under the experienced and clear-sighted politician Stephanos Dragoumis on 18 January 1910, and Venizelos left for Chania.

Venizelos was an ambitious man. His success in solving the deadlock in Greece and the leadership gap he discovered there encouraged him to prepare for a political career on the mainland, although it is difficult to establish the exact point in his career when he began to think of such a step. Most likely it was long before 1910, by which time he was already forty-six years old; but it was only in 1910 that a clear opportunity arose. As we have seen, in the early summer of 1909, on the eve of the military coup, he had put a stop to a popular movement for him to lead a reform movement in Athens. He had first intimated such a possibility at the end of 1909, in an interview with the respected editor of *Nea Imera*, Ioannis Chalkokondylis, when, speaking of the political legacy of the League's 'revolution', he proposed the formation of political clubs throughout the country, which would evolve into a 'party of reconstruction', to support the 'government of reconstruction'.[15] Besides, other Cretan politicians also wanted to continue their careers on the central stage. The persistence with which the Cretan politicians fought for their entry into the Greek parliament, whenever the Greek elections afforded them an opportunity, had two elements: the pursuit of a national cause and the fulfilment of a personal ambition. For Venizelos, this meant nothing short of a leading role. As head of the foreign affairs department of the Cretan state, together with President Michelidakis, he had already communicated with both G. Theotokis and D. Rallis at the height of the flag crisis. When he met them in Athens in December 1909, he negotiated with them in his capacity as a mediator, but he was implicitly acknowledged as their equal.

Elections for the Double Revisionary Assembly were duly proclaimed on 17 March and were scheduled for 8 August. Meanwhile in Crete, on 7 March, the Cretans held their own elections; but, as the Greek elections, with which they were initially intended to coincide, had been postponed, they made no attempt to send deputies to Athens. There was tension in the political atmosphere. Venizelos secured a small and unstable majority and was elected president of the executive committee. In Chania, at the opening of the assembly on 26 April controversy broke out, when the Muslim deputies refused to take the required oath of allegiance to the king of Greece. On 6 May the Muslims were excluded and the assembly was adjourned for forty days. When it met again on 26 June Venizelos resolved the stalemate by means of a compromise whereby the assembly admitted the Muslim deputies and immediately adjourned for another four months. Having gained four months of peace for Crete, Athens and Europe, Venizelos left for a holiday.[16]

In Greece, the electoral campaign instigated a heated debate on the character of the assembly. The old parties stood by the January arrangement that the assembly should not tamper with the regime. During the electoral campaign anorthosis became the watchword for a generation of ambitious young professionals who saw in the discrediting of the old political parties and in the forthcoming elections an opportunity to begin a political career. Among them, a significant majority, which included socialists, radicals and demagogues, clamoured for a major revision of the constitution and therefore to change the assembly into a constitutional rather than a revisionary body. These candidates and their followers regarded Venizelos as their future leader. After all, he had consistently blamed King George I for the political quandary of Greece. His career in Crete, his reputation as an uncompromising revolutionary leader and his quarrel with the high commissioner, Prince George of Greece, seemed to justify their expectation. Venizelos was indeed one of the candidates. His candidacy to a seat as deputy for Attica and Boeotia had been submitted by 'friends'.

Throughout the electoral campaign, Venizelos adopted a strategy of complete silence. Not only did he stay away from campaign meetings, he disappeared from the political scene altogether. Fleeing the dilemmas of both Crete and Athens, he travelled to Switzerland and Italy, allegedly for reasons of health. Only on the very eve of the vote, and again through the channel of 'friends', did he give an indication of his attitude in the matter. By means of a letter in the newspaper *Estia*, his friend Emmanuel Benakis assured voters that the allegation that Venizelos entertained anti-dynastic feelings was unfounded. His aim was to reassure his supporters and the king that he did not intend to renounce his January commitment to the regime.[17]

During the turbulent days that followed the 8 August elections, Venizelos gave proof of an impressive combination of resolve and flexibility, a combination which was one of the key features and the principal cause of his phenomenal political career.

POLITICAL CAREER IN GREECE

The elections resulted in an extremely unclear political landscape. Before the threat posed by the new candidates, the old parties had formed a coalition named 'the Unionists' and appeared as a united party in the 362-seat assembly. The independent candidates, however, although disunited and ill-prepared, had succeeded in winning the confidence of the electorate. The most prominent figure among them was undoubtedly Eleftherios Venizelos, by then a forty-six-year-old experienced politician with a remarkable career.

The Revisionary Assembly faced a complex political crisis. One aspect of the crisis was the domestic issue. The coalition of the old parties did not have the voting power to form a government. The independent candidates, on the other hand, were a disparate grouping of individuals, who lacked a common ideology and party discipline. The majority among them were outspokenly in favour of a radical revision of the constitution, in order to curtail royal privileges. They included some of the followers of Venizelos himself, who believed that Venizelos was party to their views. Even after his electoral triumph Venizelos, who had been elected first deputy for Attica and Boeotia, did not hasten to make his appearance in Athens. Via Rome he returned to Chania, to resign from his position as head of the Cretan government and from the leadership of his party, and he left for Athens on 30 August.[18] The sessions of the assembly began on 3 September, only to be interrupted by violent demands for its conversion into a constituent assembly. On 5 September, Venizelos addressed an impressive Athenian gathering in Constitution Square and set forth his political agenda. The highlight of his speech came when, in answer to repeated cries from the crowd in favour of a constituent assembly, he repeatedly declared himself in favour of the revisionary nature of that body and managed to prevail upon the recalcitrant crowd. But this exchange had not been deliberate. His chief aim, in this first appearance before the Greek crowds, was to impress them with a comprehensive repudiation of the entire existing judicial, social and political system. Justice, administration, social policy and the parties all came under fire from the very onset of his speech: a criticism of the prevailing social inequality, which he summed up in the following phrase: 'Law has become a spider's web, strong enough to capture the weak, but torn to shreds with insolence by the powerful.' And he concluded by announcing his intention to join forces with those of the newly elected deputies who shared his views, in order to create a political party based on a decentralised system of political clubs established throughout the country.[19]

This appearance marked the beginning of a political relationship between Venizelos and his supporters that transformed the nature of political leadership in Greece. The character of political leadership in the existing 'personality-centred' party system was transformed, as Venizelos assumed a Messianic role.[20]

In his first address to the Athenians he made no reference to the international situation of the country, although the crisis and Venizelos' involvement in it had serious international implications. Firstly, Venizelos' decision to run for the Greek parliamentary elections had rekindled the anti-Greek sentiment of the Turkish authorities, which attacked the rights of free commerce and settlement granted to Greek citizens by expelling teachers, doctors and journalists from Constantinople, Adrianople and Thessaloniki, and by compelling businessmen, merchants and landowners to abandon their property and leave for Greece or become Ottoman subjects. An anti-Greek commercial boycott began in Ioannina and Thessaloniki in June. Following an outbreak of domestic disorders, the Turks occupied Samos between July and September, as an indirect warning to the Cretans. The Porte protested to the Powers at the electoral success of Venizelos and instructed its minister in Athens, who was on leave, not to return to his post, the grand vizier Hakki Pasha having declared that, if Venizelos became prime minister and pursued an aggressive policy, any attempt to modify the Cretan status quo would be interpreted as a casus belli.[21]

Secondly and more seriously, if the crisis with the Porte did not subside and if the extremists gained the upper hand in the assembly and domestic order was not guaranteed, negotiations for an urgently needed foreign loan, which had almost reached a successful conclusion in Paris, would fail. Venizelos hastened to appease both the Porte and Europe: although the assembly stood by the legality of Venizelos' election, since he was a Greek citizen, on 4 October they annulled the election of the other four elected Cretan candidates.[22]

Immediately following his arrival in Athens, a climate of warm rapport had been established between the crown and the Cretan politician, as they exchanged public declarations of mutual confidence, so that, encouraged by his advisers, and with the first signs of a change of mind in Constantinople, King George I no longer hesitated to charge Venizelos with the formation of a government. And, as soon as he became prime minister, Venizelos lost no time in demonstrating his pacific intentions by reserving for himself the ministries of the army and of the navy and by appointing as his foreign minister Ioannis Gryparis, a career diplomat whom he had known in Crete in the late 1880s and who was then posted in the Ottoman capital, a man whom he could rely on to improve Greek–Turkish relations and avert a crisis. And on 7 October, his speech in parliament confirmed his intentions:

> Our commitment to the work of reconstruction, which cannot take place from one day to the next, but requires a long period of domestic and international tranquillity, is the best guarantee that Greece is an element of peace in the East.[23]

N. Dimitrakopoulos became minister of justice, E. Repoulis minister of the interior, L. Koromilas minister of finances and A. Alexandris minister of education. Although these men were all distinguished professionals in their respective fields, none had any prior experience in government administration, while most of them had criticised the previous political order, an unequivocal indication that Venizelos intended his cabinet to mark a clear rupture with the old political establishment. The only exception was Venizelos himself, who had the limited experience within the confines of his turbulent native island. He had brought none of his associates from Chania, with the exception of Klearchos Markantonakis, his old friend and trusted colleague, who managed his private affairs.

Venizelos was sworn into office on 6 October. Next day, he appeared before the assembly, but without the customary statement of government policy. From the onset, he made it clear that the party composition of the assembly made it difficult for him to bring before it bills that would implement his reform programme. As he declared, he would make no pertinent statement before the assembly, but would appeal to the electorate for a new mandate after the revision of the constitution, when the task of the Revisionary assembly would end.[24] Besides his commitment to peace, his statement contained little else. The discussion as to the revisionary or constituent nature of the assembly evolved into a fierce debate as to the royal prerogative for granting dissolution of parliament. It became evident that Venizelos was forcing the delegates into a vote of confidence, which would serve as a pretext to dissolve the assembly and proclaim new elections. This is indeed what actually happened: the vote of the 266 members present was cast as follows: Ayes without reservation: 157; ayes with reservation: 51; nos: 31; abstained from voting: 22; refused to vote: 5. As the quorum was 183 votes, he declared he was not satisfied with the result and asked the king to dissolve parliament, a request the king granted. On 12 October elections for a second double revisionary assembly were proclaimed, to be held on 28 November 1910. Aspreas even believed that, when the king invited Venizelos to form a government, the latter had accepted only on the secret condition that he would be given *carte blanche* to dissolve the Revisionary Assembly.[25]

CONSTITUTIONAL REVISION AND LEGISLATION

In the August elections, Venizelos had entered as an independent candidate and an absentee. The second electoral campaign of November he headed in person and as the leader of a political party. His speeches in the campaign delineated the principles of his party.

In Crete, Venizelos had been the leader of the Liberal Party, a party that had emerged during the 1880s as a result of the first struggles for political power in the Cretan parliament that was formed following the promulgation of the Pact of Chalepa in 1878. Although he had arrived in Athens alone, his career in Greece was a continuance of his career in Crete. Shortly after his arrival, Venizelos convened a meeting of his political friends at the Ermis Hotel and founded the new party: Komma Phileleftheron (Liberal Party). The name of the new party and its emblem, an anchor, he had brought with him from Crete.

The most important element for the success of the party under formation was discipline. The discredited old parties had received a fatal blow from the August 1909 coup, so that in the August 1910 elections they failed to rally their traditional following, to the advantage of the newcomers. The independent deputies proved an unmanageable corps, who threatened the cohesion of both old parties and the new party alike. Only party lists could guarantee party discipline and only party discipline could guarantee that the 'reconstruction programme' would succeed. Therefore, to the indignation of his rivals, Venizelos adopted the practice of party lists of candidates and 'party discipline' became the catch phrase of the November 1910 elections. After all, it was the experience of the August elections and the unmanageable assembly it had produced that had made Venizelos adopt electoral lists. As he put it: 'The independence of those belonging to the legion of the struggle for reconstruction is pure political anarchy.'[26] Under such circumstances, independent candidates who did not belong to Venizelos' new lists were doomed to failure.

Theotokis, Rallis and Mavromichalis, the leaders of the major old parties, considered the engineered dissolution of the assembly an unconstitutional manipulation and abstained from the November elections. The result was a landslide victory for the new party with 307 deputies in a total of 362 in the new Double Assembly, 245 of them being new members. Now Venizelos had the power to go ahead with the reform programme, a task that proceeded alongside that of constitutional revision. To the otherwise unchanged cabinet, he added an eighth ministry, the ministry of national economy, devoted to the development of the productive resources of the country. To this ministry he appointed Emmanuel Benakis, a liberal industrialist and prominent member of Athenian society, a close friend and one of his most loyal associates. The new cabinet assumed office on 11 January 1911.

On 26 January Venizelos brought before the assembly a draft proposal for the revision of articles of the constitution, prepared by a six-member committee of the assembly. Another committee of the assembly, consisting of thirty members, undertook to elaborate on its details. Stephanos Dragoumis, the leader of the major opposition party, was appointed president of this committee, Constantinos Zavitsianos, a young Corfiot deputy who had begun his career as a judge, became its secretary, and Constantinos Raktivan, an eminent lawyer, its speaker. The committee worked hard under the close supervision of Venizelos and completed its task by 14 February, when deliberations in the assembly began. The fifty-eight articles under revision were deliberated in forty-two sessions, some of the issues provoking unreasonably long and heated debates, especially when ideological matters were involved, as on the language question,[27] and the issue of the limitation of property rights. On at least five occasions – language question, freedom of the press, forced appropriation of property, council of state and electoral court – Venizelos, who assisted in all but one session, prevailed by providing well-documented and pragmatic solutions.[28] The revision process in the assembly was completed on 20 May. Although the reform process had been occasioned by the need to emerge from a political deadlock and to salvage the regime, it served as an opportunity both to expand political liberties and to improve the effectiveness of the administration. Articles 5, 6 and 12 provided additional guarantees for the rights of the individual. Article 16 ensured mandatory and free elementary education. Articles 56 and 57 guaranteed improved functioning of parliament. Article 10 introduced voting by ballot in future parliamentary elections. Article 71 prescribed the removal of the military from parliament. Article 57 instituted a council of state and article 90 a higher council of justice. Article 102 introduced tenure for civil servants.

The final article, 108, provided for a more flexible method than the existing one for revising the constitution. The revised constitution was promulgated on 1 June 1911 and became law on 2 June.

Venizelos regarded the constitution not only as a tool to 'rationalise the parliamentary system' and to 'guarantee the freedom of the individual', but also to 'facilitate the interventionist role of the state in the economy' as an instrument of financial development and social progress.[29] The most obvious example of this is the article on land reform. To continue his reform programme, in his address of 1 June marking the conclusion of the revision process, Venizelos announced that the Double assembly would not dissolve but would continue working as a legislative body and he enumerated the issues that were his immediate priorities: the passing of statutes required by the constitution itself, municipal reform bills, judicial reform bills; and bills relating to Athens university, to agriculture, labour, emigration, finances and the two budgets of the current and the coming year.[30] Thereafter, legislative bills were introduced at a remarkable pace, until parliament was prematurely dissolved in early December.

Venizelos' speech of 5 September 1910 has become famous as a clear example of the influence he exerted over massive gatherings. But it is more useful as a tool to analyse his interpretation of the political situation he had been invited to reform. Those who could not follow his condensed speech could read it in the newspapers the following day.[31] He began his speech with an impressive account of the sectors of public life which were in need of reform. Being a lawyer by profession, he started with the familiar – justice: the antiquated civil legislation, commercial law and criminal law. Next came the educational system, the church, the local authority system and central administration. His criticism centred on the absence of any kind of social and economic policy, which had resulted in the neglect of the labouring and rural classes and the failure of the state to exercise a sound fiscal policy. All this had led to increased emigration, which further curtailed the country's productivity and wealth.

What is most surprising is not only the deftness with which Venizelos solved the political stalemate and became the leading political figure in Greece, but also his complete mastery of Greece's complex social situation and his readiness to propose solutions. Forming a clear picture from Crete, with Cretan priorities occupying the centre of his mind, would have been impossible, no matter how avidly he read the Greek press. Until his involvement in Greek affairs in December 1909, his interest in Greece was limited to the political scene and to its effect on Cretan affairs. It appears that on his return to Crete in January 1910, he was determined to examine the general condition of the country. With his well-known energy and thoroughness, he began a profound study of both the international prospects and the domestic situation of Greece. Once he became convinced that he posed no threat to the regime, Emmanuel Benakis, among others, volunteered to advise him.[32] An indirect exchange of views between the two men on the political situation had begun before Venizelos' visit to Athens. The first existing letter addressed directly to Benakis is dated 20 February 1910. To this Benakis answered on 12 March, laying down a blueprint of political and social reform: tax reform, eradication of contraband, public security, improvement of communications, development of the productive forces of the country – agriculture, stock farming and foreign trade.[33] Another of his most loyal friends was Emmanuel Repoulis, a Peloponnesian journalist and politician, whose special interests included finances and administration. Repoulis had been an associate of Stephanos Dragoumis in his short-lived experiment to initiate reform in 1907. After its failure, Dragoumis' group was dissolved, Repoulis continued to criticise the regime with his articles and turned to Venizelos as soon as he appeared on the political scene, to become one of his closest advisers.

Thus, when he assumed office in Athens, Venizelos had formed a comprehensive view of the social situation of the country. In a nutshell, at the root of the domestic problem lay the antiquated judicial and educational systems, and social and economic underdevelopment. The single most severe direct consequence of this backwardness was increased emigration, which in turn perpetuated a vicious circle of stagnation.[34] Once the causes of underdevelopment were removed, then the wave of emigration would cease. In other words, economic growth would result in social growth, which in turn would bring an increase of revenues and eventually control emigration and increase national power.

> Today's governmental regime believes that, before the end of the present decade, the Greek people will see their exports doubled, their imports doubled, their national product doubled, the people's prosperity secured; they will see that emigration will cease having the unhealthy effect it has today, that foreign lands will not absorb a large part of the labour force that is so necessary to cultivate our own land, which only awaits their care in order to provide its riches in abundance.
>
> When this happens, conscription will double, therefore the military strength of Greece will also double and her position in the world will correspond to her military and economic strength . . .[35]

Two and a half months after assuming office, he had transformed this comprehensive analysis into a political agenda that he called 'the programme of reconstruction' and he used the opportunity of a massive electoral rally in the capital of the underdeveloped plain of Thessaly, Larissa, to present it to the electorate. It is a long list of qualified promises, whose salient characteristic is an attempt to balance out conflicting social forces. The measures fall into two categories: taxation and production. As he explained from the start:

> When we speak of reconstruction and when we work to achieve it, we seek to give to the Greek people the quantity of prosperity to which they are entitled, because they have been subjected to heavy taxation for many years in the hope of improving public finances, but each time they have found themselves deceived in their hopes. Because, unfortunately, in the past the direct relation between the national economy and wealth, that is between citizens and state revenues, was being overlooked.[36]

His first promise involved a reform of the taxation system: a reduction of indirect taxation on necessary goods, which burdened the weakest classes, and a shift of this burden to the wealthier classes in the form of income tax and death duties. A reform of the customs tariff would encourage sound domestic industry without stifling consumption by means of excessive import duties.

The second category of reforms was intended to revive the productive forces of the country. He announced the creation of a new ministry dedicated to the promotion of trade, agriculture and national wealth in general. He then promised to implement without delay the plans for the irrigation of Thessaly, which had been completed by previous administrations; to compile a land registry; and to pass laws that would establish a credit system for farmers and would rid them from the affliction of usury. Next, he committed himself to deal with public welfare in three domains: with regard to the rural population, he promised to solve the daunting question of land reform by means of legislation that would regulate relations among farmers and landowners and eventually, after a period of careful study, provide landless farmers with small plots. With regard to industrial workers, he undertook to pass bills that would guarantee their health, safety and social security, without unduly burdening the industrialist class. Finally, concerning the major issue of emigration, he believed that the improvement of social conditions and special legislation would limit the exodus.[37]

His long address dealt with all the issues for which he had criticised the previous administrations in his 5 September speech: local administration, public security, the administration of justice, education and military reorganisation. On all these issues he had elaborated specific proposals.[38]

There is a consistent pattern of political ethics that runs through his early electoral speeches: sacrifice of personal and partisan interests to the common cause; honesty above expediency toward rulers and ruled alike; submission of the politician to the rule of law; and the conviction that power is not an objective to be sought for its own merit, but a means for attaining a higher end. This list was appealing to the electorate, which had been disappointed by party politics and could now see an alternative positive picture of future political ethics.[39]

Once in power and with the electoral victory of November secure, he could allow himself the luxury of magnanimity toward his rivals. They were no longer considered responsible for political and moral corruption, as they had been a year before. Their weakness was neither lack of patriotism nor ignorance of the necessary reforms, but lack of political courage.[40] This was the closest he came to acknowledging the work of his predecessors. Yet, in the field of legislative reform, as in the case of the amendment of the constitution, the success of the early years of Venizelos' administration benefited greatly from the legislation voted during Dragoumis' months in office. The first innovative measures in many fields had been voted between January and August 1910 by the Dragoumis administration. Venizelos took over with similar determination in October, and started work in January 1911 with increased popular sanction. Dragoumis' legislation had focused on the structural changes of the administration, on issues of public finance and on public safety and national security. In turn, Venizelos gave precedence to matters of legislative reform, social policy and education over an expansionist foreign policy, as he assured his voters in November 1910.[41]

At the end of his first term in office, beside the constitutional revision, Venizelos was able to produce a remarkable output of legislative work. This he presented to the electorate and asked for a renewal of his mandate. Viewed as a whole, order and productivity were the key directions. In the domain of law and order, financial and security measures contained a mixture of severity and leniency with a view to effectiveness. All measures tended to enhance the control of central authority, by erasing levels of administration, by simplifying procedures and by improving communications. The result was that fugitives gave themselves up for trial, and overdue debts to the state were collected. In detail, his performance listed an impressive number of measures.

In the domain of justice, special commissions, headed by eminent jurists, began work on replacing the antiquated system with a new commercial code and new codes of civil and criminal law. Meanwhile, legislation dealt with urgent needs related: to civil law, such as rules on wills and usury; to criminal law, such as laws on fugitives, and on the conversion of small sentences to financial penalties; and to laws improving the conditions of both lawyers and judges. Other laws dealt with education, securing the financial autonomy of the University of Athens, increasing the number of primary schools and encouraging training in the fields of production and technology. One of Venizelos' major achievements was the revision of the system of local administration. The 1911 law on municipalities he regarded, as he said with a measure of exaggeration, as equal to the revision of the constitution. A number of laws and measures were dedicated directly to increasing productivity. A reform of the gendarmerie, alongside the law on fugitives, was intended to increase security in the country; while a number of public works, such as the draining of marshes, construction of roads and the improvement of postal and telegraphic communications laid the foundations for increased growth.

By means of another set of laws and specific measures Venizelos aimed at further increasing productivity and achieving social welfare and justice. The newly-founded eighth ministry, the Ministry of National Economy, dedicated exclusively to the promotion of productivity, was given ample funding and was able to produce spectacular results: it set up new agricultural schools and improved education, organised its statistical service and introduced new methods and varieties of products. A department of labour and social welfare was set up in the new ministry, to study labour issues. This, until 1910, had belonged to the domain of the Ministry of the Interior, which lacked the qualified personnel. A mixed labour council was set up, consisting of workers, industrialists, civil servants, MPs and university professors. Its size, however, rendered the council too inflexible to deal with everyday matters.[42]

A number of bills were produced initiating what Venizelos believed to be the beginning of comprehensive labour legislation: laws on the hygiene and safety of workers, on women's labour, on labour of minors, on minimum wages, on the settlement of labour disputes. Labour legislation brought a visible, albeit limited, measure of control over the state of workers' conditions. To cite but one example, although a maximum of ten to twelve working hours per day was established for most industries in 1911, an inspection a year later revealed that workers in certain provincial factories worked for fourteen or even eighteen hours.[43] Progress was slow, not because legislation was lacking nor because inspections did not reveal its violations, but because social pressure was not as strong as in other industrialised countries.

The legislation, however, which produced the most spectacular short-term results, and provided a firm basis for the future, was the major reform of the ineffective and corrupt tax system. The reorganisation of the General

Office of Public Accounts, coupled with systematic and equitable enforcement of existing legislation, new customs laws and measures against contraband, and the first laws of a major reform of the tax legislation, increased the revenues of the state. Overdue taxes were collected, while the efficiency of the tax collecting and customs services, and increased productivity, brought new revenues without recourse to heavier taxation.[44]

As it turned out, Venizelos' pre-war reform work ended with the abrupt termination of the session of the Double assembly in December 1911. But the work already completed was a part of a well-thought-out plan. Undoubtedly Venizelos had no illusions that he could complete it in a short time. And by March 1912, he was far from certain that he could proceed without interference. Nevertheless, to his electorate he gave a full description of his social and political vision: the implementation of existing legislation, the statutes required by the revised constitution such as the law on the council of state, a reform of the customs legislation, new laws on emigration, on the improvement of sanitary conditions, on education, on the institution of a land registry, on credit, labour and commerce, and of course major public works throughout the country.

Indeed, serious work was under way on several of these issues. In 1912 the minister of the interior, Emmanuel Repoulis, set up a committee headed by himself to study the issue of emigration. In the summer, the committee produced a detailed report and a bill on the matter.[45]

On other matters, such as commercial and industrial issues, balancing between industrialists and workers, between free trade and protectionism in a socially and economically equitable customs tariff, required a careful study of conflicting interests and long preparatory statistical work. By 1912, the statistical service of the new ministry, the labour committees and the workers and industrialists' unions were beginning to produce their reports, but no legislation was completed.[46]

THE LIMITS OF REFORM

Although social reform and financial progress were fundamental issues in Venizelos' political agenda, from the onset, international complications forced him to give increasing priority to issues of foreign policy and military reorganisation. In November 1910, as he had assured his voters in Larissa, and through them Greece's neighbours:

> We are, in conclusion, a government particularly inclined toward peace, because our country is in need of a long period of quiet, in order to recover and advance. Therefore, by adopting measures for our army, we do not have aggressive designs against anyone.

> The whole world is aware of the sincere joy with which the Greek people saluted the Turkish change of regime. This is not unreasonable, in view of our great interests in the neighbouring state, and it justifies the interest with which we follow events there, in an effort to remove every misunderstanding with Turkey, as with the other peoples of the Balkans, in order to encourage the development of a bond that may later assume a different form.[47]

Even as he had assumed power in Athens, he had been faced with a crisis in Greek-Turkish relations. He had dealt with it in an unequivocal way by placing Gryparis at the helm of the Foreign Ministry. He had also assured both the Porte and the Great Powers that Greece would not seek trouble by forcing a solution of the Cretan question. The Cretans, however, had remained restless. At every opportunity since the failure of their movement in September 1908, they had attempted to force a de facto union with Greece by sending deputies to the Greek parliament. Venizelos, a staunch supporter of union, now appeared determined to block it. At the risk of losing popular support, he sent them back. Although the opposition, both in Crete and in Athens, attempted to benefit from Venizelos' seemingly unpopular decision, his firm hand in the Cretan question gave him a second resounding victory in the March 1912 elections. Twice he had been obliged to use force to keep the Cretan deputies out of the Greek parliament – in December 1911, when he co-operated with the international naval forces patrolling Cretan waters to intercept seventy Cretan deputies on their way to Piraeus,[48] and in May 1912, when Venizelos himself refused admission to those deputies who had evaded international surveillance and had made their way to Athens.[49] His attitude on both these occasions had kept the peace, but at a heavy price: the normal functioning of parliament. In December 1911, before the threat of the Cretan deputies, Venizelos had prematurely ended the session of parliament, thus putting a sudden end to the reform programme he had initiated eleven months before.

Parliament was not to convene in regular sessions until after the end of the Balkan Wars. What was even worse, the implementation of articles of the constitution that were of vital importance for justice and social progress, such as the land reform and the founding of the council of state, awaited the end of the ten-year war period. The unforeseen precipitation of the Balkan crisis therefore prevented him from moving from legislation to implementation, as he had intended.

FINANCIAL AND MILITARY REFORM

Inevitably, Venizelos had fallen into the same trap he had set up himself. As the responsible head of the Greek government he had no option but to resist the very tactics he had adopted while in charge of Cretan affairs that, if yielded to, would lead to a premature war. The only way out was to temporise until Greece was diplomatically and militarily prepared. After all, he was utterly convinced that the solution of both the Cretan question and that of the partition of Macedonia would involve at best a show of strength, most probably outright military engagement. Indeed, he had dedicated himself to the task, a combination of diplomatic and military preparations, as soon as he had come to power. In this domain, as in that of public finances, he continued the policy of Stephanos Dragoumis, who had laid the foundations for a sound economy, for the invitation of foreign military missions to reorganise and train the army and the navy and for an understanding with the Ottoman Empire's Balkan neighbours.

One of his first measures was to apply to London for the dispatch of British naval officers to organise the Greek navy. The result was that a mission under Rear-Admiral Tufnell arrived in Athens on 11 April 1911. Shortly before, in mid-January, a French military mission under General Eydoux had arrived to deal with the army. Meanwhile, the revision of article 3 of the constitution enabled foreign subjects to assume positions of responsibility in the armed forces, thus greatly facilitating their task.

Venizelos, in charge of the separate ministries of the army and, until the May 1912 major cabinet reshuffle, of the navy as well, followed military affairs in person for they involved three extremely delicate areas: the thorny issue of defusing tension within the armed forces after the Goudi coup; the acceleration of Greek military preparations; and, ultimately, the orientation of Greek foreign policy.

The relationship between Venizelos and Greek military officers deserves particular attention. The Goudi coup had been aimed against all existing political parties and the crown.[50] The restlessness and conspiratorial movements of the army, the gendarmerie and the navy until Dragoumis had taken office were adequate proof that after the Goudi coup, the military had established a practice of resorting to the use of force whenever they disagreed with political developments or felt threatened.[51] Yet the particular circumstances under which Venizelos had been summoned to rescue the 'revolution' and the personality of Venizelos himself guaranteed that he, unlike other Greek leaders, would not be cowed into becoming a hireling of the Military League or any group of officers. Indeed one of his first steps upon the assumption of power had been to demonstrate beyond doubt that he was in complete control of the armed forces and to see that the military confined themselves strictly to their professional role. Indeed, article 71 of the revised constitution forbade military officers from entering parliament. Besides, the expansionist policy of the country required a long-needed and hitherto poorly-pursued programme of military reform, involving the co-operation of a trouble free military corps. One of the statements in his first appearance before the assembly was that he intended to mend divisions and restore discipline within the army.[52] Another urgent step was to establish good relations with the crown prince. Constantine, who had left Greece immediately after the August 1909 coup, had returned to Athens in the first days of September 1910, shortly after the elections. One of Venizelos' first measures was to reinstate the crown prince as head of the armed forces. Overcoming Constantine's initial obstinacy and after a heated debate in parliament, Venizelos recreated the office of inspector general of the army in June 1911, one of the first bills passed after the revision of the constitution. Constantine still refused the government's offer, yielding only by the end of March 1912. Consequently, in the event of war, he would become head of the armed forces.[53]

Constantine's reservations stemmed from his profound distrust of the French in matters of military training and equipment. The crown prince and his German-trained entourage had opposed the invitation of the French mission and were determined to undermine its task. But General Eydoux and his staff had the unconditional support of Venizelos, and the spring manoeuvres of May 1912 were so successful that even Constantine reluctantly acknowledged the progress that had been made.[54] The standing military force had been raised from 60,000 to 100,000 men, while the mobilisation was expected to produce 135,000 men.[55]

The selection of the British mission to train and organise the Greek navy had been accepted unreservedly by Greek naval officers and their training proceeded uneventfully. Tufnell trained the Greek fleet intensively in the summer months of 1911 and 1912, in the Aegean and Ionian waters, and at the end of May 1912, a co-ordinated military and naval exercise was conducted off Volos. Clearly, in the summer of 1912 the country was preparing for war. In this war, the Greek navy was expected to play a decisive role. A set of key proposals was adopted that proved to be of vital importance.

First of all, at long last, a decision was taken on the programme of naval construction. As by July 1912 what mattered above all was rapid delivery dates, the orders for all ships – two destroyers, six torpedo boats and a cruiser – were given to the German firm Vulkan, inciting strong reactions from the British. The British obtained their share by an additional last-minute purchase of four destroyers in the last days of September. When the war broke out, all six destroyers – Vulkan offering two that had been ordered by the German government – and a French-built submarine were able to join the Greek fleet in the Aegean. Together with the *Averof*, a large cruiser that had been acquired in 1911, they were a sizeable force, able to contribute effectively to the war effort.

Secondly, at the end of the summer the naval staff finalised the plans of action of the fleet. The general staff concluded that the single goal of the naval operations should be total mastery of the sea: to secure the fleet's communications, to hinder the communications of the enemy and the transport of troops from Asia, and to liberate the Aegean Islands and Crete. This could be accomplished only if the Greeks could isolate the Turkish fleet beyond the Dardanelles, by patrolling the area at close range. Limnos, a small island at the exit of the straits, suited the purpose ideally. The first task of the fleet therefore was to occupy it and transfer its naval base there.

Most critically, the selection of the head of the navy was a matter in which Venizelos had the final word. To the disappointment of his rivals, Venizelos selected Captain Pavlos Koundouriotis, a hotheaded and controversial officer, who was nearing the end of an insignificant career as aide-de-camp of King George I. On the eve of the war Venizelos appointed him commander-in-chief of the Aegean fleet and on 5 October, as the fleet was ready to sail, promoted him to the rank of rear-admiral.[56]

To the military preparation of Greece he had devoted 105 million drachmas, including the proceeds of a recent loan.[57] To Venizelos' dismay, this amounted to a significant part of Greece's resources, which he had intended to devote to the social needs of the country. As he had repeatedly remarked, at the root of a nation's well-being and strength lay a sound economy. Although he never acknowledged as much, in the domain of public finances, he continued the policy of Stephanos Dragoumis, who had laid the foundations for a sound economy. Dragoumis' administration, under the guidance of the vice-president of the National Bank of Greece, the eminent financial expert Ioannis Valaoritis, had adopted measures to stabilise the drachma and to prepare for a foreign loan. The sound management of the fiscal year 1910 had resulted in a surplus budget of 5 million drachmas after many years of deficit. Venizelos had appointed as successor to Dragoumis at the head of the finance ministry a trusted friend of both Dragoumis and Valaoritis, an ex-journalist and former consul general of Greece in Thessaloniki, the enterprising Lambros Koromilas. His predecessor's financial policy had enabled the country to contract a 150 million francs foreign loan, the first instalment of which, 110 million, was introduced in the Paris Bourse in November 1911. All these measures, together with the overall improvement of the administration, resulted in brighter prospects for the economy, reflected in two consecutive surplus budgets for the years 1910 and 1911. These funds were used to finance the preparation and the conduct of the Balkan Wars, deferring the development of the country's productive forces to a more propitious date. That date did not come before 1923, by which time Greece was up against a set of entirely new challenges and opportunities.

NOTES

1. Helen Gardikas-Katsiadakis (1992), 'I Elliniki Kyvernisi kai to Kritiko Zitima: 1908' ['The Greek Government and the Cretan Question: 1908'], *Aphieroma ston Panepistimiako Daskalo Vas. Vl. Sfyroera apo tous mathites tou* [*Studies Dedicated to the University Teacher Vas. Vl. Sfyroeras by his Students*], Athens, pp. 343–72. To underline the provisional character of the executive committee, the sectors of the administration did not have the status of ministries or secretaries of state, but of 'higher directorates'.
2. Helen Gardikas-Katsiadakis (1995), *Greece and the Balkan Imbroglio. Greek Foreign Policy, 1911–1913*, Athens, pp. 35–7.
3. From the early stages of the League's conspiratorial meetings, the junior officers had hoped that Venizelos would lead the movement for the country's revival. S. Victor Papacosma (1997), *The Military in Greek Politics. The 1909 Coup d' État*, Kent: Kent State University Press, p. 49.
4. Ibid., pp. 54, 206.
5. *Kiryx* [*Herald*], 26 August 1909; quoted in (1981), *Eleftheriou Venizelou ta keimena, 1909–1935* [*Eleftherios Venizelos' Texts, 1909–1935*], ed. S. I. Stephanou, vol. 1, 1909–1914 (hereafter: *Keimena* I), Athens, p. 142.
6. Ibid.; quoted in *Keimena* I, pp. 144–5 (see Note 5). My emphasis.
7. Venizelos to the head of the Military League, quoted in *Keimena* I, p. 141 (see Note 5).
8. Helen Gardikas-Katsiadakis (1992), 'To daneio tou 1910. Oikonomiki anorthosi kai politiki syngiria 1909–1910' ['The Loan of 1910. Financial Revival and Political Conjuncture 1909–1910'], *Mnimosini* 11, pp. 444–5.
9. *Kiryx*, 26 August 1909; quoted in *Keimena* I, p. 143 (see Note 5).
10. For a detailed and accurate account of the first meeting between Venizelos and the League's council, see George K. Aspreas (1930), *Politiki istoria tis Neoteras Ellados 1821–1928* [*A Political History of Modern Greece, 1821–1928*], vol. IIIa, Athens, p. 133 ff.
11. *Kiryx*, 26 August 1909 and other articles; quoted in *Keimena* I, p. 145 ff (see Note 5).
12. *Akropolis*, 1 September 1909.
13. Venizelos to Theotokis, Athens, 9 January 1910 and reply by Theotokis; both quoted in Aspreas, *Politiki Istoria*, pp. 141–2 (see Note 10).
14. The decision was taken on 15 January and Dragoumis was sworn into office on 18 January, after a meeting with the League's council. Aspreas, *Politiki Istoria*, pp. 149–51 (see Note 10).

15. Text of the interview in *Keimena* I, p. 157 (see Note 5). Whether deliberately or not, for a long time Venizelos refrained from using the term 'Liberal Party'.
16. Gardikas-Katsiadakis, *Greece and the Balkan Imbroglio*, p. 37 (see Note 2).
17. Helen Gardikas-Katsiadakis (1995), 'I gnorimia Venizelou kai Benaki' ['The Acquaintance of Venizelos and Benakis'], *Pepragmena tou VII Diethnous Kritologikou Synedriou* [*Proceedings of the VII International Cretological Congress*], vol. IIIa, Rethymnon, p. 82.
18. The generally accepted view that he arrived at Athens on 5 September is not convincing, since the assembly opened its proceedings on 3 September. Although he stopped at Syros on his way to Piraeus, it is hardly possible that the crossing lasted six days.
19. From his speech of 5 September 1910 in Athens, published in *Keimena* I, pp. 174–5 (see Note 5). The first such political club was the Liberal Club he founded in Athens.
20. For this interpretation of the nature of Venizelos' role as a political leader, see Mark Mazower (1992), 'The Messiah and the Bourgeoisie: Venizelos and Politics in Greece, 1909–1912', *The Historical Journal* 35 (4), pp. 885–904.
21. Gardikas-Katsiadakis, *Greece and the Balkan Imbroglio*, pp. 37–8 (see Note 2).
22. Gardikas-Katsiadakis, 'To daneio tou 1910', pp. 482–3 (see Note 8).
23. *Keimena* I, p. 189 (see Note 5).
24. Ibid. p. 188.
25. Aspreas, *Politiki Istoria*, p. 164 (see Note 10).
26. *Keimena* I, p. 229, from his speech of 26 November 1910 in Athens (see Note 5).
27. Venizelos' intervention to impose a middle-of-the-road solution to the language question briefly estranged the proponents of the vernacular (dimotiki) among the progressive liberal-socialist intellectuals who had supported him. See Rena Stavridi-Patrikiou (1988), 'I entaxi sosialiston dianooumenon sto kinima tou Venizelismou' ['The Adherence of the Socialist Intellectuals to the Venizelist Movement'], in George Th. Mavrogordatos and Christos Ch. Hadziiosif (eds), *Venizelismos kai astikos eksynchronismos* [*Venizelism and Bourgeois Modernisation*], Irakleion, pp. 318–19.
28. Nikos C. Alivizatos, 'O Eleftherios Venizelos kai o syntagmatikos eksynchronismos tis choras' ['Eleftherios Venizelos and the Constitutional Modernisation of the Country'], ibid., p. 33, remarks that certain points of his views on parliamentarism he had already formulated while participating in the drafting of the 1907 Cretan constitution. For Venizelos' frequent attendance and contribution, see pp. 34–5.
29. Ibid., pp. 39–42.
30. *Keimena* I, pp. 276–8 (see Note 5).
31. Ibid., p. 178 from his speech of 5 September 1910 in Athens.

32. For both personal and ideological reasons, the enlightened members of the local upper middle class and of the diaspora supported Venizelos. See George Dertilis (1977), *Koinonikos metaschimatismos kai stratiotiki epemvasi 1880–1909* [*Social Change and Military Intervention, 1880–1909*], Athens, pp. 227–8.
33. Gardikas-Katsiadakis, 'I gnorimia Venizelou kai Benaki', p. 81 (see Note 17).
34. Venizelos concentrated on the social and demographic consequences of emigration, which was predominantly transatlantic, ignoring the importance of the inflow of funds from emigrant workers.
35. *Keimena* I, p. 354 (see Note 5).
36. *Keimena* I, p. 204 (see Note 5).
37. Neither specific Greek legislation, nor improved domestic conditions helped in diminishing emigration. It continued unabated until the inter-war period, when it ended due to American anti-immigration legislation. See S. D. Petmezas (1999), 'Dimographia' ['Demography'], in Christos Hadjiiosif (ed.), *Istoria tis Elladas tou 20ou aiona. Oi aparches, 1900–1922* [*History of 20th-Century Greece. The Beginnings, 1900–1922*] [hereafter: Hadjiiosif (ed.), *History of Greece*], vol. Ia, Athens, p. 50.
38. *Keimena* I, pp. 204–8, from his speech of 14 November 1910, in Larissa (see Note 5).
39. See his speeches of 5 September, 14 November and 26 November 1910, in *Keimena* I pp. 174–8, 204–8 and 226–30 respectively (see Note 5).
40. Ibid., p. 227, from his speech of 26 November 1910 in Athens.
41. Ibid., p. 208.
42. George B. Leon (1976), *The Greek Socialist Movement and the First World War. The Road to Unity*, Boulder: East European Monographs, pp. 54–5.
43. Ibid., pp. 57–8.
44. *Keimena* I, pp. 343–51, from his speech of 19 February 1912 in Patras (see Note 5).
45. Alexandros Kitroeff, 'I yperantlantiki metanastefsi' ['Transatlantic Emigration'], Hadjiiosif (ed.), *History of Greece*, vol. Ia, pp. 148–9 (see Note 36).
46. See Christina Agriantoni, 'Viomichania' ['Industry'], Hadziiosif (ed.), *History of Greece*, vol. Ia, pp. 180, 199 (see Note 36).
47. *Keimena* I, p. 208 (see Note 5).
48. Katsiadakis, *Greece and the Balkan Imbroglio*, pp. 76–7 (see Note 2).
49. Ibid., p. 81.
50. Aspreas, *Politiki Istoria*, IIIa, pp. 99–100 (see Note 10). A large number of Greek officers resented the favouritism practised by Crown Prince Constantine, as commander-in-chief of the army, and the introduction of bills harmful to their professional interests. These grievances, along with the general disillusionment at the international situation, were the principal causes of the coup.
51. Papacosma, *The military*, generally (see Note 3).

52. *Keimena* I, p. 188 (see Note 5).
53. Katsiadakis, *Greece and the Balkan Imbroglio*, p. 13 (see Note 2).
54. Ibid., p. 55.
55. (1932) *O Ellinikos stratos kata tous Valkanikous polemous tou 1912–1913* [*The Greek Army during the Balkan Wars of 1912–1913*], vol. I, Athens, p. 33.
56. S. Dousmanis (1939), *To imerologion tou Kyvernitou tou theoriktou Averof kata tous polemous 1912–1913* [*The Diary of the Commander of the Cruiser Averof during the Wars 1912–1913*], Athens, p. 47.
57. *Keimena* I, p. 360 (see Note 5).

4

Protagonist in Politics, 1912–20

Thanos Veremis and Helen Gardikas-Katsiadakis

Venizelos was less devoted than Trikoupis to the principle of the superiority of parliamentary politics over all other forms of democratic governance. His own inclination was toward the Aristotelian division of politics into pure and corrupt versions. He was therefore less concerned with the political system than with its actual operation. This view of politics naturally placed the burden of state management on the persons in power, rather than on the system of politics. Success, therefore, would depend mostly on the attributes of the personalities who were placed, by choice or chance, in the key posts of power.[1] When Venizelos restored the damaged prestige of the monarchy, after the 1909 coup had challenged its legitimacy, and reinstated King George as the arbiter of parliamentary politics in 1910, he was depending entirely on the moderation and prudence of the particular monarch for the viability of the institution. He could anticipate neither the assassination of George nor the character of Constantine, who replaced him on the throne in 1913. Before the National Schism, Venizelos had encouraged a bipolar system of governance in which the head of state and the head of government shared substantial authority. His hope was that the grateful monarch would be willing to grant his consent on vital issues of reform and foreign policy.

The 1911 reform of the constitution had left intact its fundamental articles that guaranteed the character of the regime, with the king acting as an arbiter and guarantor in a system of parliamentary politics. With the advent of Venizelos to power the system regained its bipolar character, which it had lost following the end of the Trikoupis era and the death of his chief opponent Theodoros Diliyannis.

For a brief period, between 1910 and 1913, Venizelos' supremacy was unchallenged, as the united old parties had fallen into disrepute for having failed to deal with the social and political problems of the country. During this period, the bipolar system of governance had worked smoothly, as from Venizelos' arrival in Athens a spirit of complete mutual understanding had developed between monarch and premier. King George had fully endorsed his prime minister's decisions on all crucial matters, such as the reform of the constitution, the training and leadership of the army and navy and foreign policy issues.

Circumstances changed overnight, on 18 March 1913, when a mentally disturbed teacher assassinated King George during his afternoon walk in Thessaloniki. His son and successor, King Constantine differed from his father both in character and political orientation. He was an arrogant, inflexible and not very bright man, who had gained popularity as the commander-in-chief of the army during the Balkan Wars. As a German-trained military officer and as the brother-in-law of Kaiser Wilhelm of Germany, he was committed to veering the foreign policy of Greece away from its allegiance to the maritime powers of France and Great Britain toward the continental powers of Central Europe, Germany and Austria–Hungary.

Constantine's resentment at the entrustment of the training of the Greek army to French officers and his annoyance at the slightest interference of the prime minister in matters concerning the Balkan campaigns were early symptoms of the irreconcilable rift that divided the two men in 1915. By far the most serious indication was their disagreement over the conclusion of the Greek–Serbian alliance in May 1913. At that point, Venizelos had succeeded in prevailing upon Constantine to agree to an alliance with Serbia as the only way to deal with an imminent Bulgarian threat to Greek positions in Macedonia and to the city of Thessaloniki itself. To Constantine's justifiable fear that an alliance with Serbia might involve Greece in a confrontation with Austria, he had answered that, if Austria attacked Serbia, then Russia would intervene and a European war would break out. The risk of isolation in a local war involving Austria alone was remote; whereas the threat from Bulgaria was so pressing that Constantine could hardly refuse to agree to the only solution that could provide Greece with an ally.[2] In the months that followed, Venizelos avoided committing his country openly in favour of either of the two European alliance systems, both in order to promote the interests of Greece in Eastern Macedonia, the Aegean and Epirus and in order to maintain peace with his own king.

As it turned out, the clash between Constantine and Venizelos involved the issue of their earlier serious confrontation. The clash centred on the issue of foreign policy. Since the outbreak of the First World War in Europe the balance of powers in the Balkans was a matter of high priority for peripheral states and Great Powers alike. In Greece, ideological predilections influenced prognoses as to the outcome of the war. King Constantine and Foreign Minister George Streit, who had been appointed to the Foreign Ministry after the Balkan Wars, believed in the eventual victory of the German military forces and upheld a policy of permanent neutrality.

Prime Minister Venizelos, on the other hand, foresaw a victory for the Western naval powers and sought an opportunity to join the war on the winning side. The opportunity was not at hand for, although the Entente Powers appreciated the views of Venizelos, they considered Bulgaria a more vital potential ally in their efforts to control the Balkans than Greece. Until the summer of 1915, Great Britain in particular believed that it was possible to lure Bulgaria into the Entente camp and end the war immediately. In Greece the two opposing sides clashed and Streit resigned from office on 18 August 1914. Streit, however, remained a very influential factor in Greek politics, as the king's councillor. Three weeks later, on 7 September, Venizelos, too, resigned for the king rejected his plan to proceed to talks with Britain on the possibility of a future co-operation. King Constantine refused to accept his resignation. For a while, throughout the winter of 1914, as no spectacular developments took place in the region, the domestic crisis remained concealed. For Venizelos, the initial success of the British operations against the Dardanelles offered the opportunity he awaited to enter the war by putting substantial forces at the disposal of the Entente. At two royal councils Venizelos enjoyed the support of all the political leaders, but failed to prevail over the general staff and the king. On 6 March 1915 he again resigned from office.

When the clash between the crown and the prime minister (the head of state and the head of government) erupted in 1915 over Venizelos' decision to enter the war on the side of the Triple Entente, Constantine was prepared to exercise his royal prerogative and defy the authority of the majority in parliament. His predilection for the monarch's divine rights, a popularity gained during the Balkan campaigns and his prime minister's own practice of considering the king a partner in politics, rather than a mere symbol, drove Constantine to partake in decision-making that undermined the interests of the state.

Venizelos' view of the state was a synthesis of Trikoupis' intention to make it the locomotive of growth by creating a solid infrastructure, and Diliyannis' vision of agricultural self-sufficiency and considerations of welfare politics. Although the Cretan politician, it appears, inherited Diliyannis' orphaned constituency, mainly because Trikoupis' party had been inherited by Georgios Theotokis, the reformist platform he advocated upon his arrival in Athens won him the overwhelming support of those in the middle class of old Greece that had not declared their political preference before. This, however, was not a solid power basis.[3]

The National Schism (dichasmos), with all the features of a clash between conservatives and liberals, appeared strange in a country without an 'ancien régime' and a landed aristocracy that would turn to royalty as a rallying point. King Constantine owed his popularity to his performance as a commander-in-chief in military campaigns spurred by Venizelos' irredentist agenda. Ironically, Constantine, who made his mark in the military field, became the rallying force of the war-weary population of old Greece (as opposed to the newly-acquired territories) and the traditional political parties that had joined forces against a reformist Venizelos in the elections of 1910 and 1912.

By a strange twist of fate, the 1915 pro-royalist coalition against Venizelos included more or less the same parties that had been overruled by King George in 1910 in favour of the Cretan newcomer. The king had then made use of his prerogative to appoint the prime minister and, by choosing Venizelos and granting him a dissolution of the assembly at his own timing, had interfered beyond customary practice in Greek politics. Five years later King Constantine reversed his father's choice. He revived the old political parties – already past their prime in 1910 – with an anti-Venizelos platform and became their actual leader. This revival, however, was not a comeback of the former party leadership. The old personal parties had lost their influence as rallying forces for specific interests and to a large extent the leaders had lost their appeal as individual patrons in a local clientele system. New leaders, such as Gounaris, failed to impose their authority over the old political elite. The vacuum was filled symbolically and practically by the king. King Constantine became the head of a new party, which consisted of the agglomeration of most of the old parties of the old territories. Its main common ideological characteristic was the anti-Venizelist orientation of its leaders and following.

Top-to-bottom, or macro-historical approaches to the study of Venizelos' clash with Constantine abound. Ventiris, Alastos and Leon deal mainly with domestic political and Great Power inputs in the 1915–20 crisis. A micro-historical, bottom-up approach of the cleavage will reveal differences and divisions that lay dormant in Greek society and politics before the Great War. Regional, social, ethnic, even familial conflicts, activated by an extraordinary external event, the First World War, might have, under normal circumstances, remained inactive. Mavrogordatos has brought the 1915 schism into a meticulous analysis of mass politics in the inter-war period.[4] His study of a notorious paramilitary organisation of royalists, the epistratoi, constitutes a partial remedy for the absence of bottom-up works on the period of the great schism.[5] A similar analysis of the following of Venizelos is lacking.

On the eve of the National Schism, Greece had increased its territory from 25,014 to 41,993 square miles and its population from 2,700,000 to 4,800,000.[6] The inclusion of the population of the newly-acquired territories in the confines of the Greek state posed a threat to the monopoly in public offices hitherto enjoyed by the professional classes of old Greece, which formed the clientele of the old parties. The political establishment of 'old Greece' resented having to share its privileges with their new fellow-citizens and began to question the tenet of irredentism that was diminishing their significance in the state apparatus. Besides, the wars of 1912 and 1913 had cost the country heavily in financial resources and human casualties.

The royalist slogan 'A small but honourable Greece' was a synonym for maintaining the territorial status quo and the privileges of the original citizens of the independent state. This represented a revival of a similar episode in the past, when the 'autochthons' of 1844 had fought tooth and nail against extending citizen rights to Greeks who had gathered in the new state from unredeemed territories in the Ottoman Empire. Their progeny of 1916 imitated them in opposing Venizelos' irredentism and the bid of the new citizens for a share in the exercise of power.

The issue that triggered such a vehement division among Greeks was initially centred on a matter of foreign policy. Not without justification, political parties debated fiercely on the issue of whether Greece would enter the war on the side of the Entente or would remain neutral, as advocated the Germanophile Constantine, since the future of the state would certainly depend on the outcome of the great conflict. The subsequent clash of personalities between Venizelos and Constantine transformed the controversy into an acrimonious contest of personal loyalties for most of the population.

When Venizelos resigned in March 1915, as a result of the king's rejection of his plan to attack the Dardanelles by land to assist the allied naval operation, he chose not to raise the issue of Constantine's constitutional right to oppose his view of foreign policy. The general election held on 13 June 1915 conducted by the minority government headed by Dimitrios Gounaris gave the liberals 185 seats in a parliament of 310. Venizelos interpreted this victory as a popular mandate to his own choice of foreign policy. It was clear, however, that his earlier power basis had been reduced. Since his resignation and the dissolution of parliament, the king and the general staff had expanded their influence over the state apparatus. It was therefore evident that he did not have full control of the situation. Besides, after Venizelos' election victory, Constantine was unwilling to collaborate with the leader of the majority, refused to summon him to form a government and used his illness as a pretext for delaying the opening of parliament until 16 August. Eventually, Venizelos was sworn into office on 23 August.

Hitherto, both leaders hesitated to adopt unconstitutional methods to impose their policy. Acting upon the advice of moderate royalists, such as Dragoumis, Skouloudis and Gounaris, Constantine intended to avoid a violation of the constitution, but rather to coerce Venizelos into accepting his course of action or to force him out of office. And Venizelos had decided not to question Constantine's constitutional right to oppose his responsibility on matters of foreign policy.[7]

Yet, the situation in the Balkans undermined his policy. On 7 September 1915, Bulgaria signed an agreement with the Central Powers for an attack against Serbia. Greece was now confronted with the issue of honouring her treaty obligations toward Serbia. Venizelos moved a step further in his confrontation with the king. On 22 September he denounced Constantine's practice of ignoring the will of the popularly elected parliament in matters of foreign policy.[8]

On 23 September Bulgaria mobilised its forces and Venizelos overcame the unwillingness of the king to sign a decree for Greece's mobilisation. His main argument for opposing a Greek mobilisation was that Serbia, under pressure by Austria, was incapable of placing 150,000 men into the field of Greece's Macedonian borders, as stipulated by the Greco-Serbian alliance. Venizelos' suggestion that the allies provided this force instead, and its approval by France and Britain, tipped the balance, but only momentarily. When, under the influence of his advisers, the ambivalent king retracted his decision, Venizelos had already communicated his plan to the allies.[9] Eventually, Venizelos' threat of resignation worked and Constantine relented because he did not want to appear negligent of his country's security. He agreed to issue a decree of general mobilisation of the Greek army.

Doros Alastos dramatised the discussion between the two men in the following terms: 'Your Majesty, having failed to persuade you, I am very sorry but it is my duty, as representing at this moment the sovereignty of the people, to tell you that this time you have no right to differ from me . . . If you are determined to violate the constitution you must say so clearly and assume full responsibility.' The king's answer was staggering. 'As long as it is a question of internal affairs, I am bound to obey to the popular verdict; but when it is a question of foreign policy, great international questions . . . I must insist that it shall or shall not be done because I feel responsible before God.'[10]

The decree of general mobilisation came at a time when the landing of allied troops at Thessaloniki had become a matter of endless debate among the allies, while Venizelos vacillated between inviting the foreign troops and not exposing his dealings to the king. Eventually, on 30 September, without previous notification, a number of French officers landed at Thessaloniki with requests for further landing arrangements that amounted to extensive occupation of key positions. The presence of foreign troops in Thessaloniki caused much resentment, which was vented in the royalist press. A war to support Serbia against the Triple Alliance made less sense to the average Greek, who was prepared to fight, as he had done in the past, for the irredentist cause of his country. The issue was debated in parliament during the night of 4 October 1915. In a fiery speech, Venizelos once again denounced the king's unconstitutional practice of ignoring the will of the people, stated that he would honour the Greek–Serbian treaty and protect the Serbian flank, and gave his government a vote of confidence by a majority of twenty-seven.[11] Despite the vote of confidence, Constantine expressed his disapproval of the prime minister's statements and refused to abandon Greece's neutrality. Venizelos was once more forced to hand in his resignation.

A Zaimis caretaker government was followed by one under Skouloudis, who described his policy towards the Triple Entente as one of 'very benevolent neutrality.'[12] The allies increased their pressure on Athens for the fortification of Thessaloniki and by 10 December the two sides had reached an agreement and strict allied measures were somewhat eased.

The domestic situation, however, had become extremely complex. Following the resignation of Zaimis' government in November, the king dissolved parliament and proclaimed elections for 19 December. Venizelos, with the conviction that elections held in a state of mobilisation were not free elections, issued a manifesto denouncing the king for reducing the constitution to shreds and inviting his followers to boycott the elections.[13] The result was that, in comparison to the elections of June, the electorate abstained by a quota of 68 per cent. Abstention was particularly high in the areas newly acquired by Greece – Macedonia, the Aegean Islands and Crete. It is impossible to calculate the exact strength of each party and to claim, as Venizelos and his followers did, that the result meant a clear victory for the Liberal Party. Surely royalist propaganda, control of the state apparatus and the hardships imposed by the mobilisation and the embargo had taken their toll on Venizelos' earlier popularity. Whatever interpretation one is disposed to adopt, it is clear that in the new parliament a large section of the population was not represented, that King Constantine's power was unrestricted and that thereafter Venizelos felt less constrained to abide by constitutional methods.

The allies too were extremely concerned with the domestic situation. Besides, Skouloudis' policy proved damaging to Greek and allied interests. In April 1916, he turned down a demand of the Serbian troops in Corfu to use the Greek railways for their transportation to the Macedonian front. Later, when the Germans informed the Greek government that they would have to occupy Fort Rupel as a defensive measure against Entente advances in Macedonia, Skouloudis acquiesced. Accordingly, on 23 May a Bulgarian detachment under a German officer took over the fort, which was given up by its defenders without resistance.[14]

The surrender of Fort Rupel and the possible loss of Eastern Macedonia to the Bulgarians forced the commander-in-chief of the Entente forces in Thessaloniki, General Sarrail, to proclaim martial law, thus removing the city from the authority of the Greek government. The high-handed methods of the allies began to take their toll on Greek public opinion. Greek ships were detained in Mediterranean ports under allied control and no visa was issued by allied legations in Athens to individuals suspected of royalist affiliations. On 21 June the Entente demanded the demobilisation of the Greek army, the resignation of the government, the dissolution of the Greek parliament and the holding of new elections.[15] Although Greece was not at war, the population had begun to suffer its effects. The September 1915 mobilisation had already lasted for nine months when the allies issued their note.

Venizelos' abstention from the December 1915 elections marked the beginning of a protracted struggle between Venizelist and anti-Venizelist forces. Initially, the conflict involved the representatives of two institutions, the king and the popularly elected prime minister. Most Greeks became involved in a debate over the powers vested by the constitution in the two offices. At this point, the imminence of armed conflict gave the military the opportunity to interfere in political affairs, a practice they had abstained from since the dissolution of the Military League in early 1910. Some of the officers, who had played a leading role in the 1909 military coup and its aftermath, upheld the liberal argument that the king had no right to ignore the will of the electorate. Others had lost their former zeal for reform and did not wish to jeopardise their comfortable careers by opposing the king. Most members of the Military League of 1909 had been elevated to high ranks in a very short time thanks to their performance in the Balkan Wars and the patronage of Venizelos, and had adopted the conservative outlook that often accompanies high office.

Following the declaration of martial law in Thessaloniki on 3 June and as the domestic situation had become critical in Athens, on 21 June the allies demanded from the Skouloudis government a number of measures as outlined above. Athens accepted the demands, Skouloudis was replaced by Zaimis, demobilisation began and elections were announced for mid-August, later to be postponed until October. But the government's compliance with the demands of the allies did not have the intended effect of establishing a pro-Entente Venizelos administration in Athens. It only served to intensify the political tension, as groups of demobilised soldiers organised themselves into opposing reservist leagues. Captain Metaxas immediately formed the royalist National Reservists League (epistratoi). In response the Venizelist General P. Danglis founded the National League of Greek Reservists.[16]

On 27 August, with elections still to come but within sight, in front of a crowd of followers, Venizelos appealed to the king to reinstate the constitutional regime he had allegedly violated.[17] But matters were moving toward a revolution.

The 1916 revolt in Thessaloniki had a lasting effect on Greek politics. Georgios Ventiris, the most articulate of Venizelist apologists, dismissed his mentor's involvement in the plot.[18] The line of argument of Venizelos' supporters – namely that the revolt was a spontaneous act of the Macedonian population assisted by the military stationed in the province – was also promoted by Captain Neokosmos Grigoriadis, an early participant: 'Those who organised the revolt had no time to ask for advice . . . Venizelos had not been consulted.'[19]

Periklis Argyropoulos, Venizelist and former prefect of Thessaloniki, had been in contact with French officials in the city as well as with Venizelos. Early in December 1915 his friend, Alexandros Zannas, had informed him that the French command had given up hope that Constantine would enter the war on the side of the Entente and had come to the decision of allowing the Serbian king to establish his headquarters in Thessaloniki. This decision, according to Alexandros Zannas, would depose the Greek authorities from the province and present Macedonia to the Serbs. Between 4 and 7 December, Argyropoulos, Zannas and members of the local Liberal Club formed the National Defence (Ethniki Amyna) of Thessaloniki.[20]

Not long after the National Defence was founded, Venizelos divulged his worries about the morale of the officer corps to General Leonidas Paraskevopoulos, the influential commander of the 3rd Army Corps. He feared that the fighting spirit of the military had been so undermined by the king that they would be in no position to contribute, when called upon, to the allied war effort.[21]

This early indication of Venizelos' interest in a Thessaloniki-based provisional government may not have found favour with the British and was not pressed further at the time. Venizelos had, however, granted his approval to the recruitment of volunteers by the French army in Macedonia.[22]

The capitulation of the Greek Fort Rupel in Eastern Macedonia to the Bulgarians must have strengthened his resolution to rise against the government in Athens. But the attempt was destined to failure for lack of forces. Regular officers joining the National Defence between August 1916 and March 1917 numbered only 280–300 out of a total officer body of 4500. Constantine's decision to demobilise as a further guarantee of his government's neutrality caused Venizelos great apprehension as he realized the futility of a coup without support from a reduced army. The outbreak of the Thessaloniki revolt in August 1916, therefore, had taken him by surprise and Zannas, one of the instigators, risked a trip to Athens to pacify his leader's anger.[23]

When the revolt began, demobilised troops had not yet been removed from Thessaloniki. The commander of the demobilised 11th division, General Constantinos Trikoupis, chose to remain loyal to the king and turned his troops against the insurgents. Ignoring British objections, commander-in-chief General Sarrail, intervened and forced the 11th division out of the city and came to the assistance of the members of the National Defence in installing their provisional government.[24]

In September 1916 Venizelos, Admiral Pavlos Koundouriotis and the former chief of general staff Panayotis Danglis agreed to form a provisional government. On 26 September Venizelos and Koundouriotis, with a number of officers and politicians, left Athens under French protection and arrived at Chania, Crete, where they announced that their provisional government would enter the war on the allied side and defend the country against Bulgaria. In a few days they were joined by General Danglis. After visiting the major islands of the Aegean – Samos, Chios, Mytilene and Limnos – on 9 October they moved the provisional government to Thessaloniki and assumed command of the National Defence to oversee Greek participation in the allied war effort. The triumvirate, as the three men became known, had formed this government in direct conflict with the Athens political establishment.

According to a British diplomat:

> Not only has Mr Venizelos' action put fresh spirit into its promoters here [Thessaloniki], but it has encouraged recruits to come forward from Macedonia where, as I have already reported, very little enthusiasm had hitherto been manifested . . . The Committee of National Defence must now have at its disposal nearly twenty thousand men.[25]

Franco-British violations of Greece's territorial integrity throughout 1916 had offended Greek national honour and therefore increased Constantine's popularity. His policy found support in that segment of the population whose xenophobia was inflamed by the high-handed tactics of the allies. Although until September 1916 the Greek merchant marine and trade had prospered from the war, thereafter it had suffered severely. The allies detained a large number of ships and enemy torpedo attacks caused losses amounting to 66 per cent. Besides, the allied blockade of the coasts of Greece said to harbour German submarines, established in December 1916, resulted in shortages that were felt by the entire Greek population. The population of Macedonia also resented the requisition of property and material for the needs of the British and French troops.[26]

The primary aim of the provisional government was to recruit troops and to organise the war effort in Macedonia. It took care to avoid statements against the king. Any allusion to a change of king or to the abolition of the throne would divide the population and estrange the allies. But, in his effort to recruit an army, Venizelos ran into difficulties. Despite his moderation, the known anti-dynastic tendencies of many of his followers prevented moderate officers from joining the National Defence forces.

The territories under the command of the National Defence comprised Western and Central Macedonia down to Mount Olympus, the Aegean Islands, Crete, the Cyclades and the Ionian Islands. In November 1916, to prevent frontier episodes between the troops of the opposing governments, the allies drew a narrow neutral zone between Venizelos' Greece and that of Constantine.

On 19 November 1916 Admiral Dartige du Fournet notified all diplomats of hostile states to leave Athens. Several days before, he had asked Constantine's government to surrender eighteen field batteries, six mountain batteries, 4000 Mannlicher rifles as well as ammunition and fifty lorries. Following Prime Minister Spyridon Lambros' refusal to obey, the French admiral renewed his demand on 24 November. Two days later, he landed detachments in Piraeus and was faced with resistance by royalist troops. While marching to the city of Athens, du Fournet's 2500 French and British marines were attacked by royalist irregulars on the morning of 1 December. The admiral and some of his men were captured, although Constantine had assured him that the allies had nothing to fear. Once the foreign troops withdrew to their ships, the Athenian Venizelists were left at the mercy of the Reservists, a notorious royalist paramilitary group. The entire operation was led by two generals of the army: troops of the military district of Athens took orders from General K. Kallaris and the soldiers of the active defence were commanded by General A. Papoulas (later commander-in-chief of the Asia Minor expedition).[27]

Venizelos had asked the Entente to remove the barrier of the neutral zone in order to allow him to march on Athens and reunite the country, but to no avail. At the beginning of June, the imminence of the harvest in the grain-producing Plain of Thessaly brought matters to a head. If Constantine was denied the harvest, his government and the population could no longer withstand the hardships caused by the allied blockade established in December. To increase pressure, French troops overran the neutral zone and the greater part of Thessaly. Forced by an allied ultimatum, the king finally abdicated in favour of his second son Alexander, the heir-apparent, George, being politically tainted (having openly sided with his father's policies during the National Schism). On 15 June Constantine and the rest of his family left Greece on a British destroyer.[28] At about the same time French troops occupied Thessaly.[29] Venizelos returned to Athens to assume the reins of government and formed a cabinet consisting of N. Politis as minister of foreign affairs, E. Repoulis as minister of the interior, A. Michalakopoulos as minister of finance, A. Papanastasiou as minister of communications, P. Koundouriotis as minister of marine and S. Simos as minister of relief. The assembly elected in June 1915 was restored to its functions and soon soldiers of the divided army joined forces on the Macedonian front, terminating Greek neutrality de facto. The Greek army was supplied by the allies with modern weapons and was provisioned. Ten divisions were put into the field to confront the Germans and the Bulgarians on the Macedonian front.

The return of Venizelos was followed by the introduction of martial law and a thorough purge of royalists from the civil service and the army. A decree on 'certain crimes against the security of the country' authorised the deportation of interior enemies of the state. The leading royalist politicians were exiled.[30] The purge was conducted systematically in all sectors of the civil service. A decree signed by King Alexander suspended the constitutional guarantees for the protection of public servants, abolished their administrative councils and granted cabinet ministers absolute authority over dismissals and suspensions from office. Each ministry formed its own committee that evaluated the behaviour of its employees during the years of the political crisis. Of those imprisoned and dismissed for misconduct, by far the largest category was the gendarmes. The problems of security caused by the deprivation of the gendarmerie of its most able members caused the hasty reinstatement of the least fanatical royalists.[31]

In the army, the task of merging two parallel military hierarchies divided by political passion was never properly accomplished. Officers who had remained under the authority of Athens viewed their colleagues of the National Defence as a band of adventurers in search of promotion and foreign patrons. Liberal politicians, on the other hand, saw in the officers of the National Defence a stable grouping and natural allies against their royalist opponents.

In October 1916, the Thessaloniki government introduced an act according promotions to officers who had performed heroic deeds in the field of action. Since officers who had remained in Athens, known by the derogatory designation 'paraminantes' (those who had stayed behind), could not profit from this act, this had become yet another controversial issue in the army. In spite of a provision specifying that a minimum of ten years of service were necessary for an officer to reach the rank of major, Defence officers had attained that rank in four or five years. When commander of the army, General P. Danglis, admonished Venizelos about irregularities perpetrated by the Ministry of Army Affairs, the prime minister answered that there was no way of reversing accomplished deeds.[32]

In February 1918, a mutiny instigated by non-commissioned officers protesting against the war occurred in Lamia and spread to Thebes, Livadia and Atalanti. The government suppressed the revolt with the aid of a Cretan regiment and set up courts martial, which tried and executed several officers, NCOs and soldiers.[33]

In the autumn of 1918, the Greek forces in Macedonia broke German and Bulgarian resistance. Bulgaria capitulated on 30 September. The war ended with the signature of the Moudros armistice a month later. Soon after, Greek troops and ships joined the allies in their triumphant entry into Constantinople. With the eventual capitulation of the Ottoman and Habsburg Empires, the Great War had ended with the victory of the allies. The leaders of the victorious states convened in Paris to negotiate the complex post-war settlement. On 14 July 1919 the Greek Evzones marched past the Arc de Triomphe in Paris, in the allied victory celebration. Venizelos' presence at the Paris Peace Conference constituted the vindication of his huge effort to overcome royal resistance against Greece's entry into the Great War on the side of the Triple Entente.

Although the wars changed Greece's territory radically, the transformation of the economy was much slower and followed an incremental process. Despite the migration of 250,000 farm workers to the United States between 1906 and 1914, on the eve of the First World War 65 per cent of the Greek population was still occupied in agriculture. Yet one third of the grain and other basic foodstuffs were imported because of the sector's low productivity. In the Peloponnese small producers smarted from the chronic currant crisis, while the large landholdings of Thessaly, representing almost 35 per cent of all cultivated land in 1914, contributed little to the national economy. The absentee landlords – entrepreneurs who had purchased most of the land from Ottoman owners when the region was annexed to Greece in 1881 – refused to plough in capital to improve productivity. Instead, they rented out their property for grazing or tenant farming. Furthermore, the politically connected owners of çifliks (privately-owned land) were in a position to convince their political protégés who held office in the capital to maintain high tariffs on imported grain in order to protect their own low-grade production from foreign competition. The result was that the accession of Thessaly to Greece had caused the price of grain to rise rather than fall, despite expectations to the contrary.

The rise of the price of bread had produced a political alliance between landless peasants demanding the parcelling out of the large landholdings and the urban middle class, who demanded the abolition of tariffs. Although the liberals had championed redistribution of land since their advent in 1910, it was the arrival of the first Anatolian refugees in 1914 to 1917 that had compelled them to take action. The revolutionary government in Thessaloniki had begun the drafting of laws for the expropriation of the large estates in 1917, but they were actually put into effect after the 1922 influx of refugees from Turkey. The taking-over of estates for distribution to landless peasants rose from one in 1918 to sixty-three in 1920 and 1203 between 1923 and 1925.[34]

The Entente embargo on enemy trade had caused conditions of protectionism on Greek agricultural and industrial products. Furthermore, the demand for food supplies for the French and British troops, generated by the war in Macedonia, encouraged Greek producers to rise to the challenge and reap economic benefits. Merchant marine and trade had prospered, at least in the initial stages of the war, and no unemployment had occurred.

When the first census of manufacturers was taken in 1917, there were 282 large factories and 2,000 small ones, employing over 35,000 workers. Wine, olive oil and flour were the chief products, but soap, cement and chemical fertilisers were also produced.[35]

When the war ended and allied troops evacuated Macedonia, they left behind them a number of roads, and the Red Cross was spending large sums in aid for reconstruction. An American trade commissioner in Greece noted: 'The eyes of all the nations were upon little Greece, as Venizelos who had endeared himself to the Allies, ably and proudly pleaded her cause at the Paris Peace Conference.'[36]

The young King Alexander, who had succeeded his deposed father Constantine in June 1917, was not fond of the politician who was responsible for his family's misfortune, but his main argument with Venizelos concerned his intention to marry a lovely commoner, Aspasia Manou. Although the royal institution was not popular with the adherents of the Liberal Party, few were willing to embark on a republican adventure. Furthermore, the British, who exerted great influence on Venizelos' decisions, supported the royal institution because they believed a republican regime would bring Greece under French influence.[37] As Alexander insisted on going through with the marriage, Venizelos put the following options to his cabinet: a 'semi-morganatic' marriage,[38] or the risk of the resignation of the king and the imposition of a regency until the National Assembly decided on the future of the regime. Alexander and Aspasia married secretly in November 1919, against the decision of the politicians. Less than a year later, Alexander was bitten by his pet monkey and died of blood poisoning on 25 October, three weeks before the long awaited November elections. As his younger brother Paul refused to succeed him and the return of Constantine was out of the question, Venizelos had to choose between a republic and a new dynasty.

He decided to reconsider the matter after the national elections, which had been deferred on account of the international situation. He had promised to hold the elections immediately after the conclusion of the treaty. Indeed, upon returning from France on 7 September 1920, with the Treaty of Sèvres as the major achievement of his diplomacy, Venizelos informed parliament that elections would be held on 7 November of that year. On the road to the November elections a series of dramatic events dangerously complicated the issues facing the electorate.

Venizelos' triumphant departure from France was marred by an assassination attempt against him on 12 August 1920, carried out by two royalist officers at the Gare de Lyon railway station in Paris. The idol of half of Greece was not seriously injured but his more fanatical adherents embarked on a frenzy of terror against the royalists. The most prominent victim of their rampage was Ion Dragoumis, who was assassinated in broad daylight by paramilitary thugs on 13 August.

Dragoumis, a member of an old family of scholars and politicians, was perhaps the most idiosyncratic of the anti-Venizelists. At the outbreak of the Great War he had considered Greece's place was with the Entente, but nurtured a personal dislike for the Cretan statesman, whose sweeping irredentist agenda had destroyed his own project of reviving the Greek communities within the Ottoman realm. Dragoumis was something of a romantic. He lacked the ruthlessness of his contemporary politicians and his timing with political developments was slightly off. He was, nevertheless, the darling of Athenian society and well-known ladies of the time admired him for his patriotic fervour and his charm.

Dragoumis' death made a harsh impression on a large segment of Greek society on the eve of the elections and generated sympathy for the victims of state repression. Besides, the sudden death of Alexander and the problems relating to his succession gave the elections the character of a referendum.

Venizelos' electoral strategy was to ensure the participation of the populations of the New Territories annexed or occupied by Greece. The Greek population of Thrace and Smyrna regarded Venizelos as their saviour and the fact that these areas were under the control of the military made the task of the opposition arduous. To secure an even larger turnout of votes for his party, Venizelos introduced the military vote for the first time. His decision caused much controversy, given the politicisation of the army's leadership. In 1919 a group of officers had organised a league to intimidate opposition to Venizelos. The notorious chief of general staff, Theodoros Pangalos, planned a military take-over in the event of a royalist electoral victory. As it turned out, Venizelos acknowledged defeat before the announcement of the electoral returns in the army.[39]

The Liberal Party that participated in the 1920 elections was not a uniform institution. The left wing under Alexander Papanastasiou did not fall in line with the centrist tendencies of the party's charismatic leader. Whereas Papanastasiou and his republicans targeted the weak working class and the fragmented peasantry, Venizelos appealed to the multitude of small businessmen, salaried workers and small property-holders.

The platform of Venizelos' campaign was based on a wide appeal to diverse social classes in an attempt to transcend the National Schism and the pending dynastic issue. Like his previous campaigns, it was based on the national issue. The Treaty of Sèvres was the prize with which he sought to convince the population that their sacrifices throughout the protracted mobilisation period had not been in vain. Greek military presence in Asia Minor and its unresolved mission there, however, did not figure in the campaign of the liberals.

The 'United Opposition', consisting of a sixteen-man committee that included D. Gounaris, D. Rallis, N. Stratos, N. Kalogeropoulos, P. Tsaldaris and other prominent anti-Venizelists, played down foreign-policy issues and stressed two basic issues: the abuse of power by the Venizelists and the restoration of Constantine to the throne. At the same time they tried to convince the Great Powers that their party constituted no threat to their interests and sought to build bridges with them. Of all the anti-Venizelists, Gounaris was the only one who had formulated a party programme, which included the introduction of proportional representation and a vote for women.

The electoral outcome of 14 November was a blow to Venizelos and his supporters. His party won only 118 out of 369 seats in parliament. As Michael Llewellyn Smith points out: 'The results were geographically significant. The Venizelists had won only three electoral districts (Hydra, Arta and Spetses) in Old Greece . . . Venizelism was reduced to its original core in Crete, a few pockets in Epirus, the Aegean islands of Chios and Lesbos and Thrace.'[40]

Venizelos attributed his defeat to war weariness and the hardships of mobilisation. Venizelists believed that the promise of demobilisation and withdrawal from Asia Minor was the most potent electoral weapon of the 'United Opposition' and, although the royalist government failed to deliver its promise once in power, most Greeks who had cast their vote against Venizelos probably believed they would deliver.[41] The abuse of power by the Venizelists and the persecution of their adversaries were a further cause that garnered votes for the opposition.

In his letter dated 20 April 1931 to the journalist-historian Georgios Ventiris, Venizelos confided to his friend that his gravest error after Alexander's death had been not to postpone the November elections and discuss with the deposed king the possibility of installing his elder son, George, on the throne. Such a solution, he believed, would have averted future disasters and would have united the Greeks.[42]

Venizelos' *ex post facto* confession may not have been an option in 1920. The Allies had already overruled Prince George as a replacement of his father, because he had taken an active part in the November-December 1916 attack against the French expeditionary force in Athens. His letter, however, indicates his flexibility and readiness to find solutions that could prove beneficial to his ultimate goal – the unification of Greece and the Greeks.

NOTES

1. Gregorios Daphnis (1961), *Ta ellinika politika kommata, 1821–1961* [*The Greek Political Parties, 1821–1961*], Athens.
2. Helen Gardikas-Katsiadakis (1995), *Greece and the Balkan Imbroglio. Greek Foreign Policy, 1911–1913*, Athens, pp. 196–8.
3. Nikos Oikonomou (1980), 'Ta ellinika politika revmata prin apo ton El. Venizelo' ['Greek Political Currents before El. Venizelos'] in O. Dimitrakopoulos and Th. Veremis (eds), *Meletimata gyro apo to Venizelo kai tin epochi tou* [*Studies on Venizelos and his Time*], Athens, pp. 477–83.
4. George Th. Mavrogordatos (1983), *Stillborn Republic. Social Coalitions and Party Strategies in Greece 1922–1936*, Berkeley.
5. George Th. Mavrogordatos (1996), *Ethnikos Dichasmos kai maziki*

organosi. Oi Epistratoi tou 1916 [*National Schism and Mass Organisation. The Reservists of 1916*], Athens.

6. D. Dakin (1972), *The Unification of Greece, 1770–1923*, London, p. 202.
7. John Campbell and Philip Sherrard (1968), *Modern Greece*, New York, p. 119.
8. S. I. Stephanou (ed.) (1981), *Eleftheriou Venizelou ta Keimena, 1909–1935* [*Eleftherios Venizelos's Texts, 1909–1935*], vol. 2: *1915–1920* (hereafter: *Keimena* II), Athens, p. 153.
9. George B. Leon (1974), *Greece and the Great Powers 1914–1917*, Thessaloniki, p. 220.
10. Doros Alastos (1942), *Venizelos. Patriot, Statesman, Revolutionary*, London, p. 163.
11. *Keimena* II, p. 169 (see Note 8).
12. Alastos, *Patriot*, p. 167 (see Note 10).
13. *Keimena* II, p. 207 (see Note 8).
14. Vincent J. Seligman (1920), *The Victory of Venizelos. A Study of Greek Politics, 1910–1918*, London, pp. 73–7.
15. Ibid.
16. George Th. Mavrogordatos, *Ethnikos Dichasmos*, p. 71 (see Note 5).
17. *Keimena* II, pp. 226–9 (see Note 8).
18. G. Ventiris (1971), *I Ellas tou 1910–20* [*Greece 1910–1920*], vol. II Athens, p. 211.
19. N. Grigoriadis (1960), *I Ethniki Amyna tis Thessalonikis tou 1916* [*The National Defence of Thessaloniki of 1916*], Athens, p. 18.
20. P. Argyropoulos (1970), *Apomnimonevmata* [*Memoirs*], Athens, p. 180. In his 19 May 1959 article in the daily *To Vima*, Zannas also recalls that he had been in contact with Venizelos since November 1915.
21. Venizelos to Paraskevopoulos, 24 December 1915 (Nikos Petsalis Archive).
22. D. Portolos (1974), 'Greek Foreign Policy, September 1916 to October 1919', unpublished Ph.D. thesis, Birkbeck College, University of London, p. 34.
23. Incident related to the author by Zannas' widow Virginia.
24. Argyropoulos, *Apomnimonevmata*, pp. 191–2 (see Note 20).
25. Wratislaw to Elliot (Athens), no. 235, Thessaloniki, 21 October 1916, PRO FO 371/2625/210988.
26. A. Andreadis (n.d.), *Les effets économiques et sociaux de la guerre en Grèce*, Paris, p. 108.
27. S. B. Chester (1922), *Life of Venizelos*, New York, pp. 292–5.
28. Leon, *Greece and the Great Powers, 1914–1917*, pp. 439–46 (see Note 9).
29. Seligman, *The Victory of Venizelos*, pp. 83–4 (see Note 14).
30. N. Petsalis-Diomidis (1998), *I Ellada ton dyo Kyverniseon* [*Greece of Two Governments*], Athens, p. 81.
31. For a definitive account of the purges see William Edgar, 'Oi ekkathariseis tou 1917' ['The purges of 1917'] in Dimitrakopoulos and Veremis (eds), *Meletimata*, pp. 530–44 (see Note 3).

32. Panayiotis Danglis (1965), *Anamniseis, engrapha, allilographia* [*Recollections, Documents, Correspondence*], vol. 2, pp. 255–6.
33. For a detailed account of military affairs in that period, see Thanos Veremis (1997), *The Military in Greek Politics. From Independence to Democracy*, London, pp. 61–7.
34. A study of the expropriation of land is included in the basic work on Greek agriculture: A. Sideris (1934), *I georgiki politiki tis Ellados (1833–1933)* [*Greece's Agrarian Policy (1833–1933)*], Athens, pp. 176–81.
35. Eliot Grinnell Mears (1929), *Greece Today*, Stanford, pp. 32–3.
36. Ibid., p. 36.
37. Michael Llewellyn Smith (1973), *Ionian Vision*, New York, p. 136.
38. Ibid.
39. Ibid., pp. 141–3.
40. Ibid., p. 151.
41. Constantinos Zavitsianos (1947), *Ai anamniseis tou ek tis istorikis diaphonias Vasileos Constantinou kai Eleftheriou Venizelou* [*His Recollections from the Historic Dispute between King Constantine and E. Venizelos*], vol. 2, Athens, p. 100.
42. Ventiris, *I Ellas tou 1910–20*, pp. 417–21 (see Note 18).

5

Venizelos' Diplomacy, 1910–23: From Balkan Alliance to Greek–Turkish Settlement

Michael Llewellyn Smith

Anyone who writes about Eleftherios Venizelos has to confront the controversial nature of his character and reputation. Judgements of him by his contemporaries and by subsequent generations, by both Greeks and foreigners, have varied from hero-worship to anathema. But time has had its effect. It is not so difficult now to appreciate the greatness and force of Venizelos while acknowledging his limitations and his mistakes.

I shall describe Venizelos' diplomacy and foreign policy, and assess his achievement in the crucial phase of his career which stretched from his assumption of office in Greece in 1910 to the turning point in Greek foreign policy marked by the Treaty of Lausanne.

I shall argue that, though briefly attracted after the Young Turk revolution by the idea of co-existence of the Greek and other Christian minorities with Muslims, in a modernised, multinational Ottoman Empire, he soon developed a foreign policy based on the nationalist premises of the Great Idea. He pursued this by means of internal reform and alliances with the liberal Western powers, until circumstances destroyed it in fire and bloodshed in 1922. This foreign policy was consistent with Venizelos' vision of a modernised, European Greece. The dominant influence of the Great Powers in the Eastern Mediterranean and Balkans, though it sometimes entailed humiliation for Greece, justified Venizelos' willing dependence on them.

When he became prime minister of Greece in October 1910, Venizelos was already a veteran of foreign affairs. His experience as a revolutionary leader in Crete brought him into contact with the Ottoman authorities and with the representatives of the Great Powers on the island, as well as with successive Greek governments and the Greek royal family. His dispute with Prince George of Greece, the first high commissioner of the Power in Crete, over the tactics to be followed on the road towards enosis, the union of Crete with the mother country, led to the withdrawal of the prince by his father King George.[1]

On taking office in Greece, therefore, Venizelos had a deep knowledge of the Cretan question, which was itself an important aspect of Greek–Turkish relations, and a broad knowledge of the Eastern question as it engaged the interests of the Great Powers. He was experienced in administration but lacked direct experience of government on the scale of the Greek nation. His experience had taught him that the external relations of Greece were an existential question – the 'national question' – organically connected with the internal progress of the nation.

Venizelos' arrival in Athens and assumption of power mark the beginning of his diplomatic career on the wider international stage. This phase of his career ended, after triumphs and disaster, at Lausanne in 1923. The Treaty of Lausanne is a watershed in Greek politics, marking the end of the phase of expansion embodied in the Great Idea expounded by Kolettis in the 1840s,[2] and introducing the social upheaval of the exchange of populations which was to shape Greek society and politics in the inter-war years.

VENIZELOS' DIPLOMACY 1910–23

Between 1910 and 1923 Venizelos developed a diplomacy which was remarkable in its outcome and its manner. It achieved great results for the Greek nation, in the near doubling of Greek territory and population as a result of the Balkan Wars, and in the consolidation and extension of these gains in the Paris settlement after the Great War. Of course, many people, in politics, administration, the armed forces and propaganda work were associated with these achievements. But to an unusual degree they were the product of one architect, Venizelos himself. He also led Greece into the events which culminated in the Asia Minor catastrophe of September 1922 and the uprooting and expulsion of the Christian Greeks of Asia Minor. His share of responsibility for this outcome is much disputed. What is clear is that he appreciated the finality of the disaster and adjusted quickly to the new reality of Greek–Turkish relations in 1923. One of his strengths was readiness realistically to accept a new situation.

The period falls naturally into four phases: first, that in which Venizelos attempted to define his aims, moving at first cautiously but in the end boldly towards the Balkan system of alliances and agreements which were the basis of the Balkan Wars and Greece's massive accretion of territories; second, that in which, with European war, Venizelos threw in his lot and that of Greece with the Entente, calculating on victory for the Powers with which Greece's interests were most closely aligned; third, that of the Paris Peace Conference, a period of intensive negotiation and propaganda on behalf of Greek claims, in which Venizelos played a dominating role in crafting and presenting Greece's case; and finally, after the hiatus from November 1920 to autumn 1922 which Venizelos spent in exile, his return to foreign policy as the chief Greek negotiator of the Lausanne Treaty, which settled outstanding issues with Turkey in a way which, though with considerable political strains, has lasted until today.

Throughout the whole period, including when he was out of power, Venizelos was actively engaged in foreign policy. After his resignations in 1915, for example, he maintained close links with the allied representatives in Athens, pending the establishment of the provisional government in Thessaloniki. Between November 1920 and September 1922, in his absence in Western Europe and the Americas, he felt obliged to respond to the approaches of his friends and of the British government. The period is a continuum, in which Venizelos was continually engaged in the same range of foreign-policy issues concerning Greece's territory. These were the issues which he believed to be most important for the progress and development of the nation; but they also included vital points at issue between him and King Constantine, and therefore became the focus of the power struggle between Venizelists and royalists.

FOREIGN POLICY AND DIPLOMACY

Throughout this period, Venizelos' foreign-policy aims – which effectively defined the foreign policy of Greece – cannot easily be separated from his 'diplomacy' in the technical sense of the means and instruments which he used to achieve his ends. Nor can his diplomacy and foreign policy be easily separated from his underlying political philosophy and thus from the totality of his policies as a statesman.[3] Foreign policy is not the same as diplomacy, but it is difficult and in the end unsatisfactory to isolate the means from the ends and look at a statesman as diplomat pure and simple. But Venizelos' diplomacy has particular interest because of the major role he himself played in the implementation and projection of his foreign policies.

European prime ministers today normally deal with foreign affairs daily, but often at a relatively superficial level, and with a broad brush. They are usually happy enough to delegate to their foreign ministers, or to special advisers, except in high profile matters such as summit diplomacy, or in matters of acute domestic sensitivity. This was hardly the case with Venizelos, who was personally and continuously absorbed in diplomacy to the extent that this was necessary to the successful implementation of his national policy. The foreign-policy issues with which he dealt were not addenda to internal politics, they were questions which concerned Greece's national survival, progress and expansion. As such they were organically connected to those aspects of internal politics, notably economic and military development and reform, which were a precondition for a successful foreign policy. To Venizelos' chagrin, they often pushed into the background his plans for cultural and educational reforms, and in the post-war period distracted him from domestic political and economic issues.

Venizelos never served as foreign minister, but he often acted as his own foreign minister by throwing himself into the day-to-day hustle of negotiation, for example during the negotiations in London in December 1912 and January 1913, in Bucharest in July and August 1913, and in Paris in 1918 to 1920. His personal contribution was determining. At these times he made himself the main instrument of his own diplomacy.

This was an immense advantage for Greece. But there were also drawbacks. General Mazarakis in his memoirs points to the way in which Venizelos' dominance led to the departure, in some bitterness, of important collaborators, including Stratos, Zavitsianos, Demertzis and Koromilas. Others, such as Michalakopoulos, Kafantaris and Papanastasiou complained in private about his character.[4] Venizelos was dominant and did not brook opposition. He used his collaborators, such as Politis as foreign minister, and ambassadors such as Romanos and Caclamanos, to the full. But he took the big decisions himself, and sometimes without consultation. Deputy Prime Minister Repoulis and Acting Foreign Minister Diomidis first heard about Venizelos' memorandum setting out Greek claims at the peace conference through an interview given by Venizelos to *The Times*.[5]

Venizelos started by relying perforce on the professionals of the Foreign Ministry, senior ambassadors such as Ioannis Gryparis, George Streit and Dimitrios Panas. As time passed, he made sure that his own close collaborators held key positions, and he readily used them and his personal staff (for example the Cretan C. Markantonakis) as personal emissaries to deal with, or report on, difficult situations. Nikolaos Politis as foreign minister, Alexandros Diomidis as acting foreign minister, Apostolos Alexandris as ambassador to Berne and special emissary, Periklis Argyropoulos as ambassador to Stockholm and emissary, are cases in point. Generally, however, he saw the Greek diplomatic service as a tool to be used, rather than – as was often the case with Lloyd George – a machine to be bypassed.

Venizelos worked hard and was not afraid of the details of issues. But his view of diplomacy was broad and inclusive. He saw it not just as a matter of exchanges between diplomats on traditional lines, but as a wide-ranging means to support policy. It therefore included propaganda work and relations with the media and friendly and influential foreigners, such as Professor Ronald Burrows in the UK.[6] He saw also that it must rest on a common understanding by all Greeks, including the armed forces and the 'notables' in the areas claimed by Greece, of the need to project the impression of a 'civilising mission'. Only thus could his diplomatic efforts with allied leaders in Paris bear fruit. He spent a lot of time trying to persuade his political colleagues and military commanders of the importance of this, and in defensive action when they fell short.[7]

A peculiar feature of Venizelos' diplomacy is that much of his effort in dealing with British and French diplomatic and military representatives was actually devoted to internal matters of state, arising from his breach with King Constantine. From the time of his dismissal as prime minister in October 1915 until the end of the war this was necessarily so because he needed, with the allies' help, to remove the king and establish himself securely in power in Athens, as a precondition of prosecuting his war aims.[8] This is another feature of the interconnection of foreign and domestic matters in this period of Greek history, as in others.

SOURCES

The main sources for Venizelos' diplomacy are the diplomatic documents of Greece and the Great Powers; Venizelos' own letters to collaborators and speeches to parliament; and the large secondary literature about his career, starting with George Ventiris' influential book on the Greece of 1910 to 1920 and the memoirs of Penelope Delta and other friends and admirers.[9] Among recent works, the books of Svolopoulos, Mavrogordatos, and certain collections of scholarly essays and essays in diplomatic history have illuminated Venizelos' diplomacy.[10] There is no adequate, up-to-date biography. Venizelos' own contributions to autobiography consist of occasional diaries, of great interest in themselves (for example his diary of the period surrounding the decision of the Supreme Council to authorise the Greek occupation of Smyrna) but fragmentary in their illumination of his career and motives. The Greek documents leave large gaps. Some of these sources, especially Ventiris' book and Venizelos' own speeches to the Greek parliament, have been influential in forming the legend of Venizelos. There is a danger of retrospective smoothing of the rough edges of his career – the improvisations, the tactical moves – in the presentation of the superhuman figure of legend. It is not always possible to check the legend against the contemporary record.

Authoritative diplomatic accounts of the period are complicated, with detailed accounts of the day-to-day transactions and telegrams of diplomats.[11] I have tried to compress and simplify the complex day-to-day developments and linkages over territorial questions so as to bring out the underlying issues which confronted Venizelos. In such a mass of material concerning a rapidly changing situation, it is not difficult to find evidence of inconsistency in the positions he adopted. For example, he said different things at different times about whether or not Greece would claim western Asia Minor, Constantinople or Cyprus. The question is why, and the answer is usually to be found in the particular circumstances of the time and who was his interlocutor.

THE FIRST PHASE: BALKAN ALLIANCES AND THE EXPANSION OF GREECE

It is striking how rapidly Greece's prospects and achievements were transformed in Venizelos' first term as prime minister, and still mysterious precisely how it was done. He took power in a country that had lost prestige and even aspects of national sovereignty in the aftermath of the 1897 war against Turkey. The finances of Greece were placed under the control of the International Financial Commission. Greece lacked the economic resources and military power to achieve her foreign-policy ends. Indeed, Greek governments found it difficult to decide what these ends were, and whether the main threat to Greek interests came from the Turks or the Slavs.[12] It was in response to the perceived failures of national policy that the Military League which took power at Goudi in 1909 invited Venizelos to Greece. He became prime minister in October 1910.

The key developments of the early period of his administration in creating the conditions for effective diplomacy were the reform of the armed services and the re-establishment of Greece's finances. These followed from Venizelos' political dominance, reflected in his massive majority in parliament from the time of the elections in December 1910. It was the same factor which enabled him to dominate in his relations with King George.

Under Venizelos as prime minister Greece moved in three years from a position of military and financial weakness and relative diplomatic isolation to a rough equality with Slav neighbours, diplomatic and military successes, and territorial expansion. But Venizelos did not come to power with policies fully formed, nor was it obvious in the period 1908–12 what policy Greece should follow. The Balkans were in crisis arising from the Young Turk revolution of 1908, Austria's annexation of Bosnia-Herzegovina and Bulgaria's declaration of independence as a kingdom. The Macedonian question remained unresolved, with Greek and Bulgarian bands still active. The Cretan question was also unresolved. Crete was in semi-continuous agitation for union with Greece. Greece had no special, privileged relationship with any Balkan neighbour or with any of the Great Powers.

The Young Turk revolution, which raised hopes of new attitudes to constitutionalism and the rights of the Christian minorities in the empire, caused great confusion in Greece. In the shorter term, it led to an end of the current phase of struggle in Macedonia, with the withdrawal of the Greek bands across the frontier in 1909, and to renewed hopes of a settlement of the Cretan question. Within Constantinople the confusion was reflected in the differences between the Patriarch Joachim III, with his traditional approach to relations of Greek Orthodox millet with the Ottoman state, and Athanasios Souliotis-Nikolaidis, supported by Ion Dragoumis, who imagined a revived Greek community exercising its constitutional rights and realising its national aspirations within a multinational Ottoman Empire.[13]

Venizelos was affected by these uncertainties. For a time, in late 1908 and early 1909, before his arrival on the Greek political scene, he seems to have responded to events in Turkey very much on the lines of Souliotis' ideas, writing that the future of Hellenism was to be sought in a well-governed and Hellenised Ottoman Empire. He believed that the failure of the revolution and the break-up of the Ottoman Empire would be a disaster for the Greek nation, since it would mean the break-up of the main body of Hellenism. He cited the examples of Hellenism in Bulgaria and Romania to show what would happen to Greeks under other sovereignties than the Ottoman.[14] He commented in his Chania newspaper, *Kiryx* (*Herald*) in January 1909:

> All of Hellenism . . . felt very deeply . . . that the success of the Young Turk movement has saved not only the Turkish State, but also Hellenism, from dismemberment and catastrophe . . . Hellenism, never an acquisitive power, but a civilizing one, felt that the establishment of a constitutional regime in Turkey was, under a different form, the realization of the Great Idea . . .[15]

Taken literally, this is a strong affirmation of Souliotis' ideas, that the Great Idea did not have to be realised by conquest and physical expansion of the state. But as the Young Turks revealed themselves as hard-line nationalists intent on 'Ottomanisation' of the minorities, such ideas came to seem increasingly unrealistic.

THE FOUNDATIONS OF DIPLOMACY: MILITARY, FINANCIAL AND DIPLOMATIC

Thus Venizelos came to power in a largely defensive frame of mind, responding to circumstances as they arose. His main conviction was of the need to avoid war until Greece was strong enough to support it. Nor had he reached firm views on policy for the incorporation of Macedonia, still less of Asia Minor. His cautious approach meant taking a firm line with Cretan demands for enosis, rejecting demands that deputies from Crete should sit in the Greek parliament, which Turkey made clear she would regard as a casus belli. It also meant exploring the possibilities of a deal with Turkey over Crete. He took personal and firm charge of the Cretan question.

Venizelos' diplomacy was based on a foundation of financial and military reform and recovery. He and his finance minister Lambros Koromilas were able to build on the work of Ioannis Valaoritis, deputy president of the National Bank of Greece under Prime Minister Stephanos Dragoumis in 1910. Within a few months the Greek budget showed a healthy surplus and a foreign loan was contracted which allowed the programme of military reform to proceed.[16]

The weakness and demoralisation of the armed forces had been the long-running theme of Greek politics after 1897. Georgios Theotokis in his ministry of 1906 had tried to grapple with the problem with a plan for the reorganisation of the Greek navy by French experts.[17] The plan was sunk by a storm of domestic criticism. Theotokis then explored the possibility of German military assistance, without success, the Germans not wishing to complicate their burgeoning political and military relationship with Turkey. In early 1910, Colonel Zorbas, the leader of the Military League, as war minister in the Dragoumis ministry sounded out the French about a military mission to reorganise the Greek army.

The idea of foreign military assistance was therefore in the air before Venizelos arrived on the scene. It had obvious advantages, allowing Greece to tap into a superior modern system of organisation, and to procure modern equipment and training in its use. However, foreign assistance programmes were politically sensitive, arousing the resentment and obstruction of senior officers. In the Greek case, where the crown prince and his close collaborators were alumni of the German system of military education and admirers of German military discipline and technological prowess, putting the Greek army in the hands of a French mission was additionally sensitive. It therefore required strong and confident leadership.

Venizelos rapidly turned the vague openings of his predecessors into firm policy. To ensure success he himself took on the Ministries of War and Marine. The constitution was amended to permit foreign military missions. He invited Britain to send a naval mission, France a military mission, and Italy a mission for the gendarmerie. The French mission under General Eydoux arrived in January 1911 and the British mission under Rear-Admiral Tufnell in April 1911.[18]

These invitations represented a political choice. They did not at this stage predetermine Greece's position in a system of alliances, but they were an indication that in Venizelos' view Greece's interests were closer to France and Britain than to Germany.

Predictably, the work of the missions was far from straightforward. The French mission ran up against the contempt of Constantine and the German-trained officers; the British mission against the entrenched views of senior naval officers and politicians that, in order to dominate the Aegean in the context of a naval arms race with Turkey, they must have dreadnoughts rather than the light, rapid vessels favoured by the British. Where such conflicts arose, despite the considerable formal powers of the chief of the mission, the Greeks were in a position to get their own way. In 1914, for example, at a time of tension between Greece and Turkey over the Aegean islands, Venizelos simply bypassed the mission and bought two dreadnoughts, regarded as politically essential even if of questionable military value, from the United States. Despite such difficulties, as part of a wider programme of economic, military and financial recovery the foreign missions served their purpose and contributed to raising the technical standards and operating effectiveness of the army and navy.

Venizelos also attended to the machinery of diplomacy. By custom, the king stood at the head of the foreign policy process and himself played an active role in Greece's diplomacy. Greek prime ministers had tolerated George I's role, exercised for example on his annual visits to his relatives in Western Europe. Though Venizelos came to Greece from Crete with a radical reputation which did not commend him to the royal family, King George sensibly saw the need for a modus vivendi, not least to save the dynasty from the more extreme anti-dynastic ideas of radicals in the Military League. For his part Venizelos, whose attitude to the constitutional question of the monarchy was entirely flexible, seems simply to have moved into the territory occupied by King George, using his massive parliamentary majority, and where necessary the threat of resignation, to get his way. He was ready to exploit the king's experience and dynastic connections, just as he was ready, indeed determined, at some political cost, to restore Constantine to the machinery of state in command of the army. At an early stage he forced the king to get rid of his private secretary, who had close connections with the Theotokis political party.[19]

Within the Ministry of Foreign Affairs, Venizelos chose his colleagues according to their experience. Ioannis Gryparis, his first foreign minister, could be trusted to cultivate good relations with Turkey. His successor Lambros Koromilas, the former finance minister, was a more aggressive character and was to cause Venizelos problems.[20] The fact that Venizelos decided to replace Koromilas with George Streit in March 1913 despite Streit's known inclination for the Triple Alliance shows that at that stage what was later labelled 'Germanophilia' was no bar to senior office.[21]

Using these instruments Venizelos developed a foreign policy which was watchfully reactive, in recognition of Greece's weakness and isolation. But his ideas developed in response to events. From 1909 Russia, aiming to limit Austria's presumed ambitions in the Balkans, encouraged the Balkan states to co-operate in a Slav league under Russian patronage. The war between Italy and the Ottoman Empire which broke out in September 1911 gave an impetus to such co-operation: it seemed to show that if the Balkan states had been united they could have profited by Turkish troubles to expel the Turks from Europe. Bulgarian–Serbian negotiations led to a treaty of alliance with an associated military convention of 13 March 1912. This was an incentive to Greece to insert itself into a system of alliances, for fear of being left behind.

But Venizelos still believed that Greece required time, and must not be drawn into military adventures, for example, in Macedonia, before her armed forces were capable of sustaining them.[22] Until then Greece should accept and uphold the integrity of the Ottoman Empire. His active involvement in the pursuit of a Balkan system of alliances therefore crystallised only gradually.

THE MAKING OF THE BALKAN ALLIANCE

The idea of an understanding between the Balkan Christian states had been around since the time of Charilaos Trikoupis. It grew gradually on Venizelos between 1908 and 1912 as the hopes initially invested in the Young Turk revolution of 1908 were disappointed and it became clear that the Turkish leaders were set on a policy of Ottomanisation of non-Muslim communities.

By early 1910 Venizelos was canvassing the possibility of a Bulgarian alliance with *The Times*' Balkan correspondent James Bourchier, who had himself witnessed Trikoupis' premature attempt to develop a Balkan understanding during his visit to Sofia in 1891.[23] By mid-1910 he was talking to friends in terms of a network of understandings between the Balkan states, leading, by means of mutual concessions, to an alliance aimed at the expulsion of Turkey from Europe.[24] The government of Stephanos Dragoumis was meanwhile already engaged in talks with Bulgaria to explore an understanding. Thus, by the time Venizelos became prime minister matters were already some way advanced. He was strongly urged by Russian foreign minister Sazonov to seek an understanding with Bulgaria.

Bourchier, who divided his time between Athens, Sofia and Bucharest and who followed the political developments in Greece after the Goudi movement, was a firm believer in Balkan co-operation and played an active role in helping Venizelos to achieve an understanding with Bulgaria.[25] Venizelos had got to know him well in Crete during the disturbances of 1896. His close links with Bulgaria made him a useful unofficial go-between. He was involved in discussions with the king, the crown prince, Venizelos and Foreign Minister Gryparis on the Greek side, and with Bulgarian prime minister Gueshov in November 1911 and February 1912. Later he recorded that:

> The conversations with Mr Venizelos which led to his proposal of an alliance with Bulgaria took place at Athens in the winter of 1910 and spring of 1911, mainly in my room at the Grande Bretagne Hotel, where we sometimes sat up till two or three a.m. . . . Venizelos' proposal, which was known only to King George and myself (the cabinet knew nothing of it) was entrusted by me in a sealed packet to Mr Butler, who had acted as my agent in Montenegro . . . Mr Butler knew nothing of the contents of the packet which he personally took to the Bulgarian Legation in Vienna. It contained also long letters to King Ferdinand and Mr Gueshov, who shortly afterwards compared notes. The packet was sent sealed to Gueshov. The Bulgarian Cabinet was told nothing.[26]

For a long time Gueshov played cautious. Agreement with Serbia was the priority. But he responded to Venizelos' approach in February 1912. Thereafter Bourchier played a part as intermediary in the two countries' decision to put the matter of a treaty into diplomatic channels. A visit by Venizelos and Bourchier and Heinrich Schliemann, the German archaeologist, to Mount Pelion in April 1912 enabled Venizelos and Bourchier to talk through the details of the Greek–Bulgarian agreement.[27] Panas, the taciturn and effective Greek minister at Sofia, was entrusted with the negotiations and instructed to hand over a draft treaty in April. This led to difficult discussions over the Bulgarian demand for recognition of autonomy for Macedonia.

Venizelos showed his powers of persuasion in carrying the cabinet with him against opposition from Koromilas and the doubts of the king. Old hands of the Macedonia struggle with their intense suspicions of Bulgaria were convinced that there should be a prior agreement on the distribution of territory in case of war with Turkey. Koromilas represented this point of view in cabinet in early April. Venizelos argued that to insist on this would mean the breakdown of the negotiations over the issue of Thessaloniki. He carried the day.[28]

The negotiations concluded with the signature of a treaty on 30 May 1912. It provided for mutual support in case of an attack on either country by Turkey, except in the case of war arising from the entry of the Cretan deputies to the Greek parliament.[29] The negotiations which Venizelos then initiated with Serbia for a similar arrangement were concluded only in 1913.

Once he had come to the conclusion that an agreement with Bulgaria was necessary, Venizelos moved fast. He was surely right to insist that haggling over the territorial spoils should be avoided. He saw that a decisive moment had arrived. But this was a brave and a risky decision. The risk lay in his enforced reliance on the Greek army, still in his view unprepared, to reap the rewards of victory.

Bourchier's role is also interesting, not least for the difference it shows between the professional ethic of the journalist of a hundred years ago and of today. Bourchier was happy to play an active political and diplomatic role, and *The Times* allowed him to do so since his views were consistent with the newspaper's general line. It was an advantage for Venizelos to have as his confidant someone from outside the circle of professional diplomats, who were always likely, as representatives of the Great Powers, to argue in favour of stability. It was an additional advantage that Bourchier was capable of playing the role of intermediary with the Bulgarian king and prime minister. But Bourchier's role was secondary. It was Venizelos' leadership which brought about the alliance, the key diplomatic achievement of this first phase of his career.[30]

BALKAN WARS AND PEACE NEGOTIATIONS

Greece declared war on Turkey on 18 October, ten days after Montenegro's declaration of war on 8 October, which started the hostilities. Right up to the point where war was seen to be inevitable, Venizelos tried to avoid it. He still believed that Greece was not ready. He continued to believe in the possibility of an arrangement with Turkey which would resolve the Cretan question. It was only when it became clear to Venizelos that Bulgaria and Serbia and Montenegro were set on war that he accepted that Greece must join in.[31]

It is therefore a simplification to see the Bulgarian alliance, the expulsion of the Turks from Europe, and the doubling of Greek territory, as the logical outcome of a long-studied policy. Rather, Venizelos successfully and prudently kept Greek options open, in the knowledge of Greece's continuing economic and military weakness and the vulnerable position of the Greek Orthodox communities in Asia Minor, which remained, as it were, hostages to the Turks. He saw at an early stage the diplomatic advantages of an inter-Balkan understanding and was able to turn this brilliantly to Greek advantage when war broke out.

The period between the conclusion of the treaty with Bulgaria and the Treaty of Bucharest in August 1913 was critical to Greece's fortunes. It was a period of unremitting diplomatic effort in which Venizelos had to set the framework for military action, to ensure that the military, and especially King Constantine, did not distort the government's priorities,[32] and to ensure through diplomacy that military gains were turned into a confirmed territorial settlement.

The period of negotiation in London in December 1912, and in Bucharest in July–August 1913, determined in outline the favourable territorial settlement for Greece from the wars. Venizelos decided to conduct the negotiations himself although this meant leaving Greece in the hands of his colleagues for long periods of time. He was right to do so, for Greece's destiny was being decided not in Athens, but in London and Bucharest.

Greece's aim in the London negotiations was to secure a lasting peace, winning the maximum of territory in Macedonia, Northern Epirus and the islands, with secure frontiers, and stable relations with Turkey providing some guarantee of the safety of the Christian populations of the Ottoman Empire.[33] Venizelos hoped to secure these aims by negotiating first with Greece's allies on the division of the territorial spoils of war, and only then with Turkey over Crete, the islands and the status of the Christian peoples. He was, as always, prepared to strike compromises over territory, but remained firm at all stages that Thessaloniki must remain Greek, and that Greece should be confirmed in sovereignty over the main Aegean islands.

Real life proved more complicated than this negotiating scenario. Venizelos' hopes of agreeing on a prior division of the spoils ran up against Gueshov's insistence on the lion's share for Bulgaria in recognition of Bulgaria's larger army and greater sacrifices. The peace-making process was complicated by the decision of the Powers to take into their own hands the issues of the status and frontiers of Albania, and of the Aegean islands, so that two parallel and connected processes were in train in

London, one the Peace Conference of Turkey and the Balkan allies, the other the Conference of Ambassadors of the Powers.

Greece's position was not particularly strong. She was seen as a junior partner by Bulgaria, and by Serbia as less important than Bulgaria. She had no particular patron among the Great Powers, though France was generally supportive. Her armed forces and her economy were not in a position to sustain prolonged warfare.

Given these handicaps, Greece came well out of the two Balkan Wars, aided by luck and by the Bulgarians, who overplayed their hand. While looking mainly to Britain and France in hopes of support, Venizelos seems to have decided on a diplomacy of conciliation in all directions. He was determined not to alienate any of the Powers. This meant efforts to conciliate Austria and Germany, which paid off in the Bucharest negotiations in August 1913 when Germany offered precious support to Greece over the retention of Kavalla.[34]

As regards the territorial division of Macedonia, Venizelos was prepared to go to considerable lengths to preserve the Balkan alliance, to the extent of giving up the Kilkis and Serres region. He was ready to face down criticism by disappointed nationalists in Athens. His famous speech of 15 March 1913 to parliament, in which he rebuffed the request of Greek communities in Eastern Macedonia and Thrace for incorporation in Greece, should be seen in this light.[35] He was equally ready to envisage arbitration over Greek–Bulgarian differences, but was defeated by Bulgarian intransigence.

In the light of difficulties with Bulgaria, relations with Serbia acquired greater importance. Venizelos edged his way cautiously towards a treaty of alliance with Serbia directed against Bulgaria. He would have preferred to be able to reach a three-sided understanding with Serbia and Bulgaria, but this had proved impossible. Venizelos therefore approved of cautious discussion between Prince Nicholas in Thessaloniki and Crown Prince Alexander of Serbia. By April 1913 King Constantine, who succeeded his father George in March, and Foreign Minister Koromilas had come to the conclusion that war with Bulgaria was inevitable. Venizelos had not yet reached that conclusion. But he wanted to ensure the greatest possible freedom of action for Greece should it prove so, and to that end brought to a Crown Council in early May the question of a defensive alliance with Serbia. Against the strong objections of the king, who believed that such a treaty risked implicating Greece in war against Austria, Venizelos carried the day with the argument that the danger from Bulgaria was imminent. Greece's treaty of alliance and military convention with Serbia were signed on 1 June.[36]

VENIZELOS AND LLOYD GEORGE

In London, Venizelos forged the relationship with Britain and with Lloyd George which served as the basis of his policies for the next eight years. He arrived in London on 12 December 1912. It was his first visit to Britain, and incidentally the occasion on which he met his future wife Helena Schilizzi, a member of a wealthy family of London Greeks.[37] The ground had been prepared for him by John Stavridi, the Greek consul general in London. A solicitor with Liberal Party connections, Stavridi was a friend of Lloyd George. He held preliminary talks with Lloyd George (chancellor of the exchequer) and Churchill (first lord of the admiralty) about British–Greek co-operation in the new situation created by the Balkan War.[38] Lloyd George was insistent that Venizelos himself must come to London. In the intervals of the diplomatic negotiations Venizelos and Lloyd George carried these talks forward. Churchill and Prince Louis of Battenberg, the first sea lord, were also involved, and Prime Minister Asquith and Foreign Secretary Grey were kept informed.

The discussions had two dimensions. One was a deal whereby Britain would cede Cyprus to Greece in return for the use of naval facilities at Argostoli in the island of Cephalonia. Churchill, who initiated the proposal to cede Cyprus, was keen to obtain a deep-water harbour close to the Adriatic, from which in time of war the British fleet could bottle up and neutralise the Italian and Austrian fleets. The second was a proposal for a wider Anglo-Greek Entente, the elements of which would be British support for Greek aspirations and economic development, and naval co-operation in which Greece would play the role of local policeman, building up a fleet of small, rapid ships rather than the costly dreadnoughts which the Greek naval chiefs hankered after.

The talks were promising but inconclusive. Venizelos told Lloyd George at their first meeting that: 'All the national aspirations of Greece tended towards a closer union with England and that from the king down to the meanest subject everyone in Greece would welcome such an understanding.'

When he left London Venizelos summed up the position:

> He felt happy at the thought that our negotiations would result in an Entente with England, and probably with France, and that Greece's future would be very different to her past, when she had to stand absolutely alone, supported by no one, with not a single friend to care what happened to her. She would now build up a strong navy, develop her railways and commerce and with the friendship of England and France would become a power in the East which no one could ignore.[39]

The proposed understanding and the deal over Argostoli and Cyprus were too advanced for Grey's cautious foreign policy with its attachment to preserving regional balances. In any case they were blown away in the diplomatic complications caused by the Second Balkan War. But the record of the London talks shows that by 1912, given reasonable encouragement, Venizelos was ready to set Greece's course by reference to Britain and France. The idea that Greece could be of service to the liberal Western Powers, winning in return support for her national territorial and economic aspirations, directed his policy during the Great War.

DIFFERENCES WITH CONSTANTINE AND KOROMILAS

The strain of the two wars and the intense negotiations brought out differences between Venizelos and Constantine and between Venizelos and Koromilas. Both were inclined to take a tougher line with Bulgaria than was Venizelos. In the First Balkan War the problems were primarily tactical, revolving around difficult choices of where to deploy the weight of Greece's armed forces and how much force could be diverted from Macedonia to Epirus. Venizelos and Constantine had their differences here. Constantine seems to have come to see the second war against Bulgaria as something of a crusade, to be carried out to the point of crushing Bulgaria as a serious force, whereas Venizelos retained a notion of a Balkan equilibrium to be preserved by means of a friendly trio of Greece, Serbia and Romania, in which Bulgaria would still play a role. He was in any case much more conscious of the restraining influence of the Great Powers. Their difference came to a head over the timing of the armistice with Bulgaria, and over the negotiations in Bucharest about territory, in which Constantine thought Venizelos was too weak. At one point Venizelos was forced to bring matters to a head by requiring the king to accept his judgements as chief negotiator or replace him, at which point Constantine yielded.[40] The generally satisfactory terms of the Treaty of Bucharest papered over these cracks, but they were signs of trouble to come. Neither man put up easily with opposition. Constantine was stubborn and became convinced of his right to dictate the essential foreign policy decisions. Venizelos was equally convinced that as responsible prime minister enjoying a large majority in parliament his word should prevail. The scene was set for the clash over neutrality in the Great War.

Koromilas for his part, who carried large responsibilities as foreign minister in Athens while Venizelos was in London, embarrassed Venizelos on a number of occasions. He was knowledgeable and assertive, and less ready than Venizelos to make allowances for Greece's relative weakness and isolation. His remarks to the German minister in Athens in February 1913, suggesting that Greece had ambitions in Asia Minor, put Venizelos in a difficult position.[41] So did his decision to alter the contract for the procurement of the dreadnought from the Vulkan shipyard in Germany, increasing its tonnage. Venizelos felt obliged to disown Koromilas when Greece incurred the displeasure of Grey for hanging tough and withholding signature of the peace treaty in June 1913. On that occasion he told the British ambassador in Athens, in Koromilas' presence, that Greece's policy was quite simply 'to conform absolutely to the advice of Sir Edward Grey':[42] it followed that, unlike Koromilas, he was ready to remit to the Powers the responsibility of settling the status and frontiers of Albania, and of settling the fate of the Aegean islands. The phrase is suggestive of the priority Venizelos already attached to alignment with the most important of the Powers, which was to become the foundation of his diplomatic method.

This was one of the climaxes of Venizelos' career. An impoverished Greece had almost doubled in population and surface area.[43] The gains included Thessaloniki and the tobacco-growing region of Kavalla; Southern Epirus with Ioannina; and Crete, whose union with Greece was at last formally recognised. Greece's de facto occupation of the Aegean islands including Lesbos and Chios gave good hopes of their eventual annexation.

NORTHERN EPIRUS AND THE AEGEAN ISLANDS, 1913–14

The Treaty of Bucharest still left unresolved the question of Northern Epirus, which continued to preoccupy Venizelos in 1913 and 1914. In July 1913 the Powers signed a protocol establishing Albania as an 'autonomous, sovereign, hereditary principality' under their guarantee. They set up a commission to establish the frontiers of the new state. The so-called Florence Protocol of December 1913 gave a frontier which disappointed Greece in excluding from her sovereignty areas of Greek population and influence, such as Korytsa, Argyrokastro, Chimarra and Santi Quaranta. When the Greek army withdrew from Northern Epirot territories in accordance with the ruling of the Powers, a fierce struggle broke out between Muslim Albanians and Greek irregulars. The issue of Northern Epirus, where Greek interests clashed both with Italy and with the new Albania, was to remain a headache for Venizelos until he fell from power in 1920. At this stage his problem was how to handle the pressures of Northern Epirot patriots for irregular action in Northern Epirus, given the consequences this could have for Greece's interests elsewhere, especially in the Aegean islands. He won a temporary victory in late 1914 when the anarchic conditions in Albania led the Powers to invite Greece to occupy Northem Epirus.

The Aegean islands had been occupied by the reformed Greek navy during the Balkan Wars. It was Venizelos' aim and assumption that this would lead to definitive annexation. Turkey, however, refused to accept the fait accompli and embarked on an arms race which threatened to give her naval superiority, enabling her to repossess the islands. At the same time tension rose because of Turkish persecution and deportation of Greek communities of western Asia Minor.

In these difficulties Venizelos continued to look to Britain for support. Though Grey was not unsympathetic to Greece, the British interest was not in assigning the Aegean islands to Greece rather than Turkey – it was a matter of indifference to Britain whether Turkey or Greece controlled the islands, provided only that none of the Great Powers controlled them – but in maintaining peace through a stable concert of Europe.[44] In any case Grey saw the islands primarily as a bargaining chip through which to persuade Greece to be accommodating over the establishment of the frontiers of the new state of Albania. Venizelos was ready to sacrifice Korytsa and Argyrokastro in Northern Epirus provided he could secure a generous settlement in the islands which would give Greece sovereignty over all of them except Imbros and Tenedos. But differences among the Powers prevented this.

In early 1914 the situation became more dangerous: Turkey's purchase from the Armstrong-Vickers shipyard of the dreadnought *Rio de Janeiro* (renamed the *Sultan Osman*, of 25,500 tonnes, with armament superior to Greece's fleet) seemed to threaten that Turkey would solve the issue of the islands by force. Venizelos appealed to Grey, and separately to Lloyd George and Churchill, for the conclusion of an Entente with Britain aimed at preserving the status quo in the eastern Mediterranean. These overtures failed.[45]

As 1914 proceeded, therefore, though Greece remained in occupation of the islands, she was no nearer to a satisfactory and conclusive settlement. Turkish pressures and persecution of the Greek communities of Asia Minor added a new and dangerous element to the Greek–Turkish confrontation. In June 1914, ignoring the advice of the British naval mission, Venizelos bought two elderly and ineffective ships from the United States, the *Idaho* and the *Mississippi*.[46] Greece's allies Serbia and Romania kept their distance in Greece's dispute with Turkey over the islands. Britain's interest was in avoiding a regional war, not in helping Greece. In these circumstances Venizelos considered the possibility of provoking war with

Turkey in order to settle the issue while Greece retained naval superiority.[47] Realising that he would be isolated in such a course, he turned to discussions with the Turks, including on an exchange of populations between the Greeks of Asia Minor and displaced Muslims of Macedonia.[48] These discussions were still in train when the Great War broke out.

The end of the Balkan Wars marked a temporary halt in the realisation of the Great Idea. Rapid expansion had strained Greece's resources to the limits. The new territories, in which Greeks were mixed with Slavs, Albanians and Muslims, had to be integrated in the Greek kingdom. Northern Epirus, Thrace and the remaining islands of the Aegean were logically the next areas for the expansion of the kingdom. But Venizelos recognised that it was a time for consolidation of Greece's gains and peace with Bulgaria and Turkey.[49] The assumptions on which his policies were based were changed by the outbreak of the Great War.

THE SECOND PHASE: THE GREAT WAR

The outbreak of war in August 1914 interrupted this desired period of consolidation and posed acute problems for Greece and her Balkan neighbours. The Austrian assault on Serbia was not a casus belli for Greece, since the Greek-Serbian treaty was a defensive arrangement which applied only in a Balkan context. But the prospect of Turkish entry into the war on the side of the Central Powers suggested that Greece might profit by joining the other side. So Venizelos calculated. His inclinations, contrary to King Constantine's, aligned him anyway with Britain and France. He therefore immediately and remarkably offered to the entente Greece's full support with all her forces, in the case of Turkey joining the war on the side of the Central Powers. He was able to persuade the king to agree, probably against his better judgement.

Venizelos told parliament in August 1917:

> On or about 10 August, I think, I asked for and obtained the authorisation to declare that Greece not merely in consciousness of her indebtedness to the great Guaranteeing Powers, but from a clear perception of her vital interests as a nation, understood that her place was at the side of the Powers of the Entente; and that, whereas in the war that was being waged it was not possible for her to take a military part, since she could not, owing to the danger from Bulgaria, reinforce the Serbians, much less send an expeditionary force to France, nevertheless she thought it her duty to declare to the Powers of the Entente that, if Turkey went to war against them, she placed all her military and naval forces at their disposal for the war against Turkey, always presupposing that we were to be guaranteed against the Bulgarian danger . . .[50]

Venizelos explained that he made this offer before the outcome of the battle of the Marne was known, wishing to express:

> The deepest sentiments of the country and its government – their deep sentiment of the solidarity, the identity of Greek interests with the interests of the two Western Powers in the East, or more particularly in the Aegean.

He argued that if Turkey joined the war, Greece could not possibly remain neutral:

> With Turkey we were already in a state of suspended war, war for the islands, in the prosecution of which it was in our interest to have such powerful allies; and if we took no part in a war in which Turkey was involved, it meant that if Turkey was victorious one result of her victory would be the complete destruction of Hellenism in Asia Minor, and the loss to Greece of the islands adjacent to the Asiatic coast; while if Turkey was defeated the question of Asia Minor would be settled without any reference to Greek interests.

He added that joining the entente was a protection against the danger from Bulgaria, which was likely to gain territory on whichever side she fought, and even if she remained neutral.

Venizelos' offer showed that he believed that the war offered Greece an unrepeatable chance to realise her irredentist dreams. His approach soon brought him into conflict with King Constantine, who was inclined by family ties and military training to the German side, who saw Bulgaria as the main threat, and whose advisers, notably George Streit, were reluctant to offend Germany and Austria.

The allies turned down Venizelos' offer, fearing that it might provoke Turkey and possibly Bulgaria to abandon neutrality. After Turkey entered the war, the situation was changed. It now became Grey's object to induce Greece, Bulgaria and Romania to help Serbia resist the Central Powers, Greece actively, Bulgaria at least through a benevolent neutrality. This was the background to Grey's offer of 23 January of 'most important territorial compensation for Greece on the coast of Asia Minor' in return for Greek participation in the war on the side of the Entente.[51]

Grey's offer, which was designed to tempt Greece while keeping alive the possibility of Bulgarian neutrality, was prompted by Venizelos himself. Earlier in January, Elliott, the British minister in Athens, had proposed that Greece should come to the aid of Serbia. Venizelos replied that it would be impossible for Greece to enter the war solely on account of Serbia; but in view of the desperate plight of the Greeks in Asia Minor, if a rupture with Turkey were precipitated the 'magnificent compensation' which would arise from war with Turkey would enable him to carry public opinion with him in bringing Greece into the war on the side of the

Entente. This, while unspecific, was clearly a reference to Asia Minor. It was the first time that Venizelos had espoused the idea. It may be that he was prompted to do so by reports from Koromilas in Rome about Italian ambitions in the area.[52]

Grey's offer envisaged that Bulgaria would be enticed to join the Entente by Serbian compensation in the Monastir/Ochrid area. But the idea of Greek 'compensation' to Bulgaria was already in the air, and in putting Grey's proposal to the king, Venizelos, contrary to his earlier thesis about extension along a 'backbone' into contiguous areas, threw in the idea of offering Kavalla to Bulgaria as a further incentive. He wrote that hitherto there had been good reasons for Greek neutrality:

> But now the circumstances have clearly changed. At this moment when the prospects of realizing our national views on Asia Minor are opening before us, certain sacrifices in the Balkans can be made in order to secure the success of so magnificent a national policy.
>
> Above all we should withdraw our objections to concessions being made by Serbia to Bulgaria, even if these extend to the right bank of the Vardar.
>
> But if these concessions are not sufficient to draw Bulgaria into co-operation with her former allies, or at least to the maintenance of a benevolent neutrality towards them, I should not hesitate, however painful the operation might be, to recommend the sacrifice of Kavalla, so as to save Hellenism in Turkey and to secure the creation of a truly great Greece, including almost all the territories in which Hellenism has been active during its long history.[53]

Venizelos' proposals fell foul of the acting chief of general staff, the future dictator Metaxas, who set out a reasoned account of the difficulties of Greece establishing herself permanently in Asia Minor. He deployed a range of arguments, some of which foreshadowed what was to happen in 1919 to 1922, and objected to the suggested sacrifice of Greek territory in Macedonia to Bulgaria. Venizelos was not deterred. He put his proposal to the king, arguing that:

> the concessions to Greece in Asia Minor, which Sir Edward Grey recommended, may, if of course we submit to sacrifices to Bulgaria, be so extensive that another equally large and not less rich Greece will be added to the doubled Greece which emerged from the victorious wars.[54]

He conceded that until Greek forces in Asia Minor were organised there would be some risk of a local uprising; but this was 'extremely unlikely, since with the complete dissolution of the Ottoman State, our Muslim subjects will be excellent and law-abiding citizens'.[55]

Venizelos seems to have approached the question of Kavalla as against Asia Minor as a calculation of relative wealth, resources and numbers of

Greeks, ignoring the emotional charge of the sacrifice of a region so recently won by Greek arms and assigned to Greece through his own diplomacy. In assuming that the Ottoman Empire would be dissolved and that the Muslims in Greece's territory would be law-abiding, he failed to foresee that a Turkish nationalism might arise, matching that of the Christian Balkan nations.[56]

Venizelos later told the Greek parliament of his joy on receiving Grey's communication:

> the Greece that a short time before had been so small and of so little account had now come to take her place as the peer of the Great Powers in settling the fate of Turkey, which for generations had been the apple of discord among the European Powers.[57]

The British Dardanelles expedition offered him another chance to fulfil his policy. Hearing of the preliminary attack on the Dardanelles forts by the British fleet, in February he proposed to offer an army corps to occupy the peninsula, thus joining the war against Turkey and realizing Sir Edward Grey's offer of compensation in Asia Minor. In the face of the opposition of Metaxas and the general staff, and King Constantine's disagreement with his policy, he resigned.[58]

Venizelos' two resignations, the first in March and the second in October, both took place because of disagreement with Constantine over the question of war or neutrality. The first turned on participation in the Dardanelles expedition, the second on coming to the aid of Serbia, under attack by Bulgaria in October. The notional point at issue in October was the application of the Greek–Serbian treaty of 1913. Both Venizelos and the king had been cautious about this earlier, when Austro-Hungary declared war on Serbia, since the treaty was envisaged in a purely Balkan context. In Venizelos' view, but not in Constantine's, Bulgaria's attack on Serbia in October 1915 triggered Greece's obligation.

In fact the legal arguments were secondary. By now it was clear that Venizelos wanted to take the opportunity to enter the war, and the king, backed by the general staff, was determined to resist it. Britain's offer of Cyprus to the government of Zaimis a few days after Venizelos' resignation was not enough to shift Constantine.[59]

From the time of his second resignation until the end of the war Venizelos' diplomatic activity was dictated more and more by the demands of the internal struggle for power. Success in this became the necessary condition of achieving his war aims, since it was only by entering the war on the side of the Entente that Greece could hope to profit in the post-war settlement. (He soon gave up any hope he may have had of a political reconciliation with moderate royalists, allowing Greece to enter the war.) Entry into the war did not in itself guarantee territorial gains. Earlier allied offers of territory had lapsed, and allied obligations towards Italy conflicted with Venizelist hopes in Asia Minor. Venizelos therefore came to see that Greece must enter the war under his leadership, and participate actively in the fighting, so as to stake the strongest possible 'moral' claims.

Venizelos needed the confidence and support of Britain and France throughout his struggle with Constantine, which culminated in the revolutionary movement of Thessaloniki and the establishment of the provisional government in October 1916. This required a subtle diplomacy not least because republican France was more interventionist and readier to violate Greek neutrality than monarchist Great Britain. By 1917 allied hesitations and disputes were compromising Venizelos' prospects. He pressed for permission to extend his control into Thessaly as a base for recruitment, so as to build up the armed forces he could contribute to Sarrail's army on the Macedonian front. But he was forced to wait on the ponderous workings of allied policy-making, which led finally to the dethronement and exile of Constantine.

Throughout this period Venizelos' underlying worry was that the British would work for the reconciliation of Venizelist and royalist Greece. He believed that the time for compromise was past. By this time the schism had its own internal dynamic. Though some moderate royalists were ready to discuss it, reconciliation was ruled out by the vested interests of the followers of each camp, especially the officers in the armed forces.[60]

Venizelos wanted the king ousted. In April 1917 Politis told the Greek representatives in London and Paris that 'all compromise on the royal family has become impossible', referring to irreconcilable opposition between the liberal system and absolutism.[61] This was Venizelist language for the difference in political philosophy which underlay the schism. There was truth in it insofar as Constantine believed that in critical questions of national policy, war or peace, his duties as king overrode the views of the prime minister.[62] But it left out of account the power dynamics of the schism, where there was not so much to choose between the two sides. Under the stress of war and internal crisis, Venizelos' regime became increasingly autocratic and unpopular.[63]

By the time of Constantine's dethronement by the allies, Venizelos had come to feel that a republic would be better than a continuation of the Glucksberg dynasty. In April 1917 he argued that the best solution would be a monarchy with a king from the British royal family; second best a republic; and third best the British idea of a monarchy with one of the Greek princes taking Constantine's place. Venizelos described this solution as 'difficult to resist'.[64] He accepted it for the sake of relations with Britain, succeeding in having Alexander designated rather than Crown Prince George who was regarded as tainted.[65] The episode showed again his flexibility on constitutional questions. The regime which best served his nationalist foreign policy aims was to be preferred.

With Greece reunited under Venizelos' leadership in Athens, he was able to contribute actively to the achievement of allied war aims and the defeat of Bulgaria on the Macedonian front. This was to be the moral, though not legal, basis of Greece's post-war claims, backed by the personal prestige of Venizelos as a loyal adherent of the Entente. The cost in terms of economic and political disruption, and national humiliation through the allied interventions in Greek affairs, was high.

THE THIRD PHASE: THE PARIS PEACE CONFERENCE AND THE ASIA MINOR MANDATE

From the armistice on, Venizelos' energies were concentrated on making good Greece's claims at the peace conference. Starting with a visit to Paris and London in October–November 1918, he spent the greater part of his time outside Greece, mostly in Paris.

The Paris Peace Conference was the cockpit of Venizelos' efforts. Peace was dictated by the victors to the vanquished, all of whom except Germany had surrendered unconditionally. The defeated had to accept terms handed down by the Supreme Council, which was determined to keep matters in its own hands. The smaller allies, of which Greece was one, were able to make their case and to comment on the various proposals, but were still subject to the unpredictable and conflict-ridden peace making efforts of the Great Powers.[66] Thus, those who disposed of Greece's fate were the United States, Britain, France and Italy, and the key to Venizelos' diplomacy was his efforts to win the leaders of these Powers to Greece's side, or in the case of the US and Italy to neutralise their opposition.[67]

Greece's claims were put forward in a comprehensive memorandum,[68] drafted by Venizelos himself at President Wilson's suggestion in twelve hours of uninterrupted work. It followed the lines of a memo he had sent to Lloyd George when he was in London in early November. In this he had argued in favour of a threefold settlement in Asiatic Turkey: the creation of an Armenian state; the creation under the auspices of the League of Nations of an independent state of Constantinople and Eastern Thrace, to assure the freedom of the Straits; and the annexation of western Asia Minor to Greece.[69]

Venizelos argued that the large area he claimed in Asia Minor could be delimited 'without the slightest difficulty'. This could be done in such a way as to include an Ottoman population roughly equal to the 800,000 or so Greeks who remained outside the area, and the peace treaty should then encourage mutual and voluntary intermigration. He was attracted by a solution whereby Asia Minor would eventually consist of homogeneous national areas, with a strong, defensible Greek zone which would not be subverted from within.[70]

In his memorandum to the peace conference, Venizelos claimed the maximum that he realistically felt was attainable. He was predictably criticised in Athens for not going far enough. In the opening paragraphs he set out the political and philosophical justification for the claims, with an eye to President Wilson himself, the champion of self-determination:

> The complete victory of the allied and associated states affords the occasion to fix the political frontiers of the European states in exact accordance, or as approximately as possible, with their ethnical character. In this way the indispensable basis of the Society of Nations will be created.[71]

Venizelos went on to list his statistics for the distribution of the Hellenic nation within and outside the kingdom of Greece. He claimed all the islands of the Aegean, both those which were under Ottoman sovereignty, and the Dodecanese which had been under Italian occupation for six years. On cultural and historical grounds he claimed almost the whole of Northern Epirus with its mixed population of Greeks and Albanians, of whom the majority spoke Albanian. He claimed both Western (Bulgarian) and Eastern (Turkish) Thrace, despite the majority of Muslims over Greeks recognised in Greek statistics. In Asia Minor he proposed to solve the Pontus problem by incorporating the vilayet of Trebizond, where the Greeks were most densely concentrated, in the new state of Armenia. This was the best he could do for a population too distant for Greece to protect and too weak to protect itself. He had wisely refused to endorse the demands of the Pontian Greeks that Pontus should become an independent Greek republic.

In western Asia Minor Greece claimed the strip lying west of a line running from near Panderma on the Sea of Marmara to a point on the south coast opposite Kastellorizo. The zone included Smyrna and most of the vilayet of Aydin. According to Venizelos' figures, which were those of the Ecumenical Patriarchate's census of 1912, the zone contained just over 800,000 Greeks as against just over one million Turks and just over

100,000 Armenians, Jews and others. Venizelos got round these inconvenient figures by including in the zone for statistical purposes the neighbouring islands of Imbros, Tenedos, Lesbos, Chios, Samos, Ikaria, Rhodes and the Dodecanese, and Kastellorizo, where Greeks easily outnumbered Turks. He argued that these islands were geographically an extension of the mainland.[72] On this basis Venizelos was able to argue for the cession of Asia Minor on ethnographic, historical and cultural grounds.

The logic of Greece's claims purported to be primarily ethnographic.[73] It was based on President Wilson's principle of self-determination. This was the fashion of the time and it was no doubt essential that Greek claims be couched in this form. However, the principle, besides posing endless problems to the peacemakers in finding their way through incompatible sets of national statistics, did require some juggling by Greece over Asia Minor, Western Thrace and Northern Epirus, to make good all her claims even on the basis of her own figures.

Greece's claims raised a number of problems. One was how to define nationality. The Greeks' answer to this, following the French nineteenth-century thinking of Ernest Renan, was by the individual's 'national consciousness', not by race, religion or language.[74] This met the point that many of those whom the Greek state regarded as Greek were Turkish or Slav speakers. National consciousness was of course not an objective criterion, since people changed their minds about their national status according to circumstances: if a Greek band had occupied a village in Macedonia, the villagers were likely, prudently, to conclude that they were Greek; if a Bulgarian, Bulgarian. In theory these matters could be resolved by means of a plebiscite, but in contested areas fair plebiscites are difficult to arrange and do not always give the answer that the peacemakers want. But it was the criterion which best met the Greek claims set out in Venizelos' memorandum. It was also consistent with the inclusive notion of Greek identity which was the basis of Greek nineteenth-century irredentism.[75]

Another related issue was what importance to attach to the credits earned by fighting in the war on the 'right' side, the side of the Entente? If self-determination was to prevail, did they have no meaning? And what if the various promises made by the allies were found incompatible with the principle of self-determination?

These were problems intrinsic to the difficult task of peacemaking. They were appreciated by Venizelos. Since 1915 he had recognised that the various offers made to Greece by the allies having lapsed, he could not revive them on the basis of Greece's entry into the war in other circumstances. What he could and must do was to ensure by Greece's effective military participation, and by his own assiduous lobbying, and by his continuing usefulness to the Powers, that Greek claims could not be easily brushed aside. And he must try by negotiation to minimise the threat to Greek claims from Italy, which had conflicting interests both in Albania/Epirus and in Asia Minor and the Dodecanese.

For this reason, at Clemenceau's request, in late 1918, Venizelos volunteered two Greek divisions in support of a French expedition to South Russia, in support of Denikin's anti-Bolshevik forces. These Greek troops, in which Nikolaos Plastiras served as an officer, fought with distinction.[76] They can be seen as a prudent investment by Venizelos.

Of all the issues which Venizelos presented to the Peace Conference in Paris, the most important and difficult was the claim to a zone in Asia Minor. It was ambitious, laying claim to a population of some hundreds of thousands of people, of mixed Turkish Muslim, Christian Greek, Armenian, Jewish and Western European Levantine origins.[77] It would clearly require military force to be made good over time. In the longer term it would require either that the Muslim inhabitants of Greece's zone should be reconciled to Greek rule, or that they be exchanged for Greeks from outside the zone so as to make the Greek zone homogeneous. It directly impinged on the perceived interests of Italy, which claimed territory in southwestern Anatolia. In other words, the claim bristled with difficulties, but was enormously attractive both in that it incorporated in the Greek state the most substantial and prosperous of Greek communities in the diaspora, and because it extended Greek territory around the Aegean; though Greek sovereignty would not be continuous unless and until Greece obtained also the Straits zone.

Constantinople and the Straits were one of the keys to a stable settlement. The temptation to claim Constantinople was great. It was the summation of Greek nationalist desires embodied in the Great Idea, even if the ethnographic justification was doubtful. But the interests of the Great Powers in the freedom of the Straits seemed to Venizelos to be too great to make a Greek claim plausible. The Russians, with their own recognised claim to the Straits, had effectively put themselves out of the game through the Bolshevik revolution. Lloyd George might have bought a Greek claim, but neither his colleagues nor the French and Americans would do so. Since the whole basis of Venizelos' policy was co-operation with the Western allies, this precluded the claim. He therefore argued that Constantinople and the Straits should be internationalised.[78]

Cyprus, annexed by Britain in November 1914 following the Ottoman Empire's entry into the war on the side of the Central Powers, and inhabited in the majority by Greeks, was not mentioned in Venizelos' claim. He did not want complications with Britain over Cyprus to prejudice the achievement of his primary aims, including Asia Minor. In presenting his case orally, however, to the Council of Ten, Venizelos said that he was convinced that the British government would be sufficiently magnanimous to surrender Cyprus to Greece anyway: 'to sum up, Greece claimed all the islands of the Eastern Mediterranean, including . . . Cyprus.'[79]

The Paris Peace Conference was the zenith of Venizelos' diplomacy, defined as the use of diplomatic means (persuasion, lobbying, negotiation and propaganda) to achieve the ends he set out for Greece, even if the Asia Minor catastrophe in September 1922 retrospectively threw doubt on these ends. Venizelos was in his element in Paris, where his qualities of charm, will power, personal force and industry came into their own. He was master of the necessary arguments to support Greek claims. His friendship with Lloyd George gave him an advantage in this period of diplomacy by conference, in which policy was made in small conclaves of senior statesmen, with little regard for the traditional mechanisms of diplomacy.

The Lloyd George factor was crucial in assigning to Greece the mandate to occupy Smyrna. If the decision as to Asia Minor had been left to the experts, whether American or British, it would not have gone to Greece.[80] The Greek landing was authorised by the Supreme Council because of the Italians, who were landing troops in Asia Minor and threatening to pre-empt the decisions of the Peace Conference. To President Wilson's fury they had temporarily walked out of the Supreme Council because of a row over the future of Fiume. Venizelos and Lloyd George were able to take advantage of these circumstances to secure a decision by the council to authorise a Greek peacekeeping mandate and the immediate occupation of Smyrna by Greek troops, which duly took place on 15 May 1919. It was another climax to Venizelos' career.

From that triumphant point on, his difficulties accumulated and Venizelos was forced more and more onto the defensive. The occupation was marred by incidents of violence which gave a handle to Greece's critics in Paris. The voices of those on the spot who thought the occupation unwise became louder. Most importantly, Venizelos' prediction that there would be no difficulty or uprising by Greece's 'loyal Muslim subjects' proved wrong. Within the zone of occupation, after a bad start Greek forces were able to keep order, though there was intermittent activity by bands of Turkish chettes operating from outside the zone. But contrary to Venizelos' expectations, Turkish nationalism, under the leadership of Mustafa Kemal, was provoked into active life by the Greek occupation itself. The dissolution of the Ottoman Empire which Venizelos had assumed would permit Greek expansion into Asia Minor left the Anatolian heartlands of Turkey stubbornly determined to remain Turkish.[81] Finally, as time passed, it became clear that France and Italy would prefer to settle with Kemal rather than co-operate in imposing a draconian peace.

In the face of these difficulties, though sometimes disheartened, Venizelos fought a stubborn and effective rearguard action to defend the Greek occupation and ensure that in the final peace treaty with Turkey Greece's peacekeeping mandate was converted into a definite annexation. First he took steps to ensure impartial and effective administration by naming a trusted colleague, Aristidis Stergiadis, to be high commissioner in Smyrna. Second, he took every opportunity to defend the Greek case in the council and with the key decision makers. Third, he continued to offer Greek services to the allies in pacifying Turkey and in imposing the peace treaty.

DIFFICULTIES WITH ITALY AND THE UNITED STATES

In parallel with the struggle for Asia Minor, from December 1918 until the signing of the relevant treaties, Venizelos was intensively engaged in defending all Greece's other claims. Each of these, Northern Epirus, Eastern and Western Thrace, and the islands, raised different problems, and each brought Greece into opposition with Italy. In defending them, Venizelos used his familiar technique of invoking the support of Britain and France. He was frustrated by American opposition to Greece's claims both in Northern Epirus and in Thrace, where the Americans insisted on what Greeks saw as misguided arguments based partly on population statistics and partly on economic geography. He made sustained efforts to negotiate Greece's differences with Italy.

In December 1918, on his way to Paris for the Peace Conference, he held talks with Orlando and Sonnino in Rome, aimed at reaching agreement over Northern Epirus and the Dodecanese.[82] These talks were resumed in Paris. He made no progress, even though he was prepared to see the Greek claim in Northern Epirus whittled down in return for satisfaction in the Dodecanese and Asia Minor.[82] The Greek committee established by the Supreme Council divided equally on the claim (US and Italy against Britain and France) and failed to reach a decision.

After the Greek occupation of Smyrna, it became necessary to delimit the respective Greek and Italian zones of occupation. In July 1919, at Clemenceau's suggestion, Venizelos and the Italian prime minister Tittoni discussed a wider accommodation of Greek–Italian differences. The discussions concluded with an agreement. Italy would support Greek claims in Northern Epirus including Korytsa and Argyrokastro, and in Thrace, Asia Minor and the Dodecanese. Greece would support an Italian protectorate over Albania, Italian sovereignty over Valona, and the neutralisation of the Corfu channel. Italy would retain Rhodes unless and until Britain conceded Cyprus to Greece and a plebiscite were held. This temporary agreement was the nearest Venizelos got to neutralising the obstruction by Italy of Greek claims. It did not last. The agreements were subject to the provision that if Italian aspirations in Asia Minor were not satisfied, Italy would recover her full freedom of action. Italian aspirations were not satisfied by the Treaty of Sèvres, and Italy (under a successor government to Tittoni's) then denounced the agreement.[84] Thus Italian opposition continued to complicate the task of the Greeks in Epirus, Thrace and Asia Minor.

The struggle at the Peace Conference over Thrace was particularly gruelling. Here the Americans proved tenacious opponents of Greece's claims. They sympathised with Bulgaria's claim on ethnological and geographical grounds to a part of Western Thrace, including access to the Aegean. Continued uncertainty over the final disposition of Constantinople and the Straits also complicated the disposition of Eastern Thrace. But Greece also faced resistance by Bulgarians to the armistice terms and by Muslims to the prospect of Greek administration. Characteristically, Venizelos put his trust in the Peace Conference. He refused to contemplate direct action on the ground, such as the arming of volunteers in the villages so as to create 'facts', because he thought this would impact negatively on the peacemakers in Paris.[85]

The Greek committee again split 2–2, with Britain and France supporting Greece's claims, the US and Italy opposing. The period July to September 1919, when the question of Thrace was thrashed out prior to the conclusion of the Bulgarian treaty, was perhaps the most testing of Venizelos' career, as he struggled to convince the Supreme Council, and in particular the Americans, of the justice of Greece's claims. He admitted to being reduced to prostration.[86] In the event Greece secured Western Thrace, and Eastern Thrace through the Treaty of Sèvres, only to lose the latter to Turkey in the crisis of October 1922.

THE PROBLEMS INCREASE

By June 1920, when more than a year had passed since the Greek occupation and there was still no treaty, Venizelos' position was becoming increasingly difficult. He argued plausibly that the longer the delay in announcing the terms of the treaty the more difficult it would be to impose it. Delay played into Kemal's hands. The British forces of occupation in the zone of Constantinople came under pressure from Kemalist nationalist forces in the Ismid area. The allied position in the Straits zone appeared threatened. Lloyd George asked for Venizelos' help in London on 14 June, telling him that Greece could expect no help from the allies in imposing the Turkish treaty which had been agreed in principle at San Remo in April.

In reporting to Athens, Venizelos described the issue as a choice between undertaking to impose the terms of the treaty (which had not yet been signed) and seeing Greek claims whittled away in response to pressure from the French, Italians and British military circles. Therefore 'at this critical point in the history of the nation' he had undertaken to lend the British one division for Ismid, and to smash the Turkish concentrations opposite the Greek lines, without seeking any aid, even economic, from the allies. He had added that if even this lesson would not induce the Turks to sign and execute the treaty, he would undertake to increase the strength of the Greek army to such a point that it could, together with the British troops presently in Turkey, impose the treaty. But in this case he would need British economic aid and war materials, and an undertaking that Turkey would be reduced to the central Anatolian plateau. 'I succeeded in getting Mr Lloyd George to accept these proposals, and it was thanks to him that we succeeded in getting the permission given at Boulogne.'[87]

The Greek operations were successful. Greek forces occupied Bursa and advanced to a front extending to the edge of the Anatolian plateau. They also occupied Eastern Thrace and Adrianople. This was the furthest the Greek army went under Venizelos as prime minister and he now hoped for further territorial gains if Turkey did not accept the terms of the treaty.

The Treaty of Sèvres was signed on 10 August. A paper instrument, since it was never ratified or implemented, it represented the magnificent but hollow outcome of Venizelos' tireless diplomacy and of Greek military action. The Ottoman Empire ceased to exist. Turkey was reduced to her Anatolian kernel and a strip of Europe extending up to the Chatalja lines. The treaty provided for an autonomous Kurdistan in the east,[88] and an independent Armenia. The Smyrna zone was to be administered by Greece, remaining under nominal Turkish sovereignty for five years, pending definite annexation if (or rather when) so decided by plebiscite. The Straits were internationalised. Anatolia was carved up into zones of economic influence, France receiving Cilicia, Italy Adalia and the south-west. Eastern Thrace was ceded to Greece by Turkey, while Western Thrace was annexed to Greece by a separate treaty.

This should have been Venizelos' finest hour. Greece had gained, on paper, a generous Smyrna zone, almost the whole of Thrace, the islands of the Aegean including Imbros and Tenedos commanding the Straits, the Dodecanese except for Rhodes. Of the regions of Greek interest, only Northern Epirus, Cyprus, Constantinople and the Straits zone, and the Pontus fell outside this settlement, and of these Venizelos had seriously claimed only Northern Epirus.

But these were not real gains. The Turkish nationalist army remained in the field and Greece's allies were not willing, or able, to impose peace on a recalcitrant Turkey. Against these stubborn facts Venizelos' diplomacy had no answer. The remaining months until he fell from power in November 1920 illustrate the dilemma. First, in late August, the Greek commander-in-chief Paraskevopoulos urged action to crush the Turkish nationalists by an advance into the interior as far as Ankara. Venizelos uncharacteristically prevaricated. Facing a general election, he wished to demobilise rather than mobilise new divisions. He would promise to act only if Turkey failed to execute the treaty within six months. Then he changed his mind and sent a telegram to Lloyd George urging action on the lines recommended by Paraskevopoulos, with the aim of destroying the nationalist forces around Ankara and the Pontus, creating a separate state of Constantinople and the Straits, and also a separate state of the Pontus. Venizelos said that provided Britain gave the necessary financial assistance Greek forces could achieve these ends. He envisaged that British troops would cover the Greek advance by covering the line of the Sakarya river. This plea evoked scepticism in London. On 16 October Venizelos, in a further telegram, conceded that Greece would not be able to achieve the hoped for 'knock-out blow', since the nationalists would probably retire into the interior before the Greek advance. It would therefore be necessary to maintain the occupation for a fairly long time. This being so, if the allies were not ready to approve his radical solution, Venizelos proposed that they should rapidly form an interallied commission to organise the Turkish army and gendarmerie as provided in the treaty. Such a commission, he claimed implausibly, would be able to disperse the Kemalist troops.[89]

Even this appeal evoked no response. Four weeks later Venizelos fell from power.

These final throws of Venizelos illustrate the dilemma of the policy for Asia Minor which he promoted by his highly effective diplomacy. Some have argued that the aim of securing a Greek zone was reasonable, since it was in 1918 to 1919 a general assumption, not unique to Venizelos, that the allies would take part in a carve-up of Turkey and would co-operate to impose a harsh treaty.[90] But by 1920 it was clear that this assumption was false. Yet there was no alternative policy for Venizelos. Success depended on Greece enjoying allied backing which was not forthcoming.

Venizelos' diplomacy was also undermined by the dual nature of the Greek administration of Asia Minor. It was not easy to reconcile the harsh imposition of martial law and the civilising mission of enlightened administration of a loyal Muslim population. The man who had to do so was the high commissioner of the Greek zone in Asia Minor, Aristidis Stergiadis, who summed up the contradiction in his own personality.[91] Stergiadis was a Cretan lawyer of Macedonian origin who had proved his nationalist credentials in the Cretan revolutionary movement of the 1890s, and his administrative skills as governor general of Epirus in the critical post-war period from 1918 on. He was selected by Venizelos early in 1919, somewhat against his will, to represent Greece in Asia Minor. He landed in Smyrna and took charge (remaining formally responsible for his Epirus mission) a week after the violent episodes which had compromised the Greek mission in Asia Minor from the start. Stergiadis quickly got on the wrong side of the local leadership. He was determined to establish an administration impartial as between Muslim and Christian, and willing to offend Greek susceptibilities in so doing.

In doing this Stergiades was carrying out Venizelos' instructions. Venizelos saw that to allow revanchism on the part of the Greeks, whether local people or the army, would compromise Greece's position in the eyes of the allies and prejudice the provisions of the Turkish peace treaty still to be finalised. Exposed to allied leaders and their military advisers (some of whom took a dim view of the Greek occupation) he was in a position to appreciate what his colleagues in Athens and compatriots in Smyrna found difficult to understand. To the allied leaders he must present Greece on the one hand as a capable, up-to-date country exercising a civilising mission in Asia Minor, and on the other as a willing executor of the allied will in controlling nationalist bands in Anatolia and (later in 1920) imposing the terms of the Treaty of Sèvres. The language he used to his colleagues in defending Stergiadis' approach was correspondingly fierce.[92]

NOVEMBER 1920–SEPTEMBER 1922

Venizelos' fall at the elections of November 1920 led to the return of King Constantine after a plebiscite. Venizelos himself left Greece for Nice, Paris and London. He stated that he would not involve himself in the internal affairs of Greece, but found this easier to state than to put into practice, since his advice was still sought by the British government as well as by his own supporters in Greece and in Asia Minor.

As was natural, he remained loyal to his own conception of the Greek mandate in Asia Minor. Consulted by Sir John Stavridi, who was sent by Curzon to Nice to establish Venizelos' views about the return of King Constantine, Venizelos summed up his view as: 'Treaty of Sèvres must be saved at all costs.' He would prefer to see Crown Prince George become king and Constantine formally abdicate, but if this was impossible would prefer that Constantine be recognised on condition that he bind himself to carry out the treaty.[93] This was logical enough, but because of French resentment of Constantine and desire by now to settle with Kemal, the joint declaration of the allies on 2 December, at French instigation, included the statement that the restoration of Constantine to the throne:

> could only be regarded by the allies as a ratification by Greece of his hostile acts. This step would create a new and unfavourable situation in the relations between Greece and the Allies, and in that case the three governments reserve to themselves complete liberty in dealing with the situation thus created.[94]

Venizelos' views on the military tactics to be adopted in Asia Minor altered with the change of regime. The return of Constantine and the consequent chill in the relations between Greece and the allies made it all the more important in his view that Greece should put herself in the hands of the allies concerning the imposition of peace. Summoned from Nice to Paris to consult with Lloyd George, he argued strongly to Lloyd George's private secretary Philip Kerr that Greece's claims should be upheld. The allies should give economic assistance, since the Greek army was defending not only Greek but also allied interests in imposing the treaty.[95] Kerr said such assistance was impossible with Constantine on the throne again. Venizelos replied that he did not dare make suggestions to the Athens government, for fear that they would do exactly the opposite of what he suggested:

> But if I were in the position of the present Greek Government, and saw that the economic situation had reached an impasse, I would abandon all the other territories occupied at present by our army, and limit myself to the occupation and defence of those territories alone which were conceded to us by the Treaty of Sèvres, together with the Meander valley. The defence of this region could be handled by a force of three divisions, or 45,000 men.[96]

This was the first appearance of the idea of a shortening of the front, which was to dominate political discussion in 1921 and 1922.

VENIZELOS BREAKS WITH GOVERNMENT POLICY

So far Venizelos' attitude was supportive of the Greek government. However, he was soon put under pressure from Venizelist quarters in Constantinople to support an alternative strategy of autonomous action to defend Hellenism in Asia Minor should the Greek government fail to do so. Venizelos recommended three representatives to Sir John Stavridi, who put them in touch with Philip Kerr. In discussion with the three in January 1921, Kerr said that Lloyd George was 'favourably disposed to the consideration of the idea, always on the understanding that nothing was to be attempted until Constantine had failed to maintain the Treaty of Sèvres'. The scheme as expounded by the three men looked very much like a rerun of Venizelos' revolution of 1916, but in much less favourable circumstances – an attempt to restore Venizelos to power was mixed with the motive of defending Hellenism in Asia Minor. No British support transpired.[97]

By May 1921 Venizelos was predicting disaster, owing to Greece's diplomatic isolation, which he said could only be alleviated by the abdication of Constantine. By June he was convinced that to undertake an offensive and therefore to reject the offer of mediation made by the Powers on 21 June would be disastrous. He publicly broke with royalist policy in July, just before the Gounaris government, having rejected British mediation, launched its major offensive in Asia Minor. He wrote in these terms to General Danglis:

> When I maintain that our government has blundered criminally in not accepting the intervention of the Allied Powers, I do not consider that Turkey would have accepted a solution in accordance with the British point of view; but in the event of Turkey's refusal to accept such a solution, Great Britain would have appeared justified in public opinion in coming to our support in imposing the Treaty of Sèvres . . . Now that the refusal has come from us, public opinion in England will not, under any circumstances, allow the government to assist us . . . To what other result can resumption of hostilities lead than to our complete economic and military exhaustion, which will place us in the position, after a few months, of having to beg for intervention under conditions incomparably harsher than those already offered?[98]

In a second letter, written on 26 August during the Greek army's advance towards Ankara, Venizelos roundly condemned the offensive, which he claimed would not lead to victory since the Turks could withdraw and avoid the knock-out blow. The publication of his two letters made clear the breach between Venizelos and the government.[99] His criticisms do not lack force, but could be applied to his own policy before November 1920 as well as to his opponents in 1921.

Despite his criticism of the government, Venizelos' policy continued to be that no compromise was possible over Greece's claims recognised in the Treaty of Sèvres. And he still believed that it was only the dynastic issue which prevented the allies from upholding those claims. In October 1921 he tried to get the British to tell Gounaris that Constantine must go.[100] In the winter he set off for the Americas with his new wife, Helena Schilizzi. His position was awkward because he was under continual pressure from worried supporters, in Constantinople, Smyrna and Athens, to endorse plans for independent nationalist action to defend the Greek zone in Asia Minor.[101] In response to a despairing telegram from the Patriarch, he refused either to approve or disapprove the idea that the Greeks of Asia Minor should undertake their own defence. He set out both the enormous difficulties of the enterprise, and ways in which, if they decided to proceed, they might get round them. But Venizelos concluded that without Stergiadis at its head, the movement stood no chance of success.[102] He saw Stergiadis as the best guarantee that there would be a strong and experienced hand at the tiller in Smyrna.[103] This was not advice which the National Defence wanted to hear.

It cannot be claimed that Venizelos had much impact on events after he left government in November 1920, either by influencing allied governments to soften their stand towards Greece, or by deterring his hotheaded supporters from plans for independent action in Asia Minor. He was too far out of the stream of events. He remained loyal to his own Asia Minor policy but without the means to promote it.

THE FINAL PHASE: THE TREATY OF LAUSANNE AND THE END OF THE GREAT IDEA

The Greek army was defeated by Kemalist forces in August 1922 and retired towards Smyrna in disarray. At once a vast movement of refugees began to migrate from Asia Minor to Greece. The army and Greek administration were evacuated and Smyrna burned. A revolutionary movement led by Colonel Plastiras, a strong supporter of Venizelos, took power in Athens.

The new government invited Venizelos to represent it abroad. His prestige with allied governments, and in particular Britain, was regarded as an indispensable asset in the peace negotiations which would settle Greece's boundaries at the proposed peace conference with Turkey.

Turkish sovereignty over the whole of Anatolia had been settled by the outcome of the war. So had the Turkishness of its population, by the expulsion or flight of most of the Greeks. But there remained important questions for resolution. The most difficult of these for Greece were the status of Eastern Thrace, claimed by Turkey and still occupied by the Greek army, the settlement of the refugees expelled from Asia Minor and the fate of the remaining Greeks in Asia Minor.

In agreeing to represent the government, Venizelos set out his conditions, which, as always, were based on his perception of the need to re-establish Greece's credibility with the allies. He believed that only he was in a position both to appreciate how the new situation had diminished Greece's negotiating strength, and to convince the inexperienced government and revolution in Athens to swallow the bitter pill.[104] He insisted that Greece must accept allied demands even where they reduced further Greece's territorial gains from the unratified Treaty of Sèvres. This meant the abandonment of Eastern Thrace, despite the presence of strong and well-organised Greek forces in this area.[105]

Venizelos wrote that:

> The new government should be aware that the catastrophe which we have suffered is irreparable. We have not only lost Northern Epirus, but also western Asia Minor and Eastern Thrace, from the moment that the three Great Powers, formerly our allies, decided to return them to Turkey . . . no citizen with any sense could think of pursuing the war against Turkey, in the complete military and diplomatic isolation in which we find ourselves . . .
>
> The government must urgently draw a political line. If that policy includes a decision to persist in holding onto Thrace, even against the decision taken by our former allies, my heartfelt wishes will go with the nation in this struggle, but I would sadly have to decline the honour of representing my country abroad.
>
> If on the other hand the government shares my views, let me know as soon as possible, because if I can give the Powers the assurance that we will submit to their decision over Eastern Thrace, we can be pretty well sure that at least England will never authorise the Turks to cross the Straits and carry the war into Europe. Thus if there were a resumption of hostilities between Turkey and England, we would be taking part in it as the ally of Britain, and the return of the Turks to Europe would become impossible.[106]

Members of the Greek government and military were tempted to try to hold onto Eastern Thrace, which they believed they were in a position to do. The cost in terms of relations with the allies and the subsequent conduct of the peace negotiations was in Venizelos' estimation too high, and his view prevailed.

The question of Eastern Thrace was thus in effect settled before the Peace Conference began at Lausanne in November 1922. There remained the question of Western Thrace. Here Curzon and Venizelos had no difficulty in confirming the Greek sovereignty which Greece had obtained in 1920 and in seeing off the demand of the Turks for a plebiscite of the inhabitants.[107]

The negotiations at Lausanne have been seen as largely a struggle between the British and the Turks. Venizelos was able to shelter under Curzon's wing in arriving at territorial arrangements which, while falling far short of the demands of nationalists in Athens, were reasonable in the aftermath of a great defeat, and in the face of frequent opposition from France and Italy. Greece was confirmed in the possession of the Aegean islands, except for Imbros and Tenedos, which were assigned to Turkey. The islands near to the Turkish coast were demilitarised. The Dodecanese remained with Italy. The question of Cyprus did not arise.[108]

For all the bitterness of the Lausanne settlement for Greece after the high hopes of Sèvres, it was a realistic and balanced settlement, which has lasted until today as the basis of Greek–Turkish relations. Venizelos and Ismet share the credit for this achievement.[109]

THE EXCHANGE OF POPULATIONS

Of all the questions arising, the most urgent was that of the refugees. Venizelos set out his views to Nansen, the League of Nations high commissioner for refugees, on 13 October 1922 in reply to Nansen's first thoughts on what should be done. Referring to reports that Turkey had decided no longer to accept the presence of Greek populations on Turkish soil, and would propose a compulsory exchange, he urged Nansen to do all he could to get the exchange started even before the conclusion of a formal treaty, so that the work of settling Greek refugees in vacated Muslim properties could begin.[110] He told the Greek foreign minister Kanellopoulos that the Greeks of Eastern Thrace should be discouraged from hoping that they could stay, and encouraged to take up their moveable property and take the road of exile.[111] Venizelos explained the logic of this in terms which show that as early as October 1922 he foresaw the role that the refugees could play in Greek life:

> Without exaggeration, the future of Greece depends on whether we get the right or wrong solution to this question. If we fail to arrive at the right solution there will be disasters which one trembles even to think of, whereas a successful solution will contribute within a few years to our recovering from the unbearable burdens which the defeat in the war has bequeathed us, and to our

> securing, after the collapse of the Greater Greece, the consolidation of the Great Greece, of which the frontiers will never be secure if Western Thrace and Macedonia are not ethnologically as well as politically Greek territories . . .[112]

The refugee question was 'settled' by a bilateral convention signed at Lausanne on 30 January 1923, providing for a compulsory exchange of populations. The Muslims of Greece were exchanged for the Christian Greeks of Asia Minor, with the exception of the Greeks of Constantinople and the Muslims of Western Thrace. It is unclear where the idea of a compulsory exchange originated. Both Venizelos and Curzon had strong reservations about the compulsory nature of the arrangement, but given that the Turks insisted on it Venizelos soon came to see that it was necessary. The political advantage of the arrangement for both sides was that it drew a line under the expulsions of the Greeks from Asia Minor and made thoughts of returning to their homelands impossible. For the Turks this removed a perceived threat. For the Greeks it created the homogeneous nation which Venizelos had foreseen.

The signature of the convention was only the first formal step in a process which took years to work itself out; through the establishment of the refugees, their economic support, and negotiations with Turkey over various aspects of the convention including the property clauses. The political effects were as radical and lasting as the economic, shaping the pattern of Greek politics throughout the inter-war period.[113]

As we have seen, Venizelos had first considered a (voluntary) exchange of populations, under Turkish pressure, in 1914. He included in his proposals to the Peace Conference the suggestion that there should be a voluntary exchange of Muslims from Greece's zone in Asia Minor for Greeks from outside the zone. He was thus well aware, before the Lausanne negotiations, of the potential value of such exchanges in consolidating populations and eliminating sources of tension. The exchange of populations fell within this framework. Controversial, tragic in some of its effects, it was a realistic recognition of established facts created by war. It helped create the ethnically compact Greece of today. Probably only Venizelos could have negotiated it and sold it to the Greek people.

CONCLUSION: VENIZELOS' FOREIGN POLICY AND HIS DIPLOMACY

Venizelos' diplomacy between 1912 and 1923 is identified with the final phase of the Great Idea, that is the incorporation of the 'unredeemed' Greeks within the boundaries of the Greek kingdom. It took time for this policy to crystallise. We have seen how in 1908 to 1909 Venizelos toyed with the idea of safeguarding Hellenism within the boundaries of the Ottoman Empire, by support for the initial ideas of the Young Turk revolution and by good relations with Turkey. But from 1915 on it became his overriding foreign policy aim.

At the heart of Venizelos' political philosophy was the idea of the nation, its progress and liberation.[114] In foreign affairs this came from 1912 onto mean the inclusion of as many Greek communities as possible within the Greek state, through territorial expansion. This was not the only conceivable nationalist project: Souliotis Nikolaidis and Ion Dragoumis presented an alternative, but one which could not survive the behaviour, itself a product of nationalism, of the Turkish leadership. Venizelos' approach thus came to seem inevitable.

Only after 1922 and the collapse of Greek hopes in Asia Minor did Venizelos perforce accept the different approach of consolidating the nation within settled national boundaries. With this change, which Venizelos urged on his wilder supporters, Greek policy entered a new and more restrained and defensive phase.

The nationalism which underlay Venizelos' policy was in its broadest sense common to the Greek nation, including Venizelos' opponents. All Greek political parties would have described themselves as representative of the 'national idea', and Constantine as crown prince and later king was fully associated with Greece's expansion during the Balkan Wars. Indeed he sometimes pushed Venizelos to go further in the direction of nationalist assertion than Venizelos thought it possible or prudent to go. The differences between Venizelos and his opponents from 1915 on were not so much over the political philosophy of national liberation, or the idea of the nation, as over power and who should hold it, and only then over the tactics to be adopted, the alliances to be made, and the limits to Greece's ambitions posed by circumstances.

The philosophy within which Venizelos clothed his policy of national liberation was that of self-determination of nations or peoples, a concept which acquired its greatest resonance and influence at the time of the Paris Peace Conference, not least because of its endorsement by President Wilson as one of his famous Fourteen Points. The criterion adopted by Venizelos for nationality was that of national consciousness, not race, language or religion. This non-objective criterion suited Greek purposes, since it could be used to strengthen Greek claims to disputed territories in Northern Epirus, Thrace and Macedonia.

The most difficult question to answer in assessing Venizelos' diplomacy is the extent to which it was rooted in a consistent political philosophy of liberalism, and the extent to which it was opportunist. Venizelos' admirers claim the former, for which there is ample evidence in Venizelos' own speeches, with their references to the identity of interests with the liberal Powers. Others, who see him as an opportunist, point to examples early in his career when he treated the Powers on an equal footing, and was ready in 1913 to look to Germany as guarantor of his policy of Greek–Serbian–Romanian alliance.

But Venizelos was a nationalist first and political philosopher second. The hesitations of his move towards his final standpoint of alliance with the Entente were due to various factors: the complications of the relations of the Powers with Balkan countries, and the difficulty and danger of putting all his eggs in one basket, the views of colleagues such as Streit, and the countervailing force of King Constantine.

What distinguished Venizelos, apart from his personal charisma, was the clearness and force with which he imposed a unified policy of economic and military recovery, and the single-mindedness and energy with which he pursued his foreign-policy aims when opportunities presented themselves. The prime example of this is his decision, justified by the events, to engage in the First Balkan War even though in his view Greece's recovery was far from sufficiently advanced. He saw that the opportunity would not wait. As Venizelos said in parliament in 1917:

> I was in fact attempting to avoid war, not because I did not believe that nations are obliged to resort to war when their own existence and integrity are at stake, but because I thought that Greece had not been adequately prepared in the interval of barely two years since her regeneration (1910) in order to confront the chances of war with confidence and security. But war broke out because, although on the one hand it became possible to settle the Cretan question, on the other the remaining Balkan states had decided on war with Turkey, and in such circumstances it was not permissible for us to remain passive spectators.[115]

How, finally, may we judge Venizelos' foreign policy and diplomacy? Many see him primarily as a doughty fighter for the Greek nation, who carried as far as it was possible to take it the emancipation of the Greek peoples of the diaspora. If he overreached himself, and Greece's capacities, in Asia Minor, that was because in the circumstances of 1918 and 1919 it was unthinkable to reject the opportunity offered by circumstances.

Critics take a different view. Not many criticise Venizelos for his nationalist assumptions, which were the common currency of his time, though Marxist critics have accused him of imperialism. The most cogent criticism is that Venizelos accepted too easily the logic of Great Power relations and Greece's status as a pawn in the game of the Powers. He accepted a dependence that was humiliating for Greece (for example in the violations of Greek neutrality by the allies in the Great War) and which left Greece defenceless in the face of the manoeuvres, betrayals and pressures of the Powers. This viewpoint has been argued most cogently by George Leontaritis, who describes Venizelos' policy as 'expansion conceived in a vacuous framework', arguing that Venizelos had no conception of the real nature of the war, the imperialist system and the post-war crisis. Trapped in an institutionalised pattern of economic and political dependence, Greece's resources never matched the hegemonic role she chose for herself.[116] There is truth in some of these criticisms, and in the point that Venizelos entered the war with only a rudimentary conception of his war aims, relying on support from Britain and France, and failing to understand how their divergent interests, and those of the other powers, could undermine Greek aspirations. But there is also something academic about them. Venizelos had to operate in the circumstances of his time, and with the instruments at his disposal. He well understood the relationship of foreign policy and economic and political resources. He was not a creative political thinker in matters of foreign policy, but a doer. He exploited the circumstances and the tools available to the utmost.

VENIZELOS' QUALITIES AS A DIPLOMAT

Venizelos brought to diplomacy a range of qualities of which the most important were his industry and energy; concentration on the key requirements of foreign policy; persuasiveness; rapidity of mind and action; and a clear understanding of political realities and priorities against which to judge immediate tactical needs.

The evidence for Venizelos' industry is the time he devoted to foreign policy and diplomacy, even to the extent, in the view of his critics, of losing touch with political realities at home in the period 1918 to 1920. On his persuasiveness Ventiris cites the distinguished royalist diplomat and minister George Streit: 'When the two of us are alone and we disagree, Venizelos never convinces me! If there are three of us, I begin to waver. The moment he addresses several people, at cabinet meetings for instance, it often happens that I am carried away too, along with the others!'[117] Venizelos himself recounts occasions on which he seemed to have persuaded the king against his better judgement. He attributed his persuasiveness not to superior intelligence but to the sincerity with which he put forward his views.[118] Many contemporary witnesses, both Greek and foreign, spoke of his charm, even when as political opponents they saw something devilish in it.[119]

The speed of thought and action which Venizelos displayed at crucial moments of his career was a product of his temperament but also an incidental advantage of his position as prime minister. Towards the end of the period under discussion, he did not have to consult widely before making a decision. He not only represented Greece, he was seen to embody Greece. This rapidity went with a boldness of conception and action, for example in the conclusion of the Greek–Bulgarian Treaty of 1912, and in the immediacy with which he decided to throw in Greece's lot with the Entente Powers in August 1914.[120]

Venizelos' clarity of vision and judgement of fundamental aims went with a great tactical flexibility, which his opponents labelled opportunism. Opportunism can be good or bad. Venizelos' critics saw it as an aspect of lack of principle. To his supporters he was a man of strong principles, but ready to make bold and surprising concessions for tactical reasons. The latter view is surely the more convincing.[121]

When all these qualities have been listed, however, something is still missing. This is the legend of Venizelos and its effect on his diplomacy and on Greece's position. His prestige with foreign statesmen was a major asset for Greece. It did not come by accident: he had worked for it, from 1910 on, by his assiduous cultivation of Britain and France, and of the prosperous liberal Greek communities of the diaspora. This image of Venizelos the heroic and far-sighted leader was taken up abroad by admirers such as Ronald Burrows, the principal of King's College London, and his colleagues, who founded the Anglo-Hellenic League in 1913 as an instrument of propaganda on behalf of Greek interests. Venizelos was regarded as the saviour of his country, the new Pericles, the embodiment of Hellenism and the virtues of ancient Greece.[122]

Contemporary descriptions show the force which Venizelos exerted on the peacemakers through his legendary reputation and his personal charm. He was able to exploit his own position as an unhesitating supporter of the Entente.[123]

Venizelos the diplomat comes high in the scale of expertise, skills of persuasion, will power, and the other qualities of diplomacy. Venizelos the statesman must be measured by results. By that measure he outstrips other Greek statesmen in foreign policy as a result of the great expansion of the Greek kingdom in 1912 to 1923. The failure of his Asia Minor policy, for which he was in my view mainly responsible, was due to his failure to understand the dynamics of the post-war world – the conflicts and weakness of Greece's allies, their unwillingness and inability to impose a draconian peace treaty on Turkey, and the force of Turkish nationalism under Kemal, which was too much for either Greece or the allies to deal with. Venizelos overreached himself in Asia Minor, and many Greeks paid dearly. But he was probably led to take what proved an unwinnable gamble when he lost hope, after 1914, of a peaceful and prosperous future for Hellenism in Asia Minor.[124] And the catastrophe of 1922 led, through Venizelos' skilful handling of the Lausanne negotiation, to the consolidation of Greece's frontiers and population and the establishment of the refugees. These were forerunners of Venizelos' Greek–Turkish Friendship Treaty of 1930, a rapprochement which still has lessons for politicians, diplomats and journalists in the twenty-first century.

One way of assessing Venizelos' diplomacy is to consider the obstacles he had to contend with in trying to achieve his expansionary ends. They were formidable. They included:

1. the resolute insistence of King Constantine and the general staff, on a policy of neutrality in the Great War. Given the customary role of the king in foreign-policy making and the charismatic nature of his leadership, this was a formidable obstacle. In the end it led to Venizelos' fall from power in the elections of 1920, for it can hardly be doubted that it was the popularity of the king, and the unpopularity of Venizelos' oppressive administration during the latter stages of the war, that brought about that result.
2. the consistently obstructive policy of Italy, whose national aims conflicted with those of Greece in Northern Epirus/Albania, in the Dodecanese, and in Asia Minor. Venizelos devoted a great deal of time and energy to trying to establish a reasonable working relationship with Italy, and was ready to envisage compromise solutions. Except in his short-lived agreement with Italian prime minister Tittoni, in July 1919, he never succeeded. The problem was in fact insoluble, because of the determination of Italy in pursuing her claims, and the obligations which the allies had taken towards Italy in the Treaty of London of 1915, which were bound to bring her into conflict with Greece. In one way Italy helped Greece. She was such an obstructive nuisance at the Peace Conference, over Fiume and Asia Minor, that the other three of the Big Four lost patience with her, and in her absence allowed Greece to occupy Smyrna. But this proved a poisoned cup.
3. the philosophical and territorial disputes and rivalries between Greece's allies, the Great Powers, also worked against Greek interests, which lay in a rapid and draconian peace treaty with Turkey, imposed, forcibly if necessary, by all the allies working together. It is only necessary to read the proceedings of the Supreme Council to see how unlikely, indeed impossible, it was that the allies would agree to implement a rapid and draconian peace. The main reason for the

delay which so frustrated Venizelos and his colleagues was the uncertainty over the position of the United States: whether the US would take on the responsibility of a mandate for the new state of Armenia, or other responsibilities in the Turkish peace settlement. Since the answer to this lay with the American Congress, it was not within the power of the other allies to affect. They were impotent to find any way round the difficulty, and the consequent delays put paid to all hopes of a rapid peace settlement. A further cause of delay was the prior claim, for Britain, France and the US, of the German peace treaty.
4. Finally, Greece's own poverty and lack of development. Despite the rapid strides taken between 1910 and 1913, there was still a mismatch between Greece's aspirations and her means. This became increasingly serious as the Turkish treaty was further delayed, leading to frustration and a note of near desperation in some of Venizelos' comments in late 1919 and 1920.

In the light of these obstacles, it is perhaps surprising, not that Greece failed to achieve all her aims, but that she and Venizelos achieved so much.

Venizelos was a great and charismatic leader, and a man of his time. He was supremely effective in expressing the aspirations of the emerging Greek liberal society, with his belief in the power of the liberal Western ideas to shape the post-war world. He willingly accepted the imperialist assumptions of the allies' policy towards Turkey as the framework for Greece's expansion. In this sense Venizelos lived, and was proud to live, by the rules of the Great Powers.

NOTES

1. C. Svolopoulos (1974), *O Eleftherios Venizelos kai i politiki krisis eis tin aftonomon Kritin, 1901–1906* [*E. Venizelos and the Political Crisis in Autonomous Crete, 1901–1906*], Athens; see also the chapter on Crete in C. Svolopoulos (1999), *Eleftherios Venizelos: 12 Meletimata* [*El. Venizelos: 12 Studies*], Athens.
2. On Greek foreign policy and the Great Idea (Megali Idea) which formed Venizelos' education in foreign affairs, there is an extensive literature on particular episodes and periods, but no comprehensive studies apart from Douglas Dakin (1972), *The Unification of Greece 1770–1923*, London.
3. On this connection, see Svolopoulos, *12 Meletimata*, esp. Chap. 3 'Liberalism and the Great Idea' (see Note 1).
4. A. Mazarakis-Ainian (1979), *Mémoires*, Thessaloniki, pp. 185–6, slightly abridged from the Greek edition, (1948), *Apomnimonevmata*, Athens.

5. N. Petsalis-Diomedis (1978), *Greece at the Paris Peace Conference (1919)*, Thessaloniki, p. 123.
6. George Glasgow (1924), *Ronald Burrows, a Memoir*, London, contains at pp. 242–51 the letter of 17/30 November 1916 in which Venizelos invited Burrows to become the semi-official representative of the provisional government in Britain, and the enclosed letter to Grey inviting the British government to recognise him as such. On Burrows and like-minded philhellenes, see Richard Clogg (2000), 'The Ingenious Enthusiasm of Dr Burrows and the "Unsatiated Hatred" of Professor Toynbee', in R. Clogg, *Anglo-Greek Attitudes: Studies in History*, London; also R. Clogg (1986), *Politics and the Academy: Arnold Toynbee and the Koraes Chair*, London. On propaganda, see D. Kitsikis (1963), *Propagande et Pressions en Politique Internationale*, Paris.
7. See Petsalis-Diomedis, *Greece at the Peace Conference*, pp. 209–11 (see Note 5), and generally on his efforts from May 1919 to defend the Greek occupation of Smyrna from charges arising from the excesses of the Greek occupying forces in the first days of the occupation, and to awake his colleagues to the danger to Greece's position in Paris.
8. This period, and Venizelos' role, are analysed in detail in George B. Leontaritis (1990), *Greece and the First World War*, Boulder, an indispensable account, if harsh in its judgement of Venizelos' foreign policy.
9. G. Ventiris (1931), *I Ellas tou 1910–1920* [*Greece 1910–1920*], 2 vols, Athens; P. S. Delta (1986), *Eleftherios K. Venizelos: Imerologio, Anamniseis, Martyries, Allilographia* [*E. K. Venizelos: Diary, Memoirs, Testimonies, Correspondence*], ed. P. A. Zannas, Athens.
10. Svolopoulos, *O El. Venizelos* (see Note 1); George Th. Mavrogordatos (1983), *Stillborn Republic: Social Coalitions and Party Strategies in Greece, 1922–1936*, Berkeley; O. Dimitrakopoulos and T. Veremis (eds) (1980), *Meletimata gyro apo ton Venizelo kai tin epochi tou* [*Studies on Venizelos and his Time*], Athens; (1988) *Symposio gia ton El. Venizelo. Praktika* [*Symposium on El. Venizelos. Proceedings*], Athens.
11. For example, on the Balkan Wars period, Helen Gardikas-Katsiadakis (1995), *Greece and the Balkan Imbroglio: Greek Foreign Policy: 1911–1913*, Athens; on the war period, George B. Leon (1974), *Greece and the Great Powers 1914–1917*, Thessaloniki; Leontaritis, *Greece and the First World War* (see Note 8); and for the Peace Conference, Petsalis-Diomidis, *Greece at the Paris Peace Conference* (see Note 5). All these are authoritative and detailed accounts. A book which compresses the material without distortion is Harry J. Psomiades (1968), *The Eastern Question: The Last Phase*, Thessaloniki.
12. This dilemma confronted Greece with awkward choices from the 1870s on. The British ambassador who arrived in Athens in 1885 commented on the proclamation of a united Bulgaria under Alexander of Battenberg on 18 September 1885: 'It was a signal triumph for the rival Slav in whom, far

more than in their ancient oppressor the Turk, the Hellenes had long come to see their most dangerous enemy.' Horace Rumbold (1905), *Final Recollections of a Diplomatist*, London, p. 41. If the challenge for Greek policy was to match resources with ambitions in order to provide a material basis for foreign policy, the challenges for diplomacy were how to exploit international circumstances to seize opportunities for expansion, and how to time such action.

13. Thanos Veremis (1989), 'From the National State to Stateless Nation', *European History Quarterly* 19, pp. 135–48.
14. These ideas are contained in a letter of 12/25 August 1908 cited by Svolopoulos, *Venizelos: 12 Meletimata,* p. 65 (see Note 1), and in the Chania newspaper *Kiryx* on 31 December 1908.
15. Venizelos in *Kiryx*, Chania, 20 January 1909, cited in Svolopoulos, *Venizelos: 12 Meletimata,* p. 42 (see Note 1).
16. Gardikas-Katsiadakis, *Balkan Imbroglio,* Chap. 3 (see Note 11) on Acceleration of Military and Financial Preparations.
17. Theotokis' plan went with a broader and equally abortive scheme for an alliance of Greece with France and Britain, based on a misapprehension that France had already formed a Mediterranean Entente with a group of countries: D. Dakin (1962), 'The Greek Proposals for an Alliance with France and Great Britain, June–July 1907', *Balkan Studies* 3, pp. 43–60. Theotokis set the pattern for Venizelos' reforms over foreign military assistance, Constantine's command of the army, and the financing of military reforms and procurement.
18. On the French mission, see L. Paraskevopoulos (1933), *Anamniseis 1896–1920* [*Memoirs 1896–1920*], Athens, vol. I, pp. 106–7; Franchet d'Esperet (1933), 'Les rapports militaires de la France et de l'Hellénisme au cours d'un siècle', *Revue d'Histoire Diplomatique* 47, p. 284. For the British mission, see Maurice Pearton (1985), 'Britain and Greek Naval Defence 1910–1916', in *Greece and Great Britain During World War I,* Thessaloniki, pp. 17–47. Pearton gives an illuminating account of the inherent political problems in such exercises in bilateral technical cooperation. He concludes that technically the British mission was a success but that it failed in a wider sense, and that it was not an instrument for influencing Greek procurement decisions. The French military mission was more important and achieved more. Strictly speaking, though the invitations to France and Britain were diplomatic initiatives of Venizelos, the activities of the missions once they reached Greece became a part of Greece's domestic politics, since their commanders were Greek employees. In fact, of course, the missions continued to pose problems of foreign policy. See also Mark Kerr (1927), *Land, Sea and Air,* London; Admiral Kerr was chief of the British mission from 1913 on and a friend and supporter of King Constantine.
19. Gardikas-Katsiadakis, 'Venizelos kai Ypourgeio Exoterikon' ['Venizelos

and the Foreign Ministry'], *Symposio gia ton Eleftherio Venizelo*, pp. 265–82 (see Note 10).

20. Ibid., pp 273ff., gives examples: Koromilas, with deep experience of the Macedonian problem, was always suspicious of Bulgaria and of Austria. Venizelos was generally more cautious and keen to avoid giving offence to the Powers.
21. Ibid., p. 281, quotes a telegram from King George to Venizelos: 'I'll tell Streit to come via Thessaloniki. This is necessary in any case insofar as Streit inclines towards Triple Alliance whereas our interests are served by Triple Entente and he must be brought to realise this.' King George to Venizelos, 2/15 March 1913, Venizelos Archive, Benaki Museum, 173/2/22.
22. See the intriguing undated manuscript note in his papers, which must have been written at this period:

    > the policy of the government towards Turkey . . . Integrity – dismemberment. Lapse of time, awareness of community of interests may also lead to final settlement of Cretan question. But let us gain time. Time may be a remedy which today appears impossible. Even the Great Powers often buy time. Community of interests of the Balkan States. Their confederation. This would serve the interests of everyone. It would also fortify the European equilibrium. And the financial interests of the Great Powers.

    This is an undated note in Venizelos' hand in the Venizelos Archive, ELIA, cited in Gardikas-Katsiadakis, *Balkan Imbroglio*, p. 46 (see Note 11).
23. Lady Grogan (1926), *The Life of J. D. Bourchier*, London, pp. 135–6. Bourchier noted the beginning of his involvement in his diary for 26 Feb. 1910: 'Venizelos came to see me at 11 p.m., and stayed till 1 a.m.; unfolded all his views – even Bulgarian alliance; evidently means to take the helm by-and-by here.' Bourchier was an Anglo-Irish eccentric, a failed schoolmaster at Eton, deaf, anti-Ottoman in a Gladstonian way, a fearless defender of oppressed peoples and a humanitarian activist. He became a correspondent of *The Times* at a time when *Times* correspondents carried immense influence. He was regarded by the Greeks as a good and important friend until his sympathies for Bulgaria compromised him in their eyes. He ended a sad figure, arguing on behalf of Bulgaria in a naive way in the margins of the Paris Peace Conference.
24. Svolopoulos, *Venizelos: 12 Meletimata*, p. 66 (see Note 1). Therefore Dakin's judgement of Venizelos' motives seems too limited, viz. that Venizelos saw a Greek–Bulgarian understanding as a:

    > defensive arrangement which might lead to better relations with Turkey, to the improvement of matters in Macedonia, even to a solution of the Cretan problem. He had no concept of the alliance as an aggressive

instrument and he had no expectation that the Serbs would join it. Dakin, *Unification*, p. 193 (see Note 2).

25. In 1919 in Paris, when events had driven the two men far apart, Venizelos acknowledged Bourchier's 'valuable services to Crete in her struggle to obtain the realization of her national aspirations'. Grogan, *Bourchier,* p. 54 (see Note 23).
26. Ibid., pp. 135–6. Bourchier exaggerated the secrecy of the operation: Foreign Minister Gryparis was kept informed.
27. Ibid., pp. 136–9, gives extracts from Bourchier's diary entries on this exhilarating visit. Lady Grogan comments that a mountain-side afforded the best possible opportunity for private conversations which had necessarily to be conducted in very loud voices. There are many anecdotes about Bourchier's deafness.
28. Gardikas-Katsiadakis, *Balkan Imbroglio,* p. 98 (see Note 11); A. Alexandris (1947), *Politikai Anamniseis* [*Political Memoirs*], Patras, pp. 41ff.; Ventiris, *Greece 1910–1920,* vol. I, p. 93 (see Note 9).
29. In the event this clause was ignored.
30. Gardikas-Katsiadakis, *Balkan Imbroglio*, p. 46 ff. (see Note 11); E. Prevelakis (1966), 'E. Venizelos and the Balkan Wars', *Balkan Studies* 7, pp. 363–78.
31. Venizelos (1917), *The Vindication of Greek National Policy 1912–1917; a Report of Speeches delivered in the Greek Chamber, August 24–26, by E. Venizelos and others,* London, p. 66:

    > I had not wished for that war [the war against Bulgaria] any more than I had wished for the first war against Turkey . . . I had reached the point of proposing to the Porte that in return for its nominal rights of suzerainty and the payment of a small tribute it should recognize the right of Cretan deputies to take their seats in this House. I was in fact attempting to avoid war.

32. A notorious example of a dispute over strategic, that is, political, priorities, was Venizelos' insistence that the Greek army should proceed with all speed to occupy Thessaloniki, and not be diverted, as the crown prince argued on military grounds, to Monastir in order to crush the main body of the Turkish forces facing the Greek army. See Venizelos' August 1917 speech to parliament in ibid., p. 189.
33. *Instructions aux délégués plénipotentiaires du Gouvernement Royal Hellénique (1912),* Athens, 25/8 Dec 1912, AYE, A/5/n.n.; quoted in Gardikas-Katsiadakis, *Balkan Imbroglio,* p. 143 (see Note 11). The general diplomatic background is in E. C. Helmreich (1938), *The Diplomacy of the Balkan Wars 1912–1913,* Cambridge, and the Greek aspects in Gardikas-Katsiadakis, *Balkan Imbroglio,* from Chap. 6 (see Note 11).
34. Gardikas-Katsiadakis, *Balkan Imbroglio,* pp. 235 ff (see Note 11).

35. See below, Note 48.
36. Treaty of alliance and military convention in Greek White Book, Nos 2 and 4. For more details on the conclusion of the treaty see L. Hasiotis (2004), *Ellinoservikes scheseis 1913–1918* [*Greek–Serbian Relations 1913–1918*], Thessaloniki, pp. 29–42.
37. His second wife, and not the mother of his children. They married in London in 1921 after Venizelos' defeat in the Greek elections of November 1920. Helena's money helped Venizelos in his subsequent career. She built the great house on Loukianou Street, which is now the British Embassy residence: see Michael Llewellyn Smith (1998), *The British Embassy Athens*, Athens.
38. Stavridi's diary is held by St Antony's College, Oxford. The story is told in Michael Llewellyn Smith (1973), *Ionian Vision,* London, new edition C. Hurst (1998), pp. 12–18; and Helen Gardikas-Katsiadakis, 'Venizelos kai Tsortsil: oi vaseis tis anglo-ellinikis synennoisis (1912–1913)' [Venizelos and Churchill: The Foundations of the British-Greek Understanding (1912–1913)], in *Meletimata,* pp. 87–100 (see Note 38).
39. Llewellyn Smith, *Ionian Vision,* p. 17 (see Note 10).
40. Gardikas-Katsiadakis, *Imbroglio,* pp. 236–7 (see Note 11); Venizelos, *Vindication,* p. 69 (see Note 31).
41. Gardikas-Katsiadakis, *Imbroglio,* p. 162 (see Note 11).
42. Ibid., p. 175.
43. Greece's territory increased from 63,211 to 120,308 sq. km., and population from 2,631,912 to 4,718,221: Svolopoulos, *Venizelos: 12 Meletimata,* Chap. 5, p. 71 (see Note 1). The point is that the gains were substantial, in manpower (important for recruitment to the armed forces as well as for the economy), in agricultural land, and in islands giving control of maritime communications in the Aegean.
44. B. Kondis, 'The Problem of the Aegean Islands on the Eve of World War I and Great Britain', in *Greece and Great Britain during World War I,* pp. 49–63 (see Note 18).
45. Ibid., p. 51.
46. Pearton, 'British and Greek Naval Defence 1910–1916', p. 29 (see Note 18).
47. Kondis, 'Aegean Islands on the Eve of World War I', in *Greece and Great Britain during World War I*, p. 57 (see Note 18).
48. Dimitri Pentzopoulos (1962), *The Balkan Exchange of Minorities and its Impact upon Greece,* The Hague and Paris, p. 56. See also Llewellyn Smith, pp. 30–4 (see Note 38). This Greek–Turkish agreement, a new departure in the handling of national minorities, provided for their orderly and peaceful interchange under the supervision of a mixed commission, and for the valuation and liquidation of their fixed property. Essentially it was a tidying up of an existing situation. Its negotiation eased the plight of the Greeks of Asia Minor in the difficult period after the Balkan Wars, but

it was not implemented because of the outbreak of the Great War. Further and worse persecution of the Greek communities of Asia Minor was to follow in 1916. See Y. Mourelos (1985), 'The 1914 Persecutions and the First Attempt at an Exchange of Minorities between Greece and Turkey', *Balkan Studies* 26, pp. 388–413.

49. In a famous speech to parliament on 2/15 March 1913, between the First and the Second Balkan Wars, Venizelos developed the metaphor of a 'backbone' to define the limits of Greek expansion. Greek populations of eastern Macedonia and Thrace, then occupied by Bulgarian forces, had appealed for incorporation in the Greek kingdom. Venizelos replied that:

    > even if the Allies told us that they were prepared to allow us to extend our frontiers in that direction, so as to include those Greek populations, I at least as the responsible Minister would reject such frontiers as being too dangerous . . . Greece would be weaker if she were to extend in this way along the coasts without a backbone, than if her frontiers were filled out in another direction . . .

    At the time he said this, Venizelos wanted to preserve the Balkan system of alliances and was not prepared to antagonize Bulgaria. But his remarks implicitly suggest that he recognized that the hinterland of Eastern Macedonia and Thrace was predominantly Bulgarian (Llewellyn Smith, *Ionian Vision,* p. 20 (see Note 38)).
50. Venizelos, *Vindication,* pp. 73–4 (see Note 31).
51. Llewellyn Smith, *Ionian Vision,* pp. 35–48 (see Note 38).
52. N. Petsalis Diomidis, *Greece at the Paris Peace Conference*, p. 36 (see Note 5), cites Koromilas' warning of Italian ambitions, based on Ventiris, *Greece 1910–1920,* vol. I, pp. 265–6 (see Note 9).
53. Llewellyn Smith, *Ionian Vision,* p. 46 (see Note 38).
54. Ibid., p. 52.
55. Ibid., p. 53.
56. Defenders of Venizelos argue that his Asia Minor policy was based on the assumption that the allies would ensure and impose the dissolution of the Ottoman Empire and carve up Anatolia between them. This was a reasonable, though false, assumption in 1918, but hardly in early 1915.
57. Venizelos, *Vindication,* p. 81 (see Note 31).
58. Venizelos, ibid., pp. 81–5 gives his own dramatic account of the dispute, the Crown Council at which his proposal was debated, and so on.
59. C. M. Woodhouse, 'The Offer of Cyprus: October 1915', in *Greece and Great Britain during World War I,* pp. 77–97 (see Note 18).
60. Thanos Veremis (1997), *The Military in Greek Politics, From Independence to Democracy*, London, esp. Chap. 4 on The Impact of the First World War on Civil–Military Relations.
61. Leontaritis, *Greece and the First World War,* p. 15 (see Note 8).

62. Cf. the remark which Venizelos attributed to Constantine in his speech in *Vindication*, p. 105 (see Note 31):

> when it is a question of foreign affairs, great international questions, I think that so long as I believe a thing is right or not right, I must insist upon its being done or not being done, because I am responsible before God.

63. The constitutional questions at issue are analysed by Leontaritis, *Greece and the First World War*, (see Note 8) p. 68 ff (see Note 8). For the purges of the judiciary, military and civil service, and the church, see Leontaritis, pp. 63–7.
64. Ibid., pp. 15–16; Venizelos to Romanos, Paris, 22 April 1917.
65. However, much later, in 1936, answering the criticism of colleagues that he had permitted the elections of November 1920 to take place after Alexander's death, and therefore on the issue of the return of Constantine, Venizelos claimed implausibly that he could and should have negotiated with Constantine an arrangement whereby George should succeed to the throne. He suggested that this might have permitted him to win the elections and conduct the Asia Minor campaign to a successful conclusion. Ventiris, *Greece 1910–1920,* vol. II, p. 419 (see Note 9), cited by Llewellyn Smith, *Ionian Vision,* pp. 156–7 (see Note 38).
66. The most vivid brief description of the process and its defects is still Harold Nicolson (1965), *Peacemaking 1919*, New York. See also Margaret MacMillan (2001), *Peacemakers: Six Months that changed the World*, London.
67. Venizelos was the only Greek able to deal with these leaders on equal terms. He was quite ready also to deal with relatively junior officials if they carried influence: cf. his regular discussions with Harold Nicolson.
68. *La Grèce devant le Congrès de la Paix*, Paris, 1918. This memorandum of Greece's claims, drafted by Venizelos, was published simultaneously in December 1918 in French, and in English under the title *Greece before the peace conference.*
69. Petsalis Diomidis, *Greece at the Paris Peace Conference 1919*, pp. 73–4 (see Note 5): Venizelos' letter and memo of 2 November to Lloyd George are in Lloyd George Paper, House of Lords Record Office, F 55/1/11.
70. Thus Venizelos had moved away from his earlier view of Greek Asia Minor as a multi-ethnic area with a loyal Muslim population; but the two conceptions continued to feature in his thinking. He never resolved the dilemma.
71. *Greece before the Peace Conference*, London, 1918 (see Note 68). There is a large literature on population statistics. Most contemporary works are partisan and unreliable. Petsalis Diomidis, *Greece at the Paris Peace Conference,* Appendix A (see Note 5), gives a useful account of 'Hellenism in 1912'. P. Kitromilides and A. Alexandris (1984–5), 'Ethnic Survival,

Nationalism and Forced Migration: The Historical Demography of the Greek Community of Asia Minor at the Close of the Ottoman Era', in *Bulletin of the Centre for Asia Minor Studies,* vol. 5, Athens, pp. 9–44 defend the Ecumenical Patriarchate census of 1912 as a contribution to the demography of the Greeks in Asia Minor.

72. The Turks had earlier used the same argument to claim that the islands should not be separated from Turkey.
73. Politis stated that the Greek claims followed exactly the principle of self-determination: N. Politis (1919), *Les Aspirations nationales de la Grèce,* Paris. When it came to the point, Venizelos and other Greek diplomats used whatever historical, cultural or political argument came to hand in defending their case.
74. Svolopoulos, *Venizelos: 12 Meletimata,* Chap. 3, 'Liberalism and the Great Idea', pp. 46–7 (see Note 1). Venizelos' memorandum tackled the question head on over Northern Epirus, where he argued for a Greek zone including 120,000 Greeks and 80,000 Albanians:

    > One may be tempted to raise the objection that a substantial portion of this Greek population uses Albanian as its mother tongue, and is consequently, in all probability, of Albanian origin; but the democratic conceptions of the Allied and Associated Powers cannot admit of any other standard than that of national consciousness. Only the Germanic conception could substitute for this the standard of race or language.

    In support, he referred to the Souliot women, Albanian speakers, who threw themselves over a cliff rather than submit to their Albanian persecutors.
75. Isocrates' dictum "We consider Greeks those who partake in our culture"became the basis of nineteenth-century Greek irredentism' – T. Veremis (2003), '1922: Political Continuations and Realignments in the Greek state', in Renée Hirschon, (ed.), *Crossing the Aegean: An Appraisal of the 1923 Compulsory Population Exchange between Greece and Turkey,* New York and Oxford, pp. 53–62.
76. For the Greek participation in the French expedition to South Russia, see P. A. Zannas (ed.) (1979), *Nikolaos Plastiras,* Athens, pp. 1–54.
77. The numbers are disputed, but it is generally accepted that though the Greeks were the dominant element in Smyrna/Izmir, the Muslims were more numerous in the Greek zone of occupation as a whole.
78. However, in 1920, when the Turks had shown that they would not accept the treaty, Venizelos did talk of a crushing Greek blow against them which would not only impose the treaty but also drive the Turks out of Constantinople. N. Petsalis-Diomidis (1980), 'Ti Smyrni i tin Poli – mia enallaktiki lysi pou o Venizelos aperripse mallon veviasmena' ['Smyrna or the City: An Alternative Solution which Venizelos Rejected Too Hastily'], in *Meletimata gyro apo ton Venizelo,* pp. 101–18 (see Note 10) cites evidence

that Venizelos always envisaged Greece getting Constantinople in the end, and favoured an international regime for Constantinople and the Straits in 1920 over an individual mandatory power, on the grounds that an international regime was less likely to last and more likely to surrender the zone to Greece. Curzon certainly thought this was Venizelos' view. Venizelos saw Greece obtaining Constantinople by a kind of pincer movement from Eastern Thrace and the Asia Minor zone. The allies came fairly close in May 1919 to offering Greece Constantinople plus the whole of Eastern Thrace in return for abandoning the Smyrna zone, which would revert to Turkish sovereignty.

79. Venizelos before the Council of Ten, 3 February 1919, in *Papers Relating to the Foreign Relations of the United States (FRUS)*, Washington 1919, iii, p. 861. His confidence was misplaced. Not all British politicians were in favour of this imperial commitment. Gladstone thought it an absurd and unnecessary burden on Britain, and as we have seen Churchill was ready to concede it as part of the deal he envisaged in 1912 to 1913; and in October 1915 Britain actually offered Cyprus to Greece as an inducement to the Zaimis government to come into the war, but the offer was formally declined. Though the strategic value of Cyprus was questionable from the time of Britain's acquisition of Egypt up until the time of the establishment of British bases (the present Sovereign Base Areas), the Colonial Office and the chiefs of staff were always reluctant to relinquish it. The Foreign Office was sometimes readier to see it as a bargaining chip. See also I. P. Pikros, 'O Venizelos kai to Kypriako Zitima' ['Venizelos and the Cyprus Question'], in *Meletimata gyro apo ton Venizelo,* pp. 173–308 (see Note 10).
80. The US experts concluded that the area was Turkish by population, and that the Turkish hinterland required its own outlet to the sea at Smyrna; Petsalis-Diomidis, *Paris Peace Conference*, pp. 121ff (see Note 5). The British experts, Toynbee and Nicolson, recommended in April 1919 leaving Asia Minor to Turkey and assigning the whole of Thrace to Greece; Llewellyn Smith, *Ionian Vision,* p. 76 (see Note 38).
81. The story of Greece's occupation is told in Llewellyn Smith, *Ionian Vision* (see Note 38); A. J. Toynbee (1922), *The Western Question in Greece and Turkey,* London, and A. A. Pallis (1937), *Greece's Anatolian Venture and After,* London; as well as in many Greek books and memoirs. Greek general staff and Turkish general staff histories are important. The Turkish side of the story is told in Andrew Mango (1999), *Ataturk,* London, and, more vividly but less authoritatively, in Lord Kinross (1964), *Ataturk: The Rebirth of a Nation,* London.
82. Petsalis-Diomidis, *Peace Conference*, pp. 110–11 (see Note 5).
83. Ibid., pp. 116–17.
84. Ibid., pp. 251–6 analyses the Venizelos–Tittoni agreements and their negotiation. He argues that it was a mistake on Venizelos' part to allow the inclusion of the provision (clause VII) making the agreements subject to the

satisfaction of Italian aspirations in Asia Minor. But, whether or not Tittoni would have insisted on this clause, his successors would not have hesitated to find some other pretext to denounce the agreement.

85. Examples in ibid., p. 166.
86. Ibid., pp. 153–72, 256–90; in his letter of 9 August to Repoulis, Venizelos wrote that the preceding fortnight had been 'the most dramatic for our national question' and that the mental and physical strain had made him a 'wreck'. He continued that the settlement then under discussion, though not ideal, was:

    > a real miracle after the perils which our national affairs encountered. We shall have rescued the Greek acropolis of Thrace and we shall become the vigilant guards of Constantinople, and if we succeed in organising the new Greece into a state of law and order and civilisation, not only will the work of the present generation take root and become unassailable, but Constantinople will fall one day into the national embrace.

87. Llewellyn Smith, *Ionian Vision,* pp. 124–8 (see Note 38).
88. This is one of the reasons why the treaty has entered Turkish demonology, causing Turks still to believe that Western European states would like to break up Turkey.
89. Llewellyn Smith, *Ionian Vision,* pp. 131–3 (see Note 38).
90. Dakin, *Unification,* pp. 227–8 (see Note 2), argues in these terms. Leontaritis, *Greece and the First World War,* Introduction, pp. xi–xii (see Note 8), argues, more convincingly in my view, that Venizelos' assumption was unreasonable from the start, being based on a failure to understand the way imperialist Great Powers ('allies') behave, or to understand the Turks. Following his military chiefs, who were deceived by the common phenomenon of their troops being received as 'saviours' by local people, Venizelos consistently underestimated the force of Turkish nationalism.
91. The story is well told in V. Solomonidou, 'Venizelos Kai Stergiadis – Mythos kai Pragmatikotita' ['Venizelos and Stergiadis – Myth and Reality'], in Th. Veremis and G. Goulimi (eds) (1989), *Eleftherios Venizelos – Koinonia – Oikonomia – Politiki stin Epochi tou* [E. Venizelos – Society – Economy – Politics in his Age], Athens, pp. 477–536. Toynbee, *The Western Question,* pp. 162–80 (see Note 80), has an interesting and well-balanced account of Stergiadis' character in the first part of his period as high commissioner.
92. Llewellyn Smith, *Ionian Vision,* pp. 99–100 (see Note 38); Petsalis-Diomidis, *Peace Conference,* pp. 220–8 (see Note 5).
93. *Documents on British Foreign Policy 1919–1939* (DBFP), edited E. L. Woodward and R. Butler, 1st Series, xii, no. 451.
94. Ibid., no. 457.
95. For Venizelos' dealings with the allied governments on war loans and Greek debts, and for his attitude to the allies' credit embargo following

Constantine's return, see Ioanna Pepelasi-Minoglou, 'O Venizelos kai to Xeno Kephalaio 1918–1932' ['Venizelos and Foreign Capital 1918–1932'] in *Symposio,* pp. 145–63 (see Note 10). She shows that Venizelos was supportive of the Constantine regime concerning the allied credits. He seems to have considered it a personal obligation to hold the allies to what he saw as their commitments to Greece.

96. Lloyd George Papers, House of Lords Record Office F 90/1/36 gives Kerr's record of the conversation. Venizelos sent his own record to Prime Minister Rallis.
97. Llewellyn Smith, *Ionian Vision,* p. 187 (see Note 38); for the memo the three men left with Kerr, see Lloyd George Papers, House of Lords Record Office F 90/1/34.
98. Texts of letters in P. Danglis (1965), *Anamniseis, Eggrapha, Allilographia [Memoirs, Documents, Correspondence],* 2 vols, vol. 2, pp. 406–9, 410–12.
99. Llewellyn Smith, *Ionian Vision,* p. 235 (see Note 38).
100. FO 286/757 in the British Public Record Office (PRO); memo by Sir Eyre Crowe of talk with Venizelos, 13 October 1921.
101. The story of the movement of National Defence in Constantinople and Smyrna is a complex one, involving General Papoulas, the commander of Greek forces in Asia Minor, the Venizelist Ecumenical Patriarch Meletios, Colonel Kondylis and others. See Llewellyn Smith, *Ionian Vision,* pp. 257–65 (see Note 38).
102. Venizelos Archive, Benaki Museum, File 268.
103. So incidentally did the British ambassador Bentinck in the spring of 1922. Even after the disaster of September 1922, while not defending Stergiades publicly, Venizelos refrained from joining in the general vituperation, advising his sons in Paris to treat Stergiadis with courtesy. No doubt he appreciated that Stergiadis had represented him not only politically but personally, sharing some of his own characteristics while lacking his charisma.
104. See the letter from Venizelos to his friend I. Mourelos of 12/25 October 1922, from the Venizelos Archive, File 29, quoted in Svolopoulos (1988), 'O Eleftherios Venizelos kai i Antallagi Plithysmon' ['E. Venizelos and the Exchange of Populations'] in *Symposio* (see Note 10):

    > I agreed to serve the government because I saw . . . how little the people appreciated the enormity of the disaster. Even after the disaster in Asia Minor the liberal press expected that, once Constantine left the throne, nothing would prevent us throwing ourselves into the arms of our former allies . . . I judged that I should accept the charge so as to be able to say to the revolution and to the Greek people that Eastern Thrace was already lost and all we could do was to see what might still be saved so as to avoid a still greater disaster . . .

105. The Greek army had occupied Eastern Thrace in July 1920, and the area had been assigned to Greece in the unratified Treaty of Sèvres. D. Dakin,

'The importance of the Greek Army in Thrace during the Conference of Lausanne', in *Greece and Great Britain during World War I,* pp. 211–32 (see Note 18), includes an assessment of Greek forces.

106. A. Mazarakis-Ainian (1979), *Mémoires,* Thessaloniki, pp. 281–3. General Mazarakis was the Greek representative at the Mudania armistice negotiations and refused to sign what he saw as humiliating terms. Mazarakis argues the view that Greece could have held onto Eastern Thrace, and that Venizelos and the government gave up too easily. He argues that if Britain had seen Greece build up her strength and show determination not to evacuate, she would have come round to support for this (pp. 299–301). But though Curzon, other things being equal, would have welcomed this, and though he used the presence of the Greek army in Western Thrace as a useful lever in the subsequent negotiations with the Turks at Lausanne at the time of the Mudania armistice, with Kemal threatening the allied lines at Constantinople, Curzon put allied solidarity first.
107. Harold Nicolson (1934), *Curzon: the Last Phase, 1919–1925,* London, describes how Curzon outmanoeuvred Ismet on this.
108. C. Svolopoulos, 'The Lausanne Treaty and the Cyprus Problem', in *Greece and Great Britain during World War I,* pp. 233–45. Archbishop Kyrillos as president of the National Council representing the island's Greek population addressed a petition for union with Greece to the British government in March 1922. He followed this with a call for full self-government. This was rejected by Britain in January 1923, as was a fortiori the call for union. Venizelos was never prepared to push the Cyprus issue with Britain, taking the line that sooner or later Britain would cede the island to Greece without pressure, as had been the case with the Ionian islands. But strategic arguments prevailed within Whitehall.
109. A good short account is in Psomiades, *Eastern Question* (see Note 11), which also contains the text of the treaty signed at Lausanne on 24 July 1923, at Appendix 1. Nicolson, *Curzon: the Last Phase* (see Note 106), presents the viewpoint of the main architect of the treaty. Though the treaty is the basis of Greek–Turkish relations, it has not survived without strain. Greece sees Turkish actions, especially since the 1996 dispute over Imia/Kardak and the subsequent Turkish assertion that there are 'grey zones' of undetermined sovereignty in the Aegean, as revisionist and designed to subvert the treaty.
110. Venizelos to Nansen, 13 October 1922, quoted in Svolopoulos, 'Venizelos kai i Antallagi Plithysmon' (see Note 103).
111. Svolopoulos, 'Venizelos kai I Antallagi Plithysmon', pp. 113–14 (see Note 103) Venizelos to Foreign Minister, 3/16 Oct 1922, Venizelos Archive. Benaki Museum, File 30.
112. Svolopoulos, 'Venizelos kai I Antallagi Plithysmon' p. 115 (see Note 103) Venizelos to minister of foreign affairs, 17 Oct 1922, Venizelos Archive, Benaki Museum, File 30.

113. On the refugee settlement and exchange of populations, see D. Pentzopoulos, *The Balkan Exchange of Minorities* (see Note 48); S. Ladas (1932), *The Exchange of Minorities, Bulgaria, Greece and Turkey*, New York. Text of the Convention at Appendix 2 of Psomiades, *Eastern Question* (see Note 11).
114. Katerina Gardikas Alexander, 'The Changing Language of Political Contention in the Era of King George I', in Philip Carabott (ed.) (1997), *Greek Society in the Making, 1863–1913,* London, pp. 197–207, points out, however, that Venizelos' idea of the nation was not of a unified national body. In his speeches and platform from 1909 to 1912 he introduced to Greek politics a new and sharper definition of divisions within Greek society between the exploiter and exploited classes, and projected his Liberal Party as representative of the healthy strands of Greek society.
115. Venizelos, *Vindication,* p. 66 (see Note 31).
116. Leontaritis, *Greece and the First World War,* Introduction, pp. xi–xiii (see Note 8).
117. Ventiris, *Greece 1910–1929,* vol. I, p. 196 (see Note 9).
118. E. Prevelakis (1966), 'Eleftherios Venizelos and the Balkan Wars', *Balkan Studies* 7, pp. 363–78.
119. Nicolson, *Peacemaking 1919,* p. 251 (see Note 66), wrote of 'a strange medley of charm, brigandage, *welt-politik*, patriotism, courage, literature – and above all this large muscular smiling man, with his eyes glinting through spectacles and on his head a square skull-cap of black silk'. Nicolson was a hero-worshipper. He wrote to his father that Venizelos and Lenin were the only two really great men in Europe.
120. These cases are discussed by Byron Theodoropoulos in a characteristically lucid and interesting talk, 'Ta Oria tis Tolmis' ['The Limits of Boldness'], in *Symposio,* pp. 289–96 (see Note 10). Theodoropoulos cites Venizelos' offer of Greek military assistance to the British in June 1920, as going beyond the limits. He contrasts these three examples of Venizelos' boldness in thought and action with his careful and gradual preparation for the Greek–Turkish Treaty of Friendship of October 1930, and argues that Venizelos, while preserving the boldness of his vision, had learned lessons from his earlier impetuosity about how to achieve his ends. But whereas in the three earlier examples, time pressed, and Venizelos could not have achieved his aims without rapid decision and action, in the latter case there was not the same pressure.
121. For the supportive view, see Svolopoulos, *Venizelos: 12 Meletimata,* generally, and C. M. Woodhouse (1968), *The Story of Modern Greece,* London, p. 194: 'a genius in diplomacy, a humane and far-seeing statesman, and an unchallenged leader of his fellow-countrymen' (on Venizelos in 1912 to 1913). For a critical view, see Dakin, *Unification,* p. 183 (see Note 2), describing Venizelos' career as:

> at once a series of inconsistencies and yet a ruthless and calculated pursuit of national aims. Venizelos remained always the opportunist he had been in Crete. Believing like most Greeks that he alone knew what to do and how to do it, he had changed his tactics even to the extent of what appeared to be a change of principles . . . Of principles, however, he was totally devoid. If he appeared to have any – constitutionalism, tolerance, monarchy, and honesty – it was because they all provided useful means which he was always clever enough to disguise as ends.

Both passages show that foreigners are by no means exempt from partisanship in Greek political affairs.

122. Glasgow, *Ronald Burrows,* with a foreword by E. K. Venizelos, (see Note 6); R. Clogg (2000), 'The "ingenious enthusiasm" of Dr Burrows and the "unsatiated hatred" of Professor Toynbee' in Clogg, *Anglo-Greek Attitudes,* London, pp. 36–59.
123. E.g. Charles Seymour (1965), *Letters from the Paris Peace Conference,* New Haven, p. 56; and Nicolson, *Peacemaking,* generally (see Note 66). The diplomatic records show a number of occasions on which Venizelos won a point by arguing that such and such an allied decision would make his position politically untenable at home. This is a well-known diplomatic ploy, but it works.
124. In other words, the logic of expansionism took hold, once the Balkan Wars led to the expulsion of Muslims from Europe and the consequent disruption and persecution of the Greek communities of Asia Minor.

6

Reconstructing Greece as a European State: Venizelos' Last Premiership, 1928–32

Ioannis D. Stefanidis

I. DOMESTIC ASPECTS

Re-entry into politics

In May 1928, Venizelos staged a come-back in politics despite his oft-stated commitment never to do so. The survivor of the great duel that had rocked the Greek state and the country's society since 1915 was fully aware of the tremendous symbolism of his act. For nearly two decades his name defined the principal cleavage in Greek politics. His presence in the political arena was likely to rekindle old passions and open old sores.

The elder statesman had returned to Greece in April 1927. He stayed at Chania, in his native Crete, and repeatedly stated his intention not to return to politics. He did, however, express interest in public affairs, particularly through letters to Georgios Kafantaris, the leader of the Progressive liberals and minister of finance in the coalition government of Alexandros Zaimis. Venizelos' practice proved extremely irritating to his former lieutenant. Failing to secure the unconditional endorsement of his policy, Kafantaris stepped down from the party leadership and resigned his cabinet post. The majority of his followers decided to throw in their lot with Venizelos.[1]

In a brief statement issued on 23 May 1928, Venizelos announced his decision to resume the leadership of the reconstituted Liberal Party. His re-entry was a far cry from his meteoric advent in the aftermath of the 1909 military coup. He envisaged his new role as stabilising, if not outright conservative. His party, he declared, was 'the principal stronghold against the perils threatening the regime', the threat of dictatorship and social unrest. He attributed all these risks to the lack of strong government.[2] His, it seems, was an agonising decision. Apparently, he would have wished to emerge as a national leader above party politics. A few weeks earlier he had appeared ready to accept the presidency of the republic,

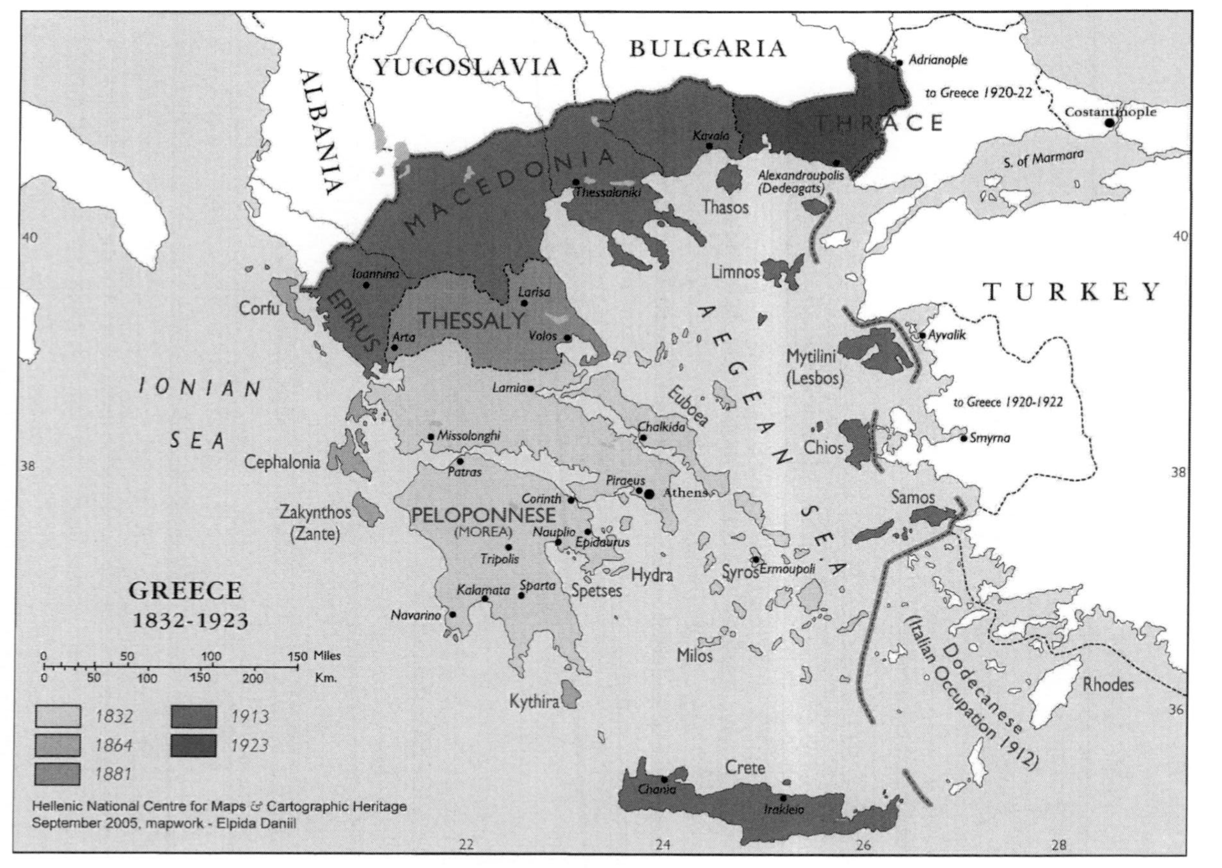

The expansion of the frontiers of Greece, 1830–1923

provided that all Venizelist groups gave him their support. What was more, shortly after his announcement of 23 May, he stated his readiness to retire for good, if the People's Party unconditionally recognised the republican regime. Panagis Tsaldaris, the party leader, declined. Venizelos also advised the president of the republic to keep the coalition government in place. Within a month, however, the Cretan leader decided to bring about its downfall.[3]

What tipped the scales against the Zaimis government, in which the Venizelist Kafantaris and Alexandros Papanastasiou served alongside the royalist Ioannis Metaxas, was its procrastination over the law constituting the senate and, ultimately, its reluctance to move quickly down the path to fresh elections. Venizelos accepted the mandate, which was coupled with a decree dissolving the parliament. He also persuaded President Pavlos Kountouriotis to sanction the plurality system for the impending elections by emergency decree. This enabled him to rally most Venizelist groups and personalities – with the exception of Kafantaris – around the Liberal Party.[4]

During the electoral campaign, Venizelos preached a combination of large-scale projects aimed at increasing production, harmonious industrial relations, and good government and reform, which would render the country 'unrecognisable' within four years.[5] Haunted by the memory of defeat in the wake of the triumph at Sèvres eight years earlier, he was genuinely surprised by the results. It was a landslide victory, unsurpassed in Greek electoral history. By the evening of 20 August 1928, the Venizelists enjoyed a resounding majority of 223 seats out of 250. The Liberal Party commanded 178 seats, while the royalist opposition had mustered only twenty-four.[6]

The realignment of Venizelist ranks soon proved little more than an electoral expedient. Papanastasiou, Andreas Michalakopoulos and the Agrarian group retained their autonomy. Venizelos himself searched beyond his traditional following. Four out of the twelve posts in his first cabinet went to non-Venizelist politicians of conservative outlook, including Interior Minister Constantinos Zavitzianos and Foreign Minister Alexandros Karapanos. He was careful not to include persons who either belonged to the Venizelist old guard or had made their name during the republican period.[7] It was only a year later, on the occasion of the senate elections, that he would turn to die-hard Venizelists and republicans, Generals Gonatas and Plastiras for instance. Perhaps he was dismayed by the adamant refusal of the royalist opposition to respond to his conciliatory overtures. Zavitzianos' resignation in July 1929 would mark the end of broad-based cabinets. Venizelos would then rely on a shrinking fraction of Venizelism, beset by the increasingly hostile opposition of militant republicans, neutrals and anti-Venizelists.

More important, perhaps, for his government's success, was the fact that Venizelos could not avail himself of the team of brilliant men who had worked with him during the 1910s. Some, notably Repoulis and Koromilas, had passed away. Others, like Kafantaris and Papanastasiou, had grown out of their leader and had their own following. Kafantaris, in particular, bitterly resented the 'old gentleman's' return and became a vociferous critic at an early stage. Michalakopoulos and, from the younger generation, Georgios Papandreou would serve with distinction at a time when loyalty rather than merit seemed to count in Venizelos' choices.

For some time, it seems, Venizelos took a personal interest in transforming the Liberal Party into a modern mass party based on a network of local organisations. His effort, however, foundered on the reaction of the party 'notables' who had traditionally relied on personal links with party 'bosses'.[8] George Mavrogordatos questions the extent of Venizelos' commitment to party reform. His 'organizational activism', he notes, 'always had an erratic, superficial, and short-lived quality'. He doubts whether the charismatic leader could 'submit himself to the routine of party administration' at a time when he had difficulty in complying with 'fixed constitutional rules'.[9]

To a lesser extent than in the 1910s, Venizelos felt the need to espouse a coherent and exact political ideology. His message, not unlike that of his principal opponents, was flexible and programmatic, in line with the catch-all strategy he adopted during the 1928 campaign. His undisputed charisma served him well on that occasion but it would prove a stumbling block when co-operation and consensus were required. Venizelos was apparently aware of the need to diversify his social basis in order to ensure stable government. He could no longer count on the entrepreneurial bourgeoisie and the diaspora to provide social leadership, as had been the case in 1910. He envisaged a role for his party at the head of 'several classes joined together in some general direction'. His success in 1928, however, would not survive the economic rocks ahead. Anti-Venizelism had already made inroads in the business class, while retaining much of its traditional clientele of petty bourgeois strata, which felt threatened by capitalist modernisation, principally state employees, artisans and the export crop-oriented smallholders of 'Old Greece'.[10] As will be seen, by the end of its four-year rule, Venizelism would experience a significant erosion of its social basis of entrepreneurs, newly constituted smallholders, and even its more recent and staunchest supporters, the refugees.

Consolidation and modernisation

Following his return to office, Venizelos' immediate task was to consolidate the young republican regime. Priority was given to the new institutions provided for by the 1927 constitution, notably the senate and the council of state. Law 3711 of 1928 established the latter as the supreme administrative court. The council of state began its function in May 1929. Constantinos Raktivan, its first chairman and former minister of justice, proved a happy choice. The new body was empowered with authority to annul acts of the executive and greatly contributed to the consolidation of the rule of law.

The senate was a hybrid representative institution. Ninety-two of its 120 members were to be directly voted for by the electorate, eighteen were to be appointed by corporate interests (including the labour confederation, the chambers of industry and commerce, and the universities) and ten by a joint session of deputies and senators, representing, in effect, the parliamentary majority. Senators had more limited legislative powers than deputies, but their votes were required for the election of the president of the republic. Law 3786 of 1929 provided for their election, which duly took place in April 1929. The results appeared to confirm the dominance of the Liberal Party. The anti-Venizelist vote sank to an all-time low and equally poor was the performance of the splinter Venizelist groups.

Then the government proceeded with the election of president. For more than five years since the proclamation of the republic, the head of state had been only temporary. The incumbent, Admiral Pavlos Kountouriotis, was elected in May 1929. Seven months later he resigned for reasons of health and old age. Despite a consensus among Venizelist leaders in favour of Kafantaris' candidacy, Venizelos went back on his earlier decision and designated the aging Zaimis. This proved a miscalculation that would mean for Venizelos the continuing alienation of his former lieutenants.[11]

Venizelos also had a qualified success in keeping the army out of politics. Speaking to his close friend and confidante, distinguished authoress of children's literature Penelope Delta in May 1928, he attributed his decision to return to politics mainly to his fear of military intervention. His source of concern was not Kondylis or other disgruntled elements but 'the purest republican officers' who, in the face of Venizelist impotence, might seize power in order to forestall a royalist restoration. Venizelos' prestige and crushing parliamentary majority actually discouraged any such tendencies among officers.[12] There was only a minor incident, the so-called 'pig-farm' conspiracy involving a few officers, mostly retired supporters of

General Pangalos. Their arrest coincided with Venizelos' visit to Ankara, in late October 1930. This episode, quite insignificant by inter-war standards, was blown out of proportion owing to the over-reaction of Minister for War Themistoklis Sofoulis.[13] Only towards the end of the government's four-year term would the so-called Military League under General Alexandros Othonaios, the army inspector general, be reactivated as Venizelos himself raised the bogey of royalist restoration.

Venizelos' four-year term was marked by acts of legislation with far-reaching consequences on Greek social and economic life. While less impressive than the record of his first government of 1910 to 1915, these acts nonetheless underscored the liberal leader's commitment to modernisation. Law 3632 of 1928 on the stock exchange and law 5076 of 1931 on corporations and banks provided a legal framework for the capital market and large-scale entrepreneurial activity, which passed the test of time. Law 3741 of 1929 on 'horizontal ownership' revolutionised the use of landed property, with mixed effects on living conditions in Greek urban centres. Law 4680 of 1930 gave the final impetus to the drafting of a civil code – a century-old undertaking. An outline was ready by November 1930 and the revised draft followed in early January 1931. This served as the basis for the final text that was adopted during the Metaxas regime.[14]

Education was one of the principal tiers of Venizelos' package of reform. In a speech in Thessaloniki, during the 1928 electoral campaign, he had stressed the need for overhauling the education system. In its current form, he warned, the system prepared 'the future army of social overthrow'. His reform was inspired by an elitist but nonetheless pragmatic approach, and, perhaps, owed much to the British model. While professing support for general, classical education, Venizelos believed that it should be reserved for 'a select few'. The mass of primary education graduates should follow education commensurate with the needs of the national economy. The proposed system intended to direct the predominantly lower middle-class and rural youth towards acquiring practical, professional skills. For Venizelos, education and social stability were intimately related. Moreover, he hoped to combat the deeply engrained mentality that had long identified secondary classical education with access to a public service post.[15]

Initiated by Education Minister Constantinos Gontikas (1928–30), the reform programme stipulated six-year compulsory education, the abolition of the so-called 'Hellenic schools' as an intermediary stage between primary (dimotika) and secondary schools (gymnasia), and more professional and technical schools at the expense of the classical gymnasia whose number was reduced. It also provided for flexible curricula, according to the specific needs of each school and its students, a list of textbooks, and school libraries. For the first time, national entrance examinations were introduced for higher education. Greek vernacular (dimotiki) was now taught in primary schools and the way opened for its use in secondary education. Under Georgios Papandreou (1930–2), the Education Ministry engaged in an extensive construction effort, which resulted in 3,167 new school buildings – twice as many as erected during a century of independent statehood.[16]

Public order was a field where much could be done to substantiate Venizelos' claim to strong and good government. Significantly, the kidnapping of two Agrarian candidates by brigands in Epirus had marred the 1928 election campaign. They were released after a handsome ransom was paid. The incident brought a long-standing social ill of modern Greece into the limelight. After the elections, Minister of the Interior Zavitsianos supervised a determined campaign against brigandage. Within months the authorities managed to annihilate or bring to justice most of the bands then active in the countryside.[17]

During the electoral campaign, Venizelos had made no secret of his intention to curb communist activity. In early 1929, Zavitsianos introduced a draft on 'measures for the security of the social regime and the protection of civil liberties', which penalised the propagation of communist or secessionist ideas. Penalties ranged from six months' to five years' imprisonment and up to two years' deportation. It also enabled the authorities to dissolve labour unions, disband public meetings and dismiss public servants and officers. Despite fierce reaction from the left wing of the Venizelist camp, the draft was passed and became the so-called Idionymon law 4229 of 1929. Between 1929 and 1932, more than 1,500 persons would receive various sentences under the clauses of this law. In July 1931, the government reintroduced deportation by administrative act – a measure formerly used to combat brigandage – as a further measure against communist activity.[18] Far from pre-empting the 'red peril' these acts proved the first in a long succession, which would extend well into the post-war period.

By penalising convictions, the Idionymon law appeared to cast doubt upon Venizelos' commitment to individual rights and liberal tenets. There is evidence that the liberal leader was genuinely preoccupied with communism as a potential but nonetheless serious threat. His critics interpreted Venizelos' policy as the reaction of the ruling élites vis-à-vis growing social problems and an assertive working-class movement.[19]

Indeed, Venizelos' return to office had been preceded by considerable labour unrest. This subsequently died down and the years 1928 to 1930 marked the lowest point of leftist activity and influence. The Communist Party (KKE) suffered under the twin impact of its slogan for autonomous Macedonia and Thrace and a leadership crisis which was not settled before 1931.[20] Its social reservoir was still quite limited as Greece lacked a sizeable industrial proletariat. The majority of non-agricultural workers were employed in artisan workshops and small business. Most of them owned some property, particularly in their village of origin, and shared a common social outlook with their petty-bourgeois employers.[21] In the case of refugees, those disenchanted with Venizelos were more likely to turn to anti-Venizelism than to the KKE. Militant tendencies were largely confined among manual workers, particularly those employed in tobacco warehouses. Despite its militancy, tobacco unionism represented a seasonal occupation threatened by modernisation, which could hardly provide the vanguard of a mass movement.[22] The disruptive potential of organised labour has been exaggerated, it seems, by both Venizelos and students of the Greek labour movement.

In line with current 'bourgeois' views, Venizelos regarded the legal arsenal against communism as complementary to a policy of satisfying a minimum of labour demands. His earlier governments had established a considerable record of labour legislation, which aimed at securing social peace by pre-empting social unrest at a time when Greece was only beginning to acquire the kernel of an industrial proletariat. Yet, after his return to power, he was reluctant to enforce labour-protection measures enacted in 1917 to 1920. While priority was given to rapid economic growth and employment, particularly for the refugees, Venizelos saw little use in raising labour costs, which remained a comparative advantage for the average small Greek enterprise.

His most important piece of social legislation was introduced towards the end of his four-year term. Despite strong reaction from conservative circles, employee organisations and organised interests, Venizelos decided to go ahead with a fairly comprehensive scheme of social insurance. He was probably prompted by the twin impact of depression and the recent reverses of the liberal vote in by-elections. With the assistance of the International Labour Bureau of the League of Nations and a team of reform-minded experts, the government prepared draft legislation establishing the Social Insurance Fund (IKA), which was tabled in May 1932. Its introductory statement revealed much about the reasoning behind Venizelos' labour policy. Social insurance was understood as part and parcel of a fairly paternalist conception of the modern state. The latter ought to care for the welfare and 'peace of mind' of the working class and provide mechanisms that could serve as 'a safety valve against violent overthrow and revolution'. Although it did not come into full effect until 1937, law 5733 was a stepping stone to the Greek 'welfare state'[23] Venizelos also intended to introduce state intervention and arbitration in labour disputes but the plan foundered on the combined reaction of employee and labour organisations.[24]

The drachma and the banking system

At the time of Venizelos' return to politics the Greek economy had already embarked on a rigorous course of stabilisation. It was linked with a loan of some £9 million, which the coalition government of Zaimis had sought to secure from the London capital market with the assistance of the League of Nations. The loan was intended to finance an extensive programme of land reclamation and improvement, particularly in Northern Greece. This would not only facilitate the settlement of rural refugee families but also lessen Greece's dependence on grain imports and thus help to reduce the trade deficit. The conditions set by the fiscal committee of the League of Nations were that the drachma should be stabilised through the adoption of the gold exchange standard and a fixed exchange rate and, significantly, a central reserve bank should be set up, endowed with exclusive issuing rights. The latter proposition put the government to the test, as it challenged the inveterate interests vested in the National Bank of Greece. In addition to being the largest commercial bank, the National Bank issued currency notes and operated as a mortgage, agricultural and industrial credit bank. Its relationship with the state was a symbiotic one. While it was run by what was in effect a state bureaucracy, its issuing rights and reserves gave its leading circles a say in the course of general economic policy.[25]

It was Kafantaris who, as minister of finance, undertook to put the Greek financial house in order. His acceptance of the proposals of the fiscal committee experts led to the signing of the Geneva Protocol, which spelled out the terms for the £9 million loan. The gold exchange standard was adopted, the drachma was stabilised against the British pound and it became fully convertible. The National Bank was obliged to transfer its issuing privilege and considerable cover to a new central bank. The agreement was effected against the fierce reaction of the National Bank and led to a cabinet crisis. In May 1928, the Bank of Greece came into being under Alexandros Diomidis, one of Venizelos' former lieutenants, as its first governor.[26]

Although Venizelos had initially expressed misgivings about the setting up of the new institution, he continued Kafantaris' policy after he came to office. This was no easy task, as the new and the former issuing banks became locked into a protracted tug of war. The National Bank reluctantly conceded part of its deposits in gold to the central bank as cover to the new banknotes. Subsequently, it did much to drain the resources of the Bank of Greece and, ultimately, undermine its role. That this effort failed was partly due to the determination of the Venizelos government to move ahead with the restructuring of the banking system initiated by Kafantaris; it was also aided by external factors, such as the conditions set by the League of Nations and the world economic crisis.[27]

Agricultural credit was also removed from National Bank control and was assigned to a new state institution, the Agricultural Bank of Greece (law 4332 of 1929). As in the case of the Bank of Greece, the step was taken with fierce resistance from the National Bank and the anti-Venizelist opposition.[28] Within its first year of operation, the bank issued loans worth 1,304 million drachmas and managed to sustain the rural economy during two difficult years. Perhaps more importantly, the new institution helped to free farmers from the exploitation of moneylenders.[29] The National Bank continued to dominate credit to industries and manufacturers.

The second round in the struggle between the state and its central bank on the one hand, and the commercial banks led by the National Bank on the other, was fought during the 1931 to 1932 economic crisis. As the government stuck to the gold standard even after Britain had abandoned it, the National Bank led a wave of speculation against the drachma, buying Greek state bonds in gold in foreign stock markets. Thus Greek capital fled abroad on the pretext of 'repatriating' the external debt. At a time when the League of Nations organs prescribed a stiff deflationary policy, the commercial banks drained central bank reserves in gold and foreign exchange and increased their own. The Bank of Greece proved unable to control the transactions of the commercial banks in exchange. The cover of currency circulation moved dangerously close to the minimum 40 per cent stipulated by the Geneva Protocol. Venizelos felt obliged to come out and denounce the National Bank as a source of 'financial anomalies'. This state of affairs contributed to the government's decision to suspend the convertibility of the drachma. The new policy, which came into effect after April 1932, terminated the efforts of the National Bank to recover its former role. For the rest of the inter-war period, the Bank of Greece would effectively control not only credit policy but also foreign trade, the rate of investment, production and economic expansion.[30]

Economic expansion . . .

Venizelos' extensive programme of land reclamation and improvement seemed well suited to the needs of a country where two thirds of the population depended on agriculture for their income. The previous government had already assigned the drainage of the Yannitsa basin to the American Foundation Company. Aware of a latent Anglo-American antagonism, Venizelos ensured that both sides shared in further development projects. Thus, he signed new contracts with the American Monks and Ulen for the Strymon valley and with the British Henry Boot and Sons Ltd for areas in Thessaly and Epirus.[31] The realisation of these projects would turn out hundreds of thousands of hectares of arable land. It would also help to combat the acute malaria epidemics plaguing Central and Eastern Macedonia, in particular.

Venizelos also continued a policy inaugurated by Papanastasiou, which was aimed at increasing grain production. Greek farmers concentrated on a few export-oriented products, mainly currants and tobacco, at a time when two thirds of domestic consumption of wheat had to be covered by imports. The state imposed a high tariff on imported wheat and other cereals and concentrated domestic production by offering artificially inflated prices. In 1930 the tithe was abolished and hence grain production became practically tax exempt. A succession of bad years and delays in reclamation projects seriously disrupted this effort during Venizelos' term. Ultimately, however, these measures combined with the slump in international prices for currants and tobacco to set off a process that would render Greece almost self-sufficient in grain by the end of the decade. Farmers were encouraged to switch to cereal, cotton, and olive and fodder crops, which were primarily directed to the domestic market.[32]

In fact, the longer-term effects of Venizelos' 'New Deal' for Greek agriculture were more significant than the immediate outcome of his four-year term in office. His policy of land reclamation and improvement was complemented by institutions which provided sustained financial and scientific support. The Agricultural Bank, the Tobacco Institute, the Cotton Institute and other agencies would have a lasting impact on agricultural production.[33]

An issue concerning the rural population was left over by the previous government and had to be tackled by Venizelos. Since the 1880s, the British-owned Lake Kopais Company had been reclaiming and exploiting large tracts of land in Boeotia. The company's tactics of exploitation had repeatedly caused unrest among the local population of tenants and share-croppers. Venizelos proposed that the National Bank of Greece or the Agricultural Bank buy out the estate. The negotiations reached deadlock, as the prospective buyers were not prepared to pay the high price sought by the company.[34] The matter would eventually be settled after the war, with quite favourable terms for the British investors.

Production and trade was to be further stimulated by an ambitious road-building programme. This was only partially realised, however, due to the reluctance of capital markets to provide credit after the world slump. Indeed, Venizelos' programme of public investment was based on the assumption that Greece would continue to secure the necessary funds from abroad, as had been the case since 1923. Attracted by a suddenly expanded domestic market, foreign investment had risen steadily after the Asia Minor catastrophe. Between 1923 and 1932, the Greek state borrowed some 950 million gold drachmas, which were channelled into refugee rehabilitation, public works, land reclamation and private investment projects. A further 600 million drachmas were lent to the private sector. During his term, Venizelos secured five loans yielding £10.5 million drachmas, four fifths of which went to infrastructure projects. At a time of monetary restrictions and falling share prices, high-yield state bonds attracted considerable capital.[35]

By 1932, the country's external debt stood at some 150 per cent of its GNP, while its servicing absorbed 81 per cent of foreign exchange receipts from exports.[36] Significantly, nearly 45 per cent of Greek foreign debt holders were Greek citizens and institutions, the largest among them being the National Bank of Greece. This proved, if anything, the continuing incapacity of the Greek state to secure revenue through taxation and its need to resort to extensive borrowing. As a result, Greece's per capita national debt was by far higher than that in any other country of south-eastern Europe.[37]

Venizelos came to office on the crest of a wave of remarkable industrial growth that was temporarily arrested under the impact of the world economic crisis and recession. The sharp increase in the price of imported goods, under the twin impact of devaluation and relatively low inflation, favoured domestic production in the longer term. The protectionist arsenal introduced in 1932 fuelled autarkic trends and prepared the ground for the expansion of import-substituting industries. Venizelos also attempted to promote industrial mergers through tax incentives and other discriminating practices. The number of industrial concerns continued to increase, as did employment in the secondary sector. Electric power, the textile industry and construction led the way. From 1929 to 1938, Greece would achieve high industrial growth rates, estimated between

5.11 per cent and 5.73 per cent annually, coming a world third after the Soviet Union and Japan.[38]

. . . and contraction

Even as Venizelos returned to office in summer 1928, the economic picture gave ample cause for concern. The benefits of stabilisation and capital flows notwithstanding, the Greek economy continued to be vexed by the issue of refugee settlement and rehabilitation, structural and fiscal problems, and state intervention and protection. Moreover, it had begun to feel the sting of adverse international trends. By 1928 the primary sector was already suffering from the decline in international prices for agricultural products. As a result, the value of production remained stagnant, despite the expansion of arable land and the increased volume of new products. The crisis hit other sectors of the economy as it reduced demand for consumer goods and led farmers to diversify their crops towards high-yield products and self-consumption.[39] The balance of payments deteriorated under the impact of declining exports and invisible revenue as emigrant and sailor remittances shrank by two thirds between 1928 and 1932.[40]

Yet, for nearly two years after the Wall Street 'crash', there was hope that the Greek economy might after all eschew the worst effects of the world crisis. This was an unrealistic prospect, partly sustained by the government's record of fiscal orthodoxy. Between 1928 and 1931, three successive budgets showed a surplus, public debt was reduced by 11 per cent, inflation was kept low and unemployment was not a serious issue. What was more, Venizelos and his associates believed that, by clinging to the terms of the 1928 stabilisation, Greece would continue to enjoy unfettered access to foreign credit.

By the second half of 1931, the policy of a balanced budget was proving illusory and painful for the Greek economy. According to Costas Costis, Venizelos' fiscal policy helped to intensify the crisis by reducing available income. Indeed, per capita taxation and taxation as percentage of the GNP were considerably higher in Greece than in the rest of southeastern Europe.[41] Moreover, the government felt compelled to impose a system of import licences and other currency restrictions that inevitably stifled foreign trade. Imports were restricted and delayed, as credit became scarce. As a result, state revenue from import duties dropped at a time when export receipts suffered from the loss of foreign markets to Greek products.[42]

The crisis was brought home on 21 September 1931, when Britain abandoned the gold standard. The British pound was no longer convertible into gold and devalued by 20 per cent. The adverse effect was immediately felt on the shares traded on the Athens stock exchange. The government intervened and dealings were suspended for a time. Yet no steps were taken to limit the rising demand for foreign exchange. The run on the drachma went on for six days and by 27 September the Bank of Greece had lost $3.6 million of its exchange reserves. Its governor, Diomidis, was forced to resign and was replaced by Emmanuel Tsouderos. An emergency law 'on the protection of the national currency' was passed. It provided for restrictions on transactions in foreign exchange, which in effect rendered the drachma non-convertible.

For another eight months, the government waged a desperate 'battle of the drachma', refusing to take the national currency off the gold exchange standard. It only switched the fixed rate of the drachma from the pound to the dollar, which, however, was itself floating. Venizelos held out against the advice of Greece's foremost economic experts, notably Kyriakos Varvaressos and Xenophon Zolotas, who advocated the immediate abandonment of the gold exchange standard. Moreover, until as late as 15 March 1932, Greek political leaders unanimously supported the government's policy. In an apparent effort to inspire confidence in a bewildered public, the Greek premier optimistically repeated that the crisis would be transient. To him the policy of the 'hard drachma' was more than a matter of honour. Venizelos firmly believed that the unravelling of the stabilisation of 1928 would spell the end of economic reconstruction and a reversion to lack of confidence, instability and inflation.

Persistence on convertibility proved grist to the mill of speculators. It encouraged demand for foreign exchange and the hoarding of imported goods in anticipation of devaluation. The Bank of Greece reacted by raising interest rates and took measures that curbed currency circulation. Indeed, commercial banks were obliged to deposit a fixed percentage of their account at the Bank of Greece. These measures, however, failed to avert the drain of foreign currency reserves, which would shrink from $38.9 million in late 1930 to $2.336 million on 26 April 1932. Speculation against the drachma was spearheaded by the National Bank of Greece, which resorted to buying Greek bonds in gold from the London stock market. According to Tsouderos, the bank's twin aim was to gain leverage vis-à-vis the Greek state, whose foreign debt in gold it was amassing, and to undermine the role of the newly established central bank as the guarantor of monetary stability.[43]

Venizelos pinned his hopes for riding the crisis on a major foreign loan. This might enable him to complete the infrastructure projects and shore up the worsening balance of payments. He soon discovered that even 'ordinary' sources of finance had all but dried out. Following the so-called 'Hoover moratorium' on all war debts and reparations in July 1931, Greece was unable to draw any more funds from the extremely favourable arrangements which Venizelos' skilful diplomacy had secured during the Hague Conference two years earlier.[44] What was more, the International Financial Commission (IFC), which had controlled certain sources of public revenue ever since the Greek defeat in 1897, refused to guarantee loans other than those supervised by the League of Nations. A number of other issues, including the renegotiation of contracts signed during the Pangalos regime with major foreign concerns, were bound to complicate an already formidable task.[45]

In January 1932, Venizelos embarked on a tour of the three states represented on the IFC, namely Britain, France and Italy. He asked for a $50 million loan in four annual instalments and a five-year moratorium on the servicing of the Greek external debt, which at the time absorbed 43 per cent of the state budget. Gaining little more than sympathy from those three governments, he then turned to the fiscal committee of the League of Nations and the Bank for International Settlements. During the ensuing contacts, the same circles as had dictated the 1928 stabilisation now privately advised that its cornerstone, the gold exchange standard, be dispensed with. Finally, the fiscal committee recommended a one-year moratorium on debt servicing and the deposit of its local currency counterpart in a special account at the Bank of Greece in order to finance the public projects in progress. Venizelos considered this proposal utterly inadequate. Finally, the council of the League of Nations, which convened in mid-April 1932, declined to take a position on the Greek recourse. This left Venizelos with no option but to reverse course. On 25 April 1932 the drachma was taken off the gold standard and became non-convertible. In the following month, Greece defaulted on its debt payments.[46]

The new finance minister, Kyriakos Varvaressos, laid out the government's new policy. The drachma was allowed to devalue (62 per cent against the dollar by the end of 1932) and stiff exchange controls were imposed. Credit came completely under the control of the Bank of Greece, which assumed the exclusive right to provide foreign exchange. A further measure, introduced on 29 July, affected all deposits of foreign exchange in Greek commercial banks. The latter were obliged to deposit their exchange reserves in the Bank of Greece and received the equivalent in drachmas. This policy, combined with high interest rates, would facilitate the progressive return of capital that had flown abroad, a process that reached its peak after Venizelos' fall from office.[47]

Venizelos also attempted to institutionalise the new course towards more control in the economy. A supreme economic council (SEC) was set up as chief advisory body.[48] Its impact, however, was marginal, as economic policy-making remained the preserve of the prime minister and his entourage.[49] Significantly, both the Venizelist splinter groups and the People's Party in opposition strongly objected to the creation of the SEC in line with their criticism of the government's policy of intervention in the economy. Yet the centre of gravity had decisively shifted in favour of the state. Borrowing and loan policy, often under quite favourable conditions, would render the state extremely competitive vis-à-vis the private sector. For the first time, taxation was used as a means for furthering the objectives of state economic policy.[50]

State intervention was coupled with protectionism. As the major trading states of the world failed to devise a concerted response to the crisis, Greece had little choice but to try and cut her losses. During 1932 foreign trade contracted by 61.5 per cent from its 1929 level. Traditional export products suffered heavily. Between 1929 and 1933 tobacco exports dropped by 81 per cent and production was cut by more than half, while currant and wine exports were halved. Government policy switched in favour of exchange-saving crops and import-substituting industries. Tariffs for most domestically produced products rose by 50 per cent to 100 per cent and quotas were imposed on most imports. These measures were in keeping with the policies adopted by Greece's trading partners, most of which had already raised import tariffs tenfold. As a result, the proportion of exports to imports rose considerably. A modicum of foreign trade was maintained mainly through bilateral clearing agreements. In 1932, Greece signed ten such agreements, which were primarily aimed at securing the traditional outlets for Greek tobacco exports in Central Europe.[51] As has been remarked, having started from monetary and exchange objectives, Venizelos' policy resulted in establishing 'the most elaborate and effective system for the protection and encouragement of domestic production'.[52]

With regard to external debt, which at the time of Greece's default stood at $515 million, mostly at the hands of British bondholders, Varvaressos successfully negotiated a rescheduling agreement. Servicing was limited to 30 per cent of interest due.[53] The sharp curtailment of debt payments and the reduced trade deficit released funds, which subsequently facilitated a swift recovery. Greece avoided deflation as the policy of the Bank of Greece secured a steady flow of credit. The collapse of the banking system – a typical feature of the slump in many European countries and the United States – was averted. Rather, the National Bank of

Greece was able to buy out many of its smaller competitors and consolidate its dominant position in commercial credit.

As was the case with other aspects of his policy, the measures adopted in mid-1932 did not come into full effect until after Venizelos was out of office. The crisis culminated only months before his term was due to expire. The depression spread from the fiscal front to that of the real economy. The GNP fell by more than one third within a year. As economic activity contracted, unemployment rose threefold (from 75,000 to 237,000) at a time when 73 per cent of working-class families lived below the subsistence level. Since the early 1920s, emigration had ceased to offer an outlet to economic discontent. However belatedly, the Greek people experienced the worst aspects of the slump.[54] According to Mavrogordatos, the economic crisis cost Venizelos the support of the business class – his staunchest ally in his modernising effort – and 'shattered the momentum of Venizelism as an agent of bourgeois transformation'.[55]

Venizelism and the refugees

The crisis also put to the test the special relationship between Venizelos and an important segment of Greek society, the refugees. The advent of 1.25 million people from Anatolia, Eastern Thrace and the Black Sea coastal regions had proved a blessing in disguise in more than one respect. The settlement en masse of refugee families in the so-called 'New Lands', primarily Macedonia and Western Thrace, decisively turned the balance in favour of ethnic homogeneity. In towns, the newcomers provided the secondary sector and services with a cheap and often skilled workforce. In the countryside, they proved the driving force behind the expansion and partial modernisation of Greek agriculture: cultivated land doubled in many areas of refugee settlement and new products, tobacco and maize in particular, were introduced. Once settled, refugees contributed to the expansion of the domestic market. Refugee rehabilitation itself stimulated certain sectors of the economy, particularly construction and public works, at a time when the world economic crisis threatened to slow down economic activity.[56]

Thanks to the work of the Refugee Settlement Commission, which was completed by January 1930, there had been considerable progress towards the settlement of refugees, particularly in rural areas. Venizelos stepped up the process whereby he hoped to turn destitute refugees into owners of land and self-employed entrepreneurs. Previous governments had secured the necessary funds. The objectives were political as well as social and economic. By giving the refugee as well as the landless peasant families a stake in land and state protection, the Venizelist governments of the period by and large retained the loyalties of these social groups. The policy of urban settlement was considerably less successful. Despite the government's efforts and owing to the slowing effect of the economic slump, by the end of Venizelos' four-year rule some 30,000 urban and 17,000 rural refugee families still lacked adequate housing.[57]

The most serious issue, which threatened to undermine refugee allegiance to Venizelism, concerned the compensation claims for properties abandoned in Turkey. According to the Lausanne Convention of 1923, the compensation of the exchanged persons for abandoned property should primarily burden the host country, while any outstanding balance should be borne by their country of origin. For five years, the matter was endlessly debated by the two sides without a mutually acceptable estimate of the respective obligations ever being reached. Eventually, in his pursuit of the Greek–Turkish rapprochement, Venizelos proceeded with the summary settlement of the mutual property claims. He was prepared to concede an outstanding figure in favour of Turkey, estimated at £125,000, in order to clear the ground for his political objectives. Moreover, having fixed a rather nominal amount of compensation in cash and bonds, Venizelos announced that no further compensation advances would be forthcoming. Clearly, to do otherwise would have been beyond the means of the Greek treasury, as the total of refugee claims amounted to 100 billion drachmas. Instead, the Greek premier chose to press ahead with the completion of refugee settlement. He took particular care of rural settlers, whose debts to the state were sliced by one third. This was followed by a clearing of debts and claims. The Ankara Convention of 1930 provoked fierce reaction from refugee organisations and afforded the opposition and various patrons, such as General Kondylis, an opportunity to dispute the Venizelist hold on the refugee vote.[58]

For nearly a decade, refugee support had enabled Venizelism to offset the predominant influence of its rivals in Old Greece. The preponderance of refugees in electoral districts of the New Lands and their compact settlements in and around Athens and other major cities rendered their vote a valuable political asset. Yet the inability of the various refugee organisations to operate effectively as pressure groups benefited a certain brand of politicians and patrons, not necessarily of refugee origin themselves. By advocating refugee demands to the fullest extent, these so-called 'prosphygopateres' were able to build up their own clientelistic networks and to monopolise the refugee vote. Until 1930, the majority of these networks owed allegiance to Venizelos' Liberal Party. The Cretan leader entrusted portfolios dealing with refugee issues, such as public works and relief, to politicians of refugee origin.[59] The Venizelist grip and swift progress towards settlement and rehabilitation, especially in rural areas, considerably reduced the chances of the left, the fledgling KKE in particular. The latter never won more than a small fraction of the refugee vote, despite the fact that persons of refugee origin were over-represented on the party's central organs.[60]

The support of the refugee masses to Venizelism was deeply rooted. It dated back to the aftermath of the Balkan Wars, when the first wave of expellees from Asia Minor had reached Greece. Venizelos was credited with the policy that had led to the Treaty of Sèvres, while his royalist opponents were held responsible for the tragic outcome of the Anatolian campaign. The sudden arrival of destitute refugee families was bound to cause a conflict of interests with native populations. Native peasants and townsfolk alike resented competition for land or employment from refugees and took exception to their cultural diversity. More often than not, it was anti-Venizelist patrons and politicians who undertook to defend native interests against a predominantly Venizelist administration; and it was Venizelos, the man who had brought the vision of Megali Idea nearer to completion, who was looked upon by refugee masses as saviour and guarantor of a better future.[61]

The downfall

For some time after Venizelos' return to office, anti-Venizelism struggled for political survival. Bereft of its natural leaders since 1922 and split between two factions, Tsaldaris' People's Party and Metaxas' followers, anti-Venizelism remained an essentially reactive force, averse to modernisation and largely dependent on traditional clientelistic networks. The core of its social base consisted of the traditional rural oligarchy and the state bureaucracy of 'Old Greece'. What was more, it lacked the charismatic leadership of its rival.[62] At the same time, as has been noted, the communist left was immersed in a profound crisis while the considerable Agrarian movement split, as its Venizelist faction returned to the liberal fold.[63]

By 1931, however, anti-Venizelism had bounced back, largely under the banner of the People's Party, and would be able to make inroads into the Venizelist camp. This quick recovery undoubtedly owed much to the economic crisis that rendered Venizelos unable to deliver his promises of sustained growth and higher living standards. In search of security and stability, the entrepreneurial middle class felt attracted by Tsaldaris' conservative blandishments. Hit by falling prices and unemployment, the new smallholders and the urban workers 'became massively available for

Agrarian radicalism' and communism. The brunt of the crisis, it appears, was borne by the commercial lower middle class, which also swayed towards anti-Venizelism. Confined to the realm of domestic and especially economic policy, Mavrogordatos notes, Venizelos' charisma 'rapidly reached its limits'. Nationalism was no longer an issue and Venizelos' foreign policy was not designed to appeal to mass instincts. As the dividing lines between the two great rival blocs seemed to blur, Venizelos increasingly turned to republicanism as a means 'to hold the Venizelist bloc and especially the Liberal Party together'.[64]

As has been remarked, within a year after his return to politics, Venizelos had all but abandoned his effort to bridge the gap with anti-Venizelism. The inclusion of General Gonatas and, initially, of Plastiras in the liberal ticket for the senate was received as an affront by the anti-Venizelist camp, who had branded the leaders of the 1922 revolt as 'murderers' of the six royalist leaders executed at Goudi.[65] The legacy of the National Schism, which had seemed to become irrelevant in 1926–7, once more threatened to dominate the political discourse. The reluctance of the People's Party to seal the regime issue by offering unequivocal recognition of the republic permitted Venizelos increasingly to identify the predominance of his party with the survival of the republican regime.

The high tide of Venizelism was over by summer 1929. The local elections of that year proved a setback for the Liberal Party. Athens was lost to the anti-Venizelists as the Venizelist vote split. A few months later, Zaimis' election to the presidency confirmed the division of the Venizelist camp. The rift between Kafantaris and Venizelos deepened and Kondylis took the chance to abandon the Venizelist camp altogether. During 1930, Papanastasiou and Kafantaris bitterly attacked Venizelos' concentration of power and his frequent references to the regime issue. Kafantaris, in particular, became the major critic of the government's economic policy, insisting on the need to maintain fiscal orthodoxy and to keep the role of the state as limited as possible.[66]

'Good and honest government' had been one the central themes in Venizelos' electoral campaign of 1928. This was more than a slogan to the Cretan leader who had always been sensitive to questions of integrity. From late 1930 and through 1931, allegations of abuse of authority and embezzlement of public funds afforded the opposition press the opportunity to subject the government to a relentless smearing campaign. Several of Venizelos' associates were implicated in scandals, ranging from a computing error in the price of bread and the adulteration of quinine tablets to conspiring with various cabals of merchants or public-works contractors. A case of discrimination in the allocation of public-works contracts

Eleftherios Venizelos as a young lawyer in Crete (late nineteenth century)

Venizelos with Cretan rebels and officers of the European powers at Akrotiri, Chania, February 1897

Cretan Executive Committee. M. Petychakis, El. Venizelos, A. Michelidakis (chairman), Em. Logiadis, Ch. Pologeorgris, 1908

Eleftherios Venizelos as a rebel leader in Therisso, spring 1905

The committee drafting the new constitution of the Cretan state, 1906–7

Venizelos (middle, with bow tie) on the day of his departure for Athens in order to assume the premiership. Municipal garden, Chania, September 1910

Venizelos and European statesmen at London City Hall during the negotiations concluding the First Balkan War, December 1912

Venizelos with King Constantine at the front during the Second Balkan War, July 1913

Venizelos and Balkan leaders at the signing of the Treaty of Bucharest, 10 August 1913

Official ceremony marking the union of Crete with Greece, Chania, 1 December 1913

Venizelos and Admiral Paul Kountouriotis on the way from Chania to Thessaloniki, September 1916

SEPTIEME ANNÉE. — N° 2167. LE NUMÉRO : 10 CENTIMES. — ÉTRANGER : 20 CENTIMES Samedi 21 octobre 1916.

•EXCELSIOR•

Journal Illustré Quotidien

ABONNEMENTS (du 1er ou du 16 de chaque mois)
France... Un an, 35 fr. 6 mois, 18 fr. 3 mois, 10 fr.
Étranger. Un an, 70 fr. 6 mois, 36 fr. 3 mois, 20 fr.
On s'abonne sans frais dans tous les bureaux de poste
Les manuscrits non insérés ne sont pas rendus

Informations - Littérature - Sciences - Arts - Sports - Théâtres - Élégances

Adresser toute la correspondance à l'ADMINISTRATEUR D'Excelsior
88, avenue des Champs-Elysées, PARIS
Téléph. : WAGRAM 57-41, 57-45
Adresse télégraph. : EXCEL-PARIS

A Salonique. — La première poignée de main du général Sarrail à M. Venizelos

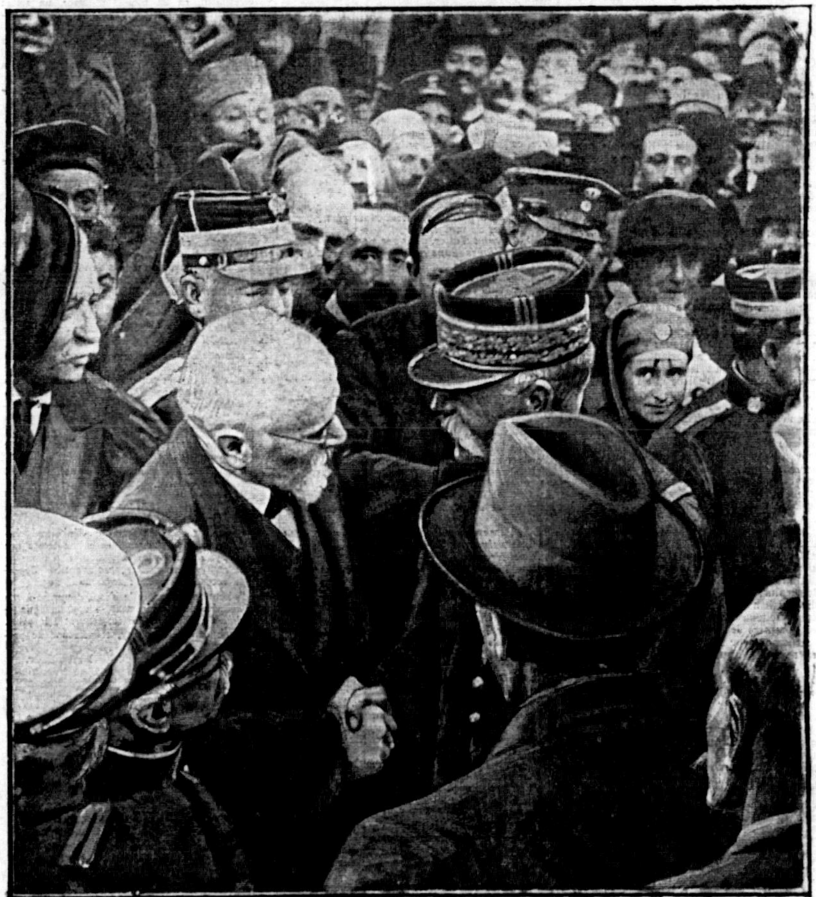

Voici le premier des documents publiés en France sur l'événement de si haute portée historique qui eut Salonique pour théâtre, le 9 octobre dernier, jour où M. Venizelos, chef du parti national, arriva dans cette ville. Le général Sarrail avait tenu à être l'un des premiers à saluer le grand Crétois au moment où il mit pied à terre. Et ce fut aux cris de : « *Zito i Gallia!* » — Vive la France! — que le chef des armées alliées traversa la foule et vint serrer la main du patriote hellène.

Venizelos is welcomed in Thessaloniki by the commander of allied forces General Sarrail, October 1916

A view of the 'anathema' against Venizelos, 13 December 1916

A meeting on the terms of armistice following the end of the First World War. Versailles, 16 November 1918

Following the award of the doctorate of law honoris causa *by the University of Oxford, 25 June 1920*

Venizelos signing the Treaty of Sèvres, 10 August 1920

The opening meeting of the Council of the Society of Nations, 1920. Venizelos is at the head of the table

A. Doxiadis, H. Morgenthau, El. Venizelos at Zappeion with orphan refugee children from Asia Minor, February 1924

Eleftherios Venizelos and Ismet Inonu during Inonu's visit to Athens, October 1931

Swearing in of the Venizelos government, July 1928

Venizelos addresses a pre-election rally in Thessaloniki, June 1933

Mourning crowds accompany Venizelos to his resting place. Chania, March 1936

Venizelos family house, Chalepa, Chania, 1925

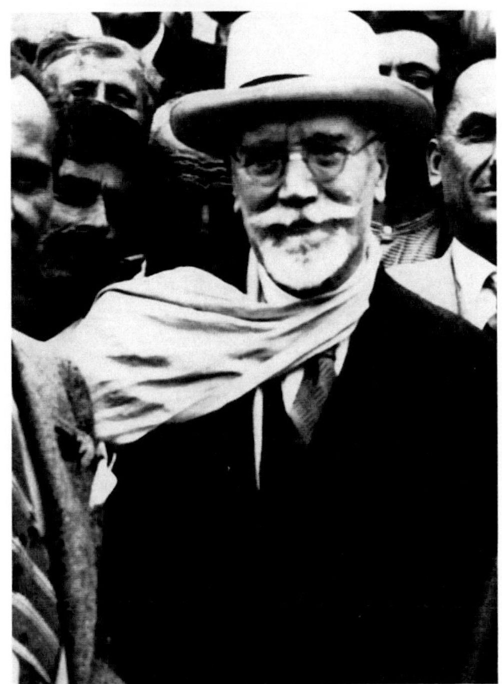

Two classic portraits of El. Venizelos, 1933 and 1930 respectively

Translating Thucydides. Oil painting by D. Kokotsis, 1927

on the island of Lesbos, which subsequently collapsed in court, cost Venizelos one of his most able associates, Minister of Communications Byron Karapanayiotis. Like Gonatas and Plastiras, Karapanayiotis was a bête noir of anti-Venizelism, as he was connected with the trial and execution of its six leaders in 1922. Although his own integrity was never directly disputed, Venizelos felt obliged to defend his ministers in public and thus bore the brand of the ensuing outcry. While most of the politicians and high officials implicated in this campaign were subsequently vindicated in court, the slogan 'Down with the thieves' remained the battle cry of the anti-Venizelist camp until the 1932 elections.[67]

Even before the full effects of the economic crisis became visible, signs of Venizelist retreat clearly emanated from by-elections. The most alarming results came from Thessaloniki and the island of Lesbos, in February and July 1931 respectively. They revealed a strong leftward trend, as the communist vote doubled or trebled, reaching 21.7 per cent in the case of Lesbos. Significantly, both districts contained a large number of refugees who were still scratching a meagre living in shanty-towns. If nothing else, the results proved the failure of social and legal measures such as the Idionymon to curb communist influence. In an effort to bolster the prospects of orderly succession between the two main 'bourgeois' blocs, Venizelos contacted the People's Party leadership, asking for an unconditional recognition of the republic. Once again, Tsaldaris declined.[68]

By mid-March 1932, with the economic crisis in full swing, Venizelos was proposing the formation of an all-party government, which could enforce the necessary harsh measures. Rebuffed by the opposition, he went it alone and reversed the policy of stabilisation. It was during the ensuing debate in parliament, on 28 April 1932, that Venizelos, accused by Papanastasiou of fatalism in the face of the crisis, responded by reciting his own epitaph:

> Dear friends, the deceased before us was a real man, with great courage, with confidence in himself and in the people whom he was called to govern. Perhaps he committed many mistakes, but he never lacked courage, he never was a fatalist, because he never expected to see his country advanced by way of fate, but he put to its service all the fire he had inside him, every power of his body and soul.[69]

During his last months in office, Venizelos was gripped by deep insecurity regarding the prospects of his party and the republican regime itself. The harsh criticism of former associates and the scurrilous personal attacks of the opposition press led him to submit to parliament a proposal for the revision of the constitution. Predicting a crisis, the liberal leader advocated the inclusion of a provision similar to article 48.2 of the Weimar constitution, which invested the president with emergency powers in case of not only external but also domestic threat to state authority. Clearly, in the twilight of his career and amidst the polarised domestic conditions fed by the deteriorating international situation, Venizelos was inclined to contemplate the curtailment of certain freedoms and liberal norms. He apparently envisaged the strengthening of the executive, including a 'temporary dictatorship' perhaps, as the antidote to the perceived 'crisis of parliamentary rule'.[70] The attempt to revise the constitution proved unsuccessful. Following the Liberals' defeat in the 1932 and 1933 elections, the proposal was abandoned.

Haunted by the Liberal set-backs in recent by-elections, Venizelos persuaded the president to authorise the postponement of the election of one third of senate members, which was due in May 1932. He subsequently had a law passed reintroducing proportional representation only for the impending national elections, after which the country should revert to the plurality system. Predictably, the Venizelist opposition supported proportional representation, as they did not exclude co-operation across the political divide. A few days later, Venizelos announced his intention to introduce a new press law, threatening severe penalties for attempts to undermine confidence in the drachma. As was the case with his proposed constitutional amendment, the measure was condemned by the entire opposition as proof of Venizelos' autocratic intentions. In May 1932, the Cretan leader responded by tendering his resignation.[71]

Papanastasiou, leader of the left-wing faction of Venizelism, formed a cabinet. He resigned, however, a few days later, as Venizelos, who still controlled the majority in parliament, did not offer unconditional support for the far-reaching economic programme of the new government. On 5 June Venizelos was back in office and presided over a long and bitter electoral campaign. Kafantaris and Papanastasiou attempted to forge a 'third force' with an up-and-coming Agrarian Party.[72] This as well as the encroachments of the anti-Venizelist camp the liberal leader attempted to stave off, by opting for tactics of polarisation. He warned his audience of the risk of renewed military interventions or even a civil war, in case the People's Party came to office. In fact, his own supporters within the armed forces, headed by Generals Othonaios and Constantinos Manettas, had revived the Military League in order to prevent a royalist come-back. Venizelos continued in this vein even after Papanastasiou publicly denounced the existence of the league. On the eve of the elections, the opposition jointly dismissed the existence of a royalist threat to the regime. Yet Tsaldaris' assurances still fell short of an unconditional declaration of allegiance to the republic.[73]

In the event, Venizelos' tactics of polarisation were not altogether without success. In the elections of 25 September 1932 his party polled twice as many votes as did all Venizelist break-away groups. Still, it was evident that his appeal had shrunk to a fraction of the social coalition which had endowed him with a resounding majority four years earlier. Most of the defectors were directed towards the left-wing Agrarian Party and the communists, who appeared to challenge 'the existing dominant division between the two bourgeois blocs' – a prospect that Venizelos had consistently sought to avert.[74] The Liberal Party secured slightly more seats than the People's Party, which now dominated the anti-Venizelist camp. Tsaldaris, however, adroitly exploited the inability of the Venizelist majority to produce a government. He rejected Venizelos' proposal for an all-party cabinet. Then, upon taking the mandate, he issued a statement 'unreservedly' recognising the republican regime. Thereupon, the Military League announced its dissolution. He then proceeded to form a cabinet with Metaxas and Kondylis.[75]

Tsaldaris' first government proved short-lived, as Venizelos was tempted to try his hand in fresh elections, which were scheduled to be waged under the plurality system. His confidence was boosted as most Venizelist leaders, with the exception of Kondylis, returned to the fold. On 16 January Venizelos formed what proved to be his last cabinet. Soon after, the Chamber of Deputies was dissolved. The electoral contest evolved into a more or less clear battle between Venizelism and anti-Venizelism. As Daphnis noted, it was too late for the former to prevail, as, for four years, 'Venizelism had attacked Venizelos', to the benefit of the anti-Venizelist camp.[76] With the issue of the regime temporarily removed, the focus of the electoral campaign shifted onto the economy. Tsaldaris' promise of a 25 per cent payment to the refugees threatened to tip the balance in closely contested districts. Venizelos, however, refused to overbid his opponent for popular favours. On 5 March 1933 the anti-Venizelist United Opposition emerged victorious in seats although the rival National Coalition had polled marginally more votes.[77] Greek politics were about to re-enter the maelstrom of extreme polarisation.

II. SAFEGUARDING THE PEACE: THE FOREIGN POLICY OF THE LAST VENIZELOS GOVERNMENT, 1928–32

The context

The return of Venizelos to Greek politics and high office in 1928, despite its controversial domestic impact, proved a watershed for the country's foreign affairs. His four-year term as prime minister confirmed the Cretan politician's reputation as an astute master of diplomacy who combined vision with the precepts of Realpolitik. Having thrived in circumstances of turmoil and war, Venizelos was able to prove his skills in time of peace.

In 1928 the systemic environment in which a small power like Greece operated had been radically transformed from that of the cataclysmic second decade of the twentieth century. The European states system had entered a period of decline, irretrievably injured by the Great War. The pre-war system of alliances had dissolved. It was succeeded by a multipolar dispensation of power, which the victors found increasingly hard to maintain. The vanquished and a number of disgruntled victors already disputed the settlement imposed by the peace treaties. Part of that edifice, the Treaty of Sèvres, had already collapsed with immediate disastrous effects on Greece. A new form of international organisation, the League of Nations, was failing to fulfil its mandate of collective security. In this case, too, Greece had reaped the bitter fruits of failure, when fascist Italy attacked and briefly occupied the island of Corfu, with impunity. Little wonder that the European powers saw fit to revert to the very diplomatic methods that the founders of the league had held responsible for the fateful summer of 1914. An elaborate system of regional and bilateral pacts purported to provide security against a violent revision of the post-war settlement. The 'spirit of Locarno' meant little more than a delicate balance that hinged upon the continuing capability of Britain and France to preserve the status quo in Europe by means of their already waning preponderance of power.

Under the circumstances, Greek foreign-policymakers faced a number of dilemmas. A fundamental choice had to be made with respect to the post-war settlement. Was Greek policy to pursue the revision of the Lausanne peace treaty or should it acknowledge the irrevocable demise of its former irredentist objectives? Was Greece to seek the protection of a Great Power and regional allies or should it try to maintain an equal distance from the 'big' and friendly terms with all her neighbours? The dictatorship of General Theodoros Pangalos appeared to opt for a revisionist course, which entailed serious concessions to potential allies such as Yugoslavia and a costly antagonism vis-à-vis Bulgaria and Turkey. The all-party government that replaced him in 1926 sought to restore Greece's credibility and overcome her diplomatic isolation. Under Andreas Michalakopoulos, a long-time associate of Venizelos, Greek diplomacy scored some successes, notably the pact of friendship with Romania and the preliminaries of an understanding with Italy. It is, perhaps, the comparison with the bleak conditions of 1923–27 that justifies authors describing Venizelos' come-back as 'the decisive turning point' in Greek foreign policy between the wars.[78]

A diplomatic tour de force*: Rome, Paris, London, Belgrade*

During a speech at Thessaloniki, on the eve of the 1928 general election, Venizelos left his audience in no doubt as to his fundamental directions in foreign affairs: a complete break with his irredentist past and abandonment of Greek territorial claims; unreserved recognition of the status quo; peaceful settlement of disputes and friendly relations with all neighbouring states, including former enemies, such as Bulgaria and Turkey; friendly relations with Italy on a footing equal with Greece's former 'protecting powers', Britain and France; strict observance of the principles and aims of the League of Nations.[79] Security, stability and credibility were vital conditions if Venizelos was to fulfil his role as a great statesman in peacetime.

His return to power was followed by a flurry of diplomatic activity, which helped to transform the diplomatic position of Greece in a matter of months. The first results of Venizelos' vigorous new course became manifest as early as 23 September 1928, with the signing of the Greek–Italian treaty of friendship, conciliation, and judicial settlement of disputes. Although this document provided for neutrality in the case that one of the signatories came under attack, Mussolini himself offered to guarantee Greek sovereignty over Thessaloniki, in particular, in case of an external threat. Given the state of tension between Rome and Belgrade, it was clear that the Italian assurance was directed against a Yugoslav attempt to get a foothold in the Aegean.[80] Venizelos, for his part, recognised the Albanian regime of self-proclaimed King Zog and effectively discouraged the irredentist agitation about the Dodecanese islands held by Italy.[81]

The understanding with Rome was then skilfully exploited by Venizelos in his attempt to improve the diplomatic position of Greece vis-à-vis Yugoslavia and its principal ally and protector, France. For some time, Belgrade had displayed hegemonic tendencies towards its weaker southern neighbour, extracting considerable concessions from the Pangalos regime. France, for her part, treated Yugoslavia as the mainstay of her system of alliances in southeastern Europe. After his Italian sojourn, Venizelos proceeded to Paris. His aim was to reassure his hosts that the Greek–Italian understanding included no secret clauses against third parties. He also left no doubt about his sincere intention to restore

Greek–Yugoslav relations on the basis of equality and mutual respect. Venizelos was equally candid about his discomfort with Yugoslav attitudes. Talking to the French prime minister and wartime associate, Aristide Briand, he pointed out that the persistent Yugoslav claims might be interpreted as a threat against Thessaloniki; if that was the case, Greece would have no option but to seek the support of Italy.[82] Venizelos' reasoning appealed to Briand and secured the favourable attitude of France during the following stage.

Still in Paris, the Greek statesman met with the Yugoslav foreign minister, Vojslav Marinković, and tried to hammer home the idea of a bilateral arrangement similar to the treaty with Italy. Above all, Venizelos sought to reverse Pangalos' commitments, which centred on Yugoslav access to the free zone of the Thessaloniki port, the passage of supplies in time of war, property rights on the Thessaloniki–Gevgelija railway line, and the recognition of Yugoslav nationality to members of the Slav-speaking community in Greek Macedonia. Talks continued in Belgrade. In the event, the Yugoslavs would drop their claims and, on 11 October 1928, two protocols were signed, which settled the questions of the Yugoslav zone at Thessaloniki and the Thessaloniki–Gevgelija railway line with full respect for Greek sovereign rights.[83]

The political accord, provided for in the Greek–Yugoslav protocol, was expedited sooner than expected, owing to Yugoslav domestic developments. In early 1929, a protracted political crisis resulted in the imposition of personal rule by King Alexander Karadjordjević. The new regime proceeded with the conclusion of a treaty of friendship, conciliation and judicial settlement of disputes with Greece, on 27 March 1929. As was the case with the Italian pact, the treaty was an act of bilateral diplomacy, which, nonetheless, confirmed the adherence of both parties to the regime established by the peace treaties and the League of Nations. At the same time, Belgrade agreed to cede all its rights over the Thessaloniki–Gevgelija line to the Greek government for 20 million francs.[84]

Venizelos' visits to Paris and London, in autumn 1928, were primarily intended to allay the suspicions of the two former allies regarding the extent of the rapprochement with Italy and to reaffirm the Greek premier's intention to work for sincere and friendly relations. Yet there was a clear limit, which the elderly statesman was determined to observe. The same man who, in the last war, had unhesitatingly thrown his nation's lot in with the Western powers, was now convinced that Greece's best interests lay away from dependence on any one power or combination of powers, which might drag her into the next war.[85] Venizelos also refused to entertain proposals for a regional pact emanating from Paris and Rome. France and her regional surrogates, Romania and Yugoslavia, were seeking a Balkan 'Locarno', as they misleadingly put it. It was intended as a means to safeguard the post-war settlement and cordon off revisionist powers. Venizelos insisted that stability could never be attained if certain countries, such as Bulgaria, were excluded.[86] He equally rejected Italian overtures regarding a triple alliance between Rome, Athens and Ankara.[87]

Relations with Paris and London were further complicated due to the issue of war debts and Venizelos' quest for external loans in his effort to meet the pressing needs of economic development and refugee rehabilitation. His attempt to broaden the pool of foreign capital by resorting to the American market and seeking the guarantee of the International Financial Commission upset British financial circles, which had up to that point enjoyed a preferential status. Moreover, the Venizelos government undertook to revise concessions to major British concerns under the Pangalos regime.[88] It took all of Venizelos' diplomatic skills to placate British interests without prejudice to Greece's chances in the international capital market and the international conference on war reparations, which was convened at The Hague in August 1929. Mustering British and Italian support, the Greek premier secured a considerable increase in Greece's share of reparations from the former enemy states, at a time when the Young Plan provided for sharp cuts across the board.[89] Unfortunately, this brilliant success was neutralised by the world economic crisis, which deprived the Greek economy of vital inflows at a critical moment.

The former Cretan rebel also ensured that Anglo-Greek relations were not compromised on account of the Cyprus question. A crown colony since 1925, the predominantly Greek-speaking island entered a period of unrest in 1929. Under the impact of the world crisis, the governor's attempt to raise taxes caused widespread discontent, which soon assumed nationalistic overtones. Encouraged by the Greek consul general, Alexis Kyrou, himself of Cypriot origin, church leaders and nationalist politicians agitated for enosis (union) with Greece. Venizelos was alarmed but failed to have Kyrou removed due to the latter's family connection to Foreign Minister Michalakopoulos. In late October, passions flared up and there was violence between Greek demonstrators and the colonial authorities. British repression provoked a spate of indignation in the Greek press and parliament. Venizelos took matters into his own hands. Greek vital interests, he warned, dictated a policy of 'undisturbed friendship' with Britain as well as Italy – a reference to the unredeemed Dodecanese. His forceful intervention staved off a diplomatic breach with London but was a boon to his domestic critics.[90]

The road to Ankara

In the aftermath of the Lausanne treaty, Venizelos had realised that the new territorial and ethnic realities offered a solid basis for burying the century-old antagonism between Greece and Turkey. In his own words: 'the treaty has definitely settled the territorial issue between the two countries. Indeed, Turkey has ceased to be an empire in order to become a nation state, while Greece has completed her national unification.'[91] There were no significant minorities which either side could use as an instrument of expansion. Their concerns, interests and objectives in the field of foreign policy were essentially compatible.

The only serious hurdle lay in the outstanding economic claims of both sides arising from the Convention for the Compulsory Exchange of Populations of 1923. After five years of bitter negotiations, the prospects for a settlement remained poor. The Turkish government appeared inclined to use the status of the ecumenical patriarch and the wealthy Greek community of Constantinople as bargaining chips. Moreover, the two governments sought to face the psychological divide between the two peoples, who had only too recently experienced the cruel realities of protracted war, occupation and ethnic cleansing.

Security considerations were paramount in Venizelos' attempt to promote Greek–Turkish conciliation. Collective security under the auspices of the League of Nations had proved a very imperfect mechanism, lacking the sanction of overwhelming power. There existed no multilateral arrangement which might credibly guarantee Greek security. As has been noted, Venizelos refused to enter into a bilateral alliance with any one Great Power and risk incurring the enmity of another. Greece faced the revisionist claims of Bulgaria, the hegemonic aspirations of Yugoslavia, and Albanian high-handedness vis-à-vis the Greek minority living in the south. Turkey was the only neighbour which appeared satisfied with the territorial status quo. The Greek government also took into account its extensive defence requirements. The incipient naval arms race with Turkey clearly militated against the urgent needs of economic reconstruction and refugee rehabilitation, the modernisation of the state and, last but not least, the survival and well-being of the Greek minority and the Ecumenical Patriarchate in Istanbul.[92]

The Greek–Turkish rapprochement was favoured by similar considerations on the other side of the Aegean. The regime of Mustafa Kemal understood security as entailing the balancing of Great Power influence in the region and rejected bilateral commitments. A legacy of suspicion towards the great European powers died hard. In Kemal's words, Turkey's national policy ought 'to work within our national boundaries for real happiness and the welfare of our nation and the country by relying above all on our own strength in order to maintain our existence'. Above all, his regime was grappling with the formidable tasks of a far-reaching domestic experiment, a peculiar mixture of modernisation, nationalism, secularism, populism and statism, against the challenge of a deep-rooted Islamic culture and anti-Kemalist uprisings.[93]

In 1928, the international diplomatic setting also appeared conducive to a rapprochement. In an effort to expand its influence, Rome saw fit to champion a Greek–Turkish understanding. The British also favoured a rapprochement in principle, mindful of possible adverse repercussions of an increase in either Italian or Soviet influence in the region. Yet they failed to take an active interest. In sum, external factors acted as accelerators at best.[94] The conciliation process was first and foremost sustained by the hard-headed realism and leadership qualities of Venizelos and his Turkish counterparts.

In the wake of his election, in August 1928, Venizelos wrote a cordial letter to the Turkish prime minister, İsmet Paşa (later İnönü), proposing a treaty of friendship, non-aggression and arbitration. According to the Greek leader, there were no outstanding issues other than those arising from the exchange of populations. The time has come, he argued, to terminate once and for all the legacy of conflict in the interest of both countries and international peace. İsmet's reply was positive.[95] Yet it would take more than two years of stiff bargaining before the two governments were able to hammer out an agreement. Turkish negotiators dug their heels on the financial issue. Any settlement was bound to affect the lot of more than a million Greek refugees. The political stakes for Venizelos cannot be exaggerated. A swing of the refugee vote could have obliterated the Venizelist majority in many regions. Yet the Cretan leader decided to maintain his course. As he later put it in parliament: 'If public opinion does not agree with me, I mean to educate it and not to be dragged by it.'[96]

In the event, Venizelos decided to brush aside Greece's economic claims from the properties of the 'exchanged' persons. He accepted a clearing agreement whereby Greece undertook to pay a considerable excess that satisfied Turkish demands over liquidated properties. This, of course, would cost him politically.[97] It was the price Venizelos was prepared to pay in order to improve the country's security and relieve its future from a sterile antagonism with her neighbour to the east. His momentous decision was vindicated by the fact that his domestic opponents, having reaped benefits from domestic resentment, followed on Venizelos' heels and further strengthened relations with Turkey.[98]

The Ankara agreements, signed on 30 October 1930, included a number of important legal instruments, which could serve as a model for peaceful relations. According to the Pact of Friendship, Neutrality, Conciliation and Judicial Settlement, any bilateral dispute, legal or otherwise, should be submitted to a commission of conciliation and, failing this, to the International Court of Justice or another, commonly agreed judicial body. This was in conformity with the peaceful settlement of disputes enshrined in the League of Nations Covenant.[99] Under the Protocol on the Limitation of Naval Armaments the two states undertook to give six-months notice before proceeding with the acquisition of new vessels 'in order to enable themselves to prevent, if possible, a naval arms race through friendly consultation'. This agreement enabled Venizelos to cancel the procurement of an expensive battleship. A tribute to his farsightedness, he initiated a balanced programme focusing on swift destroyers, submarines and air units.[100] Finally, the Convention on Settlement, Commerce and Navigation provided that citizens of the two countries could enter, reside and settle in the respective territories without limitations other than those existing for native citizens. Although this convention permitted only the individual settlement of persons and enterprises and effectively precluded the return of refugees, Venizelos hoped that, in due course, Greeks would be able to return to Asia Minor in numbers.[101]

Venizelos was quick to announce the end of the long legacy of hostility between the two states. Replying to the critics of the Ankara agreements in parliament, he proclaimed: 'The struggle between Greece and Turkey, let us call it a "trial", has lasted seven centuries. Now, a final verdict has been issued, the Treaty of Lausanne. I do not intend either to lodge an appeal or to seek a new hearing of the case; and I suggest that you do the same.' [102] Indeed, the new relationship could only take root provided that both sides respected its political and territorial cornerstone, the Treaty of Lausanne. Perhaps Venizelos did not share the elation of the Turkish foreign minister, Tevfik Rüştü, who, after the signing of the 1930 pact, envisioned the day, 'when [the Greek–Turkish] borders will lose their present worth, and will acquire a purely administrative significance'.[103] Greek and Turkish leaders above all perceived a community of interests on the two sides of the Aegean. As İsmet put it: 'Turkey and Greece are obliged to work in a spirit of understanding at any event in the Balkans and the eastern Mediterranean basin, where their interests manifestly coincide.'[104] The survival of the new spirit primarily rested on this assumption.

The art of the impossible: conciliation in the Balkans

The rapprochement with Turkey, Venizelos repeatedly stated, could serve as a model for an understanding among all Balkan states. It has been noted that the Cretan leader had no time for local security pacts designed to contain revisionist forces in the region. He knew only too well that, given the opportunity, the intervention of a great European power could easily overturn local balances. He envisaged a gradual process, which might engage all the states of the region and provide long-term stability. As a first step, he proposed bilateral treaties of friendship and peaceful settlement of disputes among all Balkan states. Second, existing frontiers should be recognised and guaranteed by all against an attack from within the region. Third, all states could pledge 'benevolent neutrality' in case of conflict between any one of them and a non-Balkan power. This scheme he confided to İsmet during his visit to Ankara in October 1930. Both statesmen realised that success hinged on Bulgarian participation.[105]

The prospect of a settlement was in line with Venizelos' view that conciliation between Bulgaria and her neighbours was an absolute prerequisite for regional peace and stability. Thus he was prepared to go some way towards meeting Bulgarian discontent with the post-war settlement, short of a revision of frontiers. The task was all the more daunting as he had to carry Belgrade and Bucharest with his plans. Apart from the Bulgarians' underlying rejection of the territorial settlement, progress stumbled upon the question of minorities.[106] Under the influence of the Internal Macedonian Revolutionary Organisation (IMRO), the Sofia government insisted upon the recognition of minority rights for ethnic Bulgarians in Greece and Yugoslavia. A similar situation existed with Romania on account of southern Dobrudja. What was more, Venizelos did not see eye to eye with his own minister for foreign affairs. Assuming this post in July 1929, Michalakopoulos came out in favour of a tough line towards the Bulgarians. It was quite doubtful, he argued, that concessions of the kind suggested by Venizelos would ever compel Sofia to reverse its policy, at least as long as IMRO remained entrenched within the government and the security apparatus.[107]

A Bulgarian démarche on the minority issue was rejected by the Greek government in early 1929. The matter was brought up again when the Greek and Bulgarian foreign ministers met at Geneva, in September 1930. Replying to his Bulgarian colleague, Michalakopoulos explained that a Greek concession of minority rights was certain to upset Greek–Yugoslav relations, as it had been the case with the Politis–Kalfov agreement of 1924. That agreement had not been implemented largely thanks to

Venizelos' defence of the Greek *volte-face* before the Council of the League of Nations. Ever since, any hint at the recognition of a Bulgarian minority in Greek Macedonia raised the alarm in Belgrade as implying the existence of a population of similar ethnic outlook in Yugoslav Macedonia. Michalakopoulos, however, did not exclude the prospect of the question being considered anew, provided that Bulgaria unequivocally and publicly recognized the territorial settlement of the Neuilly Peace Treaty as final.[108]

Determined to press ahead, Venizelos ventured to communicate his ideas to Yugoslav foreign minister Marinković, during the latter's visit to Athens in December 1930. Invoking his own record of Greek–Turkish conciliation, the Greek premier suggested that a Bulgarian minority could be recognised in southern Yugoslavia and implied that Greece would act likewise; in return, Sofia should formally declare its respect for the existing frontiers and ensure that the subversive activities of IMRO were terminated. To this end, the good offices of the Great Powers of Europe, Britain in particular, and Turkey could be forthcoming. Far from being seduced, Marinković curtly rejected the formula and stated that any hint about minorities would be interpreted as unacceptable interference in Yugoslav domestic affairs.[109]

Greek–Bulgarian difficulties were further compounded by a set of economic problems. With regard to the question of a Bulgarian commercial outlet on the Aegean coast, Sofia ignored Venizelos' offer of a free zone either at Thessaloniki or Alexandroupolis, an offer the Greek statesman had first tendered during his brief tenure of office in early 1924. His offer apparently lost some of its attraction as a viable option in view of the stiff opposition of the Greek general staff to the idea of extending the railway connection to the Bulgarian border. Some progress was achieved towards the definition of mutual financial obligations arising from the Convention of Mutual Emigration of 1919. Despite serious misgivings in the press and parliament, Venizelos upheld the agreement reached between the Greek and Bulgarian finance ministers, Kafantaris and Mollov, in December 1927. Thus, Greece undertook to meet the outstanding balance after the liquidation of property claims by ethnic Greeks and Bulgarians who had chosen to emigrate to their respective 'motherlands'. Still, Athens made this conditional upon the payment of the considerable Bulgarian war reparations. An agreement was reached on this score in January 1930, and the Bulgarian government agreed to pay an annuity of an average 11 million francs over a period of thirty-six years. As far as other bilateral issues were concerned, Sofia rejected the Greek proposal that, in keeping with the League of Nations Covenant, they be submitted to international arbitration.[110]

The Great Depression afforded Sofia an opportunity to desist from fulfilling its financial obligations. As soon as the Hoover Plan for a one-year moratorium of international debts was announced, in July 1931, the payment of Bulgarian reparations was suspended. Retaliating, the Greek government withheld all disbursements under the Kafantaris–Mollov agreement. In late 1931, the work of the Mixed Commission of Emigration, set up by the 1919 convention, was terminated without settling a number of outstanding issues. Those were subsequently referred to the finance committee of the League of Nations to little practical avail. The spiralling financial dispute precluded the renewal of the bilateral commercial agreement, which expired at the end of 1931. As a result, Bulgarian products suffered from a tenfold increase in Greek tariffs, a symptom of the protectionist mood of the depression era. The impact was severe, as Greece absorbed nearly one fifth of Bulgarian exports at the time. In a sense, Venizelos' efforts towards a Greek–Bulgarian rapprochement, like many of his domestic plans, fell victim to the world economic crisis.[111]

The crisis and the parochial outlook of the foreign policies of most European powers also precluded the fruition of the plan for European economic and political co-operation, which French prime minister Briand advanced in September 1929. The response of the Greek government was unreservedly positive and, significantly, urged the inclusion of Turkey in the process. Yet it is unlikely that Venizelos, being a pragmatist, did not realise the poor prospects of the plan. Nonetheless, he was ever ready to endorse similar initiatives on a regional level, without undue optimism, of course.[112]

This was the case with the Balkan conferences, the first of which was convened in Athens in 1930. It was championed by Alexandros Papanastasiou, former associate of Venizelos and leader of a splinter Venizelist group. Four successive annual conferences were held in various cities between 1930 and 1933 – with a last, unofficial meeting in Athens in 1934. The participants were not technically government representatives but they were expected to defend their respective national policies. Almost inevitably, progress was hampered by existing differences, mostly related to the territorial settlement of the last wars. The Bulgarian delegation straightaway raised the question of minorities. Only Albania was willing to discuss it. This led the Bulgarians to withdraw from the Bucharest conference of 1932.[113] The rise of revisionist powers on the European scene and the clinging of the status quo Balkan states to a narrow concept of security would preclude further progress towards a regional understanding along the lines envisioned by Venizelos: respect for the rights of national minorities in return for recognition of the territorial settlement.

NOTES

1. Grigorios Daphnis (1974), *I Ellas metaxy ton dyo polemon, 1923–1940* [*Greece between the Two Wars, 1923–1940*], 2nd edn, Athens, vol. I, pp. 371–3.
2. Ibid., p. 375.
3. Ibid., pp. 372, 375–80; G. Christopoulos and I. Bastias (eds) (1978), *Istoria tou ellinikou ethnous* [*History of the Greek Nation*], vol. XV: *Neoteros ellinismos apo to 1913 os to 1941* [*Modern Hellenism from 1913 to 1941*], Athens, pp. 310–12.
4. Daphnis, *I Ellas*, vol. I, pp. 381–96 (see Note 1).
5. Ibid., pp. 389–96; George Th. Mavrogordatos (1983), *Stillborn Republic: Social Coalitions and Party Strategies in Greece, 1922–1936*, Berkeley, pp. 36–7.
6. Christopoulos and Bastias (eds), *Istoria*, vol. XV, pp. 313–14 (see Note 3).
7. Daphnis, *I Ellas,* vol. I, pp. 375–6, 385–6 (see Note 1).
8. Mavrogordatos, *Stillborn Republic*, pp. 82–3 (see Note 5).
9. Ibid., p. 86.
10. G. Mavrogordatos (1982), *Meletes kai keimena gia tin periodo 1909–1940* [*Studies and Documents on the Period 1909–1940*], Athens, pp. 55–77; Mavrogordatos, *Stillborn Republic*, pp. 95–6, 181 (see Note 5).
11. Daphnis, *I Ellas*, vol. II, pp. 8–17, 20–9 (see Note 1); Christopoulos and Bastias (eds), *Istoria*, vol. XV, pp. 314–16 (see Note 3).
12. Thanos Veremis (1977), *Oi epemvaseis tou stratou stin elliniki politiki, 1916–1936* [*The Interventions of the Military in Greek Politics*], Athens, pp. 201–3.
13. Daphnis, *I Ellas,* vol. II, pp. 32–3 (see Note 1); Iphigenia Anastasiadou (1980), 'O Venizelos kai to ellinotourkiko symphono philias tou 1930' ['Venizelos and the Greek–Turkish Pact of Friendship of 1930'], in O. Dimitrakopoulos and Th. Veremis (eds), *Meletimata gyro apo ton Venizelo kai tin epochi tou* [*Studies on Venizelos and His Time*], Athens, pp. 344–6.
14. Andreas A. Gazis (1992), 'O Eleftherios Venizelos kai to idiotiko dikaio' ['Eleftherios Venizelos and Private Law'], in G. Mavrogordatos and Ch. Hadjiiosif (eds), *Venizelismos kai astikos eksynchronismos* [*Venizelism and Bourgeois Modernisation*], Irakleio, 2nd edn, pp. 58–65.
15. Daphnis, *I Ellas,* vol. II, pp. 97–8 (see Note 1); Christos Hadjiiosif (1992), 'I venizelogenis antipolitefsi sto Venizelo kai i politiki anasyntaxi tou astismou sto mesopolemo' ['The Venizelist Opposition to Venizelos and the Political Reorganisation of Bourgeois Forces in the Inter-War Period'], in Mavrogordatos and Hadjiiosif (eds), *Venizelismos*, p. 443 (see Note 14).

16. Alexis Dimaras (1992), 'Charaktiristika astikou phileleftherismou sta ekpaideftika programmata ton kyverniseon tou Venizelou' ['Traits of Bourgeois Liberalism in the Educational Programmes of the Venizelos Governments'], in Mavrogordatos and Hadjiiosif (eds), *Venizelismos*, pp. 27–31 (see Note 14); Daphnis, *I Ellas*, vol. II, pp. 84, 98 (see Note 1).
17. Daphnis, *I Ellas*, vol. II, p. 17 (see Note 1).
18. Nikos Alivizatos (1983), *Oi politikoi thesmoi se krisi, 1922–1974: Opseis tis ellinikis empeirias* [*The Political Institutions in Crisis, 1922–1974: Aspects of the Greek Experience*], Athens, pp. 347–61.
19. Ibid., pp. 385–91; Mavrogordatos, *Stillborn Republic*, pp. 145–6 (see Note 5).
20. Angelos G. Elephantis (1979), *I epaggelia tis adynatis epanastasis: KKE kai astismos ston mesopolemo* [*The Promise of the Impossible Revolution: The Greek Communist Party and Bourgeois Forces in the Inter-War Period*], Athens, 2nd edn, pp. 85–120; Mavrogordatos, *Stillborn Republic*, pp. 92–3 (see Note 5).
21. Mavrogordatos, *Stillborn Republic*, p. 144 (see Note 5).
22. Ibid., pp. 141–2, 146–52.
23. Antonis Liakos (1988), ' "Apo kratos phylax eis kratos pronoia": Oi parametroi tis ergatikis politikis sto mesopolemo' [' "From the Guardian State to the Welfare State": The Parameters of Labour Policy in the Inter-War Period'], *Symposio yia ton Eleftherio Venizelo. Praktika* [*Symposium on Eleftherios Venizelos. Proceedings*], Athens, pp. 169–79; Liakos (1992), 'O Eleftherios Venizelos kai to diethnes grapheio ergasias' ['Eleftherios Venizelos and the International Labour Bureau'], in Mavrogordatos and Hadjiiosif (eds), *Venizelismos*, pp. 262–70 (see Note 14).
24. Hadjiiosif, 'I Venizelogenis antipolitefsi sto Venizelo', p. 444 (see Note 15).
25. Bank of Greece (1978), *Ta prota peninta chronia tis Trapezis tis Ellados, 1928–1978* [*The First Fifty Years of the Bank of Greece, 1928–1978*], Athens, pp. 59–61; Christopoulos and Bastias (eds), *Istoria*, vol. XV, p. 333 (see Note 3); Mark Mazower (1989), 'I Ellada kai i oikonomiki krisi tou 1931' ['Greece and the 1931 Economic Crisis'], in Th. Veremis and Y. Goulimi (eds), *Eleftherios Venizelos: Koinonia–oikonomia–politiki stin epochi tou* [*Eleftherios Venizelos: Society–Economy–Politics in his Age*], Athens, pp. 230–1.
26. Bank of Greece, *Ta prota peninta chronia*, pp. 61–70 (see Note 25); Daphnis, *I Ellas*, vol. I, pp. 364–9 (see Note 1).
27. Christopoulos and Bastias (eds), *Istoria*, vol. XV, pp. 334–5 (see Note 3).
28. Mavrogordatos, *Stillborn Republic*, p. 168 (see Note 5).
29. Daphnis, *I Ellas*, vol. II, pp. 86–9 (see Note 1).
30. Christopoulos and Bastias (eds), *Istoria*, vol. XV, p. 335 (see Note 3); M. Mazower (1992), 'Oikonomiki politiki stin Ellada' ['Economic Policy in Greece'], in Mavrogordatos and Hadjiiosif (eds), *Venizelismos*, p. 180 (see Note 14).

31. Ioanna Pepelassi-Minoglou (1988), 'O Venizelos kai to xeno kephalaio, 1918–1932' ['Venizelos and Foreign Capital, 1918–1932'], in *Symposio*, p. 160 (see Note 23).
32. Daphnis, *I Ellas*, vol. II, pp. 90–1 (see Note 1); Chrysos Evelpidis (1950), *Oikonomiki kai koinoniki istoria tis Ellados* [*Economic and Social History of Greece*], Athens, p. 71; Christopoulos and Bastias (eds), *Istoria tou ellinikou ethnous*, vol. XV, p. 332 (see Note 3); Mavrogordatos, *Stillborn Republic*, pp. 163–8 (see Note 5).
33. Daphnis, *I Ellas*, vol. II, pp. 86–91 (see Note 1); Christopoulos and Bastias (eds), *Istoria*, vol. XV, p. 333 (see Note 3); Mazower (1989), 'I Ellada kai i oikonomiki krisi tou 1931', in Veremis and Goulimi (eds), *Venizelos*, p. 181 (see Note 25).
34. Nikos Melios and Apostolos Papadopoulos (1992), 'To kopaidiko zitima sta plaisia tou astikou eksynchronismou kai tis agrotikis metarithmisis' ['The Copais Question in the Context of Bourgeois Modernisation and Rural Reform'], in Mavrogordatos – Hadjiiosif (eds), *Venizelismos*, pp. 159–69 (see Note 14).
35. Costas Costis (1989), 'I elliniki oikonomia sta chronia tis krisis 1929–1932' ['The Greek Economy during the Years of the Crisis 1929–1932'], in Veremis and Goulimi (eds), *Venizelos*, pp. 217–18 (see Note 25); Pepelassi-Minoglou, 'O Venizelos kai to xeno kephalaio', in *Symposio*, p. 159 (see Note 23).
36. Bank of Greece, *Ta protа peninta chronia*, pp. 107–8 (see Note 25); Christopoulos and Bastias (eds), *Istoria*, vol. XV, p. 337 (see Note 3); Costis, 'I elliniki oikonomia sta chronia tis krisis', in Veremis and Goulimi (eds), *Venizelos*, p. 214 (see Note 25).
37. Evelpidis, *Oikonomiki kai koinoniki istoria*, pp. 104–5 (see Note 32); Christopoulos and Bastias (eds). *Istoria*, vol. XV, pp. 336–7 (see Note 3); Mazower, 'I Ellada kai i oikonomiki krisi tou 1931', in Veremis and Goulimi (eds), *Venizelos*, pp. 172–3 (see Note 25).
38. Olga Christodoulaki (2001), 'Industrial Growth in Greece between the Wars: A New Perspective', *European Review of Economic History* 5, pp. 72–8; Mark Mazower (1991), *Greece and the Interwar Economic Crisis*, Oxford, p. 311. See also, Christopoulos and Bastias (eds), *Istoria*, vol. XV, pp. 338–40 (see Note 3).
39. Costis, 'I elliniki oikonomia sta chronia tis krisis', in Veremis and Goulimi (eds), *Venizelos*, pp. 190–226 (see Note 25).
40. Bank of Greece, *Ta prota peninta chronia*, pp. 102–7 (see Note 25); Christopoulos and Bastias (eds), *Istoria*, vol. XV, p. 341 (see Note 3).
41. Costis, 'I elliniki oikonomia sta chronia tis krisis', in Veremis and Goulimi (eds), *Venizelos*, pp. 217–20 (see Note 25).
42. Bank of Greece, *Ta prota peninta chronia*, pp. 102–7 (see Note 25).
43. Ibid., pp. 92–101, 148; Daphnis, *I Ellas*, vol. II, pp. 103–11 (see Note 1); Christopoulos and Bastias (eds), *Istoria*, vol. XV, pp. 328–9

(see Note 3); Costas A. Karamanlis (1995), *O Eleftherios Venizelos kai oi exoterikes mas scheseis, 1928–1932* [*Eleftherios Venizelos and our Foreign Relations, 1928–1932*], Athens, 2nd edn, pp. 280–6; Mazower, *Greece and the Interwar Economic Crisis*, pp. 143–76 (see Note 38).

44. Daphnis, *I Ellas,* vol. II, pp. 72–5 (see Note 1); Karamanlis, *O Eleftherios Venizelos,* pp. 251–5 (see Note 43).
45. Pepelassi-Minoglou, 'O Venizelos kai to xeno kefalaio', in *Symposio*, pp. 161–2 (see Note 23).
46. Bank of Greece, *Ta prota peninta chronia,* pp. 98–101 (see Note 25); Dafnis, *I Ellas,* vol. II, pp. 111–15, 125–231 (see Note 1); Christopoulos and Bastias (eds), *Istoria*, vol. XV, pp. 329 (see Note 3); Karamanlis, *O Eleftherios Venizelos*, pp. 288–308 (see Note 43).
47. Daphnis, *I Ellas,* vol. II, pp. 118–25 (see Note 1); Karamanlis, *O Eleftherios Venizelos,* pp. 308–12, 316–18 (see Note 43); Mazower, 'I Ellada kai i oikonomiki krisi tou 1931', in Veremis and Goulimi (eds), *Venizelos*, pp. 264–6 (see Note 25).
48. Mazower, 'I Ellada kai i oikonomiki krisi tou 1931', in Veremis and Goulimi (eds), *Venizelos*, pp. 269–70 (see Note 25).
49. Mazower, 'Oikonomiki politiki stin Ellada', in Mavrogordatos and Hadjiiosif (eds), *Venizelismos*, pp. 171–2 (see Note 14).
50. Costis, 'I elliniki oikonomia sta chronia tis krisis', in Veremis and Goulimi (eds), *Venizelos*, pp. 217–18 (see Note 25).
51. Evelpidis, *Oikonomiki kai koinoniki istoria*, pp. 70–1 (see Note 32); Christopoulos and Bastias (eds), *Istoria*, vol. XV, pp. 329–31 (see Note 3); Mazower, 'Oikonomiki politiki stin Ellada', in Mavrogordatos and Hadjiiosif (eds), *Venizelismos*, pp. 177–80 (see Note 14).
52. Christopoulos and Bastias (eds), *Istoria*, vol. XV, p. 329 (see Note 3).
53. Bank of Greece, *Ta prota peninta chronia,* pp. 107–8 (see Note 25); Mazower, 'I Ellada kai i oikonomiki krisi tou 1931', in Veremis and Goulimi (eds), *Venizelos*, pp. 268–71 (see Note 25); Mazower, 'Oikonomiki politiki stin Ellada', in Mavrogordatos and Hadjiiosif (eds), *Venizelismos*, pp. 176–7 (see Note 14).
54. Christopoulos and Bastias (eds), *Istoria*, vol. XV, pp. 341–2 (see Note 3). For a fresh approach to the impact of the world slump on the secondary sector of the Greek economy, based on revised indices, see Christodoulaki, 'Industrial Growth in Greece between the Wars: A New Perspective', pp. 72–8 (see Note 38).
55. Mavrogordatos, *Stillborn Republic*, pp. 135–6 (see Note 5).
56. Dimitri Pentzopoulos (1962), *The Balkan Exchange of Minorities and Its Impact upon Greece*, Paris and The Hague, pp. 125–67. For a concise account of the impact of refugees on the Greek economy see Gerasimos Augustinos (ed.) (1991), *Diverse Paths to Modernity in Southeastern Europe: Essays in National Development*, New York, pp. 93–8.
57. Margarita Dritsa (1989), 'Prosphyges kai ekviomichanisi' ['Refugees and

Industrialisation'], in Veremis and Goulimi (eds), *Venizelos*, pp. 29–70; Mavrogordatos, *Stillborn Republic*, pp. 156–61, 186–91 (see Note 5); Pentzopoulos, *The Balkan Exchange of Minorities*, pp. 95–119 (see Note 56).

58. Anastasiadou, 'O Venizelos kai to ellinotourkiko symphono philias tou 1930', in Dimitrakopoulos and Veremis (eds), *Meletimata*, pp. 322–31 (see Note 13); Mavrogordatos, *Stillborn Republic*, pp. 210–14 (see Note 5); Pentzopoulos, *The Balkan Exchange of Minorities*, pp. 117–19 (see Note 56).
59. Refugee politicians Leonidas Iasonidis and Emmanouil Emmanouilidis served on Venizelos' cabinets as did a number of native Venizelists with considerable refugee following, among them Ioannis Valalas from Kastoria, and Dimitrios Dingas and Alexandros Zannas from Thessaloniki.
60. Mavrogordatos, *Stillborn Republic*, pp. 198–206 (see Note 5); Pentzopoulos, *The Balkan Exchange of Minorities*, pp. 181–95 (see Note 56).
61. Mavrogordatos, *Stillborn Republic*, pp. 206–7 (see Note 5); Pentzopoulos, *The Balkan Exchange of Minorities*, pp. 173–7 (see Note 56).
62. Mavrogordatos, *Stillborn Republic*, pp. 79–80, 323–5 (see Note 5).
63. Ibid., pp. 90–3.
64. Ibid., pp. 330–1.
65. Daphnis, *I Ellas,* vol. II, p. 15 (see Note 1).
66. Ibid., pp. 8–17, 20–9.
67. Ibid., pp. 30–9, 116–17; Yiorgos Ploumidis (1980), 'Antivenizelika phylladia kai i politiki tous, 1910–1935' ['Anti-Venizelist Pamphlets and their Policy, 1910–1935'], in Dimitrakopoulos and Veremis (eds), *Meletimata*, pp. 617–20 (see Note 13).
68. Daphnis, *I Ellas,* vol. II, pp. 45–7 (see Note 1).
69. Quoted ibid., p. 132.
70. Alivizatos, *Oi politikoi thesmoi se krisi,* pp. 49–50, 61–2 (see Note 18); Alivizatos (1992), 'O Eleftherios Venizelos kai o syntagmatikos eksynchronismos tis choras' ['Eleftherios Venizelos and the Country's Constitutional Modernisation'], in Mavrogordatos and Hadjiiosif (eds), *Venizelismos*, pp. 37–8 (see Note 14); Hadjiiosif 'I venizelogenis antipolitefsi sto Venizelo', in the same book, p. 439, who claims that 'the failure of the programme of the Liberal Party indicated that under the circumstances the modernisation of Greek society was incompatible with political democracy'.
71. Daphnis, *I Ellas,* vol. II, pp. 134–7 (see Note 1).
72. Mavrogordatos, *Stillborn Republic*, p. 142 (see Note 5).
73. Daphnis, *I Ellas,* vol. II, pp. 143–4, 147–53 (see Note 1); Christopoulos and Bastias (eds), *Istoria*, vol. XV, pp. 318–19 (see Note 3).
74. Mavrogordatos, *Stillborn Republic*, pp. 335–7 (see Note 5).
75. Daphnis, *I Ellas,* vol. II, pp. 153–61 (see Note 1).
76. Ibid., p. 19.

77. Ibid., pp. 172–82; Christopoulos and Bastias (eds), *Istoria*, vol. XV, pp. 320–1 (see Note 3).
78. Constantine Svolopoulos (1977), *I elliniki exoteriki politiki meta tin Synthiki tis Lozanis: I krisimos kambi. Ioulios – Dekemvrios 1928* [*Greek Foreign Policy after the Lausanne Treaty: The Critical Turning Point, July–December 1928*], Thessaloniki.
79. Karamanlis, *O Eleftherios Venizelos*, p. 50 (see Note 43); Svolopoulos, *I elliniki exoteriki politiki*, pp. 52, 106–7 (see Note 78).
80. Karamanlis, *O Eleftherios Venizelos*, pp. 55–7 (see Note 43); Svolopoulos, *I elliniki exoteriki politiki*, pp. 54–9 (see Note 78).
81. Karamanlis, *O Eleftherios Venizelos*, pp. 56–7, 172–6 (see Note 43); Svolopoulos, *I elliniki exoteriki politiki*, pp. 60–2 (see Note 78).
82. Karamanlis, *O Eleftherios Venizelos*, pp. 57–60 (see Note 43); Svolopoulos, *I elliniki exoteriki politiki*, pp. 122–4 (see Note 78).
83. Greece, annual report for 1928, PRO, FO 371, 13659, C1763; Karamanlis, *O Eleftherios Venizelos*, pp. 60–1, 63–6 (see Note 43); Svolopoulos, *I elliniki exoteriki politiki*, pp. 125–40 (see Note 78).
84. Daphnis, *I Ellas*, vol. II, pp. 60–1 (see Note 1); Karamanlis, *O Eleftherios Venizelos*, pp. 67–70 (see Note 43); Greece, annual report for 1929, PRO, FO 371, 14391, C5972.
85. Svolopoulos, *I elliniki exoteriki politiki*, p. 157 (see Note 78).
86. Karamanlis, *O Eleftherios Venizelos*, pp. 58–60 (see Note 43); Svolopoulos, *I elliniki exoteriki politiki*, pp. 66–7, 72 (see Note 78).
87. Anastasiadou, 'O Venizelos kai to ellinotourkiko Symphono', in Dimitrakopoulos and Veremis (eds), *Meletimata*, pp. 340–3 (see Note 13); Karamanlis, *O Eleftherios Venizelos*, pp. 94–7 (see Note 43); Svolopoulos, *I elliniki exoteriki politiki*, pp. 150–2 (see Note 78).
88. Karamanlis, *O Eleftherios Venizelos*, pp. 229–47, 255–69 (see Note 43).
89. Daphnis, *I Ellas*, pp. 71–5 (see Note 1); Karamanlis, *O Eleftherios Venizelos*, pp. 247–55 (see Note 43).
90. Daphnis, *I Ellas*, pp. 75–83 (see Note 1); Karamanlis, *O Eleftherios Venizelos*, pp. 163–72 (see Note 43); Yannis P. Pikros (1980), *O Venizelos kai to Kypriako* [*Venizelos and the Cyprus Question*], Athens.
91. Anastasiadou, 'O Venizelos kai to ellinotourkiko Symphono', in Dimitrakopoulos and Veremis (eds), *Meletimata*, p. 339 (see Note 13).
92. Ibid., pp. 310–11; Karamanlis, *O Eleftherios Venizelos*, pp. 28, 33–4, 73–5 (see Note 43); Svolopoulos, *I elliniki exoteriki politiki*, pp. 19–21, 142–3 (see Note 78).
93. Feroz Ahmad (1993), *The Making of Modern Turkey*, London, pp. 66–7; Anastasiadou, 'O Venizelos kai to ellinotourkiko Symphono', in Dimitrakopoulos and Veremis (eds), *Meletimata*, pp. 331–2 (see Note 13); Evanthis Hatzivassiliou (1999), *O Eleftherios Venizelos, i ellinotourkiki prosenggisi kai to provlima tis asphaleias sta Valkania, 1928–1931* [*Eleftherios Venizelos, the Greek-Turkish Rapprochement and the Problem*

of Security in the Balkans, 1928–1931], Thessaloniki, pp. 47–8; Svolopoulos, *I elliniki exoteriki politiki*, pp. 143–4 (see Note 78).

94. Anastasiadou, 'O Venizelos kai to ellinotourkiko symphono', in Dimitrakopoulos and Veremis (eds), *Meletimata*, p. 316 (see Note 13); Karamanlis, *O Eleftherios Venizelos*, pp. 76–8, 89–90 (see Note 43); Svolopoulos, *I elliniki exoteriki politiki*, pp. 150–1 (see Note 78).
95. Svolopoulos, *I elliniki exoteriki politiki*, pp. 145–6 (see Note 78).
96. Anastasiadou, 'O Venizelos kai to ellinotourkiko Symphono', in Dimitrakopoulos and Veremis (eds), *Meletimata*, p. 373 (see Note 13).
97. Ibid., pp. 322–6, 347–9; Karamanlis, *O Eleftherios Venizelos*, pp. 81–4 (see Note 43).
98. Anastasiadou, 'O Venizelos kai to ellinotourkiko Symphono', in Dimitrakopoulos and Veremis (eds), *Meletimata*, p. 386 (see Note 13); Hatzivassiliou, *O Eleftherios Venizelos*, pp. 111–15 (see Note 93).
99. Anastasiadou, 'O Venizelos kai to ellinotourkiko Symphono', in Dimitrakopoulos and Veremis (eds), *Meletimata*, pp. 349–50 (see Note 13).
100. Ibid., pp. 350–6; Hatzivassiliou, *O Eleftherios Venizelos,* pp. 86–98 (see Note 93); Karamanlis, *O Eleftherios Venizelos*, pp. 85–9 (see Note 43).
101. Anastasiadou, 'O Venizelos kai to ellinotourkiko Symphono', in Dimitrakopoulos and Veremis (eds), *Meletimata*, pp. 356–66 (see Note 13).
102. Ibid., p. 385.
103. Ibid., p. 340.
104. Daphnis, *I Ellas*, p. 69 (see Note 1).
105. Karamanlis, *O Eleftherios Venizelos*, pp. 128–9 (see Note 43); Panayotis Pipinelis (1948), *Istoria tis exoterikis politikis tis Ellados, 1923–41* [*History of the Foreign Policy of Greece, 1923–41*], Athens, p. 85.
106. On the issue of minorities in Greece's relations with her Balkan neighbours, see Lena Divani (1995), *Ellada kai meionotites: To systima diethnous prostasias tis Koinonias ton Ethnon* [*Greece and Minorities: The System of International Protection under the League of Nations*], Athens.
107. Karamanlis, *O Eleftherios Venizelos*, pp. 112–13 (see Note 43).
108. Ibid., pp. 103, 106.
109. Ibid., pp. 109, 131–3; Greece, annual report for 1930, PRO FO 371, 15237, C882; N. Henderson to A. Henderson, Belgrade, 21 April 1931, PRO FO 286, 1105/189; Waterlow to A. Henderson, Sofia, 7 May 1931, FO 286, 1105/189; Ramsay to A. Henderson, Athens, 20 June 1931, PRO FO 286, 1105/189.
110. Karamanlis, *O Eleftherios Venizelos kai oi exoterikes mas scheseis*, pp. 102, 105–8 (see Note 43); Consular Reports, Thessaloniki, August 1929, October 1929, PRO, FO 286, 1052; Greece, annual report for 1930, PRO FO 371, 15237, C882.
111. Karamanlis, *O Eleftherios Venizelos kai oi exoterikes mas scheseis*, pp. 108–9, 136–42, 277–9 (see Note 43); Greece, annual report for 1932, PRO, FO 371, 16774, C 1121.

112. Dimitri Kitsikis (1965), 'La Grèce et le projet Briand', *Revue d'Histoire Moderne et Contemporaine* 12, pp. 203–17; C. Svolopoulos (1988), 'L'attitude de la Grèce vis à vis du projet Briand d'union fédérale de l'Europe', *Balkan Studies* 29 (1988), pp. 29–38.
113. Karamanlis, *O Eleftherios Venizelos kai oi exoterikes mas scheseis*, pp. 142–3 (see Note 43); Prokopis Papastratis, 'Apo ti megali idea sti Valkaniki Enosi' ['From Great Idea to Balkan Union'], in Mavrogordatos and Hadjiiosif (eds), *Venizelismos*, pp. 417–38; L. S. Stavrianos (1944), *Balkan Federation: A History of the Movement toward Balkan Unity in Modern Times*, Northampton, pp. 230–7; C. Svolopoulos (1987), 'O Alexandros Papanastasiou kai i diavalkaniki synennoisi' ['Alexandros Papanastasiou and Inter-Balkan Understanding'], in G. Anastasiadis, G. Kontoyorgis and P. Petridis (eds), *Alexandros Papanastasiou: Thesmoi, ideologia kai politiki sto mesopolemo* [*Alexandros Papanastasiou: Institutions, Ideology and Politics in the Inter-War Years*], Athens, pp. 393, 395, 398; Greece, annual report for 1930, PRO, FO 371, 15237, C 882; Greece, annual report for 1931, PRO FO 371, 15970, C 1621; Greece, annual report for 1932, PRO FO 371, 16774, C 1121.

7

The Last Years, 1933–6

Ioannis S. Koliopoulos

Venizelos departed from the Greek political scene as he had entered it: in the wake of a military coup. Unlike the other great statesman of twentieth-century Greece, Constantine Karamanlis, who did everything in his power to abstain from activities that called into question constitutional legality, Venizelos more than once acted under the conviction that political requirement must occasionally be allowed to prevail over legitimate government. Unlike Karamanlis also, who prepared for himself the place in history he thought appropriate for a great statesman, Venizelos did not appear to care much about how posterity would judge his actions. From the point of view of respect for established institutions, then, Venizelos belonged to a set of new men, like Camilo di Cavour and Otto von Bismarck, who believed that their nation's interest justified all means, including revolution against legitimate authority. Like Karamanlis, however, he was neither a convinced republican nor a staunch supporter of the monarchy; both were prepared to support either the monarchy or the republic as long as the hereditary or the elected head of state did not seriously question their definition of the national interest, perhaps because both had little faith in the capacity of either regime to function properly without a strong man, in a country lacking either a strong monarchical or republican tradition.

Venizelos' electoral defeat in March 1933 caused an abortive military coup headed by Nikolaos Plastiras, a man too closely identified with Venizelos to be considered, by Venizelists no less than by anti-Venizelists, an independent agent. Plastiras had visions of his own 'march on Athens', after Mussolini's 'march on Rome', but it is very doubtful that he had kept Venizelos in the dark, although there is no evidence, either, to show that the elder statesman encouraged Plastiras in this course of action. Venizelos had little faith in Plastiras' political judgement and in his capacity to seize power in 1933, let alone to establish a Mussolinian dictatorship. The Venizelists were divided among themselves more than their opponents and had lost considerable ground in the electorate. Soon they were to lose their bases of support in the armed forces of the country, as a result of the failed coup of March 1933 and of a similarly failed coup of March 1935, which was a much more serious undertaking and had far more serious consequences than the 1933 one.

The anti-Venizelist government seized the opportunity, following the suppression of the Plastiras coup, to cashier a fair number of army officers believed to be his associates and to promote its own favourites to take the place of the dismissed men. Ever since the National Schism of 1916, governments in Greece had had frequent recourse to this means of strengthening their position vis-à-vis their political opponents. Building one's base of support in the armed forces to the loss of opponents, although condemned by everyone, had been used by opposing political camps with the same end in mind: to use this support in order to stay in power.[1]

The furore caused by the March 1933 coup had hardly subsided, when a more shocking event brought political passions to a boil: an attempt in June to assassinate Venizelos. This act against the life of the leader of opposition, as well as the circumstances in which it occurred – the would-be assassins chased Venizelos' car on the road leading from Kifissia to Athens and riddled it with bullets, with no police intervention – shocked the Venizelist political camp and convinced its leadership that it was the ruling party which was after Venizelos' life.

The motives behind the assassination attempt, maintained Venizelos in a carefully prepared assessment of the incident, were political. Ever since he had come back to Greek politics in 1928, the anti-Venizelist press had been preaching his physical destruction as the only way to free Greece from his calamitous influence, and the anti-Venizelist political leadership had never unequivocally condemned these incitements to murder. No doubt Prime Minister Panagis Tsaldaris would never have approved of political murder as a means of dealing with political opposition; all the same, he and other anti-Venizelist leaders had not come out against editorial incitement to murder, perhaps because they did not want to lose the support even of those who inspired such editorials. In addition to the moral responsibility for the attempt on his life, Venizelos charged the government of complicity in the act for allowing the director of public security, Ioannis Polychronopoulos, to involve himself in the organisation of the criminal act. Polychronopoulos' dismissal and arrest, instead of allaying Venizelos' anger, raised the volume of attacks against the government, for the arrested man was a high-ranking member of the ruling party and had been chosen by the government.[2]

The situation further deteriorated as a result of an electoral court decision, which invalidated the election of the twenty Thessaloniki members of the chamber, of whom eighteen were Venizelists. The court decided that the electoral law under which the Thessaloniki deputies had been elected was unconstitutional, because it provided for the separate election of Jewish deputies. This law, which was the work of a Venizelist government and aimed at circumscribing Jewish electoral power, had turned Thessaloniki into a Venizelist preserve by neutralising the heavily anti-Venizelist Jewish electorate of the city. The repeat election in July 1933, which was conducted after abolishing the separate Jewish electoral colleges, dashed the government's hopes of reducing Venizelist power in a Venizelist stronghold: the Venizelists won all twenty seats. The shock and revulsion caused by the attempt on Venizelos' life had turned even moderate anti-Venizelist public opinion against the government and deprived it of its two Thessaloniki seats.[3]

More disquieting than the government's losses in the Thessaloniki repeat election was the opposition's making the question of the regime an electoral issue. The reason for raising this question, according to Venizelos, was an interview the exiled king of Greece, George II, had given in the spring of the same year, in which the interviewer had been left with the impression that King George, although unwilling to press for his return to Greece, had never renounced his rights to the Greek throne. This position of the exiled monarch, which did not really represent a shift from his previous position, was seized upon by Venizelos and projected as an indication of King George's intention to reclaim the Greek throne; which, in conjuction with various statements of royalist anti-Venizelists to the same effect, constituted a threat to the republic.

Venizelos' assessment of royalist pronouncements was made for the purpose of checking centrifugal forces within the Venizelist camp, as the defence of the republic was perhaps the issue on which all Venizelist leaders agreed. All available evidence suggests that royalist pronouncements of the type mentioned above did not pose a real threat to the republic. The Popular Party of Panagis Tsaldaris and the other anti-Venizelist parties had solemnly agreed, before assuming power, to rule within the constitution of the republic and to uphold the republic. Tsaldaris was a moderate politician and a convinced parliamentarian; he was certain that what Greece really needed was not another upheaval over the regime of the country but good and honest government. No doubt old royalists felt otherwise, but Tsaldaris' position in the party was strong and secure. The only real threats to the republic at the time were actions like the one Plastiras had taken in March of 1933 or the attempt on Venizelos' life three months later, as well as attempts to make capital of royalist pronouncements by enlarging the threat these pronouncements represented.

In the autumn of 1933 and on the occasion of a rather protracted debate on the question of an amnesty for the Venizelist politicians who had been charged with complicitiy in the Plastiras coup, Tsaldaris saw the amnesty as an opportunity for an agreement with Venizelos to shelve both the Plastiras coup and the attempt on Venizelos's life, in order to defuse a rather dangerous political situation. Tsaldaris was in a position to assess the dangers inherent in a protracted confrontation between diehards of both camps and was prepared to unhook Venizelists involved in the March coup if Venizelos agreed to drop the issue of anti-Venizelist involvement in the assassination attempt. Both issues threatened to destabilise political life, since they strengthened the position of diehards in both political camps. Venizelos refused to meet Tsaldaris halfway, because he correctly estimated that a compromise like the one his opponent suggested would have strengthened moderate elements in the government and facilitated Tsaldaris' aim of governing free from pressure from anti-Venizelist extremists.[4]

For the next two years, Venizelos avoided a compromise and was set on unseating his political opponents, because he was convinced that they were scheming for the downfall of the republic and the establishment of a royal dictatorship. The dismissal of Venizelist officers involved in the Plastiras coup and the promotion of anti-Venizelists to key positions in the armed forces were proof to him of the government's aim of undermining the Venizelist base of support in the services. It was a correct assessment of the government's aim, as it rested on assumptions and practices deeply embedded in the political system since the National Schism. The assessment turned into a self-fulfilling prophecy, as it denied Venizelos the flexibility required to prevent the further deterioration of the situation. He chose instead to encourage hardline Venizelists in the armed forces to prepare for the defence of the republic, allocating to them a role no prudent political leader should and making himself a captive of men whose main concern was not so much the defence of the republic but their own narrow professional interests and dreams of glory.

Prudence, however, does not seem to have been one of Venizelos' strongest qualities, and lack of prudence at that crucial juncture proved calamitous for the country. The ageing statesman, after so many years of identification with Greece's fortunes and after all his extraordinary service to his countrymen, could not bring himself to accept a lesser role, nor could he put distance between himself and the pursuits and interests of his past associates. Venizelos had come to believe that he was indispensable to Greece, and missed an opportunity to leave behind the role of the rebel and settle for that of the elder and wise statesman.

It is not certain, of course, that Venizelos' compliance with the suggestion shelving both divisive issues would have checked the deterioration of the political situation. It is not unlikely that Venizelist diehards would have gone on with their dark pursuits even without Venizelos' encouragement or consent – one group of them at least made no secret of their impatience with constitutional government. It is equally unlikely that a gentlemen's agreement between Tsaldaris and Venizelos would have prevented old and new royalist zealots from pursuing their own ends. The greatest threat to the country's constitutional government did not emanate from the nearly twenty-year-old division between two hostile camps but from extremist elements in both camps conspiring for permanent one-party rule.

Events followed a predictable course: military officers involved in the Plastiras coup were dismissed, while Venizelist politicians charged with complicity in the coup were amnestied. It is worth noting in this respect that Venizelist hardliners did not shed many tears for the eclipse of a set of high-ranking associates of Plastiras, who lacked a proper military education and like their patron had climbed in the hierarchy through party favouritism. Equally predictable was the outcome of the other divisive issue, the attempt on Venizelos' life: short of hard evidence and with the authorities obstructing the inquiry, the Venizelists were unable to bring the culprits to justice. The inconclusive inquiry poisoned political life and pushed the two camps further apart.

In foreign affairs the government of the Popular Party tried not to depart from the policy Venizelos had initiated in 1928. Greece's bilateral pacts with Italy, Yugoslavia and Turkey, which Venizelos had negotiated and signed in the years 1928–30, were considered adequate security arrangements against revisionist Bulgaria. In the autumn of 1933, however, Yugoslavia and Romania sounded out Turkey and Greece on the signing of a joint Balkan pact, which the Greek government appeared to favour. Venizelos, too, was not opposed to a Balkan pact, as long as it did not in any way antagonise Italy and did include Bulgaria, and made certain of informing the government of these two terms, which he considered of cardinal importance. Without Bulgaria and with an irritated Italy, the proposed Balkan pact offered Greece less security than that of Venizelos' bilateral agreements, and threatened to involve the country in a war with a non-Balkan Great Power.

Dimitrios Maximos, the Greek foreign minister, was in agreement with Venizelos' appraisal of Greek security considerations and accepted his terms for a Balkan pact. Italy and Great Britain, whose governments were approached by Maximos at Venizelos' suggestion, expressed reservations about a Balkan pact which did not include Bulgaria. Without Bulgaria, the pact would further antagonise that country and force it to turn to a Great Power for protection against its neighbours. To include Bulgaria in the pact, it was necessary to meet its claims against its neighbours, at least partly; it was a prerequisite which none of Bulgaria's four neighbours was prepared to satisfy. If Bulgaria's claims against its neighbours were to be satisfied, there was no need to conclude a Balkan pact, as Bulgarian revisionism was the primary motive for such a pact. As far as Greece was concerned, its bilateral agreements of the previous period were preferable to a Balkan pact, because they did not exclude Italy from the region's security considerations and left open the prospect of eventually including Bulgaria in a regional settlement.

The Greek government, however, did not wish to keep Greece out of even a pact without Bulgaria, in order to avoid the country's possible isolation and particularly to forestall a possible Yugoslav–Bulgarian understanding, which would have been disastrous to Greek security. The Greek–Italian pact of September 1928 was perhaps a respectable counterweight to the prospect of such a Yugoslav–Bulgarian understanding. This prospect, which was not then or afterwards unrealistic, was a major preoccupation of Greek foreign policy; it had been the primary motive behind Venizelos' signing in 1912 of the Greek–Bulgarian alliance treaty before embarking on the war against Turkey, and in September 1928 the Greek–Italian pact of friendship. Incidentally, the possibility was eventually realised in 1947 by the communist regimes of Yugoslavia and Bulgaria but was cut short a year later, as a result of Yugoslavia's break with the Cominform.

The Balkan pact was eventually signed in Athens on 9 February 1934, despite Italian and British misgivings and Venizelos' objections. These reservations, however, obliged the Greek government to insist on limiting the obligation deriving from the pact to defend only the 'internal' Balkan frontiers. The four participating members guaranteed these frontiers, and invited the other two countries of the region, that is, Bulgaria and Albania, to join them in the mutual guarantee of their frontiers. This invitation was of no practical use and simply reflected the decision of the four members to postpone until a more propitious time a regional settlement including Bulgaria. The pact was a useless instrument in the hands of four governments, which knew well that Bulgaria alone posed no threat to any one of them, and that only as an ally of a non-Balkan Great Power would that country pose a real threat to their security. Venizelos believed this situation should have been avoided, but the government considered it unavoidable for the reasons already mentioned. Both assessments were correct, because they rested on a sound analysis of Greece's security considerations, but which were, however, affected by such unforeseeable factors as Italian and British policy in the Eastern Mediterranean.

Relations between government and opposition deteriorated in 1934 as a result of two issues, which reflected the government's intention to strengthen its position and the opposition's effort to defend its bases of support. The first issue concerned the electoral law of the country, which the government, following a long tradition of electoral manoeuvring, tried to change in the larger cities, in order to secure a larger return of seats in the coming general elections. The charges and countercharges were seldom untrue and disclosed some of the darkest and most ludicrous aspects of Greek representative government. It was the second issue, however, that revealed a grimmer side of Greek politics. This had its roots in 1917, when Venizelos resumed office following the exile of King Constantine. Each manipulation had favoured officers friendly to the party in office, and each prepared the way for the next manoeuvre by the opposing party. The man who made in 1934 one more such intervention in the list of promotions was a former Venizelist officer and now army minister in the government of Tsaldaris, George Kondylis, a man who had risen in the ranks through successive manipulations by his Venizelist patrons. Kondylis represented a set of officers who had climbed the ranks as the protégés of the two major parties eventually to become arbiters in the fierce struggle between the two parties, the Venizelists or liberals and the anti-Venizelists or conservatives.[5]

The armed services promotions list issue, more than any other major political issue of the time, set in motion the Venizelist machinery in the army and the navy. A major change of the proposed review of the promotions list was that seniority should be restored by cancelling promotions realised in the years 1917 to 1919, which affected most of the Venizelist military hierarchy. Two clandestine bodies of Venizelist officers, one associated with Plastiras, the 'Democratic Defence', and the other somewhat antagonistic to the Plastiras set, the 'Hellenic Military Organisation', were already planning, with Venizelos' blessing, to mount a coup in order to 'protect' the republic.

Venizelos' role in the conspiracy that launched the March 1935 military coup against the conservative government of Tsaldaris has been expertly and comprehensively charted and explained.[6] Encouraged by close associates to believe that the republic was in danger himself encouraging other associates to believe that that danger was real, the elderly statesman allowed himself to become part of a conspiracy against the elected government of the country, believing all the time that the defence of the republic against real or imaginary dangers justified the unconstitutional activities of his political and military associates. Rumours of impending coups by Kondylis or Ioannis Metaxas added fuel to the conspiracy, as the rumoured coups were expected to lead to the establishment of dictatorial rule. Like the equally bruited intention of the exiled Greek monarch to return to the country, these coups were not realistic prospects, for the simple reason that neither Kondylis nor Metaxas had the necessary backing in the officer corps to carry out a successful coup against a government which they anyway supported. These rumoured coups made easier the identification of the republic with democratic rule, whose defence justified even unconstitutional means like a military coup against a freely elected and democratic government. 'The motive for the revolution,' wrote Venizelos, shortly after the March 1935 coup, to the British minister in Athens:

> has been given by the universal conviction of the democracy that the Athens government is pursuing the dissolution of the democratic regime and the restoration of the expelled dynasty . . . Consequently, the aim of the revolution is to settle the question of the regime in such a manner as to exclude all anxiety for the democratic governance of the country, and in order that the democratic composition of the armed forces of the nation may be conserved and secured.[7]

In this pronouncement Venizelos expressed what the Venizelist press had been saying in so many words ever since the liberals were defeated at the polls. To himself and his closest associates Venizelos reserved other aims, in addition to that of defending and strengthening the republic. One such aim was to purge the armed and security services of all anti-Venizelist officers, and subsequently to close these services to anyone who was opposed to the refurbished Venizelist order. Another was to revise the republican constitution to allow the president to be elected not by parliament but directly by the people and given the power to override civil liberties in emergency situations.

What all this amounts to is not so much concern for the ostensibly harassed republic, but a covert attempt to establish one-party rule, and if necessary dictatorship. The rebels declared that they were taking action to prevent the restoration of the monarchy, and tried to persuade the public that the republic was indeed in danger. Venizelos, a resident in Crete ever since the attempt on his life in 1933, assumed the leadership of the revolt and sailed north as in 1916, when he had rebelled against King Constantine. According to the plan, after the initial coup, which was expected to lead to the government's fall, a military government would be set up in Athens; otherwise, a provisional government would be formed in Thessaloniki, and an expedition would be mounted against Athens.

The government of Tsaldaris reacted with unexpected vigour and determination, and launched what was essentially a counter-revolution against the Venizelists. Metaxas was hurriedly sworn in as minister without portfolio, while Kondylis rushed to the Venizelist North to suppress the rebellion. Rebel officers in Athens were soon isolated, and surrendered after a brief period of fighting. The same happened in the North, where the rebellion collapsed after sporadic skirmishes. Venizelos, who had meanwhile returned to Crete, was left isolated there and had no option but to flee from Greece for the last time. He and a few of his followers fled to the Dodecanese, Italian territory at the time, and subsequently to Paris.

The March 1935 coup was essentially a Greek affair. Foreign states took care to stay out of the struggle. Of the Balkan partners of Greece only Yugoslavia was favourably disposed towards the government of Greece, and heeded its request for aircraft; but the coup collapsed before Yugoslav assistance could arrive. Britain and France turned down similar requests for aircraft. Italy, which might have been interested in the return of Venizelos to power, refused to allow Plastiras to cross over to Greece from Italian territory. Allegations that Italy condoned the coup arose out of the absence of criticism of Venizelos in the Italian press and the flight of Venizelos to the Dodecanese; there is no evidence, however, that Italy was privy to the affair. The British government, which was also thought to have been involved, saw the issue as a struggle between 'ins and outs', and tried to sit on the fence until one of the contestants appeared to be winning. They considered all eventualities, and left their options open until the very end in a masterly exercise of calculated caution; so much so that the British minister in Athens, Sir Sydney Waterlow, thought that they should have shown more sympathy to the government of Greece, which was, after all, the lawful government of a friendly state.[8]

The British government could not possibly ignore the great influence which the name of Venizelos commanded in Britain, especially in parliamentary circles. Another and more cogent reason for their cautious policy seems to have been their dislike of the Greek government, which they considered inefficient, corrupt and decidedly inimical to British interests. The quick collapse of the coup in a sense relieved the Foreign Office, but it also caused some quiet resentment. The Foreign Office appeared favourably disposed towards Venizelos, if only for the sake of the days of the First World War. 'I always liked Mr Venizelos personally,' wrote Sir Robert Vansittart, permanent under-secretary of state for foreign affairs at the time:

> indeed I liked him immensely . . . I should have thought Mr Venizelos one of the most amiable and overestimated men of his day – there were many less amiable – which has dragged on now like an indifferent summer afternoon. Whether dusk is finally at hand, and whether that in itself is a cause for rejoicing I must leave to more expert local knowledge. I should not have thought it would have greatly changed the fundamental defects of Greek character and Greek politics.[9]

An immediate result of the March 1935 coup was the reopening of an issue that had remained dormant till then, the future of the monarchy. Although King George II had never renounced his rights to the throne, nor for that matter had he ceased to hope for his return to the country, there is reason to believe that the issue of the monarchy preoccupied none of the major parties seriously and would never actually have emerged under relatively normal circumstances. The republic was not in the serious and immediate danger that Venizelos claimed, at least not for the reasons he put forward; the exiled king was not in a position to endanger the republic, while Tsaldaris had no reason to do so. Others, however, like Kondylis and a set of royalist officers associated with him, *were* in a position to endanger the republic and did have reason to do so.

Venizelos, an old and broken man, issued endless and meaningless threats to the Greek government from Paris. At the same time, he was in close contact with both London and Athens. Many influential people, both Greek and British, approached him throughout the summer, and asked him whether he would recognise the restoration if King George undertook to return as king of all the Greeks. Available evidence leaves no doubt at all that Venizelos did want a reconciliation with the king, since it would do a great deal to unite the divided country, and that he was counting on a royal amnesty to all political and military leaders of the March 1935 coup.[10]

These contacts were interrupted suddenly on 10 October 1935, when Kondylis carried out the coup he had long been preparing. In the stormy meeting of the chamber on the same day, the prime minister and another hundred deputies walked out, and what was left of the chamber elected Kondylis prime minister and regent until the return of King George. At the same time, Kondylis and his followers proclaimed the end of the republic, a state of martial law, and set a plebiscite for 3 November. In great haste the British government set aside all misgivings, and recognised Kondylis and his regime; the Abyssinian crisis had just broken out, and they could not afford an estranged Greek government.[11]

The Kondylis coup was a great blow to Venizelos, who believed that if King George were to return under these circumstances, he would rely on the support of royalist officers, and that this support would seriously circumscribe his freedom of action. Nevertheless, he was prepared to countenance a trial period for the king, as long as the latter undertook on returning to Greece to be monarch of all the Greeks and to respect the liberties provided by the constitution of 1911. Venizelos, however, was convinced that such a pledge on the part of the king would not suffice to safeguard liberties and democracy without the reinstatement of more than 1000 Venizelist officers who had been dismissed as a result of their involvement in the March 1935 coup. Moreover, without the reinstatement of the dismissed Venizelist officers, Venizelos knew that his party would never be able to come to power and keep it. He was therefore prepared to recognise the restoration of the monarchy and facilitate the king's return to Greece, if in addition to the pledge to respect constitutional liberties, the king undertook to grant an amnesty to all military officers and civil servants who had been dismissed for participation in the coup, with the exception of himself.[12]

The plebiscite of November 1935 was rigged in the best Greek manner: with martial law still in place, there were blue ballot papers for the monarchy and red for the republic. By all accounts, the proceedings were a farce staged by Kondylis and the royalist officers who had overthrown the government of Tsaldaris in October, so as to secure as large a majority as possible in favour of the monarchy. It is not unlikely, in view of the instability and the frequent coups which had plagued the republic ever since its promulgation in 1924, that the Greeks would have come out in favour of the restoration of the monarchy anyway. There is reason to believe that moderates in both major political camps in Greece thought that King George had a real chance of succeeding in reuniting the country. The king himself appeared to believe that he would be able to play that role; or that was at least the impression he gave when, on returning to Greece, he dismissed Kondylis and promised to reign as a constitutional monarch.

Venizelos welcomed the king's apparent determination to dissociate himself from those who had brought him back to Greece and encouraged him to grant a general amnesty, in order to win wider acceptance and at the same time to break free from royalist extremists. The exiled leader was disappointed when King George amnestied, on 1 December, all those who had been condemned as a result of participation in the March 1935 coup and been dismissed from service, except military officers, whom he only pardoned, so as to deny them reinstatement. The refusal to reinstate dismissed Venizelist military officers reflected, thought Venizelos, the determination of his political opponents to establish one-party rule.[13]

There can be no doubt that many old and new royalists were scheming along exactly the lines Venizelos thought, but it is doubtful that the king encouraged such schemes. King George was by all reliable accounts genuinely prepared to work for a reconciliation, if only to create for the restored monarchy a broader base of support than the one the royalist extremists who had engineered his return represented. Non-reinstatement of the dismissed Venizelist army and navy officers was, from the king's point of view, an act of prudence, since the reinstatement of these officers could have been expected to reopen the delicate issue of seniority in the officer corps and of appointments to key command positions. It is also possible that King George did not dismiss, as he was encouraged to by moderates of both major parties, warnings from royalist extremists that they were prepared to stage yet another coup to prevent the reinstatement of the dismissed Venizelist officers. The king wished, rather than a confrontation like the one the moderates suggested, to terminate the political anomaly by leading the country to general elections.

The elections of 26 January 1936 – the next free political contest would be held ten years later – did not put an end to the political crisis, because neither of the two major parties won an absolute majority of seats in the chamber, and the communists held the balance with fifteen seats. The electoral results obliged Greece's political leaders to explore one of the two following alternatives: a collaboration of the two major parties; a collaboration of one of them with the Communist Party of Greece. The latter was not feasible, because the Communist Party was thought to be, and was doing all it could to support this, an agent of international communism bent on overthrowing liberal democracy and capitalism, and ceding Macedonia to Greece's neighbours. The former alternative was no more feasible, on account of the inability of the two major parties to agree on a mutually acceptable solution of the question of the dismissed military officers.

The prolonged post-electoral stalemate gave Venizelos a last opportunity to state his position on the issues involved. On 5 March 1936, the day before the chamber was to convene to elect its president, the army minister, General Alexandros Papagos, was received by the king and announced, on behalf of the heads of the armed and security forces of the country, that they would not tolerate a government resting on the support of the communist deputies. It had just become known that the leaders of the liberals and the communists had reached an agreement, which provided for communist support in the chamber for the liberal candidate, in return for the repeal of anti-communist legislation by a liberal government. King George dismissed Papagos and in his place appointed Ioannis Metaxas in the caretaker government of Constantinos Demertzis. Venizelos praised the king for his decision to dismiss Papagos, one of the royalist officers who had collaborated with Kondylis for the overthrow of the republic, and to bring Metaxas into the government.[14] The old statesman could not possibly have foreseen the events that kept Metaxas in power and allowed him to impose dictatorial rule. On 18 March 1936, in Paris, he passed away.

The incumbent prime minister, Constantinos Demertzis, decided to honour Venizelos with a state funeral in Athens. Anti-Venizelist animus, however, especially in military circles, had not been extinguished. Old resentments and passions threatened to mar what was meant to be an occasion of honour and respect for the protagonist of Greece's greatest national achievements in the twentieth century.[15] The government gave way to anti-Venizelist rancour. The funeral service took place in the Greek church of Saint Stephen in Paris, in the presence of the highest dignitaries of the French republic. From Paris Venizelos' coffin was carried by special train to Brindisi and there it was transferred to the naval vessel *Pavlos Kountouriotis*, which, accompanied by the destroyer *Psara* sailed through the Corinth Canal and southward to Chania. Thus Venizelos finally went home to Crete, to a reception marked by unprecedented public emotion and scenes of mourning by massive crowds of his followers and his Cretan compatriots. On 27 March Crown Prince Paul and four members of the cabinet joined the crowds accompanying Venizelos to his final resting place in the courtyard of the Chapel of the Prophet Elijah on the hill at Akrotiri, overlooking the city and the Gulf of Chania. Venizelos returned to rest at the place where he had hoisted the flag of union of his native island with Greece thirty-nine years earlier.

His grave has become a place of pilgrimage not only for Cretans but for all Greeks who visit his home city.

NOTES

1. The best study of the subject is Thanos Veremis (1977), *Oi epemvaseis tou stratou stin elliniki politiki, 1916–1936* [*The Interventions of the Greek Army in Politics, 1916–1936*], Athens.
2. For the attempt on Venizelos' life in June 1933 see Grigorios Daphnis (1955), *I Ellas metaxy ton dyo polemon, 1923–1940* [*Greece between the Two Wars, 1923–1940*], vol. II, Athens, pp. 220ff.

3. Ibid., pp. 227–9.
4. Ibid., pp. 230–1.
5. Veremis, *Epemvaseis*, pp. 238 ff (see Note 1).
6. Ibid., pp. 253–85. See also Th. Veremis (1987), *The Military in Greek Politics*, London, pp. 99–133.
7. See John S. Koliopoulos (1977), *Greece and the British Connection, 1935–1941*, Oxford, p. 11.
8. Ibid., p. 14.
9. Ibid., p. 15.
10. Ibid., p. 21. See also G. Pesmatzoglou (1950), *Gyro apo tin palinorthosin tou 1935* [*Concerning the Restoration of 1935*], Athens, pp. 44 ff.
11. See James Barros (1982), *Britain, Greece and the Politics of Sanctions. Ethiopia, 1935–1936*, London, pp. 112ff.
12. See John S. Koliopoulos (1980), 'O Venizelos kai i palinorthosi tis monarchias (1935)' ['Venizelos and the restoration of the monarchy (1935)'], in O. Dimitrakopoulos and Th. Veremis (eds), *Meletimata gyro apo ton Venizelo kai tin epochi tou* [*Studies on Venizelos and His Time*], Athens , pp. 551–62.
13. Daphnis, *I Ellas*, pp. 391–2.
14. Ibid., pp. 406–7.
15. On the impact of Venizelos' death, see Helen Gardikas-Katsiadakis (ed.) (2004), *O thanatos tou Eleftheriou Venizelou ston athinaiko typo* [The Death of Eleftherios Venizelos in the Athenian Press], Chania.

PART III

The Content of Political Action

8

The Experiment of Inclusive Constitutionalism, 1909–32

Ioannis Tassopoulos

INTRODUCTION

Eleftherios Venizelos' vision of state, politics and society was by no means constrained by nineteenth-century conceptions of laisser-faire liberalism.[1] He was fully aware that the state, were it to accomplish its national mission,[2] had to be active and effective, undertaking a wide range of initiatives and responsibilities and pursuing policies that extended into many fields of national life. Such a state required, however, the rational and efficient organisation of its institutions. Understanding this is crucial in our effort to reconstruct an internally coherent constitutional philosophy out of his positions on various issues and problems. But a constitutional philosophy depends on the consistent endorsement of certain political principles, as much as it relies on a sensitive and insightful perception of political realities.

Eleftherios Venizelos was not an ideologue, but he certainly was a man of ideas. As N. Alivizatos has shown, Venizelos' constitutional programme was marked by three constant priorities: the rationalisation of the parliamentary system, the guarantee of the non-abusive exercise of individual liberties under the constitution, and the facilitation of the interventionist role of the state in the economy.[3] This article follows Alivizatos' analysis, but it adopts a slightly different and more abstract formulation of the statesman's fixed constitutional ideals. Accordingly, popular sovereignty, the rule of law and effective government were the three pillars of Venizelos' constitutional edifice. Depending on the exigencies of the time, he did on occasion compromise these principles, but he never abandoned them.[4] Running the risk of a certain schematisation, we may attempt to connect each of the aforementioned principles with a particular phase of Venizelos' political career. In 1911, the rule of law marks the revision of the 1864 constitution; in 1915, with the outbreak of the National Schism, popular sovereignty takes priority; and in 1928, during Venizelos' third long term in office, he was preoccupied with effective government. These rather abstract concepts aptly offer themselves for a broader synthesis. In this regard, the key notion is that of an 'inclusive constitutionalism'. Section II of this article tries to untangle this rather complex notion, which is crucial for understanding Eleftherios Venizelos' constitutional philosophy. Subsequent sections trace the rise and fall of Venizelos' option for a more inclusive constitutionalism, in the course of Greece's political history. At the beginning, with his appearance on the Greek political scene in 1909 (section III), Venizelos was quite moderate on the issue of the regime (that is, the controversy over a monarchical or republican form of government – sections IV, V). However, in the inter-war years, following the National Schism, Venizelos abandoned the inclusive and conciliatory approach which prevailed in 1909 (sections VI, VII).

INCLUSIVE AND EXCLUSIVE CONSTITUTIONALISM

Following A. Gramsci, the notion of inclusive constitutionalism could be analysed in terms of a ruling class which establishes the idea that 'it is possible to imagine the coercive element of the State withering away by degrees, as even-more conspicuous elements of regulated society (or ethical State or civil society) make their appearance.'[5] Conversely, in exclusive constitutionalism, the ruling class fails to secure its 'political and cultural hegemony' in the above sense and has to rely on force.[6] From the normative point of view, however, inclusive constitutionalism is not analysed primarily in terms of its social underpinnings. Rather, the focus is on its power to implement in the political organisation of society its fundamental ethico-political ideal, so as to render it operationally decisive, and generally valid. As a consequence, that ideal ceases to be identified with a specific social class or group of interests, and acquires a truly constitutive character, offering a generally valid standpoint of analysis and a commonly accepted conceptual framework, which encompasses and resolves socio-political conflicts on its own terms.

The constitutional tradition of political liberalism, which is not satisfied with the mere prospect of a principle relative to a specific historical society, but aspires to universal validity and objectivity, is by definition the most inclusive one. Indeed political liberalism is grounded on the idea of multifarious self-determination (individual, social and political) of persons who have universal human rights and are equal before the law.[7] To the extent that this ethico-political standpoint offers in fact the basis for the resolution of socio-political conflicts through accommodation, incorporation and/or change, and leads to institutional adaptation by gradual growth and/or formal amendment, then, we can talk of inclusive liberal constitutionalism. The latter is consistent both with the rationalist branch of constitutionalism, associated with the written and rigid constitutions of the USA and France,[8] and with the more pragmatic and historically oriented British constitution, which relies heavily on conventions.[9] What is really distinctive of inclusive constitutionalism is not the origin of its institutions in reason or experience, but rather its rational expansion through the exercise of *prudence*.[10] As Edmund Burke noted:

> [P]rudence (in all things a virtue, in politics the first of virtues) will lead us rather to acquiesce in some qualified plan that does not come up to the full perfection of the abstract idea, than to push for the more perfect, which cannot be attained without tearing to pieces the whole contexture of the commonwealth . . . In all changes in the state, moderation is a virtue, not only amiable, but powerful. It is a disposing, arranging, conciliating, cementing, virtue . . .[11]

The following sections illustrate that the experiment of inclusive constitutionalism is bound to fail when the political system is extremely polarised and the drive to reach a consensus has vanished, leaving no space for the exercise of prudence.[12]

An example of inclusive constitutionalism is offered by the development of American constitutional law, through judicial expounding of legal principle,[13] such as freedom of speech, equality and due process of law.

On the other hand, exclusive constitutionalism is grounded on the discrimination and selection of various individuals or groups of persons, on the ground of criteria such as national origin, political creed, religion, language, race, and so on. Only those who share the decisive feature are included in the polity, while the others are excluded from the community or relegated to an inferior position. The notorious theoretical exposition of an exclusive conception is of course Carl Schmitt's acceptance of the opposition between 'friend' and 'enemy' as fundamentally important for constitutional law.[14]

The infamous decision *Dred Scott* v. *Sanford*,[15] of the American Supreme Court, is paradigmatic of an exclusive constitutional interpretation. Another example is that of the pervasive ideology which prevailed in Greece after the civil war of the 1940s and tended to exclude from normal political life anyone who was deemed to be 'left-minded'.[16]

THE HISTORICAL BACKGROUND

In July 1908, the Young Turks won power, after a successful revolt. The crisis in the Ottoman Empire provoked agitation all over the Balkans.[17] On 8 October 1908, the Cretans proclaimed their enosis (union) with

Greece, but their move was not endorsed by the Greek state, which was still financially weak, militarily unprepared and demoralised after the humiliating defeat in the 'unfortunate' war of 1897.[18] One year later, in July 1909, it became apparent that any Greek action in favour of the union with Crete would have led to immediate war with the Turks.[19] The frustration and the anger from the inability of the Greek state to meet the challenge provoked the Goudi Revolt by the Military League, on 14–15 August 1909, under the leadership of Colonel N. Zorbas.[20] The Military League demanded the reorganisation of the armed forces and the removal of clientelism from the administration of state business,[21] but, on the other hand, it explicitly disavowed more radical aims such as the abolition of the dynasty or the king's replacement.[22] When the Military League found itself in a political impasse about its future moves, it invited Eleftherios Venizelos, the eminent Cretan politician, to serve as its political adviser.[23] At the end of December 1909, Venizelos arrived in Athens.

Originally, the main target of the military revolt of 1909 were the old parties and the 'oligarchy' which ran the state and were held responsible for the predicament of the country.[24] However, as long as the political unrest continued, a more radical turn of the Goudi Revolt could not be excluded. Remarkably, the potential of such political developments found a distinct constitutional expression: would the body elected to implement the programme of the Military League be a constituent parliament or a revisionist assembly? At stake was the form of the regime. The exercise of constituent power meant that the assembly would be legally unlimited and free to replace the monarchy with a republic. On the other hand, the authority of a revisionist parliament would be bound by the constitution of 1864, which prohibited the amendment of the fundamental provisions, including the form of the regime.[25] Soon after his arrival in Athens, during his first meeting with the leadership of the Military League, Venizelos argued in favour of a revisionist parliament. He justified this position on an appraisal of both the declining political influence of the Military League and of the long-term interests of the country, which required political unity and eschewed internal strife and discord.[26]

THE DILEMMA OVER A REVISIONIST PARLIAMENT OR CONSTITUENT ASSEMBLY, 1909–10

In January 1910, during a meeting of King George with some of the most important parliamentarians, the decision was made to resolve the political crisis through the convocation of a revisionist parliament.[27] On

18 February 1910, a parliamentary resolution for the revision of the non-fundamental provisions of the constitution of 1864 was voted on with an overwhelming majority of 150 to 11, exceeding by far the majority required by article 107 of the constitution of 1864.[28] Though compliance with the procedures for the revision of the constitution was only partial, the effort to meet at least the super-majority standard set by article 107 was an important factor in support of the revisionist character of the parliament. Next, King George issued a royal address, emphasising as well that the parliament to be elected had only limited authority, which did not include the fundamental provisions of the constitution of 1864.[29] Afterwards, parliament was dissolved, and the Double Revisionist Parliament was elected on 8 August 1910, pursuant to article 107.[30] During these elections, Eleftherios Venizelos was elected a member of the Greek parliament for the first time.[31]

On 1 September 1910 the Double Revisionist Parliament was convoked and the king inaugurated its proceedings with a speech where the legal limitations to its authority were repeated.[32] Quite soon, however, it became apparent that the nature of the parliament, and the concomitant issue of the regime, were more controversial than expected.[33] So, on the day after the inauguration, the Double Revisionist Parliament decided by 148 votes to 121 that it would hold discussions about its constituent or revisionist character.[34] Moreover, there was substantial political agitation among the public in favour of a constituent assembly. At this critical moment, Venizelos tilted the scale in favour of constitutional continuity and political unity. On 5 September 1910, Venizelos addressed a massive demonstration in the centre of Athens. When he spoke in favour of a revisionist parliament, the audience interrupted him three times, asking for a constituent assembly, but Venizelos insisted and was finally able to prevail over his audience.[35]

At the end of September 1910, the king gave a mandate to form a government to Venizelos, who accepted. In the following days, Venizelos requested a vote of confidence by the parliament. During the parliamentary debates, he once again had the opportunity to clarify that the Double Revisionist Parliament was not a constituent assembly and therefore did not exercise full sovereign power, but had only the legally constrained competence to amend the constitution, within the limits set by article 107 of the constitution of 1864.[36] On these grounds, he accepted the royal prerogative to dissolve parliament.[37] Indeed, when Venizelos concluded that he did not have the support of a solid parliamentary majority, he asked the king to dissolve parliament and hold new elections on 28 November 1910.[38]

Venizelos' option for a revisionist parliament should not be assessed in the light of the subsequent political developments associated with the National Schism.[39] In 1909, his moderate position was more than reasonable. Modelled on the Belgian constitution of 1831, the constitution of 1864 was a rather liberal and progressive document for its time.[40] It had introduced popular sovereignty, that is, the democratic principle, mitigated however by the introduction of a hereditary king.[41] As a consequence, during its long application, the constitution of 1864 was open to conflicting readings, emphasising either the prerogatives of the throne, or the fundamental principle of the regime, which was popular sovereignty. Among the provisions whose literal meaning accepted a monarchical construction it was stated that: 'The king appoints and dismisses his ministers.'[42] At the same time, albeit explicit statement of the rule that the government must enjoy the confidence of parliament was not written down in the constitution, the constitution contained the 'seeds' for the gradual growth of the parliamentary system.[43] So, it was provided that parliament had the right to forward any reports addressed thereto to the ministers who were obliged to offer explanations when so requested; according to the same provision, parliament could set up investigation committees from among its members.[44] It was further provided that parliament could demand the presence of the ministers.[45] In 1875, following a fierce political conflict with Charilaos Trikoupis, one of the most prominent political figures in nineteenth-century Greece, King George accepted that he would select the prime minister from the parliamentary majority.[46] Generally speaking, during the reign of King George, who had an acute political instinct and knew when to show flexibility, the constitution of 1864,[47] though far from perfect, was clearly no impediment to the normal development of constitutional and political life in Greece. Indeed, it is quite remarkable that during the last quarter of the nineteenth century the electoral campaign and the ballot obtained an overwhelming legitimacy as the sole means for the rise to power.[48]

At that time, and under those conditions, Eleftherios Venizelos' option for constitutional continuity, political moderation, national unity and conciliatory spirit towards the throne certainly made sense. In any case, this choice was indispensable for Venizelos' political programme of 'regeneration',[49] that is, the preparation of the state of Greece for fulfilment of its national aspirations. It is submitted, however, that the option for an inclusive constitutional tradition was not merely a matter of tactical manoeuvre, which Venizelos was forced to accept under the pressure of political realities in 1909. At that time, Venizelos sincerely believed in the gradual growth of royal parliamentary democracy in

Greece. In his important speech of 5 September 1910, Venizelos emphasised his commitment to the democratic principle, but also reserved an important constitutional role for the king, who 'is a powerful factor, integrating the polity and protecting the regime from any deviation'.[50] Moreover, the king, 'having the prerogatives bestowed by the regime, possesses tremendous power to do good; further, he holds colossal power to prevent evil, by restraining his government from the devious outcomes of breaches of the law'. He also emphasised the lack of an indigenous royal family and found it 'incredibly naive to sacrifice half a century of the dynasty's assimilation in Greek national life'.[51]

These statements illustrate Venizelos' specific conception of inclusive constitutionalism in 1910. It is an evolutionary model, which emphasises not rigid rules but applied legal principles, and requires increased prudence and responsibility on the part of political actors. Characterised by flexibility, adaptability and openness, with its requirement for checks and balances to countervail illegal exercise of political power, the model became obsolete and inapt for the polarised and exclusive political culture which followed the National Schism of 1915.[52] In retrospect, Venizelos' tolerance of a bipolar political system, which came perilously close to a requirement of dual confidence (royal and parliamentary) for the formation of government, may seem particularly unfortunate.[53] On a deeper level, Venizelos could be justly criticised for underestimating the value of clear legal rules in establishing, in an unequivocal manner, the parliamentary system.[54] However, these questions do not undermine the importance of Venizelos' contribution to an inclusive and liberal constitutional tradition, which tries to integrate all the political forces of society without polarisation and ostracism.

THE CONSTITUTIONAL REVISION OF 1911 AND THE RULE OF LAW

The old parties abstained from the elections of 28 November 1910, while Venizelos did not take part as a simple candidate, but as leader of his own political movement, established on 22 August 1910. Venizelos' Liberal Party won an overwhelming majority in parliament (307 out of 362 seats).[55] On 8 January 1911, the Second Double Revisionist Parliament was convoked in Athens and in the course of approximately three months, it amended fifty-four out of the 110 articles of the constitution of 1864.[56] Compared with the lofty and ideologically ornamented speeches of the Second National Assembly of 1862, the prevailing spirit in the debates of 1911 was much more down to earth, pragmatic, oriented to a rational analysis of institutions and devoid of vague and idealised discussions of principle.[57] The shift in rhetoric reflects the difference in substance. If liberty is the keyword for 1862, the consolidation of the rule of law sets the tone in 1911.[58]

Venizelos participated actively in the debates of the Second Revisionist Parliament.[59] He had a thorough understanding of what the rule of law meant – the supremacy of the law over the administrative authorities, the ministers and the king himself.[60] It is the principle which transforms nominal freedom into a really effective one. He defended with eloquent fervour the creation, under constitutional guarantee, of a council of state, that is, of a court competent to review the legality of administrative action. If anything at all, the rule of law meant due process of law. Legal interests and rights should not depend on ministers' good will;[61] they should be fully secured under judicial protection. The petition to annul illegal administrative acts (recours pour excès de pouvoir) was clearly conceived as a facet of the rule of law and more particularly of the right to receive legal protection from the courts.[62]

Venizelos discussed legal interests and rights as bulwarks against the tyranny of the majority.[63] More than once, both in the debates about the council of state and about the creation of a court responsible to judge the legality of elections, Venizelos emphatically expressed his view of the judiciary as the institution responsible for defending the rule of law. He rebutted arguments about the risk of judicial abuses by pointing out that the courts were the least dangerous branch,[64] deprived of the power to countervail against the colossal power of an administration supported by a democratically elected legislative majority. Finally, his perception of the judicial office was by no means instrumental or mechanical. Venizelos emphasised the role of the council of state in the gradual growth of the law.[65] He also resisted vehemently the temporary suppression of judicial independence, both on the grounds that such independence, being of a fundamental nature, was beyond the reach of the Revisionist Parliament, and of the necessity to prevent an injury to the morale and confidence of the judiciary. According to Venizelos, the most harmful consequences from encroachments into judicial independence do not concern present time, but extend to the remote future.[66] Venizelos showed an acute awareness of the importance of continuity and tradition in further embedding institutional authority and stability. In this regard, the replacement of the spoils system with tenure for public servants was also serving the ideal of the rule of law in the field of public administration.[67]

Equally important was Venizelos' commitment to popular sovereignty. Confronted with parliament's reaction to a bill introducing the right of the prince and successor to the throne of Greece to be commander in-chief, Venizelos insisted that he derived his authority directly from popular sovereignty, which was fully independent from the Military League. 'All my political life,' he said, 'depends on the power which the statesmen of a parliamentary state derive and must derive from popular confidence.'[68]

Venizelos' position on effective government was multifaceted. The quorum necessary for debates to be held in parliament was reduced to one third of its members, while Venizelos discussed 'parliamentary customs' and insisted on a simplification of parliamentary procedures.[69] Another deputy developed a constitutional analysis of the prime minister's position 'who is the leader of the party supported by the parliamentary majority and is called to head the government'.[70] Relying on his charismatic personality, Prime Minister Venizelos frequently assumed an immediate legitimacy between the people and himself and verified in practice his dominant position within the Liberal Party, and on the Greek political scene in general.[71]

Moreover, Venizelos insisted on protecting the state against emergency situations, not only in case of war, but also during military conscription. As he said: 'We are not going to establish a dictatorship in emergency situations; we still have the constitutional and parliamentary regime in its entirety. But we fortify the authorities, we fortify the judiciary with the necessary means in order to handle emergency situations menacing the state.'[72]

Finally, Venizelos had the opportunity to express his moderate position regarding individual rights in the debates over the expropriation of big estates in Thessaly and the distribution of the land to farm workers. Venizelos' arguments over the agrarian problem reflect a concept of private property which defines a socio-political regime, is sanctioned by law, is not absolute, and takes into account the general interests and claims of society. In a famous passage, he declared: 'I, and please take this to mean the Liberal Party and the government of this country, will be the most secure support of the order and the social regime. But I do not want this regime to be static. I do not want it in its old form of organisation, so that it falls down in ruins. I rather want it progressive, adapting to the circumstances of the day, so that it will help the state to fulfil its high mission.'[73] At the same time, the constitution was revised to improve the protection of personal security and other individual rights (especially the right to association), while elementary education was made free and compulsory.[74]

It is noteworthy that the participants in the debates about the revision of the constitution showed more often than not a keen appreciation of the role fundamental principles play in constitutional analysis. Venizelos and other deputies exemplified an impressive familiarity with the relevant way of thinking. Popular sovereignty permeates the constitutional structure as a whole and provides the legal and political standpoint for a principled interpretation of the various institutions.[75] This was surely a constitutional system of considerable maturity. In the light of the constitutional crisis which initiated the National Schism,[76] it is hard to exaggerate the familiarity of the parliamentary political élite with constitutional arguments from first principles.

Venizelos' Liberal Party won the elections of March 1912, gaining a sweeping majority in parliament. The result was indicative of public support of his efforts for the 'regeneration' of the country.[77] Under Venizelos' leadership, Greece had nearly doubled its territory and population during the Balkan Wars of 1912 to 1913. In addition, Eleftherios Venizelos' government promoted intensely and quite impressively the modernisation of the country.[78] However, the National Schism brought an abrupt and tragic end to this period.

THE NATIONAL SCHISM AND THE PRINCIPLE OF POPULAR SOVEREIGNTY

On 21 February 1915, while the Gallipoli campaign was in full swing, King Constantine opposed Venizelos' decision for Greek participation in the First World War on the side of the Entente. As a consequence, the prime minister tendered his resignation, and the king replaced him with Dimitrios Gounaris, a leading figure of the anti-Venizelist camp. As the Liberal Party had the support of an overwhelming majority in parliament, the latter was dissolved and new elections were held on 31 May 1915. Venizelos again won the elections and the parliamentary majority. However, he was appointed prime minister only on 10 August 1915, as the king had tried to override this result on various pretexts. On 5 October Venizelos was again compelled to resign, because of the king's obstinate refusal to follow his prime minister's policy. Parliament was dissolved in October 1915 for a second time, but the liberals, who denounced this dissolution as blatantly unconstitutional, abstained from the general elections of 6 December 1915.[79] N. Alivizatos correctly characterises the National Schism as a major crisis of liberal constitutionalism, where, ultimately, the locus of sovereignty was at stake.[80]

The constitution of 1911 provided that 'the king appoints and dismisses his ministers'[81] and that 'the king has the right to dissolve parliament'.[82] Literally, both these royal prerogatives were unconditional; but this did not mean that there were no limits to the king's powers.[83] It is therefore essential to identify what these limits were, and what nature they had, that is, whether they were legally binding or not. To complicate the situation further, the interrelationship between the appointment of the prime minister and the dissolution of parliament, though important in practice, is not immediately evident.[84] In Greece of 1915 these issues were not clearly settled.

As already said, in 1875 the principle, which is a cardinal feature of the parliamentary system, was introduced that the leader whose party had the proclaimed confidence of parliament was appointed prime minister. However, in constitutional practice the king often could appoint a minority government and dissolve parliament, if the confidence of parliament was not obtained.[85] This meant that the first dismissal of Venizelos' government and the concomitant dissolution of parliament were within the king's authority, although Venizelos objected to the appointment, not of a neutral government, but of a deeply political one, under his main rival, Gounaris. The same, however, cannot be said about the second dismissal and dissolution. The rationale for this dissolution of parliament was to appeal to the electorate, in case of disharmony between the government and the people.[86] But once the popular will was expressed, the king could not further pursue his disagreement with the prime minister. After the elections, the king's refusal to yield to the responsible government, which had obtained parliament's confidence, was clearly unconstitutional.[87]

In fact, the argument of the anti-Venizelist camp, that the situation between the first and the second dissolution was substantially different, and therefore the king could justifiably make use again of his prerogative, was a sophistry. Clearly, the various incidents (the Gallipoli campaign or the Greek–Serbian treaty) of the same fundamental controversy (that is, neutrality or participation of Greece in the First World War) could not constitutionally be dubbed 'different situations', calling for repeated dissolutions of parliament.[88] Venizelos was therefore perfectly right when, after the May elections, he invoked the principle of popular sovereignty and advised the king to refrain from pursuing a personal policy against the will of the electorate. As Constantine insisted on imposing his own political agenda on the foreign affairs of the country, Venizelos was justified in concluding that the king was acting like an absolute monarch of divine right, and violating the constitutional regime.[89]

Venizelos was not innovating, when he was opting for an interpretation concerning the dissolution of parliament and the king's constitutional role, consistent with the fundamental principle of popular sovereignty. The ramifications of the parliamentary system may not have been definitely settled, but there was no ambiguity about the democratic principle.[90] Therefore, it is safe to conclude that the throne was fully responsible for the severe disruption of constitutional continuity, for the abandonment of political moderation, and for the blow to national unity.

From a narrower constitutional perspective, the king's attitude, during the first phase of the National Schism, undermined the inclusive constitutional system, and contradicted the whole methodology of gradual growth of Greece's political institutions which Venizelos had tried to cultivate upon his entrance to Greek politics. In an unprecedented way, the constitution was turned into a battleground, especially over its provisions, which had to serve as the last ditches of defence in uncompromising political conflicts.[91] Under these circumstances, political ethos and prudence are to no avail; what prevails is the striving for legal certainty, dry and precise language, exact and detailed guarantees – that is, legal positivism with all its pros and cons.[92] That philosophy has its corresponding constitutional form, favouring detailed and complete, yet long and cumbersome, provisions, which often lack the flavour of constitutional law.

In 1920, Venizelos' proposal to revise the constitution aimed, among other things, at 'regulating in a more precise manner, and on a parliamentary basis, the royal right to appoint the ministers', and at 'clearly specifying the constitutional basis of the dissolution of parliament, and of the conditions for its exercise'.[93] The attempt proved to be abortive as the Liberal Party lost the 1920 elections.[94] But the trend for textual thoroughness and precision, which had started with the proposal of 1920, has remained with us and culminated in the constitutional revisions of 1986 and 2001.[95]

In October 1916, Venizelos formed a revolutionary government in Thessaloniki and the country was divided into two states. In November 1916, the Venizelists were persecuted, as violence reigned in Athens.[96] The first phase of the National Schism ended in 1917 with the intervention of the allied Powers, the king's exile, the accession of his son Alexander to the throne, and the formation of a new Venizelos government.[97] The parliament elected in May 1915, though already dissolved, was revivified (and is therefore known as the 'Lazarus Parliament'). According to Venizelos, this move re-established the principle of popular sovereignty, which had been overthrown by the unconstitutional dissolution of that parliament.[98] It also reflected Venizelos' reluctance to exercise dictatorial power.[99]

During the Balkan Wars (1912–13) and the First World War Venizelos enforced martial law,[100] which was gradually extended to cases concerning the internal security of the country.[101] In addition, important restrictions to constitutional rights and guarantees were introduced (deportation;

violations of freedom of speech, freedom of the press, of the functional and personal independence of the judiciary)[102] and applied extensively to anti-Venizelists. It is therefore apparent that Eleftherios Venizelos, notwithstanding his truly charismatic personality did not (or maybe could not) resist the tide of the National Schism, and the pressure it exerted on the principles of political liberalism guaranteed by the Greek constitution of 1864/1911. Nevertheless, one cannot assess objectively these developments in isolation from the general trend which marks the advanced democracies of the West during the same period. A comparative inquiry reveals that France, Britain or even the USA experienced severe tensions in their political institutions and liberal principles, because of the unprecedented pressures exerted by the First World War.[103]

In any case, it should be emphasised that Venizelos tried to reinvigorate the democratic basis of his authority through the ballot. However, despite his major diplomatic successes, the liberals suffered a devastating defeat in the elections of November 1920, and Venizelos moved away from Greece. As King Alexander had already died in October 1920, King Constantine returned to the country, after a rigged referendum.

Anti-Venizelist forces had ruled for two years, up to 1922, when the revolution of that year overthrew their regime, in the aftermath of the Asia Minor disaster. In September 1922, King Constantine was forced to abdicate. Six anti-Venizelist leaders were sentenced to death and executed in November 1922. In October 1923, anti-Venizelists attempted a coup d'état, which was suppressed by loyal Venizelist forces. On 25 March 1924 the Fourth Constituent Assembly abolished the monarchy and proclaimed the republic.

THE REPUBLIC AND THE QUEST FOR EFFECTIVE GOVERNMENT

On 4 January 1926 General Pangalos, who had already concentrated legislative power in his hands with the approval of the assembly on 30 June 1925, established a dictatorship, which was overthrown on 22 August 1926. Concerning these turbulent years, N. Alivizatos notes that after a decade of continuous crises, constitutional institutions in Greece lost their old cohesion and legitimacy.[104] Moreover, the military (also separated into Venizelist and anti-Venizelist factions) increased its interventions in politics, further destabilising constitutional government.[105]

On the other hand, however, the parliament that emerged from the elections of November 1926 supported the 'ecumenical government', in which ministers from both the Venizelist and anti-Venizelist camps participated, and voted in the republican constitution of 1927. The latter provided for a president of the republic,[106] introduced a second chamber (senate)[107] and established the principle of parliamentary government.[108] Moreover, the 1927 constitution re-established the council of state as an administrative court, explicitly recognised judicial review of legislation,[109] ameliorated the protection of individual rights,[110] and guaranteed social rights, for the first time in Greek constitutional history.[111]

Nevertheless, the repercussions of the National Schism ran deep, eroding the foundations of liberal constitutionalism. In 1924, the legislative degree 'on the safeguard of the republican regime' escalated repressive steps against political dissent, while in 1929 Venizelos' government passed the well-known 'Idionymon' law, which intensified Greece's anti-communist legislation.[112]

In the elections of 19 August 1928 Eleftherios Venizelos enjoyed a landslide victory. He governed for four years, giving priority to the economic stabilisation of the country.[113] Another major contribution was the start of the functioning of the council of state in 1929, which enhanced the guarantees of the rule of law in the field of administrative action. In terms of constitutional developments, in 1932 Venizelos introduced a proposal for the amendment of the 1927 constitution, which had been drafted without his participation. In essence, this proposal provided for the introduction of a provision similar to article 48 paragraph 2 of the Weimar constitution, in which the head of the state was authorised to exercise extensive legislative and executive power.[114] Actually, during the last phase of his political career Venizelos was oriented towards the increase of executive power. He justified this need on three grounds: the worsening international situation, which, he predicted, would eventually lead to a new major war; the interventionist role of the modern state; and the peculiarities of Greece's political scene, where extreme polarisation undermined the normal operation of the parliamentary system of government.[115] In response to this situation, Venizelos considered the possibility of becoming president of the republic in a constitutional system with enhanced presidential features.[116]

In the electoral campaign of 1932, Venizelos tried to keep together his political alliance by intensifying the polarisation between republicans and royalists, and by resorting to the history of the National Schism.[117] G. Daphnis notes that Venizelos declared on 4 September 1932 that:

> the civil war, which has been carrying on for seventeen years, could only be terminated, either through an understanding between the two sides . . . or through total victory by one side over the other. This victory should be conclusive, to the point that the losing party definitely recognises its defeat and begs for unconditional peace.[118]

The withdrawal from the inclusive and conciliatory approach, which prevailed before the eruption of the National Schism, is quite remarkable.

The elections of 1932 did not give Venizelos sufficiently strong parliamentary support. In the new elections of March 1933, the plurality electoral system led to a clear anti-Venizelist majority.[119] The transfer of power from one party to the other was not smooth. Between 1933 and 1935, political life was again extremely polarised. A fruitless coup d'état by the Venizelist General Plastiras on the night of the elections in 1933, an attempt to assassinate Venizelos and his wife in June 1933, and another abortive coup d'état on 1 March 1935, badly organised by the Venizelist military, again stirred up the passions of the National Schism,[120] and led to the imposition of the Kondylis dictatorship and the restoration of the monarchy in 1935.[121] In 1936, Venizelos died in exile; that year the dictatorship of 4 August was established.[122]

G. Mavrogordatos notes that:

> the rules of the game themselves remained in contention throughout the interwar period. There were *no* secure and institutionalized mutual guarantees, offering safety to both sides, to prevent the struggle for power between anti-Venizelism and Venizelism from degenerating or escalating into civil war.[123]

Clearly, trust had given way to radical and pervasive mistrust. The age called not for Aristotelian prudence, but for Hobbesian politics.

CONCLUSION

The National Schism reversed the constitutional course of Greece, and set it on a track quite different from Venizelos' original plans. In fact, one of the main victims of the National Schism was the inclusive constitutional tradition of the country. Being subverted from within, so to speak, by the intransigence of the king on obsolete monarchical and anti-democratic interpretations of his constitutional role, the normal growth of political institutions was interrupted. Eventually, the inclusiveness of the country's considerable constitutional tradition yielded to extreme polarisation, which threatened not only the political survival but also the life of the defeated party. Under these circumstances, Eleftherios Venizelos' original project for an inclusive political system, bolstered with the safeguards and guarantees of the rule of law was abandoned and the institutional achievements of his first term in office were reversed and annulled. As a consequence, Greece's constitutional institutions entered a long period of instability and crisis, which ended only in 1975. However, the guarantees of the rule of law, introduced by Venizelos in 1911, through the revision of the constitution of 1864, held the basis for Greece's new democratic start under the constitution of 1975.[124]

Characterized by flexibility, adaptability and openness; requiring checks and balances to countervail illegal exercise of power; and adjusted to integrate all the political forces of society without polarization and ostracism, Venizelos' original option for inclusive constitutionalism remains a first rate contribution. Beyond the philosophical attraction of the ideal *per se*, Venizelos' legacy consists in his firm belief that this ideal is also deeply political, viable and auspicious.

NOTES

* I am grateful to Professor P. Kitromilides and Professor G. Mavrogordatos, for helpful comments on an earlier draft of this paper. Of course, full responsibility remains with the author.

1. See e.g., N. Mouzelis (1980), 'Oikonomia kai kratos tin epochi tou Venizelou' ['Economy and State in Venizelos' time'], in O. Dimitrakopoulos and Th. Veremis (eds), *Meletimata gyro apo ton Venizelo kai tin epochi tou* [*Studies on Venizelos and His Time*], Athens, pp. 3, 7–8; N. Tsiros (1997), *To nomothetiko ergo tou Eleftheriou Venizelou kata tin periodo 1911–1920 sta plaisia tis metarrithmistikis tou politikis kai sta koinonikopolitika dedomena tis epochis* [*The Legislative Work of Eleftherios Venizelos of the Years 1911–1920 within the Context of his Reform Policy and the Socio-Political Conditions of that Era*], Athens.
2. Before 1922 the national mission of the state was to fulfil the hopes of Greek irredentism (the Great Idea). After 1922, the aim of the state was to integrate the refugees into national life and achieve the social and economic modernisation of the country.
3. See N. Alivizatos (1992), 'O Eleftherios Venizelos kai o syntagmatikos eksynchronismos tis choras' ['Eleftherios Venizelos and the Constitutional Modernisation of the Country'], in G. Th. Mavrogordatos and Chr. Hadjiiosif (eds), *Venizelismos kai astikos eksynchronismos* [*Venizelism and Bourgeois Modernisation*] Irakleio, pp. 33, 38–42.
4. On the contrary, Venizelos' attitude towards the monarchy changed in the course of the years. See V. Papacosma, 'O Eleftherios Venizelos kai to zitima tou avasileftou dimokratikou politevmatos (1916–1920)' ['Eleftherios Venizelos and the Issue of Republicanism (1916–1920)'], in Dimitrakopoulos and Veremis (eds), *Meletimata*, p. 485 (see Note 1).
5. See A. Gramsci (1987), *Selections from the Prison Notebooks*, ed. Q. Hoare and G. N. Smith, New York, pp. 262–3.
6. Ibid., p. 258.
7. On the constitutional tradition of political liberalism, see I. A. Tassopoulos (2001), *To ithikopolitiko themelio tou Syntagmatos* [*The Ethico-Political*

Foundation of the Constitution], Athens, which presupposes J. Rawls (1993), *Political Liberalism*, New York.

8. See on the written and rigid constitution in the Continental and the American traditions A. Manessis (1980), *Syntagmatiko dikaio* I [*Constitutional Law I*], Thessaloniki, p. 150; W. Van Alstyne (1987), 'The Idea of the Constitution as Hard Law', *Journal of Legal Education* 37, p. 174.
9. See G. Marshall (1986), *Constitutional Conventions*, Oxford; E. Barendt (1998), *An Introduction to English Constitutional Law*, Oxford, p. 40.
10. See P. W. Kahn (1989), 'Community in Contemporary Constitutional Theory', *Yale Law Journal* 99, pp. 1, 7; Tassopoulos, *To ithikopolitiko themelio*, pp. 196–7 (see Note 7).
11. See L. Bredvold – R. Ross, *The Philosophy of Edmund Burke*, Ann Arbor 1967, p. 38.
12. See, on the prevalence of the politics of conflict over the quest for consensus, E. Christodoulidis (1994), 'The Suspect Intimacy between Law and Political Community', *Archiv für Rechts-und Sozialphilosophie* 80, p. 1.
13. See for legal principles, H. Hart and A. Sacks (1994), *The Legal Process*, Westbury, pp. 113, 143–58. The classic exposition of the normative importance of legal principles is R. Dworkin (1977), 'Hard Cases', in *Taking Rights Seriously*, Cambridge, p. 81. The emphasis on legal principles combined with the notion that the political community 'should show not only concern but an *equal* concern for all members' (R. Dworkin (1986), *Law's Empire*, Cambridge, p. 200) leads to an inclusive constitutional tradition.
14. See C. Schmitt (1928), *Verfassungslehre,* Berlin; Italian transl. A. Caracciolo (1984), *Dottrina Della Costituzione*, Milan, p. 283.
15. See Dred Scott v. Sanford, 60 US (19 How.) 393 (1857), discussed in A. Bickel (1975), *The Morality of Consent*, New Haven, p. 33.
16. See N. Alivizatos (1983), *Oi politikoi thesmoi se krisi (1922–1974)* [*The Political Institutions in Crisis (1922–1974)*], Athens, pp. 525–600.
17. See L. Stavrianos (2000), *The Balkans since 1453*, London, pp. 475, 525.
18. Ibid., p. 474.
19. Ibid.
20. See G. Dertilis (1985), *Koinonikos metaschimatismos kai stratiotiki epemvasi 1880–1909* [*Social Change and Military Intervention 1880–1909*], 3rd edn, Athens, p.181.
21. See G. Mavrogordatos (1983), *Stillborn Republic*, Berkeley, p. 5.
22. See Dertilis, *Koinonikos metaschismatismos,* p. 186 (see Note 20).
23. See G. Ventiris (1970), *I Ellas tou 1910–1920* [*Greece 1910–1920*], Athens, vol. I, p. 61.
24. See Mavrogordatos, *Stillborn Republic*, p. 122 (see Note 21).
25. See constitution of 1864, art. 107, par. 1. Found in all Collections of Greek constitutional documents.
26. See Dertilis, *Koinonikos Metaschismatismos*, pp. 210–12 (see Note 20); G. Ventiris, *I Ellas*, pp. 63, 64 (see Note 23).

27. See M. Davis and G. Papaioannou (1911), *To istorikon tis anatheoriseos tou Syntagmatos kai ta episima keimena. To neon Syntagma* [*The Chronicle of the Constitution's Revision and the Official Documents. The New Constitution*], Athens, pp. 6–7.
28. Ibid., p. 11.
29. Ibid., pp. 13–14, 45–6.
30. The Revisionist Parliament was 'double', as provided by article 107 of the constitution of 1864: 'Once the revision is decided, the existing parliament is dissolved and a new one is convened for this special purpose, composed of double the number of deputies, which decides about the provisions to be amended'; however, other conditions for the revision of the constitution set out by article 107 were not fulfilled. See in this respect, Nicos Alivizatos (1981), *Eisagogi stin elliniki syntagmatiki istoria* [*Introduction to Greek Constitutional History*], Athens, p. 100.
31. Ibid., pp. 100–1.
32. See Davis and Papaioannou, *To istorikon*, pp. 46–7 (see Note 27).
33. See Alivizatos, *Eisagogi*, p. 101 (see Note 30).
34. See Davis and Papaioannou, *To istorikon*, pp. 14–15 (see note 27).
35. See S. I. Stephanou (ed.) (1981), *Eleftheriou Venizelou ta keimena, 1909–1936* [Eleftherios Venizelos' Texts, *1909–1936*], hereafter: *Keimena*, vol. I, Athens, p. 173.
36. Ibid., p. 194.
37. Ibid., p. 197.
38. See Davis and Papaioannou, *To istorikon*, p. 16 (see Note 27).
39. See following text.
40. See A. Manessis (1959), *Deux états nées en 1830*, Brussels; Alivizatos, *Eisagogi*, p. 106 (see Note 30).
41. See A. Manessis (1980), 'I dimokratiki archi eis to Syntagma tou 1864', in A. Manessis, *Syntagmatiki Theoria kai Praxi* ['The Democratic Principle in the Constitution of 1864'] [*Constitutional Theory and Practice*], Thessaloniki, p. 65.
42. Constitution of 1864, art. 31.
43. See A. Dimitropoulos (1991), *I Archi tis Dedilomenis* [*The Principle of Declared Confidence*], Athens, p. 134.
44. Constitution of 1864, art. 58 (see Note 25).
45. Constitution of 1864, art. 78 (see Note 25).
46. See Dimitropoulos, *I Archi*, p. 14 (see Note 43).
47. See Alivizatos, *Eisagogi*, p. 97 (see Note 30).
48. See C. Tsoukalas (1981), *Koinoniki anaptyxi kai kratos* [*Social Development and the State*], Athens, p. 319.
49. See *Keimena*, vol. I, p. 203 (see Note 35).
50. Ibid., p. 176.
51. Ibid., p. 177. See also Papacosma, 'O El. Venizelos', in Dimitrakopoulos and Veremis (eds), *Meletimata* p. 499 (see Note 4). But see also

C. Jordan-Sima, 'O Venizelos kai to provlima tis engathidrysis avasileftis dimokratias stin Ellada' ['Venizelos and the Establishment of a Republican Regime in Greece'], in the same book, p. 505.

52. See in this respect the comment of Th. Veremis (1999), 'Venizelos' Political Philosophy', *I Kathimerini,* 24 October, p. 10.
53. Ibid.
54. See Note 8.
55. See Alivizatos, *Eisagogi*, p. 102 (see Note 30).
56. Ibid., p. 103.
57. See on the Second National Assembly, I. A. Tassopoulos (1993), *The Constitutional Problem of Subversive Advocacy in the United States of America and Greece*, Athens, p. 74.
58. See Alivizatos, *Eisagogi,* p. 106 (see Note 30).
59. See Alivizatos, 'Venizelos kai syntagmatikos eksynchronismos' in Mavrogordatos and Hadjiiosif (eds), *Venizelismos*, p. 35 (see Note 3).
60. See *Official Gazette*, Parliamentary Debates, session 77, 30 April 1911, p. 1954.
61. Ibid.
62. Ibid., p. 1955.
63. Ibid., p. 1954–55.
64. Ibid., p. 1955.
65. Ibid., p. 1953.
66. See *Official Gazette*, Parliamentary Debates, session 85, 10 May 1911, p. 2185.
67. See *Official Gazette*, Parliamentary Debates, session 92, 18 May 1911, p. 2331.
68. See *Official Gazette,* Parliamentary Debates, session 113, 14 June 1911, p. 2854.
69. See *Official Gazette*, Parliamentary Debates, session 61, 30 March 1911, p. 1459.
70. See *Official Gazette*, Parliamentary Debates, session 57, 23 March 1911, p. 1329.
71. See *Official Gazette*, Parliamentary Debates, session 113, 14 June 1911, p. 2853–4. On Venizelos' charisma, see Mavrogordatos, *Stillborn Republic*, p. 55 (see Note 21).
72. See *Official Gazette*, Parliamentary Debates, session 88, 13 May 1911, p. 2257. But he did not address the issue of legislative delegation to the executive; see Alivizatos, 'Venizelos kai syntagmatikos eksynchronismos', in Mavrogordatos and Hadjiiosif (eds), *Venizelismos,* p. 40 (see Note 3).
73. See *Official Gazette*, Parliamentary Debates, session 54, 19 March 1911, p. 1217.
74. See Alivizatos, in Mavrogordatos and Hadjiiosif (eds), *Venizelismos*, p. 40; *Official Gazette*, Parliamentary Debates, session 47, 11 March 1911, p. 992.

75. See e.g. *Official Gazette*, Parliamentary Debates, session 113, 14 June 1911, p. 2,853; *Official Gazette*, Parliamentary Debates, session 57, 23 March 1911, p. 1339.
76. See following text.
77. See Alivizatos, *Eisagogi*, p. 109 (see Note 30).
78. See G. Ventiris (1970), *I Ellas tou 1910–1920* [Greece 1910–1920], Athens, 2 vols.
79. For the full exposition of the historical events see Ventiris, *I Ellas* (see Note 23). See also Alivizatos, *Eisagogi*, p. 110 (see Note 30); G. Anastasiadis (1981), *O diorismos kai i pafsi ton kyverniseon tis Ellados* [*The Appointment and Dismissal of Government in Greece*], Thessaloniki, p. 93; B. S. Markesinis (1972), *The Theory and Practice of the Dissolution of Parliament*, Cambridge, p. 162; G. Mavrogordatos, *Stillborn Republic*, p. 26 (see Note 21).
80. See Alivizatos, *Eisagogi*, p. 115 (see Note 30).
81. Constitution 1911, art. 31 (see Note 25).
82. Constitution 1911, art. 37 (see Note 25).
83. See Dimitropoulos, *I Archi*, p. 134 (see Note 43).
84. Ibid., pp. 95–100; Markesinis, *The Theory*, p. 154 (see Note 79):

    The Diliyannis version was finally adopted according to which a minority government could be appointed provided it immediately obtained the confidence of the House or dissolved if it were censured. Had Trikoupis' doctrine been fully implemented, dissolution would have been rarely used since it would only be possible for a majority party to advise it.

    But it should be noted that Diliyannis' version of the doctrine of declared majority was not valid under the constitution of 1952: A. Manessis (1991), *Ai eggyiseis tiriseos tou Syntagmatos* [*Guarantees for the Observation of the Constitution*], Athens, p. 454, Note 73.
85. See A. Svolos (1942), *Syntagmatikon Dikaion* [*Constitutional Law*], vol. 2, Athens, p. 59; Markesinis, *The Theory*, at p. 172 (see Note 79); Anastasiadis, *O diorismos*, p. 95 (see Note 79).
86. See e.g. Anastasiadis, *O diorismos*, pp. 25–6 (see Note 79).
87. See Manessis, *Eggyiseis*, pp. 453–4 (see Note 84).
88. See Markesinis, *The Theory*, pp. 176 (see Note 79).
89. See S. Stephanou (ed.) (1969), *Eleftheriou Venizelou Politikai Ypothikai* [*Eleftherios Venizelos' Political Legacy*], vol. II, Athens, pp. 28, 39–40.
90. See Note 41.
91. See e.g. Mavrogordatos, *Stillborn Republic*, p. 316 (see Note 21).
92. To my knowledge, the best exposition of such a version of legal positivism in constitutional law is Ch. Eisenmann (1986), *La Justice Constitutionnelle et la Haute Cour Constitutionnelle D'Autriche*, Paris, pp. 11, 17–20.
93. See *Official Gazette*, Parliamentary Debates, 25 August 1920, p. 1061.
94. See Alivizatos, *Eisagogi*, p. 121 (see Note 30).

95. See Constitution 1975/1986/2001. See also, Prokopis Pavlopoulos (2001), in D. Tsatsos – Ev. Venizelos and X. Kontiadis (eds), *To Neo Syntagma* [*The New Constitution*], Athens, p. 470; Ev. Venizelos, in the same book, p. 484.
96. See G. Mavrogordatos (1996), *Ethnikos dichasmos kai maziki organosi* [*National Schism and Mass Organisation*], Athens, p. 95.
97. See Note 81.
98. See *Keimena*, vol. II: *1915–1920*, p. 312 (see Note 35).
99. See *Keimena*, vol. III: *1920–1929*, p. 125 (see Note 35).
100. See Alivizatos, *Politikoi thesmoi*, pp. 43–52 (see Note 16).
101. See N. Tsiros (2000), *Kratos – Exousia – Koinovouleftiko systima se thesmiki kai politiki krisi* [*State – Power – Parliamentary System in Institutional and Political Crisis*], Athens, p. 254; Stephanou (ed.), *Politikai Ypothikai*, pp. 619, 704, 706 (see Note 89).
102. See Tsiros, *Kratos*, pp. 257–80 (see Note 101); Alivizatos, *Politikoi thesmoi*, p. 340 (see Note 16).
103. See C. Rossiter (1979), *Constitutional Dictatorship*, Westport, pp. 75, 131, 207; Tassopoulos, *Subversive Advocacy*, p. 108 (see Note 57).
104. See Alivizatos, *Eisagogi*, p. 136 (see Note 30).
105. See Th. Veremis (1997), *The Military in Greek Politics*, London, pp. 88–9, 132–3 and the same author's contribution on Venizelos and civil military relations in the present volume.
106. Constitution 1927, art. 67 (see Note 25).
107. Ibid., arts 31, 32 (see Note 25).
108. Ibid., art. 89 (see Note 25).
109. Ibid., art. 5 (see Note 25).
110. Ibid., arts 16, 18 (see Note 25).
111. Ibid., arts 21–3 (see Note 25).
112. See Alivizatos, *Eisagogi*, p. 47 (see Note 30); Tassopoulos, *Subversive Advocacy*, pp. 105, 106 (see Note 57).
113. See Mavrogordatos, *Stillborn Republic*, p. 36 (see Note 21).
114. See Alivizatos, 'Venizelos kai syntagmatikos eksynchronismos', in Mavrogordatos and Hadjiiosif (eds), *Venizelismos*, p. 37 (see Note 3).
115. See C. Polychroniadis (1943), *Ai gnomai tou Eleftheriou Venizelou peri metarrythmiseos tou politevmatos* [*The Views of Eleftherios Venizelos on the Reform of the Regime*], vol. 2, Athens, pp. 52, 63, 110.
116. See Alivizatos, 'Venizelos kai Syntagmatikos eksynchronismos', in Mavrogordatos and Hadjiiosif (eds), *Venizelismos*, p. 38 (see Note 3).
117. See Mavrogordatos, *Stillborn Republic*, p. 41 (see Note 21).
118. See G. Daphnis (1997), *I Ellas metaxy dyo polemon 1923–1940* [*Greece between two wars 1923–1940*], vol. II, Athens, p. 149.
119. See Mavrogordatos, *Stillborn Republic*, p. 43 (see Note 21).
120. As noted elsewhere in this volume, the attempted coup of 1935 was approved by Venizelos.

121. See Mavrogordatos, *Stillborn Republic*, p. 51 (see Note 21).
122. See Daphnis, *I Ellas*, p. 395 (see Note 118).
123. See Mavrogordatos, *Stillborn Republic*, p. 322 (see Note 21). He continues:

> Concretely, and especially in Venizelist eyes, the Republic was embodied *not* in its constitution but rather in two *key*, if less dignified, documents: the army list and the electoral law, symbolizing the interdependence of military and parliamentary strategies.

124. See Alivizatos, 'Venizelos kai Syntagmatikos eksynchronismos', in Mavrogordatos and Hadjiosif (eds), *Venizelismos*, pp. 42, 43 (see Note 3).

9

Venizelos and Civil–Military Relations

Thanos Veremis

The 1967 military dictatorship in Greece came as a surprise to all foreign observers who considered the country part of a Western family of democratic regimes. The event generated a belated interest in the study of Greek civil–military relations and scholarly research sought to identify the precursors of 21 April 1967.[1] The Venizelist coup which backed the break-away Thessaloniki government of 1916 was probably the first of a series that politicised the officer corps and introduced the armed forces to military conspiracies.

The role of the military throughout the nineteenth century was of a different nature. The first mission of the regular army and its officer corps in post-independence Greece was to consolidate the authority of the centralised state and its institutions.[2] While accomplishing that task officers also embraced the ideology of Greece's expansion and were engaged in the irredentist pursuits of the Greek kingdom. Throughout the nineteenth century the military rarely challenged civilian supremacy in state policy. When they did enter the political discourse in the twentieth century, officers were initially united in their protest against the shortcomings of the crown and its supporters but were later subordinated to liberal or royalist agendas rather than acting as a corporate body. The only organised attempt against civilian authorities that conformed to the pattern of a corporate military conspiracy, namely the coup of 1935 against the government of Panagis Tsaldaris, was undermined by clientele networks and personal rivalries and failed miserably. Its failure in fact taught the military that they could never antagonise the civilian arbiters of the state effectively unless they could invoke a larger threat to the social order. Those officers who profited from this lesson came thirty-two years later to launch their successful coup.

Military interventions between 1909 and 1935 can be divided into two basic categories: those that acquired wider national significance and were endorsed by the public, and those aimed merely at promoting the private interests of various influential military figures and their clienteles. The coups of 1909, 1916 and 1922 made the army a champion of national aspirations and expansionist dreams, or an instrument to punish erring politicians. Civilian participation was considerable in these coups whose main objective was to substitute one set of civilian rulers for another. With the exception of the 1935 coup, interventions between 1923 and 1935 were usually instigated by officers with personal grievances, leaving civilians uninvolved and uninterested.[3]

The Military League of 1909 staged an effective demonstration of the officer corps' determination to rid Greece from an inept political and royal establishment and enjoyed wide popular acclaim. The protagonists of the league summoned to the helm an unknown lawyer with an impressive record in the struggle for Cretan independence. Eleftherios Venizelos advised his admirers to confine their zeal to their professional sphere, and made himself visible in Greek politics. By the end of 1910 he was already prime minister with an overwhelming mandate for reform.

The need to rely on personal contacts for professional advancement drove the less professionally secure officers to search for military patrons. The nature of patronage was flexible (except in periods of national division), which gave a client the chance to change patrons if his own failed to deliver favours. Every client became in turn the patron of lower-ranking officers, and so on. Any similarity that may appear, however, between clientele networks and the formal military hierarchy, is superficial. Unlike the latter case where each junior officer was obliged to obey all his superiors in rank, clientage hierarchies demanded exclusive loyalty, at the expense of rival networks.[4]

It is therefore easy to understand why clientelism in the armed forces had a pernicious effect on the discipline and the operability of the chain of command. Antagonisms among officers of the same political camp, but of different clientage networks were frequent. Military organisations such as the National Defence of 1916, the Revolution of 1922, the Military League, the Republican Battalions, as well as many others with less visibility, all consisted of an assortment of followers held together by a weak bond of ideology and vulnerable to dissolution at every change in the terms of patronage contracts.

Venizelist and anti-Venizelist adherents in the armed forces were preoccupied with their petty conspiracies while significant changes were occurring around them. The Asia Minor catastrophe of 1922 and the influx of one and a half million refugees into a country of barely five million, transformed Greek society. The urban centres received the bulk of the dispossessed refugees and the Greek Communist Party (KKE) found willing recruits among their numbers. The threat that the party posed to the established social order of the inter-war period may not have been formidable, but the attempt of the Comintern (Communist International) to alienate recently acquired territories from Northern Greece was an issue that caused a national outcry against the KKE. The decision of the party to fall in line with the Bulgarian slogan for a 'United Macedonia and Thrace' (under Bulgarian tutelage) during the sixth Balkan Communist Conference of 1924, caused a major split among its members and later on gave Venizelos a reason to clamp down on the Greek communists. The Communist Party's challenge addressed the entire system and could have posed a formidable threat to the socio-economic establishment of Greece. It could, in other words, have unified the fragmented military against it if the threat it posed had been credible.

In spite of their weakness in a country without a significant industrial labour force, the communists managed to transform the content of Greek nationalism, from its nineteenth-century appeal to all unredeemed Orthodox Christians in Ottoman lands, to an exclusive ideological preserve of those who allegedly could trace their ancestry back to antiquity.

Venizelos' own nationalist views were initially in line with those of the 'unredeemed' Greeks, but after the completion of the country's unification he too adopted more parochial views about the Greek nation. Gradually Greek nationalism reformuluted its theory to recast the Greeks as an exceptional people in the Balkans whose culture was threatened by hostile Slavs and alien ideologies such as communism. Under the Metaxas dictatorship (1936–40) this perception was articulated into a creed that would reappear after the war as a preserve of conservatives and right-wingers in politics.

The inter-war military clients of Venizelos naturally agreed with such views, but even anti-Venizelist officers shared this new nationalism with their adversaries. The 1916 schism between royalists and Venizelists in the army was determined by circumstances rather than ideological differences. Once privileges were granted to the victors the cleavage acquired a lasting nature. An issue that caused bitter antagonism among the military was the celebrated Army List. According to law 927 of 1917, officers who had fought with the National Defence in Thessaloniki were granted an extra ten months of service in their seniority ranking giving them the benefit of precedence over others in the seniority list. This extraordinary arrangement, which favoured a specific sector of the officer corps, was the cause of most inter-war military disputes, even among Venizelist officers.

Some of the officers in the Thessaloniki government of 1916 and the protagonists of the 1922 military regime under Colonel Nikolaos Plastiras, re-emerged between 1923 and 1926 as heads of patronage networks that promised their clients security and promotion. With royalist competition formally out of the way after the establishment of the republic in 1924, Venizelist officers shed all pretences of ideological commitment to their leader and strove to improve their own professional prospects. Officers such as Georgios Kondylis and Stylianos Gonatas retired from active service and pursued political careers, while Plastiras abstained from formal politics but continued to exert backstage influence on his clients. Theodoros Pangalos managed to usurp power briefly in 1925–6, but was overthrown by his own praetorian supporters and imprisoned. The Pangalos dictatorship had not only reaped its crop of errors on the economic and foreign policy fronts, but it had alienated both Venizelists and royalists. After the inconclusive elections of 1926, a widespread spirit of tolerance and moderation prevailed that led to the formation of a coalition government under the veteran politician Alexandros Zaimis, known as Oikoumeniki, in which all the major parties were given ministries.

On 14 December 1926 the minister of army affairs in the coalition government, General Alexandros Mazarakis, introduced a bill on the status of 2836 officers dismissed from the army between 1917 and 1923, mainly because of their anti-Venizelist activities. The Populist (anti-Venizelist) Party deputies in the government made the rehabilitation of some of these officers a condition for reconciliation. The Populists argued that since most of the officers had been dismissed en masse after the November 1923 coup, they should all be readmitted and judged along with their colleagues on active duty on the basis of their professional competence rather than their political affiliations. Liberal deputies retorted that the purpose of any decision on the issue should be the prevention of politically minded officers from undermining the unity of the army. In fact the army was already the preserve of Venizelist officers, and the concern of liberal politicians was about reinstating cashiered officers of the anti-Venizelist camp who could in time challenge their own control of the institution. After many tribulations the bill finally reinstated 341 officers and was published in the *Official Gazette* on 2 June 1927. Venizelist officers threatened the government with military action and it took the intervention of an improbable champion of legality, the longstanding friend of Venizelos, Plastiras, to dissuade his fellow republicans from launching a coup. Venizelos himself, still in retirement, wavered before siding with Plastiras in favour of the bill.[5] His subsequent return to active politics marked a departure from the conciliatory spirit of the coalition government and a polarisation between liberals and royalists.

Before discussing Venizelos' final act as a patron of his officer-clients, it is necessary to recount his previous attitudes vis-à-vis the officers. Venizelos' initial attitude towards the military was unmistakably firm. In his first term as prime minister (1910–12) he was strict in enforcing order when incidents of disobedience occurred against his benign treatment of the royal family.[6] Upon the successful conclusion of the Balkan Wars, Venizelos reminded his chief of general staff, Victor Dousmanis, a long-time royalist who later turned against him, of the decisive role of politics in winning the armed conflict, after having praised the military for their performance.[7] Subsequent involvement in the Thessaloniki coup of 1916 against King Constantine's neutralist policy made Venizelos a party to favouritism among the officer network. Thus, throughout his 1917 to 1920 term he turned a blind eye to the high-handed tactics of his clients (Kondylis, Pangalos, Hatzikyriakos, and so on) and by failing to restore order among his followers, encouraged clientelism within the army.

During the period 1917 to 1920, bitter recriminations against Venizelos abounded from his royalist detractors. Considerable criticism was also levelled by the more objective officers of this period. Professionals with impeccable records of neutrality in the Venizelist-royalist dispute, such as Generals P. Kontoyannis and A. Charalambis, bemoaned the collapse of military hierarchy and discipline.[8] Even friends who had collaborated in setting up the Venizelist government of 1917 in Athens, such as Generals P. Danglis and A. Mazarakis-Ainian, pointed out the extreme acts committed by the more fanatical Venizelist officers at the expense of their opponents on active duty, as well as Venizelos' own negligence.[9]

After the collapse of the Asia Minor expeditionary force and the expulsion of most of the Greek population of Turkey, the military coup of Plastiras and Gonatas relied on Venizelos for advice on their future course. By discouraging these and other military aspirant dictators from holding onto power permanently, Venizelos was instrumental in reviving democracy after the collapse of 1922. His letter to the leader of the '1922 Revolution', Nikolaos Plastiras, of 21 November 1922, is a superb apology on behalf of parliamentary democracy and an eloquent condemnation of the military as political arbiters.[10] In 1924 Venizelos resigned as head of the government to avoid a face-on clash with his military friends and withdrew from politics for more than four years.

The legacy of the government of National Unity (Oikoumeniki) in restoring civilian supremacy in politics was reinforced by Venizelos' election to power in 1928. However, when Venizelos began to raise the spectre of a restoration of the monarchy in 1932, republican officers susceptible to alarm rallied to his side.

Military organisations such as the National Defence of 1916, the Revolution of 1922, the Military League, the Republican Battalions (a unit that occasionally turned against the government) as well as less important ones such as the Organisation of Majors, Kondylis' Kynigoi, the League of Recalcitrant Officers and paramilitary organisations such as the Epistratoi and the Republican Defence, all consisted of a diverse assortment of adherents held together by a weak bond of ideology and vulnerable to dissolution at every change in patronage between civilians and the military. Membership was by no means a levelling element among members of unequal status, while all the problems of vertical recruitment often disrupted the organisations' effectiveness.

In March 1935 a coalition of republican officers and civilians sought to overthrow the government of Panagis Tsaldaris (a moderate conservative), allegedly to avert an impending return of the monarchy. A distinction between civilian and military conspirators does not clarify the nature of the opposition that existed between the different groupings that made up the loose republican coalition responsible for the coup of 1935. Examining the different categories of the military who were implicated is more revealing. There were roughly three such categories. First, there was a group which played a minor role in the outbreak of the coup, made up of older retired officers who somehow felt, like Nikolaos Plastiras, that an officer's mission does not cease with his career in the service. Generals Neokosmos Grigoriadis and Anastasios Papoulas, both members of Republican Defence, were two such cases. Secondly, there were officers who had been dismissed either at the fall of the dictator Theodoros Pangalos in 1926, such as Napoleon Zervas and Andreas Kolialexis, or after the attempt by Plastiras to seize power in 1933, such as Leonidas Spais, Ilias Diamesis and Miltiadis Kimisis, whose main motive was the desire to re-enter the army or navy. Their obstinate faith in Plastiras and their impatience in pressing for action soon placed them at odds with the third group, the ESO (Elliniki Stratiotiki Organosis [Greek Military Organisation]), which consisted mainly of junior officers, graduates of the military academy, with ambitious plans to reform the army into an élitist institution, independent of politics.

Although the coup was initially conceived by Venizelist politicians as a pre-emptive measure against the Populist government, the active participation of civilians in it was ultimately limited to Venizelos and a few of his close friends. Most of the politicians involved had made feeble attempts to direct different military groupings, and were either ignored by the officers or dropped out at various stages of the organisation.[11]

The conviction of Venizelos that the republican officers were still the servants of his political designs had been overtaken by events. His flight to Crete after friction with members of the government in parliament had deprived him of a clear view of newly emerging military groupings. Although old allies such as General Alexandros Othonaios were still active in the army, the latter's staff officer Colonel Stephanos Saraphis and his ESO conspirators, were outside Venizelos' influence. Contrary to what Venizelos may have thought, the members of the ESO had no intention of facilitating the return of officers who had been dismissed for collaborating with Plastiras in his failed coup of 1933. Between the members of the ESO, who were sophisticated military academy graduates, and the more traditional officers of the Republican Defence, there was no point of agreement other than their general desire to overthrow the Populist government. In fact, a large gap separated them, and Venizelos did not realise that the goals of the two groups were incompatible. It was this very rivalry among hypothetical allies that undermined his coup of 1935.

The origins of the ESO can be placed sometime in early 1932 when Venizelos was threatening his Populist opponents with military intervention. With Othonaios organising a clandestine Military League insubordination had again become rampant. Younger officers such as Lieutenants Nikolaos Skanavis and Markos Kladakis, despite being Venizelists, felt indignant at the way political patrons were corrupting the professional ethos of officers and turning them into the familiar 'condottieri' of the 1920s. By 1932 the percentage of academy graduates among junior officers had risen. Those from Evelpidon, in whom professional pride was strong, formed a separate caste within the army. They read literature, discussed international affairs and despised their seniors who had risen from the ranks. Education was at a higher premium than reckless valour, and the independence of the army from politics was their most cherished goal.[12]

In August 1934 Venizelos invited members of the ESO to Crete, and pointed out to Saraphis and Chr. Tsigantes the danger of a restoration of the monarchy, urging them to act on the same lines as the officers of the coup of 1909. Saraphis replied that if circumstances led to a revolution they would wish to have Venizelos as their leader, but without the company of civilian councillors who had brought the republican camp into disrepute. It was the first time that the military protégé of Venizelos had dared impose conditions on his patron, but the significance of the incident escaped the old statesman who retained the illusion that the army was still prepared to do his bidding. Venizelos, although out of touch with the undercurrents, sought to use the officers without compromising his own credibility as a guarantor of normal parliamentary practices.

Venizelos lost control of the coup from the outset. His message calling for its postponement was ignored; the fleet, confusing his instructions, arrived at his doorstep in Crete instead of sailing to Thessaloniki to aid General Dimitrios Kammenos who therefore delayed his action. On the whole, Venizelist officers did not take advantage of the element of surprise and reverted to defensive tactics, hoping perhaps that the government would collapse before the fighting began. In spite of his disappointment, Venizelos handled the political aspect of the coup with dexterity. He capitalised on the government's error in proclaiming martial law, while reassuring the public that the coup was a harmless incident. Venizelos rightly pointed out that the government either had to admit that it faced a serious threat, in which case only parliament could decide if martial law was the correct response, or it had to acknowledge that its measures were unconstitutional. The 2 March issue of *Kathimerini* admitted openly that dictatorship was no longer a theoretical issue but the only way of facing the danger of revolution. Formally, therefore, Venizelos appeared to be opposing a government which had infringed the constitution. His proclamation in favour of the insurgents rekindled anti-Venizelist hysteria. His effigy was burned in public, petitions were signed against him, and the more fanatical newspapers called him a 'mad dog' and demanded that he be shut up in an asylum.[13] Georgios Vlachos, owner of *Kathimerini*, wrote on 2 March: 'The republic and its imaginary perils are inventions of the old man from Chalepa and his criminal mob whose preoccupation is to seize power.'[14] In this anti-Venizelist frenzy, all those held in prison for the attempt on the life of Venizelos in 1933 (including the ex-police commissioner, Polychronopoulos), were released.

In spite of the large number of people who were mobilised, the coup of 1935 was relatively bloodless. No more than four or five soldiers and civilians were killed and a few officers were wounded. Two officers committed suicide and three more were court-martialled and executed. Among them were the leading figures of Republican Defence, Generals A. Papoulas and M. Kimissis, who had done nothing during the evening of 1 March 1935. By the time the coup erupted, Saraphis and Tsigantes had severed all their contacts with them. Their death sentence was an act of anti-Venizelist vengeance. Both Papoulas (a royalist before 1922) and Kimissis had in different ways been instrumental in the execution of the six prominent royalists in 1922 (Prime Minister D. Gounaris; the commander-in-chief of the armed forces in Asia Minor, General G. Hadjianestis; and four Ministers – all court-martialled and condemned to death as responsible for Greece's Asia Minor catastrophe). Cavalry Major S. Volanis, who was left to rebel alone against the authorities of Thessaloniki, was also executed.

Between 10 March and 14 May, when martial law was finally lifted, 1130 officers and civilians were tried. Sixty were sentenced to death, of whom fifty-five – including Venizelos and Plastiras – had already fled abroad, and two were pardoned. Fifty-seven were sentenced to life imprisonment and seventy-six were given light terms.

The failure of the coup was attributed to a variety of reasons. Undertakings on a large scale required the kind of organisation which was almost impossible to sustain in Greece. Given the traditional competitiveness between factions at all levels of Greek society, Venizelos should not have delegated authority to so many participants. Zannas failed as a co-ordinator because each group demanded autonomy of action and refused to submit its plans to his scrutiny. Venizelos was the only figure commanding sufficient authority to act as a leader of the operation, but by 1935 he was too old and tired to assume command over the conspirators. Instead he decided to mobilise all anti-government forces to act on his behalf.

Among the conspirators there were varying degrees of attachment to Venizelos, who was the general point of reference of the undertaking. Zannas, Argyropoulos and the navy were loyal to him, whereas the loyalty of ESO, Saraphis and Tsigantes was questionable.

The absence of strong common ideological grounds shared by the various groups was thinly disguised by a republican front. Diversity of aims and motives hampered co-operation and impaired the outcome of the coup. In addition to their Venizelist allegiance, individuals strove to further the interests of different and often conflicting patrons. ESO's effort to destroy the traditional clientage arrangement in the army and replace it with professional meritocracy failed dismally. Saraphis was the client of Othonaios and the Tsigantes brothers had been attached to Pangalos. The dismissed officers of the Republican Defence depended on Plastiras to return to the army; and the navy, basically loyal to Venizelos, was divided between Demestichas and Kolialexis.[15]

The collapse of the coup and Venizelos' flight from Greece signified a transformation of partisan clientele in the armed forces. After a long period of Venizelist domination the army became the preserve of royalists.

The coup had profound implications for both internal and external Greek affairs. The restoration of King George II in 1935, which came about partly in consequence of a purge of Venizelists from the army following the coup, had a direct impact on Greek foreign policy up till the Second World War.

The reinstatement of Venizelist officers who had been dismissed for their alleged involvement with the 1935 coup preoccupied Venizelos in his self-exile shortly before his death in 1936. King George was prepared to use their reinstatement as a way of securing Venizelist compliance to his rule, but, as it turned out, the dictatorship of Metaxas, inaugurated on 4 August 1936, made this compromise unnecessary. With almost 1500 Venizelists out of the armed forces, the 5000-strong officer corps under Metaxas (or, more appropriately, under King George) was ideologically the most homogeneous that twentieth-century Greece ever had.

Venizelos did not live to see the full consequences of the 1935 coup. When George II dismissed General Papagos, who was opposed to the reinstatement of cashiered Venizelist officers, Venizelos was led to believe that the monarch had at last become the king of all the Greeks. Little did he suspect that Metaxas was the candidate for the forthcoming dictatorship.[16]

NOTES

1. For a comprehensive analysis of historical research in Greece on civil–military relations see 'Note on the sources' in Thanos Veremis (1997), *The Military in Greek Politics. From Independence to Democracy*, London, pp. 189–95. Books on the subject in English are few: John S. Koliopoulos (1987), *Brigands with a Cause: Brigandage and Irredentism in Modern Greece 1821–1912*, Oxford; S. Victor Papacosma (1977), *The Military in Greek Politics: The 1909 Coup d' Etat*, Kent; Constantine Danopoulos (1984), *Warriors and Politicians in Modern Greece*, Chapel Hill; Nicholas Stavrou (1977), *Allied Policies and Military Interventions*, Athens; C. M. Woodhouse (1985), *The Rise and Fall of the Greek Colonels*, London.

   Even fewer are the articles in scholarly journals: Andre Gerolymatos (1984), 'The Role of the Greek Officer Corps in the Resistance', *Journal of the Hellenic Diaspora* 11(3), (Fall), pp. 69–79 and (1985) 'The Security Battalions and Civil War', *Journal of the Hellenic Diaspora* 12(1), (Spring), pp. 17–27; Nicos Alivizatos (1991), 'Civilian Supremacy over the Military. The Case of Modern Greece', *Revue de droit militaire et de droit de la guerre* 30, pp. 9–28; Hagen Fleischer (1978), 'The "Anomalies" in the Greek Middle-East Forces, 1941–1944', *Journal of the Hellenic Diaspora* 5(3), (Fall), pp. 5–36.
2. See John A. Petropulos (1968), *Politics and Statecraft in the Kingdom of Greece 1833–1843*, Princeton, pp. 165–72 and generally.
3. Th. Veremis (1978), 'Some Observations on the Greek Military in the Inter-War Period, 1918–35', *Armed Forces and Society* 4(3) (May), pp. 527–41.
4. Th. Veremis (1976), 'The Officer Corps in Greece (1912–36)', *Byzantine and Modern Greek Studies* 2, pp. 113–33.
5. Veremis, *The Military in Greek Politics*, esp. pp. 90–8: 'The Sensitive Issue of the Army List' (see Note 1).

6. D. Dakin (1972), *The Unification of Greece*, London, pp. 188–9.
7. Victor Dousmanis (1946), *Apomnimonevmata* [*Memoirs*], Athens, pp. 143–4.
8. P. Kontoyannis (1924), *O Stratos mas kai oi teleftaioi polemoi* [*Our Army and the Last Wars*], Athens, pp. 350–6; A. Haralambis (1947), *Anamniseis* [*Recollections*], Athens, p. 91.
9. A. Mazarakis-Ainian (1948), *Apomnimonevmata* [*Memoirs*], Athens, p. 213; P. G. Danglis (1965), *Anamniseis, etc.* [*Recollections etc.*], vol. 2, Athens, p. 253.
10. *E. Venizelos Papers* (Dossier No. 268) Benaki Museum Archive. Published in S. I. Stephanou (ed.) (1983), *Eleftheriou Venizelou ta keimena 1920–1929* [*Eleftherios Venizelos' Texts 1920–1929*], vol. III, Athens, pp. 272–4.
11. Veremis, *The Military in Greek Politics*, pp. 99–133 (see Note 1).
12. G. Daphnis (1955), *I Ellas metaxy dyo polemon* [*Greece between Two Wars*], Athens: vol. II, pp. 280–300.
13. Veremis, *The Military in Greek Politics*, p. 129 (see Note 1).
14. G. Vlachos (1961), *Politika arthra* [*Political Tracts*], Athens, p. 61.
15. Articles on the 1935 trials, *Acropolis*, 18 April – 30 July 1971; also *Estia*, 5–15 March 1935. See also Daphnis, *I Ellas*, vol. II, pp. 355–7 (see Note 12).
16. John S. Koliopoulos (1977), *Greece and the British Connection, 1935–1941*, Oxford, pp. 39–43.

10

Venizelos and Economic Policy

Christine Agriantoni

Eleftherios Venizelos did not link his name with the economy, yet it was the economy that was largely responsible for his downfall. It is history's irony, in his case, that he played a part in the emergence of a new world which, in the end, annulled him. He came to power with an ambitious reform policy, which included transforming the watchman state into the welfare state, a transformation that was already in progress in the developed countries. However, the abandonment of liberalism and the preponderance of state intervention in the economy, as well as the deflection towards autocratic means of dealing with social relations, were not necessarily part of the original plan. Venizelos was led empirically in this direction, without theoretical groundwork, which is perhaps why it is particularly interesting to explore the mechanisms that brought about this shift, which is, moreover, characteristic of European history in the inter-war period.

Eleftherios Venizelos' economic 'training' was that which secondary education and legal studies were able to provide at the time he was growing up, as well as what he gleaned from practical involvement with his family's business. We know that he was taught commercial courses at high school,[1] and while in the law school of the University of Athens, where he studied from 1881 until 1887, he must have attended lectures in political economy by the 'father of economic science in Greece',[2] Ioannis Soutzos. His spell of service in his father's firm was rather brief: he ran it himself from 1883 to 1885, after the death of his father Kyriakos, but finally sold it in order to dedicate himself to his studies and to his career as a lawyer.[3] Certainly, the whole culture of this child of a bourgeois business family guaranteed him a good sense of economic issues and solid contact with entrepreneurial praxis.[4] These conditions shaped a liberal bourgeois, a typical product of the century in which he grew up. It is also well known that, after his arrival in Greece, Venizelos moved easily and almost immediately into the higher social echelons of the major entrepreneurial families.[5]

This does not, of course, mean that Venizelos was familiar with advanced economic thinking. His own discipline was law: he practised the profession, kept abreast of international legal developments and was acknowledged for his formidable knowledge and eloquence in legal matters.[6] Although the observation of the French ambassador to Greece, de Billy, in 1918, that Venizelos, 'n'est à aucun degré un financier. Il a pour les questions d'argent une ignorance d'idéaliste',[7] surely indicates a supercilious diplomat's annoyance in a moment of hard bargaining, it nonetheless contains a dose of truth: what de Billy calls 'idealism' is the absolute submission of Venizelos' economic practice to his political ambitions, something to be expected for a great political leader and furthermore from one characterised by a sophisticated pragmatism.[8]

In addition to the political determinants, the economic policy he applied in the end certainly contained elements of his personal economic philosophy and of the views of his associates. On this last point, it should be stressed that the halo of 'charisma' that surrounds Venizelos in a way isolates him from his milieu and does not facilitate elucidation of his various collaborators' contribution to the formation of his policies. As for his economic philosophy, it is useful to pinpoint its nucleus, as this was already elaborated when he arrived in Greece, before we proceed to an analysis of his economic policy.

Venizelos in 1910 can be placed securely in the current of new liberalism, which had been taking shape since the late nineteenth century. This distanced itself from classical liberalism, incorporated the ideas of social reformism and progressivism, and sought increased government intervention in order to confront the new social problems of poverty, unemployment and dramatic inequalities, which industrialisation had created. These views did not negate Venizelos' belief in free trade, in open economies and in the regulatory power of the market. However, he was well aware that ideas about the state and its functions in society had been differentiated significantly in recent decades. Speaking of the planned expropriation of the çifliks in 1911, and replying to those who cast doubts on the state's right to do so, he declared:

> [I]t would have been impossible to find support for this issue a few decades ago, but today it is feasible . . . it is impossible for the modern concept of the state to accept the private citizen standing against the interest of society as a whole, by saying: 'I insist on . . . this property . . . because that's the way I like it.'[9]

Conscious defender of the bourgeois order,[10] Venizelos was careful from the outset to differentiate himself from the socialist current, long before the Russian revolution and the sharpening of social struggles in Greece. When parliamentary deputy P. Aravantinos, from the 'sociologists' group, applauded his positions on the state, in 1911 ('he placed the state high, as the state should stand high, according to today's concept of the state . . .'), Venizelos hastened to reply:

> [I]t might cause misunderstandings, on account of the socialistic ideas you hold. It might cause misunderstandings that in the sense of state intervention in property you go much further than I do . . . It is not possible for us to have the same concept.[11]

Recognising the 'opposition between capital and labour', to which he referred repeatedly, Venizelos believed concurrently in its transcendence and in the possibility of '[these] two forces . . . in our country . . . working together in harmony'. He sought the 'collaboration of industrial capital . . . [and] the workforce . . .' and the 'development of the social solidarity of all classes . . .'[12] The entire construction of his labour policy in his first four-year term (1910–14) was based on the expectation of this collaboration as well as on the conviction that the only way for the modern state to deal with the danger of social unrest is: 'to forestall the outbreaks through the timely satisfaction of the just demands of those classes of labourers who are society's outcasts . . .'[13]

Venizelos' views on Greek society and the possibilities of the economy differed, to a degree, from the conservative views that had hitherto held sway. It is possible that he concurred with Georgios Ventiris' view on the recent 'rise of the bourgeois' in Greece,[14] since he undoubtedly identified with the bourgeoisie: he did not hide, however, his almost archetypal antipathy for large landownership and rentier mentality, which had 'a somewhat usurious character'.[15] These identifications supplied him with motivation and confidence. 'Our country is not poor, but it is unexploited,' he was to say in one of his first public interventions, declaring also that emigration, which the previous governments had looked upon favourably, was for him a 'terrifying haemorrhage of the national organism . . .'[16] This confidence of his in the potential of the domestic economy underpinned his continuous resort to foreign borrowing, even during the last four-year term of his government (1928–32), at obvious variance with the turn of the international conjuncture at that time. He never underestimated the primacy of political power: '[H]ow will it be possible for us to live life for a moment, in opposition to the powers which possess the Mediterranean? . . . These, gentlemen, are what regulated the position of Greece and not this loan,' he said in 1918, referring to the allied credits.[17] This is a view which at the same time attests to his belief in the power of the advanced states ('these colossal bodies which are the states with which we form alliances . . .'),[18] whose trust he considered necessary to win from the outset by bolstering the prestige of the state, afterwards by its total compliance with the instructions of the League of Nations, eventually by the policy of stabilisation. Nevertheless, his views on the desirable form of the Greek economy seem to be rather traditional, ascribing a central position to trade and shipping, with a particularly ambivalent stance towards industry, which was to be modified only in the last four-year term: on declaring the opening of the conference of the chambers of trade and industry in Athens in December 1919 – a critical moment for foreign trade, it is true, which was on the verge of bankruptcy – he was to say that transit trade must constitute for Greece, far more than in the past, the principal source of wealth.[19] A little later, in September 1920, on board the *Narcissus* off the coast of Smyrna, he was to speak about the new economic prospects that the expansion of Greece opened up, in the following words, as recorded by one of the few who were present:

> Greater Greece will very quickly become rich too . . . thanks to the grain-growing plains of Thrace, of Macedonia, of Thessaly and of Asia Minor [and] completely self-sufficient . . . she will have precious metals to export . . . In terms of tobacco, she will be the premier producer in Europe. And in olive oil she will lead all . . . thanks to the enormous olive groves of Asia Minor . . . raisins, wines, carpets, figs, precious metals and above all merchant shipping . . . will ensure for the country abundant, guaranteed and stable wealth.[20]

These visions reveal that for Venizelos the concept of wealth was based on a somewhat inelastic territoriality. They illuminate from another viewpoint, beyond the Great Idea and irredentism, his commitment to the territorial expansion of Greece. We should also add, lastly, his unyielding belief in the value of the 'healthy currency' policy, a basic pillar of classical liberal thinking, which he defended to the last.

1910–14, THE ERA OF 'RECOVERY'

Venizelos' first four-year term in power is distinguished by the dynamism and the strong will of a leader, whose personality was still pristine, and of the new political personnel who surrounded him. The heralded 'recovery' had a dual content: economic development – 'our policy for the development of agriculture and wealth in general',[21] as he himself characterised it – and social justice: on this issue, with obvious political aim, Venizelos concurrently gave shape to the diffuse social protest which had been manifested in many ways in the conjuncture of the military mutiny of 1909, which had also brought him to power.

The policy of economic development was framed by two new 'productive' ministries. The Ministry of Agriculture, Trade and Industry, which had been established in 1910 (law 3824) by the government of Stepfanos Dragoumis and operated from 1 January 1911, was renamed as the Ministry of National Economy in July of that year, and entrusted initially to Emmanuel Benakis and later to Andreas Michalakopoulos,[22] who remained at its helm for three years, with the 'pro-agrarian' Alexandros Mylonas as his secretary general.[23] On the other hand, the Ministry of Transport was set up in 1914 (law 276), which included the technical services of the Ministry of Home Affairs and undertook public works, railways and telecommunications (post office, telegraph and telephone), with the engineer Dimitrios Diamantidis as first minister.[24]

The Ministry of National Economy certainly placed emphasis on agriculture. In the first year of its operation, it conducted the second – the first in 1860 – systematic census of agriculture.[25] It created the institution of prefectural agronomers, organised the forestry service, founded a plant pathology service and a veterinary microbiological institute, supported agricultural education (Averoff Farm School in Larissa) and agricultural stations, promoted the import of new varieties of crops (cotton, tobacco), the improvement of viniculture and wine-making (oenological laboratories) and so on. Special attention was paid also to developing the institution of agricultural co-operatives (law 602/1914), enabling the National Bank to multiply spectacularly its loans in the farming sector. Last, in this same period the foundations were laid for major agrarian reform, that is the allocation of the large landholdings – which was to be implemented later – with the constitutional reform of 1911, which made provision for expropriating estates for reasons of 'public benefit', and with law 3856/1911, which prohibited the eviction of tenant farmers, while one of the first measures that was taken in the new provinces was to ban the transfer of immoveable properties.[26]

To this 'developmental assault' on agriculture, questions of industrialisation – other than labour issues – played second fiddle.[27] Even though the climate of recovery and the expansion of territory accelerated industrial development, Venizelos does not seem to have had a specific industrial policy at that time. On the question of the customs tariff, until then the sole political instrument in this field, he expressed from the outset the classic liberal/anti-protectionist position and seemed, indeed, hostile to industry, declaring his opposition to the 'prohibitive duties' which led to: 'the creation of industries that had no national character and had as a result . . . the indirect taxation of the consumer through the excessive increase in the price of industrial products'.[28]

However, the review of the customs tariff, which he promised right away, was never implemented.[29] Repeating the promise two years later, he took care to appease the industrialists by stressing the gradual nature of change and adding that one of his aims was simultaneously to achieve 'the reinforcement of the viable, our truly viable industry'.[30] Such vacillation bears witness to ambivalence towards the industrial phenomenon itself, which importunately disturbed the social peace and was considered almost a necessary evil: referring to the 'struggle between capital and labour' in another context, Venizelos spoke of: '[a struggle] which, beginning in our country also *of necessity* from the creation of any industry, is destined to develop daily *of necessity*, despite the discontent it arouses in a large number of people'.[31] It bears witness also to the difficulties on the negotiations front, which he had in the meantime opened with employers, after the labour legislation had been passed.

This legislation, the first of its kind in Greece, was Venizelos' most important intervention in the industrial sector, fruit of his collaboration with the social reformists and socialists,[32] an intervention which whipped up storms, led to rescissions and in the end did not bring him the expected benefits. A series of laws in 1911 and 1912 set the terms for regulations for child and female labour and introduced regulations on working conditions and hours in industry,[33] while in 1914 trade union issues were regulated, prohibiting the formation of mixed unions of employers and workers, as had been common. In order to apply the legislation, the Labour Bureau (later Inspectorate) was founded at the Ministry of National Economy (the Supreme Labour Council had been founded in 1911).

From the outset, the labour legislation met with strong opposition from the employers, who accused Venizelos of creating a labour issue where none existed, of 'scandalising the workers' and of ruining the equilibrium of the 'democratic' and 'classless' Greek society.[34] Reaction focused mainly on the issue of working hours, in combination with the problems of implementation posed by the polymorphism of Greek industry, as well as with the difficulties industry was experiencing and the spectre of unemployment that had been looming over workers since the war. As a result, working hours were not regulated uniformly in the next two decades and formed a permanent open front of social and political argument.[35] Decrees for application of the 1911 law were voted in sporadically for specific trades, while when Greece signed the international labour convention at the 1919 Washington conference, which imposed the eight-hour working day, it managed to obtain postponements for its gradual application.

Indications of Venizelos' annoyance and withdrawal to more conservative positions on labour issues were manifested as early as 1914. In a way, the law on unions passed in that year can be considered as such,[36] and certainly a little later, in September 1914, he was to support the curtailment of the right to strike for transport workers (strikes by railway and tram employees had preceded this, as well as of workers in the gas industry, typographers and so on), returning to classically conservative positions on the structures of Greek society:

> There is a misunderstanding on their part concerning the social question in Greece. A working class does of course exist here, but our industry is so small . . . that those who say that usually today's worker is tomorrow's capitalist are right.[37]

This stance demonstrates that his patience was running out after the rash of strikes in that year and, primarily, that the Great War, which had just broken out, was already creating compulsion and leading to clampdowns. Venizelos' about-turn did not go unnoticed. After exchange of fire with Spyros Theodoropoulos,[38] he was also accused of opportunism by parliamentary deputy C. Sokolis: 'Not long ago [the government] presented labour bills which . . . it confesses today outran the needs and the ideas of the Greek people . . . And we come today to bring before Parliament a dictatorial bill . . .'[39]

The said bill, which Venizelos supported, was 'on measures to secure the necessary transport and public order in the state', which foresaw the mobilisation of workers in transport services, post offices and so on in the event of strike. The industrialists, who felt vindicated and requested that gas and electricity workers be included too, commented: '[A]fter the strike . . . Venizelos began to understand that his social policy to date was not correct. Since then he has begun . . . to pay attention to the objections too.'[40]

At the budgetary level, Venizelos' first four-year premiership brought limited interventions in the taxation system and the spectacular inauguration of his policy of foreign loans. Initially, the Ministry of Finance was entrusted to Lambros Koromilas, whose prudent management and attempted 'good housekeeping' of the public accounts was praised by Andreas Andreadis.[41] Later, it passed to Alexandros Diomidis, one of Venizelos' most constant collaborators on economic issues, until his fall in 1931.[42] The 50 per cent cut in the tax on sugar was certainly an important relief for the working classes,[43] but the amendment to the law on income tax, which the then minister of finance, Athanasios Eftaxias, had introduced in 1909, rather favoured affluent taxpayers in the end. Eftaxias' tax on net income (which concerned only those incomes not taxed in another way) was replaced in 1911 – a proposal by Koromilas – by a tax on imputed income, on the basis of the rent paid and a series of other standard-of-living indices. The change was justified by reference to taxpayers' protests over the checks that Eftaxias' law imposed, but if the new law really got rid of 'all inquisitionist character', as the liberal Andreadis claimed, it also left margins of manoeuvre for taxpayers without analogous monitoring opportunities for tax-inspectors.[44]

To the arsenal of legislation relating to the economy in this period should be added law 3937/1911 'on conventional interest . . .', the first legislative measure that sought to strike at usury, as well as law 146 'on unfair competition', also the first of its kind in Greece.

The policy of foreign borrowing was inaugurated with the loan of 1911, procedures for which had been set in motion by the Dragoumis government in February 1910. The loan (of 110 million francs), which was underwritten by Greek, French and British banks, was finally issued in June 1911 and was intended for railway, water-supply and harbour projects. However, apart from one part of it, which was devoted to paying back bank advances, it was in the end absorbed in the expenses of the Balkan Wars.[45]

The cost of these two wars is estimated at 414 million drachmas (414 million gold francs).[46] The budget surpluses of the years 1910 and 1911, the contribution of the National Bank, which financed the state through domestic loans and discounting treasury bonds and bills of exchange, the operation of the International Financial Control and of law 3642/1910 enabled the financing of war outlays without increasing the fiduciary issue and without forfeiting the parity of the drachma. Nevertheless, by the end of the wars, the accumulated obligations and the increased administrative costs of the new provinces had put the treasury in a difficult situation – and the crisis in the National Bank's relations with the state was due to a degree to the pressure exerted on it at that time. In the end, the Greek state proceeded in 1914 to contract the largest foreign loan in its history, of 500 million francs, which was negotiated by the governor of the National Bank himself, Ioannis Valaoritis, with the same banks. The issue of the loan, on favourable terms for the lenders, was highly successful (the first instalment of 250 million francs was issued in Paris in 1914 and was covered three times), which fact bears witness to the renewal of trust by financial circles in the future of Greece.[47] However, the outbreak of war in August 1914 prevented the second part of the loan from materialising.

The crisis in relations between the state and the National Bank was created in the summer of 1914, when Ioannis Eftaxias, the anti-Venizelist governor of the NBG from March 1914, put obstacles in the way of granting of advance payments to the state for the purchase of military vessels in America. Indeed he tried, inopportunely and unsuccessfully, to guarantee that the NBG's issuing privilege in the new provinces would be negotiated in exchange.[48] Venizelos accepted the a priori guarantee of the privilege – given, moreover, that the idea of the sole issuing bank seems to have ripened – leaving to negotiation under his arbitration the details of the contract between the NBG and the Ministry of Finance. Not long after, however, in November 1914, he voted in a law which stipulated that the members of the board of the NBG had to be approved by the government in power. Ioannis Eftaxias was dismissed and his position was taken by Alexandros Zaimis. At the same time, the contract extending the NBG's privileges was signed, with which, however, the state secured its interests (state exemption from paying interest on the loan in inconvertible banknotes, participation in the profits from circulating banknotes, increase in taxation of the NBG). With this gesture Venizelos on the one hand defined the state's relations with the largest private financial institution and on the other showed who had the upper hand.

1917–20, ALL FOR THE WAR

This period, which corresponds to the stepping-up of the war effort, represents a critical turning point. The liberal management was abolished de facto, albeit provisionally, since in the first phase of the unification of the state, after the interlude of the provisional government in Thessaloniki, a 'basically dictatorial regime' was installed.[49] State control of the economy expanded significantly, new views on the Greek economy began to take shape, while attitudes to social protest hardened decisively.

Emergency measures regulating the operation of the economy began to be adopted from late 1914. Restrictive measures on trade included direct government intervention in trade for supplying the country with coal and grain, a process that led to the founding of a separate Ministry of Food-Supply and Self-Sufficiency by the government of Spyridon Lambros in early 1917;[50] a ban on the trading of certain commodities (war material) or on the export of those that the country must not be without; the safeguarding by law (1918) of the state's right to regulate, during the war and for eight months after the armistice, the production and trade of goods essential for food-supply, fuel, and so on; control on imports (law 1772/1919), which remained in force until 1922;[51] intervention in monetary transactions: granting banks the right to refuse withdrawals from deposit accounts (summer 1914) – a measure which had been imposed for the first time in September 1912 (mobilisation) for

12 months; a ban on the export of gold[52] (reintroduced in 1917 and in 1918)[53]; and, finally, exchange control (for the first time by legislative decree of 20 Jan. 1917), a consequence of the negotiations for the allied credits which was abolished in July 1920.

The allied credits and the adventures of the drachma after the war are crucial constituents of economic developments as well as of debates in economic theory in inter-war Greece.[54] The securing of economic support from the Entente Powers, in view of Greece joining the war on their side, was of decisive importance for the policy of the Venizelos government from June 1917.[55] Greece had already spent 757 million drachmas on sporadic mobilisations in the period of neutrality and her economic abilities were nil. The negotiations, lasting several months, were held at a particularly difficult time for Venizelos: the National Schism, food shortages due to the embargo (which was lifted on 16 June 1917), the anti-war sentiments of a large section of the population made his position insecure and did not allow for radical measures to secure domestic resources. Britain and France, for their part, were already indebted to the United States, were worried about the devaluation of their own currencies and, at the time of this late entry of Greece into the war, did not have unlimited resources, despite their wish to support Venizelos. They put pressure on the Greek government to raise funds from domestic sources by increasing taxes or resorting to internal loans and the issue of paper money. This position was strengthened by the ascertainment that there had been a significant increase in wealth in Greece during the course of the war. A report by the French ambassador, Roger Clausse, estimated the profits from shipping, trade, stock appreciation, rising value of ships, emigrant remittances and supplies to allied forces, at 1.8 billion drachmas.[56] The report from Sergent, French government emissary and deputy governor of the Bank of France, who arrived in Greece in September 1917,[57] noted also the spectacular rise in deposit accounts in the large banks and of their assets available abroad, in the price of agricultural produce, in the profits from shipping and trade, the country's positive balance of trade and so on. At the same time, he recognised the necessity of allied credits, because of the high requirements of military expenditure, which was calculated at about 1 billion drachmas. These positions were reinforced by the striking fact that, in contrast to other currencies, the drachma remained at par.

On the basis of law 3642/1910, which had introduced a kind of gold exchange standard, the National Bank of Greece continued to issue banknotes during the war, backed by foreign currencies bought at par with gold. The drachma was first linked to the franc, from February 1915 it was linked to the pound sterling and last, in 1916, it was linked to the dollar. But as a recent study has pointed out,[58] in reality the gold standard was hampered during the war, as was the operation of law 3642, and the maintenance of parity of the drachma was in a way artificial. In the meantime, per capita fiduciary circulation tripled between 1914 and 1918, exacerbating the inflation that had appeared from 1914.

In the final phase of the negotiations, Venizelos himself visited Paris and London, in November 1917.[59] He tried to secure immediately available credits and not book credits, as the allies proposed, and greater flexibility in the use of credits obtained, avoiding the setting up of a control commission. On both issues the agents of the responsible ministries, and primarily John Maynard Keynes, then in charge of foreign payments at the British Treasury and adviser to Chancellor of the Exchequer A. Bonar Law, were resolute. In the end, Venizelos achieved very little in his efforts to improve the terms of liquidation of the book credits, but he did negotiate a ceiling (250 million) on the sums that the NBG would advance toward the costs of the allied armies in Greece.[60]

On 3 December 1917 the Protocol of Versailles was signed and on 10 February 1918 the final agreement with which France, Britain and the USA opened to Greece credits up to 750 million francs, in equal portions, in order to cover delayed debts and for military expenditure in the year 1918. The credits were to be opened gradually, after the approval of the relevant expenditures by the Inter-Allied Financial Commission, with representatives from all four countries, which was installed in Athens. Against these credits, banknotes to the value of 817.8 million drachmas were issued.[61]

The second part of the agreement concerned the supply of foodstuffs and munitions from France and Britain, which would be paid off after the war, and after these countries had decided what the burden of cost to Greece would be in the end.[62] The last part of the agreement covered the advance payments that the NBG would grant for the expenses of allied troops in Greece and which were to be paid off within two years of the end of the war.

These transactions with the allies were a harsh experience for Greece and for Venizelos personally. On many points agreement was reached under pressure, and things were left unclear and demanded renegotiation, for example with regard to whether the agreement Venizelos himself had made in September 1917 with the Wheat Executive Committee in London, for the supply of grain, included the victualling of troops or only civilians;[63] and whether the costs for supplies of material in Greece should be reckoned in with the 750 million francs or not. The British, always more 'tight-fisted' and suspicious, had a very restricted notion of the term 'delayed debts', which the credits would cover,[64] while for the costs of the allied armies, which the NBG paid in drachmas, the most serious problem that arose was determining the exchange rate of the currencies, given that the value of the franc was depreciating continuously.

From February 1918, the operation of the Inter-Allied Financial Commission also caused friction. The occupation of Greece and the British–French blockade were recent experiences, and the Venizelos government, 'stained' by returning to power with foreign help, did not want in any way to appear to be conceding sovereign rights. The ministers in Athens refused to facilitate the work of the commission. The foreign representatives for their part accused Venizelos of running his domestic policy with the allied credits, by increasing, for instance, army rations and fares on the state-run railways.[65] Relations with the Inter-Allied Commission headed for crisis. After Michalakopoulos' démarche to London in late April 1918, Keynes cynically proposed to his colleagues delaying the opening of credit until the Greek government became more 'co-operative'.[66] Venizelos exploded with rage in front of the ambassadors of the Powers in Athens, threatening to resign, but proposing, in the end, compromise and collaboration with the Inter-Allied Commission.[67] Even so, the delays went on, frustrating obstacles to the financing of the army.[68]

These long months of negotiations give the impression that, whereas for Venizelos the political priority was clear – with the result that in the end, helped by his inveterate optimism, he committed the country's economy beyond its limits – on the side of his allied partners the economic criterion seems always to have been uppermost, as well as the tendency to take every opportunity of reinforcing their control of Greece. That Venizelos was aware of the dangers is borne out by his 'corrective' interventions in the negotiations. Nonetheless, he tried to reassure parliament in March 1918, when Stratos expressed the concern that the nature of the allied credits would cause inflationary note issue and devaluation of the currency.[69] 'These fears, gentlemen, are groundless,' Venizelos replied. He accepted that the swelling of fiduciary circulation 'brings the increase of prices', but argued that this increase would have happened even if the 'loan was made directly as a foreign loan in gold bullion', since the high prices were due to 'the inability of the country to use wealth in more productive sectors, as long as the war lasts'. He tried to avoid loss of confidence in the currency: 'I ask: how could we accept that the banknotes, which are issued today against credits granted by the very governments of three of the richest states in the world . . . would have lesser value at home . . .?' and to inspire optimism about the country's post-war potential:

> I foresee that by the end of the war there will be plenty of money accumulated in the country, on account of military spending by our own army and by foreign forces in the country; these expenditures are also high that not only will they make available the resources necessary for the development of the country's productive potential but will also allow the state to locate domestic sources of adequate borrowing in order to cover all her needs.

However, the end of the war was not to come quickly for Greece. In November 1918, shortly after the capitulation of Germany, Venizelos, already in Paris, sought to secure new credits for 1919.[70] The related negotiations[71] led to the signing of a new agreement on 19 March 1919, in which France and Britain opened new book credits in Greece for 1919, totalling 100 million francs (including the remainder of the 750 million), on about the same terms as previously.[72] In a letter to Venizelos, a few days before the agreement was signed, Keynes warned (on behalf of his minister) that 'there will be no question of further credits', and ended with the following words:

> [T]hose of us who are in touch with these matters are all greatly impressed with the financial strength of Greece. We feel sure that there is hardly any country in Europe which will find itself in a better position than will, by prudent management, the Hellenic government . . .[73]

This assessment was soon to be proved fallacious. Serious problems had begun to beset the fragile Greek economy as soon as hostilities ceased, with the depreciation of commodity stocks, the drop in profits from shipping, the reduction in foreign currency reserves and then the rampant speculating in foreign exchange by capitalists and banks. The 'strong drachma', which permitted the above assessment, did not last beyond the summer of 1919, since, along with everything else, the NBG began converting the foreign currency reserves of law 3642, which it had in dollars, into pounds sterling and francs (currencies devalued in relation to the dollar). When the drachma began losing ground against the dollar, Venizelos tried to restore it to parity by reinforcing state intervention in the foreign exchange market.[74] This was the first manifestation of his fixation on keeping a 'strong currency', and it was fruitless. At the end of 1919 the drachma was finally linked to the pound and devalued, while the needs of the Asia Minor campaign had already stretched financing with domestic funds to the limits.[75] From 1920, the issue of uncovered banknotes began,[76] a practice which continued even after Venizelos' fall from office in November 1920.

It is well known that, on the pretext of this political change in November 1920, the allies only partly liquidated the book credits of 1918 to 1919.[77] Several years later, and after much negotiation, Greece finally gave up her relevant demands, receiving in return the stabilisation loan of 1928.[78] The fate of the allied credits was certainly not the only cause of the serious monetary and exchange instability that bedevilled the Greek economy in the years to come, even though they certainly exacerbated the consequences of the inflationary note circulation. Nonetheless, the fact that the major devaluation of the drachma took place after the elections in November 1920 allowed pro-Venizelists and anti-Venizelists at the time, such as Diomidis and Eftaxias respectively, to support this view.[79]

Beyond borrowing from abroad, Venizelos was at first hesitant to use other means available to fiscal policy in order to confront the needs of the war effort, in other words, an increase in tax revenues, given the climate of political strife and the anti-war mood pervading when he returned to power in June 1917. In the end, however, he did not avoid it. To raise additional domestic funds was one of the terms of the allied credits, and was also the basis of the Sergent report, and so in the autumn of 1917 old taxes were increased and new ones imposed.[80] But since the potential of the existing taxation system, which unfairly burdened the working classes, was limited, the government soon pushed ahead with taxation reforms.[81] The first step in this direction was law 1043 of 6 November 1917, which levied the 'extraordinary profits' tax, with retroactive effect from 1915.[82] At the same time, the bill on income tax was submitted, with a proposal from the Minister of Finance M. Negrepontis, which was finally voted as law in 1919 (law 1640/3 Jan. 1919). The taxation reform of 1919 was completed with law 1641, which amended and codified the tax on inheritances and gifts, and law 1642, which levied tax on the automatic appreciation of real estate. However, law 1640/1919 remained a dead letter for several years, at first because of the ineptitude of public services and subsequently due to anomalous circumstances, and in the end was subjected to a host of amendments, exceptions and favourable exemptions (Kafantaris estimated 150 amendments in 1933).[83] The fact remains that between 1914 and 1920 the per capita taxation burden increased by about 25 per cent in constant prices,[84] something which did not improve the popularity of Venizelos.

The above describes the framework of state pressures on economic life in wartime. The difficulties of the transition to a peacetime economy, at an international level, and particularly the prolongation of the war for

Greece, not only did not favour the 'withdrawal' of the state in the post-war period, but also possibly strengthened Venizelos' statism, as he became alienated from both the entrepreneurial and the labouring classes. His relations with business circles were in any case difficult to balance; on the one hand employers objected to controls and taxation,[85] while on the other they welcomed measures to suppress workers' activism. During 1918 and 1919 these relations were good, in the climate of euphoria created by high profits and an upswing in business activity. The Great War had changed conceptions of Greek industry, in which unprecedented state interest was expressed at that time. The first systematic census of industry was organised; an 'industrial commission' composed of employees, professors and industrialists was set up in the Ministry of National Economy, which attempted a kind of planning;[86] as well as a 25-member fuel committee to boost the output of lignite; while the government financed prospecting to locate oil deposits.[87] Further, in the autumn of 1918 a delegation of Greek industrialists and other businessmen, led by A. Michalakopoulos and with the participation of several entrepreneurs, supporters or friends of Venizelos, was sent to London, to gather information and to negotiate possible collaborations.[88] In the following year, however, things changed considerably for the worse. Many business plans remained on paper or were derailed into speculating ventures (particularly in foreign exchange), while the businessmen's official bodies requested unlimited issue of banknotes in order to face money shortage, and at the same time abolition of all controls.[89] Finally, in the same period, the state sector of the economy was expanding in the field of infrastructure networks and technical projects, with the founding of the Greek state Railways in 1917.[90]

Even more drastic was Venizelos' estrangement from the working classes. The significant reduction in real wages – since the increases in wage rates did not offset the rise in the cost-of-living index from 1914 – and the technological changes which made obsolete a host of skills; the most characteristic example being the spread of cigarette-making machines in the tobacco industry – led to radicalisation of the workers' movement. Because national ambitions demanded the support of the Western socialist parties and in particular of the British Labour Party, Venizelos at first sought the collaboration of the labour unions in Greece and complied in the unification of the movement with the founding of the General Confederation of Greek Workers (GSEE), in the autumn of 1918.[91] For the same reasons, the government accepted (and parliament ratified) the international labour conventions voted on in Washington in 1919.[92] But the mobilisations activism did not stop, the policy of class collaboration was not bearing fruit – particularly since the Russian revolution had affected the political landscape generally and favoured radicalisation – and so the government proceeded to persecutions of union leaders, exiles and suppression of protest. Things were particularly bad in 1919 to 1920, when devaluation of the drachma and soaring inflation brought the workers into dire straits. The rift deepened with the passing of law 2111 'on offences against freedom of work', in 1920, which endeavoured to protect strikebreaking, and law 2112 'on termination of contract of employment' which settled dismissals, while law 2151 of the same year amended law 281/1914 on labour unions, by trying to make it difficult to exercise the right to strike.[93]

Obvious in Venizelos' speeches was the prominence of the anti-communist – anti-Bolshevik syndrome, which emerged in this period in all Western countries, under the strains created by the ongoing war. This turned out to be critical, both for the development of his own views and as a tool of coercion and menace: '[L]abour policy is not only a task of justice . . . it is also a task of political foresight . . . if we want to pre-empt, so that our wonderful working people . . . will not one day stray towards Bolshevism,'[94] he said in parliament in 1919, addressing the employers ('that great class of my friends'). And shortly after, he was to add more threateningly to the other side: '[O]n the now most acute struggle of the classes proper care must be taken, if we do not wish to see subversive . . . theories developing at home.'[95]

Defending the new labour bills of 1920, referred to above, and which his left wing denounced as against the workers, Venizelos declared:

> The aim of the bills is . . . to forestall all those abuses which were provoked . . . to ensure that the workers' interests are defended by the workers themselves . . . because we are in danger of creating a new exploiter . . . who, usually not belonging to the working class at all . . . propels the working class . . . into acute opposition to the rest of society, with the aim of actually overturning social order . . .

And he concludes with a vivid description of the two-front struggle in which he had placed himself, in the following words:

> I would be entirely unworthy of all the great confidence that the Greek people has shown in me . . . if, simply in order to prolong my remaining days in power, I allow social order to be put in jeopardy, through slackening the reins and handing them over to Bolshevik elements, or I turn towards the right and reverse my liberal and labour policy . . .[96]

Ten days later he lost the elections of 1 November 1920.

1928–32, 'AGAINST THE WIND'

The last period of government by Venizelos was inaugurated by yet another conflict concerning the National Bank, so setting the seal on the central role that economic issues were to play in this phase. Banking reform had already been set in motion by the Zaimis government with the Geneva Protocol (15 Sept. 1927) and the founding of the Bank of Greece (12 May 1928) when Venizelos – for reasons feigned or real, it matters not – expressed publicly his disagreement with certain aspects of the agreements pertaining to the National Bank.[97] Thus he led the 'conflict of authority',[98] which had been created ipso facto from the moment of his return to Greece, to its final resolution, forcing the resignation of Georgios Kafantaris, minister of finance in the Zaimis government, and finally assuming power in July 1928.

After endeavouring to renegotiate in toto the stabilisation agreements with the Financial Committee of the League of Nations (FC/LoN), without success,[99] Venizelos in the end imposed his view on the matter of the gold reserve of the National Bank. He maintained that the appreciation of this reserve, with the stabilisation rate of the drachma, and after the two increases of the issue ceiling in 1914 and 1920, was due exclusively to the 'law of stabilisation' and consequently the state ought to have a share in this.[100] With the contract of 3 June 1929, the National Bank did in fact concede half of this appreciation (560 million drachmas) to the state, with which the government reinforced the Agricultural Bank, which was founded in 1929 in the form of a non-profit public benefit institution specialising in agricultural credit.[101] Moreover, this move completed the process of rationalisation and specialisation of the banking system, which also enabled the National Bank to take a more dynamic turn to lending to businesses and eventually to emerge benefited by the reorganisation of the banking landscape, despite the fact that it adopted a tactic of undermining the new central bank.[102]

Venizelos' last four-year term began in auspicious circumstances. His economic strategy in this period is presented thoroughly in another chapter in this volume.[103] Here will be discussed only the basic axes that determined his government's actions, as well as the development of the economy itself, with the aim mainly of identifying the constants and the changes in policy, in relation to the point of departure of this essay.

Foreign borrowing remained the unchanged element and central axis of Venizelos' policy – based on the idea of the open international economy and the free movement of capital. It was this element that was overturned unexpectedly by the international crisis of 1929. The previous governments (all Venizelist) had followed an analogous policy: the stabilisation loan of £9 million was part of the 1927 agreement with the FC/LoN and had already been issued successfully in London and New York when Venizelos took over the government.[104] Earlier loans, however, had been made mainly in order to confront the major and urgent needs of rehabilitating refugees and returning the drachma to the gold exchange standard. Venizelos placed more emphasis on using loans to finance ambitious projects for the country's economic development. So in late 1928, moves were made to obtain a new loan of up to £22 million, to carry out drainage and other anti-flooding works in Macedonia and road-building works.[105] It is worth noting, however, that for Venizelos this borrowing had a moral basis, just as had the allied credits of the war: then the moral basis was the mobilisation on the side of the allies, now Venizelos linked Greece's need of loans with the Asia Minor defeat and the refugee problem, as well as with the Great Powers' fulfilment of their obligations after 1920:

> Without this injustice [meaning the economic embargo of 1921–2], Greece would not find herself in need either of contracting the refugee loan, nor of the tripartite, nor of the productive . . . Her foreign debt would be half of today's . . .

he told the council of political leaders on 25 March 1932.[106] This moral dimension was a reminder, in other words, of the priority that Venizelos always accorded to politics in managing economic affairs.

The cornerstone of the policy of foreign borrowing was maintaining the stability of the drachma, which is why Venizelos was led into the hopeless 'battle of the drachma' from September 1931, when the pound abandoned the gold standard. At the climax of the domestic economic crisis, in January 1932, he visited the capitals of the member states of the International Financial Commission, seeking a third loan of $50 million, together with a five-year deferment of payment, this time in order to support the drachma as well as to continue the major public works. In the 'Memorandum' he then handed over to the governments of the said countries, is described with clarity the central position that foreign borrowing held in his scheme for the development of the Greek economy. Venizelos said that in normal international economic circumstances, and given that Greece had stabilised her currency and had secured the basic precondition for balancing the state budget, the free movement of capital would enable the maintenance of stabilisation, notwithstanding the deficit in Greece's foreign accounts. Indeed, this deficit could be perpetuated without problem, provided the loan capital was used productively and for purposes of increasing the national income, 'so as to cover in the end the deficit in our balance of payments'.[107]

Venizelos' demands were considered unrealistic by the International Financial Commision which pointed out the contradiction between the demand for a new loan and the intention of declaring a moratorium on previous debts.[108] The final report of the FC/LoN after the Neimeyer mission, on the situation of Greece in March 1932, shifted the possibility of lending (a sum of only $10 million) to a vague though 'near future', and recommended drastic cut-backs – judging it necessary 'to reduce temporarily the expenditure on irrigation works'.[109] The FC/LoN also recommended deferment of debt payments for one year. When Venizelos had exhausted all possibilities of securing a new loan, he was forced at the Council of the League of Nations to accept the inevitable, that is, for the drachma to abandon the gold exchange standard (April 1932). And considering the degree to which he himself had promoted the national currency as the 'country's flag', its downfall inevitably dealt an irreparable blow to his prestige.[110]

Nonetheless, Venizelos' insistence was not merely a result of theoretical 'rigidity' or awareness of the great burden that devaluation of the drachma would place on the national debt. Contemporary perceptions of the 1929 crisis should be taken into account. The duration and the depth of the crisis sparked off by the crash of the New York stock exchange in 1929 were not immediately appreciated at an international level. Indeed, it seems that in an initial phase the central banks accepted the fall of Wall Street with relief, because it brought a general respite in the currency market.[111] International trade and movement of capital (beyond the USA) – particularly the long-term loans to Europe and the developing countries – showed signs of recovery in the first half of 1930. Some indications may in fact have inspired hopes of overcoming the difficulties quickly: the Hague Conference in 1930, at which the issues of war reparations and war debts were finally decided, had produced positive results – Venizelos secured a relatively high share in the reparations (from Hungary and Bulgaria),[112] something which possibly also renewed trust in his personal diplomacy.[113] Even in early 1931 the country had succeeded in securing the second part of the productive loan, albeit with difficulty.

In the domestic economy, the recession was felt first of all in agriculture, but this sector suffered from chronic problems and had for some time been an object of special attention from the state. Speaking in May 1930 about the tobacco crisis, Venizelos attributed it to the over-production or to the damage of the crop by rain, and made no connection whatsoever with the international environment.[114] Bankruptcies in the sectors of trade and manufacturing/industry were attributed to the sea of small enterprises which had flooded these fields, especially after the arrival of the refugees.[115] The correlation of individual indications and the realisation of the dimensions and the global nature of the crisis, and of the consequent recession, seem to have come later. In his interview in the newspaper *Eleftheron Vima*, for New Year 1932, Venizelos referred to the 'seeds of worsening' which 'had been bequeathed to the world by the year 1930 and the last months of 1929, when the great stock-exchange crisis exploded in America', expressing, of course, his optimism that Greece would 'effectively weather the storm'.[116] In the 'Memorandum' of January 1932, he dated the 'deterioration of the international crisis' from the summer of 1931,[117] with the crucial turning point for Greece the pound's abandonment of the gold standard. And in March 1932 he addressed parliament, opening with these words:

> Gentlemen deputies, since the month of October of the year 1929 . . . the whole world has been beset by an economic crisis, the extent and intensity of which has perhaps never been seen before. Until the month of September 1931, Greece, without anyone of course being able to claim that she did not feel the repercussion of this crisis at all, was going ahead with the task of its economic reconstruction with a firm step . . .[118]

The abandonment of the gold standard in April 1932 spelt the collapse of a fundamental element of liberal, open economy and brought the drastic reinforcement of state interventionism and of introversion in the Greek economy. Interventionism of course, and to some degree introversion too, had already covered considerable ground on the other fronts of the Greek economy and especially the rural economy. The priority that had been given to this last is the second basic axis of Venizelist policy in the four years 1928 to 1932. Of itself the double effort of allocation of large landholdings[119] and rehabilitation of the refugees, which changed the landscape of the northern regions of the country, in practice constituted a manifestation of organised rural colonisation under state supervision. At the instigation of the pro-agrarians, and in particular of Alexandros Papanastasiou, the first state bodies for intervention in production, the Independent Currant Organisation and the Central Committee for Protection of Domestic Grain Production (KEPES), had already been founded, in 1924 and 1926 respectively. The protection of cereal production in particular aimed at the country's self-sufficiency in grain, since grain imports placed a significant burden on the balance-of-trade deficit.

Venizelos continued this policy: the relevant legislation was completed in 1929 to 1930 and KEPES supported the producers during the crisis. In 1931 the Cotton Institute was set up, to promote cotton-growing in order to cover the needs of the domestic textile industry.[120] In other words, the fiscal difficulties and the monetary instability of the 1920s had already set in motion policies of introversion and self-sufficiency, which had not yet been so named, while Venizelos declared 'state intervention necessary' in order to support the producers in a period of falling prices (which he of course considered temporary), and discussed the possibility of creating monopolies in the trade of certain staples. Indeed the parliamentary committee set up to consider this in late 1928, proposed in 1930 the founding of a state controlled monopoly for the export of tobacco, but the plan did not go ahead because of objections from the liberal minister of the national economy, Panagis Vourloumis (of an old Patras merchant family) and, possibly of the still dynamic commercial interests in the tobacco sector.[121] Nevertheless, Venizelos did discuss such ideas for other products. In May 1930 he said in Thessaloniki: 'I think that we could perhaps found also an organisation which would undertake the monopoly of all the country's olive oil,'[122] and added that he had discussed with the industrialist Andreas Hadjikyriakos the idea of setting up an analogous monopolistic industry in this sector. It is also known that in early 1932, in the depths of crisis, he charged the deputy governor of the National Bank of Greece, Alexandros Koryzis, with the preparation of a plan for the organisation of the country's entire foreign trade under state control.[123]

The major draining and irrigation projects in the plains of Macedonia, which absorbed a large part of the loan resources, and the founding of the Agricultural Bank, were another two acts of the liberals which aimed at the development of the rural economy. Venizelos was censured by the press at home and by foreign observers for the way in which the land reclamation works were carried out, as well as the road-making works, which were granted to the firm of Pafsanias Makris. He was criticised mainly for commissioning them in toto and not in sections, and therefore of inelastic allocation of resources.[124] Venizelos himself insisted to the last on their importance for increasing national income, which he believed would be noticeable within five years. The works – completion of which was slowed down by interruption of financing – did indeed significantly increase the productive possibilities of agriculture, which followed a rising course throughout the rest of the 1930s. However, in conditions of recession, the expansion of cereal cultivation did not have any impact on economic growth.

Major public works in the rural sector, as well as networks of new technologies imported to Greece in the same period,[125] were conditions that favoured the dissemination and the acceptance of the large economic conglomerates, the gigantism of which was a dominant trend in the development of the international capitalist economy from the early twentieth century. Venizelos appears to have accepted these new ideas, indeed in the sphere of domestic industry he supported the policy of mergers as well as of cartels, which the National Bank of Greece promoted, under its flag of 'rationalisation'[126] – just as it supported, in some cases, the monopolistic control of the market by some companies,[127] while it also adopted measures that favoured the larger businesses.[128]

Industry did not carry the same weight in Venizelist economic policy as agriculture, but it was certainly an object of more energetic interest than in previous periods, perhaps because Venizelos awaited from industry relief of unemployment, which reached alarming proportions during the crisis. The regime of law 2948/1922 had already secured a more favourable framework for the development of industry, while from 1926 the new customs tariff of 1924 was applied, with increased protectionist dimensions even though, as always, this was in order to generate cash.[129] The Venizelos government reinforced this framework by reducing the tax on profits of corporations and by strengthening the preferential treatment of domestic industries in supplies for the state, which had been introduced by law 2948/1922, as well as by systematic efforts to support at least some industrial exports.[130] From the autumn of 1931, the restrictions on imports finally brought advantages to industry and hit commercial interests – even though Venizelos does not seem to have moved over himself to the dogma of self-sufficiency, as his former close collaborator Diomidis had in the same period.[131] There is no doubt that the creation of strong economic conglomerates and monopolist situations in a period of economic difficulty reinforced the discontent of the working classes, without securing for Venizelos the support of businessmen, who observed with dismay the infiltration of the *économie dirigée* into the common vocabulary and their affairs, as well as the radicalisation of labour demands, for which they always considered the labour policy of the liberals responsible.

On this front, Venizelos' policy in this period, freed of the necessity of consensus imposed by wartime conditions, openly adopted repression. The tendencies that appeared in embryo in 1919 and 1920 crystallised with the voting in of the famous Idionymon, special law 4229/1929 'on measures of security of the social regime'. Concurrently, however, and although he showed no special zeal in applying labour legislation, so as not to 'impede the creation of new industries',[132] Venizelos did not abandon the building of the welfare state and his government drafted the first law on social security, which was passed but not applied while he was in power. He refused, however, to include the relief of unemployment in the law, arguing that:

> [T]here will be nothing more calamitous for Greece than if we establish as state obligation the provision of assistance to the unemployed. We shall cause desertion of the countryside, desertion of the fields, in order to invite all those people who have no desire to work to the cities, to come to register in the lists of the state.[133]

He argued, moreover, that one of the causes of the crisis of the British pound and the difficulties of Great Britain was 'that there operates the system of state assistance to the unemployed'.

When Venizelos lost the election in March 1933 and left politics for good, 'economic nationalism', the turn towards self-sufficiency and the abandonment of liberalism, had become the dominant reality in Greek economic life. Together with this development, and the parallel reinforcement of state interventionism, the possibility of the subversion of parliamentary rule acquired a strong presence in political discourse and on the political horizon of the period.

In a macroscopic evaluation, the most durable traces of Venizelist modernisation in the Greek economy and society were the transformation of the landless peasants of Thessaly and Macedonia into small landowners, the labour legislation and the major rehabilitation works in the agricultural sector, together with the networks of modern infrastructures in the cities. In the urban sector of the economy, although industrialisation expanded considerably, its structures were not modified perceptibly. Venizelist modernisation did not put industry at the centre of the economic development of Greece, while the great sharpening of social contrasts, consequence of the influx of refugees and the economic difficulties of the inter-war years, negated the promise of social justice. Finally, the state undertook the regulation of labour relations but eventually reinforced also its own repressive character.

NOTES

1. Lilly Macrakis (1992, *Eleftherios Venizelos 1864–1910*, Athens, p. 130) attests that such classes were taught in the Antoniadis Lykeion, which Venizelos attended in Athens, and also at the grammar school in Syros, from which he graduated.
2. M. Psalidopoulos (1989), *I krisi tou 1929 kai oi Ellines oikonomologoi* [*The 1929 Crisis and the Greek Economists*], Athens, p. 139.

3. Macrakis, *El. Venizelos*, pp. 161–3 (see Note 1).
4. Kyriakos Venizelos was an 'affluent and educated bourgeois', as described by Lilly Macrakis, *El. Venizelos*, p. 115 (see Note 1).
5. Indicatively: Helena Venizelos (1995), *A l'ombre de Venizelos,* Paris; Penelope Delta (1988), *Eleftherios K. Venizelos. Imerologio-Anamniseis-Martyries-Allilographia* [*El. Venizelos. Diary-Recollections-Testimonies-Correspondence*], ed. P. A. Zannas, Athens.
6. Macrakis, *El. Venizelos*, pp. 187, 191 (see Note 1).
7. De Billy (from Athens) to Foreign Minister Pichon, undated copy attached to a letter from Pichon to the ministry of finance, Paris 16 May 1918, Archives du Ministère des Finances (AMF), B 31857.
8. Venizelos himself had no qualms about admitting his lack of credentials concerning special budgetary or even financial issues. See analogous thoughts of Panagis Vourloumis (1985), 'I oikonomiki politiki tou Eleftheriou Venizelou' ['The Economic Policy of El. Venizelos'], *Epikentra*, pp. 72–7 (grandson of minister of national economy of the same name in the last four-year term of the Venizelos government), as well as C. Hadjiiosif (1988), 'I Venizelogenis antipolitefsi ston Venizelo kai I politiki anasyntaxi tou astismou ston mesopolemo' ['Venizelist Opposition to Venizelos and the Political Recovery of the Bourgeoisie during the Interwar Period], Mavrogordatos and Hadjiiosif (eds)., *Venizelismos kai astikos eksynchronismos* [*Venizelism and Bourgeois Modernisation*], Irakleio, p. 442.
9. S. I. Stephanou (ed.) (1981–4), *Ta keimena tou Eleftheriou Venizelou 1909–1935* [*E. Venizelos' Texts, 1909–1935*], 4 vols, Athens (hereafter: *Keimena*), vol. I, pp. 263–4 (Parliament, 19 May 1911). See comparable remarks on Venizelos' views of the new role of the state (but in the post-war period) in N. Alivizatos (1995), *Oi politikoi thesmoi se krisi: 1922–1974* [*Political Institutions in Crisis 1922–1974*], Athens 3rd edn, pp. 47–8.
10. '[I]n every case I shall be the safest support of order and of the social regime. But I do not want that regime immobile . . .', *Keimena*, vol. I, p. 274 (Parliament, 19 May 1911) (see Note 9).
11. Ibid., p. 272.
12. *Keimena*, vol. I, p. 357 (speech in Syros, 25 Feb 1912) and vol. II, p. 695 (Parliament, 27 Jan. 1920) (see Note 9). For Venizelos' unreserved acceptance of class inequalities see George Th. Mavrogordatos (1983), *Stillborn Republic. Social Coalitions and Party Strategies in Greece, 1922–1936*, Berkeley and London, pp. 111–16.
13. *Keimena*, vol. I, p. 274 (see Note 9).
14. G. Ventiris [1931] (1970), *I Ellas tou 1910–1920* [*Greece in 1910–1920*], (2nd edn) Athens, vol. I, p. 21ff. See also G. Th. Mavrogordatos (1988), 'Venizelismos kai astikos eksynchronismos' [*Venizelism and Bourgeois Modernisation*], in Mavrogordatos and Hadjiosif (eds), *Venizelismos,* pp. 9–19 (see Note 8).

15. The excerpt is from a comment on the landowners of Thessaly, who 'made mainly an investment of money . . . without any activity whatsoever, without any risk whatsoever . . .', *Keimena,* vol. II, p. 692 (Parliament, 27 January 1920) (see Note 9).
16. *Keimena*, vol. I, pp. 205–6 (speech in Larissa, 13 Nov. 1910) (see Note 9).
17. *Keimena*, vol. II, p. 464 (Parliament, 28 March 1918) (see Note 9).
18. Ibid., p. 462.
19. For his speech to this conference, the military attaché of the French legation to Greece informed the Ministry of Trade, Archives Nationales (AN), F12 9241, Athens 15 Dec. 1919.
20. Lieutenant General D. Vakas (1950), *O Venizelos os polemikos igetis* [*Venizelos as a War Leader*], Athens, p. 409.
21. *Keimena,* vol. I, p. 349 (speech in Patras, 19 Feb. 1912) (see Note 9). Venizelos' election campaign speech in Larissa, in November 1910, was devoted almost exclusively to the basic directions of his economic policy.
22. D. Gatopoulos [1947] (2002), *Andreas Michalakopoulos*, Athens, p. 35, mentions that the politician from Patras, who had studied law at the University of Athens, subsequently proceeded to 'special economic studies', without being more specific about these.
23. Subsequent leader of the Agrarian Party.
24. See A. Karadimou-Gerolympou and N. Papamichos (1988), 'Rythmisi tou chorou: politikes protovoulies kai thesmikes rythmiseis' '[Space Regulation: Political Initiatives and Institutional Interventions], in Mavrogordatos and Hadjiosif (eds), *Venizelismos,* p. 116 (see Note 8).
25. S. Petmezas (2002), 'Agrotiki oikonomia' ['Rural Economy'], in C. Hadjiiosif (ed.), *Istoria tis Elladas tou 20ou aiona* [*History of 20th-Century Greece*], Athens, vol. I-1, pp. 53–85; *Keimena*, vol. I, p. 349 (see Note 9); Ch. Evelpidis (1944), *I georgia tis Ellados. Oikonomiki kai koinoniki apopsis* [*Greek Agriculture. Economic and Social Aspects*], Athens.
26. Petmezas, 'Oikonomia', in Hadjiosif (ed.), *Istoria* pp. 81, 83 (see Note 25).
27. It is characteristic that in 1915, after the change in government, the industrialists requested that what had been done for agriculture by the previous government be done for industry. See *Viomichaniki kai Viotechniki Epitheorisis* [*Industrial and Manufacturing Review*] [henceforth: BBE], vol. 2, May 1915, p. 14.
28. *Keimena*, vol. I, p. 205 (speech in Larissa, 15 Nov. 1910) (see Note 9).
29. Even though a law was also passed (3512/1910) 'on study of a general review of the tariffs of customs duties'. See C. Hadjiiosif (1993), *I giraia selini. I viomichania stin elliniki oikonomia 1830–1940* [The Old Moon. Industry in the Greek Economy 1830–1940], Athens, p. 280.
30. *Keimena*, vol. I, p. 352 (speech in Patras, 19 Feb. 1912), 356 (speech in Syros, 25 Feb. 1912) (see Note 9).
31. Ibid., p. 576 (Parliament, 30 Sept. 1914, my emphasis).

32. A. Liakos (1988), 'O Eleftherios Venizelos kai to Diethnes Grapheio Ergasias' ['El. Venizelos and the International Labour Bureau'], in Mavrogordatos and Hadjiiosif (eds) *Venizelismos*, pp. 255–70 (see Note 8), and Liakos (1993), *Ergasia kai politiki stin Ellada tou mesopolemou* [*Work and politics in Greece in the Interwar Period*], Athens.
33. Law 3934/1911 "on workers' health and safety and on working hours', law 4029/1912 'on labour of women and minors', law 551/1914 'on compensation for workers injured by accident' and law 281/1914 'on unions'. See also S. Moudopoulos (1988), 'O nomos 281/1914 gia ta epaggelmatika somateia kai I epidrasi tou stin exelixi tou syndikalistikou kinimatos' ['Law 281/1914 on Trade Unions and its Impact on the Evolution of the Trade Union Movement'], in Mavrogordatos and Hadjiisosif (eds), *Venizelismos*, pp. 225–53 (see Note 8), G. D. Lixouriotis, 'Prostateftikos nomothetikos paremvatismos kai I emphanisi tou ergatikou dikaiou stin Ellada: I periptosi tis paidikis ergasias' ['Protective Legislative Interventionism and the Beginnings of Labour law in Greece: The Case of Child Labour'], in the same book, pp. 205–23.
34. A torrent of articles in the publication of the Association of Greek Industrialists and Manufacturers (AGIM): *BBE* 1(4) (August 1914), p. 106 'Social Legislation') and no. 3 (July 1914), 'Labour Issues', 65–6, and so on (see Note 27). In early 1912, AGIM submitted 'a long and detailed memorandum' to Venizelos, concerning the labour bills that had been put to parliament, requesting a deferment so that the issues could be studied better: *BBE* 1(1), May 1914, p. 5.
35. Liakos, *Ergasia kai politiki*, p. 266 (see Note 32).
36. It was suggested by socialists of the time and has been by later researchers that law 281/1914 was aimed at surveillance of union activity. See S. Moudopoulos, 'O nomos', in Mavrogordatos and Hadjiisosif, *Venizelismos* (see Note 8) with thorough analysis of the discussion in A. Liakos, *Ergasia kai politiki*, pp. 160–5 (see Note 32).
37. *Keimena*, vol. I, p. 574ff. (Parliament, 30 Sept. 1914)(see Note 9).
38. Founder of the Athens Labour Centre, parliamentary deputy of the Liberal Party in 1911, one of those who shaped social policy, see A. Liakos, *Ergasia kai politiki*, pp. 105, 297 (see Note 32).
39. *Keimena*, vol. I, p. 577 (see Note 9).
40. *BBE*, vol. I, October 1914, p. 179 and April 1915, pp. 357–61 (see Note 27).
41. A. M. Andreadis (1939), *Erga* [*Works*], vol. II, Athens, p. 45.
42. Co-governor of the National Bank from 1916, provisionally foreign minister in 1917, and governor of the National Bank of Greece from 1923, Diomidis was considered the embodiment of Venizelos' intervention in the economic sector. See the almost negative portrait of him by D. Tsoungos (1932), *Oi oikonomikoi mas igetai* [*Our Economic Leaders*], Athens, pp. 55–66.

43. *Keimena*, vol. I, p. 348 (speech in Patras, 19 Feb. 1912) (see Note 9).
44. Andreadis, *Erga*, p. 544, (see Note 41); Athanase J. Sbarounis (1933), *L'impôt sur le revenu en Grèce. Etude historique, critique et comparée*, Athens, p. 27ff.
45. Andreadis, *Erga*, pp. 552–4 (see Note 41), C. P. Costis (in collaboration with G. Kostelenos) (2003), *Istoria tis Ethnikis Trapezas tis Ellados 1914–1940* [*History of the National Bank of Greece 1914–1940*], Athens, p. 92.
46. According to A. Andreadis, *Erga*, p. 554 (see Note 41). E.-J. Tsouderos (1919), *Le relèvement économique de la Grèce*, pp. 68–9, adds another 271 million, following Lefeuvre-Méaulle (*La Grèce économique et financière*, Paris, 1915) as does Costis, *Istoria*, p. 93 (see Note 45).
47. Costis, *Istoria*, p. 95 (see Note 45).
48. See ibid., pp. 96–117. Eftaxias succeeded Venizelos' friend, Ioannis Valaoritis, who was killed in May 1914.
49. See G. B. Leontaritis (1990), *Greece and the First World War: From Neutrality to Intervention, 1917–1918*, Boulder, p. 59.
50. In 1914 the Provisioning Commission was set up, while the National Bank was charged with supplying grain on behalf of the government. The Ministry of Food-Supply was led initially by the industrialist Epameinondas Charilaos, then by Ioannis Drosopoulos (under the last Zaimis government) and from June 1917 (Venizelos government), by E. Embeiricos.
51. Costis, *Istoria*, p. 138 (see Note 45).
52. Ibid., p. 122, see also *BBE*, vol. I, September 1914, p. 146 (see Note 27).
53. N. S. Pantelakis (1988), *Symmachikes pistoseis. Kratos kai Ethniki Trapeza (1917–1928)* [Allied Credits. The State and the National Bank (1917–1928)], Athens, p. 39.
54. Psalidopoulos, *I krisi*, p. 30 (see Note 2).
55. For the credit from the allies see E.-J. Tsouderos (1924), *Les crédits alliés (1918–1919)*, Athens; N. Pantelakis, *Pistoseis* (see Note 53); and G. B. Leontaritis, *Greece*, pp. 194–247 (see Note 49). There is a wealth of material in the AMF archives, files 31855–60, 31864–71.
56. Leontaritis, *Greece*, p. 209 (see Note 49).
57. Sergent's report is dated 22 Oct. 1917, see AMF, B 31856.
58. Costis, *Istoria*, pp. 128–9 (see Note 45).
59. It should be clarified that, in addition to the minister of finance, M. Negrepontis, the persons involved in handling these issues and who conversed with or accompanied Venizelos, were Th. Lekatsas (representative to the Inter-Allied Financial Commission) and Greek amabassador to Paris, Athos Romanos.
60. Venizelos' proposed 'corrections' to the protocol of December 1917 are enumerated in A. Bonar Law's letter to his French counterpart Klotz, 22 Dec 1917, in AMF, B 31856. See also, Leontaritis, *Greece*, p. 232ff. (see Note 49), Pantelakis, *Pistoseis*, p. 58ff (see Note 53).

61. Law 1235/4 April 1918 added a clause to law 3642 which permitted the issue with these credits as cover, see Tsouderos, *Les crédits alliés*, pp. 11–12 (see Note 55). When Tsouderos was writing in 1924, 578.3 million were still in circulation, without cover of course. See also Psalidopoulos, *I crisi*, p. 56 (see Note 2). It should be added that these credits were to be paid off fifteen years after the signing of the peace.
62. With regard to this issue, a second agreement was contracted with France and Britain on 1 June 1918 in London, see in relation AMF B 31856, 'Ravitaillement, Convention 1 June 1918, Londres'.
63. Agreement was finally reached on the supply of the Greek army at the conference held in London 4–9 March 1918.
64. They meant specifically only the debts of the provisional government in Thessaloniki and 'not, of course, the entire Greek national debt!', see 'Note britannique' of 16 July 1918 sent by the French minister of foreign affairs to his colleague the minister of finance, 20 June 1918, in AMF B 31857.
65. A relevant bill was submitted to parliament but was later withdrawn. For the issue, see the analytical report from the French representative to the Inter-Allied Commission, Montréal, to Minister Pichon, Athens 20 April 1918, in AMF B 31857.
66. Letter from Keynes to the French economist J. Avenol, London 8 May 1918, and attached 'Memorandum', in AMF B 31857.
67. Venizelos' threats of resignation had lost their effectiveness by that time.

    'The Greek government has committed itself to proceed to mobilisation, and if it does not do so, it loses not only its credibility but also its credits, to which it owes its popularity, since thanks to these it is able . . . to avoid taxation . . .'

    This was said in Keynes' 'Memorandum' (see Note 66). The episodes are described by Montréal (see Note 65) as well as de Billy (copy of his letter attached to a document of 16 May 1918) in AMF B 31857. Venizelos' proposed compromises in 'Annexe à la lettre No 108' (undated), in the same file.
68. In September 1918 Venizelos, in the 'Aide mémoire sur la situation financière du Gouvernement Hellénique', Athens 11/24.9.1918, which he delivered to de Billy in Athens (in AMF B 31857) recorded these delays, as a result of which the NBG issued banknotes without cover. In similar spirit, M. Negrepontis, Greek minister of finance, protested to Montréal, Athens 29.8/11.9.1918, AMF B 31857.
69. *Keimena*, vol. II, pp. 462–8 (Parliament, 28 March 1918) (see Note 9).
70. AMF, B 31857, 'Conversation avec M. Venizelos, 28.11.1918'.
71. Venizelos corresponded personally with Keynes, in the framework of the new negotiation. After the first draft agreement, of 1 March 1919, Venizelos requested an increase in the sums, since he could not proceed more quickly with demobilisation, and an advance payment in cash immediately. Keynes, under the 'instructions' of his minister, doubted the expediency of keeping

276,000 men armed, hinted at the suspicion that the Greek government was already selling off munitions without keeping entries up to date in the reciprocal accounts, and lastly referred to the loan of 25 million dollars which Greece had indeed just contracted, in order to refuse the requests. See in AMF, B 31858, the draft agreement of 1 March 1919, Venizelos' letter to Keynes (Paris, 5 March 1919) and Keynes' reply to Venizelos, (31 March 1919). Venizelos turned to Sergent, asking him to use his influence on the 'Trésorerie Britannique' (ibid., Paris 13/26 April 1919), but to no avail.

72. The text of the 'Accords financiers avec la Grèce pour 1919', again in three parts, is in AMF B 31858. Another agreement between Greece and France, on 30 July 1919, concerned the military supplies specifically for the Ukraine campaign and the manner of settling them (see the text in the same file).
73. AMF, B 31858, Keynes to Venizelos, 10 May 1919.
74. The government undertook the management of law 3642, see Costis, *Istoria*, p. 145 (see Note 45). At the conference of the chambers of trade and industry, in November 1919 (see Note 19), Venizelos defended the state's right to keep control of foreign exchange after the war as well, an attitude which probably caused the great displeasure of mercantile and banking circles.
75. In September 1919 a domestic lottery loan of 300 million drachmas was issued, without great success, see Th. Veremis and C. Costis (1984), *I Ethniki Trapeza sti Mikra Asia (1919–1922)* [*The National Bank in Asia Minor (1919–1922)*], Athens, p. 112.
76. The Venizelos government signed two contracts with the National Bank of Greece, which made provision for increasing the right of issue, in May and September 1920, by 700 million drachmas in all, see Costis, *Istoria*, p. 151 (see Note 45). According to Psalidopoulos, *I Crisi*, p. 57 (see Note 2), the unsecured issues in 1919 and 1920 reached a total of 900 million drachmas.
77. About *half the share* of Britain and *one third* the share of the USA had been liquidated by October 1920, see Tsouderos, *Les crédits alliés*, p. 9 (see Note 55), with the text of the allied notification of 8 Dec. 1920: 'au cas où le roi Constantin remonterait sur le trône, la Grèce ne recevra de la part des Alliés aucun appui financier . . .' The French had already refused to liquidate their own credits (through withdrawals of the NBG, as anticipated in the agreement) before the November elections, when their approval was sought in July 1920 for the first widening of the NBG's issuing right (see previous Note). They argued that Greece could not request widening of the fiduciary circulation on the one hand, and on the other the liquidation of credits, which would have meant restriction of this circulation. A specious argument, which is why neither Britain nor the USA used it then. Venizelos himself protested later, in November 1922, to the French prime minister at this stance, obliging the services of the Ministry of Finance to give explanations. See the 'Note au Ministre' of 17

Nov. 1922, AMF B 31862. Moreover, in view of the refugee loan of 1924, Venizelos never ceased putting pressure on the allies to pay the rest of the credits. See Ioanna Minoglou-Pepelasi (1989), 'Oi diapragmatefseis gia to prosfygiko daneio tou 1924' ['Negotiations for the Refugee Loan in 1924'], in Th. Veremis and Y. Goulimi (eds), *Eleftherios Venizelos. Koinonia-Oikonomia-Politiki* [El. Venizelos. Society-Economy-Politics], Athens, p. 335. See also a memorandum of 21 Jan. 1925, from Venizelos to Churchill, at that time chancellor of the exchequer, published in *Keimena*, vol. III, p. 371ff (see Note 9).

78. Psalidopoulos, *I Krisi*, p. 56 (see Note 2).
79. Diomidis (1922) 'heatedly' argued this view in: *Ta oikonomika tis Ellados pro kai meta tin 1 Noemvriou 1920* [*The Finances of Greece Before and After 1 November 1920*], Athens but later he referred only to the essential problem of the successive issues of banknotes ('sudden and massive violation of every legal rule'), on account of the prolongation of the Asia Minor campaign, see (1928) *I nomismatiki mas astheneia kai ta mesa pros therapeian aftis* [*The Disease of our Currency and the Means for its Recovery*], Athens, pp. 10–12. Eftaxias expressed his views in an interview in the newspaper *Eleftheros Typos* in May 1921, which the French legation in Greece transmitted *in* extenso to the French Ministry of Finance on 10 May 1921, see AMF B 31855. This issue is discussed by Costis in Veremis and Costis, *I Ethniki Trapeza*, pp. 119, 132 (see Note 75).
80. For instance, taxes on alcohol, olive oil, matches and so on were raised, and taxes were also levied on stock-exchange dealings, train and steamship tickets. Stamp duty was imposed on diplomas amongst other things, and there were various taxes on tobacco (export, land tax, on cigarette-making machines). Montréal sent analytical reports to the French Ministry of Finance, see specifically the report of 29 Sept. 1918, in AMF B 31857.
81. In his introduction to the work by Athanase J. Sbarounis, *L'impôt sur le revenu en Grèce . . .*, p. VIII (see Note 44), G. Kafantaris readily concedes that the experience of war was the impetus for adopting the reform.
82. This law was abolished from 1 Jan. 1920, to be revived for a period in 1922, in the form of an 'extraordinary tax' on the profits of 'sociétés anonymes', see Sbarounis, *L'impot*, p. 43 (see Note 44). Venizelos, however, boasted of this taxation in his pre-election speech in Patras, in October 1920 ('[W]e did not neglect to take what belonged to the state from those who made excessive profits during the war . . .'), *Keimena,* vol. III, p. 88 (Patras, 21 Oct. 1920) (see Note 9).
83. According to Psalidopoulos, *I Krisi*, pp. 58–61 (see Note 2), the continual modifications aimed at improving the return of taxes, since the reform was made hurriedly and without calculating correctly the country's 'standard of taxation morality'.
84. According to A. Aggelopoulos (1928), 'I phorologiki epivarynsis tis Ellados apo tou 1914 mechri simeron' ['Fiscal Charges in Greece from

1914 up to today'], *Miniaia Oikonomiki kai Koinoniki Epitheorisis*, 45, (31 Jan. 1928), pp. 784–93.

85. It is indicative of this that in the very stringent cash-flow conditions of the autumn of 1917, Negrepontis asked the shipowner L. Embeiricos – who was known to Venizelos – to persuade the shipowners to grant a loan to the government. Embeiricos requested exemption from the extraordinary profits tax, which request Venizelos refused categorically, see Leontaritis, *Greece*, p. 225 (see Note 49).
86. *BBE*, 5(1-2), May–June 1918 (see Note 27). Minister of national economy at that time was K. Spyridis, who succeeded E. Repoulis.
87. 'And we had no hesitation about the state taking a share of the expenses . . .', Venizelos was to say in his pre-election speech in Patras on 21 October 1920 *Keimena*, vol. III, p. 81 (see Note 9).
88. Information on this delegation is in AN F12 9241, where there are numerous relevant reports by de Billy from Athens. The list of members is in the letter dated 6 September 1918.
89. 'Rarely did a prevailing social class show major blindness and deepest ignorance of its class interests,' commented Diomidis, (*I nomismatiki mas astheneia,* p. 11 (see Note 79)), referring to the AGIM's demand for the issue of banknotes in 1919.
90. The GSR included the Piraeus-frontier line (which had been linked up with the Macedonian line in 1914, at the expense of the state) and the Thessaloniki network. The body was reorganised in 1920 (law 2144 'on the administration of the railways of the Greek state') and work was completed with the Macedonia network (which the allies handed over to Greece in February 1920).
91. See George B. Leon (1976), *The Greek Socialist Movement and the First World War: The Road to Unity*, Boulder and Leon (1980), 'To elliniko ergatiko kinima kai to astiko kratos 1910–20' ['The Greek Labour Movement and the Bourgeois State'], in O. Dimitrakopoulos and Th. Veremis (eds), *Meletimata gyro apo to Venizelo kai tin epochi tou* [*Studies on Venizelos and his Time*], Athens, pp. 49–84. The GSEE soon split, however, into pro-Venizelists and socialists. Shortly after the inaugural congress of the GSEE, in October 1918, the Socialist Labour Party of Greece (SEKE) was founded, which was renamed the Communist Party of Greece (KKE) in 1924.
92. Liakos, *Ergasia kai politiki*, p. 239ff (see Note 32).
93. Moudopoulos, 'O nomos', in Mavrogordatos and Hadjiiosif (eds), *Venlizelismos*, pp. 250–3 (see Note 33). C. Hadjiiosif, 'To prosfygiko chock' [The refugee shock], in Hadjiosif (ed.), *Istoria tis Elladas*, vol. II-1, p. 15 (see Note 25).
94. *Keimena*, vol. II, p. 623 (Parliament, 26 Nov 1919) (see Note 9).
95. Ibid., p. 693 (Parliament, 27 Jan 1920) (see Note 9).
96. Ibid., p. 696.

97. See Olga Christodoulaki, 'I metarrythmisi tou trapezikou systimatos kai i idrysi tis Trapezas tis Ellados' ['The Reform of the Banking System and the Foundation of the Bank of Greece'], in Hajiiosif (ed.), *Istoria tis Elladas*, vol. II-1, pp. 251–67 (see Note 25).
98. Mavrogordatos, *Stillborn Republic,* p. 37 (see Note 12). Kafantaris had already resigned, in May 1928, from the leadership of the Liberal Party, when Venizelos returned from Europe and settled in Chania, from where he began to intervene in political life again.
99. For the sounding out of the FCLN for the purpose of reconsideration of the Geneva Protocol, see the note of the president of the FC, de Chalendar, dated 6 Nov 1928, in the AMF B31868.
100. See mainly Venizelos' letter to Kafantaris, dated 3 July 1928, in the newspaper *Eleftheron Vima*, which is also published in *Keimena*, vol. III, pp. 455–7 (see Note 9).
101. AMF B31868, the French ambassador in Athens to the Foreign Ministry in Athens (15 Jan 1929), in which are the basic outlines of the agreement that had already been made; Costis, *Istoria*, pp. 400–1 (see Note 45).
102. Costis (1986), *Oi trapezes kai i krisi 1929–1932* [*The Banks and the 1929–1932 Crisis*], Athens.
103. See Ioannis Stefanidis, 'Reconstructing Greece as a European State: Venizelos' Last Premiership, 1928–32' in this volume.
104. The League of Nations' loan was named 'tripartite', since one third was made available for covering budget deficits, one third for stabilisation and one third for refugee rehabilitation. Ioanna Pepelasis Minoglou (2002), 'Between Informal Networks and Formal Contracts: International Investment in Greece during the 1920s', *Business History*, 44(2) (April) pp. 40–64.
105. D. Stephanidis (1930), *I eisroi xenon kephalaion kai ai oikonomikai kai politikai tis synepeiai* [*The Influx of Foreign Capital and its Economic and Political Impact*], Thessaloniki, p. 256; A. N. Petsalis (1931), *To daneion ton paragogikon ergon kai ta dimosia oikonomika tis Ellados* [*The Productive Works' Loan and the State Finances of Greece*], Athens. The originally envisaged sum of £22 million was in the end given in two instalments: the first, of £4 million, was issued in London in December 1928 and the second, of £4.6 million, in March 1931. It was never possible to negotiate the rest.
106. *Keimena*, vol. IV, p. 454 (from the publication of the speech in the newspaper *Eleftheron Vima*, 27 March 1932) (see Note 9).
107. 'Memorandum sur la répercussion de la crise mondiale sur la situation économique et financière de la Grèce (remis aux Ministres par M. Vénizélos le 24.1.32)', in AMF B 31871.
108. The French were particularly sensitive to the issues of the earlier loans, in which they had a greater participation, and for the same reason showed greater hesitation regarding the abandonment of the gold standard and

devaluation of the drachma, which the British had proposed. See the note from the French finance minister to the foreign minister, Paris 4 Feb 1932, in AMF B 31871. Analytical presentation of the 'battle of the drachma' in Mark Mazower (1991), *Greece and the Inter-War Economic Crisis*, Oxford.

109. 'Text of report adopted by the Financial Committee' in AMF B 31871.

110. In his official announcement, which was published in the newspapers on 28 September 1931, and in his speech to the Athens Chamber of Commerce and Industry Venizelos had made dire predictions about the dangers that the possible devaluation of the drachma – which he characterised as 'the country's economic flag, around which I summon all to rally' – harboured for the economy, see *Keimena*, vol. IV, p. 370 (speech to the AGIM, 28 Sept 1931) (see Note 9). His official announcement ended with the phrase 'I give the Greek people my personal assurance . . . that we can maintain the integrity of our national currency' (ibid., p. 366).

111. See Philippe Gilles (2004), *Histoire des crises et des cycles économiques*, Paris, p. 160. Venizelos was later accused in parliament of not foreseeing in time the effects of the crisis and in his reply he referred to the president of the USA a few months before the crash, see *Keimena*, vol. IV, p. 524 (Parliament, 28 April 1932) (see Note 9). His close collaborator Alexandros Diomidis, who paid for the confusion of September 1931 with his dismissal, on a trivial pretext, from his position as governor of the Bank of Greece, said a few months later that with the episode of the British pound 'the world woke up suddenly' from the 'simple view' that the international crisis, though serious, would be usual and passing. See Diomidis (1933),'Ta katholika phenomena tis kriseos kai i epidrasis afton eis tin exelixin ton idiotikon kai dimosion oikonomikon' ['The General Manifestations of the Crisis and their Impact on the Evolution of Private and Public Finances'], in Diomidis, *I oikonomiki erevna ton megalon technikon zitimaton* [The Economic Investigation of Big Technical Issues], Athens, p. i.

112. G. Mitrophanis (2004), 'I dimosia oikonomia' ['Public finances'], in V. Panayotopoulos (ed.), *Istoria tou Neou Ellinismou, 1770–2000* [History of Modern Hellenism 1770–2000], vol. 7, Athens, pp. 123–40. See also D. Stephanidis, *I eisroi*, p. 209ff (see Note 105).

113. In his historic speech to parliament on 30 March 1932, when the Niemeyer report had just been made public, Venizelos referred to the success in The Hague: 'if the spirit of justice is shown to us, which was shown at least at the last moment in the Hague Conference . . .', *Keimena*, vol. IV, p. 465 (see Note 9).

114. *Keimena*, vol. IV, 181 (speech in Thessaloniki, 13 May 1930) (see Note 9). A little further on, when speaking about the 'fall in prices' of olive oil too, he said somewhat vaguely that 'this is a more general phenomenon' (ibid., p. 182).

115. Concentrated discussion on these issues in the publications of the Athens

Chamber of Trade and Industry, the Bank of Athens and so on, from the last quarter of 1929 on. See also M. Mazower, *Greece*, p. 187ff (see Note 108).

116. The interview is republished in *Keimena*, vol. IV, pp. 420–1 (see Note 9).
117. From July 1931 dates the Hoover moratorium, which kick-started new negotiations of Greece with Bulgaria, and which in the end suspended payment of reparations (15 April 1932). See AMF B 31870 and G. Mitrophanis 'I dimosia oikonomia', in Panayotopoulos (ed.), *Istoria* (see Note 112).
118. *Keimena*, vol. IV, p. 437 (see Note 9).
119. It should be remembered that rural reform, after the constitutional provision in 1911, which has been discussed, was inaugurated legally in 1917 to 1919, by the Venizelos government, but because of the war and the political upheavals was finally implemented after 1922.
120. S. Petmezas, 'Agrotiki oikonomia', in Hadjiiosif (ed.), *Istoria* (see Note 25)
121. M. Mazower, *Greece*, p. 171 (see Note 108). Measures to relieve the tobacco crisis were limited in the end to the state purchasing old stocks, the adoption of measures to restrict cultivation on unsuitable ground and a reduction in land tax.
122. *Keimena*, vol. IV, p. 182 (see Note 9).
123. M. Mazower, *Greece*, pp. 270–1 (see Note 108).
124. See a relevant letter from the French ambassador in Athens to his minister 11 Feb 1932, in which he also relays the comments of the anti-Venizelist newspaper *Proia* (AMF B 31871). For the road-construction contract and the flaws in the execution of these works see Ioanna Pepelasis Minoglou (1998), 'Phantom Rails and Roads. Land Transport Public Works in Greece during the 1920s', *The Journal of Transport History* 19 (1) pp. 33–49.
125. The project for the water supply of Athens, which Venizelos had begun in his first four-year term but did not manage to finish then, had been commissioned since 1925 from the American firm Ulen and Co., while the first high-voltage electricity network in the Athens area had been commissioned at the same time from the British Power and Traction Company. In 1930, the Venizelos government commissioned the German firm Siemens and Halske to construct the first telephone network.
126. In order to exercise long-term industrial credit, the NBG had set up in 1927, together with the Hambros Bank in London, the company Hellenic and General Trust – but in crisis conditions lending was restricted to a small number of firms.
127. As in the case of the Société Anonyme of Chemical Products and Fertilizers which, shaken by the rural recession, was supported by state guarantee in order to take a loan in 1930 and by customs protection in 1931. See Costis, *Oi Trapezes*, p. 29 (see Note 102) and Mavrogordatos, *Stillborn Republic*, p. 135 (see Note 12).

128. Exemption from the requirement of an operating permit for existing large companies, and so on, see C. Hadjiiosif, *I giraia selini, p.* 285 (see Note 29).
129. At least according to the words of Kafantaris under the coalition government, see Mazower, *Greece*, p. 134 (see Note 108).
130. Repeated negotiations were held between Greece and France, throughout the four-year term, on wine exports, on which France imposed quotas. Venizelos was involved personally in these negotiations, in collaboration with the industrialist-magnate Epameinondas Charilaos, who controlled the Greek Wine and Spirits Company. Naturally, the fact that this industry was linked with the problematic agricultural sector of currant-growing played a role in the importance attached to it. Copious material on these negotiations in AN F10 2111–3.
131. Who supported, from late 1931, the 'most extreme restriction of imports' and the 'persistent effort to satisfy our needs ourselves . . .', see 'Ta katholika phenomena', p. vi (see Note 111).
132. Liakos, *Ergasia kai politiki*, p. 312 (see Note 32): the excerpt is from a letter from Venizelos to Albert Thomas in 1928.
133. *Keimena*, vol. IV, p. 410 (speech at the 'Parnassos' hall, 7 Dec 1931, published in the newspaper *Eleftheron Vima* of 8 Dec 1931) (see Note 9).

11

Modernisation and Reaction in Greek Education during the Venizelos Era

Alexis Dimaras

This chapter focuses on the evolution of primary and secondary education during the Venizelos era.[1] For the greater part of the period under review, vocational education was essentially non-existent as a structural part of the system. As for the tertiary level, the Venizelos governments attempted two major legislative interventions: one at the very beginning (1911) of the period and another at the very end (1932). The main axis of both was the power relations between the government and the professorial establishment (in July 1931 a law had been passed which established the post of a government delegate in universities). During the years that intervened, many related matters were discussed, dominant among them being those concerning the living, schooling and study conditions of students. However, all this did not directly affect (nor did it lead to different interpretations of) the factors which, on other levels, shaped and expressed educational policy in each period.[2] Important to future developments and to the linking of the system to goals of national prestige and economic development were the founding of the University of Thessaloniki (1925–6), the granting of university status to the Polytechnic School (1929) and to the School of Fine Arts (1930), as well as the earlier (1920) founding of two post-secondary institutions (the Agronomy School and the Commercial School) which later evolved into universities.[3]

The forming of a general educational policy is related to many factors, is the result of consecutive processes, the blending of diverse trends, and the compromise of different pressures which it is almost impossible to identify. Moreover, the roles of various advisers remain dubious – usually forever – while they themselves rarely appear under their own name. In any case, concerning Venizelos, we at least have one direct indication of personal concern when, in 1918, he said: 'You should know that I consider our educational reform to be the greatest title of glory of my premiership and my greatest service to the motherland.'[4]

It seems that the only solid responsibility – but also the most decisive participation – of each prime minister had been in the selection of the person to whom he entrusted the Education Ministry portfolio. Here too, one can observe an essential change with the Venizelos government: up until his era, this post was held, as a rule, by politicians of no particular prestige or charisma. Their terms of office were relatively short.[5] With Venizelos in power things changed both in terms of individuals and terms of office: the selection of Apostolos Alexandris as the first minister of education in 1910 and of his successor, Ioannis Tsirimokos, represented a radical change compared to the past, since they both had clear ties to the modernising group of demoticists, the supporters of the use of the spoken language.[6] The period of the government of 1917 to 1920 was covered in its entirety (three years and four months) by Dimitrios Dingas.[7] It was under this government that, vis-à-vis primary schooling, a decisive change was implemented in the educational approach and in language teaching, of which Venizelos was very proud. As in the case of a prime minister, so too in the case of a minister, the main evaluation criterion remains his choice of associates. And it is evident that the conscientious Dingas, who was devoted to reform, was overshadowed by the three 'great men' of educational demoticism – Alexandros Delmouzos, Dimitris Glinos, and Manolis Triantaphyllidis – whom he had appointed (obviously with the approval, if not the urging of Venizelos) to high posts in the ministry. For all three ministers, that was the first time they had been members of a cabinet. Finally, in the period 1928 to 1932, Venizelos used two ministers who were experienced members of previous cabinets: Constantinos Gondikas, who was responsible for drafting the basic bills of the reform and for effectively supporting them in parliament, and Georgios Papandreou, who continued his work until 1932.

But the third Venizelos government also marked an important exception to yet another general rule: in early January 1930, when Papandreou succeeded Gondikas, the change of minister did not bring about a change in the government's educational policy. Not that the new minister did not emphasise policy elements other than those on which his predecessor had focused his attention. But the main direction which had been set by Gondikas was also followed by his successor, and indeed, with consistency and decisiveness. The three major issues, which, as will be developed further on, were dealt with legislatively in 1931 (school buildings, textbooks and the secondary school curriculum), all lie fully within the spirit of the main reformative framework of the laws of 1929. It is this smooth succession which constitutes the exception: up until then – but also since then and up until very close to our time – the replacement of a minister (even without a change of government) meant – almost automatically – a change of policy. Sometimes this occurred for obvious political reasons, but often it seemed inexplicable. This phenomenon was so widespread that the view was held that, basically, Greece didn't have a governmental but a ministerial educational policy. The exception – which could perhaps be attributed to a personal wish of Venizelos – becomes even more interesting when juxtaposed with what took place during the previous Venizelos government, in 1912, when Tsirimokos introduced the reform, making only marginal reference to the proposals of his predecessor.

Apart from these specific events, and regardless of the extent of Venizelos' personal involvement in the major or minor issues of educational policy, there are certain more complex matters which remain – possibly forever – unclarified. These refer to the interrelation – or lack thereof – between the more general and broader goals of the government and its educational policy.

Today, for example, we know that, following 1922, the most deprived (also in terms of education) strata of the population belonged, in their majority, to the Venizelist side. However, we do not know whether the governments of the time were aware of this correlation and whether the policies which they followed in education aimed either at maintaining this relation or overthrowing it. Similarly, there are no facts or direct statements attesting to a connection between educational and demographic policy in relation, for example, to the New Territories, the refugees and/or the minorities.

It can be safely claimed that education in Greece had preserved certain features of the late nineteenth century unchanged: it was bookish, it relied too heavily on learning by rote, it was not practical enough, and it placed inordinate importance on ancient Greece at the cost of modern Greece. This was the case not only immediately after the reformative efforts of the Venizelos governments, but also many years later. Furthermore, judging by the level of illiteracy at the end of the period being reviewed, the overall picture is not a positive one: according to the 1928 census, of the population aged fifteen and older, 63.5 per cent of the women and 25.9 per cent of the men were illiterate.[8] Of course, in 1928, special circumstances (the annexation of the New Territories, the exchange of populations, and so on) do not allow direct comparisons with the past or the acknowledgement of achievements. In 1907, the percentages were 82.6 per cent for women and 50.2 per cent for men. However, when carrying out such assessments, it should not be overlooked that in the twenty-two years covered in this review, it was only during the last four that a consistent educational policy was implemented. The only other intervention of some duration – the regulation, in 1916, of language teaching in the first years of primary school – was, of course, a necessary, but not a sufficient condition for the overthrowing of the main negative features of the system.

THE ROAD TOWARDS A LIBERAL EDUCATIONAL POLICY

The conventional and symbolic significance taken on by the Goudi revolt in all aspects of modern Greek life is expressed in education through the so-called 'educational demoticism' movement, that is to say, the linking of the demands for the recognition of vernacular Greek (demotic) as a common, national language to those in favour of the modernisation of the school system.[9] The movement had its own conventional starting point in Photis Photiadis' 1902 essay 'To glossikon zitima k'i ekpaideftiki mas anagennisis' ['The Language Question and our Educational Renaissance']. If this was its 'first' theoretical manifestation, its actual beginning was marked by the founding of an Anoteron Dimotikon Parthenagogeion [Higher Municipal Girls' School] in Volos, in 1908.

The ideological context within which this school operated and its unique psysiognomy are illustrated succinctly, and with absolute clarity, in two references to the school made by its principal, Alexandros Delmouzos:[10]

> The Municipality [of Volos] founded . . . the Higher School for Girls with a particular purpose and for girls from a particular social class. It was to educate *Greek women of a practical and illuminated mind, who would later be able to set up a fine household and educate their children in the right way.* It is for this reason that the proposal for its foundation asked that their higher general education be humanitarian, national and modernistic, but offering also practical knowledge and abilities, of the kind needed to run a household and raise children.[11]

In the second reference, Delmouzos cites one of the general principles on which the curriculum of the girls' school was based:

> [The students] were to acquaint themselves with Greek civilisation as it evolved through its three great periods: antiquity; its continuation, Byzantine; and the modern period. The basis, however, the starting point and the finish line was modern Hellenism, our contemporary society and its problems . . . The immediate and chief linguistic aim [of the school] was the demotic language.[12]

Everything, therefore, that was linked to the founding and the organisation of this school showed that things were changing: it was founded on an initiative of the municipality and not the central government, which had absolute control of the system; it was located in the provinces and not in Athens, which was the centre of almost all cultural activities;

it was intended for girls, who formed an appreciable minority in terms of their participation in education; it met the demand of the (new) bourgeois segment of society to extend the education of its children; it operated outside statutory forms (the official system did not provide for such post-primary schools) and thus enjoyed the freedom to formulate its own curriculum; its principal belonged to the younger generation (Delmouzos was twenty-eight when he assumed the post) and had had recent contact with German progressive pedagogy. Moreover – and perhaps more significantly – it was at the Volos school that the barrier of the language question was surmounted and that the demotic was treated as an integral part of the educational and pedagogical – and therefore the social – modernisation of Greece.

The linking was complete and absolutely clear: the school, whose 'starting point and finish line was modern Hellenism', also had the demotic as its main teaching object and instrument. Equally clear was the break with the scholastic past but also with the educational establishment (in the broadest sense of the term). Thus, educational demoticism took on a specific ideological content which extended beyond and above language. To begin with, there was the indirect acknowledgement of the fact that there existed a modern Greek civilisation with elements worthy of comprising the axis of a national educational/cultural programme. Moreover, Delmouzos made clear at the Volos school that the starting point from which to approach modern Greek civilisation would not be a general outlook which was cut off from life but, rather, society itself. Taking this even further: this modern Greek society was not to be approached only in an abstract and descriptive way, but also by focusing on 'its problems'. All this would lead to the formation of citizens possessing critical thought; who would be proud of the world in which they lived; aware of the problems surrounding the society to which they belonged; and, as such, inclined to contribute to their solution.

The opposition – a combination of diverse interests of equally diverse origins and manifestations – also forged its position: educational demoticism (in its linguistic and educational expression, but especially in a combination thereof) constituted a threat to the nation analogous to the internal and external menaces coming from other directions. It was these views that formed the basis of the polemic that soon began on the school of Volos and was marked by violence. Their most epigrammatic, populist and quaint formulation can be found in a quote by the bishop of Dimitrias, Germanos Mavromatis, who headed the prosecution of the school:[13] 'In the conscience of all the people, demoticism,[14] anarchism, socialism, atheism and freemasonry are one and the same.'[15]

The quote is taken from the trial that took place in 1914 in Nafplion (because tempers in Volos were still heated). The accused were charged because:

> at various times from September 1908 to late March 1911 . . . mainly in the Workers' Centre and the Volos Girls' School, they tried by word of mouth, by teaching and by printed pamphlets to attract converts to so-called religious doctrines, that is to say atheism, actions with which the preservation of political order is irreconcilable . . . and they achieved their aim in part by drawing many to these beliefs . . .

that is to say they were charged with violating 'the law regarding vilification and the press'.[16] Accused were, among others, leaders of the local workers' union, Doctor Dimitris Saratsis (who had recommended the founding of the Girls' School to the municipal council, but who had also played a leading role in the setting up of the workers' centre), and Alexandros Delmouzos.

The Nafplion Trial ended with the accused being acquitted. However, as was to happen in subsequent cases, the modernising effort had been quashed: the Volos school closed in 1911 as a result. But the conflict it had provoked had contributed decisively to defining the field of conflict between the old and the new, conservatism and modernisation, as well as the choice of symbols of each side.

THE SPREAD OF MODERNISING TRENDS

In conjunction with the general climate that prevailed after Goudi, the events surrounding the Volos Girls' School had hastened (and, conceivably, facilitated), the emergence of other movements advocating change in various fields and levels of the educational system. There is, for example, the case of primary school teachers, who, during the last two decades of the nineteenth century, had started a rudimentary trade union and had ensured – despite certain subsequent indirect upsets – an appreciable improvement in their professional situation.[17] In 1909 one can observe an increased mobility in the field, leading, among other things, to disruptive trends stemming mainly from the desire of the provincial unions to shake off the suzerainty of their Athenian colleagues. In this context, a demand was then expressed which appears to have differentiated the type of claims put forth: its character was hierarchical – and therefore social – since the teachers demanded the right to be elected to the position of inspector.

Another field in which significant changes took place was that of the university student body: during the first months of 1910, a relatively small group of students founded the Phoititiki Syndrophia (Students' Society) which aimed to 'help establish the living Greek language in all forms of our written communication'. Of course, this movement falls primarily within the category of the linguistic fight – and it is significant that a manifesto written by the society was published in the journal *Noumas*, the militant publication of the demoticists. Both the breadth of its aims and their interdependence is discernible in the society's texts. Thus, for example, explaining their motives in the foreword to its statutes, the founders note:

> We finally felt that without sincerity we would not be able to achieve anything good and brave. And we saw that there was no greater insincerity than to ignore the language of our mothers. We saw that it was cowardly to hide and be ashamed of ourselves instead of proud.[18]

This reference to pride immediately brings to mind what was noted above concerning the recognition of the values of modern Hellenism at the Volos school.

It is worth noting that the society drew its dynamism (possibly in terms of numbers as well) from the students of the faculty of philosophy, the professors of which were the leaders of all movements defending purist language (katharevousa): the tendency to overthrow the status quo came, in this case, from within.

Among the private initiatives that marked the turn in educational interests and aims, I should also mention that the Union of Greek Women, which had set up an educational department as early as 1897, became particularly active at the turn of the century – and especially from 1908 onwards – in the field of pre-school education and the education of women. Regardless of the fact that this upper-middle-class charitable society continued to define its activity according to broader national – and not specifically social – needs, the modernity of its actions is obvious. Aiming in the same direction, though from a totally different starting point, was the Women Workers' Sunday School, founded in 1911 by the Athens Workers' Centre. One is reminded of the – albeit informal – relationship between the Volos Workers' Centre and the Girls' School.

A totally different case in terms of importance, for various reasons, was the founding in 1910 of the Ekpaideftikos Omilos (Educational League), which aimed to 'found a model primary school in Athens and help, in time, to reshape Greek society'. Here again we see the link between social and educational issues. After all, the language used in the league's founding texts – perhaps even more so than the names of those who signed them (among them, A. Delmouzos, Ion Dragoumis, and Ph. Photiadis) – does little to hide the fact that this effort fell within the broader movement of educational demoticism.[19]

The league functioned without crucial changes in its aims until 1927. During this period, the uncontested leadership belonged – rarely collectively and mostly successively – to the three 'great men': Dimitris Glinos, Alexandros Delmouzos and Manolis Triantaphyllidis.[20] And, touching upon the symbolism specified in this chapter, I should note that these three expressed the three main axes of the movement respectively: the social, the pedagogical and the linguistic.

STATE VACILLATION UNTIL 1916

For the first few years of the century, and up until the point when Eleftherios Venizelos assumed the reins of government in 1910, the state had continued to move at the long-established, slow pace of the past. Among the few pre-Venizelist acts that could be considered as modernising I could mention the increase in the teaching hours allocated to modern Greek (one hour a week, also, to teach from anthologies, mainly of excerpts of modern Greek literary texts) in the first two years of (the four-year) secondary school and the addition of chemistry (one hour a week) to the last two years.

More drastic – and historically more interesting – was the establishment, in April 1910, of a new state educational foundation, the Secondary Education Teacher Training College. Its purpose was 'the theoretical and practical pedagogical instruction of . . . secondary education teachers'. In this instance, the ministry seems to have had two different goals simultaneously. One is obvious and is the one stated: to satisfy an earlier demand for the pedagogical instruction of teachers who, at university, were taught only the subjects of their chosen field.

The second goal is not immediately obvious. The Secondary Education Teacher Training College, which possibly aimed initially at state intervention to prevent students straying from the established equilibrium (this was the time of the Students' Society and of intense linguistic-educational clashes), finally had the opposite result: it was used as a counterweight to university conservatism in order to attract secondary education teachers to the modernising position which the state was trying to promote after Goudi. This drastic turn was also marked by the change implemented by the government in its leadership: the first director, Nikolaos Exarchopoulos, assistant professor at the faculty of philosophy, was replaced in 1912 by Dimitris Glinos. As a consequence,

Exarchopoulos assumed a clear and aggressive position against educational demoticism and personally against its leaders.[21]

Meanwhile, the government had finally accepted the proposal to include in the constitution, during the revision of 1911, an article on the protection of the state's 'official language', that is, on the imposing of katharevousa. This provision complemented another by which 'it was expressly forbidden . . . to render in any other linguistic form' the text of the holy scriptures. Amid the fever of the linguistic battle, these arrangements disappointed and discouraged the supporters of educational demoticism, regardless of whatever balance was secured by Venizelos,[22] and regardless of the fact that the constitution also introduced the purely liberal concept of compulsory and free schooling at the primary school level.

Nevertheless, it was also at that time that efforts began on the part of the Ministry of Education to collaborate with those who favoured and promoted linguistic-educational modernisation – and these met with a positive response. In January 1912, the president of the Central Educational Council of the Ministry (under Minister Apostolos Alexandris) sent out a circular to the Educational League in which he requested the opinions of the recipients regarding the reformation of the programmes for primary schools and girls' secondary schools. The league replied with a long memorandum which was published in its *Bulletin*. We know its authors from other sources: one part was written by Delmouzos and the other by Glinos. What we do not know is whether it was submitted for approval to the other members of the Educational League. In any event, this act of the ministry and its publication lent prestige to the league and consolidated its reputation.

Later on, the replacement of Alexandris by Ioannis Tsirimokos at the Ministry of Education (31 May 1912),[23] also marked the deeper involvement of the leaders of educational demoticism in the forming of an educational policy, culminating in the close collaboration between the new minister and Dimitris Glinos, which began immediately: he was assigned, as has already been noted, the direction of the Secondary Education Teacher Training College (an act which possibly also had intentional symbolism) and was asked to help in the planning of educational reform, a reform which would constitute part of the government's 'restorative' effort. The collaboration was a fruitful one and the bills proposed to parliament by Tsirimokos in November 1913 – and especially their long and detailed preambles – were the work of Glinos.

In 1913, therefore, modernising positions regarding education had been clarified: they emerge consummately in the bills and pointedly in their preambles. A typical example is this reference to the autonomy of primary schools:

> It is an act of depriving the people of intellectual sustenance when this school's programme is adapted in any way to the programme of the higher schools . . . Worse than anything else is that a primary school should degenerate into a preparatory pre-secondary school.[24]

This position referred to older legislative-reformative proposals (at least as early as 1880), but the tone now had an explicitly social perspective. Also more explicit, compared to earlier reports of this kind, was the perception regarding the stratification of society and the function of the educational system in relation to it: the system had to offer every social class 'the general education needed by it'.[25]

In other respects – and especially in terms of their structure – the bills of 1913 systematised and focused earlier proposals rather than introducing new schemes:

> The distinctive marks of the system [we propose] are the following: 1. A primary education which is integrated, unified and common to all Greek children, consisting . . . of only one six-year cycle. 2. The beginning of secondary education after the end of this cycle. 3. Secondary education schools in parallel, that is, independent of each other, each with its own special and self-contained curriculum, shorter for the middle class and lengthier for the one aimed at the higher [social] class.[26]

However, this effort (just like the ones made repeatedly from 1877 onwards)[27] did not bear fruit, even though it had been made in a generally reformative climate, and despite the fact that it consciously avoided any reference to language teaching. Obviously, criteria similar to those that had directed Venizelos towards accepting constitutional reform regarding language had led him to abandon the effort for educational reform. Once more, the balance of power had tipped towards the conservatives. The opposition to the government's linguistic-educational intentions and, especially, to the advisers the government had chosen, was especially powerful, even within the Liberal Party. Thus, up until the revolt of 1916, besides the establishment of the Secondary School Teacher Training College, state reform manifested itself in only two programmes: one regarding primary education and another regarding secondary education (with the former in place until 1964 and the latter until 1931); and the remodelling of the Educational Council, which, for the first time, was free of the suzerainty of university professors. Other than that, a small indication of the state of affairs is a census concerning the hygiene of school buildings carried out in 1916: in a total of 1166 school buildings inspected throughout the country, 346 (30 per cent) were judged 'hygienic' and 449 (43 per cent) 'unhygienic' – the rest were judged 'moderately hygienic'.[28]

THE REACTION AND ITS REACTIONS

Thus, from Goudi to Thessaloniki, the powers resisting modernisation had three important successes to their credit (the closing of the Volos Girls' School, the passing of constitutional articles regarding language, and the abandonment of the Tsirimokos bills) and had defined the field of the polemic, its starting point always being the language question.

Even notable scholars, such as Georgios Hadjidakis, professor of linguistics at Athens University, centred their arguments on the language question: when it was announced that the Educational League had been set up with the aim of founding a school, Hadjidakis – using a tactic mentioned above – commented only on the teaching of language. In the event, he wrote that should the proposed 'linguistic form' prevail, 'what will our relation be to the church, to older literature, to legislation and to our establishment as a whole?'[29]

But the leadership of the Reaction was then taken on by another university professor, the classicist Georgios Mystriotis. Already a familiar name from the great conflicts of the early twentieth century concerning the language question, his struggle reached its zenith during the time of the voting for the constitution.[30] It was then that he founded a committee 'for the lawful protection of the national language', having, on another occasion, termed the proposal for the recognition of the demotic as a 'national issue of a magnitude never before encountered in the Greek world, [for] the present struggle aims at splitting up and wiping out our entire race'.[31]

In the few discussions that focused their interest elsewhere, those opposed to modernisation usually supported the view that the main orientation and the basic structures of the educational system were fine as they stood, and that the intervention needed should be exclusively in the direction of improving its conditions and rendering its function more effective. The following observation of Hadjidakis' is typical: 'Our first and foremost duty should be to examine . . . in what way and how quickest to find financial resources, to build schools, to educate teachers and to acquire blackboards',[32] and not to intervene in matters of language teaching.

I should note that now the attention of conservatives also turned, obviously for various reasons, to secondary schools: numbers had grown, signs of independence on the part of young people had multiplied, the movement of secondary school graduates towards university had increased, and the social role of this group had gained in importance.[33]

MODERNISERS IN THE GOVERNMENT

The revolt of 1916, a decisive event for the future of Greece, also acted as a catalyst for educational matters. In May 1917, the Thessaloniki government, following a proposal by Dimitris Glinos as the president of a three-member educational council, issued a decree according to which the reading books of the early primary school classes 'have to be written in the common spoken (demotic) language, free of any archaism or idiomatic expression'.

After the government moved to Athens, the decree was ratified by law and since then had been inplace without interruption – albeit with variations – thus constituting perhaps the most important intervention in the development of modern Greek educational programmes. And that was because the (Athenian) law of 1917, complemented the following year by another, led to still more innovative measures: the approval of many books and the selection of one from a number proposed by the teachers' council of each school; the general – and not analytical – description of their content in the relevant proclamations regarding their authorship (giving more freedom to prospective authors of text books); the absence of binding teaching instructions, which encouraged initiative; the commissioning of books by competition rather than assignment; the use of specialised manuals for specific geographical areas.[34]

Generally speaking, the interventions of 1916 to 1918 were limited to the issue of language teaching at primary school level (and subsequently also to the issue of the relevant textbooks) and hence did not constitute an 'educational reform' in the sense of a radical and general institutional change of the system. However, they did act as a catalyst for its orientation, perhaps an even greater one than the major, statutory reforms that were later enacted.

Certainly, the people involved also contributed greatly to this development. These were Dimitris Glinos, as secretary general of the Ministry of Education, and two of his – for the time being – colleagues, Alexandros Delmouzos and Manolis Triantaphyllidis, as 'higher supervisors of primary school education'. Their personalities (and the power which they drew quite possibly directly from Venizelos) were such that they overshadowed the minister, Dimitrios Dingas, who, however, seems to have supported them unreservedly.

Now, the three 'great men' of educational demoticism channelled their energies in specific directions: the 'rules' of the demotic (it was then that the first version of Triantaphyllidis' *Grammar* was published in pamphlet form), the 'illumination' of teachers (through local conferences, the republication of the informative *Bulletin* of the Education Ministry, and articles in the *Bulletin of the Educational League*), and the publication of new textbooks. This latter activity – a revolutionary change in the approach to the subject – marked a modernising turn in the major content of Modern Greek pedagogy.[35]

OVERTHROW

As is obvious from the above, from the early years of the Venizelos governments, the basic periodization of educational history coincides with that of general political history. Accordingly, the overthrow that resulted from the 1 November 1920 election directly influenced educational issues. Moreover, the tenacity with which the establishment had for years opposed any modernisation led to the same consequences of this change in the balance of power. And since the entire reformative-modernising effort revolved around primary school textbooks, that was where the attack of the conservative reaction centred.

The new education minister, upon assuming his post, formed a committee (the leading role in which seems to have been played by Nikolaos Exarchopoulos) 'to examine the teaching of language in primary schools'. The committee submitted its report in early February 1921, and its findings were most damning. Amongst its proposals, the most famous was the one demanding that 'the readers written according to those laws [of 1918] should be immediately ejected from all schools and burnt as being works of falsehood and malicious intent'. The passion with which the committee addressed the issues is revealed in its proposal 'to prosecute criminally those culpable of the sudden and underhand acts carried out towards the degeneration of the Greek language and of education'.[36] Other educational and social characteristics of the readers have only a secondary place in the report.

Those 'culpable', however, were not criminally prosecuted – they had already been fired from their posts – and it is not known whether the books were burnt. Nevertheless, another proposal of the committee, to reinstate the use of the books which had been approved 'before 1917', soon became law.

But, in 1921, the return 'to things as they were before 1917' could not constitute a generally acceptable solution, especially since the earlier inaction essentially led to a regression to the conditions of the 1890s.[37] Almost ten more years were to elapse until, within a new constitutional framework, the government acquired the composition, the orientation and the majority that would allow for the first effective reformative intervention in education since the 1830s.

Thus educational changes were limited to the 'improvement' of numbers (though not always of the ratios) and to certain aspects of the infrastructure: more pupils, more teachers, a larger participation of women, technically improved textbooks, more school buildings. Pupils, however, attended classes with the same aims and subjects, teachers used the same methods, women were still a small minority in all areas, the content of textbooks was based on the old pedagogical principles, and most school buildings were unsuitable. This inertia exacerbated the situation, precisely because other factors had changed considerably.

THE NEW EFFORT AND THE CLARIFICATION OF TENDENCIES

In the early 1920s, the educational system was also faced with the major problems that had emerged following Greece's national misadventures. Together with the abrupt changes in numbers (especially in terms of pupils) and the needs which resulted (teaching personnel, buildings, and so on), there also occurred, naturally, a major cultural restructuring. But since the national and political situation were developing at a rapid pace, the pre-requisites were soon created for modernising interventions in educational issues and for the 'return of the demoticists', as it was termed. In October 1923, within the framework of the political-partisan restructuring which led to the establishment of the republican regime, the Ministry of Education entrusted Alexandros Delmouzos with the direction of a prestigious institution: the Marasleio Teacher Training College in Athens. The following year finally saw the opening of a Pedagogical Academy under Glinos. The students of the academy trained at the Marasleio. The Marasleio's own students trained at the 'Protypo' (Model School), whose principal was Michail Papamavros, one of the most militant and active advocates of educational demoticism.

Thus, based on the Volos experience (1908–11) and the period between 1916 and 1920, they all began once again 'to set up, in time, a true school, using our own life experience',[38] by focusing on the teaching personnel. The academy aimed to 'mould' educators, each of whom, 'with love and faith, sees in the young souls the possibility of a better humanity and places his entire self at the service of its creation'.[39] For its part, the Marasleio was based on the 'belief that the school is not an instrument which slavishly serves society, but rather one of the most important factors in individual, social and national progress'.[40]

The effort made at both institutions was intensive and arduous, not only because it had to deal with external reaction, but also because it entailed the organisation of new state institutions (even the teacher training colleges were acquiring a new structure); practical approaches which had not actually been tested and which had only a strong theoretical-ideological foundation; and – at the Marasleio – collaboration with personnel that had been selected by others, based on different criteria.

These challenges would presumably have been met with the enthusiasm and hard work of those in charge, in a climate of concern over the older methods, which had grown out of the previous reformative efforts, even though it appeared that most teachers' 'psychology was opposed' to new ideas, and that 'they had been forced to change the form, while the spirit remained the same'.[41] The motive for change originated with the children, who had clearly indicated, with their attitude and the interest shown in class, that they preferred schoolbooks written in the demotic. The return to old methods revealed to society the value of that which had been abolished.

But the reaction, also basing itself on political instability, was quick to launch an attack, using methods that had been tried in previous years. It promoted (or provoked) a 'scandalising' of society (just as in Volos, and just as in 1921 in the reader report), mainly in matters which were unrelated to the essential aims of the attempted change. In 1924, various organisations (among them, representatives of the church, the Technical University, the Archaeological Society, but also employees of the National Bank, the Panhellenic Pharmaceutical Society and the Athenian Periodicals Association) held a 'national conference to fight against the enemies and corrupters of religion, language, family values, property, morality, national consciousness and the motherland'. The confusion of concepts here too (just as in the assessment made a decade earlier by the Bishop of Dimitrias) was complete – and obviously intentional.

Equally tried were the direct actions against Delmouzos and the Marasleio. In 1925, the newspapers printed a series of vitriolic articles against the 'scandals' that were going on in the Teacher Training College. According to a description of the time, besides the use of the demotic and the falsification of national history in the lesson,[42] teaching systems were implemented through which 'the students were led to anarchy and dissoluteness, expressed through impudence and insensitivity'.[43] There followed administrative, as well as police and ecclesiastical inquiries, which allowed some to conclude that the 'reformers . . . have communist tendencies' and that their effort 'presents tangible evidence to prove their wish to overthrow of the bourgeois regime'.[44] In 1926, political developments also led to the dismissal ('due to cutbacks') of Delmouzos, Glinos and their direct associates. Thus ended in failure and to the great disillusionment of its protagonists yet another attempt at modernisation.

The work of these pioneers was, indeed, completely obliterated. When, some years later, governmental educational policy began to follow similar lines no trace could be found of these 'avant-garde' school units.

Educationally speaking, events in the years leading up to the Venizelos government of 1928 were the result of a period of reassessment and the gradual emergence of a new dynamic. One of the most important of these was the founding in 1924, under the Papanastasiou government, and the opening in 1926 of Greece's second university, at Thessaloniki.[45]

This was the realisation of an earlier plan which aspired, among other national aims, to the creation of a modernist cultural centre which would function as a barrier to the spread of the conservatism of the University of Athens and especially its faculty of philosophy. And indeed the faculty of philosophy at Thessaloniki was able to assemble from the outset many advocates of educational demoticism. In fact, two of the three 'great men' of the Educational League ended up in Thessaloniki as elected professors. Triantaphyllidis, who had since 1921 dedicated himself exclusively to scholarship following the disappointments of 1916 to 1920, was in Thessaloniki from the opening of the university in 1926, while Delmouzos went there in 1929, after the split of the Educational League.

This split, which occurred in 1927, was the second important event that marked the course of educational issues. It was certainly precipitated by the disillusionment brought on by the frustrating of the second effort of the demoticists to influence developments through state channels. But its roots ran deeper and were related to the general national, social and political restructuring of the period. Thus, at one of the league's general assemblies, which extended to nine sessions, from 16 February to 24 March, 1927, approximately 120 of its members were called upon to choose between the two diametrically opposed views of their leaders:[46]

Glinos, who had by then joined the Communist Party of Greece, claimed that 'a political orientation had to be given to the league's action, and that its direction could be none other than "no limit towards the Left" '. On the other side, Delmouzos put forward the view that the league:

> should in no way become politicised; on the contrary, its obligation was to remain firm in regard to its main principle, that is, that education is a national matter and that demoticism, far removed from partisan rivalries,

> will aspire to set foundation in Greek schools for the living tradition of the nation. . . .[47]

The majority chose Glinos' view, and Delmouzos resigned from the league; he was followed by the members who shared his views. The league continued by promoting its (new) ideas – it even published its own periodical – for two more years, presided over by Glinos, until early 1929, at which time it fell into decline and broke up.

In 1927, besides the Education League, and only a few months later, another collective educational body, the Teachers' Federation of Greece (DOE) also split. Certain representatives walked out of the annual general assembly, 'having observed . . . the permanent turn of the assembly towards communism' and simultaneously expressing their intention to spearhead the founding of a 'National Teachers' Federation'.[48] Nine years later, in 1936, in order to justify the imposition of the dictatorship, Ioannis Metaxas would include, in his proclamation of 4 August, the argument that communism 'was infiltrating . . . education, corrupting a large part of the body of educators, from the university down to the teachers of elementary education . . . thus undermining hope for a better future for the Greek race'.[49] The true extent of this 'infiltration' which, as noted above, also influenced the actions of the Teachers' Federation is impossible to measure. But regardless of the numbers, it is obvious that the incidents of 1927 described here significantly influenced the assessment of this infiltration.

THE REFORM OF 1929 TO 1932 AND ITS ELIMINATION

Within this general national-social and specifically educational context,[50] the Liberal Party formulated its programme for the elections of 19 August 1928. Their triumph allowed the Venizelos government to put together, by the end of its term in office, an educational reform which would go down in history for many different reasons:

1. It was the first out of a succession of reformative proposals – approximately one century after the forming of the system – which succeeded in being ratified by parliament and becoming a law of the state.
2. It was the first reform to be developed continuously and consistently through a succession of legislative adjustments over a three-year period.
3. It was the first reform to be supported by two successive ministers of education – Constantinos Gondikas and Georgios Papandreou as of January 1930 – without its main orientation being altered.[51]

4. It brought about radical changes such as the generalised co-education of boys and girls at all levels of instruction, and the building (according to figures of the time) of 3167 schools, thanks to a loan that the government had taken out with a Swedish company.[52]
5. It included innovative regulations (which will be discussed below) in relation to the curriculum of secondary education and textbooks. Following their abolition by the next regime, these regulations still remain unrealised goals in the early twenty-first century.

The Reform of 1929 to 1932, therefore, constitutes the most significant turning point in the history of modern Greek education after the 1830s. However, a rational assessment of the situation would require one to take into account the fact that the decisive modernising interventions in education should be considered within a broader politico-economic context, which, at its base, expressed different ideological approaches. This contradiction raises questions concerning the intentions of the authorities, the co-ordination of their executives, the awareness of the social effects of certain educational measures, possible compromises in order to achieve a balance, amongst other things. Comprehensive and convincing answers seem not to have been formulated as yet by researchers specialising in this area.

The modernist innovations of the reform were facilitated by the new framework created for education by the constitution of 1927; not so much by its specific provisions or omissions – it did not contain an article on the protection of katharevousa, like the one before (and the one after) it – which allowed for radical interventions in education, as by the general spirit of its respective clauses (freedom of teaching, decentralisation, state protection of intellectual work, and so on). The provision, for example, for a minimum six-year compulsory education, which generally expressed a concern for the spread of 'education of the people', did not constitute the starting point for the (modernising) extension of primary schooling from four to six years. Nor did it call for the equally important abolition of lower secondary schools. Both these measures – with the consequent extension of the gymnasium period of study from four to six years – had been proposed as early as the previous century, and had prevailed in the New Territories and in many centres of Hellenism abroad. Even the drastic reinforcement of the vocational-technical sector of the system, which appeared here as an indirect constitutional recommendation, had been included in the plans of 1913, with no reference to it in the constitution in force at the time.

On the other hand, major, unprecedented and innovative adjustments of the measures that made up the reform were not covered – because such coverage was not required. Such was the case of the (new, six-year) gymnasium curriculum, which was published in 1931. It contained modernist elements which, directly or indirectly, fully or partially impinged on the character of the system: the teaching of ancient Greek authors (in certain classes exclusively) in translation; the authorisation of the School Teachers' Council to take crucial decisions, such as the increase or decrease of teaching hours; the setting of rules for and the upgrading of 'school life' (with 'free activity afternoons'); the setting up of 'special classes for groups of pupils who display an obvious gift for and remarkable progress in certain lessons' and elective courses; a limiting of details in the description of the subjects to be taught and the fixing of a relatively simple 'framework', and more. Equally important and unprecedented were many of the provisions of the law of the same year regarding textbooks. Perhaps the most significant among them was the removal of any sense of (state) monopoly. The ministry approved more books for each subject and the teachers' councils would select one, following a proposal by the teachers justifying their choice. Besides the course books, the use of companion books and 'free reading' was established.[53]

The reform as a whole, on the level of planning and specialisation, was not based on direct proposals by the traditional leaders of educational demoticism. As mentioned above, they had taken their own, individual paths. It is possible that Delmouzos helped unofficially. However, the reform stands as a clear expression of the principles of educational demoticism and it is, therefore, indicative of their widespread dissemination that the early regulations were based on the proposals of two other – less prominent – men: Evangelos Kakouros, who held a top administrative post in the Ministry of Education, and Miltos Koundouras,[54] a member of the newly-established Educational Advisory Board. Similar conclusions can be drawn from the observation that the greater part of the reformative interventions had already been formulated as positions, proposals or demands by the executives of the system (directors and deputy directors of teacher training colleges, and primary and secondary education inspectors) in three major conferences held in 1930. Equally interesting, of course, is the fact that some of the most innovative demands expressed at these conferences (such as the abolition of religious instruction) were not included in the state regulations.

Mention was made above of the apparent contradiction between the orientation of the educational policy and the broader social policy of the Venizelos government of 1928 to 1932. Furthermore, an overall view of the educational regulations of that time seems to present a similar picture. For, alongside the often very progressive modernising and liberal measures, one may observe the enactment of others which carry different intentions. The imposition of university entrance exams was judged on the whole as restricting the rise of the general level of education. Yet, even if this is seen merely as the completion of a measure that had begun to be broadened in 1927,[55] other measures, stemming directly from governmental initiatives, expressed similar 'anti-popular' tendencies. Among them, I should mention the appointment of a governmental delegate to universities,[56] and the intervention to limit the number of gymnasiums and, consequently, the percentage of the population with access to them and any subsequent social improvement.

The government's stance on the issue of the demotic is interesting from many viewpoints. On a legislative level, the educational reform was not a linguistic one. Despite the absence of any constitutional protection of katharevousa, the language issue remained silently in the margins. Any expansion in the teaching of the demotic took place indirectly – and, apparently, with great hesitation – in adjacent regulations, such as the description of the modern Greek curriculum for gymnasiums or in matters relating to textbooks. Obviously, society and its ruling class were not yet ready for the big plunge and the government did not dare (or simply did not wish) to take it. The rationale which had led to the compromise of 1911 was valid again in 1931. The educational reform of 1929 to 1932, despite its important modernising features, was kept within its bourgeois limits.

All this took place before May 1932. After that, the change in the political landscape soon led to the deconstruction of the reform. The Educational Advisory Board – the executive body of modernisation – was abolished in January 1933, the legislation concerning schoolbooks was changed in November, and, in 1935, all the innovative features of the gymnasium programme were amended. The definitive blow was dealt in 1936 and after by the dictatorship of 4 August, which adapted to its purposes the entire educational system and used its mechanisms and structures for the benefit of the social groups from which it drew its support and which it served. Modernising tendencies came to the fore again as late as 1963 to 1964, reinstating many principles and regulations which were representative of the actions of Venizelist circles and governments.

NOTES

1. This chapter draws extensively on earlier contributions I wrote for the collective work (2003–4), *Istoria tou Neou Ellinismou – 1775–2000* [*History of Modern Hellenism – 1775–2000*], ed. V. Panayotopoulos, Athens, as well as on my contributions, in Greek, to various collective works: (1980), 'Protheseis

ton proton kyverniseon Venizelou (1910–1913) sta ekpaideftika' ['The Intentions of the First Venizelos Governments (1910–1913) in Education – Indications from Legislative Texts'], in O. Dimitrakopoulos and Th. Veremis (eds), *Meletimata gyro apo ton Venizelo kai tin epochi tou* [*Studies on Venizelos and his Time*], Athens, pp. 21–47; (1988), 'Charaktiristika astikou phileleftherismou sta ekpaideftika programmata ton kyverniseon Venizelou' ['Characteristics of Bourgeois Liberalism in the Educational Programmes of the Venizelos Governments'], in G. Mavrogordatos and Ch. Hadjiiossif (eds), *Venizelismos kai astikos eksynchronismos* [*Venizelism and Bourgeois Modernisation*], Irakleio, pp. 21–32; (1988), 'Ideologikes taseis kai Venizelismoi stin ekpaidefsi' ['Ideological Trends and Venizelisms in Education'], *Symposio gia ton Venizelo* [*Symposium on Venizelos*], Athens, pp. 330–7.

2. See generally Anny Brychea and Costas Gavroglou (1982), *Apopeires metarrythmisis tis Anotatis Ekpaidefsis – 1911–1981* [*Attempts at Reform in Higher Education – 1911–1981*], Thessaloniki.
3. Today (2004) the official names of these institutions in English are: Aristotle University of Thessaloniki; National Technical University of Athens (Athens Polytechnic School); Athens School of Fine Arts; Agricultural University of Athens; Athens University of Economics and Business.
4. Quoted by Pavlos Nirvanas, one of the members of the committee of 1918 on readers in the demotic. The statement was made on the occasion of the publication of these readers. *O Noumas* 16 (1919), p. 16.
5. As always, the exceptions, such as the appointment of Theotokis by Trikoupis, only prove the rule.
6. See also Note 22.
7. Dimitrios Dingas (1876–1974), a close associate of Venizelos from the outset, was 'minister' of justice of the Thessaloniki government. One of the five ministers of education to serve in the Venizelos governments, Dingas' term of office was the longest; the shortest (a year and a half) was that of Constantinos Gondikas (without that reflecting on the significance of his work, as will be explained below). For comparison purposes, I should mention that in the interim period of 1915 to 1917, the Ministry of Education was held by eight ministers, with an average term of office of three and a half months.
8. Indicative of the caution with which data of the time should be viewed is the fact that in 1931 the minister of education mentions a 58 per cent rate of illiteracy among women and 23.5 per cent among men.
9. A very good introduction to the issue is the first part of Anna Frangoudaki's (1992), 'Diglossia and the Present Language Situation in Greece: A Sociological Approach', *Language in Society* 21, pp. 365–81. The combination of the language question and the problem of education are elucidated in E. P. Papanoutsos (1978), 'Educational Demoticism', *Comparative Education Review* 22, pp. 46–50.

10. See Note 20.
11. A. Delmouzos (1950), *To Krypho Scholeio 1908–1911* [*The Clandestine School 1908–1911*], Athens, p. 29. The title of the book, which is a full record of the work that took place in Volos, refers directly to the popular legend according to which, in the years of the late Ottoman period, the Christians organised schools which functioned clandestinely at night in churches.
12. Ibid., p. 31.
13. More so than in other cases, in almost all the quotations in this chapter, precisely because the issue of language is of primary importance, translation clouds the immediate clear impression of the general stance of the author, which emerges from the words, grammatical forms and syntactical constructions of the various periods of the Greek language he might use. These cannot be rendered into another language without adulterating the meaning of the text.
14. In the text, the term is malliarismos (an abstract noun deriving from the adjective – which later became a noun – malliaros = hairy). The origin of the term is doubtful. It was probably a reference to the hairstyle of certain young authors of the time, who wrote literature in the demotic. In any case, it was widely used perjoratively by the opponents of the demotic from the early twentieth century.
15. *I diki tou Nafpliou (16–28 April 1914)* [*The Nafplion Trial (16–28 April 1914)*] – Shorthand Records, Athens, 1915, p. 17.
16. Ibid., pp. 2–3.
17. One of the most typical cases is that of the 'Association of Greek Primary School Teachers', which was founded in late 1892. To be eligible for membership one could not hold higher qualifications than those of an ordinary teacher. This excluded school inspectors and the directors of teacher training colleges who also had general powers regarding the functioning of all schools. One essential and positive intervention on the part of the government in the regulation of the working conditions and the pay of teachers took place in 1895 with the passing of a basic law on primary school education.
18. All relevant documents of the period 1910 to 1911 are included in Miltos Koundouras (1986), *Kleiste ta scholeia – Ekpaideftika Apanta* [*Close the Schools – Complete Educational Works*], ed. Alexis Dimaras, vol. II, Athens, pp. 281–311. The quote is on p. 281.
19. It is significant that, of the league's thirty-eight founding members (politicians, businessmen, men of letters and some involved in education), most had, to a greater or lesser extent, direct or indirect relationships with or leanings toward Venizelos personally or the Liberal Party.
20. Dimitris Glinos (1882–1943), Alexandros Delmouzos (1880–1956), Manolis Triantafyllidis (1883–1959). All three were graduates of the faculty of philosophy of the University of Athens. They pursued postgraduate studies in Germany and formed the league's leadership from 1912 to 1920. In 1912,

Glynos was called upon to collaborate with the minister of education and, in 1916, he was appointed president of the Educational Council established by the Thessaloniki government. From 1917 to 1920, all three served in the highest posts of the Ministry of Education, organising and promoting the teaching of the demotic at primary school level. In 1921, a disillusioned Triantaphyllidis withdrew from public life. The other two were reassigned to important posts in the ministry, in the sector of teacher training, during the period 1923 to 1925. The split of the league in 1927 marked Glynos' turn to the left – in 1936 he rose to the position of a leading cadre of the Greek Communist Party. Delmouzos was elected professor at the newly-established 'modernist' University of Thessaloniki (where Triantaphyllidis had also become a professor) in 1928. Thus, neither of them openly participated in the planning or the implementation of the 'reform of 1929'.

21. Nikolaos Exarchopoulos (1873–1960), was – as were all the leaders of demoticism – a graduate of the faculty of philosophy of the University of Athens and had pursued – as they had – postgraduate studies in Germany. Initially he had been favourably disposed towards the new education movement and was a member of the 'Sociologists', but he held conservative views concerning the language question. From 1912, when he was elected to the chair of pedagogy of the faculty of philosophy at Athens University, and especially following the death in 1916, of his colleague Georgios Mystriotis, who was a professor of classics (see below), Exarchopoulos rose to become a fanatical leader of the conservative linguistic-educational side. In 1929, he was also elected a full member of the Academy of Athens.
22. A fuller analysis of the issue can be found in Anna Frangoudaki (1977), *O Ekpaideftikos dimotikismos kai o glossikos symvivasmos tou 1911* [*Educational Demoticism and the Linguistic Compromise of 1911*], Ioannina. See also generally, Rena Stavridi-Patrikiou (1999), *Glossa, ekpaidefsi kai politiki* [*Language, Education and Politics*], Athens.
23. Apostolos Alexandris (1879–1961) was made minister of education in the first Venizelos government (October 1910). A few months earlier, he had signed the founding declaration of the Educational League, but withdrew his signature shortly before assuming his ministerial post. Ioannis Tsirimokos (1867–1934), Venizelos' main political associate from the outset (speaker of the house 1911–12) and a defender of the principles of demoticism, was the brother of Markos Tsirimokos, an active founder-member of the Educational League.
24. All the relevant texts of 1913 are included in Philippos Iliou (ed.) (1983), *Dimitris Glinos – Apanta (1910–14)* [*Dimitris Glinos – Complete Works 1910–14*], vol. II, Athens, pp. 183–372. The quotation is on p. 191.
25. Ibid., p. 236.
26. Ibid., p. 235.
27. See Note 37.

28. *Deltion tou Ypourgeiou ton Ekklisiastikon kai tis Dimosias Ekpaidefseos* [*Bulletin of the Ministry of Ecclesiastical Affairs and Public Education*], No. 3 (March 1919), p. 14 – cited in Alexis Dimaras (ed.) (1974), *I metarrythmisi pou den egine* [*The Reform That Never Was*, vol. II (1895–1967)], Athens, pp. 116–17.
29. From an article by Hadjidakis in the newspaper *Athinai* (4 May 1910). It is cited in Dimaras, *I metarrythmisi*, pp. 70–2 (see Note 28). Nevertheless, Hadjidakis (1848–1941) kept the discussion at a scholarly level. Totally opposed to Psycharis' views in favour of the exclusive use of the vernacular, he believed that the solution of the language question lay in the 'middle way', and that it would come about gradually. Hadjidakis also clashed with Triantaphyllidis. He strongly rejected any ideological advancement of modern Greece which would be at the expense of its classical heritage.
30. Georgios Mystriotis (1840–1916) had played a leading role in the great linguistic riots of 1901 and 1903. The former (during which there were fatalities among the demonstrators) were triggered by the translation of the Gospel into the demotic and the latter by a performance at the Royal (now National) Theatre of Athens of Aeschylus' *Oresteia* in a modern Greek translation, which was not even in the demotic. Throughout this time, Mystriotis had instilled in university students (not only of the faculty of philosophy where he was professor) the conviction that all action towards the dissemination of the demotic constituted a grave threat against religion and the nation. Some of them had become leaders of the conservative social powers that opposed linguistic – and, therefore, educational – reform. The matter is especially complex, since it combines with the lively political, governmental and regime-related disputes of the time, inter-ecclesiastical differences, as well as the threat of 'Panslavism' which was being put forth. For a comprehensive presentation and analysis of the events of 1901, see Philip Carabott (1993), 'Politics, Orthodoxy and the Language Question in Greece – The Gospel Riots of November 1901', *Journal of Mediterranean Studies* 3, pp. 117–38. I should add, as a further fact indicative of the complexity of the issue, that two of those who, in later years, would become leaders of demoticism (Glinos and Triantaphyllidis), participated in the events of 1901 on the side of the supporters of katharevousa.
31. From a speech made in the aula of the University of Athens in 1911. The quotation can be found in Dimaras, *I metarrythmisi*, p. 85 (see Note 28).
32. From a pamphlet published in 1920 on the occasion of the establishment of the teaching of the demotic at primary schools. The quotation can be found in ibid., p. 129.
33. Another discernibly reserved position came from the small group of Greek educators who, in the mid-1870s, and on Greek scholarships, had pursued postgraduate studies in Germany (mainly under the successors of Johann Herbart, such as Wilhelm Rein and Tuiskon Ziller). Upon returning to Greece, they had been involved primarily in the organisation of teacher

training according to the principles they had learnt in Germany. They were all opposed to demoticism, rigid in their focus on the established German pedagogy of the time, and – since positions of power were few – they developed intense personal rivalries among themselves. As individuals and as the bearers of ideas, they held sway over the issues of primary education until at least the early twentieth century.

34. The problem of schoolbooks is one of the most acute and long-lasting in the Greek educational system. It preoccupied the central authorities from the years of Capodistrias to the early twentieth century. The search for a balance between state control and the pluralism that resulted from freedom of expression and of teaching has not produced any results in all these years, particularly since significant financial interests are involved in the matter. At least since the years of the Metaxas dictatorship (1936–40) and afterwards, the system of a single and obligatory teaching manual per subject and school-year has prevailed. As is apparent from all that is noted here, the Venizelos governments (mainly during 1917 to 1920 and 1928 to 1932) had a notably more liberal approach to this matter.
35. These were *To Alphavitari me ton ilio* [*The Primer with the Sun*], as it came to be known, because its cover showed a boy gazing at a big sun; and *Ta psila vouna* [*The Tall Mountains*], which described the life of a group of children who, at the urging of their teacher and under the care of one of their parents, decide to spend a few summer weeks in the mountains, camping. The story often refers indirectly to the principles of the New Education Movement. The creation of the *Primer* is attributed chiefly to Delmouzos. The latter was a work of Zacharias Papantoniou (1877–1940), the son of a teacher, who, at the time, was already a well-known journalist, writer and art critic. During that period (1918), he was appointed Director of the Greek National Gallery, a post he held until his death. In any event, in the writing of *Ta psila vouna*, Papantoniou must have collaborated with the educators of the Ministry.
36. The committee's report was published by the Ministry of Education in the spring of 1921 in a 160-page booklet, in a printing of 20,000 copies – a quantity which was obviously excessive (it is significant that primary-school teachers numbered fewer than 10,000 in the entire country and that the *Bulletin of the Educational League* was published in fewer than 1000 copies) and demonstrates the partisan-political influence attempted here. This is also evident in the extreme language used ('the burning of the books,' 'the criminal prosecution' of the legislators and authors, terming the reform a 'sudden and underhand act' and a work of 'malicious intent', for example). The committee's findings are cited in Dimaras, *I metarrythmisi*, pp. 130–1 (see Note 28). For the reactions of those who proposed the reform, see the following paragraphs in the main text.
37. The first significant and relatively comprehensive modernist proposal for educational reform in the new Greek state dates back to 1877 (the G. Milissis

bills). The effort was unsuccessful. From then, and up to the period being reviewed here, proposals with similar aims were made by various governments, but always without reaching the stage of ratification by parliament. Most important among them is the one of 1889 (the Trikoupis government), the one of 1899 (the Theotokis government), and the one of 1913 (the Venizelos government – as described above). This constant postponement of reform meant that every time the starting point for change were the main principles of the system which had been set up in the 1830s.

38. A. P. Delmouzos (1929), *Oi protes prospatheies sto Marasleio* [*The First Efforts at the Marasleio*], Athens, p. 7.
39. From the speech made by D. Glinos at the opening of the Pedagogic Academy (5 Nov. 1924). Cited in Dimaras, *I Metarrythmisi*, vol. II, pp. 139–41. The quotation is on p. 139.
40. A. Delmouzos (1925), *Marasleio kai zoi* [*Marasleio and Life*], Athens, p. 12.
41. Delmouzos, *Oi protes*, p. 9 (see Note 38).
42. The accusations of the 'unpatriotic' teaching of history were caused by the claim of a teacher (Roza Imvrioti), reported in the newspapers, to 'examine the history of the revolution of 1821 as the product of the uprising of the bourgeoisie, influenced by the revolution of the respective social classes of the West, and not by the general revolt of the enslaved nation'.
43. From the report issued by the Educational Advisory Committee of the Ministry of Education which carried out the inquiries. Dimaras, *I Metarrythmisi*, vol. II, p. 150 (see Note 38).
44. Ibid.
45. For a general (but not very scholarly) history in English of the first thirty-five years of this university see Basil D. Kyriazopoulos (1961), *The Aristotelian University of Thessaloniki*, Thessaloniki.
46. Despite research, the facts concerning the membership of the league remain quite doubtful. It is calculated, however, that in 1927 the active members were no more than 500 – perhaps only 350. For comparison purposes, I should note that the total of secondary education teachers was approximately 3000.
47. From the concise description of the facts surrounding the split in E. P. Papanoutsos (1978), *A. Delmouzos – I zoi tou – Epilogi apo to ergo tou* [*A. Delmouzos – His Life – Selections from his Work*], Athens, pp. 94–104.
48. Dimaras, *I Metarrythmisi*, vol. II, pp. 45–6 (see Note 38).
49. Ibid., pp. 183–4.
50. C. Krimbas, who has studied cultural and academic influences in Greece from the founding of the modern Greek state onwards, has shown that, vis-à-vis countries chosen by the élite for postgraduate studies, Germany and German-speaking countries in general dominated in the humanities and the sciences, up to the mid-1960s. Krimbas also makes the very interesting observation that this exclusivity takes on a special meaning when seen in the light of the powerful political influence exerted on Venizelos by Britain

(as was the case previously with Trikoupis). Costas Krimbas (1993), 'Ideologikes epidraseis stin Anotati Paideia' ['Ideological Influences on Higher Education'], in C. Krimbas, *Thravsmata Katoptrou* [*Fragments of a Mirror*], Athens, pp. 169–83.

51. Constantinos Gondikas (1872–1938) and Georgios Papandreou (1888–1968) were close associates of Venizelos from the outset. Gondikas had taken on the Ministry of Education from April to October 1923, in the Stylianos Gonatas cabinet. In January 1930 he left the ministry to fill the post of director of the recently-founded Agricultural Bank. As for Papandreou, regarding his interest in education, it is worth noting that later, when he was prime minister in 1963 to 1965, he took on the Ministry of Education once again and proceeded to yet another major educational reform.
52. For comparison purposes, I should mention that it has been calculated that, in the previous 100 years, the corresponding number had been 1474.
53. Concerning the difference between this programme and the ones that preceded and followed it, one need only repeat what was noted above regarding the school books of 1918: 'Their features are completely different' from those presented this time.
54. Evangelos Kakouros (1886–1945), a graduate in philosophy from the University of Athens, pursued postgraduate studies in pedagogy and psychology, and translated Georg Kerschensteiner's *Begriff der staatsbürgerlichen Erziehung* into Greek (1926). A supporter of educational demoticism, he held higher executive posts in the Ministry of Education from 1922 to 1935. Miltos Koundouras (1889–1940), also a philosophy graduate of Athens University and a founding member of the Students' Society in 1910, did his postgraduate study in Germany, where he attended classes given by the educational reformer Georg Kerschensteiner. He visited many 'progressive' schools and was greatly influenced by the work of Paul Geheeb.
55. Although the measure (which was linked to the establishment of a numerus clausus) was totally in keeping with the declared intention of the government to limit the number of university graduates, in the long run it did not seem to affect society's drive towards tertiary studies. It is indicative that from the very first year of its imposition, Athens and other large cities witnessed the emergence of private, fee-paying cramming schools (phrontistiria), which are still flourishing in the early twenty-first century.
56. Seen from a different viewpoint, of course, the placing of a governmental delegate in universities could be considered as an action which would guarantee the systematic implementation of the modernist educational policy at the tertiary level as well.

12

Venizelos and Church–State Relations

Andreas Nanakis

To form a comprehensive picture of Venizelos' relations with the church, we must begin our investigation of the subject in his birthplace, Crete, for his view of the church was shaped by his personal experience of the stance and activities of the Orthodox Church in Crete. The Church of Crete naturally played its part in the crisis in relations between Venizelos and Prince George, high commissioner of Crete, and in the division that followed – a reflection in miniature of the future breach between Venizelos and King Constantine.

In Crete, the demographic situation was clearer than in other regions of the Ottoman Empire.[1] The more numerous Christians (about 202,000) and the minority Muslim community (about 72,000 according to the 1891 census) became involved in armed clashes during the nineteenth century, a phenomenon rare in other parts of the Ottoman Empire. After the Ottoman conquest of the island in 1669, the cultural identity of the Orthodox population had been preserved by the Church of Crete, acting under the jurisdiction of the patriarchate of Constantinople. It is no exaggeration to claim that the Church of Crete played a role of decisive importance in the shaping of events in Crete under Ottoman rule.

It was against this historical and geographical background that Venizelos defined his relationship with the church and clarified his attitude to it through his collaboration with members of the hierarchy. The church's activity in Crete was to define for Venizelos a policy to which he later steadfastly adhered. The Venizelist faction that emerged in the bosom of the church included eminent prelates with whom Venizelos had closely collaborated.

THE CHURCH OF CRETE

It is highly revealing of the stance adopted towards the church by liberal and radical forces that in 1880 to 1882 the Christian communities of Chania, Rethymnon and Kissamos rejected the bishops elected by the local synod of Crete. Their rejection was connected with the confrontation between the traditional centre of the Orthodox community in Constantinople and the new national centre in Athens when, under the Trikoupis government, attempts were made to appoint bishops within the Ottoman Empire who were exponents of the national ideology. The liberal radical forces of Crete, while refusing to accept the bishops so appointed, did not turn completely against the local church but confined their judgement to the affair of the bishops.[2] It is significant that the *Lefka Ori* in Chania, in which Venizelos later wrote a column, and also the similarly oriented newspapers *Aptera*, also in Chania, and *Nea Rhadamanthys* in Rethymnon, did not turn against the church or its work and role in Crete. No trace can be found, for example, of the theoretical principles and terminology associated with the kind of anti-clericalism that had sprung from the Enlightenment.[3] The criticism was concentrated exclusively on the question of episcopal elections in Crete.

At that time the Church of Crete was governed, as it still is today, by a local synod consisting of eight bishops who, together with the metropolitan of Crete, deal with affairs as a local church depending canonically on the Patriarchate of Constantinople.[4] The Christians of Crete sought through repeated insurrections to extend their privileges and assume a dominant role in the affairs of the island consonant with their superior numbers. The slogan 'freedom or death', used in the uprisings of the early nineteenth century, developed into the overtly political message 'union or death', naturally under the influence of the aims and aspirations of the national centre, Athens. In these developments, which led to the proclamation of the autonomous Cretan state in 1898 and its unification with Greece in 1913, Venizelos played a leading and decisive role. An equally decisive factor, however, was the activity of the Church of Crete, with which Venizelos closely collaborated. Indeed, when tendencies and factions were created and formalised in Cretan society, Venizelos won some devoted supporters within the bosom of the church – and not only amongst the ranks of the lower clergy, but at the highest level of its hierarchy. There were questions of major importance on which the majority of the bishops were aligned with Venizelos.

During the uprising of 1897, when Venizelos was at Akrotiri, Chania, Nikiphoros, the bishop of Kydonia is known to have undertaken on behalf of the Greek consulate at Chania to keep the general commander of Kydonia, Hadji Michalis Yannaris, informed and to direct his actions. On 21 November 1897, Venizelos addressed a signed letter written in his own hand to Bishop Nikiphoros, in which he wrote: 'It is essential that the said letter be sent as a matter of urgency . . . Therefore, in the absence of any other immediate and secure opportunity, I request Your Eminence to send the said letter by special post . . . I kiss Your Eminence's right hand.'[5] On 19 October 1897, another bishop, Dionysios Kastriyannakis of Rethymnon, blessed the flag of Cretan independence at Arkadi and delivered a fiery speech on national unification, in which he declared that 'love of freedom and the restoration of our national unity has started to become a reality'.[6] The bishop of Petra, Titos Zographidis, too, led a band of rebels in the capture of the fortress of Spinalonga.[7] The archimandrite Chrysanthos Tsepetakis involved himself in the struggle for national unification at Akrotiri and said in a speech to the insurrectionary forces on 25 March 1897:

> We acknowledge no other nation than the Greek, with which we are connected by the same blood, the same language, and the same history. We beseech you warmly, with tears in our eyes, Our Father who art in heaven, that we may be united with Greece in mind and spirit, and that you will unite us politically to the shame of our unjust foes.[8]

During the insurrection of 1897, which led to the withdrawal of the Turkish forces from Crete, as in the uprisings that had preceded it, Venizelos witnessed the local church standing at the side of the rebels and actively seeking to secure the demands of the Christians. This was no coincidence. The confrontation between the Christian and Muslim communities had brought the local Church of Crete to an early self-awareness and an appreciation of its national identity. Amongst the basic factors in this were the presence of the Greek state – through its consulates, the education network, the Cretan graduates of the national university who settled on the island – and the experiences of the previous bloody rebellion of 1866, or the stories that were told of earlier uprisings. Above all, however, there were the general expectations placed by the whole of Europe in the idea of the nation state, which assumed the dimensions of a messianic religion in the minds of the insurgents. In the minds of the young priests of the Church of Crete – men born in Crete and usually educated at the Patriarchal Theological School in Chalki, contemporaries of Venizelos – who were called upon at the end of the nineteenth century to serve the Orthodox tradition in their birthplace, Crete, the religious tradition had now become a national tradition.

In Crete, doubt had been cast on the validity of the traditional cultural worldview of Orthodoxy as a political aspiration at an early date, through the confrontations and armed clashes between Christians and Muslims, and it had even been questioned by the clerics who, in theory at least, were called upon to serve the Orthodox idea. Because of their education, these figures of the church had the potential for change, in contrast with the graduates of the Theological School of Athens, whose actions were those of subjects at the behest of the political authority in the national centre.

Venizelos collaborated with the clerics who gave expression to the idea of the nation. The assembly held at Armenoi in June 1897 was presided over by Dorotheos Klonaris,[9] bishop of Kissamos, who proposed I. Sphakianakis, one of Venizelos' close collaborators, as president of the following assembly to be held at Melidoni in October of the same year. These events effectively bound Venizelos to the church and they proceeded together to play a leading role in furthering the formation of the modern Greek state. It is no coincidence that Eleftherios Venizelos delivered the funeral oration for one of the leading figures in the uprising of 1866, Archimandrite Parthenios Peridis.[10] The positive image and opinion of the church that crystallised in Venizelos' mind was associated not only with his personal experience but also with the attitude to the church adopted by the social forces in Crete represented by the liberals.

After the arrival of Prince George as high commissioner of the Cretan state in December 1898, Venizelos brought this experience to his participation in the executive – that is, the government – in the capacity of councillor (Minister) for justice. The presence of the Cretan Muslims made it impossible to adopt the religion of 'the Eastern Orthodox Church of Christ' as the official religion of Crete.[11] The proposal to this end was rejected by the constitutional assembly, by 134 votes to twenty-two. Article 7 of the Cretan constitution declared that 'Cretans of all religions are equal before the law and enjoy the same rights.' One of the most dynamic representatives of nationalism in Crete, Dionysios, bishop of Rethymnon, signed one of his encyclicals on the issue as 'desiring with all my heart this coexistence between the Cretan Christians and the Cretan Muslims for the good of our common fatherland'.[12]

After the constitution had been voted on, the Cretan republic was called upon to settle the issue of the head of the local church, a question which had arisen during the insurrection of 1897.[13] The death of Timotheos of Crete in 1897 was followed by a long vacancy, until the Patriarchate decided in May 1898 to appoint as metropolitan of Crete the bishop of Lampi and Sphakia, Evmenios Xiroudakis, who was connected with the faction opposed to Patriarch Joachim III. Following the traditional outlook of the church, the new metropolitan believed in enlightened despotism. In contrast, the pro-Joachim faction enjoyed a good working relationship with ordinary people who, under the general regulations of 1860, acquired an institutionalised role in the administrative structures of the church. Venizelos played a prominent role in resolving the problem that arose when the majority of the insurrectionary forces refused to recognise the new metropolitan.

The reasons for their rejection lay in the fact that the new constitution of Crete had not yet been adopted and the new metropolitan could not be installed, like his predecessors, on the basis of a berat from the sultan. However, the installation of Evmenios without the issuing of a berat was not a solution. One very important aspect of the issue was the confrontation between the supporters of Joachim and the anti-Joachim faction, to which Evmenios belonged.[14] The bishops who have been mentioned above, Dionysios of Rethymnon, Titos of Petra, Dorotheos of Kissamos, and a little later Dionysios' successor Chrysanthos, all of whom worked closely with Venizelos, were also the most dynamic exponents in Crete of the idea of Greek nationalism.

The need to regularise the legal status of the Church of Crete by drawing up a charter required the recognition of the metropolitan, so that a meeting of the synod under his presidency could constitutionally be convened to approve the charter. Venizelos in the end withdrew all his reservations regarding the recognition of Evmenios and in May 1900, Prince George signed the decree installing the metropolitan.[15] After this, in October 1900, Venizelos, as councillor for justice signed a convention with Evmenios of Crete,[16] acting as representative of the Patriarchate. According to this convention the patriarch elected the metropolitan of Crete, who was then recognised by the Cretan state. The resolution of the metropolitan issue was followed in December 1900 by the approval and publication of the charter of the Church of Crete, which was in the main the work of two men: Dionysios of Rethymnon and Venizelos, who attended the synod and, as representative of the state, signed the charter in the official codex of the local synod.[17]

The result of all this was the creation of an autonomous local church administered by its provincial synod and reporting to the Ecumenical Patriarchate. This unusual religious regime in Crete was later preserved by Venizelos. In 1928, when the regulation of the position of the church in the Greek state was finalised by a patriarchal and synodic enactment, the law of the state was not 'applied to Crete because of the ecclesiastical regime in force there'. It is no coincidence that Venizelos was the prime minister under whom the enactment of 1928 and law 3615/1928 were both signed. Venizelos thus preserved the distinctive ecclesiastical regime of Crete, to the formulation of which he had himself greatly contributed.

Venizelos' confrontation with the high commissioner, Prince George, his dismissal from the office of minister, and the Theriso movement that followed in 1905, all led to a cooling of relations between Venizelos and the Church of Crete. A few days after Venizelos was dismissed as councillor for justice in 1901, Dionysios of Rethymnon wrote him a letter of encouragement:

> My dear Eleftherios, your dismissal has fallen like a thunderbolt on myself and all those who admire you and truly love the fatherland. I pity with all my heart, not yourself, but this unhappy land, for which your departure is a terrible blow. You have great patriotism, and in your heart the fire of love for our people and the fatherland burns so pure that I have no doubt that you will not allow yourself to be dominated by any thoughts or ideas other than those dictated by the true interests of the nation and Crete. Men cast down those whom God has appointed to a high place.[18]

Venizelos' dismissal was followed by the electoral confrontation of 1903, in which the prince triumphed. In March 1903, the newspaper *Patris*, which supported the prince, appeared with the headline 'The Destruction of the Venizelists'.[19] This is the first occurrence of the term 'Venizelist'. Two years later, the confrontation developed into a complete breach with the Theriso movement.[20]

In all these developments with regard to Crete, the majority of the bishops of the synod of the Church of Crete aligned themselves firmly with Venizelos. This same year Prince George and Metropolitan Evmenios attempted, unsuccessfully on account of the reaction of the priesthood, to appoint as bishop of Kissamos the prince's friend, Archimandrite Gabriel Manaris.[21] This development is of considerable importance in demonstrating Venizelos' influence on the synod. However, the crowning event, which reveals Venizelos' connections with the leadership of the local church, was the Theriso movement of March 1905. Venizelos, of course, had supporters in the ranks of the church other than the bishops mentioned above. It is significant that the seminary of Chania, in the Aghia Triada monastery, sided with the rebels of Theriso. For this, its scholarch, Archimandrite Chrysanthos Tsepetakis, later bishop of Rethymnon, was dismissed by the prince, along with some other teachers. About one year before the Theriso movement, in March 1904, another legendary figure of the Cretan church, Archimandrite Parthenios Kelaidis, whose career goes back to the uprising of 1866, sent a memorandum to the prince in which he brought him face to face with his responsibilities. 'In consequence of this contrived division, we shall find ourselves, Your Highness, on the verge of civil war,'[22] wrote Kelaidis. The Theriso movement was brought to an end by the resignation of Prince George in September 1906.

Throughout the entire advance of the Christian population towards independence, a majority in the Church of Crete played a decisive role, that overcame the resistance of those forces opposing the administrative regime which sought to replace the traditional forms of organisation. Venizelos, who was born and bred in Crete, was completely familiar with the role played by the clergy in these developments. It is highly significant that, as is clear from the above, the most powerful exponents of Venizelos' views were to be found amongst the ranks of the pro-Joachim bishops of Crete.[23]

In contrast, the opposition to Joachim III in Crete, led by Metropolitan Evmenios, aligned itself with Prince George. The schism at the social and ecclesiastical level, which first occurred in Crete during the formation of the Cretan state and the period of Cretan autonomy (1898–1913), was repeated in the rest of Greece, where it was focused on the dilemmas confronting the modern Greek state during the First World War.

THE PATRIARCHATES OF ALEXANDRIA AND JERUSALEM

When he became prime minister of Greece, Venizelos enjoyed close relations with the church hierarchy and other clerics in Greece and throughout the Orthodox world: that is, with the Ecumenical Patriarchate, the senior Patriarchates of Alexandria and Jerusalem, and the Archbishopric of Cyprus. I now turn to a review of these, before examining his relationship with the church of Greece.

Venizelos was not only an exponent of the idea of creating a powerful nation state in the Balkans, an idea shared by Ioannis Metaxas and King Constantine, but by opting for the Entente, he reverted to Thucydides' 'mighty state of the sea'. As was to be expected, the wider world of Hellenism, which resided in both near and remote historical centres, reflected the schism in the national centre, Athens, and gave its support to one of the two factions – the Venizelists or the anti-Venizelist supporters of King Constantine. The leadership of the Greek Orthodox Churches expressed one or the other tendency and showed corresponding sympathy or antipathy to the personalities, political developments and events of the day. Any attempt to consider or define the relations between Eleftherios Venizelos and the church cannot, of course, confine itself solely to the autocephalous Church of Greece.

The Patriarchate of Alexandria governed a robust and sizeable Greek community that numbered about 100,000 in Egypt.[24] Of these, 70,000 were Greek subjects, while 30,000 were Greek Egyptians. In 1927, about 37,000 Greeks lived in Alexandria and 25,000 in Cairo. This Greek bourgeoisie of the Patriarchate of Alexandria were amongst the most powerful supporters of Venizelos and the liberals. Consequently, after the demise of Patriarch Photios (1900–26), they took action in May 1926 and elected as their patriarch Meletios Metaxakis, a dynamic bishop who was not merely an exponent of Venizelism but was completely identified with Venizelos, his policy and his party. In a consular report of the time, we read that '[A]s I have already had the honour of communicating to Your Highness, in many communities, the struggle has become one between Venizelists and anti-Venizelists.'[25]

The Patriarchate of Jerusalem functioned on the basis of regulations that ensured the domination of the patriarch.[26] The long patriarchate of Damianos (1897–1931), his strong personality, his relations with the Porte and the circumstance that the patriarchate was organised as a monastic fraternity in which the patriarch-abbot exercised full control, all enabled Damianos to survive two major crises, in 1908 and 1918, and remain in office.[27] Two leading figures in the fraternity, Meletios Metaxakis and Chrysostomos Papadopoulos, who fled or were expelled in 1918, were supporters of Venizelos. Through documents or reports many pages long, signed by Archimandrites Nikodimos, Ioakeim, Ippolytos and others, the members of the Brotherhood of the Holy Sepulchre turned to Venizelos, Meletios or Chrysostomos for a resolution of problems in Jerusalem. This clearly demonstrates a general tendency to support Venizelos in the ranks of the brotherhood.[28]

THE CHURCH OF GREECE

After the Goudi coup (1909) and Venizelos' assumption of the office of prime minister, he was called upon to collaborate in church affairs with the autocephalous church of the Greek state. In Athens, the church of Greece was unilaterally declared independent in 1833 and was not recognised by Constantinople until 1850. Thereafter, like all the national churches, it came under state control. The canon law of the church was infringed at its very foundation and since that time the metropolitan bishop of Athens and chairman of the synod has in practice been appointed by the government in Athens. The social, intellectual and economic condition of the clergy was very depressed and, despite the endeavours of the ecclesiastical leadership, no substantial initiatives were taken by the state to improve matters. Political forces in the national centre claimed for themselves responsibility for the formulation of ecclesiastical policy in both domestic and foreign affairs. An upgraded church, which would undoubtedly enjoy very strong popular support, would become a substantial factor in the life of the state. The Church of Greece had been required to confine itself to ministering to the religious needs of the people. Now incorporated into the state power structure, the church, through the legal framework of its own charter, served the ends of state-building and national integration of the modern Greek state.[29] Despite occasional attempts, the body of the hierarchy found it impossible to meet in its entirely to discuss and take decisions about major church issues. Significant here is a protest about this matter made by bishops from areas liberated during the Balkan Wars. Writing to the minister of religious affairs in the Zaimis government in October 1915, they note that 'even in the most adverse times of Turkish enslavement, the Patriarchates, and especially the Ecumenical Patriarchate itself, summoned the so-called great Synods'.[30]

Thus, the ecclesiastical reality with which Venizelos found himself faced in Greece was completely different from that he had known in Crete. Since 1902, Theoklitos Minopoulos had been archbishop of Athens.[31] Minopoulos was born in Tripoli in 1848 and graduated from the Theological School of Athens, after which he went to Germany for further education. In 1892 he became bishop of Monemvasia and Sparta. After the Goudi coup in 1909 the Mavromichalis government brought forward two important laws relating to the church 'concerning the general ecclesiastical fund and the administration of monasteries',[32] and 'concerning parish churches and their property, concerning the qualifications of parish priests and their salaries'.[33] The latter assigned the administration of parish churches to five elected individuals, four of whom were to be laymen and the fifth the parish priest of the church, appointed after a vote by parishioners.

Venizelos swore in his first government on 6 October 1910, but a number of major issues relating to the church, particularly the question of the independence and canonical status of the church of Greece, remained unresolved. The need to pass legislation dealing with other, equally serious problems faced by the Greek state, such as the review of the constitution, the strengthening of the army and the Balkan Wars of 1912–13 that followed, relegated the resolution of ecclesiastical problems to the margins.

In dealing with the general issue of the church, the government of Venizelos did not deviate from current Greek practice. Law 201 of 1852 had promulgated the charter of the church of Greece, and had established as the highest ecclesiastical authority not the general body of the hierarchy but a synod of five members. Venizelos was acting within the general spirit of the policies followed by previous Greek governments, though with an inclination to acquiesce with the hierarchy. On 10 February 1914, five bishops who had not been members of the synod sought an audience with King Constantine and Venizelos, and handed to them a memorandum on the reconstitution of the church, signed by nineteen bishops out of the total of thirty-two in the church of Greece. This initiative led to the formation of a legislative committee. Although the Venizelos government could have called an assembly of the bishops to consider jointly the settlement of the problem of the church, it avoided doing so. It was helped in this course by the fact that it was impossible to call a convocation of all the prelates within the Greek state; for after the Balkan Wars and the expansion of the state, about half of it fell within the jurisdiction of the Patriarchate of Constantinople and any convocation of the bishops therefore presupposed canonical permission from the Phanar. The government followed the precedent established by previous constitutional models for relations between the Greek state and the church and proceeded on its own initiative, without consultation, to form the legislative committee. This consisted of six bishops, three from the church of Greece and three from the New Territories, and eleven laymen. Theoklitos of Athens was appointed chairman of the committee, with Gennadios of Thessaloniki as his deputy.[34]

The committee held its official inaugural meeting on 31 May 1914 and its work lasted for over a year. On the basis either of existing laws or of new legislation passed for the purpose, it submitted to the Ministry of Ecclesiastical Affairs a number of draft laws relating to: (1) a new charter, (2) parish churches and parish priests, (3) the governance of monasteries, (4) the general church fund, (5) preachers, (6) seminaries, (7) church courts and church penal procedure.[35] Both sides, church and state, had reached the conclusion that after the work of the committee was completed and the draft legislation submitted to the government in May 1915, the bishops should be convoked to study it and make recommendations. However, I. Tsirimokos, the minister of ecclesiastical affairs in the new Venizelos government that emerged from the elections of 31 May 1915, sent a circular letter to the bishops within the Greek state, asking them for their views and for any amendments they might have.[36] This displeased the bishops who, with very few exceptions, failed to reply to the minister.

It is clear that the Venizelos government, like all preceding governments of Greece, was reluctant to convoke the hierarchy. The general body of bishops in the Greek state could not meet as a synod, of course, since the canonical status of the new territories had not been regulated. However, with the agreement of the Patriarchate, the bishops could have held a convocation to discuss this issue.[37] The hierarchy, annoyed at this failure, circumvented the legal restrictions and the bishops of the autocephalous Church of Greece and the Greek dioceses of the Ecumenical Throne in Thessaloniki and Ioannina met in Athens to discuss the settlement of church affairs. All this, taken in combination with the consequences for Greece of the political and military developments of the First World War and the schism, resulted in the failure to lay before parliament the draft legislation prepared by the committee.[38]

THE GREEK PROVINCES OF THE ECUMENICAL THRONE AND THE LAST VENIZELOS GOVERNMENT

After the expansion of the Greek state into Epirus, Macedonia, the Aegean islands and Crete, all of which fell within the ecclesiastical jurisdiction of the Ecumenical Patriarchate, the primary issue that arose was the settlement of ecclesiastical jurisdiction in the liberated regions, which were called the New Territories. One of the views expressed relating to the canonical status of the Greek provinces of the Ecumenical Throne was that the settlement of the ecclesiastical problem should be deferred until after the stabilisation of the new frontiers of the Balkan national states. The more optimistic anticipated the entry of the Greek army into Constantinople and the incorporation of the city into the Greek state, which might lead to the abandonment of the autocephalous status of the church of Greece and the unification of the church of Greece with the ecclesiastical centre of the Ecumenical Patriarchate.

The settlement of the problem was deferred also in view of the idea mooted at the signing of the Treaty of Sèvres concerning the creation of an international state in the region of Constantinople.[39] The consideration given to the creation of such an international state gave birth to views on the status of the church within it.[40]

During this transitional period, the prelates Ioakeim of Nikopolis, Vasilios of Dryinopolis, Neophytos of Paramythia, and Spyridon of Vella and Konitsa, later archbishop of Athens, submitted a memorandum to the Patriarchate on 1 October 1913, in which they expressed the view that the New Territories 'should not be completely independent under the Great Church, but should occupy a middle ground, in which they would be subject politically to the Greek kingdom and ecclesiastically to the Patriarchate'.[41] A similar view was also expressed by Evmenios of Crete and the provincial synod of Crete, who requested in writing that the current ecclesiastical regime in Crete be maintained.[42] The delay in settling the issue of the New Territories was due to the pressing need to attend to other major problems of a political, military and ecclesiastical nature. The ecclesiastical issues that delayed the settlement of the problem of the Greek provinces of the Ecumenical Throne were the vacancy of the patriarchal throne (1918–21) and the subsequent election of Meletios

Metaxakis, which was not recognised by Athens up to the time of the Asia Minor disaster of 1922; the brief patriarchate of Gregory VII (December 1923–November 1924); and the election and dethronement of Constantine VI (December 1924–May 1925).

Meanwhile, a bill, published in the *Government Gazette* 234/ 3–9–1925, had been promulgated in parliament 'Concerning the formation of an advisory committee to study and report on the most suitable administrative system for the metropolitan sees of the New Territories'.[43] According to article 4, the findings of this committee would be submitted to the full body of the prelates of the New Territories, which would meet in Thessaloniki for ten days for this purpose. The committee drew up 'a draft charter of the Orthodox Church in the New Territories', article 7 of which stated that 'the administration of the church is exercised (1) by the synod of all the bishops, meeting in Thessaloniki, (2) by a permanent seven-man synod with its headquarters in Thessaloniki, and (3) by the bishops of each metropolitan see or bishopric, who form the spiritual and ecclesiastical authority of the province to which they have been appointed'.[44]

The final settlement of the Greek provinces of the Ecumenical Patriarchate was to be made in 1928, under the last Venizelos government. In this year, the patriarchal and synodic enactment concerning the administration of the holy metropolitan sees of the New Territories[45] was signed by Patriarch Basil and the Holy Synod.[46]

Under the conditions put forward by the enactment it is very clear that the Greek provinces of the Ecumenical Patriarchate were ceded temporarily to the autocephalous Church of Greece, to whose administration they were subject. However, the general provisions of the 1928 enactment make it plain beyond dispute that the general settlement of the question of the New Territories made under Venizelos' government involved the unequivocal spiritual and canonical dependence of the dioceses of the region upon the Ecumenical Patriarchate.[47] The Greek state differed from the other Orthodox Balkan states in ecclesiastical matters by virtue of the fact that two churches had jurisdiction within it – the Ecumenical Patriarchate and the Church of Greece. The new charter of the independent Church of Greece,[48] law 5187/1931, was passed in the final term of office of the Venizelos government (4 July 1928–26 May 1932).

Before considering the 1931 law, the earlier charters of the church of Greece need to be considered. Law 200 of 1852, 'Concerning bishoprics and bishops, and concerning the clergy under the bishops', which had made the church completely dependent on the state and had maintained the clergy in ignorance, came to an end in 1923.

The 'charter-law of the autocephalous Church of Greece'[49] published in December 1923 by N. Plastiras, the leader of the 1922 coup, made the synod of the diocesan bishops the highest ecclesiastical authority of the church of Greece. At this point, for the first time in the history of the Greek state, the hierarchy acquired the fundamental and basic right, stipulated by the holy canons of the church, to convene in regular meetings. The synod met in Athens as of right, for one month, beginning on 1 October every year.[50] The new charter passed by the Venizelos government in 1931 maintained the canonical right of the hierarchy of the church of Greece that was established for the first time by the 1923 charter, but only in part. For though it recognised the hierarchy of the church of Greece as the supreme ecclesiastical authority, it allowed it to meet as of right from 1 October only every third year.[51] Under the 1923 law, the convening of an extraordinary meeting of the synod required the issuing of a presidential decree. The 1931 law maintained the body of the holy synod under law 200 of 1852 and the legislative decree of 1925, though with only nine members. Four of these came from the autocephalous Church of Greece and four from the New Territories; they were invited in order of seniority under the chairmanship of the incumbent archbishop of Athens.[52] To elect the metropolitan bishops, all the current metropolitans sent their ballot slips with the names of two candidates to the synod, which drew up a short-list of the three candidates receiving the most votes. The short-list was submitted to the state, which appointed the metropolitan.[53] The election of the archbishop of Athens was conducted in accordance with the canons and by the full quorum of the body of the hierarchy convened by a decree for the purpose.[54] The 1931 law, like its predecessor of 1921, retained the state representative, but decisions taken by the synod in his absence were now lawful, provided he had been invited to attend.[55]

THE EXCOMMUNICATION OF VENIZELOS AND THE OUTCOME OF THE SCHISM IN THE CHURCH

In September 1916, after the capture of the Greek regions of Eastern Macedonia by the Bulgarians, the Ethniki Amyna (National Defence) coup took place in Thessaloniki, followed by the formation of a provisional government by Venizelos, Danglis and Kountouriotis.[56]

The Thessaloniki coup met with a favourable response amongst the hierarchy of the Greek provinces of the Ecumenical Patriarchate. The majority of the clergy supported the government in Thessaloniki. The schism over the course to be followed by Greek nationalism occurred at a very difficult time for the synod of the church of Greece. The metropolitan of Athens, Theoklitos Minopoulos, was reluctant to take the decision to associate the body of the synod officially with the excommunication of Eleftherios Venizelos. Arsenios of Larissa brought all his influence to bear on the synod. In so doing, he gave expression to the feelings of reserve officers.[57] The synod and the clergy participated in the excommunication of Venizelos in 1916, amidst the fierce emotions and bitterness of the political schism and out of a fear that they might be accused of colluding with the government and state of Thessaloniki, which included Epirus, Macedonia, the Aegean islands and Crete.

Theoklitos' responsibility, as head of the independent Church of Greece, lay in his unwillingness to distance himself from events and prevent the church from becoming officially identified with a specific political grouping, choosing instead to participate in the excommunication. Given the organisational structure of the church of Greece, which had existed ever since the formation of the modern Greek state and the role determined for it by the governing political forces of the day, one wonders whether Theoklitos and the synod in fact had the option of distancing themselves and refusing to participate in the events played out on the field of war. The church had a specific role within the structure of the state: to minister to the religious needs of the people and to accept the current political regime in the national centre; a role that effectively gave it no room for manoeuvre.

When Venizelos came to Athens after his triumph in June 1917, the excommunication made it impossible for him to collaborate with the chairman of the synod, Theoklitos of Athens. The solution to the problem was sought in a device whereby the state, following the usual tactic of the civil authority in Greece, would exercise control over the church but the process of political intervention would be given the semblance of regularity. In order to allow the church to express a view on the matter, the minister, I. Dingas, attended a meeting of the ecclesiastical council of the hierarchy, in Thessaloniki, on 18 June 1917, and asked for its opinion.[58] The council of the hierarchy stated its view that the government might suspend or even rescind article 13 of law 201 determining the formation of the synod of the church of Greece and convene a new synod with bishops who had not participated in the excommunication, under the chairmanship of the senior archbishop. This synod would constitute an extraordinary ecclesiastical court of twelve members, in accordance with the canons, which would try the members of the clergy that participated in the excommunication. This new synod of the church of Greece would be competent to invite bishops from the New Territories to serve in the twelve-man ecclesiastical court.

The recommendations of the ecclesiastical council of the hierarchy were followed by the Venizelos government. On 11 July 1917 it published a legislative decree by which 'an ecclesiastical court is convened consisting of thirteen members, namely the active members of the Holy Synod and the others who hold metropolitan sees, archbishoprics or bishoprics within the state, both those subject to the autocephalous Church of Greece and those in the New Territories . . . The special ecclesiastical court is presided over by the senior archbishop.'[59]

The sessions of the ecclesiastical court, fifty in all, were held between 2 August and 20 November 1917, and it was decided that Theoklitos should be dethroned and retire to a monastery. The other priests who had participated in the excommunication received lesser penalties.

Perusal of the names of the bishops who were condemned reveals that the larger part of the hierarchy of the church of Greece agreed with or succumbed to the pressure of the reserve officers and took part in the excommunications declared by cities and townships. This aligned the hierarchy of Old Greece with King Constantine and the royalist camp, which agreed to support the king's view of the stance to be adopted by Greece in the First World War. However, it is an undisputed fact that the hierarchs of the church of Greece looked upon the king as representing continuity with the Byzantine emperor, with whose name were linked legends and traditions that acted as strong ideological antibodies sustaining the Greek people and Hellenism throughout the period of Ottoman domination. Constantine had been styled XII, as successor to the last Byzantine emperor.[60] The interpretation offered to Venizelos in 1916, by Meletios Metaxakis of Citium, of the devotion to the king of another section of Hellenism, the Greeks of Cyprus, is very characteristic and revealing:

> For Cypriots, King Constantine continues to be the resurrected king of marble, and whoever irreverently speaks his name is guilty of an act of impiety against the most sacred shrines of the Greek people. However, it is possible to accelerate developments, and for Cypriots to arrive at the point of national evolution at which they can distinguish between the fatherland and the king.[61]

The king also represented state legitimacy, with which the church of Greece had never come into conflict since its foundation. At the same time he was an expression of the stability of a regime associated with the security provided by Greece's neutrality during the First World War. The majority of those condemned by the court, moreover, served in agricultural and pastoral regions on the mainland and had suffered the consequences of the naval blockade by the Entente Powers and the bombardment of Athens. This contrasted with the experience of the Greeks of Macedonia, who had suffered the consequences of the occupation of Greek areas by the Bulgarian army, collaborating with the Central Powers.[62]

MELETIOS METAXAKIS AS METROPOLITAN OF ATHENS, AND HIS EXPULSION

After the condemnation and dethronement of Theoklitos of Athens on 26 February 1918,[63] the metropolitan of Thessaliotis raised the question of the election of the next metropolitan of Athens. The short list of three was composed of the archimandrites Chrysostomos Papadopoulos, (a university professor) and Iakovos Vatopedinos, and the metropolitan of Citium, Meletios Metaxakis, who was chosen by the state and enthroned on 8 March 1918.[64]

As metropolitan of Athens, Meletios Metaxakis entered the arena in the national centre at a very interesting period: a new world was coming into being, marked by the end of the empires – with the concomitant dissolution of the Ottoman Empire – and the redrawing of the borders of the Balkan states. It was a troubled time, but one which can be examined through a personality of the breadth and dynamism of Meletios. His election, of course, was not unconnected with his political support for Venizelos, as expressed in a letter dated 18 November after the National Defence coup. 'The metropolitan of Citium . . . is entirely at the disposal of the provisional government and, through me, seeks guidance from His Excellency Mr Venizelos.'[65] Venizelos had triumphed in Greece and, after the excommunication, the independent Church of Greece, a national church like those of the other Balkan states, was now, through the election of Meletios, presided over by an archbishop well-disposed to Venizelos and the Liberal Party.

Meletios Metaxakis was born in Prasa of Lasithi in Crete, in 1871,[66] and went to Jerusalem in 1889. He was ordained deacon in 1892, studied at the School of the Holy Cross and, under Patriarch Damianos, served as under-secretary and chief secretary at the Holy Sepulchre. Before assuming the throne of Athens, Meletios had distinguished himself for his handling of a number of major crises in the church. In 1907 he went to Cyprus as representative of Jerusalem, in order to resolve, along with the representative of Constantinople, Vasileios of Anchialos, and Photios of Alexandria, the recent problems of the archbishopric of Cyprus. In 1908, the synod of the Patriarchate of Jerusalem unanimously deposed

Damianos, on the grounds of the compliance he showed with the Arabs.[67] Meletios went to Constantinople and issued a memorandum in 1909 which helped the Porte to solve the crisis.[68] In 1910, while he was in Constantinople, he was elected metropolitan of Citium, a post he occupied until 1918, when he became metropolitan of Athens. In Cyprus he founded a seminary and a commercial high school, and published an ecclesiastical newspaper.

As metropolitan of Athens, Meletios submitted a memorandum 'Concerning the situation of the Church and What Needs to be Done' to the Holy Synod in 1920. In this he sought to lay the basis for the emancipation of the church from the bonds imposed on it by the state which had remained in place ever since its foundation.

Meletios took the view that laws concerning the church should originate with the ecclesiastical authority and then be submitted to the government as recommendations. He expressed a similar opinion during the debate in the synod on amendments of the draft legislation concerning parishes.[69] In December 1919 he submitted a draft bill to the synod, designed to settle a number of issues relating to the church of Greece, asking the synod to study possible ways in which to regulate the affairs of the church and then make proposals. He raised the matter once again in the synod in March 1920, asking for its recommendations so that he could submit the draft bill to the government and lay it before the hierarchy, which would be convened for the purpose, in accordance with the decision taken by the legislative committee.[70] The vote on the draft bill and the settlement of the affairs of the church of Greece were postponed until after the end of the war and the signature of the peace treaty.

Because of the circumstances in which Meletios was installed as metropolitan of Athens and head of the church of Greece, his prelacy was linked with the period when Venizelos held power. Meletios was destined to follow the fate of Venizelos and his government, which was rejected at the elections held on 1 November 1920. On 17 November 1920, the new, anti-Venizelist government of Dimitrios Rallis notified Meletios in writing that his predecessor's dismissal from the throne was unconstitutional and invalid.[71] Consequently, Meletios was asked to resign from the metropolitan throne and leave the metropolitan residence,[72] which he did after submitting letters of protest.[73]

After this, a convocation of the ecclesiastical body was sought, to give the church's blessing to the decisions taken and to proclaim the innocence of the condemned prelates. To this end, the synod asked the government to convene the hierarchy of the church of Greece. On 3 December, under the presidency of the senior archbishop, Dionysios of Zakynthos, the hierarchy convened for the first time in the history of the autocephalous Church of Greece,[74] and condemned the penalties imposed by the supreme ecclesiastical court in 1917 as 'anticanonical, invalid and non-existent'.[75]

THE STANCE ADOPTED BY CONSTANTINOPLE DURING THE SCHISM AND THE ELECTION OF MELETIOS METAXAKIS AS PATRIARCH

The political schism and the division of the national centre into Venizelists and anti-Venizelists naturally influenced the course of Greek nationalism,[76] and of Hellenism as a whole. It is indicative of the intensity of the schism that, after the fall of Venizelos, the two bodies in Constantinople (the Holy Synod and the Mixed Council) held an extraordinary meeting at which they expressed their gratitude to him in writing.[77]

The pro-Venizelist climate in Constantinople is also described in a note sent to the prime minister, D. Rallis (in office from 4 November 1920 to 23 January 1921), by Christos Androutsos, a graduate of the school at Chalki and royalist professor in the Theological School of Athens:

> Constantinople is suffering, understandably enough, from Venizelitis, which is being exploited by various people, unwittingly serving foreign interests. This situation will pass of itself in time and because of the furtherance of the national question. I therefore consider any spying or corrective mission to be superfluous. It is enough for some good person amongst the Greek authorities here to direct matters. The fragmented Patriarchate is already beginning to find its way . . . The rest will follow automatically. Details in person.[78]

By a curious quirk of history, Constantinople, which over the centuries had been the cultural and ecumenical centre of Hellenism and the focus of the loyalty of the Orthodox peoples, and which had acted in the context of privileges,[79] was gradually transformed into a second national centre, after the creation of the autocephalous churches of the Balkans and its collusion, verging on identification with the Greek state, during the period of the schism. Amidst the uncertainty and agony about the future of the Asia Minor campaign and of its flock in the peninsula – that is in fact about its own future – Constantinople remained loyal to Venizelos and his party even after his defeat in the elections of 1920. It sought an escape from the gloomy landscape of the Asia Minor front. The general leaning towards the person of Meletios Metaxakis and his election to the patriarchal throne were the product of the agony arising from these concerns. Because of its history and its association with the ecumenical traditions of Greek culture, Constantinople, as an ecclesiastical centre, was not identified with the elections in the national centre. During the schism, Athens, the leading city of classical Greece, selected as the capital of the modern Greek state by the new Bavarian king, Otho and his father, under the influence of European classicism, claimed for itself, as national centre,[80] the right to determine the course of Hellenism as a whole. This became evident through the many initiatives taken, as we shall see, to prevent the election of Meletios as ecumenical patriarch, and subsequently the efforts to ensure that his election was not recognised.

After the demise of the great patriarch Joachim III, in November 1912, the Greek embassy in Constantinople first had thoughts of Meletios as patriarch at the beginning of 1913.[81] His candidature, however, foundered on the general regulations. Germanos V of Chalcedon, leader of the anti-Joachim faction, was elected in January 1913. The patriarch, who was about eighty years old, resigned in October 1918, since his age prevented him from caring for the refugees and bringing pressure to bear on the Porte regarding the persecution of the Christian communities. In June 1919, it was decided at the Patriarchate to form a committee of bishops and laymen, which in October 1919 submitted a memorandum on the need for a patriarchal election. In the same month, members of the two bodies 'warmly proclaimed themselves in favour of the indefinite deferment of the election'.[82]

A characteristic feature of the stance adopted by Constantinople in the matter of the patriarchal election was its complete acquiescence with the suggestions and recommendations made by the Venizelos government. The change of government in Athens, after Venizelos' defeat in the elections of November 1920, marked a new relationship between Constantinople and Athens – one of initial reservation that subsequently evolved into rejection and overt conflict between the two centres of Hellenism.

On 12 April 1921 the Patriarchate issued an encyclical setting in motion the procedures for the election of a patriarch. In October 1921 the decision was taken in Constantinople finally to announce the patriarchal election, amidst the scepticism created by King Constantine's ineffective summer military campaigns in the interior of Asia Minor.[83] For Constantinople, the patriarchal election served as a deus ex machina, which was called upon to resolve the impasse of the emerging drama. It was anticipated that the patriarch elected would take initiatives as religious and political leader of Greeks in Thrace and Macedonia and would make contact with political figures of the Entente. At a period when international legitimacy was to be based on the formation of nation states, even if this involved slaughter and movements of population, the expectation in Constantinople (one of the many possibilities entertained during this transitional period involved the creation of an independent state in Asia Minor) was that the new patriarch would take political steps to save his flock. There were, of course, those who followed developments with considerable scepticism, and demanded a neutral stance of all the Powers in Constantinople.

The electoral convention, consisting of clergy and laymen, met in the Patriarchate, in the courtyards of which were officers of the guard, wearing civilian dress. The most likely victor in the elections was Germanos of Amaseia, since nine bishops had delegated him to vote in the final ballot for a candidate from the short list of three in the church. Some members of the guard asked him 'to withdraw his candidature in favour of Meletios . . . and indicated that, if he refused to sacrifice himself in favour of Metaxakis, he would be excluded from the popular ticket and would not, therefore, be able to go to the church as a candidate'.[84] This meant that during the voting by the convention of clergy and laymen to establish the short list, at which the lay members were in the majority, Germanos of Amaseia would receive no votes and would not be voted onto the short list from which the bishops who came to the church would elect the patriarch. In the election to the short list, Germanos received seventy-eight votes out of 100 and the archbishop of Caesarea, Nikolaos and Meletios seventy-three each. In the church Meletios was elected patriarch with sixteen votes, Germanos Karavangelis of Amaseia receiving two votes.[85]

In the eyes of the government in Athens, Patriarch Meletios Metaxakis was identified with the figure and the political choices of Venizelos. The fears felt in the national centre regarding Patriarch Meletios' stance were founded on the clear evidence of his career and general policy, which were informed by liberalism. It was for this reason that, as we have already seen, when metropolitan of Athens, he was not invited to swear in the Rallis government that succeeded Venizelos after the 1920 elections, and was subsequently induced to resign from his position as metropolitan. Athens was naturally, therefore, opposed to his election and ascent to the patriarchal throne. Events also marked the complete break between Athens and Constantinople, which became independent of the national centre. The fact of the election had an overtly political dimension, both in the repeated delays and in the final choice of Meletios. Meletios was a dynamic figure. This is clear from his career as a whole. After he had resigned as metropolitan of Athens, he had become active in the organisation of the Greek community in America, where he was at the time of his election to the throne of Constantinople.

After the new political situation created in Turkey by the rise to power of Kemal Ataturk, Meletios was regarded as the most dynamic representative of Greek nationalism in the church. During the negotiations for the Treaty of Lausanne, the Turkish delegation asked that he withdraw from Constantinople. On 10 July 1923, fourteen days before the signing of the Treaty of Lausanne, Meletios took leave of absence and went to Mount Athos for health reasons, and on 20 September he resigned from the post of ecumenical patriarch. In 1926 he was elected patriarch of Alexandria, in which city he passed away in 1935.

CONCLUSION

To sum up. In his childhood and early youth in Crete and during the rebellion of 1897, Venizelos had become aware of the true situation of the Church of Crete. As councillor of the Cretan state, Venizelos drew up the charter of the provincial synod of the Church of Crete and published it in the *Government Gazette* of the Cretan state. In the Cretan state, the rift between Venizelos and Prince George, and the Theriso movement that followed in 1905, created a major local schism, a forerunner of the National Schism that followed with the coup of the 'National Defence' in Thessaloniki in 1916. In the Cretan schism, during which the term 'Venizelists' was used for the first time in a newspaper headline of 1903, Venizelos enjoyed the support of a large part of the clergy and the majority of the bishops. This strengthened his positive relations with the church.

Consequently, when he became prime minister of Greece, he had already formed a clear positive picture of the church and the role it could play in achieving the national aims of the Greek state. The subsequent course of events was not to contradict this picture. There was a strong group of Venizelist bishops in the church, on whom Venizelos relied. The expansion of Greece created a new ecclesiastical and political reality, with provinces of the Ecumenical Throne within the new Greek state. The settlement of the question of the church was to be made by the final Venizelos government in 1928. The provinces remained under the canonical spiritual jurisdiction of the Patriarchate, and their administration was ceded only temporarily to the church of Greece. An exception was made in the case of the Church of Crete, which continued to enjoy the ecclesiastical self-government elaborated by Venizelos and Dionysios of Rethymnon.

The resolution of the issues affecting the church of Greece and the work of the legislative committee formed for this purpose in 1914 were not brought to completion, on account of military preparations and campaigns. The conditions of the times naturally relegated the settlement of ecclesiastical matters to the background.

The political schism, as to whether Greece should side with the Entente, as Venizelos wished, or remain neutral, in accordance with King Constantine's view, led also to an ecclesiastical schism. In December 1916, the church of Greece, despite all its scepticism, soul-searching and hesitation, finally succumbed to pressure from the military and participated in the excommunication of Venizelos. Even if it had not done so, the devotion to the king of the majority of the bishops was unquestioned.

After the National Defence coup of 1916 in Thessaloniki, Venizelos, given his strong support in the political sphere and the support of the majority of the prelates there, summoned the hierarchy of the New Territories to a meeting. By so doing, he created a strong counterweight to events in Athens. Venizelos' political influence over the state of Thessaloniki was strong and unquestioned – especially given that the danger to the Greeks in this second state came from the allies of the Central Powers, with whom the king was colluding. When he assumed the office of prime minister of the entire state in June 1917, Venizelos called a meeting of a twelve-member ecclesiastical court consisting of bishops well-disposed toward himself, in order to try the bishops who had participated in the excommunication. Theoklitos of Athens and Arsenios of Larisa were dethroned and other bishops were punished.

Meletios Metaxakis of Citium became metropolitan of Athens with the support of the Venizelos government. The fall of this government and the return of King Constantine also swept away Meletios of Athens, who was called upon to resign, and Theoklitos was restored as metropolitan of Athens by royal decree. The effects of the political changes of that troubled period on the affairs of the church were a consequence of the domination of the state in the structure and organisation of the church.

The initiatives taken by Athens to ensure that Patriarch Meletios was not recognised by the Greek Orthodox patriarchates of Alexandria and Jerusalem and the archbishopric of Cyprus, and the attitudes adopted by them provides us with a picture of the strong support enjoyed by Venizelism in the Greek Orthodox communities there. The political change in Athens that followed the coup of Plastiras in 1922 led to the recognition of Meletios and subsequently to his resignation from the patriarchal throne in order to pave the way for the signing of the Treaty of Lausanne.

It may also be concluded that the political schism extended also to the body of the church – naturally enough, since the membership of the two was mutually interpenetrating. The support found by Venizelos in the ecclesiastical world was by no means negligible or less than that enjoyed by the followers of Constantine.

During the last period of his government (1928–32), Venizelos settled the issues affecting the Greek provinces of the Ecumenical Patriarchate, through a patriarchal and synodic enactment of 1928, and created two church jurisdictions: that of the autocephalous Church of Greece, created by the tome of 1850 and the enactments of 1866 in the case of the Ionian islands and of 1882 for Thessaly; and that of the Ecumenical Patriarchate with the New Territories, Crete and Mount Athos, to which were added the Dodecanese after their incorporation into Greece in 1947.

During this same period, Venizelos also passed a new charter for the autocephalous Church of Greece. The charter 5187/1931 only partially restored the canonical rights of the church of Greece. It may be confidently concluded that the final Venizelos government, in defining its relations with the church of Greece through the charter of 1931, did not persist in the previously existing political perception that the state should exercise tight control of the church, which had prevailed from 1852 to 1923, and had been strengthened by the law of 1925. However, it did preserve the political preconditions that made it possible for the state to intervene in the work of the Church of Greece, which it perceived as an auxiliary to secular policies.

NOTES

1. Th. Detorakis (1990), *Istoria tis Kritis* [*History of Crete*], Irakleion, p. 401.
2. A. Nanakis (1992), *To episkopiko zitima 1880–1882 kai i Ekklisia tis Kritis* [*The Episcopal Question 1880–1882 and the Church of Crete*], Katerini.
3. Ibid., pp. 65–6.
4. From 1967 the Synod of the Church of Crete consisted of seven prelates who were called metropolitans, while the metropolitan of Crete assumed the title of archbishop.
5. A. Nanakis (1998), *I Ekklisia tis Kritis stin epanastasi tou 1897–1898. Apo tin ethnarchiki stin ethniki syneidisi* [*The Church of Crete in the Revolution of 1897 to 1898. From Ethnic to National consciousness*], Thessaloniki, pp. 39–112 esp. pp. 113–14, for Venizelos' letter to Nikiphoros.
6. Ibid., pp. 17–32, 28.
7. Ibid., pp. 121–40, 122–4.

8. *Imerologion kai praktika tou epanastatikou stratopedou Akrotiriou* [*Diary and Proceedings of the Revolutionary Camp at Akrotiri*], Chania 1949, p. 157.
9. Historical Archive of Crete (Chania), Historical Collection, No. 40: To N. K. Papadakis (of Aptera) from Dorotheos of Kissamos, 14 June 1897.
10. A. Vidalakis (1970), *Parthenios Peridis*, Athens, Th. Tzedakis (1975), in *Proceedings of the Third International Congress of Cretan Studies*, vol. III, Athens, pp. 321–59, esp. p. 340, for evidence for the funeral oration delivered by Venizelos.
11. *Government Gazette of the Cretan State*, year I, no. 13, Chania, 20 February 1899, p. 11, A. Nanakis (1995), *To Mitropolitiko zitima kai i ekklisiastiki organosi tis Kritis (1897–1900)* [*The Metropolitan Question and the Ecclesiastical Organisation of Crete, 1897–1900*], Katerini, pp. 120–3.
12. A. Nanakis (1997), *Ekklisiastika Kritis* [*Ecclesiastical Affairs of Crete*], Thessaloniki, pp. 239–55.
13. Nanakis, *To Mitropolitiko zitima*, pp. 31–9 (see Note 11).
14. C. Spanoudis (1902), *Istorikai selides. Ioakeim III* [*Historical pages. Joachim III*], Constantinople, rep. edn by A. Nanakis (2000), Thessaloniki.
15. Nanakis, *To Mitropolitiko zitima*, pp. 132–3 (see Note 11).
16. Ibid., pp. 135–49.
17. Ibid., p. 248.
18. G. Stavrakakis (1968), 'O episkopos Rethimnis kai Avlopotamou Dionysios (1856–1910)' [The Bishop of Rethymnon and Avlopotamo Dionysios (1856–1910)], *Kritiki Estia* 189, pp. 543–51.
19. *Patris*, 20 March 1903.
20. C. Svolopoulos (1974), *O Eleftherios Venizelos kai i politiki krisis eis tin aftonomon Kritin, 1901–1906* [*Eleftherios Venizelos and the Political Crisis in Autonomous Crete, 1901–1906*], Athens.
21. Nanakis, *To Mitropolitiko zitima*, pp. 171–3 (see Note 11).
22. St. Kelaidis (1930), *O Parthenios G. Kelaidis kai i politiki aftou allilographia* [*Parthenios Kelaidis and his Political Correspondence*], Chania, pp. 295–6.
23. Nanakis, *To Mitropolitiko zitima*, pp. 171–3 (see Note 11).
24. Historical Archive of the Greek Foreign Ministry [AYE] 1930, Political Correspondence: Regulations for the Patriarchate of Alexandria, Cairo 15 November 1929, prot. no. 3112: P. Metaxas to the Ministry of Foreign Affairs.
25. AYE 1925, 1926, 1927, Death of Patriarch Photios. Appointment of Meletios as Patriarch of Alexandria, Cairo, 5 January 1926, prot. no. 29: consular report to the Ministry of Foreign Affairs.
26. AYE 1929, B/36, B Political Correspondence: Jerusalem file: regulations of the Orthodox Patriarchate of Jerusalem.
27. See *Ekklisiastikos Kyrix*, XI (1920), pp. 180–2, 451–5, 522–4.

28. AYE 1918/AAK, 5. El. Venizelos Archive: Jerusalem 12 February 1918, Deacon Constantios to 'My venerable teacher', addressed to Chrysostomos Papadopoulos; AYE ibid.: report on the condition of the church of Sinai and . . . Jerusalem, 28 February 1918, by Archimandrites Nikodimos, Ioakeim and Ippolytos to Meletios, and AYE ibid., Jerusalem, 20 February 1918, Archimandrites Nikodimos, Ioakeim and Ippolytos to Venizelos.
29. Varnavas Tzortzatos (1967), *I katastatiki nomothesia tis Ekklisias tis Ellados* [*The Constitutional Legislation of the Church of Greece*], Athens, p. 76. See also generally Ch. Frazee (1969), *The Orthodox Church and Independent Greece*, Cambridge.
30. Th. Strangas (1969), *Ekklisias Ellados istoria ek pigon apsevdon* [*History of the Church of Greece from Truthful Sources*], vol. I, Athens, p. 626.
31. V. Atesis (1953), *Epitomos episkopiki istoria tis Ekklisias tis Ellados* [*Concise Episcopal History of the Church of Greece*], vol. II, pp. 20–36.
32. *Ieros Syndesmos* [*Holy League*], Athens, 1 November 1909, with the text of the draft law.
33. Ibid., Athens, 1 February 1911, with the text of the draft law.
34. Gennadios of Thessaloniki (1928), 'I Ekklisia ton neon choron' ['The church of the New Territories'], *Grigorios Palamas* 12, p. 23.
35. Ibid.
36. Ibid., p. 24; Th. Strangas, *Ekklisias Ellados*, pp. 620–1 (see Note 30).
37. Gennadios, 'I Ekklisia', pp. 24–5 (see Note 34).
38. Tzortzatos, *I katastatiki nomothesia*, pp. 375–426 (see Note 29), with the text of the draft charter for the Orthodox Church of Greece, drawn up by the committee.
39. E. Allamanis and K. Panayotopoulou (1978), 'I mikrasiatiki ekstrateia apo to Maio tou 1919 os to Noemvrio tou 1920' ['The Asia Minor campaign from May 1919 to November 1920'], in G. Christopoulos and I. Bastias (eds), *Istoria tou ellinikou ethnous* [*History of the Greek Nation*], vol. XV, Athens, p. 18.
40. *Ekklisiastiki Alitheia* 40 (1920), pp. 427–9.
41. A. Angelopoulos (1982), *I ekklisiastiki istoria ton Neon Choron 1912–1928* [*The Ecclesiastical History of the New Territories 1912–1928*], Thessaloniki, p. 18.
42. Ibid., p. 19.
43. Draft charter of the Orthodox Church in the New Territories and its appendices (1) concerning parish churches and parish priests, (2) concerning seminaries, (3) concerning preachers, (4) concerning the church fund and (5) concerning monasteries and their administration, drawn up by a committee composed of the Metopolitans Gennadios of Thessaloniki, Spyridon of Ioannina, Titos of Crete, Chrysanthos of Trebizond, Iakovos of Mytilini, Dionysios of Mithymna and Anthimos of Maroneia, and C. Rallis, professor at Athens University. Printed at the expense of the prelacy of the New Territories. The text of the draft charter of the 'Orthodox Church of the New

Territories' appears in Tzortzatos, *I katastatiki nomothesia*, pp. 427–59 (see Note 29).

44. Tzortzatos, *I katastatiki nomothesia*, p. 429 (see Note 29).
45. Ibid., pp. 52–6.
46. Ibid., p. 53.
47. C. J. Vavouskos (1973), *I nomothetiki ypostasis ton mitropoleon ton Neon Choron* [*The Legislative Status of the Dioceses of the New Territories*], Thessalomiki, p. 26.
48. Tzortzatos, *I katastatiki nomothesia*, pp. 161–81 and 182–7 (see Note 29).
49. Ibid., pp. 124–56.
50. Ibid., pp. 136–8: articles 24–5.
51. Ibid., pp. 166–7: article 3.
52. Ibid., p. 168: article 4.
53. Ibid., pp. 172–3: article 10.
54. Ibid., pp. 173–4: article 12.
55. Ibid., p. 169: article 6.
56. G. Leontaritis (1978), 'I diethnis thesi tis Ellados stis paramones tou A'Pagkosmiou Polemou' ['Greece's International Position on the Eve of the First World War'] and N. Oikonomou (1978), 'Apo tin aphixi tou Venizelou stin Athina os to telos tou polemou' ['From the Arrival of Venizelos to the End of the war'], in Christopoulos and Bastias (eds), *Istoria tou ellinikou ethnous*, vol. XV, pp. 8–46 and 46–52 (see Note 39).
57. G. Th. Mavrogordatos (1996), *Ethnikos dichasmos kai maziki organosi. Oi epistratoi tou 1916* [*National Schism and Mass Organisation. The Reservists of 1916*], Athens, p. 107.
58. Angelopoulos, *I ekklisiastiki istoria*, pp. 64–5 (see Note 41).
59. Strangas, *Ekklisias Ellados*, pp. 719–20 (see Note 30).
60. G. Th. Mavrogordatos (1983), 'O Dichasmos os krisi ethnikis oloklirosis' ['The Schism as a Crisis in National Integration], in D. Tsaoussis (ed.), *Ellinismos kai ellinikotita* [*Hellenism and Hellenicity*], Athens, pp. 72–3.
61. AYE 1916–17, Thessaloniki Archive A/6/9: 'Attempt to draw Cyprus into the Thessaloniki Uprising', Limassol, 6 December 1916, Meletios of Citium to Venizelos.
62. Mavrogordatos, 'O Dichasmos', in Tsaoussis (ed.), *Ellimismos*, pp. 75–9 (see Note 60).
63. Statement of Theoklitos Ch. Minopoulos, metropolitan of Athens and president of the holy synod of the Church of Greece, to the special ecclesiastical court, at the hearing of the charge made against him by the Ministry of Ecclesiastical Affairs, Athens, September 1917.
64. Strangas, *Ekklisias Ellados*, pp. 758–60 (see Note 30).
65. AYE (see Note 61), Alexandria 18 November 1916, prot. no. 43, the representative for national defence to N. Politis.
66. *Ekklisiastikos Pharos* 34 (1935): a special issue dedicated to Meletios of Alexandria on the occasion of his death; Methodios of Axomi, ibid., 53

(1971), pp. 390–523; A. Phytrakis (1973), *O Oikoumenikos Patriarchis Meletios Metaxakis* [*The Ecumenical Patriarch Meletios Metaxakis*], Athens.

67. AYE 1920, B/35 Jerusalem (Holy Sepulchre) file, memorandum 'Concerning the Holy Sepulchre, December 1917, Meletios of Citium and Meliton [Ayiotaphitis]. See also, *Skiera selis tis istorias tis Ekklisias Ierosolymon o enochos* [A Dark Page of History of the Church of Jerusalem. The Culprit] (anon.), Athens 1920.
68. M. Metaxakis (1909), *Ai axioseis ton aravophonon Orthodoxon tis Palaistinis* [*The Demands of the Orthodox Arab-speakers of Palestine*], Constantinople.
69. Strangas, *Ekklisias Ellados*, p. 865 (see Note 30).
70. Ibid., p. 863.
71. Ibid., p. 924.
72. Ibid.
73. Atesis, *Epitomos episkopi istoria*, vol. II, pp. 42–52, with the relevant texts.
74. Strangas, *Ekklisias Ellados*, p. 951 (see Note 30).
75. Ibid., p. 959.
76. Th. Veremis (1989), 'From the National State to the Stateless Nation 1821–1910', *European History Quarterly* 19, pp. 135–48.
77. *Ekthesis ton pepragmenon tou D. E. Miktou Symvouliou apo 23 Dekemvriou 1919 mechri tis 22 Noemvriou 1920* [*Report on the Proceedings of the Permanent National Mixed Council from 23 December 1919 to 22 November 1920*], Constantinople, 1920, p. 6.
78. AYE A/18/4: File Defence Officers in Constantinople, handwritten note, Chr. Androutsos to Prime Minister Rallis.
79. P. Konortas (1988), 'I exelixi ton ekklisiastikon veration kai to Pronomiako Zitima' ['The Evolution of Ecclesiastical Berats and the Question of Privileges'], *Ta Istorika* 9 (December), pp. 259–86.
80. P. M. Kitromilides (1983), 'To elliniko kratos os ethniko kentro' ['The Greek State as National Centre'], in Tsaoussis (ed.), *Ellinismos kai ellinikotita*, pp. 148–50 (see Note 60).
81. See A. Nanakis (1991), *I chireia tou Oikoumenikou Thronou kai i eklogi tou Meletiou Metaxaki, 1918–1922* [*The Vacancy of the Ecumenical Throne and the Election of Meletios Metaxakis, 1918–1922*], Thessaloniki, p. 95.
82. G. Skalieris (1922), *I eklogi patriarchou kata to ekklisiastikon politevma tou Oikoumenikou Thronou* [*Patriarchal Election According to the Ecclesiastical Regime of the Ecumenical Throne*], Athens, p. 10.
83. N. Oikonomou (1978), 'Oi stratiotikes epicheiriseis Iouniou-Septemvriou 1921' ['Military Operations June – September 1921'], in Christopoulos and Bastias (eds), *Istoria tou ellinikou ethnous*, vol. XV, pp. 174–86 (see Note 39).
84. AYE 1920, B35, 14: File Appointment of Patriarch Meletios Metaxakis, Constantinople 3 December 1921, prot. no. 8496, Votsis to the Ministry of Foreign Affairs.

85. A. Nanakis, *I chireia tou Oikoumenikou Thronou*, p. 100 (see Note 81) and M. Staikos (1998), *Germanos Karavangelis Mitropolitis Amaseias kai Exarchos Kentroas Evropis 1924–1935* [*Germanos Karavangelis Metropolitan of Amaseia and Exarch of Central Europe 1924–1935*], Thessaloniki, vol. I, pp. 100–1.

PART IV

Offstage

13

Venizelos' Intellectual Projects and Cultural Interests

Paschalis M. Kitromilides

I

Venizelos was an intensely public man, consumed by politics. By his own admission he had no personal life, he only lived for politics, which he understood as a service to his country.[1] Yet this pervading political commitment, the intense politicisation of life at the expense of personal feeling and motivation, could by no stretch of the imagination be equated with the attitude and mentality of latter-day populist politicians, who appear similarly consumed by politics, but lack Venizelos' moral understanding of the character of public life. Venizelos was not evincing a twentieth-century posture of the public man; rather he could be seen to be carrying on a nineteenth-century tradition of statesmanship. With a host of great nineteenth-century political leaders he also shared another characteristic of European statesmanship, the immersion of the public personality in historical culture, understood as a kind of training-ground of responsible political action and decision. Incidentally, this had been the understanding of the purposes of their task by many nineteenth-and early twentieth-century historians as well. The understanding of history as a reading of the past detached from the commitments of the present had to wait for the critique of the 'Whig interpretation of history' in order to come into its own.

The clearest evidence of this orientation of Venizelos' intellectual interests comes from the composition of his library, which, despite its dramatic adventures survives in large part to provide the modern scholar with clues and hypotheses.[2] The collection is made up of many categories of books, including a remarkable section of modern European literature, mostly books of French literary works which apparently belonged to Madame Venizelos, who was responsible for the removal of the library from their residence in Athens to the family home in Chania following her husband's death.[3] Venizelos' own immediate interests are reflected in the extensive holdings of the library on contemporary – that is, early twentieth-century – European history, politics and diplomacy, with a special focus on Greece and her Balkan neighbours. All this is predictable enough and does not call for comment. What impresses, however, is the extensive presence of the great nineteenth- and early twentieth-century historians. Guizot occupies pride of place among them, but Hippolyte Taine, Ernest Lavisse, Seignobos, Aulard are also there.[4] British historical scholarship is not as extensively represented but Carlyle, Trevelyan and Toynbee[5] do appear as also do, quite predictably, J. Marriott, with his diplomatic history of the Eastern question[6] and, revealingly, John Morley, with the life of Gladstone.[7] The outstanding presence in Venizelos' library, however, is that of François Guizot. The collection of his works is impressively extensive.[8] This kind of evidence is quite suggestive in connecting Venizelos' historical and political thought with what has been described by his contemporary observer of European historical scholarship, G. P. Gooch, as 'the political school', the school of conservative liberal historian-statesmen whose main figures were Guizot, Mignet and Thiers.[9]

II

Such had been the substratum of historical culture that apparently formed the broader background to Venizelos' political understanding and judgement. It was this deep interest in history that motivated his most serious intellectual project, a translation of Thucydides into modern Greek. The translation, which occupied Venizelos for many years during the period of his political exile between 1920 and 1928, was an essentially political project. This is made plain especially by the commentary on the text, a meticulous task that Venizelos undertook concurrently with the translation. In a way he appears to be seeking in Thucydides a form of confirmation of his own political judgements and decisions. The translation also provided an occasion for Venizelos to express his views on the language question, which had for so long caused much ideological controversy in Greek culture and so much pointless upheaval in Greek education.[10] The fact that, by means of his translation, Venizelos appeared to be taking sides in the controversy of the language question has led most of those who have commented on his Thucydides project to attempt to examine and appraise the work in the perspective of the history of linguistic controversy in Greece. Thus Venizelos' Thucydides has been placed in a continuum of modern Greek attempts to render the ancient Athenian classic in the modern language, stretching from Ioannis Vilaras in 1815 through A. A. Pallis in 1915 to I. Th. Kakridis in 1937. All these attempts were linked with deeply ideological positions on the question of the appropriate language of modern Greek education and culture. Venizelos' project has been interpreted as a testimony of a similar nature.[11]

In fact the subject could be considered from an alternative perspective, a perspective that might reveal Venizelos' deeper political motivations rather than mere linguistic preferences as the primary factor in this important project. To recover this perspective his project should be placed in the tradition of modern Greek statesmen-historians, who self-consciously sought in Thucydides a model of political judgement. In this, the forerunner of Venizelos' Thucydides is not in fact Ioannis Vilaras, a genuine Enlightenment radical, but Spyridon Trikoupis, the diplomat-historian of the Greek war of independence. In the prolegomena to his *History of the Greek Revolution*, Trikoupis invoked the authority of Thucydides in order to justify his own project of undertaking the daring task of writing the history of his own times, narrating the deeds and conflicts of his contemporaries. Such a project did not prevent Thucydides from being unanimously acclaimed as a model of fairness and thus Trikoupis considered his own task as a viable and legitimate one.[12] Thucydides was furthermore invoked by Trikoupis as a methodological model in writing contemporary history. On the basis of Thucydides' statement concerning the need of exercising his personal judgement in ascertaining the truth, Trikoupis advanced his own claims of criticism in contemporary history.[13]

I think that it would not be an exaggeration to suggest that Venizelos shared Trikoupis' view of history as the domain of exercising political judgement, and this stimulated his interest in Thucydides as the political historian par excellence. Venizelos had a lively interest in the classics, as testified again by the extensive collection in his library. The choice, however, of devoting his years of political exile after 1920 to the ambitious project of rendering Thucydides into modern Greek, was primarily motivated, I think, by a deeply felt need to reach by means of reflection on the text of the greatest ancient Greek historian a kind of sobering appraisal of the previous decade of modern Greek politics. In other words Venizelos found in Thucydides an Archimedean point for self-reflection and self-examination over his involvement in what turned out to be the most critical decade in the history of the Greek state: a decade of achievement and pride, but also of deep passions, civil discord and fatal decisions – very much a re-enactment of the historical set-up laid out by 'Thucydides mythistoricus'.[14]

III

According to his personal secretary of 1917 to 1924, Venizelos had a long-held desire to translate Thucydides.[15] His chance finally came after the electoral defeat of November 1920. He began preliminary work after his settlement in Paris in early 1921. In December 1921, Venizelos and his new wife Helena went on a tour of the Americas. While in California, he had the opportunity of progressing with his translation. The work was continued during their subsequent visits to Cuba and Peru. During the months of this tour Venizelos devoted as much time as he could to the project, working systematically from 7 a.m. to 12.30 p.m. whenever he could, and sometimes later in the day.[16]

The couple returned from America in May 1922, and soon after, following the Asia Minor disaster, Venizelos was recalled to public duty and charged to lead the Greek delegation at the Lausanne peace conference from November 1922 to June 1923. In January 1924 Venizelos assumed a brief premiership lasting only a few weeks, returning to Paris in March of the same year. From 1924 to 1927, during his residence in Paris and London, he occupied himself with his work on Thucydides.

Venizelos did not limit himself to the task of translation. Either concurrently or following the completion of the translation he wrote a methodical commentary on the text. According to the editor of the surviving scholia Venizelos' commentary must have extended to the entire text of Thucydides. Unfortunately, only a fragmentary part of the commentary has survived, in eleven hand-written notebooks covering the main part of books I–IV of Thucydides' *History*. By some strange coincidence the comments on the opening sections of each of books I–IV have not been preserved.[17] Even in this form the commentary is a valuable source on the text and on Venizelos' understanding of it.

He appears to have worked quite methodically and systematically, consulting a wide range of dictionaries and also translations in other modern European languages of which he had a reading knowledge, in order to render the meaning of the ancient text as precisely as possible. On the basis of this extensive research Venizelos was even able to suggest a correction in a passage of Thucydides' text referring to an epidemic in the Athenian navy (Book I, 112, 4).[18] Venizelos refers to his work on Thucydides on several occasions in his correspondence and thus allows us glimpses into the progress and character of it. In a letter from Paris to the great linguist G. N. Hadjidakis in Thessaloniki, dated 12 November 1926, Venizelos mentions that he had been at work on the translation for about twenty months.[19] This is a valuable piece of information in helping us date the main part of his work on the translation in the period following his return to Paris after the brief premiership of January to March 1924. In another letter to the French neo-Hellenist Hubert Pernot in Paris, dated 15 January 1925, Venizelos asks the French professor to lend him or to borrow on his behalf from the library of the Sorbonne two books by the well-known classical scholar Alfred Croiset. One of these was Croiset's own edition of Thucydides. Apparently Venizelos needed the books for his work, and as they had been published decades earlier they were out of print and unavailable in bookstores, as he explains to Pernot.[20] All this suggests how conscientious was Venizelos' work on the translation and commentary.

Some additional evidence on the progress of Venizelos' Thucydides project is supplied by the relevant notes entered by Venizelos in an appointment diary he kept during his residence in London in the first half of 1926. On the basis of these entries we can see him daily at work on his commentary throughout the month of January and the first part of February 1926. During 1–4 January 1926 he was writing his commentary on Pericles' funeral oration (Thucydides II, 35–46). Work on Thucydides seems to have been interrupted on 13 February but Venizelos returned to it the following May. Between 13 and 20 May 1926 he commented on the third book of Thucydides.[21]

On three blank pages between the alphabetical index of addresses and telephone numbers and the main body of the 1926 diary, Venizelos inserted some bibliographical notes, apparently concerning books that had come to his attention and provoked his interest: these were mostly books on international relations but several titles on ancient history and the classics appear as well. These bibliographical notes reflect in a nutshell, as it were, the intellectual universe of a great statesman. From this last stage of Venizelos' work on Thucydides we possess an excellent visual record, the portrait painted in Paris by the Cretan painter Dimitris Kokotsis (1894–1961). This is the only portrait for which Venizelos consented to pose. The sitting took place on 3 May 1927 and apparently Venizelos agreed to allow the painter, who was in Paris for the purpose of an exhibition of his work, to paint him while checking his translation against Thucydides' original text.

By the time Venizelos returned to active politics in 1928 the translation had been completed and supplemented by its extensive commentary. The comments were mostly of a philological nature and they are a valuable testimony of Venizelos' conscientious dialogue with Thucydidean scholarship in his effort to elucidate and understand the original in order to render it correctly and precisely into modern Greek. The text of the translation was transcribed in a clean manuscript, but Venizelos continued to make corrections in subsequent years. Following Venizelos' death in 1936, Madame Venizelos gave the text of the translation to her husband's close diplomatic collaborator and biographer, Dimitrios Caclamanos, who edited it for publication. The work appeared in two handsomely produced volumes by Oxford University Press in 1940. The Greek type used for typesetting was designed by Victor Schrolderer of the British Museum. A frontispiece of Venizelos' portrait by John Sargent adorns the first volume, while a facsimile of a page of Venizelos' manuscript appears in the second volume.[22]

Venizelos' translation of Thucydides is by any standards a remarkable intellectual accomplishment. As indicated by the eloquent testimony of the surviving commentary, it was the product of the most serious devotion of the translator to the task, which was carried out upon a scholarly infrastructure of the highest professional standard. The translation is written in learned but eminently readable modern Greek, which manages to preserve and transmit to the modern readership the magnificence and serenity of the original. In this connection the editor's characterisation of Venizelos' accomplishment represents an apt judgement of the overall result:[23]

> Venizelos, in undertaking to render this work into modern Greek, realized that he had to respect, as far as possible, the sobriety and the conciseness of the original, avoiding prolixity and redundance, but at the same time bringing it to the level of contemporary understanding.

The publication of the work was highly acclaimed in international scholarly circles.[24] The *Manchester Guardian* devoted a leading article to it, drawing a parallel between the author and the translator. The article characteristically appeared under the title 'Two Greeks'.[25]

IV

The Thucydides project was certainly Venizelos' most significant and serious intellectual pursuit, a lasting monument to a rare combination of scholarship and statesmanship that integrated him in the most appropriate way in a distinctly European tradition of political leadership. Venizelos was a truly cultured man and his interests extended beyond scholarship and the classics into the broad domain of the arts. An area of artistic expression in which his profound immersion in the cultural tradition of his native Crete acted as a stimulus of a lively interest was that of folk music. During his Parisian exile he wrote to his close friend Costis Foumis, in Chania, mentioning enthusiastically that the well-known Greek composer Peter Petridis had told him that he intended to collect motifs of Cretan folk music in order to integrate them in a musical composition of his own. Venizelos added, with obvious satisfaction, that he had heard from another leading Greek composer, Manolis Kalomoiris, that the Cretans, along with the Epirots, were the most musical people of Greece and that 'their musical sense is worthy of great note'.[26] Against this background we can appreciate one of Venizelos' most seemingly idiosyncratic gestures in his later years. This was his response to a proposal to be recorded singing Cretan folk songs and ballads in the context of ethnomusicologist Melpo Merlier's remarkable initiative for a large-scale recording of Greek folk music. On the afternoon of Sunday, 11 January 1931, Venizelos, incumbent prime minister of Greece, took the time to go to the basement of the Alambra Theatre on Chalkokondyli Street in central Athens, to record two Cretan folk songs ('Digenis' and 'Haros') with the technicians of the Paris-based Pathé record company who were working for the Merlier project.[27] The original recordings of Venizelos' voice are kept in the music folklore archive of the Centre for Asia Minor Studies in Athens and were reproduced on commercial records several decades later.

The Venizelos government supported the Merlier project to collect the folk poetry and music of Greece and of the refugee population that had been relocated in Greece from Asia Minor after 1922, with a grant of 500,000 drachmas. In this initiative the suggestion came from Foreign Minister A. Michalakopoulos, but obviously the involvement in the Merlier project of Venizelos' devoted personal friend, authoress Penelope Delta, who was also Melpo Merlier's close friend and enthusiastic supporter, and of Hubert Pernot, the Sorbonne neo-Hellenist and Venizelos' supporter in Paris, must have contributed significantly to the government's decision.

V

Government support for the arts under Venizelos was not limited to music. As part of the liberal programme of reform and modernisation, modern art was encouraged already by the pre-1920 Venizelos governments. Venizelos himself showed a preference for modern painting in his time and encouraged by means of state purchases of works of art, the work of his contemporary artists, who were attempting to renew academic painting in Greece through the introduction of new aesthetic tastes emanating primarily from France.[28] In December 1917 Venizelos opened an exhibition by the 'Art Group', a group of young painters and sculptors who sought to renew Greek art by moving away from the conservative aesthetic of the academic painting of the Munich School that had dominated the world of art in Greece throughout the nineteenth century. To encourage their initiative Venizelos had the Liberal Club buy works of all artists participating in the exhibition. In September 1919, apparently at Venizelos' initiative, the Art Group exhibited their work in the Parisian art gallery La Boétie while the proceedings of the Peace Conference were under way in the French capital. The show was once more opened by Venizelos himself, who took time off from the strenuous diplomatic race that led up to the Treaty of Sèvres to show his support of the Greek artistic avant-garde.[29] One of the members of the Art Group was Constantine Parthenis (1878–1967), a particularly imaginative and talented painter, profoundly influenced by impressionism and already experimenting with forms of abstraction. Parthenis turned out to become the exponent of Venizelist ideas in the realm of the visual arts. He was particularly inspired by the dynamism of the Venizelist programme, which combined reform with active pursuit of national goals. This vision found expression in Parthenis' artistic parallel between the age of Pericles and the age of Venizelos, in a work exhibited in Paris in 1919, and again in his big retrospective show at Zappeion in Athens in January 1920. The exhibition was the occasion of a rally of Venizelist politicians and intellectuals and in March Venizelos awarded the National Prize for Excellence in Arts and Letters to Parthenis.[30]

When Venizelos returned to active politics and to the premiership in 1928 Parthenis was once again enlisted to provide artistic expression for liberalism. In 1930, under Venizelos' personal supervision, the seat of the Greek parliament was moved to the former royal palace and Parthenis was charged to decorate the parliament assembly hall with a 'democracy frieze', but unfortunately the project was never executed. Venizelos' last premiership was marked by a policy of encouragement and munificence toward the arts, carried out by the secretary of state for education, George Papandreou. The liberals planned to build a 'palace of the arts' and sought to find an appropriate piece of land for a new National Gallery building. The arts policy of the liberals was executed by Zacharias Papantoniou, a distinguished writer and art critic, who had been appointed director of the National Gallery by the Venizelos government in 1918. Papantoniou remained in his position until 1940 and in the period 1928 to 1932 he acted as an intermediary between the government and the art world, securing support for the work of painters, contributing to the renewal of the School of Fine Arts with a new law in 1929 (law 4366/1929, 11 July) and enriching the collections of the National Gallery. His most remarkable purchase, for which he enlisted Venizelos' personal approval, was the 'Concert of the Angels' by El Greco, which was secured for the National Gallery at an auction in Munich in 1931.[31]

All these measures in support of the arts were certainly an integral component of the logic of modernisation that formed the basic philosophy of Venizelism. They, nevertheless, represented quite a novelty for Greek public life. This explains the acclaim with which Venizelos was hailed by Greek intellectuals and artists, including some of the most distinguished personalities in Greek cultural life at his time, such as the national bard Costis Palamas[32] and other well-known poets including George Drosinis[33] and Sotiris Skipis.[34]

NOTES

1. P. S. Delta (1978), *Eleftherios K. Venizelos*, ed. P. A. Zannas, Athens, p. 10.
2. In 1917 Venizelos had already a good library of classical and modern authors in his house in Athens, on Lykavittou Street. The library followed him in his subsequent peregrinations and was greatly expanded during his residence in Paris in the 1920s, when he was working on his translation of Thucydides. The library was finally relocated in specially furnished quarters in the basement of the neo-classical mansion built by Madame Helena Venizelos, the president's second wife, on Loukianou Street in Athens, in 1932. After Venizelos' death the library was sent to Crete and housed in the family home in Chalepa, the beautiful suburb of Chania. The house was requisitioned by Nazi military forces during the German occupation of Crete in 1941 to 1944 and the books were thrown onto the street outside the house, to make space for military personnel. They were rescued by the young Cretan scholar N. B. Tomadakis, subsequently professor of Byzantine literature at the University of Athens. Tomadakis deposited the books in the municipal library of Chania, where the Venizelos library is still housed.
3. Michael Llewellyn Smith (1998), *The British Embassy Athens*, Athens, p. 26.
4. E.g. Hippolyte Taine (1909), *Les origines de la France contemporaine*, Paris; Charles Seignobos (1924–6), *Histoire politique de l'Europe contemporaine*, Paris; Ernest Lavisse (1922–5), *Histoire générale du IVe siècle à nos jours*, Paris; F. V. A. Aulard (1913), *Histoire de la Révolution française*, Paris; Venizelos' French books include two works by Maurice Barrès, personally presented in 1917 to the president by the author, with warm dedicatory notes. These were *Les diverses familles spirituelles de la France* (Paris, 1917) and *Le voyage de Sparte*, Paris (n.d.). See L. G. Manolikakis (1964), *Eleftheriou K. Venizelou mnimi. Aphieroseis sto Venizelo* [*Remembrance of Eleftherios K. Venizelos. Dedications to Venizelos*], Chania, p. 242.

5. E.g. Thomas Carlyle (1917), *The French Revolution. A History*, London; Arnold Toynbee (1916), *The New Europe: Some Essays in Reconstruction*, London; G. M. Trevelyan (1922), *History of Britain in the Nineteenth Century*, London.
6. J. Marriott (1918), *The Eastern Question. A Historical Study in European Diplomacy*, Oxford.
7. John Morley (1903), *The Life of Gladstone*, London.
8. François Guizot's works in Venizelos' library include the following titles: *Histoire de la civilisation en Europe* (Paris, 1872); *Mémoires pour servir à l'histoire de mon temps* (Paris, 1858–67); *De la démocratie en France* (Paris, 1849); *Essais sur l'histoire de France* (Paris, 1868) and so on.
9. G. P. Gooch (1959), *History and Historians in the Nineteenth Century*, Boston 1959, pp. 178–96. For a more up-to-date approach cf. Jean Walch (1986), *Les maitres de l'histoire 1815–1850*, Paris and Ceri Crossley (1993), *French Historians and Romanticism*, London and New York.
10. See especially Venizelos' article in *Eleftheron Vima*, 12–13 December 1926, which prefaced the publication of his translation of Pericles' funeral oration. This was the first public presentation of his work on Thucydides. The views expressed by Venizelos provoked the vehement reaction of one of his great admirers, Greece's former ambassador to London the bibliophile John Gennadios, who replied with a hostile article in *Proia*, 23 June 1927.
11. On Venizelos' position on the language question see the comprehensive appraisal by Emmanuel Kriaras (1982), 'O Eleftherios Venizelos kai i dimotiki glossa' ['Eleftherios Venizelos and the Vernacular'], *Praktika tis Akadimias Athinon* 57, pp. 547–71; Kriaras (1986), *Prosopa kai themata apo tin istoria tou dimotikismou* [*Persons and Themes from the History of Demoticism*], vol. I, Athens, pp. 179–206. On the translation of Thucydides see esp. pp. 192–5. See also C. A. Papachristos (1952), 'O Eleftherios Venizelos kai i metaphrasi tou Thoukydidou' ['Eleftherios Venizelos and the Translation of Thucydides'], *Paideia kai zoi* (March–April), pp. 117–23, 154–60. For an interesting comparison of two famous modern Greek renderings of Thucydides see Daniel P. Tompkins (1978), 'Reciprocities between a Text and Two Translations: Thucydides, Venizelos and Kakridis', *Journal of the Hellenic Diaspora* 5(1) (Spring), pp. 69–79.
12. Spyridon Trikoupis (1860), *Istoria tis Ellinikis Epanastaseos* [*History of the Greek Revolution*], 2nd edn, London, vol. I, pp. xi–xii.
13. Ibid., pp. xiii–xv.
14. Cf. Francis M. Cornford (1907), *Thucydides Mythistoricus*, London. Reprinted Philadelphia, 1971.
15. Andreas Michalopoulos (1957), in *Thoukydidou Istoriai*, trans. El. Venizelos, ed. by S. I. Stephanou and C. D. Stergiopoulos, Athens, pp. xxxi–xxxii.
16. Ibid.
17. Evi Zachariadou-Holmber (1991), *Scholia Eleftheriou Venizelou stin*

istoria . . . tou Thoukydidi [*Eleftherios Venizelos' Commentaries on the History . . . of Thucydides*], Athens. This is a remarkable work, the product of great labour transcribing Venizelos' hand-written comments from his notebooks. By the same author see also *Lessons Unlearned. Thucydides and Venizelos on Propaganda and the Struggle for Power* (Minneapolis, 2003).

18. E. K. Venizelos (1927), 'Diorthosis eis chorion Thoukydidi A, 112, 4 *λιμοῦ γενομένου*' ['An Emendation to a Passage in Thucydides A, 112, 4'], *Athina* 39, pp. 3–5.
19. Benaki Museum Historical Archives, No. 173/273. Obviously Venizelos had been at work on Thucydides for much longer (since at least 1921) but when he wrote to Hadjidakis he could have been referring primarily to his commentary on books I–IV.
20. M. I. Manousakas (1980), 'Anekdota grammata tou Eleftheriou Venizelou ston Hubert Pernot (1920–1928)' ['Unpublished Letters by Eleftherios Venizelos to Hubert Pernot'], in Odysseas Dimitracopoulos and Thanos Veremis (eds) (1980), *Meletimata gyro apo ton Venizelo kai tin epochi tou* [*Studies on Venizelos and his Time*], Athens, pp. 641–51, esp. pp. 646–7. Apparently Venizelos was referring to the work *Thucydide. Histoire de la guerre de Peloponnèse. Texte grec avec un commentaire critique*, by Alfred Croiset (Paris, 1886). As noted by the editor of the letter, M. I. Manousakas, the second book which Venizelos mentions only by its title, *Essais sur Thucydide*, was not by Croiset but by Jules Girard and had been published in Paris in 1884.
21. Benaki Museum Historical Archives, No. 173/264.
22. D. Caclamanos (ed.) (1940), *Θουκυδίδου Ιστορίαι κατά μετάφρασιν Ελευθερίου Βενιζέλου*, Oxford, vol. I, pp. vii–xix. The work was reprinted photographically in 1946.
23. Ibid., p. xii.
24. Reviews of the work appeared in *The Classical Review* 56 (1942), pp. 29–31 (A. Gomme); *Revue des Etudes Grecques* 43 (1941), p. 285 (Polymnia Lascaris); and *The Journal of Hellenic Studies* 63 (1943), p. 137.
25. *Θουκυδίδου Ιστορίαι κατά μετάφρασιν Ελευθερίου Βενιζέλου*, vol. II, p. iv (see Note 22).
26. Benaki Museum Historical Archives, No. 173/274/1927.
27. P. S. Delta, *Eleftherios Venizelos*, pp. 341–8 (see Note 1). The opposition press reacted unkindly to this expression of Venizelos' personal cultural interests and many ironic comments were published in anti-Venizelist newspapers, which overlooked the fact that Venizelos' démarche was kept completely private.
28. On Venizelos' ties with the Greek artistic world see the comprehensive survey by Aik. Patsouma (2005), 'O El. Venizelos kai i neoelliniki techni' ['Eleftherios Venizelos and Modern Greek Art'], Conference Proceedings: *Eleftherios Venizelos kai elliniki poli* [*Eleftherios Venizelos and the Greek*

Town], Athens, pp. 325–33. My remarks are indebted to this study. I am grateful to Dr Patsouma for making available to me a pre-publication draft of her article.

29. For more details see K. Perpinioti (1994), 'Omada technis' ['Art Group'], in D. Pavlopoulos (ed.), *Se anazitisi tis ellinikotitas. I 'Genia tou '30'* [*In Search of Greekness. The 'Generation of '30'*], Athens, pp. 63–6; and A. Kotidis (2000), *Constantinos Maleas*, Athens, pp. 105–21. Of special interest is the personal testimony of a member of the 'Art Group', the painter Pericles Vyzantios (1963), 'Prin apo miso aiona' ['Half a Century Ago'], *Zygos* 90 (May), pp. 19–20. I am grateful to Dr Marilena Kassimati, curator of the National Gallery of Greece for her help during my research on Venizelos' ties with the world of the arts.
30. For general appraisals of Parthenis' art and its ideological significance see Z. Papantoniou (1966), *Kritika*, Athens, pp. 77–92 (reprinting a review of Parthenis' 1920 show) and Alexander Xydis (1976), *Protaseis gia tin istoria tis neoellinikis technis* [*Propositions for a History of modern Greek Art*], Athens, vol. I, pp. 70–84.
31. For details see E. Mathiopoulos (1994), 'Enas Greco tin epochi tou Venizelou' ['An El Greco in Venizelos' Age'], *To Vima*, 18 September, p. C18.
32. Palamas expressed profusely his admiration for the president in the dedications he wrote in the presentation copies of his books, which survive in Venizelos' library. See Manolikakis, *Eleftheriou Venizelou mnimi*, pp. 154–5 (see Note 4).
33. Ibid., p. 68.
34. Ibid., pp. 191–2.

Contributors

Christine Agriantoni, Ph.D., University of Paris – X (Nanterre); professor of history, University of Thessaly

Alexis Dimaras, Ph.D., University of London, educational historian

Helen Gardikas-Katsiadakis, Ph.D., King's College, University of London; director of research, Centre for the Study of Modern Greek History, Academy of Athens

Leonidas Kallivretakis, Ph.D., University of Paris – IV (Sorbonne); director of research, Institute for Neo-Hellenic Research, National Hellenic Research Foundation

Paschalis M. Kitromilides, Ph.D., Harvard University; professor of political science, University of Athens; and director, Institute for Neo-Hellenic Research, National Hellenic Research Foundation

Ioannis Koliopoulos, Ph.D., University of London; professor of modern history, University of Thessaloniki

Michael Llewellyn Smith, D.Phil., University of Oxford; former British ambassador in Warsaw and Athens

A. Lilly Macrakis, Ph.D., Harvard University; dean, Hellenic College, Brookline, Massachusetts

Andreas Nanakis, metropolitan of Arkalochori, Castelli and Viannos, Church of Crete, Th.D., University of Thessaloniki; professor of ecclesiastical history, University of Thessaloniki

Ioannis D. Stefanidis, Ph.D., The London School of Economics and Political Science; associate professor of diplomatic history, School of Law, University of Thessaloniki

Ioannis Tassopoulos, Ll.D., Duke University; associate professor of constitutional law, University of Athens

Thanos Veremis, D.Phil., University of Oxford; professor of political history, University of Athens

Index

Abdul Hamid II, 23
Academy of Athens, 341
Adalia, 164
Adrianople, 97, 164
Adriatic, 148
Aegean, 4, 38, 109, 110, 116, 121, 142, 152, 153, 158, 160, 163, 165, 183, 190, 217, 220, 222, 224
Aegean Islands, 110, 121, 124, 125, 131, 142, 146, 150, 151, 171, 356, 359
Aeschylus, 342n30
Aghia Kyriaki, 18, 19
Aghia Triada monastery, 351
Aghioi Anargyroi, 40
Agrarian Party, 214, 215, 308
Agricultural Bank, 202, 203, 204, 300, 304, 345
Agronomy School, 319
Ahmet Zog, King of Albania, 217
Akropolis, newpaper, 44, 83, 111
Akrotiri, 58, 59, 60, 61, 62, 63, 64, 65, 71, 82, 246, 347, 348
Alambra Theatre, 383
Alastos, Doros, 2, 59, 118, 120
Albania, 12, 13, 146, 150, 151, 152, 158, 160, 163, 177, 186, 217, 220, 225, 239
Alexander, Crown Prince of Serbia, later King Alexander I of Yugoslavia, 147, 157, 218
Alexander, King of Greece, 126, 128, 129, 130, 131, 185, 262, 263
Alexander of Battenberg, 179n12
Alexandria, 12
  Patriarchate of, 352, 361, 366, 367, 369, 371
Alexandris, Apostolos, 98, 137, 320, 327, 341n23
Alexandroupolis, 224
Ali Pasha, Ottoman vizier, 21
Alivizatos, N., 251, 260, 263
Amari, 15
America, 20, 63, 113, 128, 136, 160, 161, 162, 163, 169, 178, 203, 219, 253, 267, 292, 303, 317, 366, 380
American Foundation Company, 203
Anastasakis, I., 35
Anatolia, 4, 128, 160, 162, 164, 166, 170, 184, 209, 211; *see also* Asia Minor
Anchialos, 361
Andreadis, Andreas, 44, 290, 291
Androutsos, Christos, 363, 372
Anglo-Hellenic League, 176
Ankara, 165, 168, 198, 210, 219, 220, 222
Anoteron Dimotikon Parthenagogion of Volos, 322, 324, 329
Anthimos, bishop of Maroneia, 370n43
Anthopoulos, Kostakis Pasha, 24
Antoniadis Lykeion, 41, 306
Apokoronas, 20, 23, 29, 30, 55, 57
Aptera, newspaper, 347, 369
Arabia, 12, 362
Arathi, 62
Aravantinos, P., 285
Arc de Triomphe, 127
Archanes, 66, 67, 82
Archimedes, 379
Argostoli, 148, 149
Argyrokastro, 150, 151, 163
Argyropoulos, Periklis, 123, 137, 281
Aristotle, 50, 115, 265
Arkadi, 348
Armenia, 58, 60, 61, 157, 158, 159, 160, 164, 178
Armenoi, 66, 349

Armstrong-Vickers shipyard, 151
Arsenios, bishop of Larissa, 359, 367
Arta, 24, 131
Art Group, 384
Asia, 110
Asia Minor, 4, 125, 130, 131, 135, 139, 141, 146, 150, 151, 152, 153, 154, 155, 156, 157–72, 173, 174, 176, 177, 183, 184, 185, 186, 187, 188, 189, 192, 204, 211, 222, 263, 274, 277, 280, 287, 296, 301, 313, 357, 363–5, 380, 383; *see also* Anatolia
Askyphou, 19
Aspreas, G., 99
Asquith, H. H., 148
Asty, newpaper, 73, 83
Atalanti, 127
Athens, 1, 19, 22, 23, 26, 35, 38, 41, 42, 43, 44, 45, 46, 47, 51, 55, 57, 61, 62, 66, 67, 72, 73, 74, 75, 76, 78, 87, 88, 89, 90, 91, 92, 94, 95, 96, 97, 99, 100, 101, 102, 105, 107, 108, 109, 112, 113, 115, 117, 121, 122, 123, 124, 125, 126, 127, 129, 131, 132, 135, 136, 138, 144, 146, 147, 149, 150, 153, 157, 158, 164, 166, 167, 169, 170, 171, 206, 210, 212, 219, 224, 225, 232, 234, 235, 239, 241, 242, 243, 246, 254, 255, 257, 262, 277, 284, 287, 294, 295, 306, 307, 308, 309, 311, 313, 314, 315, 316, 317, 322, 324, 325, 329, 330, 332, 334, 340, 341, 345, 347, 349, 352, 353, 354, 355, 356, 357, 358, 359, 361, 362, 363, 364, 365, 367, 370, 371, 377, 378, 380, 383, 385
Athos, 366, 368
Attica, 95, 96
Aulard, Alphonse, 378
Austria, 12, 116, 120, 140, 143, 147, 148, 152, 153, 181
Austria-Hungary, 116, 155
Averoff Farm School, 288
Avraam, N., 70
Axomi, 371
Aydin, 158
Balkans, 4, 22, 35, 41, 87, 107, 108, 111, 116, 117, 120, 122, 134, 135, 139, 140, 143, 144, 146, 147, 148, 149, 151, 152, 154, 155, 173, 174, 179, 183, 184, 211, 219, 222, 223–5, 238, 239, 242, 253, 260, 262, 277, 291, 352, 356, 357, 361, 363, 378
Balkan Wars, 116, 135, 145–7, 151–2, 277, 354, 355
Bank for International Settlements, 207
Bank of Athens, 317
Bank of France, 293
Bank of Greece, 201–2, 206–8, 300, 316n111
Barrès, Maurice, 385
Basil, Patriarch of Constantinople, 357
Bavaria, 364
Belgian constitution, 256
Belgrade, 217, 218, 222, 224, 232
Benaki Museum, 181, 189, 190, 387
Benakis, Emmanuel, 95, 100, 102, 288
Benghazi, 34
Bentinck, Sir Charles, 189n103
Berlin, 24
Berne, 137
Biliotti, Alfred, 57, 81n59, 82n79
Bismarck, Otto von, 234
Black Sea, 209
Blanc, Paul, 81n64
Boeotia, 95, 96, 203
Bolsheviks, 160, 299
Bonar, A., 294, 310
Bosnia-Herzegovina, 22, 76, 140
Boulogne, 164
Bourchier, James, 73, 143, 144, 145, 181n23, 182n27
Boutsounaria, 27
Bratianu, Ioan, 5, 6, 7
Briand, Aristide, 218, 225
Brindisi, 246
Britain, 12, 17, 31, 35, 44, 61, 72, 78, 81, 92, 109, 116, 117, 120, 123, 124, 125, 126, 128, 129, 136, 138, 142, 147, 148, 149, 151, 152, 153, 155, 156, 157, 160, 161, 162, 163, 164, 165, 167, 168, 169, 170, 171, 175, 176, 178, 179, 180, 183, 187,

Britain (*cont.*)
190, 191, 198, 201, 202, 203, 204, 205, 207, 208, 216, 217, 219, 221, 224, 238, 239, 240, 241, 242, 243, 253, 263, 291, 293, 294, 295, 296, 298, 306, 311, 312, 316, 317
British Museum, 382
Bucharest, 137, 144, 146, 147, 149, 150, 223, 225
Bulgaria, 60, 88, 116, 117, 120, 122, 124, 126, 127, 140, 143, 144, 145, 146, 147, 149, 152–5, 157, 158, 159, 163, 176, 179, 181, 182, 184, 216, 217, 219, 220, 224, 225, 238, 239, 275, 302, 317, 358, 361
Bulletin of the Education League, 331, 343
Bulletin of the Education Ministry, 331
Burke, Edmund, 253
Burrows, Ronald, 138, 176, 179n6, 192n122
Bursa, 164
Butler, 144
Byzantium, Byzantine civilization, 48, 322, 360, 385n2

Caclamanos, Dimitrios, 80, 83, 137, 382
Cairo, 12, 352
California, 380
Canevaro, Admiral F. N., 66
Capodistrias, 343n34
Carlyle, Thomas, 378
Cavour, 234
Centre for Asia Minor Studies, 383
Cephalonia, 148
Chairopoulos, editor, 89
Chalepa, 24, 26, 28, 29, 30, 38, 42, 48, 51, 52, 53, 57, 58, 62, 91, 99, 280, 385n2
Chalikoutides, 34
Chalis, Vasilios, 38
Chalki School of Theology, 78, 348, 363
Chalkokondylis, Ioannis, 94
Chamberlain, Joseph, 35, 44, 52, 78
Chania, 12, 15, 16, 18, 19, 20, 23, 24, 27, 33, 35, 37, 38, 39, 40, 42, 43, 45, 48, 49, 54, 56, 58, 59, 60, 61, 62, 64, 65, 66, 67, 68, 71, 73, 76, 78, 79, 80, 87, 88, 90, 94, 95, 96, 98, 124, 140, 180, 193, 246, 315, 346, 347, 351, 377, 383, 385n2
Charalambis, A., 277
Charilaos, Epameinondas, 310, 318
Chatalja, 164
Chester, S. B., 61
Chimarra, 150
Chios, 124, 131, 150, 159
Chronos, newspaper, 89
Chrysanthos, metropolitan of Trebizond, 370n43
Chrysanthos, bishop of Rethymnon, 350
Chrysostomos [Papadopoulos], archbishop of Athens, 353, 361, 370
Churchill, Winston, 148, 151, 187, 313
Cilicia, 164
Circassians, 34
Clausse, Roger, 293
Clemenceau, Georges, 35, 160, 162
Commercial School of Athens, 319
Communist Party of Greece [KKE], 200, 211, 274, 275, 277, 314, 334, 341n20
Constantine VI, Patriarch of Constantinople, 357
Constantine, King of Greece, 76, 109, 113, 115, 116, 117, 118, 119, 120, 121, 123, 124, 125, 126, 128, 129, 130, 136, 138, 142, 146, 147, 149, 152, 153, 155, 156, 157, 166, 167, 168, 169, 173, 174, 177, 180, 185, 189, 240, 241, 260, 261, 263, 277, 312, 346, 352, 354, 360, 364, 367, 368
Constantinople, 12, 17, 18, 22, 28, 29, 44, 58, 97, 98, 127, 139, 140, 157, 160, 163, 164, 165, 168, 169, 172, 186, 187, 188, 189, 190, 220, 346, 353, 355, 356, 361, 362, 363, 364, 365, 366, 372; *see also* Istanbul
Constantinos, deacon, 370
Corfu, 100, 121, 163, 216
Corinth canal, 246
Costis, Costas, 205, 313n79

Cotton Institute, 203
Crete, 2, 4, 5, 11, 12, 13, 14, 15, 16, 17, 18, 19, 20, 21, 22, 23, 24, 25, 26, 27, 28, 29, 30, 31, 33, 35, 36, 37, 38, 39, 40, 41, 42, 43, 44, 45, 46, 47, 48, 49, 50, 51, 52, 53, 55, 56, 57, 58, 60, 61, 62, 63, 64, 65, 66, 67, 68, 69, 70, 71, 72, 73, 74, 75, 76, 78, 79, 81, 82, 83, 87, 88, 89, 90, 91, 93, 95, 96, 98, 99, 101, 107, 108, 110, 118, 121, 125, 127, 129, 131, 134, 135, 140, 141, 142, 144, 145, 146, 150, 166, 174, 181, 182, 192, 193, 195, 210, 212, 214, 216, 219, 221, 223, 241, 242, 246, 253, 254, 274, 278, 346, 347, 349, 350, 351, 352, 354, 356, 359, 361, 366, 368, 369, 370, 383, 385
Crimean War, 17
Croiset, Alfred, 381, 387
Crowe, Eyre, 189
Cuba, 380
Curzon, Lord, 167, 171, 172, 190
Cyclades, 125
Cyprus, 2, 139, 148, 149, 155, 160, 161, 163, 165, 171, 187n79, 190n108, 219, 352, 360, 361, 362, 367, 371n61

Dakin, Douglas, 181n24
Damianos, Patriarch of Jerusalem, 353, 361, 362
Danglis, Gen. Panayotis, 123, 124, 127, 168, 189, 277, 358
Daphnis, G., 215, 264
Dardanelles, 110, 117, 119, 155
Dartige du Fournet, Admiral, 125
Daskaloyannis *see* Diyenakis, C.
De Billy, 285, 307, 311, 314
De Chalendar, 315
De Noailles, Comtesse, 35
Delcassé, Th., 81
Delmouzos, Alexandros, 320, 322, 323, 324, 326, 330, 332, 333, 334, 335, 337, 340n20, 343n35
Delta, Penelope, 138, 197, 383
Demertzis, Constantinos, 137, 246
Demestichas, 281
Denikin, Gen. A. I., 160
Diamantidis, Dimitrios, 288
Diamesis, Ilias, 278
Diliyannis, Theodoros, 30, 89, 115, 117, 270
Dimitrakopoulos, N., 98
Dingas, Dimitrios, 230, 320, 330, 339n7
Dingas, I., 359
Diomidis, Alexandros, 137, 201, 206, 290, 297, 305, 309, 316
Dionysios, metropolitan of Mythimna, 370n43
Dionysios, bishop of Zakynthos, 362
Dionysios, bishop of Rethymnon, 348, 349, 350, 351, 366
Diyenakis, Constantinos (Daskaloyannis), 37
Dobrudja, 223
Dodecanese, 158, 159, 160, 162, 163, 165, 171, 177, 217, 219, 242, 368
Dorotheos, bishop of Kissamos, 349, 350, 369
Dousmanis, Victor, 277
Dragoumis, Ion, 129–30, 140, 173, 326
Dragoumis, Stephanos, 52, 81, 94, 100, 102, 104, 108, 110, 111, 120, 141, 144, 288, 291
Drosinis, George, 385
Drosopoulos, Ioannis, 310

East, 14, 44, 54, 98, 153
Eastern, Rumelia, 76
Ecumenical Patriarchate, 158, 355, 356–7, 358, 368
Eftaxias, Athanasios, 290, 291
Eftaxias, Ioannis, 291, 292, 297, 310, 313
Egypt, 11, 12, 13, 17, 31, 34, 187, 352
Ekpaideftikos Omilos (Education League), 325, 327, 329, 334, 335, 341
El Greco, 385
Eleftheros Typos, newspaper, 313
Eleftheron Vima, newspaper, 302, 315, 318, 386
ELIA, 181

Elliot, Sir Francis, 132, 153
Embeiricos, E., 310
Embeiricos, L., 314
Embros, newspaper, 83
Emmanouilidis, Emmanouil, 230
England, 1, 2, 148, 168, 170, 185, 344
Entente, 117, 119, 121, 122, 123, 125, 127, 128, 129, 135, 148, 151, 152, 153, 154, 155, 157, 159, 174, 176, 180, 181, 260, 293, 352, 361, 364, 367
Epirus, 15, 116, 131, 146, 149, 150, 151, 152, 158, 159, 160, 162, 163, 165, 166, 173, 176, 186, 199, 203, 356, 359, 383
Ermoupolis, 40
Estia, newspaper, 73, 95
Eton, 181
Euphrates, 12
Europe, 2, 5, 6, 12, 17, 19, 20, 30, 59, 61, 63, 64, 65, 88, 95, 97, 116, 134, 135, 136, 142, 143, 144, 146, 151, 155, 158, 164, 170, 181, 188, 191, 192, 205, 208, 216, 217, 220, 223, 224, 225, 284, 287, 296, 302, 315, 348, 364, 377, 378, 380, 382
Evmenios [Xiroudakis], bishop of Lampi and Sphakia, later archbishop of Crete, 349, 350, 353, 352, 356
Evzones, 127
Exarchopoulos, Nikolaos, 326, 327, 331, 341n21
Eydoux, Gen., 108, 109, 142

Ferdinand, King of Bulgaria, 144
Firkas, 76
Fiume, 161, 177
Florence, 150
Foumis, Costis, 26, 39, 40, 45, 49, 53, 55, 62, 63, 65, 66, 70, 79, 81, 382
Foumis, M., 78, 81, 83
France, 17, 35, 51, 72, 73, 92, 108, 109, 116, 120, 121, 123, 124, 125, 126, 128, 129, 131, 138, 141, 142, 147, 148, 149, 152, 156, 157, 159, 160, 162, 163, 164, 167, 175, 171, 176, 178, 180, 185, 186, 207, 216, 217, 218, 225, 242, 246, 253, 263, 285, 291, 293, 294, 295, 296, 308, 310, 311, 312, 313, 315, 316, 317, 318, 377, 383, 384
French Academy of Moral and Political Sciences, 50
Fres, 23

Gallipoli, 260, 261
Gare de Lyon, 129
Gavriilidis, Vlassis, 83
Gedeon, Manuel, 77
Geheeb, Paul, 345n54
Geneva, 201, 202, 223, 300, 315
Gennadios, John (Eothen), 83, 386
Gennadios, metropolitan of Thessaloniki, 355, 370n43
George I, King of Greece, 89, 91, 92, 93, 94, 95, 98, 110, 115, 116, 118, 131, 134, 139, 142, 144, 147, 181, 282
George, Crown Prince, later George II, King of Greece, 126, 157, 167, 236, 243, 244, 245, 246, 254, 255, 256, 281, 282
George, Prince of Greece, High Commissioner of Crete, 47, 48, 68, 69, 70, 72, 73, 74, 75, 79, 82, 91, 95, 131, 134, 346, 349, 350, 351, 353, 366
Germanos, metropolitan of Chalcedon, later Germanos V, Patriarch of Constantinople, 364
Germanos [Karavangelis], metropolitan of Kastoria, later of Amaseia, 365
Germanos [Mavromatis], bishop of Dimitrias, 323, 333
Germany, 45, 109, 116, 122, 125, 126, 127, 141, 142, 144, 147, 149, 153, 157, 173, 178, 186, 296, 317, 323, 341, 342, 343, 344, 345, 354, 385
Gevgelija, 218
Gibbons, H. A., 59
Girard, Jules, 387
Gladstone, William, 181, 187, 378
Glinos, Dimitris, 320, 326, 327, 330, 332, 334, 335, 340, 342, 344

Glucksberg dynasty, 156
Gonatas, Col. Stylianos, 195, 212, 213, 276, 345
Gontikas, Constantinos, 198, 320, 335, 339n7, 345n51
Gooch, G. P., 378
Gospel, translation of, 342n30
Goudi, 108, 139, 144, 212, 254, 322, 324, 326, 329, 353, 354
Gounaris, Dimitrios, 118, 119, 120, 130, 168, 169, 260, 261, 280
Government Gazette, 357, 366
Gramsci, A., 252
Gramvousa, 11, 13
Great Idea [Megali Idea], 87, 135, 140, 152, 169, 172, 211, 266n2, 287
Great Powers, 12, 17, 19, 20, 28, 30, 33, 39, 52, 56, 58, 59, 60, 61, 62, 63, 64, 65, 66, 67, 68, 69, 70, 71, 72, 73, 74, 75, 76, 87, 88, 97, 107, 116, 117, 118, 122, 130, 134, 135, 138, 140, 145, 146, 147, 149, 150, 151, 152, 155, 157, 160, 168, 170, 174, 175, 177, 178, 181, 188, 216, 220, 224, 238, 239, 262, 263, 294, 301, 329, 361, 365, 367
Greater Greece, 172
Gregory VII, Patriarch of Constantinople, 357
Grey, Sir Edward, 148, 149, 150, 151, 153, 154, 155, 179
Grigoriadis, Gen. Neokosmos, 123, 278
Grogan, Lady, 182
Gryparis, Ioannis, 52, 54, 55, 81, 98, 107, 137, 143, 144, 182
Gueshov, 144, 146
Guizot, François, 378, 386

Habsburg Empire, 127
Hadjianestis, Gen. G., 280
Hadjikyriakos, Andreas, 304
Hadjidakis, Georgios, 329, 342n29, 380, 387
Hague Conference, 207, 219, 302, 316
Hakki Pasha, vizier, 97
Hambros Bank, 317n126
Hanotaux, 81n68
Hatzikyriakos, Admiral A., 277
Henderson, A., 232
Henderson, N., 232
Henry Boot and Sons, 203
Herbart, Johann, 342n33
Hobbes, 265
Holland, Robert, 83n92
Holy Sepulchre, 353, 361, 372
Hoover moratorium, 317
Hoover Plan, 225
Hungary, 302
Husein Pasha, 145
Hydra, 131

Iakovos, metropolitan of Mytilene, 370n43
Iakovos, Vatopedinos, 361
Iasonidis, Leonidas, 230
Ibrahim Pasha, 11
Idionymon, 199, 264, 305
Ikaria, 159
Iliakis, Yangos, 47
Imbros, 151, 159, 165, 171
Imerologion Akrotiriou, 62, 81
Imia/Kardak, 190
IMRO [Internal Macedonian Revolutionary Organization], 223, 224
Imvrioti, Roza, 344
International Financial Commission, 207
Ioakeim, bishop of Nikopolis, 356
Ioakeim, Archimandrite, 353, 370
Ioannina, 97, 355, 370
Ionian Sea, 109
Ionian Islands, 125, 190, 368
Iorga, Nicola, 7n5
Ippolytos, Archimandrite, 353, 370n28
Irakleion, 15, 65, 66, 68
Islam, 13, 14
Ismail Hakim Pasha, 15, 18, 19
Ismet Pasa, 221
Ismid, 164
Istanbul, 220; *see also* Constantinople
Italy, 71, 72, 95, 142, 148, 150, 153, 156, 157, 158, 160, 162, 163, 164, 171, 177, 188, 207, 216, 217, 218, 219, 221, 238, 239, 240, 242
Izmir, 186; *see also* Smyrna

Japan, 205
Jerusalem, Patriarchate of, 352–3, 361, 369, 370, 372
Jews, Jewish, 160, 236
Joachim III, Patriarch of Constantinople, 140, 349, 350, 352, 364

Kafantaris, Georgios, 137, 193, 195, 196, 197, 201, 202, 212, 214, 224, 225, 297, 300, 313, 315, 318
Kairoi, newspaper, 44, 73, 83
Kakouris, A., 35
Kakouros, Evangelos, 337, 345n54
Kakridis, I. Th., 378
Kalapothakis, 83
Kalfov, 223
Kallaris, Gen. K., 125
Kalogeropoulos, N., 130
Kalomoiris, Manolis, 383
Kamboi, 57, 59, 60
Kammenos, Dimitrios, 280
Kanellidis, 44
Kanellopoulos, 171
Kapsalis, Ioannis, 44, 77
Karamanlis, Constantine, 234
Karapanayiotis, Byron, 213
Karapanos, Alexandros, 195
Karatheodori, Alexandros (Pasha), 24, 29, 30, 57
Karavangelis, Germanos *see* Germanos [Karavangelis]
Kassimati, Marilena, 388n29
Kastellorizo, 158, 159
Kastoria, 230
Kastrinakis, Dionysios *see* Dionysios, bishop of Rethymnon
Katelouzos, Sophoklis, Elefteriou, 45, 46
Katelouzou, Maria, Elefteriou, 45, 46, 56
Kathimerini, newspaper, 280
Kavalla, 147, 150, 154
Kelaidis, Parthenios, 351
Kemal, Mustafa (Ataturk), 6, 161, 162, 164, 165, 167, 169, 176, 190, 220, 221, 366
Kerofilas, C., 59
Kerr, Philip, 167, 168, 180, 189
Kerschensteiner, Georg, 345n54
Keynes, John Maynard, 294, 295, 296, 311n66–7, 312n73
Kick, 317
Kifissia, 235
Kilkis, 147
Kimisis, Gen. Miltiadis, 278, 280
King's College, 176
Kiryx, newspaper, 74, 90, 91, 111, 140, 180
Kissamos, 11, 346, 351
Kitromilides, P. M., 266n
KKE *see* Communist Party
Kladakis, Markos, 279
Klima, 57
Klonaris, Dorotheos *see* Dorotheos, bishop of Kissamos
Kokotsis, Dimitris, 381
Kolettis, I., 135
Kolialexis, Andreas, 278, 281
Kolymbari, 62
Kondylis, Col. George, 189n101, 197, 210, 212, 215, 240, 241, 242, 243, 244, 246, 265, 276, 277, 278
Konitsa, 356
Kontaratos, I., 90
Kontoyannis, P., 277
Kopais Lake Company, 203
Koran, 14
Koromilas, L., 98, 110, 137, 141, 143, 144, 147, 149, 150, 153, 181, 184, 196, 290
Korytsa, 150, 151, 163
Koryzis, Alexandros, 304
Kotsabasis, 63, 65
Koumis, 37
Koumoundouros, Alex., 41, 43
Koundouras, Miltos, 337, 345
Koundouriotis, Admiral Pavlos, 110, 124, 126, 195, 197, 358
Koundouros, Manousos, 29, 57, 60, 66, 70, 81
Kourmoulides, 14
Krapi, 29
Kriaris, A., 35
Krimbas, C., 344–5n50
Kurdistan, 164

Kurds, 34
Kydonia, 23, 26, 45, 48, 51, 53, 347
Kyrillos III, archbishop of Cyprus, 190n108
Kyrou, Alexis, 219
Kythira, 20, 39, 40

La Boétie, gallery (Paris), 384
Labour Party of Greece, 314
Lambros Spyridon, 125, 292
Lamia, 127
Language question, 100, 112n27, 322, 327–30, 331, 342n29–30, 378–9
Larentzakis, Antonis, 48
Larissa, 103, 106, 113, 288, 308, 359, 367
Lasithi, 15, 361
Lausanne (Treaty and Convention), 2, 134, 135, 136, 171, 172, 177, 190, 210, 216, 222, 366, 368, 380
Lavisse, Ernest, 378
'Lazarus Parliament', 262
Le Temps, newspaper, 73, 82
League of Nations, 157, 200, 201, 202, 207, 216, 217, 218, 220, 222, 224, 225, 287, 300, 302
Lefeuvre-Meaulle, 310
Lefka Ori, newspaper, 26, 35, 49, 50, 52, 53, 54, 78, 80, 81, 347
Lefkorites, 26, 49, 54, 55
Lekatsas, Th., 310
Lenin, 191
Leon, George, 118; *see also* Leontaritis, George
Leontaritis, George, 175, 185
Lesbos, 131, 150, 159, 213
Levantines, 160
Liberal Club, 112n19, 384
Liberal Party (of Greece), 25, 26, 51, 53, 99, 112, 121, 129, 130, 148, 191, 193, 195, 196, 197, 210, 212, 215, 230, 257, 259, 260, 262, 309, 315, 328, 335, 340, 361, 384
Lilimbakis, 44
Limassol, 371
Limnos, 110, 124
Livadia, 127
Lloyd George, David, 137, 148, 151, 157, 160, 161, 164, 165, 167, 168, 185, 189
Locarno, 216, 219
Logiadis, Emmanuel, 88
London, 2, 12, 108, 137, 146, 147, 148, 149, 156, 157, 164, 165, 166, 176, 177, 179, 183, 201, 206, 217, 218, 219, 243, 294, 295, 298, 301, 311, 315, 317, 380, 381, 386
Louis of Battenberg, Prince, 148
Loutraki, 48

Macedonia, 60, 87, 89, 108, 116, 120, 121, 122, 123, 124, 125, 126, 127, 128, 140, 141, 143, 144, 145, 146, 147, 149, 152, 154, 156, 157, 159, 166, 172, 173, 181, 184, 200, 203, 209, 218, 223, 224, 245, 275, 287, 301, 304, 306, 314, 356, 358, 359, 361, 364
Mahmud Pasha, 27
Mahmud II, Sultan, 12
Makris, Pafsanias, 304
Malaxa, 58
Manaris, Gabriel, 351
Manchester Guardian, 382
Manettas, Constantinos, 214
Manos, Constantinos, 83n95
Manou, Aspasia, 129
Manousakas, M. I., 387
Maraslio Teacher Training College, 332, 333
Marinkovic, Vojslav, 218, 224
Maris, M. I., 44
Markantonakis, Antonis, 39
Markantonakis, Klearchos, 56, 98, 137
Markantonakis, Spyros, 39
Markoulakis, Ioannis, 39
Marne, 153
Marriott, J., 378
Mavrogordatos, G. Th., 118, 138, 196, 209, 212, 265, 266
Mavromatis, Germanos *see* Germanos [Mavromatis]
Mavromichalis, Kyriakoulis, 89, 91, 92, 100, 354
Maximos, Dimitrios, 238

Mazarakis-Ainian, General Al., 137, 190, 276, 277
Meander valley, 167
Mediterranean, 87, 122, 134, 151, 161, 180, 222, 240, 286
Meletios [Metaxakis], metropolitan of Citium, archbishop of Athens, Patriarch of Constantinople, Patriarch of Alexandria, 189n101, 353, 357, 360, 361–6, 367, 369, 370n28, 371n66, 372n67 and 84
Melidoni, 67, 349
Meliton, Ayiotaphitis, 372
Merlier, Melpo, 383
Metaxakis, Meletios *see* Meletios [Metaxakis]
Metaxas, Gen. Ioannis, 123, 154, 155, 195, 198, 211, 215, 241, 242, 246, 275, 282, 335, 343, 352
Metaxas, P., 369
Methodios, metropolitan of Axomi, 371
Michalakopoulos, A., 126, 127, 137, 195, 196, 216, 219, 223, 288, 295, 298, 383
Michelidakis, Antonios, 88, 94
Mignet, 378
Milissis, G., 343n37
Military League, 89–94, 122, 142, 214, 215, 259, 274
Milonoyannakis, Y., 62, 65
Milos, 38
Minopoulos Theoklitos *see* Theoklitos [Minopoulos]
Minos Association, 38
Missolonghi, 38
Mitsotakis, Constantinos, 23, 26, 35, 49, 62, 79
Mitsotakis, Th., 78, 79
Moatsos, Errikos, 76, 78, 79
Moatsos, Iakovos, 26, 49
Moatsos, Spyros, 46
Mohamed, Ali, 11, 12, 13
Mohammed, 39
Mollov, 224, 225
Monastir, 154, 182
Monemvasia, 37, 354
Monks and Ulen, 203
Monson, 81
Montenegro, 18, 22, 144, 145
Montreal, 311, 313
Morley, John, 378
Moudros [Mudros], 127
Mournies, 16, 37, 38, 39, 43, 77
Mourelos, I., 189n104
Mudania, 190
Munich, 385
Munich School of painting, 384
Muslims, 12, 13, 14, 15, 16, 17, 18, 19, 23, 25, 26, 28, 29, 30, 32, 39, 47, 50, 58, 69, 70, 78, 95, 134, 143, 150, 152, 154, 155, 158, 160, 161, 163, 166, 171, 172, 185, 186, 192, 346, 348, 349
Mussolini, 217, 234
Mustafa Pasha Giritli, 12, 13, 16
Mygiakis, I., 35
Mylonas, Alexandros, 288
Mylopotamos, 14, 15, 67
Mystriotis, Georgios, 329, 341n21, 342n30
Mytilene, 124, 370

Nafplion, 325
Nansen, 171, 190
National Bank of Greece, 44, 110, 141, 201, 202, 204, 206, 208, 288, 291, 293, 300, 304, 305, 309n42, 310n50, 333
National Defence [Ethniki Amyna], 123–7, 274, 275, 277, 358, 366, 367
National Gallery [of Greece], 343, 384, 388
National Schism [Ethnikos Dichasmos], 115, 117–19, 130, 235, 237, 251–2, 256, 257, 260–3, 264, 265, 363, 366
National Teachers' Federation, 335
Nazi, 385
Nea Ephimeris, newspaper, 35, 44, 80
Nea Imera, newspaper, 94
Nea Rhadamanthys, newspaper, 347
Near East, 12
Negrepontis, M., 297, 310, 311, 314
Neimeyer, 302, 316

Neologos Constantinoupoleos, newspaper, 82
Neophytos, bishop of Paramythia, 356
Neuilly, 224
New York, 301, 302
Nice, 166, 167
Nicholas, Prince of Greece, 147
Nicolson, Harold, 5, 185, 187, 191
Nikiphoros, bishop of Kydonia, 347, 368
Nikodimos, Archimadrite, 353, 370n28
Nikolaos, metropolitan of Caesarea, 365
Nikolopoulos, Spyros, 83
Nikopolis, 356
Nirvanas, Pavlos, 339
Northern Epirus, 162, 170
Noumas, periodical, 325

Ochrid, 154
Official Gazette, 276
Olympus mount, 125
Omonia Square, 43
Oresteia, 342n30
Orlando, 162
Othonaios, Gen. Alexandros, 198, 214, 279, 281
Otho, King of Greece, 364
Ottoman Empire, 4, 11, 12, 13, 14, 15, 16, 17, 19, 20, 21, 22, 23, 24, 26, 28, 29, 30, 31, 35, 46, 47, 57, 60, 62, 64, 68, 87, 89, 97, 98, 108, 119, 127, 128, 129, 134, 140, 143, 146, 154, 155, 158, 160, 161, 164, 173, 181, 184, 340, 346, 347, 360, 361
Oxford, 183, 382

Palamas, Costis, 385, 388
Pallis, A. A., 378
Panas, Dimitrios, 137, 144
Panderma, 158
Pangalos, Gen. Theodoros, 90, 198, 207, 217, 218, 219, 263, 277, 281, 130, 216, 276, 278
Papadaki, Anthoula, 79n46
Papadakis, Giorgos, 48, 79
Papadakis, N. K., 369
Papagos, Gen. Alexandros, 245, 246, 282
Papamavros, Michail, 332
Papanastasiou, A., 126, 130, 137, 195, 196, 203, 212, 213, 214, 225, 303, 334
Papandreou, Georgios, 196, 199, 320, 335, 345, 384
Papantoniou, Zacharias, 343n35, 384
Papavasiliou, professor, 78n19
Papayannakis, 74
Papoulas, Gen. A., 125, 189n101, 278, 280
Paraskevopoulos, Gen. Leonidas, 123, 132, 165
Paris, 2, 4, 5, 17, 20, 97, 110, 127, 128, 129, 135, 137, 138, 156, 157, 160, 161, 162, 163, 166, 167, 173, 179, 182, 189, 217, 218, 219, 242, 243, 246, 291, 294, 296, 307, 310, 312, 316, 380, 381, 382, 383, 384, 385
Parthenis, Constantine, 384, 388
Patras, 113, 304, 308, 310, 313, 314
Patris, newspaper, 351
Patsouma, Aik., 388n28
Paul, Crown Prince, later King of Greece, 129, 246
Pearton, M., 180n18
Pediada, 14
Pelion mount, 144
Peloponnese, 11, 102, 127
People's Party, 195, 208, 211, 212, 213, 214, 215; *see also* Popular Party
Pericles, 176, 381, 384, 386
Perides, Parthenios, 349
Pernot, Hubert, 381, 383
Perrot, Georges, 14
Peru, 380
Pervolia, 18
Petra, 348, 350
Petrides, Peter, 383
Petychakis, Minos, 88
Phaliron, 92
Phanar, 355
Photiadis, Ioannis (Pasha), 24
Photiadis, Photis, 322, 326

Photios, Patriarch of Alexandria, 352, 361, 369
Pichon, 307, 311
Piedmont-Sardinia, Kingdom, 17
Piraeus, 107, 112, 125, 314
Pistolakis, N., 62, 65
Pistolakis, Stelios, 79
Plastiras, Gen. Nikolaos, 160, 169, 195, 212, 213, 234, 235, 236, 237, 238, 240, 242, 265, 275, 276, 277, 278, 279, 281, 358, 367
Ploumidaki, Styliani, 37, 38
Ploumidakis, Agathoklis, 38
Ploumidakis, Ioannis, 38
Politis, N., 126, 137, 156, 186, 223, 371
Poloyiorgis, Ch., 26, 49, 53, 88
Polychronopoulos, Ioannis, 235, 280
Polytechnic School, 319
Pontus, 158, 165
Pop, George, 83
Popular Party, 236, 238; *see also* People's Party
Prasas of Lasithi, 361
Prophitis Ilias, 42, 63, 246
Proia, newspaper, 317, 386
Prussia, 12, 17, 65
Psiloritis, 39
Psycharis, Ioannis, 342

Raktivan, Constantinos, 100, 197
Rallis, C., 370n43
Rallis, Dimitrios, 88, 89, 93, 94, 100, 130, 189, 362, 363, 365, 372
Ramsay, 232
Rangabe, Alexandros, 87, 88
Rawls, John, 4, 6
Red Cross, 128
Refugee Settlement Commission, 209
Rein, Wilhelm, 342n33
Reinach, 73
Reineck, A., 63
Renan, Ernest, 159
Renieris, Markos, 44
Repoulis, E., 98, 102, 106, 126, 137, 188, 196, 314
Rethymnon, 15, 786, 346, 348, 349, 350, 351, 366
Reuf Pasha, 22
Rhodes, 159, 163, 165
Romania, 5, 7, 140, 149, 151, 153, 216, 219, 223, 238
Romanos, Athos, 137, 310
Rome, 96, 153, 162, 217, 218, 219, 221, 234
Rupel Fort, 122, 124
Russia, 17, 19, 22, 23, 41, 63, 72, 116, 143, 144, 160, 174, 186, 285, 299
Rüştü, Tevfik, 222

Saint Stephen (Paris), 246
Sakarya, 165
Salisbury, Lord, 81, 82
Samos, 30, 97, 124, 159
San Remo, 164
Santi Quaranta, 150
Saraphis, Gen. Stephanos, 279, 280, 281
Saratsis, Dimitris, 324
Sardinski, Nikolakis (Pasha), 24, 27, 28, 29
Sargent, John, 382
Sarrail, Gen., 122, 124, 156
Savvas, Ioannis (Pasha), 24, 34
Sazonov, 144
Schilizzi, Helena (Madame Venizelos), 148, 169, 183n37, 377, 380, 382, 385n2
Schliemann, Heinrich, 144
Schmitt, Carl, 253
School of Fine Arts, 319, 384
Schrolderer, Victor, 382
Sea of Marmara, 158
Secondary Education Teacher Training College, 326, 327, 328
Seignobos, 378
Selino, 37
Serbia, 22, 60, 116, 120, 121, 123, 143, 144, 145, 147, 149, 151, 152–5, 174, 261
Sergent, 297, 312
Serres, 147
Sèvres (Treaty), 3, 129, 130, 163, 164, 166, 167, 168, 169, 170, 171, 189, 195, 211, 216, 356, 384
Shakir Pasha, 28, 55

Siemens and Halske, 317n125
Sifakas, A., 62, 65
Simon, J., 78
Simos, S., 126
Skanavis, Nikolaos, 279
Skipis, Sotiris, 385
Skouloudis, Stephanos, 94, 120, 121, 122
Slavs, 139, 143, 152, 159, 179, 218, 275
Smith, Sir Michael Llewellyn, 131, 183
Smyrna, 130, 138, 158, 161, 162, 164, 165, 166, 169, 177, 179, 186, 187, 189, 287; *see also* Izmir
Sofia, 143, 144, 223, 224, 232
Sofoulis, Themistoklis, 198
Softazade, A., 73, 81
Sokolis, C., 290
Sonnino, 162
Sorbonne, 381, 383
Souda, 58, 59
Souliot women, 186n74
Souliotis-Nikolaidis, Athanasios, 140, 173
Soutzos, Ioannis, 284
Soutzos, Kyriakos, 284
Soviet Union, 205, 221
Spais, Leonidas, 278
Spanish Inquisition, 52
Sparta, 354
Spetses, 131
Sphakia, 19, 29, 54, 57, 349
Sphakianakis, Ioannis, 67, 70, 71, 349
Spili, 65
Spinalonga, 348
Spyridis, K., 314
Spyridon [Vlachos], metropolitan of Ioannina (ex Vella and Konitsa), later archbishop of Athens, 356, 370n43
St Antony's College, 183
Stavridi, John, 148, 167, 168, 183
Stergiadis, Aristidis, 162, 166, 169, 189
Stillman, William, 33, 78, 80, 81
Stockholm, 137
Straits, 158, 160, 163, 164, 165, 170, 187
Stratos, N., 130, 137, 295
Streit George, 116, 117, 137, 143, 153, 175, 181
Strymon, 203
Students' Society, 326
Sublime Porte, 12, 13, 18, 19, 22, 23, 24, 25, 31, 52, 68, 81, 88, 89, 93, 97, 107, 182, 353, 362, 364
Suda, 88
Svolopoulos, Constantinos, 72, 138
Sweden, Swedish, 336
Switzerland, 95
Syngros, A., 81
Syria, 12
Syros, 20, 38, 40, 41, 77, 78, 112, 306, 307

Taine, Hippolyte, 378
Tenedos, 151, 159, 165, 171
Tevfik Bedri Bey, 48
The Guardian, 82
The New York Times, 59, 82
The Times, 63, 73, 78, 80, 81, 82, 137, 143, 145, 146, 156, 181
The Tribune, 73
Thebes, 127
Theodoropoulos, Spyros, 290
Theoklitos [Minipoulos], archbishop of Athens, 354, 355, 359, 360, 361, 367, 371
Theotokis George, 87, 88, 93, 94, 100, 111, 117, 141, 143, 180, 339, 344
Therisso, 37, 38, 40, 72, 74, 75, 83, 350, 351, 366
Thessaliotis, metropolitan of [Efthymios Platys], 361
Thessaloniki, 97, 110, 116, 120, 121, 122, 123, 124, 127, 128, 132, 136, 147, 150, 181, 182, 198, 213, 217, 218, 224, 230, 235, 236, 242, 262, 273, 275, 277, 280, 292, 311, 314, 316, 319, 329, 330, 334, 339, 341, 355, 357, 358, 359, 366, 367, 370, 371, 380
Thessaly, 15, 24, 65, 87, 102, 103, 126, 127, 128, 156, 203, 259, 287, 304, 306, 308, 368
Thiers, Adolphe, 378
Thomas, Albert, 318

Thrace, 130, 131, 147, 152, 157, 158, 159, 162, 163, 164, 165, 170, 171, 172, 173, 184, 186, 187, 188, 189, 190, 200, 209, 275, 287, 364
Thucydides, 50, 80, 352, 378, 379, 380, 381, 385, 386, 387
Timotheos, metropolitan of Crete, 349
Tinos, 31
Titos [Zographidis], bishop of Petra, later metropolitan of Crete, 348, 350, 370n43
Tittoni, 162, 163, 177, 187, 188
To Vima, newspaper, 132
Tobacco Institute, 203
Tomadakis, N. B., 40, 76n1, 385n2
Topanas, 38, 56
Tourkokritikoi (Turco-Cretans), 11, 13, 14, 20, 61, 69
Toynbee, A. J., 179, 187, 192, 378
Trebizond, 158, 370
Trevelyan, George, 378
Triantaphyllidis, Manolis, 320, 326, 330, 331, 334, 340-341n20, 341, 342
Trikoupis, Charilaos, 27, 41, 54, 55, 56, 115, 117, 143, 256, 270, 339, 344, 345, 347
Trikoupis, Gen. Constantinos, 124
Trikoupis, Spyridon, 379
Tripoli, 354
Tsaldaris, P., 130, 195, 211, 213, 214, 215, 235, 236, 237, 238, 239, 240, 242, 243, 244, 273, 278
Tsepetakis, Chrysanthos, 63, 348, 351
Tsigantes, Chr., 279, 280, 281
Tsirimokos, Ilias, 355
Tsirimokos, Ioannis, 320, 321, 327, 329, 341
Tsirimokos, Markos, 341
Tsouderos, Emmanouel, 66, 206, 311
Tufnell, Admiral, 108, 109, 142
Turhan Pasha, 30
Turkey-Turkish, 2, 4, 6, 13, 14, 15, 20, 21, 25, 28, 29, 30, 35, 37, 39, 40, 41, 42, 43, 44, 46, 48, 49, 52, 55, 56, 57, 58, 59, 60, 62, 63, 65, 66, 68, 72, 74, 76, 82, 88, 89, 97, 107, 110, 128, 135, 136, 139, 140, 141, 142, 143, 144, 145, 146, 147, 151, 152, 153, 154, 155, 157, 158, 159, 160, 161, 162, 163, 164, 165, 166, 168, 169, 170–2, 173, 174, 176, 177, 178, 180, 181, 182, 183, 186, 188, 190, 191, 210, 216, 217, 220–2, 223, 224, 225, 238, 239, 254, 277, 354

Ukraine, 312
Ulen, 203, 317
Union of Greek Women, 325
United States, 127, 142, 151, 157, 163, 178, 187, 208, 293
USA, 33, 253, 263, 294, 302, 312, 316

Valalas, Ioannis, 230
Valaoritis, Ioannis, 110, 141, 291, 310
Valona, 163
Vamos, 30, 57
Van der Brule, 73
Vansittart, Robert, 243
Vardar, 154
Varvaressos, Kyriakos, 206, 207, 208
Vasilios, metropolitan of Anchialos, 361
Vasilios, bishop of Dryinopolis, 356
Vasos, Col. Timoleon, 62, 65
Veli Pasha, 14
Venezuela, 35
Venizelos, Agathoklis, 39
Venizelos, Aikaterini, 35
Venizelos, Eleni, 39
Venizelos, Evanthia, 39
Venizelos, Hadji Nikolos, 37
Venizelos, Katingo, 39
Venizelos, Kyriakos, 20, 37, 38, 39, 40, 41, 42, 56, 77, 78
Venizelos, Maria, 56
Venizelos, Mariyo, 39
Venizelos, Sophoklis, 56
Venizelos, Styliani, 39
Ventiris, G., 118, 123, 131, 138, 175, 286
Veremis, Thanos, 313
Verovic, Georgios Pasha, 30
Versailles, 294
Vienna, 144

Vilaras, Ioannis, 378, 379
Vlachos, Georgios, 280
Volanis, S., 280
Volos, 109, 322, 323, 324, 325, 329, 332, 333, 340
Votsis, 372
Vourloumis, Panagis, 304
Vryses, 20
Vulkan shipyards, 109, 150

Wall Street, 205, 302
Washington, 289, 298
Waterlow, S., 78, 232, 242
Weber, Max, 3, 5
Weimar, 264
West, 117, 160, 263, 298, 299, 344
White Mountains, 39
Whitehall, 190
Wilhelm II, Kaiser of Germany, 116
Wilson, President W., 157, 158, 159, 161, 173
Women Workers' Sunday School, 325

Xiroudakis, Evmenios *see* Evmenios [Xiroudakis]

Yamalakis, Nikolaos, 70
Yanitsa, 203
Yanitsarakis, Hussein, 70
Yannaris, Hadji Michalis, 347
Yennadis, Nikolaos, 60, 61, 62, 63, 67
Yennadis, Stephanos, 67
Young Turks, 76, 89, 134, 140, 143, 173, 253
Yugoslavia, 217, 218, 219, 220, 223, 224, 238, 239, 242

Zaimis, Alexandros, 74, 87, 121, 122, 155, 187, 193, 195, 197, 201, 212, 276, 292, 300, 354
Zanna, Virginia, 132
Zannas, Alexandros, 123, 124, 132, 230, 281
Zappeion, 384
Zavitsianos, Constantinos, 100, 137, 195, 199
Zervas, Gen. Napoleon, 278
Ziller, Tuiskon, 342n33
Zographidis, Titos *see* Titos [Zographidis]
Zolotas, Xenophon, 206
Zorbas, Col. Nikolaos, 90, 141, 254
Zouridis, N., 35, 62
Zygomalas, George, 40, 42
Zymbrakakis, Gen. Epameinondas, 89, 90